DISCARD

```
KF
569     Bergfield
.B474   Principles of real estate
        law
```

Principles of
Real Estate Law

Principles of Real Estate Law

Philip B. Bergfield, J.D.
Professor of Real Estate and Law
California State University, Los Angeles

McGraw-Hill Book Company
New York St. Louis San Francisco Auckland Bogotá Düsseldorf
Johannesburg London Madrid Mexico Montreal New Delhi
Panama Paris São Paulo Singapore Sydney Tokyo Toronto

PRINCIPLES OF REAL ESTATE LAW

Copyright © 1979 by McGraw-Hill, Inc. All rights reserved. Printed in the United States of America. No part of this publication may be reproduced, stored in a retrieval system, or transmitted, in any form or by any means, electronic, mechanical, photocopying, recording, or otherwise, without the prior written permission of the publisher.

1 2 3 4 5 6 7 8 9 0   DODO   7 8 3 2 1 0 9

This book was set in Times Roman by BookTech, Inc. (ECU).
The editors were Marjorie Singer and M. Susan Norton;
the cover was designed by Albert M. Cetta;
the production supervisor was Donna Piligra.
R. R. Donnelley & Sons Company was printer and binder.

Library of Congress Cataloging in Publication Data

Bergfield, Philip B
    Principles of real estate law.

    Includes index.
    1. Real property—United States.   I. Title.
KF569.B474   346'.73'043   78-12099
ISBN 0-07-004890-8

To Mary Delle

Contents

Preface   xi

CHAPTER 1 Introduction   1

The Function of Law / Meaning of "Property" / Possession as an Incident of Ownership / Limitations on Right of Use / Transfer of Ownership / The Privateness of Property / Constitutional Protection of Private Property / Questions

CHAPTER 2 The Physical Components of Real Estate   13

Land / Fixtures / Appurtenances / Questions

CHAPTER 3 Description of Real Property   26

Meaning and Function of Description / Adequacy or Sufficiency of Description / Land Surveying / Types of Descriptions / Description by Metes and Bounds / Rectangular Survey System / Description by Reference to a Map or Plat / Questions

CHAPTER 4	Origins of Private Ownership of Real Property	37

The Colonial Period / Acquisition of the Public Domain / Private Claims to Public Lands / Transfer of Public Lands by Sale / Transfer of Public Lands by Gift / Land for Homesteaders / Questions

CHAPTER 5	Ownership Interests in Real Estate—Estates	55

Classification of Estates / Estates in Fee Simple / Life Estates / Estates in Fee Tail / Estates for Years / Estates from Period to Period / Estates at Will / Estates at Sufferance / Future Interests / Questions

CHAPTER 6	Co-Ownership of Real Estate	69

Nature of Co-Ownership / Forms of Co-Ownership / Joint Tenancy / Tenancy in Common / Rights and Duties of Joint Tenants and Tenants in Common / Termination of Joint Tenancies and Tenancies in Common / Tenancy by the Entirety / Community Property / Dower and Curtesy / Simultaneous Death / Questions

CHAPTER 7	Incidents of Ownership	81

Trespass to Land / Negligence / Nuisance / Fences / Party Walls / Landslides / Trees / Surface Water / Lateral and Subjacent Support / Boundary Lines / Liability to Persons Entering Property / Duty Owed to Persons Outside the Land / Questions

CHAPTER 8	Easements, Profits, and Licenses	99

Easements / Profits / Licenses / Questions

CHAPTER 9	Real Estate Contracts	114

Nature of a Contract / Classification of Contracts / Elements of a Contract / Performance of Contracts / Real Estate Contracts / Options / Questions

CHAPTER 10	Deeds, Wills, and Intestate Succession	135

Transfer Resulting from Sale / Deeds / Transfer by Inter Vivos Gift / Transfer by Will / Transfer by Intestate Succession / Escheat / Questions

CHAPTER 11	Eminent Domain	152

General Characteristics of Eminent Domain / Taking of or Damage to Property / Public Use / Necessity / Excess Condemnation / Just Compensation / Taking Less than an Entire Parcel / Taking Less than Fee Interest / Taking Leased Property / Uniform Relocation Assistance Act / Uniform Real Property Acquisition Policy / Uniform Eminent Domain Code / Questions

CONTENTS

CHAPTER 12   Adverse Possession and Accretion   174

General Characteristics of Adverse Possession / Essential Elements of Adverse Possession / Open, Notorious, and Visible Occupation / Hostile and Adverse Occupancy / Claim of Right or Color of Title / Continuous and Uninterrupted Possession / Payment of Property Taxes / Nature of Adverse Possessor's Title / Mistaken Boundaries and Adverse Possession / Accretion / Questions

CHAPTER 13   Title Closing and Settlement Procedures   183

Real Estate Escrows / Real Estate Settlement Procedures Act / Questions

CHAPTER 14   Recording and Other Methods of Title Protection   201

The Recording System / Constructive Notice Other than from Recording / Torrens System of Title Registration / Abstracts of Title and Lawyer's Opinions / Title Insurance / Adjudication of Title to Real Property / Questions

CHAPTER 15   Mortgages, Deeds of Trust, and Installment Contracts—Part I   219

The Mortgage Market / Primary and Secondary Markets / Insured, Guaranteed, and Conventional Loans / Home Mortgage Disclosure Act / Uniform Land Transactions Act / The Underlying Obligation / Mortgage as a Security Device / Deed of Trust / Priorities / Rights of the Mortgagor / Rights of the Mortgagee / Questions

CHAPTER 16   Mortgages, Deeds of Trust, and Installment Contracts—Part II   248

Foreclosure / Equity of Redemption / Statutory Right of Redemption / Deficiency Judgments / Deed in Lieu of Foreclosure / Installment Sale Contract / Truth in Lending Law / Equal Credit Opportunity Act / Questions

CHAPTER 17   Mechanics' Liens   274

Persons Entitled to Mechanics' Liens / Nature of Services for Which Lien May Be Had / Property Interest Subject to Lien / Physical Property Subject to a Lien / Procedure for Obtaining a Lien / Operation and Effect of a Lien / Prevention and Extinction of a Lien / Enforcement of a Mechanics' Lien / Priority of Mechanics' Liens / Questions

CHAPTER 18   Homesteads   292

Objective of Homestead Laws / Types of Homesteads / Persons Entitled to Homesteads / Property Subject to Homestead / Acquisition of Homestead Exemption / Operation

of Homestead Exemption / Transfer or Encumbrance of
Homestead Property / Rights of Survivors of Head of Family /
Termination of Homesteads / Probate Homesteads / Questions

CHAPTER 19 Restrictive Covenants and Conditions   303

Private Restrictions on Land Use / Methods of Creating
Restrictions / Restrictive Covenants / Conditions / Questions

CHAPTER 20 Zoning   315

Development Planning and Zoning / Purposes of Zoning /
Source of Zoning Power / Zoning Authority of Local
Governments / Constitutionality of Zoning / Nature of
Comprehensive Zoning / Zoning Procedures / Relief from
Zoning Regulations / Nonconforming Use / Enforcement of
Zoning Laws / Building Codes / Questions

CHAPTER 21 Pollution Control and Environmental Protection   332

Development of Environmental Law / Federal Environmental
Legislation / Coastal Zone Conservation and Management /
National Environmental Policy Act (NEPA) / Council on
Environmental Quality (CEQ) / Environmental Protection
Agency (EPA) / Guidelines for Preparation of Environmental
Impact Statements / Draft EISs, Review of Comments, and
Final EISs / Judicial Review of Federal Agency Action / State
Environmental Legislation / Questions

CHAPTER 22 Real Property Taxes   353

Nature of the Real Property Tax / The Assessment Process /
The Tax Levy / Payment and Collection of Taxes / Real Property
Tax Liens / Sale of Tax-delinquent Property / Redemption
from Tax Sale / Tax Deed / Questions

CHAPTER 23 Landlord and Tenant—Part I   365

Landlord-Tenant Relationship / Characteristics of a Lease /
Types of Leasehold Interests / Rights and Obligations of
Parties / Questions

CHAPTER 24 Landlord and Tenant—Part II   393

Tort Liability of Landlord and Tenant / Transfer of Leased
Property / Transfer of Tenant's Interest / Termination of the
Landlord-Tenant Relationship / Landlord's Remedies to Regain
Possession of Premises / Questions

Glossary   411

Index   431

Preface

This is a book about ownership and use of real estate—a book that examines the rights and the duties, the benefits and the burdens that arise from owning a unit of space on the earth's surface. These rights and duties find expression in a large and varied body of rules of social behavior known as real estate law. By identifying and examining the policy factors that induce and justify these rules, and by separating the legal relations arising from ownership into their essential elements, the text not only invites but also encourages students to approach real estate law analytically rather than to regard it as a collection of definitions and principles to be committed to memory. Because the characteristics of real estate and its ownership can only be expressed in terms of the law that creates and gives recognition to them, a working knowledge of legal terms is necessary. This requirement, of course, is not unique to the study of real estate—every discipline or area of learning is plagued by a terminology of its own that must be understood and used when that discipline is being examined and explained. As a ready reference for the student, a selected glossary of real estate terms has been included in the text. It is not intended that the definitions contained in the glossary be memorized but instead that they be used as points of departure for analysis of the concept for which the defined word is a label. Some students find a glossary to be a useful aid in reviewing material, either for examination purposes or as a means of consolidating their knowledge.

The text presupposes no prior knowledge of real estate. It is designed to enlarge the awareness and learning not only of students at all levels—university, college, adult and continuing education—but also to prepare prospective licensees, to increase the professional skills of practicing brokers and salespersons, loan officers, and mortgage bankers, and to enhance the knowledge of present and prospective investors, homeowners, and other persons desirous of understanding the meaning of ownership and use of real estate.

For the student with no prior knowledge of real estate, Chapters 1 through 4 introduce him or her to the nature of real estate as a form of wealth, its essential elements and characteristics, society's recognition of the right to own this scarce resource, and the way in which private ownership evolved in this country. The material in the 24 chapters is organized and presented in such a way that, by selective use of the chapters, the text will meet the requirements of courses both in real estate principles and real estate law. In addition, the text will serve as a useful supplement for courses in real estate finance (Chapters 15 and 16, "Mortgages, Deeds of Trust, and Installment Contracts"; Chapter 17, "Mechanics' Liens"; and Chapter 18, "Homesteads"), real property management (Chapter 7, "Incidents of Ownership"; Chapter 8, "Easements, Profits, and Licenses"; Chapter 19, "Restrictive Covenants and Conditions"; and Chapters 23 and 24, "Landlord and Tenant"), as well as courses in urban affairs, public administration, and environmental matters (Chapter 7, "Incidents of Ownership"; Chapter 20, "Zoning"; Chapter 21, "Pollution Control and Environmental Protection"; and Chapter 22, "Real Property Taxes"). In addition, through the use of proposed model and uniform laws, the probable trend in changes in the law relating to real estate and the rationales for those changes are revealed to the reader.

Students at all levels and practitioners and professionals alike need clearly to understand that ownership of real estate is possible only because the law recognizes and protects the rights that ownership embraces. It is the law that formulates and declares the rules that define and regulate all aspects of real estate; it is the law that determines what types of interests in real estate may be owned, that describes how those interests may be acquired and disposed of; and, most importantly, it is the law that regulates the manner in which an owner may use and enjoy the property that he owns.

The core of an analysis of ownership of real estate is not an owner's legal relationship to his land, but the legal relations between an owner and society. These relations are twofold. On the one hand, an owner expects and receives protection for his or her property interests from the machinery of society; on the other, an owner finds his rights curtailed by society for the protection of other owners' interests. While the balance struck between individual rights and the social interest is a function of social and political ideologies at any given time and place, the prevailing desire has been to preserve individual rights as long as they continue to be consistent with the social welfare as currently perceived. It is the function of law to reconcile individual rights with the social change that is constantly altering the pattern of rights.

Viewed historically, private ownership of real estate has become more and more regulated. Beginning with the early common law of private and public nuisance (Chapter 7, "Incidents of Ownership") which prohibited an owner from using his

PREFACE

land in a way that interfered with other owners' use and enjoyment of their lands, zoning laws (Chapter 20, "Zoning") were enacted to further regulate an owner's use of his land in the interest of more efficient land utilization and the public interest. More recently legislation designed to regulate the use of land to prevent adverse effects on the environment has been passed (Chapter 21, "Pollution Control and Environmental Protection"). Few, if any, economic goods are today more closely regulated with respect to use and enjoyment than real estate. These regulations reflect a growing realization that society has an interest in the manner in which a valuable and limited resource is used—the realization of a greater need for regulation in today's society than in a less complex society of a few decades ago. Today, individuals who demand the right to use their lands free from regulation and control are vastly outnumbered by property owners who welcome protection against harmful and antisocial uses and conduct by others.

In its examination of the rights and duties incident to ownership of real estate, the book draws freely on all areas of the law. In so doing, the material discussed cuts across disciplinary lines of traditional law-school teaching areas. In addition to presenting the material typically included in a law school course in real property (Chapter 2, "The Physical Components of Real Estate"; Chapter 3, "Description of Real Property"; Chapter 4, "Origins of Private Ownership of Real Property"; Chapter 5, "Ownership Interests in Real Estate—Estates"; and Chapter 6, "Co-Ownership of Real Estate"), the text embraces such subject areas as constitutional law (Chapter 1, "Introduction"; Chapter 11, "Eminent Domain"; Chapter 20, "Zoning"; and others), contracts (Chapter 9, "Real Estate Contracts"; Chapters 15 and 16, "Mortgages, Deeds of Trust, and Installment Contracts"), torts (Chapter 7, "Incidents of Ownership"; Chapter 12, "Adverse Possession and Accretion"), real property security interests (Chapters 15 and 16, "Mortgages, Deeds of Trust, and Installment Contracts"; Chapter 17, "Mechanics' Liens"; Chapter 18, "Homesteads"), probate and administration of estates (Chapter 10, "Deeds, Wills, and Intestate Succession"), taxation (Chapter 22, "Real Property Taxes"), environmental law (Chapter 21, "Pollution Control and Environmental Protection"), landlord and tenant (Chapters 23 and 24, "Landlord and Tenant"), and other subject areas (for example, Chapter 8, "Easements, Profits, and Licenses"; Chapter 13, "Title Closing and Settlement Procedures"; Chapter 14, "Recording and Other Methods of Title Protection"; Chapter 19, "Restrictive Covenants and Conditions") to the extent that they are relevant to an understanding of the rights enjoyed and the obligations borne by owners of real estate.

To make *Principles of Real Estate Law* more effective as a teaching tool, a detailed and comprehensive Instructor's Manual has been developed to accompany the text. The Instructor's Manual contains briefs of reported cases from the various jurisdictions which have been selected to illustrate principles examined in the text, supplemental materials to be used as desired to amplify text discussions, answers to end-of-chapter review questions, and a collection of true-false and multiple-choice questions and answers to be used for testing purposes. In addition, the Instructor's Manual contains suggestions for the grouping of chapters for courses of varying length and differing emphasis.

To Professors Michael S. Bottelo, El Camino College; Michael L. Galonska,

University of Connecticut; and Carroll L Gentry, Virginia Western Community College who reviewed the manuscript in its entirety and made many helpful suggestions, I wish to extend my sincere thanks. I have also profited from valuable comments and suggestions by real estate instructors at this institution and others and wish to acknowledge their contributions. And finally, to the many students whose classroom comments and reactions have been invaluable in the development of the text, I wish to express my gratitude.

Although most pronouns appearing in the text are masculine in gender, they are intended to embrace all persons without regard to sex. They are used merely for convenience and facility of expression. Anyone reasonably acquainted with the field of real estate will be well aware of the important role of women as buyers, sellers, investors, and users of real estate and their significance as successful practitioners and professionals in the field.

Philip B. Bergfield

Principles of
Real Estate Law

Chapter 1

Introduction

THE FUNCTION OF LAW

Law is a body of rules adopted by an organized society to regulate and control human behavior. These rules of human conduct are enforced by the machinery of government created for that purpose and by the threat of public sanctions should the rules be broken or ignored. The enforcement machinery and sanctions are designed to compel persons to abide by the rules by which society is governed.

To attain the objective of regulating human activities through rules of social conduct, an extensive and sometimes complex system of legal rights and duties has been established.

Legal Rights and Duties

A legal **right** is an interest or claim that is recognized by law and which the law will protect. A legal **duty** is the reciprocal or correlative of a legal right. There cannot be one without the other. For every legal right belonging to a person or persons, there is a corresponding legal duty or obligation owed by other members of society to respect that right and not to interfere with the enjoyment of it. If a person fails or refuses to abide by the legal duty owed by him, the one whose legal right has been violated is entitled to a **remedy** that is prescribed by law and made available through the enforcement machinery of society. Only to the extent that the breach of a duty can be remedied does the existence of a legal right have meaning and value. And only to the extent that those who owe legal duties are aware of them and abide by the obligations they impose can the corresponding legal rights be exercised and enjoyed by the holders of those rights. Human nature being what it is, there is always the risk that someone who owes a duty will fail to comply with his obligation because of ignorance of its existence, indifference toward it, negligent conduct on his part, or willful disregard for the other person's rights.

The characteristics of legal rights and the nature and scope of the corresponding duties that they command vary considerably, depending largely on the particular subject matter to which those rights and duties relate. When, for example, two parties enter into a contract, the reciprocal rights and duties resulting from their agreement extend only to the parties themselves. By contrast, legal rights that arise from the ownership of property impose duties on all other members of society.

Sources of Law

The rules of social behavior that constitute law are pronounced by constitutions, statutes, and court decisions.

The large body of rules that the courts have formulated in settling disputes, sometimes referred to as "judge-made" law, makes up what is known as the **common law.** Despite the very large role that courts play in the lawmaking process, however, lawmaking by the federal and state legislative bodies is the principal source of our law.

While courts are constrained by the doctrine of **stare decisis,** which says that precedents should be respected and followed, legislative bodies are not. Hence, within the limits of constitutionality, the bringing about of distinct changes in existing law is the province of the Congress and the state legislatures. Presumably, these changes are wrought after the kind of investigation and debate that is not possible in ordinary judicial proceedings.

Real Estate Law

Within the general body of rules that make up the law are some that particularly relate to and regulate human conduct with respect to the economic good called "real estate." These rules, appropriately enough, are collectively known as "real estate law."

Real estate law defines and deals with rights and duties of people who acquire, use and enjoy, and dispose of a form of wealth with physical and legal characteristics peculiar to it. As a starting point for identifying and understanding these characteristics, it is useful to examine the concept **"property,"** which is basic to the law of real estate.

MEANING OF "PROPERTY"

The word "property" has two distinct but related meanings. In the strict legal sense, "property" refers to the valuable *rights* that a person may lawfully have with respect to a thing or an object. But the term is not always used in its strict legal sense. As frequently used by lawyer and layman alike, the word "property" refers to the *thing* that is owned—the subject matter in which valuable rights exist.[1] It is in this latter sense that the term "property" is more popularly and commonly used.

Property as a Thing Owned

The law divides property, in the sense of things or objects owned, into two distinct categories, one of which is known as **real property** and the other as **personal property.** The particular classification into which a given thing or object falls will depend upon the physical characteristics of the thing itself.

The terms "real property" and "personal property" derive from events in legal history rather than from an attempt to attach meaningful labels to different types of property. The early common law of England considered lawsuits that arose out of the wrongful withholding of possession of land to be "real" actions— "real" in the sense that, if the owner proved his

---

[1] The California Civil Code, sec. 654, for example, says that "In this code, the *thing* of which there may be ownership is called *property.*" [Emphasis added.]

The Code of Georgia Annotated, sec. 85-111 reads: "The term 'property' is used not only to signify things real and personal owned, but to designate the right of ownership and that which is subject to being owned and enjoyed."

INTRODUCTION

case, possession of the land itself was restored to him. On the other hand, if a cause of action arose from the wrongful withholding of something other than land, the action was said to be a "personal" one in which, instead of receiving the return of the thing withheld, the owner was awarded a sum of money as damages resulting from the wrong. As legal history evolved, the thing or object that was the subject matter of litigation took on the name of the type of action that was brought to resolve the controversy.

The concept of real and personal property is very much a part of our legal system and, while there are many legal principles that are common to the two categories, each has a body of law that is peculiar to it. Because the physical characteristics of real property and personal property differ significantly, important distinctions exist in the law relating to the two categories of property.

Real Property While the wording of the many definitions of real property varies somewhat, the essence of all of them is that real property consists of land, those things that are attached to the land, and that which is appurtenant or belongs to the land.[2] While definitions of real property frequently employ the word "immovable" to describe one of its characteristics,[3] it is important to recognize that the word "immovable" is used in a legal sense rather than an absolute one. Because they are attached to land, buildings by definition are real property, but we know that small buildings often are moved bodily from one location to another. Similarly, soil, rock, and gravel of which land is composed can readily be moved from a site that is being excavated to one that is being filled. Nevertheless, in legal contemplation these items are considered to be immovable. What is in fact immovable in the absolute meaning of the word is the *location* of a *unit of space* on the land mass. Because of its fixity, a parcel of land is entirely at the mercy of the neighborhood and environment in which it is located—it cannot be physically relocated to a more desirable site on the landscape. This vulnerability of land to its surroundings is undoubtedly the most significant consequence of its immovability.

As a unit of space on the landscape, a parcel of land can neither be consumed nor destroyed. It is a form of wealth that continues to exist indefinitely. Nor can land, like some things that are owned, be concealed from creditors or the tax collector.

The rights and duties that pertain to a given parcel of land are determined by the law of the state in which the land is situated—the "law of the situs." From the standpoint of an owner, the law with respect to real property may be more favorable in one state than in another, but the owner cannot escape the impact of less favorably real property laws by moving his place of residence to another state. Regardless of an owner's place of residence, any land owned by him is governed by the law of its situs.

---

[2] For example, a Florida statute says that " 'Real property' shall include all lands, including improvements and fixtures thereon, and property of any nature appurtenant thereto or used in connection therewith, and every estate, interest and right, legal or equitable therein, including terms for years and liens by way of judgment, mortgage or otherwise and the indebtedness secured by such liens." Florida Statutes, sec. 421.031(12).

An Illinois statute in very similar language provides: " 'Real Property' shall include land, lands underwater, structures and any and all easements, franchises and incorporeal hereditaments and estates, and rights, legal and equitable, including terms for years and liens by way of judgment, mortgage, or otherwise." Illinois Annotated Statutes, ch. 67½, sec. 91.10(f).

And, as the term is used in the Uniform Eminent Domain Code, " 'real property' means land and any improvements upon or connected with the land; and includes an easement, servitude, or other interest therein." Sec. 103(19).

[3] For example, California Civil Code, sec. 658 defines real property as consisting of "land; that which is affixed to land; that which is incidental to land; and that which is *immovable by law* . . ." [Emphasis added.]

Personal Property Definitions of personal property commonly are residual in character as, for example, in the definition: "Every kind of property that is not real is personal."[4] As thus defined, personal property includes a vast array of things, tangible and intangible, that are capable of being owned under our system of law.

In most cases, personal property will be totally consumed or its usefulness terminated in a relatively short period of time. Also, unlike real property, personal property may be moved from one location to another and frequently is capable of being concealed from both creditors and the tax collector. As we shall see in Chapter 2, "The Physical Components of Real Estate," the distinction between real property and personal property becomes particularly significant when controversies arise over fixtures—a *fixture* being a thing that once was personal property but which, if found to meet certain criteria prescribed by the law, changes into real property.

"Real Property," "Real Estate," and "Land" Used Synonymously The supreme courts of two major states have said that "Real estate at common law and in its generally accepted meaning is synonymous with real property"[5] and that " 'lands' are synonymous with 'real estate' and 'real property'."[6] A Florida statute provides that "The terms 'land,' 'real estate,' 'realty,' and 'real property' may be used interchangeably."[7] And a Michigan statute says that "The words 'land,' 'lands,' 'real estate,' and 'real property' mean lands, tenements,[8] and real estate and all rights thereto and interests therein."[9]

Since "real estate" and "real property" are but different names for the same thing, the definition of one of them necessarily describes the essential characteristics of the other. *Real estate*, then, like *real property*, consists of land, those things attached to land, and that which is appurtenant or belongs to land.

Although in its broad meaning the word "land" is used synonymously with "real estate" and "real property," it is apparent from the foregoing definition that the term is sometimes used in a more restrictive sense. As used in its narrower meaning, "land" refers to one of the elements or components of real estate and as such is commonly referred to as being "raw" or "unimproved." The characteristics of land as one of the components of real estate are examined in Chapter 2.

Whether the word "land" is intended to convey its broad or narrow meaning in a statute, court decision, or other writing ordinarily is readily apparent from the context in which the word is used.

Property as Rights of Ownership

In its strict legal sense, "property" is defined as the exclusive right to possess, use and enjoy, and dispose of an object or thing of value in a manner consistent with prevailing rules of law. When used in this sense, "property" means **ownership**, which is often defined as being a bundle of rights or privileges pertaining to an object or thing that is owned. More specifically, "ownership" is the right of complete and exclu-

---

[4] California Civil Code, sec. 663.
Wisconsin Statutes Annotated, sec. 70.04 states: "The term 'personal property' . . . shall include all goods, wares, merchandise, chattels, and effects, of any nature or description, having any real or marketable value, and not included in the term 'real property,' as defined above." The definition referred to is contained in sec. 70.03 which reads: "The terms 'real property,' 'real estate,' and 'land,' when used in this title [Chapter 70, "General Property Taxes"], shall include not only the land itself but all buildings and improvements thereon, and all fixtures and rights and privileges appertaining thereto."

[5] *Dabney v. Edwards* 5 Cal. 2d 1, 6, 53 Pac. 2d 952, 966 (1935).

[6] *City of Waukegan v. Stanczak* 6 Ill. 2d 594, 605, 129 N.E.2d 751, 757 (1955).

[7] Florida Statutes, sec. 192.001(11).

[8] "The word 'tenement' is of greater extent than the word 'land,' and in its most extensive signification comprehends everything which may be holden, provided it is of a permanent nature." 63 Am. Jur. 2d 301.

[9] Michigan Statutes Annotated, sec. 2.212(9).

INTRODUCTION

sive control over a thing that is owned, which includes the right to possess it, to use and enjoy it, and to transfer all rights pertaining to it to another person or persons.[10] The owner of a thing has the largest quantity of rights and privileges with respect to the thing owned that the law permits an individual to have. As the term is popularly conceived, "ownership" is the right by which something *belongs* to a person.

Although the bundle of rights idea is commonly used to explain the nature of ownership, it would be a serious mistake to conclude from such usage either that ownership consists solely of rights and privileges or that the rights and privileges that ownership embraces are without limitation. The law, in response to the demands of society, imposes certain duties or obligations on the owner of property. Consequently, so that it may reflect the burdens or responsibilities of ownership as well as the benefits, the notion of a "bundle" must be expanded from simply a "bundle of rights" to a "bundle of rights and duties." These rights and duties, as we have seen, exist only because and to the extent that they are recognized, protected, and enforced by the law.

Although the fact of ownership arises because something belongs to or is owned by a person, as the *Restatement of the Law of Property* points out,[11] "ownership" refers to the legal relations between persons with respect to a thing rather than to the owner's relationship to the thing itself. It is with these relations between an owner of real estate and all other persons in society that this book is concerned.

"Ownership" and "Title" Both in popular and legal usage, the word "title" means ownership. In referring to the word "title," one court has said that "A common meaning is complete ownership, in the sense of all rights, privileges, powers, and immunities an owner may have with respect to land."[12] Similarly, the *Restatement of the Law of Property* states that "In common and legal speech, the word 'title' normally . . . signifies . . . ownership . . ."[13]

As we shall see in Chapter 13, "Title Closing and Settlement Procedures" and in Chapter 14, "Recording and Other Methods of Title Protection," the word "title" is also used to refer to the totality of evidence upon which the fact of ownership is based.

POSSESSION AS AN INCIDENT OF OWNERSHIP

The right of possession of real estate is unquestionably the single most important incident of its ownership. The law of real property, it has been said, developed around the concept of possession.

A landowner's right to possession carries with it the right to use his land, and it is the use or uses to which land may be put that imparts value to it. Without the right of use, the other incidents of ownership would be of little worth because when one is deprived of the use of what he owns, little remains to him but a barren title. A landowner's right of use includes the power to exclude other persons from possessing and using the property that he owns.

Exclusive but Not Absolute Use

While the law accords the owner of real estate the right of *exclusive* use of his property free from interference by others, that right is not and never has been an *absolute* one—that is,

---

[10] The California Civil Code, sec. 654 says that "The ownership of a thing is the right of one or more persons to possess it and use it to the exclusion of others."

[11] Introductory Note to Chapter 1.

[12] *Smith v. Bank of America National Trust and Savings Association,* 14 CA2d 78, 85, 57 Pac. 2d 1363, 1367 (1936).

In the *Restatement of the Law of Property,* a "right" is defined (sec. 1) as a legally enforceable claim that one person has against another; a "privilege" (sec. 2) as the legal freedom of a person to do or not to do a certain act; a "power" (sec. 3) as a person's legal ability to alter a legal relation by doing or not doing a particular act; and an "immunity" (sec. 4) as a person's freedom against having a legal relation altered by another person doing or not doing an act.

[13] Sec. 10, note on use of the word "title" in the *Restatement.*

without qualification or limitation. As we shall see in the chapters that follow, an owner must exercise his right of exclusive use of his land with a proper regard for public policy and a reasonable concern for the rights of others. No owner has unrestricted freedom in the use of his land. His use is always subject to reasonable regulation.

Arriving at a reasonable compromise between an owner's unrestricted use of land and conflicting social interests has long been and continues to be a problem for the courts and the legislatures. From an earlier posture that permitted an owner to do whatever he pleased with his property regardless of the effect on others, the attitude of society and the law has changed to one that limits an owner's use whenever necessary to protect social interests. Changing notions regarding the use of land arise from changing conditions of modern society, many of which result from a growing population concentrated in limited land areas.

Present or Future Possession

While the right to possess and occupy real estate is a significant feature of its ownership, an owner's title is not impaired simply because he deprives himself of the right to *present* possession of his property. As we shall see in Chapters 23 and 24, an owner, as a landlord, may transfer his right of possession and occupancy for an agreed period of time to another person, a tenant, for a consideration known as rent and still retain ownership of the property. The owner continues to have the right of possession of the property in question, but it is a right to *future* rather than *present* possession, because the owner chose to sell his right to immediate occupancy and use of his property.

LIMITATIONS ON RIGHT OF USE

Legal devices for controlling use of land are many and varied. As we shall see in Chapter 19, "Restrictive Covenants and Conditions," land use controls may result from agreements between private parties and thus be voluntarily assumed by a property owner or, as discussed in Chapter 7, "Incidents of Ownership," Chapter 20, "Zoning," and Chapter 21, "Pollution Control and Environmental Protection," the controls on land use may be imposed on land by the law as incidents of its ownership. Limitations on the use of land are necessary not only for the protection of the interests of neighboring property owners but also to protect the health, safety, morals, and general welfare of the community as a whole.

Publicly imposed land use controls developed late in the history of the United States, mostly after the turn of the twentieth century. Prior to that time, land was in abundance, the economy was primarily agrarian, and there was little motive for regulating the use of land. Moreover, during the first century of the nation the belief in the inviolability of private property was especially strong. Public control of land use began to develop as the western frontier disappeared and urban areas increased in number and in size.

It is sometimes said that the right to own and use property is a "natural" right—a right that belonged to individuals long before the U.S. Constitution was adopted. Instead of creating and granting the right to own and use property to individuals, the Constitution provides for the protection of a natural right that was already in existence. But it does not follow from the fact that property rights are protected by constitutional guarantees that an individual's use of his property is immune from governmental regulation. No rule of law is better settled than the one that says that all property is held subject to the right of the state reasonably to regulate its use under the **police power.** In accordance with this rule, an owner may be restricted in the use and enjoyment of his property when restriction is required in the public interest. The rule is based on the notion that all property is held on the implied condition or obligation that the use of it shall not be injurious to the equal rights of other owners in the use and enjoyment of their property or to the larger interests of society.

Nature of the Police Power
It has been said that because of the inability to foresee the ever-changing social, economic, and political conditions in which the power is exercised, the police power is incapable of precise definition. It can, however, be described as the inherent power of the state to enact legislation to promote the health, safety, morals, and general welfare of society. It is the power of the state to subject the rights of individuals to reasonable regulation. That all rights of individuals are subject to the police power is well settled and, consequently, both persons and property are subject to restraints and limitations that reasonably serve to further and protect the public health, safety, morals, and general welfare.

The Police Power and the Constitution The police power is not a constitutional grant of authority to the states because the states existed and possessed that power before the federal constitution was adopted. The courts have many times said that the Constitution presupposes the prior existence of the police power.

The police power is vested in the legislative branch of state governments and each legislature has the power to regulate the rights and duties of all persons within its jurisdiction for the public convenience and public good. Except as otherwise provided by the United States Constitution, a state's exercise of the power is free from interference by the federal government. Generally speaking, the role of the federal government is limited to assuring that in exercising the police power the states do not invade the sphere of federal sovereignty, do not impede the exercise of any authority vested in the federal government, and do not deprive a citizen of any right guaranteed to him by the federal constitution.

While it may be technically correct to say that, within the scope of the enumerated powers granted to it by the Constitution, the federal government exercises no police power, it does exercise legislative powers that are typical of what in the case of a state would be termed police powers. It has been said that a more accurate way of stating it is not to say that the federal government has no police power, but that it possesses whatever police power may be necessary for the proper exercise of any attribute of sovereignty that is specifically granted to it by the Constitution.

Inhibits rather than Compels Use The police power, as it relates to real estate, is negative or inhibitory in character. That is to say, an owner of real estate cannot, under the police power, be compelled to devote his property to a particular use, no matter how beneficial that use may be to him or to the public. An owner can, however, be forced to refrain from putting his property to a use that is deemed to be detrimental to the public.

Standard by Which Power Is Tested The basic standard by which the police power is tested is that the power extends only to regulations that are reasonable under the circumstances of their imposition. The test of reasonableness usually applied by the courts is that the exercise of the power must not be arbitrary or capricious. Generally speaking, however, a legislature's discretion in the exercise of the police power is very broad, both in determining what interests of the public require protection and what measures are necessary to provide that protection. As discussed in Chapter 20, "Zoning" and Chapter 21, "Pollution Control and Environmental Protection," the public interest is today conceived as being very extensive. Consequently, many restrictions on the use of land and the type of structures that may be erected on it, now sustained as valid exercises of the police power, at an earlier time were in most jurisdictions regarded as invasions of the constitutional rights of property owners.

Limitations on Exercise of Power The principal limitations on a state's exercise of the police power are contained in the due process provisions and the equal protection clause of the Fourteenth Amendment to the U.S. Constitution. It is firmly established that the Fourteenth Amendment was not intended to interfere with, impair, or take away from the states the right properly to exercise the police power. It is equally well established, however, that the extent of a state's exercise of the police power is limited by the Fourteenth Amendment. In other words, the validity of any exercise of the police power must ultimately be tested against the provisions of the Fourteenth Amendment.

TRANSFER OF OWNERSHIP

An owner's right to transfer title to property is an important incident of his ownership of it. The transfer of ownership is a two-part transaction in which (1) the transferor's interests in designated property are extinguished and (2) those interests are established in the transferee. A transfer, in other words, involves both the *disposition* of ownership of the subject matter of the transaction by one person and the simultaneous *acquisition* of ownership of it by another.

In real estate law, the verbs **transfer, convey,** and **alienate** and the nouns **transfer, conveyance,** and **alienation** are synonymous and used interchangeably.

May Be Voluntary or Involuntary

The transfer or conveyance of title to real estate may result from a voluntary act on the part of an owner or it may occur despite his intention or desires. A voluntary transfer occurs when an owner willingly sells his property (Chapter 9) or makes a gift of it during his lifetime or upon his death (Chapter 10). Ownership of real estate is transferred contrary to an owner's volition when it is taken from him by eminent domain (Chapter 11), when title is acquired by an adverse possessor (Chapter 12), or when a lien to which the property may be subject is foreclosed (Chapters 16, 17, and 22).

Policy Favoring Free Transferability

It has long been the policy of society to favor the free transferability or alienability of property. "The underlying principle which operates throughout the field of property law is that freedom to alienate property interests which one may own is essential to the welfare of society."[14] This principle or policy is reflected in the legal sanctions that are brought to bear when parties to real estate transactions attempt to impose socially undesirable restraints on the alienation of real estate.

A **restraint on alienation,** as the term is used in law, is a limitation imposed by a transferor of real estate on the transferee's right to convey an interest or interests in the property he acquired from the transferor. Restrictions on the right to transfer real property interests may take many forms and, depending upon the type of interest involved and the nature of the restriction, a particular restraint may or may not be valid and enforceable.

As we shall see in Chapter 5, "Ownership Interests in Real Estate—Estates," an estate in **fee simple absolute** is the largest ownership interest recognized by the law. An inherent and inseparable attribute of ownership of a fee simple absolute is the right of the owner to transfer it. The law will not permit that right to be impaired by persons who transfer title by sale or gift and at the same time seek to maintain control over the transferee's right to transfer all or part of his interest in the property. Consequently, if A, who owns Blackacre in fee simple absolute, makes an otherwise effective transfer of it to B with the restriction that "B shall have no power to sell, give, grant, mortgage, or otherwise transfer any interest whatsoever in Blackacre to any person," the restraint on B's right of alienation will be void and B will be free to transfer whatever interest or interests he may

---

[14] *Restatement of the Law of Property,* Introductory Note to "Restraints on Alienation," which is Part II of Division IV, "Social Restrictions Imposed upon Creation of Property Interests."

desire. The traditional rationale for holding such a restraint unenforceable is the so-called repugnancy theory which says that the restraint is repugnant to the inherent characteristic of a fee simple interest.

A more meaningful justification for holding such a restraint unenforceable is that it is contrary to society's desire to promote the free transferability of one of its most important resources. As an Illinois court put it: "Restraints on alienation keep property out of commerce, they tend to concentrate wealth, they may prevent the owner from consuming the property except as to the income from it, they may deter the improvement of the property and they may prevent creditors from satisfying their claims. Against these and other social and economic disadvantages to the public, the only benefit that would accrue from such restraints is the satisfaction of the capricious whims of the conveyor."[15]

Not all restraints on the alienability of interests in real estate are unenforceable. As we shall see in Chapter 24, "Landlord and Tenant," a landlord and a tenant may covenant or agree that the tenant shall not assign the lease or sublet the property without the landlord's consent, and such a restraint on the tenant's right of alienation ordinarily is valid and enforceable. The justification for enforcing the landlord's restraint on the tenant's right to alienate his leasehold interest is the landlord's desire to have some control as to the person with whom he must deal with regard to the obligations created by the lease and to protect his interest in the physical premises.[16]

THE PRIVATENESS OF PROPERTY

In both popular and legal usage, the term "private property" means private *ownership* of property—which in turn signifies that something belongs to a particular person or persons rather than to a public or governmental entity.

A number of theories have evolved that seek to explain or justify the concept of private ownership of property. An early theory that regarded private property as a natural right succumbed to the notion that private property is a legal arrangement created by man. A labor theory which held that things of value were created by man had little acceptance with respect to land, which is a product of nature. More modernly, private property has been explained by a social welfare theory which holds that society has granted the right of private ownership of things because society is better off when its members have such a right. This theory assumes that society's recognition of private property affords an inducement to economic activity and a stimulus to the accumulation of wealth.

Historically, all of the land in the United States was owned by one government or another. As the country grew in size and population, ownership of much of the land passed from public to private ownership. The various methods by which the movement of land from public to private ownership took place are examined in Chapter 4, "Origins of Private Ownership of Real Property."

Basic to our system of private property is society's assumption that it is highly desirable for individuals to have a high degree of freedom to use the things they own. It is recognized, however, that if society is to survive, this freedom cannot be absolute. Therefore, in the interests of promoting the public health, safety, morals, and general welfare, society has deemed it desirable to impose certain controls or limitations on the right of private ownership of property.

As noted above, the use of land by private owners has increasingly been subjected to regulation as urban areas have grown and larger numbers of people seek to occupy a limited amount of space. But the power of government

---

[15] *Gale v. York Center Community Coop., Inc.* 21 Ill. 2d 86, 92, 171 N.E.2d 30, 33 (1960).

[16] *Restatement of the Law of Property,* sec. 410, Comment a.

to interfere with private ownership of property is not an unlimited one. Ever since the birth of the nation, private property has been accorded protection from undue intervention by overzealous public authorities.

CONSTITUTIONAL PROTECTION OF PRIVATE PROPERTY

The federal constitution and all state constitutions protect the right of private property from governmental action. An individual's right to use that which he owns is a fundamental right safeguarded by all constitutions. Because constitutional provisions are interpreted and applied by the courts, the exact nature and extent of any constitutional guarantee is a function of the judicial philosophy prevailing at the time a decision is rendered.

The right of private property did not originate with the Constitution but was a right that existed at the time of its adoption. The Constitution reaffirmed the prior existence of the right by expressly providing for its protection.

Constitutional protection for private property rights is afforded by (1) the due process of law requirement, (2) the guarantee of equal protection of the laws, and (3) the prohibition against unreasonable search and seizure.

Due Process of Law

Two amendments to the U.S. Constitution protect an owner from being deprived of his property without **due process of law.** The Fifth Amendment, which states that "No person . . . shall be deprived of life, liberty, or property, without due process of law . . . .," limits the power of the federal government, while the Fourteenth Amendment provides that no state shall "deprive any person of life, liberty, or property without due process of law . . . ." As the term "property" is used in these amendments, it refers not only to the thing that is owned but to all rights of ownership as well.

The guarantee of due process of law is one of the most important protections afforded an individual by the federal constitution. It has been said that without such a guarantee the right of private property as we know it today could not exist. It should be recognized, however, that the right of private property as guaranteed by the Constitution is not an absolute right but is, as we have seen, one that is subject to reasonable regulation and limitation through the exercise of the police power. In our society, all property is held subject to the implied condition that it shall not be used in a way that is injurious to society.

It is often difficult to determine whether there has been an unconstitutional deprivation of private property rights in any particular case. Reasonable restrictions may always be imposed on property without violating due process, and emergency or temporary limitations commonly are sustained by the courts. The question that arises in due process cases is whether a restriction imposed on property under a given set of circumstances constitutes a bona fide exercise of the police power, or whether the restriction wrongfully deprives a property owner of his constitutional rights.

The Constitution's due process of law provisions protect the rights of individuals in two ways, one of which is procedural, the other substantive.

Procedural Due Process Under **procedural due process of law,** a person must (1) be given notice of the intention to deprive him of his life, liberty, or property, and he must (2) be afforded a hearing in which he has the opportunity to defend himself against the deprivation. The idea underlying procedural due process is revealed in the often-repeated statement that "every person is entitled to his day in court."

No particular form of procedure or proceeding is required to satisfy the guarantee of due process of law. All that is required is that the notice which is given and the opportunity to be heard be consistent with essential fairness.

Substantive Due Process Under **substantive due process of law,** an individual is guaranteed

INTRODUCTION

that, in addition to being entitled to notice of a proceeding and an opportunity to be heard in defense of his interests, he shall not unreasonably or arbitrarily be deprived of his life, liberty, or property. Substantive due process imposes a limitation on the government's exercise of power and is a guarantee against arbitrary legislation. It requires that the objective of a law be neither unreasonable nor capricious and that the means selected have a real and substantial relation to the objective sought to be attained.

Equal Protection of the Laws

The Fourteenth Amendment to the U.S. Constitution provides that no state shall "deny any person within its jurisdiction the equal protection of the laws." Although the term "equal protection of the laws" has not been precisely defined, it has repeatedly been said that the provision means that no person or class of persons shall be denied the same protection of the laws that another person or persons in the same situation enjoy with respect to life, liberty, property, or the pursuit of happiness.

While the constitutional equal-protection provision does not require states to treat all owners of property identically, it does require that all property owners in like circumstances be treated alike, both as to privileges conferred and obligations imposed by legislation. Consequently, when the validity of a state law is challenged, the issue raised is whether the law has established reasonable classifications of persons and situations. As we shall see in Chapter 20, "Zoning," a person whose freedom to use his land has been curtailed by statute may seek to have the statute declared unconstitutional as applied to him because of his inclusion in an unfair or unreasonable statutory classification. But unless the classification is found to be arbitrary in view of the statute's objective, the courts will sustain the statute.

Although the equal-protection clause of the federal constitution does not affect a state's proper exercise of the police power, it is well settled that the police power is subordinate to the constitutional provision and that any attempted exercise of the power that is discriminatory because it denies a person or class of persons the equal protection of the laws is invalid.

Unreasonable Search and Seizure Prohibited

The Fourth Amendment to the U.S. Constitution affords the owner or occupant of real estate protection against unreasonable searches of his premises and seizures of his property by federal and state officials. The amendment provides that "The right of the people to be secure in their persons, houses, papers, and effects, against unreasonable searches and seizures, shall not be violated . . ."[17] Although the amendment only mentions "houses," the term has been construed as including any dwelling or office.[18] The protection provided by the amendment is referred to by the courts as a *right of privacy*.[19]

Questions involving the scope of the amendment's protection most commonly arise in connection with the efforts of law enforcement officers to hunt out and apprehend criminals. The amendment is not violated when a search warrant based on probable cause has been issued and which particularly describes the premises to be searched and the things to be seized. Nor is the amendment violated if, at the time of an arrest, a search is made to locate and seize products of the crime or to discover weapons that might endanger the safety of arresting officers.

The protection afforded an occupant of real property is not limited solely to searches to obtain evidence of criminal activity. In recent

---

[17] The Fourth Amendment further provides that ". . . no warrants shall issue, but upon probable cause, supported by oath or affirmation, and particularly describing the place to be searched, and the persons or things to be seized."

[18] *Gouled v. United States,* 255 U.S. 298, 41 Sup. Ct. 261 (1921).

[19] See, for example, *Wolf v. Colorado,* 338 U.S. 25, 69 Sup. Ct. 1359 (1949).

years, the importance of "administrative searches" or inspections to discover health, fire, or housing code violations has increased. Inspections of this type typically are not for the purpose of obtaining criminal evidence, but rather are for the protection of the public health and safety. In response to the question whether a search warrant is required before making such inspections, the U.S. Supreme Court has held[20] that administrative inspections are searches to which the protection of the Fourteenth Amendment applies. Therefore, in the absence of an occupant's *consent* or an *emergency situation,* a search warrant must be obtained before his premises can be inspected.

[20] *Camara v. Municipal Court of the City and County of San Francisco,* 387 U.S. 523, 87 Sup. Ct. 1727 (1967) (involving a residence); *See v. City of Seattle,* 387 U.S. 541, 87 Sup. Ct. 1737 (1967) (involving commercial premises).

QUESTIONS

1 What is the purpose of law? How is that purpose achieved?
2 What is meant by the statement that for every legal right there is a corresponding legal duty?
3 What is the doctrine of *stare decisis?*
4 Differentiate between the two meanings of the word "property."
5 With respect to their basic characteristics, how does real property differ from personal property?
6 Explain what is meant by the term "ownership."
7 What is the meaning of the word "title" as that word is commonly used with respect to real estate?
8 Explain why the right of possession of real estate is considered to be the single most important incident of ownership of it.
9 What is meant by the statement that an owner's exclusive right to use his property is not an absolute right?
10 What is meant by the statement that the right to own property is a natural right?
11 Describe the nature of the police power.
12 As it relates to real estate, the police power is said to be negative or inhibitory in character. Explain.
13 What are the principal limitations on the exercise of the police power by a state?
14 What is a "restraint on alienation?"
15 What is the distinction between procedural due process of law and substantive due process?

Chapter 2

The Physical Components of Real Estate

When a parcel of real estate is transferred from one owner to another, that parcel is identified by reference to its boundary lines and the location of those lines on the earth's surface. Generally speaking, the descriptive language contained in a deed or other document of transfer merely refers to measurements and directions of boundary lines without separately specifying the physical components of which a parcel of land enclosed by those lines is composed. Under such circumstances, the physical characteristics of the space that is acquired by the transferee are determined by operation of law. In other words, unless otherwise expressly excluded by the language of a deed or other instrument, there are certain physical elements of space that are included in every transfer of title because they are part of the real estate itself.

From the legal point of view, the physical elements of which real estate is composed are (1) the land, (2) fixtures or those things that are attached to the land, and (3) appurtenances or those things that belong to the land. These are the material elements which in combination make up the economic good known as real estate and which pass automatically in any transfer of real property without the need to be specifically indicated in the transferring document.

LAND

Although the term is often used in a much broader sense, the word **land** as used for the purposes of this chapter refers to land in its *raw* or *unimproved* state only.

In its raw or unimproved state, a parcel of land has three distinguishable physical features: (1) the *surface* of the land, (2) the *airspace* above the surface, and (3) the *subsurface* beneath it. Therefore one who holds title to a plot of land not only owns the surface of the earth but the airspace above and the earth below the surface as well. As expressed in an ancient doctrine of the common law, the ownership of land extends from the "depths of the earth to the highest reaches of the heavens." While this early common law doctrine is, in a general way, still indicative of the physical nature of land, the doctrine has been modified and limited both by legislation and by judicial decision.

The Surface
A significant attribute of ownership of land is the owner's right to possess, use, and enjoy his land to the exclusion of all other persons. Though this right is said to be an exclusive one, it is neither absolute nor unlimited. As we shall have further occasion to see, the use to which real property may be put is regulated by numerous controls that have been imposed by law and by public policy. Aside from those limitations, however, an owner of land may do as he sees fit with his property.

An important aspect of an owner's right to use and enjoy his land is his right to prevent entry upon it and subsequent use of it by any person without the owner's express or implied permission. An unlawful entry upon another person's land or the interference with an owner's possession of it is a legal wrong known as a **trespass.** In addition to being an actionable civil wrong, known as a **tort,** for which damages may be had, a trespass in some instances is a criminal act as well.

The Airspace
Limitations on Ownership The common law notion that a landowner owned the airspace above his land "to the highest reaches of the heavens" was not seriously challenged until the early 1920s when the flight of aircraft became more common. Following a series of both state and lower federal court decisions, the question of rights to airspace was finally decided by the U. S. Supreme Court in 1946.[1] The court in its decision said that "The landowner owns as much space above the ground as he can occupy or use in connection with the land. The fact that he does not occupy it in a physical sense—by the erection of buildings and the like—is not material."

As is evident from the court's statement, the height to which the airspace above his land is owned by a landowner is not a fixed distance. As the owner of a parcel of land, he owns the airspace above the surface of it to the extent that he can reasonably and beneficially use and enjoy the airspace. Exactly what constitutes "reasonable and beneficial" use and enjoyment of airspace depends upon the facts and circumstances of each case.

Some states by statute have sought to define the limitations on the ownership of airspace more precisely. For example, California[2] has stated that ownership of the airspace is vested in the surface owner subject to the right of flight as prescribed by federal authorities.

Both federal and state statutory law and judicial decisions have declared national sovereignty and control over the navigable airspace and the right of passage by aircraft in such space. In resolving airspace controversies, the courts have endeavored to balance the respective interests of both navigable and nonnavigable airspace owners without unduly limiting the development of aviation on the one hand or hampering the rights of landowners on the other.

Invasions of Airspace Like his ownership of the surface, a landowner's ownership of the airspace above the surface gives him the exclusive right to its use and enjoyment. Any unprivileged interference with the use or possession of an owner's airspace constitutes a legal wrong in the nature of a nuisance or a trespass that may be remedied by the landowner.

For example, where the branches of trees

---
[1] *United States v. Causby,* 328 U.S. 256 (1946).

[2] California Public Utilities Code, sec. 21402.

with trunks located on A's property overhang into the airspace above B's property, B is entitled to have a court order A to remove the intruding branches and to recover any damages he sustained. In some jurisdictions and under certain circumstances, B may resort to **"self-help"** and remove the offending branches himself.

Despite the fact that the operation of aircraft when carried on in furtherance of the public interest may not be enjoined by a landowner, the noise, vibration, etc., may interfere with his rights of reasonable and beneficial use to such an extent that his property is considered to have been "taken" for a public use. Depending upon the particular facts of the case, the property interest that is taken for a public purpose may either be **title** to the airspace or it may merely be the right of use in the nature of an air **easement**.[3] In either case, the landowner has a constitutional right to be compensated for the taking of his property rights in the airspace that is owned by him.

Separation of Surface and Airspace Following are three ways to separate surface and airspace.

By Sale or Lease To the extent that a landowner owns the airspace above his land, he may sell it or lease it while retaining the ownership and use of the surface. For example, in Chicago the Prudential Mid-America Building rises 40 stories over the Illinois Central Terminal; in Boston the 52-story Prudential Tower sets atop the Massachusetts Turnpike; and in New York the 59-story Pan-Am Building occupies the airspace above Grand Central Terminal. Construction of these "air-borne" buildings necessitates the acquisition of surface easements by the purchaser or lessor of the airspace for supporting columns and possible service installations.

Statutes in some jurisdictions[4] authorize state agencies to lease the airspace above state highways for uses that do not interfere with the flow of traffic. Legislation in other states[5] permits municipalities to lease airspace above streets and alleys. As the need for more space in urban areas increases, the utilization and development of airspace is a logical direction in which to turn. Consequently, it is reasonable to assume that planners and developers will look increasingly to the feasibility of making use of the unoccupied space above highways, freeways, expressways, bridge approaches, and similar surface uses of land.

By Subdivision Just as a landowner can divide the surface of his plot of land into a number of smaller parcels, he can also subdivide the airspace that he owns above his land's surface. An owner can either sell the airspace layer by layer or he can divide it into cubes or other configurations of space. This process is sometimes referred to as "horizontal" subdividing as distinguished from "vertical" subdividing, which occurs when the surface area is separated into parcels.

Horizontal subdivision and sale of units of airspace have given rise to an increasingly popular form of ownership of real property known as the **condominium.** The condominium form of ownership results when ownership of the surface land is separated from the airspace above it and the airspace is subdivided into individually owned units. In a condominium arrangement involving apartment-type units, the airspace within a unit is owned separately by the occupant while the land, supporting walls, and all common areas are co-owned by all of the owners of the subdivided units of airspace collectively.

By Condemnation By means of **condemnation,** public authorities may acquire either title

---

[3] The nature of an easement is discussed in Chapter 7.

[4] California, Connecticut, Massachusetts, and Washington, for example, have such statutes.

[5] For instance, Illinois and Wisconsin.

to or an easement in a landowner's airspace that entitles the authorities to use that airspace for some public purpose. As we shall have more occasion to see in Chapter 11, condemnation is a court proceeding by means of which a private owner's real property is taken for a public purpose and for which payment of an amount equal to the property's market value is made to the owner.

The Subsurface

The owner of a parcel of land not only owns the surface of the earth and the airspace above it, but he owns the earth beneath the surface as well. Ownership of a parcel of land has been likened to ownership of an inverted pyramid of space with its vertex at the center of the earth and its base somewhere out in the airspace.

The question as to ownership of the subsurface area of a parcel of land is significant not only because of the support it affords the surface of the land but also because of the fact that the earth below the surface may contain valuable minerals. Since minerals in place in the subsurface are a part of the real property itself, ownership of them passes to a buyer of land even though the deed which transfers title to a parcel of land makes no specific mention of the minerals.

While oil and gas and solid materials such as coal, ores, and metals are all classified as minerals, oil and gas, because of their distinct physical characteristics, are treated differently from solid minerals in some states.

Solid Minerals As long as solid minerals such as metals and ores remain in their natural place in the earth, they are legally part of the real property and belong to whomsoever owns the land in which they are located. Once the minerals have been mined and brought to the surface, however, they are said to have been severed from the real property and by that act they are converted into personal property. The significance of this conversion from real to personal property is that the mined or extracted minerals will no longer pass with the transfer of the land unless the document of transfer specifically indicates that they are intended to do so.

Separation of Surface and Subsurface Rights In addition to the right of an owner to use and enjoy his property, a significant incident of ownership is the owner's right to dispose of his property if he so chooses. An owner of land may transfer the entire parcel that he owns, or if he so desires, he may divide the parcel and transfer only part of it. The owner can, as we have seen, divide the surface of his land into several smaller parcels and dispose of some of them while retaining ownership of others. We have seen also that a landowner can dispose of portions of the airspace above his land while retaining the rest of the airspace and the other components of his property. Now we see that a landowner has the legal ability to separate ownership of the surface from ownership of the subsurface. The owner can effect this separation either by retaining ownership of the surface and transferring title to a specified layer of the subsurface to another person or, conversely, he may transfer the surface and retain the subsurface.

Right to Extract Instead of transferring ownership of a subsurface stratum of mineral-bearing land to another person, the landowner may simply grant that person the *right to extract* minerals either for a stated period of time or until the minerals are depleted. In such a case, the landowner continues to own both the surface and the subsurface of his land while the other person has the exclusive right to penetrate the subsurface and remove the minerals, which is an interest technically known as a *profit à prendre*. More commonly, the owner of the *profit à prendre* is said to own the "mineral rights" in the property.

Right of Surface Entry The reason for owning the subsurface of land or the mineral rights in the land is, of course, to explore for and exploit any minerals that might be found there. In order that exploration and extraction may be accomplished, the owner of the minerals must have some means of access to them. A well-drafted document transferring mineral rights would make reference to the transferee's right to enter the premises and, where the right is granted, indicate the manner of entering upon the surface to exercise the mineral rights. Unfortunately, however, documents sometimes fail to make mention of these matters. When a document that creates mineral rights is silent concerning the **right of surface entry,** the owner of the mineral rights is said to acquire that right by implication. This means that the law presumes that the parties intended to provide for the right of entry but overlooked making an express provision for it. This presumption arises from the fact that mineral rights are of little value if the minerals cannot be removed. From the legal point of view, an implied right of surface entry is just as effective as if the document had expressly granted the right.

Where the right of surface entry is implied, there is, of course, no agreement between the parties as to where and how the exploitation operation will be carried on. Under such circumstances, it is said that the owner of the mineral rights may enter upon the surface and carry on his operations in any "reasonable" manner, with the issue of "reasonableness" being a question of fact for jury determination.

The implied right of surface entry for the purpose of exploring for and exploiting minerals can be defeated by a provision in an instrument conveying mineral rights that *expressly* denies the right of entry. Under such circumstances, the owner of the mineral rights will have to use the surface of adjoining properties as a base for his exploration and exploitation operations.

Oil and Gas Because of their migratory character, oil and gas differ from other types of minerals found in the earth's crust. When a pool or reservoir is tapped by a well drilled on the surface of one owner's land, the well may drain oil and gas from areas of the reservoir that are located beneath the land of other owners. This fact has given rise to the question, not presented where solid minerals are concerned, as to whether and how a landowner can own the oil and gas that underlays his land.

Among the states that produce petroleum in commercial quantities, two distinct theories concerning the nature of a landowner's rights to oil and gas beneath his land have been developed, namely, (1) the ownership-in-place theory and (2) the nonownership theory.

Ownership-in-Place Theory According to the **ownership-in-place theory**, a landowner owns all substances, including oil and gas, that underlie the surface of his land. Unlike his ownership of the solid minerals in place beneath the surface, however, his ownership of the underlying oil and gas is not absolute but is subject to the "right of capture" by adjacent landowners.

The ownership-in-place theory has been adopted by a number of petroleum-producing states.[6]

Nonownership Theory The **nonownership theory** holds that ownership of land does not carry with it ownership of the oil and gas beneath the surface, but merely gives to the landowner the exclusive right to drill on his premises. According to this theory, no person owns oil and gas while it is still in the ground, but each overlying landowner has the exclusive right to extract the oil by operations conducted on his land. Of course, no one may go upon another's land to drill for oil without that landowner's permission.

States that subscribe to the nonownership theory[7] have rejected the ownership-in-place theory as being illogical.

The Rule of Capture The so-called **rule of capture** says that a landowner acquires ownership of oil and gas that he produces from wells

---

[6] For example, the theory is adhered to by Alabama, Arkansas, Colorado, Kansas, Michigan, Mississippi, Montana, Ohio, Pennsylvania, Texas, and West Virginia.

[7] For example, California, Illinois, Indiana, Louisiana, Kentucky, and Oklahoma.

on his land, even though part of that oil and gas may have migrated from the subsurface of adjoining lands. The landowner who captures the oil and gas has no liability to the owners of lands from which the oil and gas have been drained, provided, of course, that the wells themselves do not trespass upon their properties. Under the rule of capture, and in the absence of any statutes regulating drilling practices, an owner may drill as many wells as he pleases on his land and not be liable to other landowners whose lands are drained by his operations. Each adjacent landowner has the right to do likewise.

The term **correlative rights** is sometimes used in connection with oil and gas rights. As used in that connection, the term refers to the rights of owners of land that overlies a common supply of oil and gas and subjects each overlying owner to the duty to all other overlying owners not to waste the substance extracted nor to injure or spoil the common reservoir. The doctrine of correlative rights complements the rule of capture by defining reciprocal standards of fair play to be followed by all who take oil and gas from a common source.

Consequences of the Theory Adopted Both of the theories relating to oil and gas rights give an overlying landowner the exclusive right to drill a well on his land and extract oil and gas. And, within the constraints of the doctrine of correlative rights, both theories permit a landowner to own the oil and gas that he brings to the surface, despite the fact that it may have been drained from beneath another's land. In view of the similarity in the substantive features of the two theories, the question arises: what difference does it make which of the theories is adopted by a given state?

Perhaps the most significant consequence of the selection of one theory over the other has to do with oil and gas interests being classified as real property or as personal property. Classifying the interests as real property (as the ownership-in-place theory does) or as personal property (as the nonownership theory does) has significance regarding the type of instrument required to transfer title to oil and gas interests separately from the overlying land. Classification as real or personal property also has a bearing on the remedies that are available to owners for the protection of their respective interests.

Regardless of which theory a state may adopt, the transfer of ownership of land that overlies a reservoir will also transfer the oil and gas interest without the need for the instrument of transfer to expressly so state. Under the ownership-in-place theory, the oil and gas interests pass as part of the real property. Under the nonownership theory, they pass as an appurtenance to the land.

Separate Ownership of Oil and Gas Rights
We have seen that a landowner's rights with respect to oil and gas underlying his land include the right to drill wells, to extract and dispose of the oil produced, and to exclude others from drilling on his property or sharing the ownership of the oil that has been extracted. It is quite uncommon, however, for the owner of land to do the actual drilling for and extracting of oil and gas from his land. More commonly the oil and gas resources are developed by some person other than the landowner in accordance with the provisions of an agreement authorizing that person to do so.

An **oil and gas lease** is the typical arrangement for the exploitation of oil and gas resources by someone other than the owner of the land where they are located. The lessor in such a lease is the person who owns the land and the oil and gas rights, but who is not engaged in or familiar with the oil and gas extraction business. The lessee who acquires the oil and gas rights in the lessor's land, on the other hand, will commonly be a person or firm engaged in the business of producing petroleum. Such a person or firm is generally not interested in owning the oil-producing land but only in owning the rights to produce oil from it. The effect of the leasing arrangement is to separate the development rights in oil and gas from the land in which it is located.

Subject to controls imposed by conservation laws, an oil and gas lease gives the lessee the exclusive and unlimited right to explore for oil and gas by drilling wells, to extract the oil and gas when found, and to acquire ownership of it as personal property. In exchange for having granted the lessee such rights, the lessor receives, depending on the particular terms of the lease, compensation which may include: (1) a bonus of a stated number of dollars per acre upon execution of the lease; (2) an annual rental of a stipulated amount per acre which is paid for the lessee's privilege of postponing the beginning of drilling operations; and (3) royalties in the form of a percentage of the amount of oil and gas produced once operations have begun.

The owner of oil and gas rights has the same right of surface entry for purposes of exploration and exploitation as is possessed by the owner of solid mineral rights, whose rights were described above.

FIXTURES

A second major physical component of real estate is known as a fixture.

Nature of a Fixture

A **fixture** is something that originally was personal property but which has been attached to real property in such a manner as to be regarded in law as a part of the real property itself. Fixtures include all those things that laymen generally refer to as "improvements," such as houses, outbuildings, patios, fences, and so forth, but the term is not limited to such major items. Included in the term is any item of personal property, large or small, that has been so affixed to real property as to lose its personal property characteristics and become a part of the real estate to which it is attached.

Controversies Involving Fixtures Controversies involving fixtures are not uncommon. They frequently arise between landlords and tenants, buyers and sellers of real estate, and creditors with security interests in real or personal property. The issue involved in fixture cases is not whether a fixture is or is not real property, because by definition fixtures are real property. The issue in fixture cases centers on the question whether the particular thing or things in controversy are in fact fixtures. For example, a buyer of a house may contest the seller's right to remove certain equipment when he vacates the premises, the buyer claiming that it is a fixture. Or a tenant may insist on his right to remove a certain item that he installed in the leased premises, contending that the item never became a fixture.

Whether an article that is attached to real property has become a fixture or not is a question of fact to be determined by the jury in each case. To assist a jury in arriving at its determination, certain tests for distinguishing a fixture from personal property have been developed, both by court decisions and by legislation. Although a number of different tests have been developed, the primary factor in determining the character of the item involved in a controversy is the *intention* of the party at the time he attached the article to the real estate.

Importance of Intent

Determining a person's intention is frequently not an easy task. A person's actual intention is a mental or subjective matter that can only be ascertained by some outward manifestation by him. His manifestation may take the form of words or acts which may clearly express his intention, or his words and acts may require interpretation. Where disputes involving fixtures arise, the problem ordinarily is one of determining a person's intent as reflected by his actions rather than by his words.

The courts rely on several factors to assist them in ascertaining the intention of a person who has attached something to real estate. The relevant factors include such matters as: (1) the manner or method of attachment of the item in question, and its removability without injury to the premises; (2) the extent to which the attached article is specifically adapted to the use and operation of the premises; and (3) the nature of the person's legal interest in the premises at the time he attached the item to the real property. Although each of the foregoing factors is generally considered in every case, they are not necessarily accorded the same weight.

Common versus Divided Ownership

Most controversies that involve the question whether an article is a fixture or is personal property fall in one of two general categories: (1) the so-called *common ownership* cases and (2) the *divided ownership* cases.

Common Ownership In common ownership cases, the same person owns both the real property and the personal property that he attaches to it. The ready example of such a situation is the homeowner who installs certain equipment in his home and later, after entering into a contract to sell his home, removes the equipment. If the language of the sales agreement neither expressly includes nor excludes the sales transaction, the courts are inclined to find that the installed equipment is a fixture. In doing so, the courts adopt the view that there is no reason to believe that, at the time of making the installation, the owner had any intention other than to make the installed item a permanent part of the real estate.

Divided Ownership In divided ownership cases, the owner of the personal property attaches it to real property that belongs to another person. For example, a tenant may install something in his leased premises to make them more attractive or comfortable for his use. When his lease expires, the tenant attempts to remove the installed item but the landlord objects and claims that the attached article has lost its character as personal property of the tenant and has become a fixture that belongs to the landlord. In cases such as this, there is a strong public policy opposed to finding the installed item to be a fixture. It is obvious, the reasoning behind the policy goes, that the tenant had no intention of enriching his landlord by making a gift of the installed item to him.

Trade Fixtures

The policy that opposes forfeiture of articles installed by tenants and the enrichment of landlords that would result is the basis of the **trade fixture** doctrine. According to that doctrine, if an installed item qualifies as being a trade fixture, it retains its character as personal property and remains the property of the tenant. This doctrine was early recognized by the courts in the United States and is the subject of statutory provision in a number of states.[8]

Limited to Landlord-Tenant Relationship The trade fixture doctrine is limited to the landlord-tenant relationship but is broader than the term "trade" would suggest. As the language of California's trade fixture statute[9] indicates, the doctrine includes any item attached by a tenant "for the purposes of trade, manufacture, ornament, or domestic use."

Loss of Trade Fixture Status An attached article loses its status as a trade fixture and consequently cannot be removed by a tenant if its removal would cause material damage to the landlord's premises. Under such circumstances, the thing that has been attached is sometimes said to have become an "integral part" of the premises.

---

[8] Among them are California, Georgia, Idaho, Illinois, Louisiana, Oklahoma, and Rhode Island.
[9] California Civil Code, sec. 1019.

Whether an installed article can be removed without material damage to the premises is a question of fact in each case in which the issue arises.

Time for Removal   An item that qualifies as a trade fixture may be removed at any time during the period of the tenant's lease or within a reasonable period of time after the lease has expired. If not removed within the allowable time period, the right of removal is forever lost—which is the same as saying that the item has lost its status as a trade fixture and has become a part of the real property.

Where a tenant has a lease for a definite or fixed term, some courts hold that a trade fixture must be removed before the term of the lease has expired. On the other hand, if the tenant's term is not for a fixed period, as where it runs from month to month, these courts allow him a reasonable period of time after expiration of the lease to remove the trade fixture. Other courts, however, apply the reasonable time rule to all tenants, whether their leases run for fixed periods or not.

Quite aside from the trade fixture doctrine, the provisions of some leases expressly give the tenant the right to remove items installed by him. Where this is the case, courts normally allow the tenant a reasonable time after expiration of the lease to remove installed items.

As is always true with regard to "reasonableness," what constitutes a reasonable period of time after a lease has terminated is a question of fact to be determined in each case.

The Mistaken Improver

Status as a Trespasser   There are times when an occupier of real property improves that property in the good-faith but mistaken belief that he owns it. Such an innocent but **mistaken improver** is legally a trespasser who must relinquish possession of the land he occupies to its rightful owner. The question that arises when the trespassing improver is ousted from the land is whether he may remove the improvements he has made to the land or whether those improvements have become the property of the owner of the land.

At common law the rule was that the improvements, whether made by an innocent trespasser or a willful one, belonged to the owner of the land. In many states today, however, the harshness of the common rule has been ameliorated with respect to the mistaken improver who acted in good faith.

Good-Faith Improver   A **good-faith improver** is a person who makes improvements to land acting in the honest but erroneous belief, due to a mistake of law or fact, that he is the owner of the land. The good-faith improver's mistake about ownership of the property he improves might arise where he owns one lot in a subdivision but through error builds on another, where a mistake is made in the location of a boundary line, or where the deed to the property that he improves turns out to be invalid.

The term "improvement" refers not only to buildings and other structures but to other things as well. Improvements include such things as repairs necessary to preserve a building, substantial additions or alterations to buildings, preparing land for a building site, preparing land for agricultural purposes, and planting orchards and hedges.

Good faith requires that the improver honestly and reasonably believed that he owned the land he improved. He must be free from any intent or scheme to defraud the party whose land is improved. In every case the burden is on the good-faith improver to establish that he acted with no knowledge that the land he improved belonged to another. In addition, he must have exercised at least the degree of diligence with respect to the situation that a reasonable person would have exercised under the circumstances. To qualify as a good-faith improver, his mistake must not have resulted from negligence on his part.

Statutes[10] and court decisions give relief to the person who, in the good-faith belief that he is the owner, mistakenly improves real property that belongs to another person. The relief afforded the mistaken improver under such circumstances falls into three categories: (1) the right of setoff, (2) the right of removal, and (3) the adjustment of rights and equities.

Right of Setoff If the landowner brings an action against the mistaken improver for **damages** arising from the wrongful occupancy of his property, the improver is permitted to setoff against the damages awarded the amount by which the improvements he made enhance the value of the land. Obviously, if the owner only brings an action for restoration of possession and does not seek money damages for the wrongful occupancy, the right of setoff is not available to the mistaken improver.

Right of Removal In those instances where the right of setoff is not available to or suitable for the good-faith improver, statutes in some states give him the right to remove the improvements he has made, providing he pays the landowner for all damages that result from the installation and subsequent removal of the improvements.

It might happen, however, that the improvements are of a type that either cannot be removed at all or would be valueless when removed—as, for example, a drainage canal, irrigation ditch, or concrete driveway. If the improvements are of this type, and if the right of setoff is not available to the good-faith improver, a third form of relief may still be available to him.

Adjustment of Rights and Equities Some states permit a good-faith improver to bring an action to have the court adjust the rights and equities of the parties. In adjusting the parties' rights and equities, the court may exercise any of its legal or equitable powers and grant any of a number of forms of relief. For example, the court might order that title to the improvements be quieted in the owner of the land on the condition that he pay the improver the value of the improvements. Or, where the owner does not want the improvements and they cannot be removed economically, the court may grant title to the land to the improver on the condition that he pay the landowner the market value of the property. Where no remedy can be devised which would fully protect the landowner against pecuniary loss, the court may deny the improver any relief at all.

No Relief Available to Willful Trespasser Neither the willful trespasser who improves property nor the mistaken improver who is unable to establish his good faith is entitled to recover his improvement or its value. He will, of course, be liable to the landowner for any damages resulting from his trespass and occupancy. And, in those instances where the landowner does not want the improvements that the willful trespasser made to the land, the trespasser will be required to remove them or bear the cost of having them removed.

APPURTENANCES

The third component of real estate, in addition to land and fixtures, consists of those things which are said to be incidental or appurtenant to the property. Such things are generally referred to as **appurtenances** and belong to the particular parcel of land to which they are incidental. A thing is deemed to be incidental or appurtenant to land when it may legally be used for the benefit of that land.

Although appurtenances are of many different types, easements and water rights are among the more common. An easement is an interest that one landowner has in another person's land that benefits the land to which the easement belongs. Because of the scope of the subject, easements are discussed separately in Chapter 8.

---

[10] In Alabama, California, Florida, Illinois, Michigan, Ohio, Texas, Virginia, and Wisconsin, for example.

A brief survey of appurtenances in the form of water rights follows.

Water Rights

American law has classified landowners' rights with respect to water in streams or watercourses in two categories: (1) riparian rights and (2) rights arising from prior appropriation. Most states recognize either one type of right or the other, but there are several states in which both categories of water rights are recognized. An important factor in determining the nature of water rights in a given locality is the annual amount and the regularity of rainfall.

Owners of lands along a stream or in an artesian basin have ready access to water therein and it is inevitable that controversies will arise as a result of the various owners' use of the same natural resource. A landowner's need for water is, of course, dependent upon the use to which he puts his land.

Riparian Rights The principal feature of the doctrine of **riparian rights** is that owners of lands bordering on a stream or watercourse have equal right to the use of the water in the stream. These rights arise out of the fact of ownership and possession of bordering lands, which are known as **riparian lands.**

In applying the principle of equal rights to the use of water by riparian owners, two theories have been developed: (1) the natural flow theory and (2) the reasonable use theory.

Natural Flow Theory Under the **natural flow theory** of riparian rights, each riparian owner has an equal right to have the water in the stream flow as it is accustomed to flow by nature, qualified only by the equal rights of other riparian owners to make use of the water as the stream flows past their lands. For domestic purposes such as drinking, cooking, bathing, etc., each owner of riparian lands has an unlimited right to use water from the stream. But when the water is taken for purposes of irrigation, manufacturing, or other nondomestic use, the limitations placed upon a riparian owner's use of water come very close to those imposed by the "reasonable use" approach to water rights.

Reasonable Use Theory The fundamental right of a riparian owner under the **reasonable use theory** is the right to be free from any unreasonable interference with his use of water in the stream. The theory permits each owner to make beneficial use of water on his riparian lands for any purpose, providing such use does not unreasonably interfere with beneficial uses by other riparian owners. Reasonableness of use by a riparian owner is a question of fact to be determined from the circumstances of each case.

Riparian Lands The determination of reasonableness of water use is significantly influenced by whether the use occurs on riparian lands. Because of this significance, it is useful to note the characteristics of riparian land.

To be considered riparian, land must be in actual contact with a stream. Physical adjacency with the watercourse is an indispensable requisite of riparian land. In addition, the land bordering on the stream must be within the **watershed** of that stream. The watershed is the drainage area which contributes to the quantity of water in the stream.

California and a few other states further restrict riparian land to the smallest area presently fronting on a stream that has ever been held by any owner in the chain of title.

Prior Appropriation The doctrine of **prior appropriation** is the basis of a system of water rights that is very different from riparian rights. The doctrine was evolved by settlers in the arid and semiarid states to meet their needs arising from a shortage of water.

Basis of the Doctrine The two fundamental principles of prior appropriation are: (1) that the basis of the right to water is not land ownership but rather the beneficial use to which water is put; and (2) that the basis of the division of water between users when there is not enough for all is not equality of right but priority of use.

The doctrine operates as follows. A western stream typically has many irrigators who acquired their rights to the use of water at different times. When the mountain snowpack melts, the level of the stream is high and the supply of water plentiful, but the quantity of water decreases appreciably during the dry summer. To cope with the diminished flow, the rights of users (appropriators) to take water from the stream are cut off in the inverse order in which those rights were originally acquired. That is to say, the last irrigation ditch to be constructed and opened onto the stream is the first one to be shut off from a supply of water. The first ditch that was opened by the first appropriator is never closed. The right of a senior or prior appropriator extends to later appropriators both upstream from him and downstream. A senior or prior appropriator may take water that is needed by a junior or later appropriator downstream from him, while a junior appropriator located upstream from him must let the water go past unused when it is needed by the prior appropriator. There is no prorating of water among appropriators in times of scarcity. The consequences of the water shortage are borne by junior appropriators.

Obtaining the Right of Appropriation Water codes in the appropriation states establish procedures for obtaining appropriative rights. In all but three of the appropriation states[11] a permit system is in effect.

The typical procedures require the filing of an application for a permit to appropriate and the publication of notice of the fact that an application has been filed. Thereafter a hearing on the application is held, at which time persons who may be affected by the proposed appropriation may be heard. If the outcome of the hearing is favorable a permit is granted,

[11] Alaska, Colorado, and Montana.

upon issuance of which the appropriator may commence construction work on his water diversion facility. This facility is inspected following completion and, if approved, a certificate or license is issued to the appropriator by an administrative official.

State Water Systems The fifty states fall into three groups with respect to the system of water rights adopted by them. Some recognize only riparian rights, others only appropriative rights, while others have adopted both systems.

Riparian Rights Only With the exception of Mississippi, all states east of the Mississippi River, Arkansas, Iowa, Louisiana, Minnesota, and Missouri to the west, and Hawaii define water rights in accordance with riparian law. The doctrine of prior appropriation has no application in these states, although in recent years there has been agitation in some of them for shifting from the law of riparian rights to a system employing appropriation concepts.

Appropriative Rights Only Alaska, Arizona, Colorado, Idaho, Montana, Nevada, New Mexico, Utah, and Wyoming have rejected the common law doctrine of riparian rights as being unsuitable to their climatic conditions and geography. The sole basis of the right to use water in these states is prior appropriation.

Both Appropriative and Riparian Rights California, Kansas, Mississippi, Nebraska, North Dakota, Oklahoma, Oregon, South Dakota, Texas, and Washington recognize in varying degrees both riparian rights and the doctrine of prior appropriation. Each state with this dual system of water rights has devised its own method of reconciling the operation of the two systems.

Prescriptive Rights A **prescriptive right** to water arises from the continued wrongful use of water over a period of time. For water rights to be acquired by prescription, certain essential conditions must be met. (1) There must be a *wrongful taking* by a user of water to which another person has rights. (2) The taking must not only be in violation of the rights of the other person, but it also must be carried on in such a manner as to put that person on **notice** of the fact of the taking. (3) The use that is made of the wrongfully taken water must be *beneficial* to the taker. And finally, (4) the wrongful use must be *continued without interruption* for the period of the local statute of limitations that applies to the recovery of real property. Once these elements have been met, the taker acquires the legal right to continue using the quantity of water that he originally took wrongfully.

The right that is acquired by prescription is the right to use water for nonriparian rather than riparian purposes. But the prescriptive right is clearly distinct from prior appropriation, which also permits nonriparian use of water.

Underground Streams Water which flows in underground streams is subject to the same rules as water in streams that flow on the surface of land.

Percolating Waters Percolating waters include all subsurface waters other than those flowing in underground streams. There are several types of percolating waters, including (1) underground lakes and pools, (2) waters of unknown source that seep through the soil, (3) artesian waters, which are under considerable pressure, and (4) water contained in geological formations known as aquifers, which hold substantial amounts of water that move through the formations.

Under the early common law rule, which is still the prevailing view in a number of states,[12] percolating waters are regarded as part of the land in which they are located, and the landowner has substantially unrestricted rights of use. In the majority of jurisdictions, however, the theory of reasonable use is applied to percolating waters.

QUESTIONS

1 Indicate the three physical elments or components of real estate as envisioned by the law.
2 Describe the nature of the legal wrong known as a "trespass."
3 Comment on the extent to which a landowner owns the airspace above his land.
4 Aside from the support it provides for the surface of land, what is the significance of ownership of the area beneath the surface of a parcel of land?
5 Explain what is meant by the expression "implied right of surface entry" as used in connection with ownership of mineral rights in a parcel of land.
6 As they apply to oil and gas rights, how do the ownership-in-place theory and the nonownership theory differ?
7 What is meant by the "rule of capture" with respect to oil and gas rights?
8 What is a fixture, as the term is used in real estate law? Give an example.
9 Give an illustration of a situation in which a controversy might arise as to whether a given item is a fixture or not.
10 What factors are considered by the courts in determining whether a person who attached something to real estate intended that it become a fixture?
11 What is a trade fixture? What is the most significant difference between it and a fixture?
12 Give an example of a situation in which a person who mistakenly improves another's property could be said to have acted in good faith.
13 What is the principal characteristic of the doctrine of riparian rights?
14 Describe the characteristics of the doctrine of prior appropriation as it applies to water rights.
15 Describe the manner in which a prescriptive right to water is acquired.

---

[12] For example, Alabama, Connecticut, Illinois, Maine, Massachusetts, Montana, Ohio, South Dakota, Texas, and Vermont.

Chapter 3

Description of Real Property

Before ownership of a parcel of real estate can be legally transferred from one person to another, the identity of that parcel must be clearly established. A parcel of real property is identified by describing it in such a manner that it can be distinguished from all other units of land on the land mass. As far as the parties to a transaction are concerned, there is generally very little uncertainty in their minds as to the identity of the physical property to be transferred. Problems arise, however, as a result of carelessness or ineptitude in describing the parcel by the one who drafts the instrument by which title is transferred. Indefiniteness of descriptions constitutes one of the principal reasons for holding transfers of real estate invalid.

MEANING AND FUNCTION OF DESCRIPTION

The term "description" as commonly used in land conveyancing refers to the physical property rather than to the legal interest that is being transferred. Furthermore, it is not necessary that the buildings and other improvements on the land be described, but only the land on which they are situated. A valid transfer of an accurately identified parcel of land conveys everything within its boundaries that is real property as defined by the law.

The function of a description is to locate and identify a specific unit or parcel of land. If an instrument is to be valid and capable of transferring title to real property, that instrument must contain what is known in the law of conveyancing as a "sufficient" description.

ADEQUACY OR SUFFICIENCY OF DESCRIPTION

A description of real estate is said to be legally "sufficient" when the language it contains will enable a competent surveyor to physically lo-

DESCRIPTION OF REAL PROPERTY

cate the particular parcel on the landscape. Ideally the description of real property would be complete and unambiguous in all details, thus rendering any other identifying evidence unnecessary. Some descriptions satisfy this desired degree of perfection. Often, however, the description is less than ideal but is still adequate enough to meet the test of legal sufficiency. But if the description falls short of what is legally deemed to be sufficient, the document containing that description is void and the attempted transfer of title is totally ineffective. The courts, however, are reluctant to declare a deed void, and where it is possible for them to do so they will hold a conveyance to be valid even though the language of a description is ambiguous.

Clarification of Ambiguities

Words frequently have more than one meaning; if they are not carefully selected when used to describe real estate they may give rise to ambiguities. While ambiguities alone do not generally operate to render a conveyance void, they do require legal interpretation of their meanings. In order to clarify the meaning of an ambiguous description, a court action may be necessary. The modern tendency of the courts is to allow liberal interpretation of land descriptions and to admit **parol** (oral) **evidence** to explain ambiguities and determine the intention of the parties to the conveyance. A deed will not be declared void for want of sufficiency of description if it is possible, through the use of any legal rule of construction or interpretation, aided by parol evidence, to identify the premises intended by the parties to the transaction.

While parol evidence is admissible to determine which lands are included in a description, parol evidence cannot be used to transfer land that is not embraced by the language of the description. Regardless of the intentions of the parties, a deed cannot transfer title to any property other than that which the deed identifies.

Parol evidence may not be used to supply parts of a description that are missing entirely from an instrument of transfer. Parol evidence is admitted only when it tends to explain some doubtful descriptive word or phrase so that when aided by such explanation the description will identify the land intended to be conveyed. For example, where a deed describes property as "my house and lot on Oak Street," parol evidence is admissible to show that the party who executed the deed owned only one house on Oak Street and that the parties had been negotiating for the purchase and sale of that house and lot. In such a situation, the parol evidence serves to identify the particular property the parties had in mind and referred to in the deed.

LAND SURVEYING

Surveying of land involves the determination of the shape, area, and the position of a parcel of real estate on the land mass by locating its boundaries. Land surveys are either original surveys or resurveys.

An original survey of a parcel of land includes the preparation of a land description, the drawing of maps, and the designating of boundary lines on the ground with markers or monuments. These monuments may take the form of fences, walls, streams, roads, corner markers, or other natural or artificial boundary indicators. Original surveys occur when new and smaller parcels are created from a larger tract. Surveys of public lands and private subdivisions are original surveys.

Resurveys are made for the purpose of locating boundary lines from descriptions in existing documents in situations where original monuments have been removed or destroyed or when disputes as to the proper location of a boundary line arise between adjacent landowners. A resurvey that retraces the boundary lines of a parcel of land will indicate to a prospective purchaser whether structures on the land he is contemplating buying encroach upon adjoining properties or vice versa. Unless the original survey markers are still intact, a resurvey is necessary to demarcate the boundaries of a parcel when an owner wishes to install a fence, plant a hedge, or make other improvements on his property.

TYPES OF DESCRIPTIONS

No particular method of describing real estate is required by law. The basic requirement, we have seen, is simple enough—that the description be adequate to enable a qualified surveyor to locate the parcel of the land mass. Although documents employing various informal methods of describing property have repeatedly been upheld by the courts, they are not the types of descriptions that are used when deeds or other legal instruments are professionally drafted. A professionally drawn deed will normally describe or identify a parcel of real estate by one of the following forms of description: (1) by metes and bounds, (2) by the rectangular survey system, or (3) by reference to a subdivision map.

In addition to employing one of the foregoing types of formal descriptions, deeds sometimes contain a so-called being clause. This is simply a clause inserted immediately following the description of real property that reads: "Being the same premises as conveyed to the grantor by a deed dated October 14, 1968 and recorded October 15, 1968," or some equivalent language.

DESCRIPTION BY METES AND BOUNDS

The oldest method of identifying a parcel of land is the one by which the boundary lines of the parcel are expressly described. In the original American colonies, the boundary lines of private properties were designated primarily by reference to such monuments as streams, tidewater shorelines, trees, rocks, highways, and fences. Unfortunately, when those natural or artificial features of the landscape became obliterated by the passage of time or the construction of improvements, it was frequently difficult to locate a true boundary. Furthermore, deed descriptions indicating such boundaries often tended to be complicated and were frequently subject to errors of interpretation and identification. Nevertheless, and despite earlier problems, as a consequence of historical use, in a majority of states east of the Alleghenies land is still generally described by express reference to boundary lines.

Meaning of "Metes and Bounds"

The method of identifying a parcel of land by reference to the boundary lines that enclose it is known as description by **metes and bounds**. The word "metes" refers to measurements or distances, while the term "bounds" is concerned with directions. The direction that a measured boundary line takes is also known as a "course."

The expression "metes and bounds description," as commonly used by a surveyor, refers to a description of the entire perimeter of a parcel of land in which each course and distance is separately set forth, one after another, in the sequence in which a person would travel if he were to walk around the parcel following its boundary lines. The direction of travel may be either clockwise or counterclockwise, but once the direction is selected it must be consistent for the remainder of the description and must terminate at the point where the tracing of the perimeter began. At each point along a boundary line where the angle of direction is changed or a corner is reached, a permanent monument will be placed by the surveyor for future reference by subsequent surveyors and users of the property.

Need for a Fixed Starting Point

In all types of descriptions there is the absolute necessity for boundary lines to be tied to a fixed and determinable point on the earth's sur-

DESCRIPTION OF REAL PROPERTY

face. In metes and bounds descriptions, this fixed and ascertainable point is the starting or initial point from which the remainder of the description flows. The series of described boundaries that commence at a fixed monument and pursue a given direction of travel must be complete and return to the point of beginning so as to enclose the area of the parcel of land being described. If the description as written does not "close," an attempted conveyance of real estate will be ineffective because of the failure to properly identify the parcel of land intended to be transferred.

Sequence of "Calls"

A metes and bounds description is made up of a sequence of "calls," which are instructions that tell the reader how to trace out on the ground the boundary lines of a parcel of land.

A metes and bound description might read as follows: "Beginning at a point 680 feet west of the southwest corner of Orange Avenue and 37th Street in Golden City, California; thence 715 feet west to county road number R5; thence northerly 512 feet along said road to the southern property line of the Mariposa Ranch; thence east 685 feet along said property line; thence southerly to the point of beginning."

The foregoing description contains a sequence of four calls which flow in a clockwise direction of travel around the parcel's perimeter.

The first call designates a starting point at which an artificial monument is set by the original surveyor. The call then sets forth a *distance* (715 feet), a *course* (west), and an *adjoiner* (county road number R5).

The second call contains a double course indication (northerly; along said road), a distance indication (512 feet), and an adjoiner (the southern property line of the Mariposa Ranch).

The third call sets forth a distance (685 feet) and another double course indication (east; along said boundary).

The fourth call contains a course (southerly) and "closes" the description by terminating the boundary line at the point of beginning.

RECTANGULAR SURVEY SYSTEM

Before the federal government could dispose of its public lands to states, railroads, settlers, and others, it was necessary for those lands to be surveyed in order that the parcels intended for transfer could be identified. Because of the American colonies' problems with land boundaries, the Continental Congress was acutely aware of the significance of dependable land surveys. As soon as the "western" lands had been ceded to the federal government, the Congress appointed a committee to recommend a plan for subdividing and disposing of the public lands. In May of 1784 the committee, chaired by Thomas Jefferson, submitted its plan to the Congress. After due consideration and certain revisions, the plan became the basis of an ordinance passed on May 20, 1785, which was the first law pertaining to the survey of public lands. That ordinance and subsequent legislation (notably in 1796 and 1850) created the system of land survey and description that is known as the rectangular survey system.

Applicable to Public Lands

The **rectangular survey system** is the dominant method of land survey and is applicable to the states in the continental United States that were created out of the public domain, as well as Alaska. The system was never applied to the original colonies because of the difficulty of changing land descriptions where so many boundaries and parcels would be affected.

The rectangular survey system is a grid-type system of surveying constructed in the following manner.

Initial Point

The system begins with the establishment of an independent **initial point** which serves as the place of origin for surveys of land located within a certain area. Initial points are established by astronomical observations and are carefully marked on the earth's surface by suitable monuments. Frequently an initial point is located atop a prominent hill in the area that it serves.

Principal Meridian

A **principal meridian** is a line that extends due north and south through an initial point and conforms to a true meridian of longitude. There are 34 principal meridians in the continental United States, each of which has been given a distinctive name or number. (See Table 3-1.)

Base Line

A **base line** runs due east and west from an initial point on a true parallel of latitude. A base line and a principal meridian are at right angles to each other, touching or crossing at the initial point. (See Figure 3-1.)

Surveys in the area of each of the 34 initial points and their intersecting base lines and principal meridians are based upon them and land descriptions make reference to them.

Standard Parallels

Standard parallels, which are also known as "correction lines," run due east and west from the principal meridian at intervals of 24 miles both north and south of the base line. These lines conform to true parallels of latitude and thus are always equidistant from each other and the base line. Standard parallels are identified in accordance with their numerical order north and south of the base line, bearing such names as "First Standard Parallel North," "First Standard Parallel South, " and so forth. (See Figure 3-2.)

Guide Meridians

Guide meridians are lines that run true north from the base line and each standard parallel at intervals of 24 miles both east and west of the principal meridian. Although all guide meridians have bearings that run true north, the meridians are not parallel to each other. All meridians, including guide meridians, converge as they approach the north pole, the rate of convergence depending upon the distance north of the equator. Meridians in Alaska converge more rapidly than those in southern California or Florida, for example.

Because of the convergence of meridians, a guide meridian that starts on a base line at a distance of 24 miles east of the principal meridian, for instance, will be something less than 24 miles east of the principal meridian when that guide meridian reaches the first standard parallel north. The same is true of all other guide meridians that commence at 24-mile intervals on all of the standard parallels whether the parallels are north or south of the base line.

As a result of the convergence of guide meridians, the 24-mile square tracts or quadrangles that the guide meridians and the standard parallels enclose are not true squares but are more in the shape of a trapezoid. The east, south, and west boundaries are 24 miles in length, but the northern boundary is something less. To compensate for this convergence and to prevent the quadrangles from becoming increasingly smaller as one progresses north, guide meridians are commenced anew on each standard parallel at measured intervals of 24 miles. It is for this reason that standard parallels are referred to as "correction lines"—they attempt to correct the effect of convergence. If the corrections were not made and the guide meridians were extended without interruption, they would continually approach each other as they continued north, ultimately meeting at the north pole.

Guide meridians are numbered and designated in a similar fashion to the standard parallels, and bear such names as "First Guide Meridian East," "Second Guide Meridian East," and so forth. (See Figure 3-2).

Townships

The 24-mile quadrangles formed by standard parallels and guide meridians are divided into 16 tracts of land called **townships,** each of which is approximately 6 miles square.

DESCRIPTION OF REAL PROPERTY

Table 3-1. Principal Meridians and Area They Govern

Meridians	Governing surveys (wholly or in part) in States of—	Longitude of initial points west from Greenwich ° ′ ″	Latitude of initial points ° ′ ″
Black Hills	South Dakota	104 03 16	43 59 44
Boise	Idaho	116 23 35	43 22 21
Chickasaw	Mississippi	89 14 47	35 01 58
Choctaw	do	90 14 41	31 52 32
Cimarron	Oklahoma	103 00 07	36 30 05
Copper River	Alaska	145 18 13	61 49 21
Fairbanks	do	147 38 26	64 51 50
Fifth Principal	Arkansas, Iowa, Minnesota, Missouri, North Dakota, and South Dakota.	91 03 07	34 38 45
First Principal	Ohio and Indiana	84 48 11	40 59 22
Fourth Principal	Illinois*	90 27 11	40 00 50
Do	Minnesota and Wisconsin	90 25 37	42 30 27
Gila and Salt River	Arizona	112 18 19	33 22 38
Humboldt	California	124 07 10	40 25 02
Huntsville	Alabama and Mississippi	86 34 16	34 59 27
Indian	Oklahoma	97 14 49	34 29 32
Louisiana	Louisiana	92 24 55	31 00 31
Michigan	Michigan and Ohio	84 21 53	42 25 28
Mount Diablo	California and Nevada	121 54 47	37 52 54
Navajo	Arizona	108 31 59	35 44 56
New Mexico Principal	Colorado and New Mexico	106 53 12	34 15 35
Principal	Montana	111 39 33	45 47 13
Salt Lake	Utah	111 53 27	40 46 11
San Bernardino	California	116 55 17	34 07 20
Second Principal	Illinois and Indiana	86 27 21	38 28 14
Seward	Alaska	149 21 24	60 07 36
Sixth Principal	Colorado, Kansas, Nebraska, South Dakota, and Wyoming.	97 22 08	40 00 07
St. Helena	Louisiana	91 09 36	30 59 56
St. Stephens	Alabama and Mississippi	88 01 20	30 59 51
Tallahassee	Florida and Alabama	84 16 38	30 26 03
Third Principal	Illinois	89 08 54	38 28 27
Uintah	Utah	109 56 06	40 25 59
Ute	Colorado	108 31 59	39 06 23
Washington	Mississippi	91 09 36	30 59 56
Willamette	Oregon and Washington	122 44 34	45 31 11
Wind River	Wyoming	108 48 49	43 00 41

*The numbers are carried to fractional township 29 north in Illinois, and are repeated in Wisconsin, beginning with the south boundary of the State; the range numbers are given in regular order.
SOURCE: Bureau of Land Management, U.S. Department of the Interior.

Ranges Townships are formed by lines that begin at 6-mile intervals on the base line and the standard parallels and run due north to terminate at the next standard parallel. These north-south lines are generally referred to as **range lines** and, since they conform to true me-

Figure 3-1 (Bureau of Land Management, U.S. Department of the Interior)

DESCRIPTION OF REAL PROPERTY

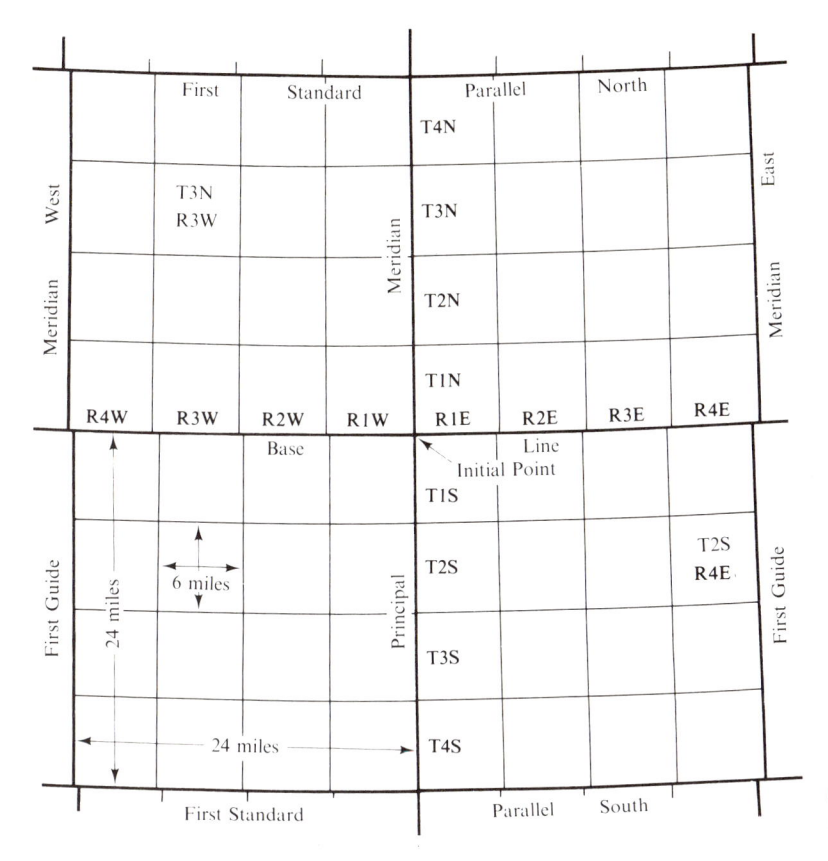

Figure 3-2 Formation and identification of townships

ridians, they are parallel to the guide meridians. The 6-mile-wide strips of land running north and south, parallel to the principal meridian and guide meridians that are formed by the range lines, are called **ranges.**

Each range or strip of land has its own designation which is derived from its position relative to the principal meridian. Ranges that lay east of the principal meridian, for example, are numbered consecutively starting at the principal meridian and extending eastward to the limits of the area served by that meridian. The first range east of the principal meridian is designated as "Range 1 East" (R1E), the next as "Range 2 East" (R2E), with the designations continuing in that fashion to the eastern limits of the area. Ranges laying west of the principal meridian are similarly numbered with their designations being "Range 1 West" (R1W), "Range 2 West" (R2W), and so on, from the principal meridian to the western limit of the area served. (See Figure 3-2.)

Tiers To conclude the formation of the 6-mile-square townships, latitudinal or horizontal lines, sometimes called *township lines,* are run due east and west from points located at intervals of 6 miles on the principal meridian. These lines intersect both the range lines and guide meridians at right angles and form the 6-mile-square tracts of land known as **townships.** These horizontal lines form layers or **tiers** of townships that run in an easterly and westerly direction. The tiers of townships are stacked both north and south of the base line and each row is given an individual designation. The tiers of townships located north of the base line are numbered consecutively beginning with the base line and continue northward to the limits of the region. The first tier north of the base line is designated as "Township 1 North" (T1N), the next as "Township 2 North" (T2N), and so on. Similarly, those tiers that lay south of the base line are designated as "Township 1 South" (T1S), "Township 2 South" (T2S), and so forth. (See Figure 3-2.)

Identification of Townships Because of the designations given to them, each township can be individually and specifically identified according to its distance and direction from any given initial point. A township situated seven tiers north and four ranges west of the intersection of a base line and a principal meridian, for example, is identified or described as being "Township 7 North, Range 4 West" (T7N, R4W) of the particular base line and principal meridian that serves as the initial point.

Size of Townships A township is the basic unit in the rectangular survey system and is also the largest unit used when identifying or describing a parcel of land by means of that system. Being roughly 6 miles on each side, a township contains approximately 36 square miles and 23,040 acres of land.

Sections

Each township is subdivided into 36 units known as **sections.** A section is approximately 1-mile-square and contains 640 acres of land. Sections are formed by the running of parallel lines, known as *section lines,* from north to south and from east to west through each township at intervals of 1 mile. The technique of subdividing a township is such that all sections

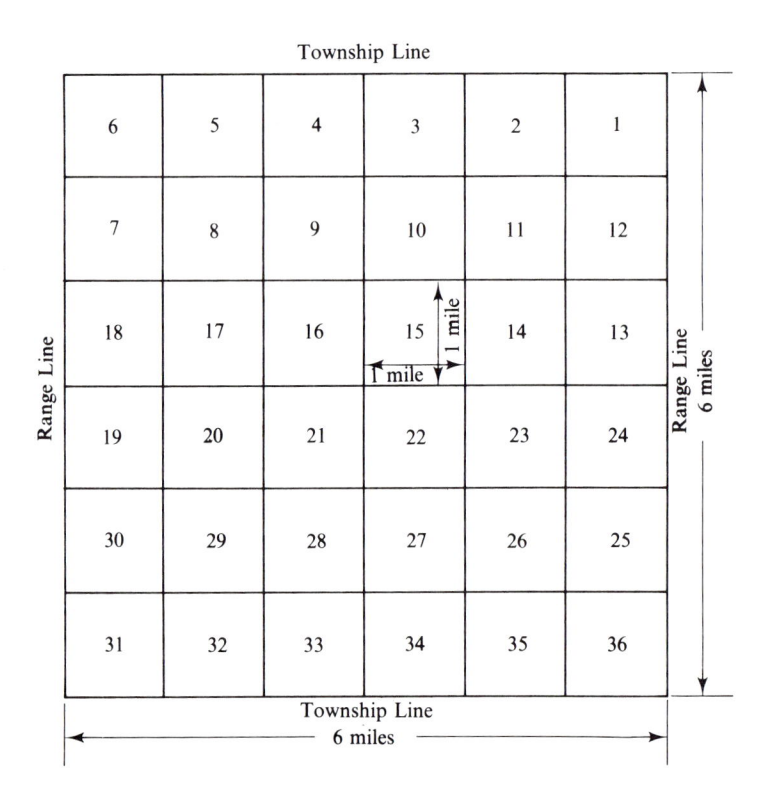

Figure 3-3 Method by which sections are numbered

DESCRIPTION OF REAL PROPERTY

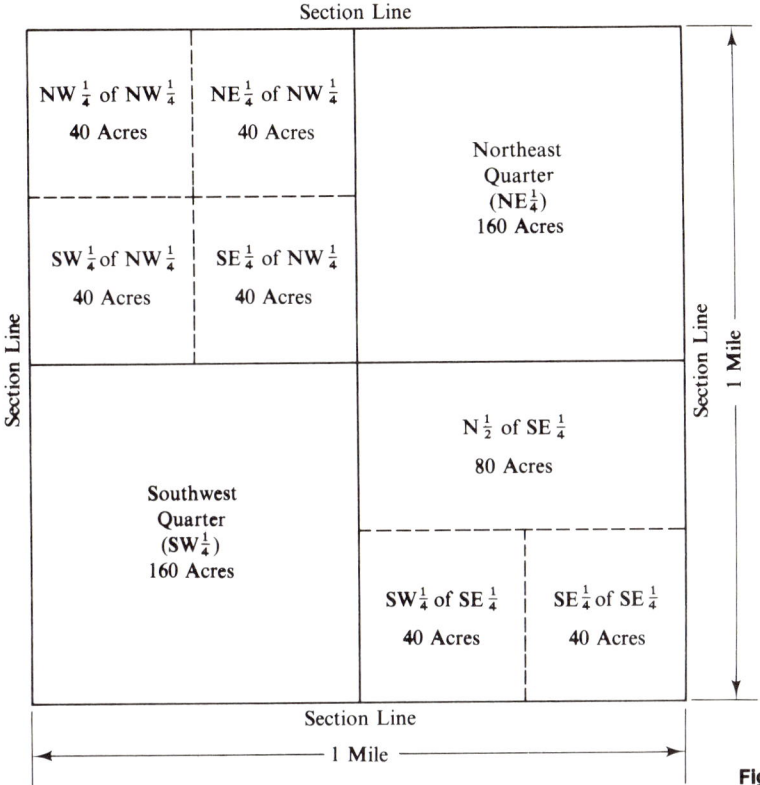

NW¼ of NW¼ 40 Acres	NE¼ of NW¼ 40 Acres	Northeast Quarter (NE¼) 160 Acres
SW¼ of NW¼ 40 Acres	SE¼ of NW¼ 40 Acres	
Southwest Quarter (SW¼) 160 Acres	N½ of SE¼ 80 Acres	
	SW¼ of SE¼ 40 Acres	SE¼ of SE¼ 40 Acres

Figure 3-4 Subdivisions of a section

are 1 mile on each of the four sides, except for those six sections along the western border of a township which are made to bear the effects of the uncorrected convergence of meridians.

Identification of Sections Sections are identified by the numbers from 1 through 36, beginning in the northeast corner of each township and running as illustrated in Figure 3-3.

Subdivisions of Sections Subdivisions of sections are described according to the position of the parcel within a section.

A section is first subdivided into quarter sections by drawing straight lines from points on section boundaries that are midway between the corners of the section. The 160-acre parcels thus formed are designated in accordance with their positions within the section as, for example, the "Northeast Quarter" (NE¼), the "Southeast Quarter" (SE¼), and so on. (See Figure 3-4.) A given 160-acre parcel of land would be described as: "NE¼ of Section 15, T7N, R4W, Third Principal Meridian, Illinois."

Tracts of land smaller than 160 acres are formed by subdividing a quarter section in the same manner as a section is subdivided. That is to say, a quarter section is in turn divided into quarters, each of which bears a designation according to its position within the quarter section. (See Figure 3-4.) A particular 40-acre tract of land would be described as: "SW¼ of NE¼ of Section 15, T7N, R4W, Third Principal Meridian, Illinois." Smaller units of land would be formed and described in the same fashion.

While the foregoing illustration divides land units into quarters, it is obvious that half units can be formed and described as well. (See Figure 3-4.)

DESCRIPTION BY REFERENCE TO A MAP OR PLAT

Identification of Subdivided Parcels

When an owner decides to subdivide a tract of land and sell it in small parcels, he will have the land surveyed and divided into blocks of land which will in turn be subdivided into lots. To facilitate identification of the parcels to be sold, a letter, number, or name is assigned to each block, and the lots within each block are then consecutively numbered. Thereafter, the map or plat of the subdivision is filed with the local recorder's office where it is reproduced in a book of maps or a plat book and used for reference when describing parcels of land that are included in the recorded map.

A parcel of land within a subdivided tract might be described as follows: "Lot No. 4 in Block B of the Eldorado Tract as shown on a map recorded at pages 24 and 25 of Book of Maps No. 75 in the office of the recorder of Los Angeles County, California." (See Figure 3-5.)

Matters Incorporated in Description

A description that identifies a parcel of land by reference to a recorded map incorporates into that description all matters which appear on the face of the map, including such things as the location of streets, parks, and easements. Boundaries of lots as reflected by courses and distances indicated on the referenced map are as much a part of a parcel's description as if they were expressly recited in the deed itself. These matters are said to have been incorporated into the deed by reference.

Location of the Subdivided Tract

The entire tract or subdivision which appears on a recorded map must itself be described so as to identify and locate it on the land mass. Unless that tract is an area of land that is susceptible to description by the rectangular survey system, the boundary lines that enclose the subdivided area will be designated by metes and bounds.

QUESTIONS

1. What is the function of a description of land in a deed or other document?
2. What is required for a description of real estate to be legally sufficient?
3. What is parol evidence?
4. What is a land survey? How does an original survey differ from a resurvey?
5. What is a so-called being clause that sometimes appears in deed descriptions of real property?
6. What do the words "metes" and "bounds" mean when used in connection with descriptions of land?
7. What is a "call" as that term is used in connection with metes and bounds descriptions?
8. In the rectangular survey system, how does a principal meridian differ from a base line?
9. Explain why, in the rectangular survey system, standard parallels are referred to as "correction lines."
10. In the rectangular survey system, what is a range? How does it differ from a tier?
11. Which is larger, a township or a section? How many miles square is each?
12. In what corners of a township are Section 1, Section 31, and Section 36 located?
13. Which of the following parcels of land is larger: Parcel A described as the SE¼ of the NW¼ of Section 10 or Parcel B described as the SE¼ of the NW¼ of the NW¼ of Section 20? How much larger?
14. Which of the parcels in Question 13 is situated north of the other? Which one is located west of the other?

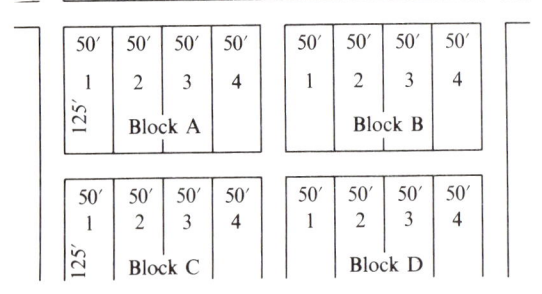

Figure 3-5 Map of Eldorado Tract

Chapter 4

Origins of Private Ownership of Real Property

In all instances, titles to lands which are today privately owned can be traced to prior ownership by a sovereign power. While some private titles are traceable to grants from foreign nations that at one time owned and controlled areas of the United States, the great bulk of private titles have their origins in transfers from the federal government. Through purchase or treaty, the federal government acquired legal title to approximately three-fourths of the area of the United States. By one arrangement or another, much of the public domain has come to be privately owned. This chapter traces the evolution of land titles in the United States from public to private ownership.

THE COLONIAL PERIOD
Ownership of the territory colonized by England was acquired by right of discovery and the ability of the British navy to defeat the claims of other nations. Through charters or grants to trading companies and proprietors, England created 13 separate colonial governments whose laws were required to be in harmony with her own. Within the prescribed boundaries of each colony, companies and proprietors were given governing authority and control over the land.

While neither England nor the colonial governments recognized the Indians' ownership rights to land, they did recognize the Indians' right to occupy the lands in their possession. The Indians relinquished their right to occupy land within the colonies through treaties requiring them to sell their lands. Both governors and proprietors purchased Indian land on behalf of the king and also issued licenses authorizing individuals to buy these lands. In some instances, individuals purchased Indian land without license and later sought to obtain official confirmation of their titles. The Indians' failure to understand the full significance of the sale of their rights and squatting by whites on Indian land gave rise to unrest and warfare on the frontier.

During the century and one-half preceding 1776, administrators of the American colonies seemed bent on getting land into private ownership as rapidly as possible. The principal interest was not to raise revenue from the granting of land to private owners but rather to encourage men of capital to settle on the land and develop it. The features of colonial land policies by which private owners acquired title to land varied from one region to another.

The South

The usual method of acquiring private ownership of land in Virginia and the southern colonies was by means of the **headright system,** which was designed to encourage men of wealth to settle workers on the land. For each new immigrant brought to a colony and settled on the land for a period of 3 years, 50 acres of land was granted to the person responsible for bringing the settler to the land. Although that person received a title in fee simple to the land, a "quitrent" or annual rental was required to be paid by him during the seventeenth century. Many of the immigrants brought to some of the colonies were indentured servants who, when later freed from their indentures, discovered that they were unable to acquire land under the headright system and either had to rent it or buy it on long-term credit.

New England

The colonies of Connecticut, Massachusetts, and Rhode Island, which controlled the land-granting process in New England, made grants of townships to groups of 6 to 80 persons who were men of affairs well known to the legislative assembly. No quitrents were demanded from these proprietors, but certain lots within each granted township were reserved for a minister, a church, and a school. After making free grants of land to the first settlers in the township and to those who would build sawmills and gristmills, the proprietors held the remainder of their townships (which in later years were 6-miles-square) for future sale.

New York

The land policy of New York emphasized making large grants to favorite individuals and families. These grants of land were mostly settled and developed by tenants.

Pennsylvania and Maryland

The proprietary colonies of Pennsylvania and Maryland were interested in raising revenue; as a consequence much of their land was disposed of through the sale of both large and small tracts to private individuals.

Termination of Colonial Grants

Having previously ordered a halt to all settlement of lands west of the Appalachians, the British government in 1774 issued instructions terminating all grants of land by colonial governors. Thereafter land was to be sold at public auction with a minimum bid of sixpence per acre, and no sales were to be made until the lands involved had been surveyed.

ACQUISITION OF THE PUBLIC DOMAIN

After the Declaration of Independence in 1776 and the Treaty of Paris in 1783, England's sovereignty over the colonies ended. Thereafter questions involving ownership and control of public lands were to be resolved between representatives of the new states and the central government created by the Articles of Confederation.

Land beyond the Appalachians

Significant among the early problems to be resolved was the claim to lands located west of the Appalachians. England's grants of land to most colonies had only vaguely described the boundary lines. Grants to Massachusetts, Con-

ORIGINS OF PRIVATE OWNERSHIP OF REAL PROPERTY

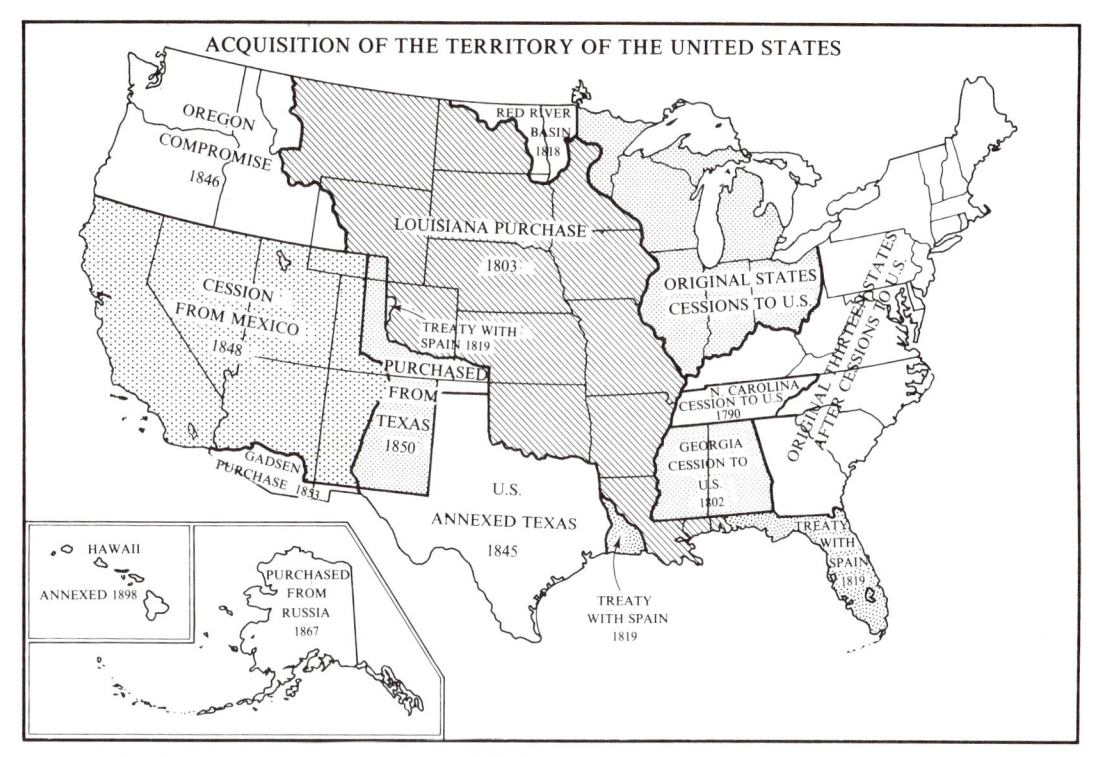

Figure 4-1 *(Bureau of Land Management, U.S. Department of the Interior)*

necticut, New York, Virginia, North and South Carolina, and Georgia gave them land between designated parallels of latitude extending from "sea to sea." These "sea to sea" grants were terminated at the Mississippi River in 1763, when England recognized Spain's claim to all lands west of the Mississippi. There remained, however, the huge area between the Appalachians and the Mississippi to which seven of the original colonies laid claims.

Following independence, the issue of who owned the public lands between the Appalachians and the Mississippi was resolved in favor of the central government, and the seven states with colonial claims surrendered those claims.

Land in the Northwest Territory

England had further limited the colonies' claims to land when, in 1774, it transferred the area north of the Ohio River to the province of Quebec. By the terms of the Treaty of 1783, however, ownership of the territory between the Ohio River and the Great Lakes, later to be known as the Northwest Territory, was acquired by the new central government.

The Louisiana Purchase

The Louisiana Territory, an area extending from the Mississippi River to the Rocky Mountains, was purchased by France from Spain in 1800. Shortly thereafter Napoleon changed his plans with respect to the area and in 1803 sold the entire Louisiana Territory to the federal

Table 4-1. Acquisition of the Public Domain, 1781-1867

Acquisition	Area Land	Area Water	Area Total	Cost*
	Acres	Acres	Acres	
State cessions (1781-1802)	233,415,680	3,409,920	236,825,600	†$6,200,000
Louisiana Purchase (1803)‡	523,446,400	6,465,280	529,911,680	23,213,568
Red River Basin§	29,066,880	535,040	29,601,920	....
Cession from Spain (1819)	43,342,720	2,801,920	46,144,640	6,674,057
Oregon Compromise (1846)	180,644,480	2,741,760	183,386,240	....
Mexican Cession (1848)	334,479,360	4,201,600	338,680,960	16,295,149
Purchase from Texas (1850)	78,842,880	83,840	78,926,720	15,496,448
Gadsden Purchase (1853)	18,961,920	26,880	18,988,800	10,000,000
Alaska Purchase (1867)	362,516,480	12,787,200	375,303,680	7,200,000
Total public domain	1,804,716,800	33,053,440	1,837,770,240	85,079,222

*Cost data for all except "State Cessions" obtained from: Geological Survey, *Boundaries, Area, Geographic Centers* (Washington, U.S. Government Printing Office, 1939), pp. 249-151.
†Georgia Cession, 1802 (56,689,920 acres). See: Donaldson, Thomas, *The Public Domain, Its History, with Statistics* (Washington, U.S. Government Printing Office, 1884), p. 11.
‡Excludes areas eliminated by Treaty of 1819 with Spain.
§Basin of the Red River of the North, south of the 49th parallel.
NOTE—All areas except Alaska were computed in 1912, and have not been adjusted for the recomputation of the areas of the United States which was made for the 1970 decennial census.
SOURCE: U.S. Department of the Interior, Office of the Secretary, Areas of Acquisitions to the Territory of the United States (Washington, U.S. Government Printing Office, 1922).

government for 3 cents per acre. Increasing the public domain by 523,446,400 acres, the Louisiana Purchase practically doubled the area of the United States.

The Red River Basin

A provision of the Convention of 1818 between the United States and Great Britain established the boundary line between the Louisiana Purchase and the British-owned territory to the north. The agreement provided that the international boundary would be drawn from a point on the Lake of the Woods west along the 49th parallel to the Rocky Mountains. By virtue of this agreement, some 29 million acres within the basin of the Red River of the North were added to the public domain.

The Acquisition of Florida

Spain ceded East and West Florida to the United States in 1819 in exchange for an agreement by the United States to pay the claims of its citizens against Spain. These claims amounted to 5 million dollars, which represents the cost of Florida. The transfer added 43,342,720 acres to the public domain.

The Annexation of Texas

Having obtained its independence from Mexico in 1836, Texas was admitted to the union in 1845. Although the admission of Texas added some 246,776,000 acres to the territory of the United States, the act of admission specifically provided that all public lands within its borders would be retained by Texas. Five years after its annexation, Texas sold 78,842,880 acres of its western lands to the United States. This addition to the federal public domain later became part of the states of Colorado, Kansas, New Mexico, Oklahoma, and Wyoming.

Cession from Mexico

Boundary disputes between the United States and Mexico led to war which ended with the Treaty of Guadalupe Hidalgo in 1848. By the terms of the treaty, Mexico sold to the United

States for 16 million dollars all of what is today California, Nevada, Utah, Arizona north of the Gila River, New Mexico west of the Rio Grande, and parts of southwestern Wyoming and southwestern Colorado. The sale by Mexico added 334,479,360 acres to the public domain of the United States.

The Oregon Compromise
In 1846 the United States and England agreed to end their joint occupation of the Oregon region. By treaty the two countries divided the Oregon country at the 49th parallel, England taking the area north of it and the United States the area south, except for the southern tip of Vancouver Island. The resolution of the Oregon question added 180,644,480 acres to the public domain of the United States.

The Gadsden Purchase
Southern congressmen and promoters interested in a railroad to connect New Orleans with San Diego, together with persons dissatisfied with the territory obtained from Mexico in 1848, demanded additional land from Mexico. James Gadsden, a railroad promoter, was placed in charge of negotiating the acquisition of additional territory. After extended negotiations, Mexico in 1853 agreed to sell for 10 million dollars a tract of land south of the Gila River which increased the public domain by 18,961,920 acres.

The Purchase of Alaska
Alaska was purchased from Russia in 1867 for $7,200,000 and added 362,516,480 acres to the public domain.

Alaska was the last territorial acquisition to increase the public lands of the United States. The later acquisition of Hawaii, Puerto Rico, the Philippines, Guam, Samoa, and smaller Pacific islands added nothing to the public lands.

PRIVATE CLAIMS TO PUBLIC LANDS

The Congress, the federal courts, and the General Land Office were confronted with a very troublesome and time-consuming problem arising from private claims to land within the public domain. These claims resulted from grants of land by the governments of England, France, Spain, and Mexico in areas formerly under their control which later became part of the federal public domain. The grants from these governments, ranging in size from town lots to thousands of acres, were rarely surveyed and their boundaries were vague and ill-defined.

Treaty Provisions
There was nothing in the Treaty of Peace of 1783 to guarantee any of the property rights of settlers in the area which the United States acquired from England. This absence of guarantee was remedied, however, in the Jay Treaty of 1794, in which the United States agreed that all settlers in the area surrendered by the British should continue "to enjoy, unmolested, all their property of any kind" the same as though they were United States citizens.

Similar assurances regarding property rights were given by the United States in subsequent treaties with France, Spain, and Mexico concerning land in the territories acquired from them.

Legislative Enactments
Throughout the nineteenth century, Congress was confronted with an estimated 30,000 to 35,000 private claims involving some 45 million acres of land. Many general and specific acts passed by Congress afforded claimants the opportunity to present their claims before commissions and courts. Although claimants complained of Congressional actions that compelled them to prove, at considerable expense and inconvenience, their rights to land, such proof was necessary because the records of prior governments were in such confusion that it was impossible to determine land titles and boundaries without adjudication of claims. Only after available documents were examined and the testimony of witnesses was heard could private ownership of land located within the public domain be determined.

TRANSFER OF PUBLIC LANDS BY SALE

The Land Ordinance of 1785

Because of the federal government's pressing need for revenue to retire its sizable public debt, the sale of the "western lands," as the land in the Northwest Territory and that between the Appalachians and the Mississippi River were called, became a matter of first importance. After debating various proposals for the disposal of these lands, Congress passed the Land Ordinance of 1785. The ordinance, besides adopting the rectangular survey system for identifying public land parcels, provided that the surveyed lands should be sold at public auction with a minimum bid of $1 per acre. The ordinance also provided that section 16 of every township should be reserved "for the maintenance of public schools within said township." A similar "public school provision" was also contained in subsequent land legislation and became a standard feature of federal land policy.

The Land Ordinance of 1785 placed no limitations on the quantity of land that any individual or company could purchase, nor was there any requirement that the land purchased must be settled on or improved. Squatters already on land being offered for sale were given no preferential rights to that land regardless of any improvements they had made on it. Like all others seeking to acquire title to the land, squatters were required to compete at public auction.

Sales on Credit

To increase the flow of revenue from the sale of public lands, Congress passed the Act of 1796. That act retained the provisions of the Land Ordinance of 1785 requiring sale at public auction but, to meet the objective of raising additional revenue, Congress increased the minimum bid to $2 per acre. A significant feature of the Act of 1796 was that it provided for the granting of credit to purchasers of public lands. The act provided that only one-twentieth of the purchase price need be paid at the time of sale, with half of the balance of the purchase price payable in 30 days and the other half one year later. The act continued the policy of cash sales of public lands and allowed cash buyers a 5 percent discount on the purchase price. The smallest parcel of land that could be bought under the act was a 640-acre tract.

There was no rush to purchase public lands following passage of the Act of 1796. Disappointment with buyers' reactions to the act induced Congress to liberalize its provisions in 1800. In addition to permitting purchases of smaller 320-acre tracts, the act substantially liberalized the terms of credit. After a down payment of one-twentieth of the purchase price at the time of purchase, a buyer was permitted to pay one-fourth of the balance in 40 days, a second fourth in 2 years, and the third and fourth installments in 3 and 4 years, respectively. The outstanding debt of a purchaser of land was subject to 6 percent interest on all but the first installment. A discount of 8 percent was allowed on three-fourths of the balance due if paid in advance of due date.

In 1804 Congress further liberalized the credit purchase system by reducing the minimum tract size to 160 acres and abolishing interest charges on all installments until they became overdue. This liberalization resulted in a substantial increase in public land sales.

Cash Sales

The purchase of public lands on credit ended with the Act of April 24, 1820. Beginning with July 1 of that year, full cash payment was required at the time of purchase. The act again reduced the minimum size of tract that could be purchased to 80 acres and lowered the minimum bid from $2 to $1.25 per acre. Any land offered at public auction which was not sold was thereafter available for private purchase at $1.25 per acre.

Although the government hoped that competitive bidding for land would yield prices in excess of the minimum of $1.25 per acre, competitive bidding was thwarted by both speculator and settler groups. Land speculators with substantial capital were the first to form buyers' combinations in which prospective buyers agreed not to bid against each other. Later, drawing upon the experience of the speculators, settlers who had entered upon and improved public lands before they were offered for sale formed settler associations with the same objective. By intimidation and otherwise, speculators were dissuaded from bidding on lands in which settler associations were interested. Thus both settlers and speculators frustrated the will of Congress by preventing competitive bidding at auctions.

Squatters and Preemption

The term "squatter" was applied both to settlers who entered upon unoccupied public lands before they were offered for sale and those who entered unoccupied lands owned by nonresident speculators. Although some commentators have made "squatterism" a term of reproach, squatting on public lands was twice legalized by acts of Congress.[1] Prior to 1841 squatters protected their interests at public land auctions through the activities of their settler associations. After 1841 squatters' interests were protected by the Preemption Act.

Settlers detested auction sales of public lands which government officials hoped would yield prices in excess of the minimum of $1.25 per acre because of competitive bidding. Settlers wanted the right to buy public lands, without competitive bidding, at a price of $1.25 per acre and were given that right by the Preemption Act of 1841.

The Preemption Act permitted settlers to acquire ownership of not more than 160 acres of surveyed public land provided they (1) inhabited and improved the land, (2) erected a dwelling on it, and (3) paid $1.25 an acre for it. Persons who already owned 320 or more acres of land were ineligible to participate and no one was entitled to exercise his right to preemption more than once.

The preemption law fell into disrepute because it was continually abused by persons who acquired land under it by fraudulent means. After repeated recommendations by the General Land Office which administered it, the act was repealed in 1891.

TRANSFER OF PUBLIC LANDS BY GIFT

Grants to Soldiers and Veterans

Until the Civil War, land grants and bounties were used to establish military outposts on the frontier and to reward soldiers in the various wars. Whether offered in advance of service or as a reward for service previously rendered, the bounty was purely military and not intended as a land measure. Nonetheless, military bounties had a profound impact on public land policies in the regions to which they applied.

The Revolutionary War During the Revolutionary War both the United States and the individual states relied heavily on bounties to induce enlistments. Despite the fact that the Continental Congress had no land subject to its jurisdiction until 1784, it made promises of grants of land as early as 1776. The various states that had holdings of lands made grants of land bounties both to their troops in the Continental Army and their own state troops.

Officers and soldiers in the Continental Army who had received warrants for land from Congress were required to wait until Congress had obtained lands in which the bounties could be located. Because of the delay in making lands available and the need of warrant holders for money, many of them were forced to sell their warrants for as little as 5 or 10 cents per acre.

The War of 1812 Even before the War of 1812 had been declared, Congress passed two

---

[1] Squatting was legalized on surveyed public lands by the Preemption Act of 1841 and on unsurveyed lands by the Homestead Act of 1862.

acts providing for military land bounties in order to stimulate enlistment in newly created regiments. Congress created military tracts in Michigan Territory, Illinois Territory, and Louisiana Territory which opened 6 million acres of land to entry by warrant holders.

Although Congress made an effort to prevent the transfer of military warrants, ways around such restrictions were readily discovered and the concentration of speculators' ownership of land in military tracts resulted.

The War with Mexico The technique of using land bounties to attract enlistments and reward soldiers was revived by President Polk's request to Congress for a declaration of war against Mexico in 1846. Congressional efforts to make land warrants nontransferable proved ineffective; many were dumped on the market and promptly fell into the hands of speculators.

The Bounty Land Act of 1850 Because there were some veterans who were not included in prior military bounty legislation, Congress passed the Bounty Land Act of 1850 which extended benefits to officers and soldiers who had served in any wars since 1790, including wars with the Indians.

Civil War Veterans Not until 1872 were veterans of the Civil War given some advantage with regard to claims to land as a reward for their services. By the provisions of the Soldiers and Sailors Act of June 8, 1872, honorably discharged veterans were permitted to count their time in service toward the 5-year period that homesteaders were required to live on their claims prior to receiving title.

Spanish-American War Veterans For veterans of the Spanish-American War and the War for Philippine Independence, Congress provided that persons with 90 days of service in the army or navy should have the same rights as were previously granted to Civil War veterans.

Grants to States

Grants for Schools The states created from the public domain (see Figure 4-2) received federal grants of public lands to assist them in establishing their public school systems. Because political and economic conditions differed at the various times that states were admitted to the union, the quantity of land granted for school purposes was not the same for all states. The first states to be admitted received one section (640 acres) in each township in the state. States which entered the union later bargained with Congress at the time of their admission and were able to obtain two sections, and still later four sections, of land for school purposes. These lands, ranging from 668,678 in Indiana to 8,711,324 in New Mexico, were sold by the states to private individuals to raise revenue for the establishment and maintenance of public schools.

The states were also given public lands for the establishment of universities and other institutions of higher learning. Except to the extent that the land was used for an institution's buildings and grounds, the lands were sold by the states to raise revenue to carry out the purpose for which the grants had been made.

Congress accompanied its grants to the states with the provision that the land should not be sold by them for less than the federal government charged private parties for its public lands.

State Improvement Grants An 1841 act of Congress granted 500,000 acres to each public-land state and to every new state thereafter admitted to aid them in the construction of "roads, railroads, canals, improvements of water-courses, and draining of swamps." States which had received grants for canals, roads, or river improvements prior to passage of the act were to have the acreage deducted from the 500,000-acre grant.

The federal government's injunction against

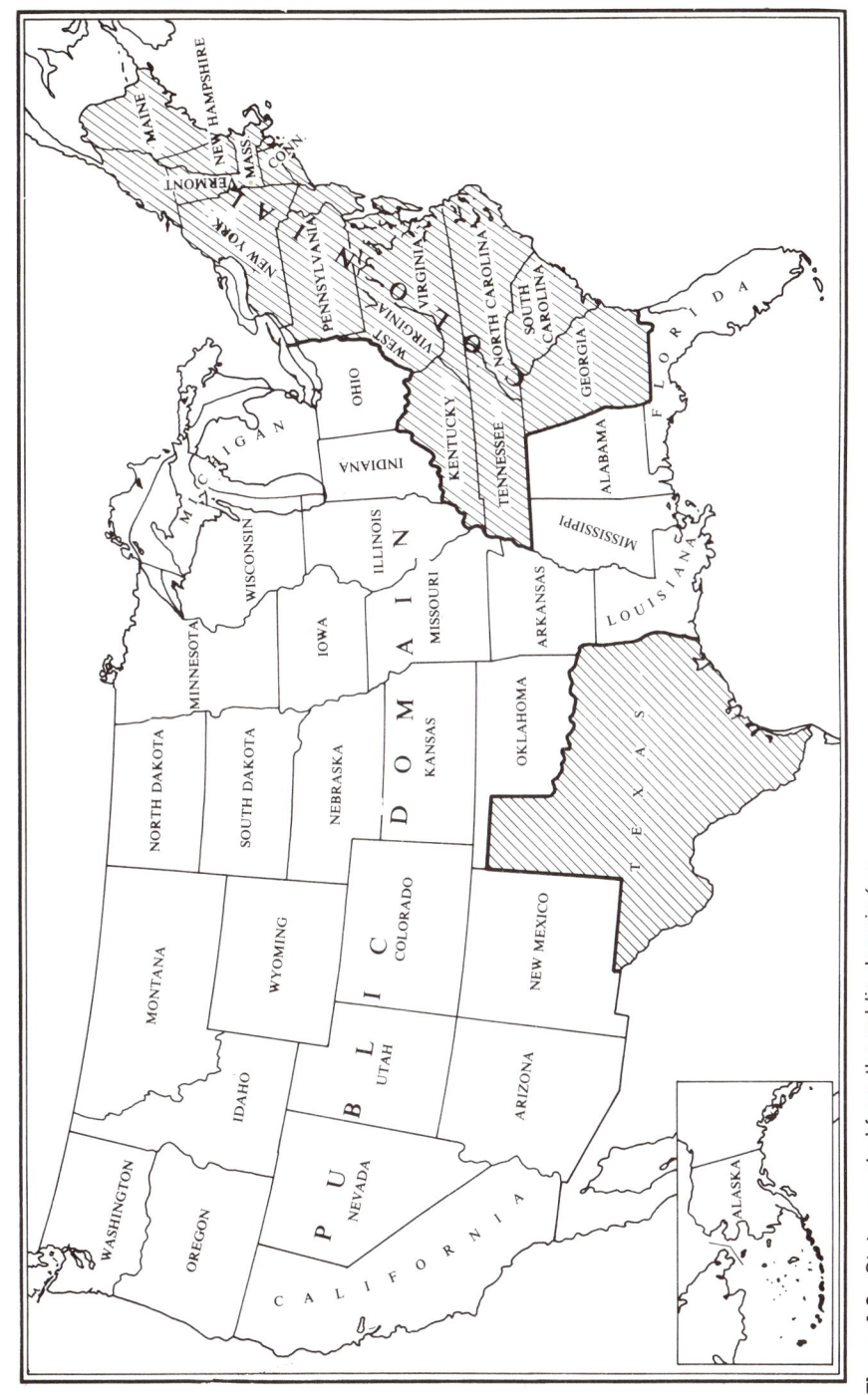

Figure 4-2 States created from the public domain (unshaded portion) *(Bureau of Land Management, U.S. Department of the Interior)*

selling granted lands for less than it charged for the public lands applied to these internal improvement grants. There was no limitation imposed, however, on the amount of acreage that could be sold to one buyer. The states were permitted to select the land for their grants from the surveyed public lands within their boundaries to which there were no other claims.

The act was repealed in 1889, and those states that were admitted to the union following its repeal received no improvement grants.

Grants of Swamp Lands Beginning in 1849, Congress passed a series of Swamp Lands Acts that were to result in the federal government granting some 65 million acres to selected states which contained such lands.

The general Swamp Lands Act of September 23, 1850, enabled specified states to reclaim the swamp and overflowed lands by granting to them "the whole of these swamp and overflowed lands, made unfit thereby for cultivation." The vagueness of the term "swamp and overflowed lands unfit for cultivation" in the Swamp Lands Act posed problems about which particular lands were granted. It early appeared that the states were more than liberal in the selection of lands they considered swamp or overflowed, and they included much land that clearly could not be so regarded. Many states followed the practice of using agents to select the lands and allowed them a portion (ranging from 10 to 50 percent) of the land for which the states received grants from the federal government. In some instances the selecting agents were in the employ of groups of speculators and investors.

State Land Policies The land policies pursued by the states ranged between two extremes. At the one extreme were the states which sought to obtain as much revenue as possible from the sale of their lands in order to promote the purpose for which the lands had been granted. At the other extreme were the

Table 4-2. Grants to States, 1803–1976

State	Common schools	Other schools	Other institutions	Railroads	Wagon roads	Canals and rivers	Miscellaneous improvements (not specified)	Swamp reclamation	Other purposes	Total
	Acres	Acres	Acres	Acres	Acres	Acres	Acres	Acres	Acres	Acres
Alabama	911,627	383,785	181	2,747,479		400,016	97,469	441,666	24,660	5,006,883
Alaska	106,000	112,064	1,000,000						103,351,187	104,569,251
Arizona	8,093,156	849,197	500,000						1,101,400	10,543,753
Arkansas	933,778	196,080		2,563,721			500,000	7,686,575	56,680	11,936,834
California	5,534,293	196,080					500,000	2,193,967	400,768	8,825,108
Colorado	3,685,618	138,040	32,000				500,000		115,946	4,471,604
Connecticut		180,000								180,000
Delaware		90,000								90,000
Florida	975,307	182,160		2,218,705			500,000	20,333,074	5,120	24,214,366
Georgia		270,000								270,000
Idaho	2,963,698	386,686	250,000						654,064	4,254,448
Illinois	996,320	526,080		2,595,133		324,283	209,086	1,460,164	123,589	6,234,655
Indiana	668,578	436,080			170,580	1,480,409		1,259,271	25,600	4,040,518

OWNERSHIP INTERESTS IN REAL ESTATE—ESTATES

Iowa	1,000,679	286,080		4,706,945			1,196,392	49,824	8,061,262
Kansas	2,907,520	151,270	127	4,176,329		321,342		59,423	7,794,669
Kentucky		330,000	24,607						354,607
Louisiana	807,271	256,292		373,057			9,504,641		11,441,261
Maine		210,000							210,000
Maryland		210,000							210,000
Massachusetts		360,000							360,000
Michigan	1,021,867	286,080		3,134,058	221,013	1,250,236	5,680,312	49,280	12,142,846
Minnesota	2,874,951	212,160		8,047,469			4,706,591	80,880	16,422,051
Mississippi	824,213	348,240		1,075,345			3,348,946	1,253	6,097,997
Missouri	1,221,813	376,080		1,837,968			3,432,521	48,640	7,417,022
Montana	5,198,258	388,721	100,000					276,359	5,963,338
Nebraska	2,730,951	136,080	32,000			500,000		59,680	3,458,711
Nevada	2,061,967	136,080	12,800			500,000		14,379	2,725,226
New Hampshire		150,000							150,000
New Jersey		210,000							210,000
New Mexico	8,711,324	1,346,546	750,000		100,000			1,886,848	12,794,718
New York		990,000							990,000
North Carolina		270,000							270,000
North Dakota	2,495,396	336,080	250,000					82,076	3,163,552
Ohio	724,266	699,120		80,774	1,204,114		26,372	24,216	2,758,862
Oklahoma	1,375,000	1,050,000	670,760						3,095,760
Oregon	3,399,360	136,165		2,583,890			286,108	127,324	7,032,847
Pennsylvania		780,000				500,000			780,000
Rhode Island		120,000							120,000
South Carolina		180,000							180,000
South Dakota	2,733,084	366,080	250,640					85,569	3,435,373
Tennessee		300,000							300,000
Texas		180,000							180,000
Utah	5,844,196	556,141	500,160					601,240	7,501,737
Vermont		150,000							150,000
Virginia		300,000							300,000
Washington	2,376,391	336,080	200,000					132,000	3,044,471
West Virginia		150,000							150,000
Wisconsin	982,329	332,160		3,652,322	302,931	1,022,349	3,361,283	26,430	10,179,804
Wyoming	3,470,009	136,080	420,000				500,000	316,431	4,342,520
Total	77,629,220	16,707,787	4,993,275	37,128,531	3,359,188	6,102,749	7,806,555	64,917,883	109,780,866	328,426,054

SOURCE: Bureau of Land Management, U.S. Department of the Interior.

states which wanted to have those lands privately owned and developed as soon as possible, selling them at low prices and on long-term credit. At the outset, legislatures and administrative officers were strongly oriented toward the latter policy, and the land resources of the states were dissipated. With some exceptions, this early experience reflects an inclination on the part of the states to rush into selling or leasing lands without due consideration of the effects of such action. All too often legislators and public officers appeared to be shaping policies that would primarily benefit them personally.

Gradually a growing sense of responsibility and a greater interest in the purposes for which the grants were made led to improved management of state lands. In addition, federal acts were later passed that either prescribed minimum sales prices that states must charge or required that lands must first be appraised and then be offered at public auction for no less than the appraised figure.

Grants to Railroads

Rights-of-way through the public lands, ranging in width from 60 to 100 feet, were granted by Congress to the railroads as early as 1835. A later general law authorized railroads to use earth, stone, and timber from adjacent public lands and to have land in addition to rights-of-way for depots and water tanks.

The First Financing Grant The first act of Congress to grant land to railroads for use other than as rights-of-way and depot sites was the Chicago and Mobile Act of 1850. That act granted to the states of Illinois, Mississippi, and Alabama a 100-foot-wide right-of-way from Chicago to Mobile, together with one-half of the land in the even-numbered sections within 6 miles of the right-of-way. The granted lands were to be sold to raise funds to help finance construction of a railroad. Since the state of Illinois was barred by its constitution from building a railroad, it transferred the grant it had received to a group of eastern investors who incorporated as the Illinois Central Railroad. Alabama and Mississippi transferred their rights under the act to the Mobile and Ohio Railroad.

Additional Grants to States for Railroads
The success of the Illinois Central and the Mobile and Ohio railroads in financing the construction of their railroads with the aid of federal land grants led to numerous later requests for federal aid to railroads. In 1852 and 1853, two land grant acts gave public lands to Missouri and Arkansas for the building of railroads. Shortly thereafter, in 1856 and 1857, several measures were passed approving land grants to states for seven railroads in Alabama, four in Florida, two in Louisiana, and one each in Iowa, Michigan, and Wisconsin. Later, between 1862 and 1871, Congress made additional grants for railroads to Arkansas, California, Iowa, Louisiana, Michigan, Minnesota, and Missouri.

The Pacific Railroad Act Although grants to states for railroad construction continued to be made, popular attention increasingly turned to proposals for the building of railroads through the western territories to the Pacific coast.

After the introduction of many bills and extensive discussion of routes to the Pacific, Congress on July 1, 1862, passed the Pacific Railroad Act, the provisions of which were later liberalized on July 2, 1864. The act chartered the Union Pacific Railroad and granted to it a 400-foot-wide right-of-way through the public lands plus 10 odd-numbered sections (increased to 20 sections by the Act of 1864) of land for each mile of railroad from Omaha on the Missouri River to the western border of Nevada. The Central Pacific Railroad, a company chartered in California, was also granted a 400-foot right-of-way and 10 sections per mile to build from near San Francisco to the California-Nevada border or 150 miles east of it if it reached the border before the Union Pacific did. The two railroads were also permitted to take timber and stone for construction from the public lands.

A provision in the Pacific Railroad Act of 1862 stated that all lands not sold or otherwise disposed of by the railroads within 3 years after completion of construction "shall be subject to settlement and preemption, like other lands, at a price not exceeding one dollar and twenty-five cents per acre, to be paid to said company." This provision would appear to mean that the Union Pacific and the Central Pacific railroads were required to sell by 1872 (the transcontinental railroad was completed in 1869) all of the lands they had received by grant or the lands still unsold would become public domain and be subject to preemption by settlers. The courts, however, prevented the unsold land from reverting to the public domain by holding that the railroad companies had "disposed of" their lands by placing a blanket mortgage on them.

In the two railroad acts of 1862 and 1864, some 2,720 miles of right-of-way and some 34,560,000 acres of the public lands were given to the two railroads.

The Northern Pacific Railroad The Northern Pacific Railroad Company was incorporated by an act of Congress on July 2, 1864, for the purpose of building a railroad from Duluth on Lake Superior to Tacoma on Puget Sound with a branch to Portland, Oregon. The act granted a right-of-way 400-feet wide plus 20 sections of land (12,800 acres) for each mile of railroad in the states in which it was built and 40 sections (25,600 acres) per mile in the territories it crossed. The gift of land, estimated at 45 million acres, was by far the largest single land grant made by Congress.

Other Transcontinental Railroads Two additional grants for transcontinental railroads were made by Congress. By provisions of the Act of July 27, 1866, Congress granted to the Atlantic and Pacific Railroad a 200-foot right-of-way through the public lands from Springfield, Missouri to the Pacific. The other provisions of the grant were the same as those extended to the Northern Pacific Railroad. Plagued by financial difficulties, bankruptcy became inevitable for the Atlantic and Pacific, and part of its land grant was taken over by the Frisco Line.

The other land grant for a transcontinental railroad was made to the Texas Pacific Railroad on March 3, 1871, for a line from the eastern border of Texas to San Diego on the Pacific. The Texas Pacific was given the same grants that the Northern Pacific had received. The railroad was never built beyond El Paso, however, and in 1885 Congress declared the grant forfeited for noncompliance with its conditions.

Table 4-3. Grants to Railroads, 1850-1976

State	Acres
Arizona	7,790,128.85*
Arkansas	23,249.94
California	11,589,796.56
Colorado	3,757,673.39
Idaho	1,321,750.67
Iowa	4,383.11
Kansas	4,057,683.78
Louisiana	1,001,943.40
Minnesota	1,905,559.14
Missouri	490,705.87
Montana	14,739,697.12
Nebraska	7,272,623.25
Nevada	5,086,603.65
New Mexico	3,355,179.07
North Dakota	10,697,490.35
Oregon	13,656,085.50
Utah	2,230,085.01
Washington	9,617,384.26
Wisconsin	13,739.94
Wyoming	5,749,051.12
Total	94,360,813.98

*Includes O&C acreage, title to which was revested in the United States by the Act of June 9, 1916 (39 Stat. 218).
SOURCE: Bureau of Land Management, U.S. Dept. of the Interior.

LAND FOR HOMESTEADERS

The Land Reform Movement

The demand for free land for settlers originated with an intellectual element among labor leaders in the 1830s and developed into a land reform movement. Early leaders of the movement maintained that every person had a right to share in the public lands, that they belonged to the people and should be freely distributed to them in small tracts. The government, they argued, had an obligation to reserve the public lands for grants to actual settlers instead of allowing them to be acquired by speculators who bought them for resale to the land-hungry rather than for development.

The land reform movement, especially with respect to free **homesteads** for settlers, increasingly gained important converts among newspapers and leading members of Congress who advocated land reform in one form or another. Congress was besieged by an increasing number of petitions calling for free land from northern legislatures and various citizen groups. Westerners who wanted rapid settlement and development of the public lands felt that free homesteads was the answer.

Despite these demands, an act passed by Congress in 1860 was vetoed by the President who, notwithstanding the many precedents of free grants to individuals and states, could find no constitutional authorization for free homesteads. Following the election of a new president and a change in the party in power, a homestead measure was enacted on May 20, 1862, and became law on January 1, 1863.

The Homestead Act of 1862

The Homestead Act of 1862 provided that any person who was the head of a family or 21 years of age, who was a citizen or had filed a declaration of intent to become a citizen, was entitled to acquire up to 160 acres of land. The act did not permit homesteading on unsurveyed public lands, and it was not until 1880 that homesteading on such lands was made legal. Homestead land was free to those who met the residence and improvement requirements of the act and paid an original filing fee of $10 plus two commissions of $4 each.

A homesteader was required to reside on the land and cultivate it for a period of 5 years before he could gain title to the land. Each qualified settler was entitled to only one homestead. The Homestead Act specifically provided for the continuation of the preemption law, thus making it possible for a settler to acquire both a 160-acre preemption and a 160-acre homestead, though not at the same time because a period of residence was required for both of them.

The homestead law contained a "commutation" clause which permitted settlers to change their homestead claims to preemption and obtain title after 6 months' residence upon payment of $1.25 per acre. This provision enabled settlers to obtain title to land without waiting for 5 years in those cases where they wanted to sell the land or use it as security for loans.

The Kinkaid Act

Because 160-acre homesteads were considered to be economically infeasible in the semiarid regions of the Great Plains, Congress in 1904 passed the Kinkaid Act. The act provided that in the western two-thirds of Nebraska settlers could acquire homesteads of 640 acres by living on them for 5 years and making improvements worth $1.25 for each acre. Lands along the Platte River and other streams suitable for irrigation were excluded from the act.

The Kinkaid Act stimulated a rush for homesteads and the transfer of public lands to private hands. Proving to be too small for stock-raising operations, many homesteads were sold and combined into more feasible ranching units.

The Enlarged Homestead Act of 1909

In the semiarid western states, legislatures, railroads, and other groups were interested in developing the states more intensively than the livestock industry had done. After searching for the best method of more effectively using the land, advocates of an enlarged 320-acre homestead unit suitable for dry farming prevailed. Advocates of such units secured the passage of the Enlarged Homestead Act of 1909.

The Enlarged Homestead Act authorized homesteads of 320 acres on nonirrigable, nonmineral lands containing no merchantable timber in the states of Arizona, Colorado, Montana, Nevada, New Mexico, Oregon, Utah, Washington, and Wyoming. Not wishing to be classified as semiarid states, California, Idaho, Kansas, and North and South Dakota requested to be excluded from the act. The Department of the Interior was charged with designating the public lands unsuitable for irrigation and thus available for private entry under the act. To acquire title to the land that was entered, a settler was required to reside on it for 5 years with continuous cultivation of crops other than native grasses.

Because of the success of the Enlarged Homestead Act in stimulating settlers to enter the land, California and Idaho in 1910, North Dakota in 1912, and South Dakota in 1915 requested to be included among the states covered by the act.

In 1921 Congress reduced the period of time that a homesteader had to be in residence on his claim from 5 to 3 years. In addition, the homesteader was permitted to be absent from his land for 5 months each year, presumably to seek employment elsewhere during the winter months.

The Stock Raising Homestead Act

The Enlarged Homestead Act had been in effect for only a short while before agitation began for stock-raising homesteads of 640, 1,280, and even 2,560 acres. Yielding to mounting demands, Congress in 1916 enacted the Stock Raising Homestead Act. The act authorized homesteads of 640 acres on land that was "chiefly valuable for grazing and raising forage crops," that contained no merchantable timber, that was not susceptible to irrigation from any known water source, and that was of such a

Table 4-4. Disposition of Public Lands, 1781–1976

Type of disposition	Acres
Disposition by methods elsewhere classified[a]	303,500,000
Granted or sold to homesteaders[b]	287,500,000
Granted to States for:	
Support of common schools	77,600,000
Reclamation of swampland	64,900,000
Construction of railroads	37,100,000
Support of miscellaneous institutions[c]	21,700,000
Purposes not elsewhere classified[d]	117,500,000
Canals and rivers	6,100,000
Construction of wagon roads	3,400,000
Total granted to States	328,300,000
Granted to railroad corporations	94,300,000
Granted to veterans as military bounties	61,000,000
Confirmed as private land claims[e]	34,000,000
Sold under timber and store law[f]	13,900,000
Granted or sold under timber culture law[g]	10,900,000
Sold under desert land law[h]	10,700,000
Grand Total	1,144,100,000

[a] Chiefly public, private, and preemption sales, but includes mineral entries, script locations, sales of townsites and townlots.

[b] The homestead laws generally provide for the granting of lands to homesteaders who settle upon and improve vacant agricultural public lands. Payment for the land is sometimes permitted, or required, under certain conditions.

[c] Universities, hospitals, asylums, etc.

[d] For construction of various public improvement (individual items not specified in the granting acts), reclamation of desert lands, construction of water reservoirs, etc.

[e] The Government has confirmed title to lands claimed under valid grants made by foreign governments prior to the acquisition of the public domain by the United States.

[f] The timber and stone laws provided for the sale of lands valuable for timber or stone and unfit for cultivation.

[g] The timber culture laws provided for the granting of public lands to settlers on condition that they plant and cultivate trees on the lands granted. Payments for the lands was permitted under certain conditions.

[h] The desert land laws provide for the sale of arid agricultural public lands to settlers who irrigate them and bring them under cultivation.

NOTE—Data are estimated from available records.

SOURCE: Bureau of Land Management, U.S. Dept of the Interior.

character that 640 acres were "reasonably required for the support of a family." Homesteaders were required to make permanent improvements that would enhance the value of the land for stock raising, such as fencing and digging wells, in the amount of $1.25 for each acre.

Sheepmen and cattlemen predicted that the breaking up of the public range lands into stock-raising homesteads as small as 640 acres would damage the range lands' carrying capacity. Shortly after adoption of the Stock Raising Homestead Act, influential individuals, livestock associations, and government officials urged its repeal and the substitution of a policy of leasing the public range lands. The movement for repeal culminated in passage of the Taylor Grazing Act of 1934.

The Taylor Grazing Act authorized the establishment of grazing districts on 80 million acres of public lands that were chiefly valuable for grazing and the raising of forage crops. The Secretary of the Interior was authorized to establish district boundaries, to issue permits for the use of the range lands, and to determine the number of livestock allowed within the grazing districts. Lands proposed for inclusion in the districts were withdrawn from all forms of private entry.

Termination of Private Entry

On November 24, 1934, all public lands in North and South Dakota and 10 intermountain and west coast states other than Washington were withdrawn from all forms of private entry. On February 5, 1935, the public lands in 12 additional states were withdrawn.

Table 4-5. Comparison of Federally Owned Land with Total Acreage of States as of June 30, 1975

State	Public domain	Acquired other methods	Total	Acreage not owned by Federal Government	Acreage of State*	Percent owned by Government†
Alabama	29,291.6	1,094,058.7	1,123,350.3	31,555,049.7	32,678,400	3.438
Alaska	352,388,859.3	18,874.4	352,407,733.7	13,073,866.3	365,481,600	96.423
Arizona	30,831,388.1	309,997.6	31,141,385.7	41,546,614.3	72,688,000	42.843
Arkansas	1,072,199.6	2,201,379.5	3,273,579.1	30,325,780.9	33,599,360	9.743
California	42,779,081.2	2,498,684.8	45,277,766.0	54,928,954.0	100,206,720	45.184
Colorado	22,899,710.2	1,083,488.4	23,983,198.6	42,502,561.4	66,485,760	36.073
Connecticut	0	9,420.2	9,420.2	3,125,939.8	3,135,360	.301
Delaware	0	40,540.2	40,540.2	1,225,379.8	1,265,920	3.202
District of Columbia	0	10,209.0	10,209.0	28,831.0	39,040	26.150
Florida	370,914.1	3,140,086.7	3,511,000.8	31,210,279.2	34,721,280	10.112
Georgia	0	2,229,375.0	2,229,375.0	35,065,985.0	37,295,360	5.978
Hawaii	0	405,529.8	405,529.8	3,700,070.2	4,105,600	9.878
Idaho	32,928,354.7	813,113.4	33,741,468.1	19,191,651.9	52,933,120	63.744
Illinois	437.2	562,208.5	562,645.7	35,232,554.3	35,795,200	1.572
Indiana	432.0	485,927.0	486,359.0	22,672,041.0	23,158,400	2.100
Iowa	340.8	223,954.8	224,295.6	35,636,184.4	35,860,480	.626
Kansas	26,341.0	686,176.8	712,517.8	51,798,202.2	52,510,720	1.357
Kentucky	0	1,349,133.7	1,349,133.7	24,163,186.3	25,512,320	5.288
Louisiana	24,842.2	1,033,409.4	1,058,251.6	27,809,588.4	28,867,840	3.666
Maine	0	131,151.0	131,151.0	19,716,529.0	19,847,680	.661
Maryland	0	202,445.1	202,445.1	6,116,914.9	6,319,360	3.204

Table 4-5 (Continued)

State	Acreage owned by the Federal Government — Public domain	Acquired other methods	Total	Acreage not owned by Federal Government	Acreage of State*	Percent owned by Government†
Massachusetts	0	84,747.2	84,747.2	4,950,132.8	5,034,880	1.683
Michigan	296,612.1	3,116,645.1	3,413,257.2	33,078,902.8	36,492,160	9.353
Minnesota	1,258,011.1	2,153,895.3	3,411,906.4	47,793,853.6	51,205,760	6.663
Mississippi	2,363.1	1,646,356.1	1,648,719.2	28,574,000.8	30,222,720	5.455
Missouri	2,647.3	2,147,284.0	2,149,931.3	42,098,388.7	44,248,320	4.859
Montana	25,189,793.9	2,475,794.2	27,665,588.1	65,605,451.9	93,271,040	29.662
Nebraska	244,555.5	449,620.7	694,176.2	48,337,503.8	49,031,680	1.416
Nevada	60,615,797.0	204,456.0	60,820,253.0	9,444,067.0	70,264,320	86.559
New Hampshire	0	710,498.1	710,498.1	5,058,461.9	5,768,960	12.316
New Jersey	0	131,045.5	131,045.5	4,682,394.5	4,813,440	2.723
New Mexico	24,263,994.7	1,838,093.8	26,102,088.5	51,664,311.5	77,766,400	33.565
New York	0	246,594.7	246,594.7	30,434,365.3	30,680,960	.804
North Carolina	0	1,968,584.6	1,968,584.6	29,434,295.4	31,402,880	6.269
North Dakota	209,122.5	2,111,779.4	2,320,901.9	42,131,578.1	44,452,480	5.221
Ohio	220.0	330,141.8	330,361.8	25,891,718.2	26,222,080	1.260
Oklahoma	150,444.1	1,389,708.1	1,540,152.2	42,547,527.8	44,087,680	3.493
Oregon	30,996,404.6	1,373,812.0	32,370,216.6	29,228,503.4	61,598,720	52.550
Pennsylvania	0	669,121.5	669,121.5	28,135,358.5	28,804,480	2.323
Rhode Island	0	7,225.1	7,225.1	669,894.9	677,120	1.067
South Carolina	0	1,141,794.9	1,141,794.9	18,232,285.1	19,374,080	5.893
South Dakota	1,600,313.3	1,695,698.5	3,296,011.8	45,585,908.2	48,881,920	6.743
Tennessee	0	1,788,330.9	1,788,330.9	24,939,349.1	26,727,680	6.691
Texas	0	3,195,599.4	3,195,599.4	165,022,000.6	168,217,600	1.900
Utah	34,312,310.6	543,825.1	34,856,135.7	17,840,824.3	52,696,960	66.145
Vermont	0	277,321.7	277,321.7	5,659,318.3	5,936,640	4.671
Virginia	0	2,384,709.0	2,384,709.0	23,111,611.0	25,496,320	9.353
Washington	11,138,273.1	1,450,169.3	12,588,442.4	30,105,317.6	42,693,760	29.485
West Virginia	0	1,069,463.2	1,069,463.2	14,341,096.8	15,410,560	6.940
Wisconsin	10,138.4	1,810,575.5	1,820,713.9	33,190,486.1	35,011,200	5.200
Wyoming	29,223,242.2	606,320.4	29,829,562.6	32,513,477.4	62,343,040	47.848
Total	702,866,435.5	57,548,375.1	760,414,810.6	1,510,928,549.4	2,271,343,360	33.479

*Does not include inland water.
†Excludes trust priorities.
SOURCE: Inventory Report on Real Property Owned by the United States Throughout the World, published by General Service Administration.
SOURCE: *Public Land Statistics*, Bureau of Land Management, U.S. Dept. of the Interior.

QUESTIONS

1 What was the nature of the headright system of acquiring private ownership of land that existed in some of the American colonies?
2 When, from whom, and at what price per acre did the United States government purchase the Louisiana Territory? What area of the country did it include?
3 How many acres of public land in Texas came into the public domain when Texas was admitted to the union?
4 What was the nature of the public school provision of the Land Ordinance of 1785? What effect

did the ordinance have on surveys of public lands?
5 How did the Preemption Act change the system of acquiring title to public lands that preceded the passage of the act?
6 In the history of land titles in the United States, what was a military bounty?
7 Describe the two extremes of land policies that were pursued by the states during their early periods of statehood.
8 For what purpose were public lands granted to railroads at no cost by the federal government?
9 Why did the President in 1860 veto an act of Congress providing free land to homesteaders?
10 How did homesteading and preemption differ as means of acquiring title to public lands?

Chapter 5

Ownership Interests in Real Estate—Estates

The word **estate** originally referred to the position or status of a landholder in the feudal society of early England, but that meaning has long been lost. As the term "estate" is used today in real estate law, it refers to the *nature*, the *quantity*, and the *quality* of an ownership interest that a person is permitted to have in real property. Although much of the law with respect to estates is rooted in history, the character and quality of estates today are matters that are entirely within the control of the courts and legislatures. There are no interests in real property that the law will protect except those that are defined and recognized by the courts and the legislatures.

Not every legally recognized interest that a person has in real estate amounts to an estate. The term "estate" refers only to *ownership* interests as distinct from interests in real estate that are security for a debt or interests that merely give a right to use the property. In this chapter we are concerned with the characteristics of the several types of ownership interests in real estate that are recognized and protected by the laws of the various states.

Protected Right of Possession

We have previously observed that a very significant incident or attribute of ownership is the owner's right of possession of the thing owned. Therefore, since an estate is an ownership interest in real estate, it entitles the owner to possession of that property. An owner's right of possession, we have seen, includes the privilege of occupying his property and using and enjoying it to the exclusion of all other persons. The particular interest that a person owns in real estate may entitle him to the present occupancy of the premises or, in some instances, his right of possession may be deferred until some time in the future. In either case, however, the owner's interest is one that is presently recognized by the law and one which the courts will presently enforce and protect. It is an owner's claim to the law's present protection of his right of possession that is the central characteristic of the ownership interest known as an estate.

CLASSIFICATION OF ESTATES

Not all estates in land are alike. As an aid to understanding the different features of the various types of ownership interests recognized by the courts and legislatures, it is useful to classify estates according to certain differences in their basic characteristics.

Estates differ primarily in (1) the *duration* of the period of time that an owner's right to possession of his property continues, (2) the point in *time* when an owner may enter into possession of his property and enjoy it, and (3) the *number of owners* entitled to possess and enjoy the property. Estates also vary as to the degree or extent to which they may be enjoyed, with some being *qualified* or *limited* with regard to the use that an owner may make of his property.

Freehold versus Nonfreehold Estates

Estates are frequently classified as being either **freehold** estates or **nonfreehold** estates. The classification is purely historical and of feudal origin. Feudalism was essentially a system of government and social order, the basis of which was ownership of land. Under the feudal system as it existed in England, land was held by a person known as a tenant under a superior or overlord by means of a relationship known as tenure. The particular form of tenure by which a tenant held his land was determined by the nature of the services that the tenant was obliged to render to his lord. For example, military tenure required that the tenant render military services in return for the land that he held; socage tenure required fixed payment of money or products instead of knight or military service. The theory of tenure has little practical importance today; it is merely a concept of academic interest.

At early common law, freehold estates were those that traditionally were held under one of the "free" varieties of tenure. Historically, a freehold estate was always associated with a right enduring for an uncertain period of time and today, as in the past, freehold estates include estates in fee simple, estates in fee tail, and life estates, all of which are of uncertain duration.

The early common law did not consider *nonfreehold* estates to be real property. Nonfreehold estates, or estates less than a freehold, developed as chattel or personal property interests in land and were not subject to feudal law. Estates less than freeholds were part of the law of landlord and tenant, and the tenant's interest was known as a **leasehold.** Although the tenant's leasehold was an interest in land, it was considered to be personal property and was called a **chattel real.** Leaseholds are still considered to be personal property or chattels real for certain purposes. Despite the fact that statutes and court decisions have tended to blur the historical distinctions between freehold and leasehold interests, they have not been entirely obliterated.

Nonfreehold estates include estates for years, estates from period to period, estates at will, and estates at sufferance.

ESTATES IN FEE SIMPLE

There are two types of estates in fee simple: (1) the fee simple absolute and (2) the fee simple defeasible.

Fee Simple Absolute

The estate most commonly encountered today is the **fee simple absolute.** To own an estate in real property in fee simple absolute is to have the greatest quantity of ownership rights recognized by law. It is the largest interest in real estate that an owner can have. No other ownership interest has as many legal rights accruing to it as the fee simple absolute.

While an estate in fee simple absolute is indeed the largest ownership interest in land that is known to the law, the term "absolute" is not to be taken in its literal sense. Taken literally, the term would appear to mean that an owner of a fee simple absolute may use his property in any manner and for any purpose that he desires, regardless of the consequences of such use on the rights of other members of society. This clearly is not the case. Even this highest form of land ownership is subject to limitations which the law imposes on the use to which an owner may put his land.

An estate in fee simple absolute is what the layperson refers to when he says that he "owns" Blackacre. The layperson, however, seldom if ever uses the full term "fee simple absolute" to describe his ownership interest. In common usage, the abbreviated terms "fee simple" or simply "fee" are used by an owner when referring to his estate in fee simple absolute. In keeping with this common usage, when the terms "fee" and "fee simple" are used in this book without any qualifying adjective, they will refer to an estate in fee simple absolute.

Potentially Infinite Duration An estate in fee simple absolute is an ownership interest of potentially infinite duration. The duration of the estate is said to equal that of the land itself. A fee simple is often referred to as an "estate of inheritance" because it will endure beyond the lifetime of the present owner. Upon the death of the present owner, his estate or ownership interest does not come to an end but passes to his descendants either by virtue of the terms of his will, if he leaves one, or in accordance with the laws of succession if he dies without having executed a will.

Like other owners of interests in real estate, the owner of a fee simple interest may transfer ownership of that interest to another person during his lifetime by means of a sale or a gift. In effecting such a transfer, the transferor's ownership terminates at the moment of transfer, but that same ownership interest of potentially infinite duration is established in the transferee as a new owner. Thereafter the new owner may possess and enjoy the property himself, or he in turn may pass the interest on to another person. And so it goes from one owner to another with the fee simple estate enduring beyond the lifetimes of any and all successive owners.

Presumption of a Fee Simple Absolute No particular words or phrases need be used to transfer a fee simple absolute interest from one owner to another. Statutes in a substantial majority of the states provide that, unless a document, whether it be a deed or a will, transferring real estate reflects an intent to convey a lesser interest, it is presumed that a fee simple absolute was intended.[1] The presumption is defeated, of course, if the transferor does not in fact own a fee simple absolute interest, because no one can transfer title to a greater interest in real property than he in fact owns.

Fee Simple Defeasible

General Characteristics Although the fee simple absolute is by far the most common of all ownership interests in real property, there is another type of fee simple sometimes encountered known as a **fee simple defeasible**. As the word "defeasible" suggests, a fee simple defeas-

---

[1] California Civil Code, sec. 1105, for example, provides that "A fee simple title is presumed to be intended to pass by a grant of real property, unless it appears from the grant that a lesser estate was intended."

Florida Statutes, sec. 689.10 states that "Where any real estate has heretofore been conveyed or granted or shall hereafter be conveyed or granted without there being used in said deed or conveyance or grant any words of limitation, such conveyance or grant, whether heretofore made or hereafter made, shall be construed to vest the fee simple title or other whole estate or interest which the grantor has power to dispose of at that time in the real estate conveyed or granted, unless a contrary intent shall appear in the deed, conveyance, or grant."

ible is an estate that can be annulled or lost to its owner under certain circumstances. However, except for the limitations on the use of the property that are expressly imposed by the document that transfers title, the owner of a fee simple defeasible has all the rights and privileges with respect to his property that are enjoyed by the owner of a fee simple absolute. The owner of a defeasible fee may use the property himself, he may lease it, sell it, give it away during his lifetime, or he may transfer it to others upon his death. But the use to which the property may be put is always subject to the limitations that are imposed on it by the provisions of the deed or will that made the fee simple estate a defeasible one.

Upon the occurrence of the act or event defined and prohibited by the document that transfers title, the owner's estate either expires automatically or may be terminated by action taken by the party entitled to do so. Like a fee simple absolute, a defeasible fee is of potentially infinite duration, but unlike the absolute fee, a fee simple defeasible may be completely lost to its owner upon the occurrence of a particular act or event.

The principal object of a transferor (who may be either the grantor in a deed or the testator of a will) when creating a defeasible estate is to limit or control the use to which real estate may be put after he no longer has title to it. The prohibited use may be most any type of limitation that the transferor desires to impose, providing, of course, that it neither violates a statute nor is contrary to public policy.

Types of Defeasible Fees Estates in fee simple defeasible take any of three forms, distinguishable primarily by the manner in which the estates may be terminated.

A defeasible fee may be either (1) a fee subject to a condition subsequent, (2) a fee simple determinable, or (3) a fee subject to an executory limitation.

Fee Subject to a Condition Subsequent If a fee simple is **subject to a condition subsequent,** the owner of the estate is exposed to the possibility of losing his title upon the happening of some act or event that occurs after he acquires ownership of the property. The particular **condition** to which the fee is subject must be clearly stated in the instrument of conveyance; when that prohibited condition or event occurs, the transferor or his successor in interest may cause the owner's defeasible estate to be terminated. For example, if the title to a fee simple in real estate is transferred subject to the condition that the premises never be used for the sale of alcoholic beverages and the premises are subsequently used for that purpose, the transferor or his successor can take steps to terminate the owner's estate in the property.

Despite the fact that the prohibited act or event may have occurred, the owner's interest in the property will continue until the transferor takes positive steps to exercise his right to terminate that ownership interest. The person who is entitled to cause the owner's estate to come to an end must take action to terminate it within a reasonable time after the condition subsequent has been breached or his right to terminate will be forever lost. The usual manner of exercising the right is by bringing an **action to quiet title** to the property.

The right of a transferor to terminate the transferee's ownership interest when the prohibited event occurs is known as a **power of termination** or a **right of entry.** In most jurisdictions, this right may be transferred from one person to another the same as any other interest in real property.

The exercise of the power of termination causes the estate that is subject to the condition that has been breached to be forfeited. This means that the owner who has breached the condition subsequent is completely divested of his ownership of the property and title to it is vested in the person who exercised the power of

OWNERSHIP INTERESTS IN REAL ESTATE—ESTATES

termination. Because of this forfeiture feature and the law's general dislike of forfeitures, conditions subsequent are not favored. The courts are inclined to strictly construe the language used in a document by a transferor and, where possible, will interpret the language as being a statement of purpose rather than a condition subsequent. By thus interpreting the language, any possibility of a forfeiture is nullified. However, where the language used in an instrument of conveyance is clearly and unequivocally stated, a provision subjecting an estate to a condition subsequent will be enforced even though doing so results in a forfeiture of title.

Fee Simple Determinable A **fee simple determinable** is similar to a fee subject to a condition subsequent in that both of these defeasible estates are subject to possible termination and forfeiture upon the happening of a certain prohibited act or event. Unlike the fee subject to a condition subsequent, however, which terminates only when the grantor or his successor takes positive steps to bring the estate to an end, a determinable fee terminates *automatically* upon the happening of the contingency to which it is subject. When the contingent act or event occurs, the forfeited estate reverts to the transferor or his successor by operation of law.

The transferor's interest in the property prior to the occurrence of the named contingency is known as a **possibility of reverter.** Like other legally recognized property rights, a possibility of reverter is transferable from one owner to another.

Unless the language of the instrument creating a defeasible fee permits no such interpretation, the courts prefer to construe an estate as being subject to a condition subsequent rather than being a determinable fee, thus avoiding the automatic termination and forfeiture of the estate.

Fee Subject to an Executory Limitation In the foregoing discussion we saw that when a fee simple defeasible was terminated the estate reverted to the transferor, his successors, or his heirs. It is possible, however, for the instrument that creates a defeasible fee to provide that, upon the occurrence of the stated act or event, the estate will pass to some person or persons other than the transferor, his successors, or his heirs. When this is the case, the defeasible fee is said to be **subject to an executory limitation.**

LIFE ESTATES

General Characteristics

Duration A **life estate** is an ownership interest in real estate whose duration is measured by the life or lives of one or more persons. The measuring lifetime may be that of the person who owns the life estate and who is called a **life tenant** or it may be the lifetime of a person who owns no interest in the property at all. For example, land may be conveyed by its owner O "to A for his life," or it may be conveyed "to A for the life of B." In the former case, A's ownership interest continues as long as he lives. Upon his death his estate terminates and he has nothing to leave his descendants by will or succession. In the second situation, however, the ownership interest of life tenant A continues until the death of B. Therefore, if B should die before A does, A's ownership interest terminates and his right of possession of the property is at an end. On the other hand, if the life tenant A should die before B, A's ownership interest continues and that interest will pass to his heirs. The ownership interest to which A's heirs have succeeded will, of course, terminate upon the death of B. It is the lifetime that is designated by the creator of the life estate, no matter whose lifetime it may be, that measures the duration of a life tenant's ownership interest. When the measuring lifetime ends, so does the life estate.

Where the duration of a life estate is measured by the lifetime of someone other than the life tenant, it is technically referred to as being a life estate *pur autre vie* (for the life of another). Those estates which are measured by the lifetime of the life tenant himself are sometimes said to be "ordinary" life estates.

Followed by a Future Interest When the owner of a fee simple estate conveys a life estate to another person, the fee simple owner carves a lesser estate out of a larger one—an estate of limited duration is created from one of infinite duration. This necessarily means that there is something "left over" that will continue when the life estate comes to an end. The ownership interest that follows a life estate or is left over is known as a **future interest.** The nature of future interests is discussed later in the chapter.

Objective in Creating a Life Estate Life estates today are primarily created in connection with family settlements and estate planning. A husband, for example, may at the time of his death leave certain real property to his wife for her lifetime and to his children upon the wife's death. It is becoming more common in situations of this type, however, for the husband to establish a trust according to the terms of which a trustee holds title to the property for the use of the wife during her lifetime and then, upon her death, the trustee conveys the title to the surviving children.

When Life Tenant's Possession Commences In the absence of a provision to the contrary, a life tenant's right of possession of the property in which he has an estate commences when the deed creating the life estate is legally delivered to him. The terms of the deed may, however, provide for the right of possession to commence at some time in the future such as, for example, upon the death of the fee owner who created the life estate. It is also possible for two or more life estates to be created to follow one after the other, in which case each successive tenant's right of possession would be deferred until the life estate that immediately precedes his estate terminates.

Methods of Creation

Creation by Express Provision A life estate is commonly created by the express language of a deed or a will. Where created by an express provision in a deed, the life tenant's ownership interest **vests** at the moment that the transferor's deed is legally delivered to the life tenant. In the case of creation by will, the life tenant's interest comes into existence upon the death of the testator, not when the will is executed.

A deed may create a life estate either by an express grant in favor of a named person or the deed may expressly reserve a life estate to the transferor who conveys all other interests in the land to a named transferee. For example, suppose that O, the owner of Blackacre in fee simple by deed grants a present life estate to A for A's lifetime. In that case O has, by operation of law, retained to himself a future interest in Blackacre the possession of which is deferred until A's death. The reverse of this situation arises when O by deed grants Blackacre to A in fee simple but by the express language of the deed reserves to himself, O, a present life estate in the property. In this case A's right of possession of Blackacre is postponed until the death of O.

Whether created by a grant, a reservation, or by will, no particular language is required to create a valid life estate. All that is required is that there be evidence of the transferor's intention to create such an interest. The term "life estate" may never actually appear in the language of the instrument that creates the interest, although in the interests of clarity and certainty it may be desirable to do so.

Creation by Implication Life estates may be created by implication in some states. For example, if a transferor executes a deed that conveys a fee simple interest and deposits that deed with some person other than the transferee named in the deed with instructions that the deed be delivered to the transferee upon the

OWNERSHIP INTERESTS IN REAL ESTATE—ESTATES

transferor's death, a life estate is said to have been reserved to the transferor for his lifetime by implication. In legal contemplation, while an ownership interest passes to the transferee at the time the deed is deposited, the transferee's right of possession of the property is delayed until termination of the life estate belonging to the transferor.

Rights of Life Tenant

Right to Transfer A life tenant's rights with respect to his ownership interest can be limited or defined by the provisions of the instrument that creates the life estate. In the absence of any express provisions in a transferring document to the contrary, the life tenant's estate is transferable. The life tenant cannot, of course, convey an interest in the property that would continue after the death of the person whose lifetime measures the duration of the life estate. Like any other owner of an interest in real estate, a life tenant cannot transfer an interest greater than the one he owns.

If the duration of the life estate is measured by the lifetime of the life tenant himself, he obviously has no interest that he can leave by will. The life tenant can, however, sell his interest or lease it, but the interest that the buyer or the lessee acquires will terminate upon the death of the life tenant.

When a life estate's duration is measured by the lifetime of some person other than the life tenant himself, the interest of the life tenant can be transferred either by deed during the life tenant's lifetime or by will at the time of his death. For the life estate to be transferable by will, the life tenant must of course predecease the person whose lifetime measures the duration of the estate. Thereafter, the interest of the person named in the will, like that of any other life tenant, expires upon termination of the measuring lifetime. For example, suppose that O, the owner of Blackacre in fee simple, by deed transferred a life estate to A for the lifetime of B. A thereafter executes a will leaving all of his property to his son S. If B dies before A, the life estate terminates and S will receive no interest in Blackacre when his father, A, dies. On the other hand, if A predeceases B, his son S will receive a life estate in Blackacre which will continue until the death of B.

Right to Mortgage In addition to being able to sell or lease his interest in real property, a life tenant may mortgage it. Whether or not such an interest, because of its uncertain duration, represents a desirable security for a debt depends upon the facts in a particular situation and the creditor's evaluation of them.

Right of Possession and Use A life tenant has the same right of possession and use of real property as an owner in fee simple, subject only to certain duties imposed upon him by law for the protection of the owner whose interest and right of possession commences upon termination of the life estate.

Duties and Liabilities of a Life Tenant

Duty Not to Commit Waste A life tenant's use and enjoyment of his estate is subject to the duty imposed on him by law not to commit waste. **Waste,** as that term applies to life estates, is an act or a failure to act on the part of the life tenant which results in a substantial and permanent reduction in the market value of the property. The concept of waste is designed to protect the owner whose interest in the property follows that of the life tenant.

Despite the apparent inclusiveness of the foregoing definition, not all voluntary acts which depreciate a property's market value constitute actionable waste. For example, where land has traditionally been used for the production of timber, a life tenant may continue such activity. Also, open mines on the land may be worked by a life tenant, even to the point of exhaustion, but in the absence of specific statutory authorization no new mines may be opened by him.

Permissive Waste A life tenant's omission or failure to act may give rise to what is known as "permissive" waste. Permissive waste results when the tenant fails to make the repairs necessary to prevent the property from injury or decay. A life tenant is liable for any decrease in the value of the property due to his neglect or indifference in properly maintaining the premises.

Inspection of the Premises While the owner of a life estate has the right to occupy and possess real property free from interference by other persons during the period of his ownership, the owner of the succeeding estate may enter upon the premises from time to time and inspect them to ascertain whether waste is being committed. If the life tenant is committing waste, the person whose interest is being injured may bring an action against him for damages or an injunction or both.

In some jurisdictions[2] a life tenant who commits waste may, at the court's discretion, be liable for a penalty payment of three times the amount of damages actually suffered by the property.

Duty to Pay Taxes In some states[3] a life tenant is under an obligation to pay annual property taxes and a proportionate share of any special assessments levied for improvements that benefit his property.

Duty to Pay Interest on Mortgage It sometimes happens that real property is encumbered by a mortgage or deed of trust at the time a life tenant's right to possession begins. In such a case, the life tenant is required to make interest payments on the secured debt, but he is under no obligation to pay anything toward amortization of the principal. It is the responsibility of the owner of the estate that follows the life estate to make payments to retire the principal of the debt.

---

[2] For example, see California Civil Code, sec. 732.

[3] See, for example, California Civil Code, sec. 840.

Termination of Life Estates

Automatic Termination A life estate terminates automatically upon the death of the person whose lifetime measures the estate's duration, whether that person is the life tenant himself or some other person. For example, where the duration of the life estate is measured by the lifetime of the life tenant, he has no interest, as we have seen, that will descend to his heirs upon his death. On the other hand, where the measuring lifetime is that of someone other than the life tenant, the life tenant has an interest that will descend to his heirs, providing always that the life tenant dies before the person whose lifetime determines the estate's duration.

Termination by Merger Under certain circumstances, a life estate may terminate before the death of the person whose lifetime measures the estate's term. For example, a life estate will be terminated by the merger of the life estate with the interest in the land that follows the life estate. Such a merger occurs when the life tenant acquires ownership of the succeeding interest or when the owner of that interest acquires title to the life estate.

Termination by Defeasance A life estate, like an estate in fee simple, can be created subject to the possibility of termination upon the occurrence of some specified act or event; in other words, it may be a defeasible estate. Upon the happening of the prohibited act or event, the life estate comes to an end even though the lifetime that measures its duration continues. For example, if O transfers a life estate to A subject to the condition that the premises never be used for the sale of alcoholic beverages, A's use of the premises for that purpose during his lifetime will cause his estate to be terminated.

ESTATES IN FEE TAIL

Characteristics of a Fee Tail

The **estate in fee tail** was devised centuries ago

to keep a family's lands within the family and to perpetuate the landed aristocracy in England. A fee tail was created by a grant of Blackacre by O to "A and the *heirs of his body.*" The transferee of the estate, A, had no power to subsequently transfer an estate in fee simple absolute because he owned no such estate. A's interest in Blackacre was a life estate for his lifetime followed by a similar life estate in the eldest son that survived him. If the holder of a fee tail died without leaving an heir of his body, Blackacre reverted to O or to O's heirs.

Limited Recognition Today

A majority of the states have statutes providing that language in instruments that formerly would have created an estate in fee tail now creates a fee simple instead. Statutes in some of the states[4] provide that it is the transferee who is named first in the transferring document (A in the foregoing illustration) who acquires the estate in fee simple. Other states[5] adopt the view that the first-named transferee takes only a life estate which is followed by a fee simple in favor of his immediate lineal heirs.

ESTATES FOR YEARS

Characteristics of the Estate

An **estate for years,** which is also known as a **tenancy for years,** is an ownership interest in land the duration of which is measured by a fixed or definite period of time. An estate for years is created by the execution of a lease or rental agreement which gives rise to a landlord-tenant relationship. Although the interest acquired by the tenant is called an estate "for years," the term is a misnomer and can be misleading. The actual duration of the tenant's interest may be for a number of years, a single year, or for periods of less than a year, such as a number of weeks or months.

The essential characteristic of an estate for years is that it must endure for a definite period of time. It must begin at a fixed point in time and end at a fixed point in time, but the duration of the particular period for which it continues is of no consequence to the existence of the estate. Some states, however, have statutes[6] establishing a maximum period of time for which leases will be valid.

In most states oral leases for periods not exceeding one year are enforceable, while leases for longer than one year must be in writing to be enforceable.

Landlord-Tenant Relationship

A lease which creates an estate for years is both a conveyance of an interest in real property and a contract between a landlord and a tenant defining their respective rights and duties. An estate for years involves a continuing relationship between the tenant, who has a present possessory interest in the property, and the landlord, who remains the owner of the property but whose right to possession and use of the property is deferred until expiration of the lease period. The landlord-owner's interest in the land is known as a **reversionary interest.** Upon expiration of the tenant's estate for years, the right of possession of the premises that the tenant acquires by reason of the lease reverts to the landlord-owner. The incidents of the landlord-tenant relationship are discussed in detail in Chapter 22.

Although an estate for years is a possessory interest in land, it is not at common law considered to be real property but instead, as we previously noted, is called a "chattel real" and is governed by the rules of law applicable to personal property. For example, if the provisions of a will leave all of a testator's real property to A and all of his personal property to B, B rather than A would be the recipient of any estates for

---

[4] For example, Alabama, California, Maryland, New Hampshire, and New York.

[5] For example, Arkansas and Illinois.

[6] For example, California Civil Code, secs. 717 and 718 limit leases of land for agricultural and horticultural purposes to 51 years and leases of town and city lots to 99 years.

years that the testator owned at the time of his death. Under the right conditions, a lease can have considerable value.

ESTATES FROM PERIOD TO PERIOD

An estate or **tenancy from period to period,** also known as a **periodic tenancy,** is an interest in real property that endures from week to week, month to month, or year to year. Although the estate may be created by express language, it more frequently arises when property is rented with no limitation placed on the duration of the tenancy and rent is paid on a weekly, monthly, or annual basis. Thereafter, the landlord-tenant relationship will continue from one rent payment period to another until one of the parties gives appropriate notice of termination to the other party.

The characteristic feature of an estate from period to period is its continuity. Unlike an estate for years which expires at the end of a definite period, an estate from period to period continues for successive periods until steps are taken to terminate it. As long as an estate from period to period continues, the relationship between the landlord and the tenant is practically identical to the relationship that arises from an estate for years.

ESTATES AT WILL

An **estate at will,** also known as a **tenancy at will,** is an estate that has no fixed period of duration and is terminable at the whim or will of either the owner or the occupant of the property. Such an estate also terminates by operation of law upon the death of either party or upon conveyance of the property by the owner. At common law the estate can be terminated without any period of notice whatsoever, but statutes frequently require the giving of 30 days' notice.[7]

[7] California Civil Code, sec. 789, for example, requires the owner to give the occupant 30 days' notice of termination.

An estate at will arises, for example, when a prospective tenant takes possession of real property with the permission of the owner but for some reason an intended lease is never executed or, if executed, the lease is invalid.

ESTATES AT SUFFERANCE

An **estate at sufferance,** or **tenancy at sufferance,** is an interest in real property which exists when a tenant wrongfully remains in possession or "holds over" after his right to possession has ended. Under such circumstances, alternative courses of action are available to the landlord. Under one alternative, he may treat the tenant as a trespasser and bring a legal action to evict him. The other alternative permits the landlord to treat the tenant's holding over as a decision by him to extend the lease under which the premises were previously occupied. The problems of the holdover tenant are discussed in greater detail in Chapter 22.

FUTURE INTERESTS

General Characteristics

The discussion of ownership interests in real estate to this point has been concerned with the characteristics of estates that have to do with the *duration* of the interest (fees simple, life estates, estates for years, and estates at sufferance) and the *quality* of the interest (absolute or defeasible).

Estates may also be classified and considered in terms of the *time* when the owner of the interest has the *right of possession* of the property and hence the right to use and enjoy it. The owner of an estate may either have the right to presently possess and occupy the property or his right to enter upon and possess the premises may be postponed until a later point in time. When an owner is not entitled to possession and enjoyment of property until some time in the future, his interest in that property is said to be a **future interest.**

Future interests arise as a consequence of es-

OWNERSHIP INTERESTS IN REAL ESTATE—ESTATES

tates of shorter duration having been carved out of a fee simple absolute. We have seen, for example, that when O, the owner of an estate in fee simple absolute, conveys Blackacre to A for A's lifetime, some interest in Blackacre is "left over" to O. By conveying a life estate, O did not relinquish his fee simple absolute, but during A's lifetime O has no right to possession of the property because he transferred that right to A. During the lifetime of A, O's interest in Blackacre is a *future* estate in fee simple absolute. Upon A's death, O will again be entitled to possession of Blackacre for a potentially infinite period of time or until he again carves out and transfers a lesser present possessory interest to some other person. Future interests, of course, are not confined to interests which follow life estates. They arise whenever a lesser estate is created out of a larger one.

It should be noted that although O's right to possession is deferred until sometime in the future, he owns his fee simple interest *now*. This means that the law will afford *present* protection to O's ownership interest in Blackacre.

Future interests are inheritable and most of them are transferable from one owner to another by deed as well.

Types of Future Interests

A future interest may take the form of a reversion, a power of termination, and a possibility of reverter, or a remainder.

Reversions, possibilities of reverter, and powers of termination have certain characteristics in common and taken together are referred to as reversionary interests. A **reversionary interest** is a right of future possession that is left over or reserved to a transferor after he has conveyed to another person a less than fee simple interest that gives that person the right to present possession of the property. All other future interests are classified as **remainders**.

Reversionary Interests

Reversion   A **reversion** is a future estate that a transferor retains when he conveys less than his entire interest in Blackacre. It is the residue of an estate that is left over when a transferor transfers an estate or estates of shorter duration than the estate he owns. If, for example, O, the owner of Blackacre in fee simple absolute, transfers an estate to A for A's lifetime, a residue is left with O. This residue or interest that is left over is a reversion and O, the owner of it, is called a **reversioner.** During the existence of A's life estate, O's interest is a reversion in fee simple absolute. Upon A's death, the right of immediate possession of Blackacre "reverts" to O by operation of law, that is, without the need for any action on O's part. As soon as O is entitled to possession of Blackacre, his reversion comes to an end and he is then the owner of a present estate in Blackacre in fee simple absolute. He is thereafter free, of course, to again carve out lesser estates from his fee and to create in himself a new reversion.

A reversioner can sell or make a gift of his reversion during his lifetime or it can pass to his heirs by succession or to his devisees by will upon his death. No matter to whom or by what means the interest is transferred, it continues to be a reversion. Any transferee, like the original reversioner, will have a present interest and right to possession of Blackacre upon expiration of the intervening possessory estate.

A reversion is said to be a reversionary interest that is not subject to any **condition precedent.** This means that there is nothing which must occur before the reversioner is entitled to possession of the property except the natural expiration of the estate that gives its owner the right of present possession.

Power of Termination   A power of termination, we have seen, is a future interest that is retained by a transferor when he conveys an estate that is subject to a condition subsequent. This interest of the transferor is also known as a right of entry. The effect of a provision in a document of conveyance that gives the transferor the right to enter the property and take possession of it upon breach of a stated condition is to enable the transferor or his successors to terminate the transferee's interest in the property. A transferor who has a power of termination or right of entry is required to take affirmative steps to bring the transferee's estate to an end; it does not terminate automatically. Failure on the part of the transferor to exercise his power or right within a reasonable time after the condition is breached by the transferee may operate as a waiver of that right and preclude him from terminating the transferee's estate.

When the transferor exercises his power of termination, he changes his previous future interest into a present possessory one. Upon termination of the transferee's defeasible estate, the transferor's interest in the property becomes a fee simple absolute with the right of immediate possession.

Possibility of Reverter When the owner of a fee simple absolute transfers a fee simple determinable, which is a slightly lesser estate than he owns, a residue is left to the transferor. Because the interest that was transferred is a determinable fee, there is, as we have seen, the possibility that the transferor will again be entitled to possession of the property at some uncertain time in the future. The transferor's right to possession will arise if and when the condition occurs that makes the fee a determinable one and thus causes the estate to come to an end. Although the prohibited act or event may never occur, the possibility is always there and it is for this reason that the reversionary interest that belongs to the transferor of a determinable fee is called a possibility of reverter.

When the act or event upon which a fee simple determinable is conditioned occurs, the estate comes to an end automatically. Upon termination of the determinable fee, the transferor's possibility of reverter terminates also and his interest becomes a present possessory estate in fee simple absolute.

Remainders
Like a reversion, a **remainder** is a future interest in real property which entitles its owner to possession upon termination of the estate of another person who is presently entitled to possession of the property. Unlike a reversion, which returns the right of possession to the person who transferred a present interest, a remainder is a future interest that belongs to someone other than the transferor of the present interest, who is known as a **remainderman.** In creating a remainder, a transferor completely divests himself of any ownership interest in real property by simultaneously transferring a present interest to one person and a future interest remaining after termination of the present interest to a different person. For example, where O conveys Blackacre "to A for his lifetime and thereafter to B," A acquires a present life estate which is followed by B's remainder in fee simple. No interest was retained by the former owner, O, and consequently he has no interest in the property.

Unlike a reversionary interest, which is a residue of a larger estate that returns the right of possession to a transferor by *operation of law,* a remainder is an interest newly created in a transferee and arises *only* by reason of an *act of the transferor.* The same instrument, either a deed or a will, that creates and transfers a present estate in land simultaneously creates and transfers a remainder. Ownership of the remainder passes to the remainderman at the time of delivery of the deed or, if the transfer is by will, upon the death of the testator.

Remainders have traditionally been classified as being either vested or contingent.

Vested Remainder A remainder is said to be *vested* when its owner would be entitled to take possession of the property subject to the remainder upon termination of an existing possessory interest. For example, if O, the owner of Blackacre in fee simple, conveys a life estate to A and a remainder to B who is living at the time of the conveyance, B's interest is said to be a *vested remainder.*

Classes of Vested Remainders The *Restatement of the Law of Property*[8] classifies vested remainders as being either (1) indefeasibly vested, (2) vested subject to open, or (3) vested subject to complete defeasance.

A remainder is *indefeasibly vested* when the remainderman is certain to acquire a present interest or right of possession at some time in the future, and once that interest is acquired it cannot be divested. For example, where O, the owner of Blackacre in fee simple, transfers the property "to A for life, remainder to B," who is living at the time of the transfer, B acquires an indefeasibly vested remainder.

A remainder is *vested subject to open* when the remainder is created in favor of a class of persons, such as the children of a named person. All of the named person's children who are living at the time of the conveyance have vested interests, but if another child is subsequently born to that person, the class "opens up" to include the newborn child. The effect of this "opening up," of course, is to dilute the interest of the other children. Suppose, for example, that O, the owner of Blackacre in fee simple, transfers the property "to A for life, remainder to the children of B." At the time of the transfer, B has two children. These two children have a vested remainder in the property that is subject to being opened up to include as co-owners any children thereafter born to B.

A remainder is *vested subject to complete defeasance* when it is created in favor of a definite remainderman who is not certain to acquire a later right to possession because his interest in the property could expire before the preceding estate comes to an end. Such a remainder is created where O, the owner of Blackacre in fee simple, conveys a life estate to A and a remainder to B, both estates being subject to the condition subsequent that the property shall not be used for a certain prohibited purpose. B's remainder interest in the property is vested, but is subject to being lost if either he or A breaches the condition to which the transfer by O was subject.

Contingent Remainder Although the term "contingent remainder" is widely used to describe a type of future interest in real property, the *Restatement of the Law of Property* does not use the expression. Many courts and writers, however, continue to use the term to refer to a remainder whose owner could not be identified if the preceding interest were to end or, even though there were an identifiable remainderman, some event must occur before he is entitled to his interest. The *Restatement*[9] prefers to use the term "remainder subject to a condition precedent" as more clearly describing the nature of the interest to which it refers. A remainder of this type arises, for example, where O, the owner of Blackacre in fee simple, transfers the property "to A for life, remainder to B if, but only if B shall attain the age of 21 years." If B is only 16 years old at the time of the transfer of Blackacre, the interest that he acquires is a remainder subject to a condition precedent, that condition being that he attain the age of 21 years.

The law favors the vesting of interests and, in the absence of a clearly expressed intention of the parties to the contrary, the courts will construe a remainder as being vested. This means that conditions contained in a document of transfer will be viewed as being *subsequent* to the vesting of the interest rather than *precedent* to it, whenever a reasonable interpretation of the language of the document permits it.

Transferability and Duration of Future Interests
In most jurisdictions all types of future interests are transferable from one owner to another,

---

[8] Sec. 157(1), (2), (3).

[9] Sec. 157(4).

whether they be reversionary interests or remainders, and whether they be vested or defeasible.

Some states[10] have adopted statutes that limit the life of future interests in real property to periods ranging from 21 to 40 years from the date of their creation.

[10] For example, Connecticut, Florida, Illinois, Iowa, Kentucky, Maine, Maryland, Massachusetts, Michigan, Minnesota, Nebraska, New York, Ohio, and Rhode Island.

QUESTIONS

1. What is the modern meaning of "estate" as that term is used in connection with real property?
2. Indicate the principal ways in which estates in real property differ.
3. What is the estate that entitles its owner to the greatest quantity of rights recognized by law? Is the owner of such an estate free to use his property without limitations?
4. Explain what is meant by the statement that an estate in fee simple absolute is an estate of potentially infinite duration.
5. What is the essential difference between an estate in fee simple absolute and a fee simple defeasible?
6. Why, when transferring real estate to a new owner, would one who has an estate in fee simple absolute transfer a fee simple defeasible instead of the entire interest?
7. Point out the basic similarity and the essential difference between a fee subject to a condition subsequent and a fee simple determinable.
8. A deed transfers a parcel of real estate "to A for the life of B." What is the interest that each of them has in the property following the transfer?
9. As compared with an owner of an estate in fee simple absolute, what is the principal limitation on a life tenant's use of his property?
10. With respect to life estates, what is permissive waste?
11. What is the essential characteristic of an estate for years? How is such an estate created?
12. Give an example of the manner in which a reversion may be created.
13. Give an example of the manner in which a remainder may be created.
14. Name three kinds of reversionary interests in real estate.
15. How do a remainder that is indefeasibly vested and a remainder subject to a condition precedent differ?

Chapter 6

Co-Ownership of Real Estate

We have seen that it is possible for more than one person to have ownership interests in the same parcel of real estate at the same time. One person, for example, may own the surface of Blackacre while another owns a portion of the subsurface and still another owns the airspace over the land above a certain height. We have also seen that one person may own a present possessory interest in the form of a life estate or an estate for years at the same time that another person owns a remainder or reversionary interest in the same property. Each of these persons is the sole owner of his particular interest in Blackacre and he alone has the right to use and enjoy the interest he owns. As the sole owner of his particular interest in the property, he is said to own that interest in **severalty.**

NATURE OF CO-OWNERSHIP

In contrast to ownership in severalty is ownership of the same property interest by two or more persons at the same time. These persons are said to hold their interest in **co-ownership.**

The term "co-ownership" does not apply to situations where two persons own separate or successive interests in the same parcel of land because each of them is the sole owner of whatever his interest may be. Co-ownership of real estate refers to the situation where a particular interest, whether it be a fee simple, a life estate, a reversion, or other interest is simultaneously or concurrently owned by two or more persons. Each of the co-owners owns an *undivided* proportionate share of the entire interest, with no one of them owning any specific or identifiable part of it. Each co-owner has a right to share in the possession and enjoyment of all of the property equally with all of the other co-owners.

Co-ownership is sometimes referred to as *concurrent* ownership and also as **cotenancy. Co-owners** are also called **cotenants.**

Co-ownership of real estate may arise from

the voluntary acts of co-owners as, for example, where A and B pool their funds and invest in a parcel of property. On the other hand, A and B may become co-owners involuntarily by inheriting a parcel of real estate from a deceased parent. In any event, whether a particular form of co-ownership is created voluntarily or involuntarily, the incidents of that co-ownership are the same.

FORMS OF CO-OWNERSHIP

Ownership of property by two or more persons may take any of several forms, each form differing somewhat in its legal characteristics and consequences from the others. These various forms of co-ownership were conceived and developed as society's response to perceived needs and have evolved in accordance with changing economic conditions and social philosophies. Some of the early forms of co-ownership have fallen into disuse and are today practically extinct, while those remaining have in many instances been altered by statute to meet the requirements of modern society.

The following forms of co-ownership are commonly encountered in one jurisdiction or another today: (1) joint tenancy, (2) tenancy in common, (3) tenancy by the entirety, and (4) community property.

JOINT TENANCY

General Characteristics

Right of Survivorship The outstanding characteristic of the **joint tenancy** form of co-ownership is the **right of survivorship.** According to that right, upon the death of one of the joint tenants his interest in the co-owned property, instead of descending to his heirs or devisees, belongs to the co-owning joint tenant or joint tenants who survive him. As each joint tenant dies, his interest passes to the surviving joint tenants as co-owners until only one tenant remains, at which time the property is no longer co-owned. If A, B, and C own Blackacre as joint tenants, upon A's death Blackacre will belong to B and C as surviving joint tenants, despite the fact that A may have left heirs. Thereafter, upon the death of B his interest goes to C who survived him and, since there is no longer any one remaining who co-owns the property with C, he is the owner of Blackacre in severalty.

The right of survivorship is rooted in the common law notion that the joint tenants comprise a single legal entity which owns the property. In accordance with this notion, upon the death of one joint tenant the property continues to be owned by the entity minus the deceased joint tenant. Eventually the entity will be comprised of only the one who lives the longest and at that point he will be the sole owner of the property. In the foregoing illustration, the entity was originally made up of A, B, and C. Upon A's death the entity continued with B and C as its members. On B's death the entity was reduced to C, the sole survivor, and at that point the fictitious entity ceased to exist.

Intent to Create Must Be Clear The joint tenancy was a favored form of co-ownership at early common law because it well served the interests of overlord and tenant in the feudal system. At early common law, when land was transferred to two or more persons and the nature of their co-ownership was not specified or was unclear, the presumption arose that a joint tenancy was intended to have been created. With the passage of time, however, the joint tenancy form of co-ownership fell out of favor, primarily because the right of survivorship came to be regarded as unfair to the heirs or devisees of a deceased joint tenant. The loss or forfeiture of one tenant's interest upon his death was offensive to certain notions of justice. As a result, shortly after the Revolutionary War legislatures in this country reexamined

CO-OWNERSHIP OF REAL ESTATE

and revamped the law concerning joint tenancies.

Today over half of the states[1] have statutes providing that a conveyance of real property to two or more persons shall not create a joint tenancy unless the intent to do so is clearly indicated in the instrument of conveyance. Statutes in other states[2] have either abolished the joint tenancy form of co-ownership entirely or have eliminated its chief characteristic, the right of survivorship.

Applicable to All Property Interests Both real and personal property may be co-owned by two or more persons as joint tenants. As far as real property is concerned, any ownership interest can be held in joint tenancy, whether that interest be a fee simple, a life estate, a reversion, or some other estate.

Creation of a Joint Tenancy

Common Law Unities At common law a joint tenancy was created only when four so-called *unities* were present, namely: (1) the unity of *time*, (2) the unity of *title*, (3) the unity of *interest*, and (4) the unity of *possession*. If any one of the four unities was missing, a joint tenancy was not created and the form of co-ownership among the transferees was held to be another type of co-ownership with differing incidents.

Unity of time means that the interests of the co-owners must vest or commence at the *same* point in time. For the *unity of title* to be present, the co-owners must acquire their interests by the *same* deed, will, or other instrument of transfer from the *same* transferor. The *unity of interest* requirement is met if the interests acquired by the co-owners are *equal*—that is to say, the share of each co-owner must be the same in all respects as that of every other co-owner. And finally, the *unity of possession* requires that each of the co-owners must have an *undivided* interest in the entire co-owned property and must have an *equal right to possess* all of the property, not just certain specified parts of it.

Most states that recognize the joint tenancy form of co-ownership still require that the four common law unities be present if a joint tenancy is to be created. Virtually all of them also require that the unities must continue to exist if the joint tenancy is to continue. There is a growing tendency among the states, however, to relax the requirement that all four of the unities must be present and this is particularly true with respect to the unity of time.

TENANCY IN COMMON

General Characteristics

Preferred over Joint Tenancy Co-ownership in the form of **tenancy in common** is the most usual type of concurrent estate encountered today. In more than half of the states it is favored over all other forms of co-ownership. This preference frequently is reflected by a statutory presumption that a tenancy in common is created unless the parties to a real estate transaction clearly indicate a different intent.[3] Generally speaking, where one or more persons are co-owners of an interest in real property, the courts will find them to be tenants in common unless special circumstances compel a different conclusion.

---

[1] Among them California, Illinois, Indiana, Massachusetts, Michigan, Minnesota, New Jersey, New York, and Wisconsin.

[2] Among them Alabama, Arizona, Florida, Kentucky, Pennsylvania, Tennessee, Texas, Virginia, and Washington.

[3] For example, Michigan Statutes Annotated, sec. 26.44 provides: "All grants and devises of lands, made to two or more persons, except as provided in the following section, shall be construed to create estates in common, and not in joint tenancy, unless expressly declared to be a joint tenancy." Sec. 26.45 states: "The preceding section shall not apply to mortgages, nor to devises of grants made in trust, or made to executors, or to husband and wife."

No particular language is required to create a tenancy in common.

No Right of Survivorship A tenancy in common differs significantly from a joint tenancy in that there is *no* right of survivorship among tenants in common. Upon the death of each co-owner, his interest passes to his heirs or devisees rather than belonging to the surviving co-owners. It is this lack of forfeiture of a deceased tenant's interest that has caused the law to favor tenancies in common over joint tenancies and to require an express and clear declaration of intention in order that a joint tenancy may be created.

Unity of Possession Only A characteristic feature of a tenancy in common is that the only common law unity that is required for it to exist is the *unity of possession.* By virtue of this unity, each tenant in common has an equal right to possession of the entire co-owned property and cannot be excluded from any part of it by the other co-owner or co-owners.

Because the *unity of interest* is not a requirement of a tenancy in common, the respective shares of the co-owners need not be equal. This means, for example, that where A and B own Blackacre as tenants in common, A can own an undivided two-thirds or three-fourths interest in the property and B the other one-third or one-fourth interest. Where there are more than two tenants in common, their ownership interests may be any combination of fractions or percentages of the whole.

When property is transferred to two or more tenants in common without their respective shares having been specifically designated, they are deemed to hold the property in equal shares.

Applicable to All Property Interests As is true of a joint tenancy, interests which are co-owned by tenants in common may be any type of legally recognized property interest, such as a fee simple, a life estate, a future interest, and so forth. Both real and personal property may be co-owned by tenants in common.

RIGHTS AND DUTIES OF JOINT TENANTS AND TENANTS IN COMMON

Aside from the right of survivorship, the property rights of joint tenants and tenants in common are essentially the same.

Right of Possession

As we have seen, all co-owners, whether joint tenants or tenants in common, have the same rights of possession of the entire co-owned parcel of real estate. No cotenant may exclude the other from possession of the property either by physically ousting him from the premises or by granting the exclusive right to possession of the property to a third person by means of a lease. However, where one cotenant assumes exclusive possession of the property without objection of his cotenants, he ordinarily is not liable to them for the rental value of their interests in the property, nor need the cotenant who occupies the premises without objection from the others make available to them their proportionate share of whatever the land produces during his sole occupancy of it.

Obviously two persons cannot occupy the same space at the same time. Hence it is necessary that the co-owners agree upon some method whereby they can distribute the benefits of possession among themselves. Where the property is not conducive to each cotenant's occupying an agreed part of it, the co-owners may lease the entire parcel to a lessee and allocate the rent in accordance with their proportionate shares in the property. Where such an arrangement cannot be agreed upon, the remedy remaining to the co-owners is to terminate their co-ownership.

Right of Contribution

A co-owner who pays more than his proportionate share of necessary expenses and maintenance costs of the property is entitled to **contribution** or indemnity from the other co-owners. Necessary expenses include the cost of repairs, taxes, interest, insurance, and other charges. A co-owner's right to contribution for maintenance and repair costs does not extend to improvements that he makes to the property.

To be entitled to contribution, a co-owner must make a demand upon the other cotenants for their share of the expense prior to the time that he makes payment. His demand for prior payment is not required, however, where immediate or emergency action is necessary or where the other co-owners are not reasonably available.

A co-owner's right to contribution is enforced by means of a lien which he acquires on the interests of the other co-owners.

Duty Not to Commit Waste

Every co-owner is under a duty not to commit waste to the co-owned premises. Waste, as we have seen, is conduct which is detrimental to the property in that it depreciates its market value. Where waste is committed by one cotenant, others have a cause of action against him for an injunction or damages or both, depending upon the particular circumstances of the case.

TERMINATION OF JOINT TENANCIES AND TENANCIES IN COMMON

Termination by Severance

A joint tenant may terminate or "sever" his co-ownership interest by transferring that interest to some other person. In other words, a joint tenant is not forever "locked in" to his joint tenancy to be freed only by his cotenant's death. When a joint tenant transfers his interest in co-owned property, he is said to have destroyed the unity of title and thereafter, lacking that essential element, the co-ownership ceases to be a joint tenancy. For example, if A and B own Blackacre as joint tenants and A by deed conveys his interest to C, the joint tenancy form of co-ownership is thereby said to be severed or terminated. As a result of A's conveyance, Blackacre is co-owned by B and C, but their co-ownership is in the form of a tenancy in common rather than a joint tenancy.

Consent of Co-Owners Not Required The so-called **right of severance** is an absolute right that belongs to every joint tenant and may be exercised by him without the need to consult his cotenants or obtain their consent to his action. It should be noted, however, that it is only the *form* of co-ownership that is severed or destroyed by a cotenant's action and not the *fact* of co-ownership. A severance changes the severing cotenant's interest from a joint tenancy interest into a tenancy in common interest, but the property continues to be co-owned as an undivided unit.

Effect of Severance on Cotenants Where three or more joint tenants own a parcel of real estate and one of them exercises his right of severance, his action does not affect the relationship existing among the other cotenants, but only changes the character and the ownership of his interest.

For example, if A, B, and C own Blackacre as joint tenants and A conveys his interest to D, the joint tenancy is severed only with respect to the undivided one-third interest acquired by D from A. The joint tenancy relationship between B and C is unaffected and continues as before with respect to the undivided two-thirds interest owned by them. Following the conveyance by A to D, the status of ownership of Blackacre is as follows: B and C as a fictitious entity or unit own an undivided two-thirds interest as joint tenants. This fictitious unit becomes a tenant in common with D who owns an undivided one-third interest in the property. If B should die, his survivor, C, will take the entire two-thirds interest that previously was owned by the fictitious unit composed of B and C. Thereafter, Blackacre will be co-owned by C and D as tenants in common, C having a two-thirds interest and D one-third.

Right Applies to Joint Tenants Only The right of severance is an incident only of the joint tenancy form of co-ownership. In fact, as we have seen, the effect of exercising the right of severance is to convert an interest into a tenancy in common interest. It should again be noted that only the *form* of co-ownership is changed by severance. The co-ownership of the property continues until it is brought to an end by some appropriate means.

Termination by Partition

Both joint tenants and tenants in common may terminate their co-ownership relationship by means of a **partition.** A partition of co-owned property may be brought about either by an agreement among the co-owners or by the action of a court.

Voluntary Partition A partition by agreement, also known as a *voluntary* partition, is accomplished by co-owners agreeing to divide physically the co-owned property into as many parcels as there are co-owners and distributing those parcels among themselves. Following distribution, each former co-owner owns his individual parcel in severalty.

It is not always possible to bring about the voluntary partition of real estate. The co-owners may be unable to agree on the manner of carving out and allocating parcels from the whole property or the property itself may be of such a character that it is not susceptible to physical division, as where an office building or an apartment house has been inherited by cotenants. If voluntary division of the co-owned property is not possible, the cotenant desiring to terminate the co-ownership relationship may bring a legal action seeking a partition.

Judicial Partition Judicial partition provides the means by which persons who find themselves in an unwanted co-ownership situation can terminate that relationship. While the courts prefer to divide physically (partition "in kind") the property among the co-owners, partition proceedings today normally result in a judicial sale of the co-owned property and a division of the proceeds among the co-owners in accordance with their proportionate shares. All jurisdictions today permit partition by sale in a proper case. At the discretion of the court, the sale may be either public or private.

Partition Is an Absolute Right Every person co-owning real estate either as a joint tenant or a tenant in common is entitled to a judicial partition as a matter of absolute right. The reason for seeking to have the co-owned property partitioned is entirely immaterial to the exercise of the right. Furthermore, the fact that the partition may result in a financial loss to the other cotenants will not prevent one co-owner from exercising his right.

Like other rights belonging to individuals, a co-owner's right of partition may be *waived* by an agreement entered into by all of the co-owners.

Termination by Transfer between Cotenants

Both joint tenancies and tenancies in common are terminated when one of two co-owners transfers all of his interest in co-owned property to the other cotenant. By means of such a conveyance, the transferee becomes the sole owner of the property.

The transfer between cotenants may be effected either by gift or by sale.

Termination by Survivorship

By virtue of the right of survivorship, when one of two joint tenants dies the co-ownership is terminated. The cotenant who survives the **decedent** becomes the owner of the property in severalty. As we have seen, this is the case even though the deceased joint tenant may have attempted to dispose of his share of the co-owned property by will.

By contrast, since the right of survivorship is

not one of its incidents, a tenancy in common is not terminated upon the death of one of two-co-owners. The heirs or devisees of a deceased tenant in common succeed to his interest in the property and become tenants in common with the surviving cotenant.

Termination by Agreement
The joint tenancy form of co-ownership can be terminated and converted into a tenancy in common if all of the joint tenants enter into a contract whereby they agree among themselves to eliminate the right of survivorship.

Termination by Involuntary Transfer
The involuntary conveyance of a joint tenant's interest has the same legal effect as his voluntary transfer of that interest. For example, where a judgment creditor of one of two joint tenants levies on the debtor tenant's interest and thereafter purchases the tenant's interest at the execution sale, the debtor's interest terminates and the creditor becomes a tenant in common with the other cotenant.

It should be noted, however, that the mere giving of a mortgage or deed of trust by a joint tenant on his interest in co-owned property does not terminate a joint tenancy. Nor is a joint tenancy terminated by a creditor obtaining a judgment lien against one cotenant. In either instance, the joint tenancy is not terminated until a foreclosure or execution sale of the joint tenant's interest in the property takes place. It is the forced sale of the cotenant's interest in the co-owned property that brings about a severance of the joint tenancy relationship.

TENANCY BY THE ENTIRETY

The form of co-ownership known as a **tenancy by the entirety** can exist only between husband and wife. Tenancy by the entirety had its common law beginnings in a social setting in which the husband and wife were considered to be one—the concept of spousal unity—and consequently only one estate existed with only one owner. With the passage of time, however, the tenancy by the entirety has undergone substantial change and in more than half of the states today it is no longer a recognized form of co-ownership. In these states a conveyance to a husband and wife will create either a joint tenancy or a tenancy in common, depending upon the language of the instrument of conveyance.

With varying statutory modifications, the tenancy by the entirety is recognized by approximately twenty jurisdictions.[4]

A tenancy by the entirety is like a joint tenancy in that an important incident of both types of tenancies is the *right of survivorship.* According to the prevailing view, upon the death of one tenant by the entirety, the surviving spouse succeeds to the full ownership of the property.

A tenancy by the entirety differs from a joint tenancy in that one tenant by the entirety cannot convert it into a tenancy in common by means of severance.

At common law the husband had the exclusive control and right to possession of property held in tenancy by the entirety, together with the right to use the rents and profits from such property entirely for his own purposes. Today, however, the majority of states that recognize tenancies by the entirety give the spouses equal rights in the control and enjoyment of the property.

COMMUNITY PROPERTY

Origin of the Community Property System
Co-ownership of property in the form of **community property** is limited to the husband and wife relationship. The community property concept is believed to have originated in the

---

[4] Alabama, Arkansas, Delaware, Florida, Indiana, Kentucky, Maryland, Mississippi, Michigan, Missouri, New Jersey, New York, North Carolina, Oklahoma, Oregon, Pennsylvania, Rhode Island, Tennessee, Vermont, Virginia, Wisconsin, and Wyoming.

customs of certain Germanic tribes and spread throughout western Europe as a result of the extensive migrations of those tribes. In the course of history, community property became the marital property system of Spain and was introduced by the Spaniards in those areas of America which they claimed and colonized.

The community property system today is the basis of marital property right in eight states. In five of them—Arizona, California, Louisiana, New Mexico, and Texas—the system is a continuation of Spanish law which was in effect at the time of statehood. The other three states—Idaho, Nevada, and Washington—voluntarily adopted the system in the early stages of their settlement.

The community property system in each of these jurisdictions is today defined and regulated by statute, with substantial variations existing among the various states. But despite these statutory differences, the basic principles of the community property system are the same in all eight states.

Nature of the Community Property System

The community property system defines the respective rights of husband and wife with regard to marital property interests. It is based on the notion that expenditures of time and energy of both members of the "community" or marital union contribute to the economic well-being of that union. Wealth accumulated by reason of the spouses' mutual and individual contributions of time and energy during marriage is considered to be owned *equally* by each spouse regardless of the nature of the services rendered, the respective levels of skills and earning power, or the fact that one spouse earns no salary or wage at all. Each spouse owns a one-half interest in the community property acquired by the marital union, subject only to each state's statutory rules with respect to control and management of the co-owned property. The respective interests of the spouses in community property clearly are not dependent upon the relative values of their contributions to the wealth accumulated by the union.

Separate versus Community Property

The community property system requires that all wealth accumulated by married persons be classified as either community property or **separate property.** Classification is important because where property is found to be *community* property, it is owned in equal shares by the two spouses. On the other hand, if an item of wealth is determined to be *separate* property, it is owned entirely by the spouse whose property it is found to be.

Community property consists of the salary or wages of either spouse received during marriage, the rents, dividends, or other income derived from community property, and property purchased with the income or proceeds of community property.

Separate property is property owned by either spouse before marriage, property acquired by either spouse by gift, inheritance, or devise, and the income and proceeds derived from separate property.

Presumption of Community Property The determination of whether marital property is the separate property of one of the spouses or is community property belonging to both depends upon an analysis of the circumstances under which the particular property was acquired. To assist in making this analysis and determination, there exists a general presumption that all wealth acquired during marriage is community property. Like other presumptions of fact, this presumption is rebuttable. The presumption is refuted by evidence sufficient to satisfy an unprejudiced mind that the property is separate in character. A common method of rebutting the presumption is to trace the property back through its various wealth forms to its separate property origin. Tracing property back through its various forms is facilitated by the doctrine which states that separate property produces separate property and community property produces community property.

Division of Community Property

Whether a particular article of wealth is community property or separate property is a significant fact to be determined at the time of dissolution of the marital union by divorce or when one of the spouses dies.

Dissolution of Marriage by Divorce In the course of divorce proceedings the court must determine what property is the separate property of each of the spouses and what is community property. The court has no jurisdiction over the separate property of either of the spouses in a divorce proceeding. That property belongs to the party whose separate property it is found to be and is not subject to division or distribution by the court. On the other hand, if the property is found to be community property, it is subject to the court's jurisdiction and will be divided equally between the spouses.

Death of One of the Spouses All community property states permit the husband to dispose of his half of the community property by will, and all states except New Mexico give the wife the same right. In none of these states, however, does a deceased spouse have any testamentary rights with respect to the surviving spouse's half of the community property.

Where a decedent spouse leaves no will disposing of his or her half of the community property, statutes in California, Idaho, Nevada, and New Mexico give the decedent's half interest to the surviving spouse. Texas divides the decedent's interest between his or her descendants and the surviving spouse. In the remaining community property states, the decedent's interest passes entirely to his or her descendants.

DOWER AND CURTESY

Dower

At common law when a woman married she acquired certain rights in land owned by her husband during their marriage. These rights of the wife were known as **dower.** The wife's dower consisted of a life estate, following the death of her husband, for her lifetime in one-third of all real estate owned by the husband. The wife's dower rights did not, however, give her any estate in the husband's real property until his death.

Inchoate Dower As long as the husband lived, the wife's dower interest in real estate owned by him was said to be *inchoate.* She had no interest which she could sell, mortgage, or lease. During the husband's lifetime, her interest amounted to no more than an expectancy to be realized if her husband died before she did. If the wife predeceased the husband, her incipient right or expectancy automatically terminated. During the wife's lifetime, however, the husband could not alone convey his real property and defeat his wife's inchoate dower. Unless the wife released her dower interest in the property, it continued to attach to the property even though title to the property was acquired by a third party. The common method of releasing an inchoate dower interest was for the wife to join her husband in the execution of a deed to property being transferred.

Consummate Dower If the wife survived the husband, the wife's inchoate dower became *consummate.* Her former expectancy ripened into a reality and thereafter she owned a life estate for her lifetime in one-third of the real estate that her husband owned at the time of his death.

Dower Abolished or Altered At a time when a man's wealth was largely in the form of real estate, dower provided a reasonable measure of economic security for a widow. In many instances today, however, real property is not the principal asset in a husband's estate, and common law dower fails to provide the economic security a widow requires. In view of the limited protection that dower would afford today, the majority of states either have completely abolished the wife's common law dower or have extensively altered her dower rights.[5]

In those states where marital property interests are regulated by the community property system, common law dower has been abolished.[6] The wife, as we have seen, owns one-half of the community property, real and personal, both during the husband's lifetime and at the time of his death.

Statutes in some states[7] have changed the wife's interest from a life estate in one-third of the husband's real property to a fee ownership of one-third.

In a minority of the states[8] common law dower still exerts a significant influence despite minor modifications arising from statutory provisions.

Curtesy

At common law a husband acquired a life estate in all (not just one-third) of the real property owned by his wife. His rights in her land were known as **curtesy**. The husband's curtesy interest in his wife's property did not arise, however, until a child had been born to the union.

Curtesy Initiate and Curtesy Consummate

Following the birth of a child, the husband's interest in his wife's real property was known as curtesy *initiate* and this interest merely changed in name to a curtesy *consummate* upon the death of his wife. Like a wife's dower, the husband's curtesy was only an expectancy during the wife's lifetime and it automatically terminated if the husband predeceased the wife.

If the husband outlived his wife, at the time of her death his expectancy became a reality in the form of ownership of a life estate for his lifetime in all of his deceased wife's real property. The fact that the common law did not permit a married woman to convey her real property without her husband joining in the transfer protected the husband's expectancy from being defeated by a sale of the wife's property without his consent.

Curtesy Abolished or Altered In the great majority of states today, curtesy has completely ceased to exist.

In the community property states the husband owns one-half of all of the community property both during the wife's lifetime and at the time of her death. As to the wife's separate property, she may in all states except Texas convey her real property without her husband joining in the deed. Where the wife dies without leaving a will disposing of her separate or community property, the various state statutes confer a share of her property to her surviving husband.

A few states by statute have changed the husband's interest in his wife's property upon her death from a life estate in all her real property to a fee simple interest in some portion (usually one-third) of the property.[9]

In a minority of jurisdictions[10] curtesy is still the source of a life estate for the husband, although statutes have substantially changed the common law. In some of these states[11] the requirement of the birth of a child before a cur-

---

[5] For example, Illinois Revised Statutes ch. 3, sec. 18 provides: "There is no estate of dower or curtesy. All inchoate rights to elect to take dower existing on the effective date of this amendatory act are hereby extinguished."

[6] California Civil Code, sec. 173, for example, provides: "No estate is allowed the husband by tenant in curtesy upon the death of his wife, nor is any estate in dower allotted to the wife upon the death of her husband."

[7] For example, Florida Statutes Annotated, sec. 731.34; Minnesota Statutes Annotated, secs. 507.02, 525.16(2).

[8] Alabama, Alaska, Arkansas, Delaware, Georgia, Hawaii, Kentucky, Maryland, Massachusetts, New Jersey, Ohio, Oregon, Rhode Island, Tennessee, Virginia, West Virginia, and Wisconsin.

[9] For example, Minnesota Statutes Annotated, secs. 507.02, 525.16; Pennsylvania Statutes, Tit. 20, sec. 12.

[10] Alabama, Arkansas, Delaware, Hawaii, Maryland, Massachusetts, New Jersey, Ohio, Oregon, Rhode Island, Tennessee, Virginia, West Virginia, and Wisconsin.

[11] Delaware, New Jersey, Oregon, and Virginia.

tesy initiate is created has been abolished. Statutes in most of the minority jurisdictions give the husband a life estate in only a portion (usually one third) of the wife's real property instead of all of it as permitted by the common law. In all but four of the minority states[12] the husband's curtesy cannot be defeated by the wife conveying her property by deed or will without the husband's consent.

SIMULTANEOUS DEATH

The Problem of Survivorship

Three of the forms of co-ownership that we have examined involve the concept of survivorship. We have seen that where one of two joint tenants or tenants by the entirety predeceases the other, the property belongs entirely to the surviving co-owner with no interest passing to the decedent's heirs or devisees. We also saw that in community property states when one spouse dies without disposing of his or her one-half of the community property, the surviving spouse becomes the sole owner of the property. Because the rules with respect to survivorship are clear, problems of ownership of property rarely arise where evidence of the fact of death of one co-owner before the other can be readily established. Frequently, however, both co-owners are killed in the same disaster under circumstances that make it impossible to determine the time sequence in which they died. Because the various methods used by the states to resolve the question of ownership were considered to be based on arbitrary and unrealistic presumptions, the National Conference of Commissioners on Uniform State Laws and the American Bar Association in 1940 approved the **Uniform Simultaneous Death Act** and recommended its adoption by state legislatures.

Uniform Simultaneous Death Act

With local variations, additions, or omissions, the Uniform Simultaneous Death Act has been adopted by all the states except Alaska and Ohio. The purpose of the act as stated in its preamble is to provide for "the disposition of property where there is no sufficient evidence that persons have died otherwise than simultaneously, and to make uniform the law with reference thereto." If there is sufficient evidence to show that one of the parties survived the other, even where the deaths occur substantially at the same time, the act is not applicable.

Joint Tenancy and Tenancy by the Entirety Section 3 of the uniform act provides: "Where there is no sufficient evidence that two joint tenants or tenants by the entirety died otherwise than simultaneously the property so held shall be distributed one-half as if one had survived and one-half as if the other had survived. . . ."

A number of states omit the phrase "or tenants by the entirety" from their statutes because that form of co-ownership is not recognized by them.

Community Property A section was added to the Uniform Simultaneous Death Act in 1953 which provides that "Where a husband and wife have died, leaving community property, and there is no sufficient evidence that they have died otherwise than simultaneously, one-half of all the community shall pass as if the husband had survived [and as if said one-half were his separate property], and the other one-half thereof shall pass as if the wife had survived [and as if said other half were her separate property]."

This section of the uniform act obviously has significance only in the small minority of states that recognize the community property system.

QUESTIONS

1 Explain what is meant by the term "co-ownership" of real estate. How does it differ from "co-tenancy?"

---

[12] Arkansas, Hawaii, Tennessee, and Wisconsin.

2 Indicate how two persons could become co-owners without voluntarily entering into a co-ownership relationship.
3 List four forms of co-ownership of real estate.
4 What is the outstanding characteristic of the joint tenancy form of co-ownership? How does it operate?
5 List the four unities that are required to be present at common law for a joint tenancy form of co-ownership to be created.
6 Why have some states either abolished the joint tenancy form of co-ownership entirely or substantially changed its characteristics?
7 With respect to the joint tenancy form of co-ownership, what is meant by the requirement that there must be a unity of interest?
8 Why do more than half of the states favor tenancies in common over all other forms of co-ownership?
9 What is the nature of a co-owner's right of contribution? How is it enforced?
10 From the standpoint of their effects on co-ownership of real estate, what is the difference between the right of severance and the right of partition?
11 Compare a joint tenancy with a tenancy by the entirety. What is the principal similarity? The primary difference?
12 Discuss the basic concept underlying the community property system.
13 From the point of view of ownership of property by a married couple, what is the difference between separate property and community property?
14 Describe common law dower.
15 Describe common law curtesy.
16 To what forms of co-ownership does the Uniform Simultaneous Death Act apply? What problem does it seek to resolve?

Chapter 7

Incidents of Ownership

Ownership of real estate involves both legal *rights* that enable an owner to use and enjoy his property and legal *duties* which restrict his use and enjoyment. In defining the rights that one owner has with respect to his property, the law at the same time is describing the duties that he owes to all other owners who enjoy similar rights in their properties. In other words, the respective rights and duties of landowners are reciprocal in that one owner's rights create duties in other owners, and vice versa. For example, the right of landowner A to be free from activities of his neighbor, landowner B, that interfere with A's enjoyment of his property is the counterpart of the duty that A owes to B not to interfere with B's enjoyment of his property by similar conduct.

Occupancy of adjoining parcels of real estate by different owners gives rise to the potential for conflicts of interest between them. When a conflict does occur, the rights of each occupant must be limited to some extent so that the interest of the other may be given reasonable recognition by the law. In the mutual adjustments that take place, each owner suffers some degree of curtailment of his freedom with respect to the use of his land.

Adjoining landowners are not at liberty to ignore common boundary lines and intrude upon each other's property. Nor may they carry on activities on their own lands in a manner that is likely to cause harm to neighboring property or that interferes with another person's comfortable use and enjoyment of his land. Adjoining property owners must not, through their acts or their failure to act, injure a neighbor's land or structures. They may excavate on their own lands, but they are obliged to do so with care.

A landowner's rights and duties with respect

to his land do not pertain only to other owners whose properties adjoin his. Under certain circumstances, a landowner's rights and obligations that are incidents of the ownership of property extend both to properties farther removed and to persons who may not own property at all.

TRESPASS TO LAND

Nature of the Wrong

A **trespass** is an unlawful invasion of an owner's or occupant's right of exclusive possession of his land. Any unlawful entry upon another's land or any interference with his present possessory interest constitutes a trespass. A trespass occurs not only when a person himself wrongfully enters and walks upon another's land, but also when he permits materials such as mud, debris, or water to flow upon another owner's land. The form of the instrumentality by which the trespasser "enters" the property is not material.

A trespass may be committed on the vertical surface of another's premises as well as upon the horizontal surface of his land. For example, where dirt or debris is piled against another person's buildings, walls, or fences located on or near a boundary line, or where wires or other things are attached to those structures, such conduct constitutes a trespass.

In view of the fact that an owner's right of exclusive possession extends to the airspace above the surface of his land and the earth beneath the surface, an entry or interference with the owner's possession of those areas is also a trespass.

Type of Intent Required

For someone entering upon land to be liable for trespass, it is not necessary that he intend to interfere with another's possession of the land. To be liable for trespass, the actor need only intend to enter upon a particular parcel of land, without regard to whether he knows or should know that he is not entitled to do so. If a person is upon another's land, and he is there intentionally, it is immaterial that he honestly and reasonably believes that he is entitled to be there. His presence there makes him a trespasser. A person's mistake of fact or law neither excuses his entry nor relieves him of liability for trespass, unless his mistake was induced by the owner of the land which he entered.

Defense of Property against Trespass

Right of Self-Help The importance attached to an owner's interest in the exclusive possession of property is deemed to justify his use of reasonable means to defend that interest. An owner is privileged to defend his peaceful possession and enjoyment of his property and that privilege is based on the same policy considerations that justify self-defense. Where circumstances are such that time does not permit a possessor to resort to the processes of the law, he may engage in self-help to protect his possession. In an appropriate case, a possessor who resorts to self-help is privileged to resist a trespass by the use of force which, were it not for the trespass, would amount to an assault or battery.[1] The use of force ordinarily is not justified unless a request has first been made of the intruder to desist from trespassing, but a request is not required where the intruder's conduct clearly indicates that the request would be disregarded.

Degree of Force Permitted An owner or occupier may order a trespasser to leave his land; if the trespasser refuses the owner may use such force as is reasonably necessary to expel him. The reasonableness of the force used in a particular instance is a question of fact for the jury. The law does not give an occupier of land the right to punish a trespasser and, if the occupier attempts to do so, he becomes a wrongdoer himself and the trespasser, in order to protect

---

[1] Harmful or offensive contact is the essence of *battery*, while apprehension of such contact is the basis of *assault*. Mere words, however threatening, insulting, or abusive, will not amount to an assault.

himself from bodily harm, may defend himself in any manner necessary under the circumstances. A possessor of property is prohibited from using a deadly weapon or an instrument likely to inflict great bodily harm when ejecting a trespasser, except where the trespasser has put him in a position where he is reasonably apprehensive of death or bodily harm.

Despite the tradition that "A man's home is his castle" and that one may kill in defense of his dwelling, most jurisdictions today adopt the view that a householder may not intentionally shoot a trespasser until he attempts to force an entry in such a manner as to lead a reasonably prudent person to believe that the intruder intends to commit a felony or to inflict some serious personal injury on the occupants of the house.

NEGLIGENCE

When exercising his right to use and enjoy real property, an owner or occupier must always act with due regard for the public good and the rights and welfare of others. This limitation on the rights of a possessor of land is the fundamental principle upon which liability is based when an occupier's use of property results in injury to another person, either because of the occupier's willful misconduct or his negligence.

Nature of Negligence

Negligence has been defined[2] as "conduct which falls below the standard established by law for the protection of others against unreasonable risk of harm." The primary wrong upon which an action for negligence is based consists of the breach of one person's duty to protect another person against injury. The basis of negligence is behavior that should be recognized as exposing others to unreasonable danger.

Act or Omission Negligent conduct by an owner or occupant of real estate may take the form of either an act on his part or his failure or omission to act when he is under a duty to do so.

No Intent Required Intent is not a material element in negligence. The word "intent" denotes that one who acts does so with the desire to cause the consequences that follow or with the belief that the consequences are substantially certain to result from his act. In negligence, the actor does not desire to bring about the consequences that follow his act or omission. His action merely creates a sufficiently great risk of the occurrence of such consequences that a reasonable man would anticipate and guard against them.

NUISANCE
General Characteristics

Interference with Use and Enjoyment The law of nuisance is concerned with protecting the right of landowners and land occupiers to use and enjoy their properties. It has been the traditional means used by the courts to balance competing interests of landowners. Basic to the common law of nuisance is the long-held notion that an owner must use his real property in such a manner as not to unreasonably interfere with other persons' enjoyment of their properties. No owner of land, not even the owner in fee simple absolute, is entirely free to use his land in any way he may desire.

Not all activity interfering with an occupant's enjoyment of his land, however, is actionable as a nuisance. Practically all human activity, particularly in areas of high population concentration, interferes to some extent with other people in society—the interference ranging from trifling annoyances to serious injuries. So that an organized society may function, each member is expected and required to tolerate a certain amount of annoyance, inconvenience, and interference with the use and enjoyment of his property. The law imposes liability for invasion of an owner's interest in the enjoy-

---

[2] *Restatement (2d) of the Law of Torts,* sec. 282.

ment of his property only when the harm that he sustains is greater than he ought to be required to bear under a given set of circumstances.

Definition of a Nuisance A **nuisance** may be defined as the wrongful interference by one person with the use or enjoyment of land in the possession of another. The term "nuisance" describes both the *conduct* of one person and the *effect or consequences* of that conduct on another or other persons. The basic issue in nuisance controversies involves the reasonableness of the conduct, without regard to the intent or negligence of the person whose conduct is the subject of complaint. Whether conduct in a given case is reasonable or not is determined by looking at the consequences flowing from that conduct.

The law of nuisance requires that consideration be given to both the social value of one person's activities that may disturb another person and the conflicting social value of the other person's freedom to use and enjoy his land without interference. The utility of one person's activity must be weighed against the gravity of the harm to another person caused by that activity.

Nuisance Per Se versus Nuisance in Fact Nuisances are classified as being either nuisances per se or nuisances in fact.

A **nuisance per se** is a use of property which is at all times and under any circumstance a nuisance, regardless of location or surroundings. It is an activity or a structure which, because of its inherent characteristics, in and of itself is hurtful to the health, morals, tranquillity, or sense of decency of owners or occupants of real estate. Any activity, operation, or structure that is by statute declared to be a nuisance is a nuisance per se.

The difference between a nuisance per se and a **nuisance in fact** lies in the nature of the proof required to establish the existence of a nuisance. The liability for committing a nuisance and the remedy available to the injured party are the same in both cases. In the case of a nuisance per se, only its existence need be established to entitle the injured party to relief. Where a nuisance in fact is alleged, however, not only must the interference constituting a nuisance be proved, but the harmful consequences to the complainant must also be established. By far the greater number of nuisance actions involve nuisances in fact.

Public or Private Nuisance A nuisance as defined above may be either public or private.

A **public nuisance** is an unreasonable interference with an interest common to the public at large, including activities which are injurious to the health, safety, morals, or welfare of the general public. Public nuisances include such activities as polluting a water supply, operating a plant that emits noxious odors, or maintaining a structure that endangers passersby on streets or highways. Statutes commonly make public nuisances misdemeanors as well as civil wrongs.

A **private nuisance** is an unreasonable interference with the use or enjoyment of land in the possession of another person. The distinction between a public and a private nuisance does not turn on the difference in the *kind* of activity that causes interference, but rather on the *scope or extent* of the injurious consequences of a particular activity.

An activity, operation, or structure may be a private nuisance without being a public nuisance; conversely, it may be a public nuisance without being a private one. On the other hand, an activity may, under certain circumstances, at the same time be both a public and a private nuisance. A public nuisance affecting an entire community is also a private one with respect to any member of the community who suffers an injury that is different in *kind,* as distinguished from different in degree, from that which is suffered by the community at large. For example, effluent discharged into a stream may not only kill fish and for that reason be a public nuisance, but it may also cause injury to an individual's cattle and be a private nuisance.

Distinguishing between public and private nuisances is important because of the remedies available to the injured parties, as we shall see later.

Nuisance and Trespass Distinguished Although both nuisance and trespass are violations of a landowner's property rights, they are different types of legal wrongs. A *trespass* arises from the unlawful *physical* interference with a present *possessory interest* in real property, while a *nuisance* is an unreasonable interference with a person's interest in the *use and enjoyment* of real property. Where there is no actual physical invasion of property, the interference complained of by an occupier is a nuisance rather than a trespass.

Nuisance and Negligence Distinguished Nuisance and negligence are distinct wrongs and differ in both their nature and their consequences. Liability for negligence, as we have seen, is based on one's failure to exercise due care in a particular fact situation, whereas a person may be liable for the commission of a nuisance despite his exercise of care and skill in carrying on an activity which interferes with the rights of another.

Activity Constituting a Nuisance

The Resulting Harm An essential factor in nuisance cases is the nature and the extent of the harm that results from conduct or activity. Where conduct causes the physical destruction of property or physical harm to one's person, that conduct is more likely to be held to be a nuisance than where the resulting harm is less tangible. Conduct or activity will, however, amount to a nuisance even though it causes no physical injury but instead results in the lessened comfort and enjoyment of one's use of land due to such things as noise, foul odors, excessive dust, or flashing and annoying lights.

Ordinary Sensitivity Test Conduct or activity that any particular person finds offensive or discomforting to him may not necessarily amount to a nuisance in the eyes of the law. The test is not whether the act complained of causes discomfort or annoyance to the *particular* sensitivities of the complaining party, but whether it would have offended a person of *ordinary* sensitivities.

Offensive to Aesthetic Sense Traditionally, activity which merely offends one's aesthetic sense or activity that only has a depressing mental effect was not considered to constitute a nuisance. More recent decisions, however, have held that activities which caused depressed feelings or were unsightly or disagreeable could amount to a nuisance. The establishment of a mortuary or funeral home in a purely residential area, for example, has been held to be "conducive to depression and sorrow and deprive a home of the comfort and repose to which its owners are entitled."[3]

Remedies for Nuisance

Private Nuisance If he can do so without committing a breach of the peace or causing unnecessary injury, a person who is injured by a private nuisance may remove or **abate** the nuisance himself. Such remedial action by a wronged person, we have seen, is known as self-help. We have also seen that the problem with resorting to self-help is the fact that, while he is in the process of abating the nuisance, the injured party might go beyond the limitations of his right to abate and cause harm or injury to the other party. To avoid this risk, the injured party may, instead of engaging in self-help, bring a civil action for an injunction or damages or both, depending upon the circumstances of the particular case.

In all situations other than those involving a nuisance per se, the party who seeks injunctive relief must establish that he will sustain irrepa-

---

[3] *Brown v. Arbuckle,* 88 Cal. App. 2d 258, 260 (1948).

rable injury if the nuisance is permitted to continue. Once the complainant has established the irreparable nature of his injury, the court will invoke the doctrine of "balancing the equities" or "balancing the hardships" before making its determination. A complainant's request for an injunction will be denied by the court if the harm to the creator of the nuisance as a result of the injunction would be substantially greater than the injury sustained by the complaining party if the injunction were denied. However, if the nuisance is the result of willful action by the one committing the nuisance, the courts will refuse to balance the hardships and will issue an injunction ordering abatement of the nuisance, irrespective of the disparity in the relative harm sustained by the parties as the result thereof.

One who has suffered discomfort or annoyance by reason of the existence of a nuisance is entitled to recover money damages. In making his claim for such damages, it is not necessary that the complainant prove that he sustained actual *physical* injury to his person or his property. Damages are recoverable for discomfort, annoyance, and mental distress whether or not there has been any physical injury to person or property.

Public Nuisance The remedy for a public nuisance is a civil action for abatement brought by a properly authorized public body or officer. It is the duty of the government to protect the property rights of its citizens by putting an end to public nuisances.

If it is necessary for effecting the abatement of a public nuisance, a building or other structure may be demolished or removed by public authorities.

In addition to making a public nuisance a civil wrong, statutes in some states also make a public nuisance a misdemeanor and thus subject the person responsible for the nuisance to criminal liability as well.

Defenses to Nuisance Actions

Lack of Negligence As previously pointed out, the type of conduct, whether it be intentional, negligent, or otherwise, that gives rise to a nuisance is not material to its existence. It is the *consequence* of conduct rather than the *type* of conduct that creates a nuisance. This being the case, it is no defense to a nuisance action to show that the activity complained of was conducted with due care or in a nonnegligent manner.

Doctrine of "Coming to the Nuisance" Under the common law doctrine of "coming to the nuisance," a person who moves into an area where a nuisance is already in existence cannot be heard to complain of the nuisance. A majority of the states today have rejected the doctrine as a defense in nuisance actions. If an occupant's use of his land is in fact a nuisance, any party who is injured thereby is entitled to a remedy regardless of whether he arrived in the vicinity before or after the commencement of the nuisance.

Other Nuisances and Other Injured Parties It is no defense to a nuisance action for the defendant to show that in the complainant's neighborhood there are other sources of discomfort or other activities that constitute a nuisance. Nor, where a complainant is injured by a nuisance, does the fact that other persons in the neighborhood do not complain justify the defendant's conduct, nor does such fact serve to mitigate the complainant's damages.

Acquiescence or Consent The equitable principle that anyone who consents to an act is not wronged by it applies to activity alleged to constitute a nuisance. One who acquiesces in the erection of a structure or the installation of facilities with knowledge of the use to which they will be put and the probable consequences of that use cannot later be heard to say that they are a nuisance. However, where the fact of the commission of a nuisance can only be established by actual use of the structure or by operation of the facility, and the complainant had no previous reason to believe that it would interfere with his comfort and enjoyment, he

INCIDENTS OF OWNERSHIP

will not be deemed to have consented to the nuisance.

Statute of Limitations An action for nuisance may be barred by reason of a complainant's lack of diligence in seeking relief. Statutes in all states limit the period of time within which actions for legal wrongs must be brought. Failure to commence a legal action within the statutory period results in the loss of the right to bring the action at all. The period of time within which a nuisance action must be commenced varies somewhat in length from state to state.

The defense that an action is barred by the lapse of time requires a showing as to when the wrong complained of occurred. That is the point in time at which the **statute of limitations** begins to run.

"Continuing" versus "Permanent" Nuisance In determining when the statute of limitations begins to run in nuisance actions, the courts distinguish between "continuing" nuisances and "permanent" nuisances.

If the nuisance is such that it could be stopped at any time by the person committing it, the nuisance is said to be "continuing." A continuing nuisance is viewed as being a new and separate wrong every day that it recurs. The person injured by a continuing nuisance is entitled to bring successive actions for relief from each recurring wrong until the nuisance has been abated. Where conduct that amounts to a nuisance is recurrent in character, the statute of limitations commences to run for each new injury at the time that injury occurs.

If a nuisance is held to be "permanent," the statute of limitations begins to run at the time that the nuisance is first committed. In such a situation, the injured party has a single cause of action for all damages resulting from that nuisance. Many courts consider a nuisance to be permanent when the probability of its enduring is great. For example, the construction of a building partly on the land of another has been held to be a permanent nuisance.

FENCES

Fences Are Fixtures

A *fence* has been described as "a visible, tangible obstruction between two portions of land so as to separate and shut in land and set it off as private property."[4] Like other things that are attached to real property, fences are fixtures and are thus a part of the land upon which they are located. Being a part of the real property, fences are transferred along with the property to which they attach without the need for specific mention of them in the document of transfer.

Duty to Construct a Fence

Unless he is under statutory duty to enclose it, the owner of land may leave his land unfenced should he choose to do so. Fencing statutes are generally designed to resolve problems arising in connection with the raising and management of livestock. Statutes range from those requiring a stock raiser to "fence livestock in" if he is to avoid liability for their actions to statutes that require adjacent landowners to "fence livestock out." Practically all states today have statutes regulating the rights and duties of landowners and tenants relative to trespassing livestock.

Some grazing states[5] have statutes requiring landowners to "fence livestock out," and their failure to do so will prevent their recovering damages from the owner of trespassing and injury-inflicting livestock. Other states[6] have "herd or stock laws" or "fencing district" statutes which permit certain localities by popular vote to require local stock raisers to contain their livestock in designated areas by erecting fences. Still other states[7] have passed statutes

---

[4] 22 California Jurisprudence 2d 100.
[5] For example, Arizona Rev. Stat. Ann., sec. 54-102 and Oregon Rev. Stat., sec. 608.15 are statutes of this type.
[6] Arkansas Stat. Ann., secs. 78-1301 to 78-1364 and New Mexico Stat. Ann., secs. 47-31 to 47-31-12 are such statutes.
[7] Illinois Stat. Ann., ch. 8, sec. 1, ch. 54, sec. 20 and Iowa Code Ann., sec. 188.2, for example, contain such provisions.

that prohibit domestic animals from running at large and make their owners liable for failure to restrain them.

Injuries Caused by Fences

Individuals are sometimes injured by contact with fences and bring suit against the owner to recover for the injuries they sustained. In such instances, the fence owner's liability to the injured party will be determined in accordance with the law of negligence.

Barbed wire fences are frequently involved in damage suits. While the courts have often declared that barbed wire fences do not render their owners liable for nuisances per se, a number of states[8] have enacted statutes that regulate the manner in which this type of fence may be constructed.

Division Fences

A **division fence** is a fence that is erected on the boundary line between the lands of two owners. While its main purpose normally is to prevent livestock from straying from one owner's land to the other's, a division fence also serves to demarcate the boundary line between the two properties and to prevent inadvertent trespasses by the respective owners.

All but six states[9] have statutes defining the rights and duties of adjoining landowners with respect to division fences. Although the statutes vary in many details, in general they require adjoining landowners to contribute equally to the costs of erection and maintenance of division fences.

Some states[10] have statutes that create local bodies, commonly called "fence viewers," with powers to resolve controversies arising in connection with the erection and maintenance of division fences. The statutory powers of the viewers include such matters as the right to determine the sufficiency of such a fence, the need for repairs, the sector that each landowner shall maintain, the payments to be made by each, the necessity for a division fence, and the time period within which the fence shall be erected or repaired.

When one landowner builds a fence at the boundary line with an adjoining property that is entirely on his own property, it is often called an "exterior fence." Such a fence is constructed and maintained entirely at the expense of the owner of the land upon which the fence is situated. However, if the adjoining landowner later encloses his land, in so doing using the other owner's exterior fence as a part of the enclosure, the exterior fence becomes a division fence and the landowner enclosing his land must bear one-half of the cost of the construction of the division fence and one-half of the expense of its subsequent maintenance.[11]

Spite Fences

The term **spite fence** is generally used to refer to a fence or similar structure that is of no beneficial use to the one erecting it but that is built for the purpose of annoying the occupant of adjoining land. In most jurisdictions, if a fence serves a useful purpose to its builder, his motive in building it is immaterial even though it causes injury to an adjoining property owner or occupant by cutting off light and air or obstructing his view. When, however, the fence serves no beneficial purpose to its builder, the trend of recent decisions is to hold such a structure to be an unlawful spite fence and permit its abatement as a nuisance.

Statutes in some states[12] provide that fences

---

[8] For example, Idaho Code Ann., sec. 35-301, Massachusetts Ann. Laws, ch. 86, sec. 6, and Montana Rev. Code, sec. 46-1404 regulate the construction of barbed wire fences.

[9] Arizona, Florida, Georgia, Maryland, New Mexico and South Carolina.

[10] For example, Alabama, Illinois, Massachusetts, Minnesota, and Wisconsin have such statutes.

[11] California Civil Code, sec. 841, Idaho Code Ann., sec. 35-105, and Washington Rev. Code, sec. 16.60.020 are examples of statutes referring to the sharing of costs under such circumstances.

[12] For example, California, Connecticut, Indiana, Kentucky, Maine, Massachusetts, Minnesota, New Hampshire, New York, Rhode Island, and Wisconsin.

or similar structures that exceed a certain height and which are *maliciously erected* for the purpose of annoying the occupants of adjoining lands are private nuisances.[13] Under these statutes malice on the part of the builder must have been a dominant motive in erecting the structure. As the term is used in these statutes, "malice" has been defined as conduct that is willful and intentional, and done in a spirit of mischief with the intent to vex, annoy, or injure another person.

PARTY WALLS
Physical Characteristics
A **party wall** is a wall that is located at the boundary line of adjacent properties and is designed to serve simultaneously as the exterior wall of structures on each of the adjoining properties. The party wall may be built astride the boundary line or it may be located entirely on the land of one owner.

The importance of party walls and hence the frequency of controversies involving them have decreased appreciably in recent years because of changed construction methods. More and more the exterior walls of an urban building are merely a shell carrying none of the structure's load.

Ownership Interests
When a party wall is located partly on the land of two adjoining property owners it is regarded as being divided longitudinally into two strips, each owner owning that portion of the wall resting on his land. For the support of structures on his land, each owner is said to have an easement in the part of the wall that is located on his neighbor's side of the boundary line and owned by him. The adjoining owners thus have cross-easements which entitle each of them to rely on the other owner's part of the wall for

---

[13] For example, California Civil Code, sec. 841.4 provides that "Any fence or other structure in the nature of a fence unnecessarily exceeding 10 feet in height maliciously erected or maintained for the purpose of annoying the owner or occupant of adjoining property is a private nuisance."

support of buildings and other structures. The cross-easements come to an end when the two adjoining buildings cease to exist because of fire, age, or some cause not resulting from an act of one of the owners. One owner's easement in the party wall does not terminate, however, when only the other owner's building is destroyed.

When a party wall is situated entirely on the land of only one owner, it is subject to an easement of support in favor of the building on the adjoining land.

Party Wall Agreements
Although not essential to its creation, a party wall commonly is created by an express agreement between adjoining landowners. Where this is the case, the provisions of the party wall agreement define the respective rights and duties of the parties with regard to the cost of construction and maintenance of the wall. If no *express* agreement exists between the parties, an agreement with respect to a party wall may be *implied* from their conduct. Rights and obligations arising from an implied agreement are determined by the courts from the circumstances of each case.

A party wall is created by implication, for example, when the owner of two buildings with a common supporting wall conveys the two buildings to different persons or conveys one of the buildings and retains the other one.

LANDSLIDES
A landslide occurs when there is a downward movement of rock and earth on a slope. The term includes both the downward movement of dry earth or debris and the slippage of wet soil and rock in the nature of mudslides. An owner who permits dry or wet earth or debris to slide or wash from his property onto that of a neighbor may be subject to liability for nuisance or trespass, depending upon the circumstances of the case and the jurisdiction in which the activity occurs.

Retaining Walls

To avoid liability for failure to keep his soil off adjacent lands, it may be necessary for a landowner to build a *retaining wall* on his property. A retaining wall is a structure designed to withstand lateral pressure and prevent the movement of soil and rocks. Retaining walls become particularly significant when one landowner fills in his lot and raises it above the level of adjoining land, thus creating the possibility that soil and rocks on his property will slide or fall onto adjoining land.

An owner who erects a retaining wall to prevent his land from sliding must, of course, build the wall entirely on his own property. If the wall encroaches on an adjoining lot, the owner of that lot may obtain a mandatory injunction requiring its removal.

An owner who raises the level of his land by filling it in cannot use a wall located on his neighbor's land for purposes of containing the filled soil. The owner of the wall may obtain an injunction against such use of his wall and may also recover any damages sustained by him by reason of injury done to his wall or property.

Unlike the situation where division fences are involved, the landowner who fills in his lot cannot compel an adjoining owner to participate in the cost and maintenance of a retaining wall erected by the former to contain the filled soil.

TREES

Trees on Boundary Lines

Co-Owned by Adjoining Landowners Trees whose trunks straddle the boundary line between adjoining properties (sometimes called **line trees**) belong to both of the adjoining owners as tenants in common. As a general rule neither of the landowners may cut down such a tree without the consent of the adjoining owner, nor may he remove any portion of a tree that extends over his property if injury to the tree would result from his action.

A landowner who destroys or injures a boundary line tree will be liable to the adjoining property owner in damages, the amount of which is measured by the difference between the market value of the adjoining owner's land immediately before and the market value immediately after the destruction or injury to the tree.

Trees near Boundary Lines

Owned in Severalty Trees whose trunks stand entirely on the land of one adjoining landowner belong to him exclusively, despite the fact that the tree's branches may overhang or its roots may penetrate the land of another owner. The owner of the tree owns the fruit that it yields even though that fruit is borne by the branches overhanging the neighboring property. The neighbor has no right to take fruit from the overhanging branches nor can he prevent the tree's owner from coming upon his property to gather the fruit from those branches. By permitting the branches to overhang his property, the neighbor is deemed to have granted an implied license to the tree's owner to enter the premises to gather fruit.

Remedies for Intruding Branches and Roots
To the extent that branches extend over an owner's land or that roots penetrate his subsurface area, they constitute a nuisance. The owner of the land who is affected by the nuisance may abate or terminate it either by (1) bringing a court action to compel the removal of the branches or roots or (2) by resorting to self-help and removing the offending branches or roots himself.

Removal by Injunction To be entitled to a mandatory injunction ordering the removal of encroaching roots or branches, a landowner must show that they interfere with his use and enjoyment of his property. If he can additionally establish that the intrusion caused actual damage to his property, the landowner may also recover money damages.

Removal by Self-Help Where the remedy of self-help is pursued, the aggrieved landowner may remove the offending branches or roots up to the boundary line of his property. In exercising his privilege to abate or terminate the nuisance caused by branches or roots, the landowner must be careful not to cut beyond the property line because such action would be a trespass by him and would render him liable for any resulting injury to the tree. In most jurisdictions, a landowner may pursue the remedy of self-help even though the roots or branches cause no actual damage to his land.

A landowner who removes branches which overhang his property has no right to keep either the wood or the fruit from those branches. His right of removal of the branches is based upon his right to abate the nuisance caused by them and not upon his acquisition of a property right in the offending branches.

SURFACE WATER

Surface water is water resulting from falling rain and melting snow that is diffused over the surface of the ground. It continues to be regarded as surface water until it reaches some well-defined channel in which it joins the flow of other waters.

The right of a landowner to use and even wholly to consume the surface waters within the boundaries of his land has never been seriously questioned. Surface water gives rise to problems, however, when it flows across boundary lines of different owners' properties. The solutions to problems created by surface waters are based upon two diametrically opposed concepts—the natural flow doctrine and the common enemy doctrine.

Natural Flow Doctrine

Under the **natural flow doctrine**, a landowner (1) cannot refuse to receive surface water that would naturally drain upon his land by erecting diversionary dikes or similar devices; (2) cannot cause surface waters to flow onto the land of another person where they would not naturally flow; and (3) cannot alter the manner or rate of flow of surface water upon land that would naturally receive such water.

Despite the fact that the natural flow doctrine imposes substantial handicaps on land development, it has been adopted by a number of states.[14] Almost any regrading of a parcel of land for construction purposes will change its surface contour and could easily be held to violate the prohibitions of the doctrine. Some courts are inclined to soften the harshness of the natural flow doctrine by holding that no liability is incurred by one who interferes with the natural flow of surface water when the damage resulting from such interference is slight.

Common Enemy Doctrine

According to the **common enemy doctrine**, every landowner may regard surface water as an "enemy" and is entitled to deal with this enemy in any manner that will reduce injury to his land to a minimum, without regard to the effects of his action on his neighbors. The common enemy doctrine permits an owner to build a dike upon his land that will cause surface waters to back up on another owner's land rather than allow the water to flow onto his land as it would otherwise do. An owner may also cut drainage channels across his land that will cause surface waters to be collected and discharged onto the lands of other persons.

The harsh effects of the common enemy doctrine have been softened by some courts, which have held that the waters involved in a particular controversy were streams rather than surface waters and hence not subject to diversion to another owner's land.

LATERAL AND SUBJACENT SUPPORT

An owner of land has the right to both lateral and subjacent support for his land. **Lateral sup-**

---

[14] For example, Alabama, California, Colorado, Georgia, Illinois, Iowa, Kentucky, Louisiana, Maryland, Michigan, Mississippi, Nevada, North Carolina, Ohio, Pennsylvania, Tennessee, and Texas.

port for a parcel of land is afforded by those properties which adjoin it on all sides. The supported lands and the supporting lands are divided by planes resulting from the establishment of boundary lines. **Subjacent support** is the support that the surface of the land receives from its subsurface or underlying area—the supporting land is beneath the supported land.

The *right* to have land supported is a right that is inherent in the possession of land and passes automatically to successive possessors of the supported land. At the same time, the *duty* to support adjoining lands passes to successive possessors of supporting lands without the need for that obligation to be specifically mentioned in the document of transfer.

Lateral Support

Common Law Rule The common law rule of lateral support imposed on an owner who excavated on his land is the duty to support adjoining land in its *natural condition*. If the adjoining land subsided as a result of an excavation made by a neighbor, the excavator's liability for the resulting damage was absolute. He was liable for injury to adjoining land regardless of the degree of care and skill employed by him in making the excavation. Negligence was not a factor in the excavator's liability.

At common law the excavator's liability attached only to land in its *natural condition*. If the land which subsided as a result of the excavation were improved with a building or other structure, the excavator was not required to support it. Under such circumstances the excavator was required only to give notice of his intention to excavate and the adjoining landowner had the responsibility of protecting his own land and buildings or accept the consequences of his failure to do so. In the absence of negligence on his part, the excavator was not liable for subsidence due to the weight of the structure on the land. If, however, the excavator were negligent in excavating on his property, he was liable for all subsidence that resulted from his negligence.

While the common law rule may have been adequate at an earlier time, it is not suited to modern urban conditions where excavations for buildings commonly extend to the boundary lines between lots. The necessities of modern conditions have led to the enactment of statutes and building codes defining property owners' rights and duties with regard to lateral support.

Statutory Provisions The type of lateral support statute or ordinance most commonly encountered imposes liability for support on landowners based on the depth to which an excavation is made. Generally speaking, the obligation to furnish support is placed on the nonexcavating owner of the structure on adjoining land in the case of shallow excavations and on the excavator when excavations go deeper than a certain level. While the statutes differ somewhat as to the depth at which the responsibility for support shifts from one adjoining landowner to another, the depths most frequently appearing in the statutes are 9, 10, and 12 feet. These statutes also provide for the giving of notice in writing of a landowner's intent to excavate and the granting of permission to enter adjoining premises to carry out the statutory duty of support.

Subjacent Support

Problems involving subjacent support arise when there has been a horizontal subdivision of land with one person owning the surface and another person having an interest in a subsurface layer or stratum. Under such circumstances, the upper layer of land is of course dependent upon the lower layer for support. The property interest of the subsurface owner may be as much as a fee simple estate in a specifically described layer of land or it may merely be a right to explore for minerals below the surface and to extract such minerals as may be found.

In its evolution, the law of subjacent support developed many features that are similar to those found in the common law relating to lateral support. For example, the obligation of an owner of a lower layer of land to support the surface of the land in its *natural condition* is absolute. Since the lower owner's liability is absolute, there is no need for the surface owner to establish that injury to the surface is due to the lower owner's negligence.

If the surface of the land has been improved with structures, the subsurface owner is not liable for subsidence damage unless it can be shown that the land in its natural state would have been damaged for lack of subjacent support. In many instances the weight of the upper layer of land alone is so great that the existence of surface structures is relatively insignificant.

BOUNDARY LINES

Location of Boundaries

Ascertained by Description and Survey The owner of a parcel of land owns only that portion of the land mass that is described or identified in the instrument by which he acquired title. The exact location and the precise dimensions of his plot of land are ascertained by an accurate survey based on the legal description of the property as set forth in the document of conveyance. When pinpointing the parcel at a specific location on the landscape, a surveyor "stakes out" its boundary lines. If the surveyor's temporary stakes or markers are promptly replaced with more permanent "monuments," such as walls or fences, disputes as to the location of boundary lines seldom occur. Boundary disputes normally arise when temporary markers have been moved or destroyed and one adjoining property owner erects walls, fences, or other structures relying on what appears to be or is assumed to be the boundary line between contiguous properties.

When land was less intensively used, and perhaps still today in some rural areas, the correct description of a parcel of land in a deed and the exact location of its boundary lines on the ground were not of great importance. The location of a property line a foot or two one way or the other mattered little; the land was not valuable enough to justify the time, trouble, and expense involved in establishing ownership of a small strip of land. But as urbanization proceeded and land values commenced to be calculated in dollars per square foot rather than per acre, a boundary line which was a mere few inches off became a matter of considerable importance. A strip of land several inches wide, when used for a multistory building in a downtown area, can be of considerable value and consequently warrant the expense of litigation when its ownership is in dispute.

Boundary disputes are not limited, however, to land whose value is measured in terms of inches or square feet. They arise in many situations not involving sites for large buildings for a variety of reasons. In the case of residential, agricultural, and recreational properties, the problem of exact location of boundary lines probably arises most often in connection with the erection of fences or walls and the planting of trees or hedges intended to demarcate property lines and prevent intrusions on an owner's property. Although prudence would suggest that a careful and professional survey be made before the expense of a boundary indicator is incurred, many instances occur where the survey is either not done at all or is done in a nonprofessional manner by the owner or some other amateur.

It is not necessary, however, that the location of boundary lines be established in all instances by a professional survey that correctly stakes out the perimeter of a parcel of land as identified in a deed or other document of conveyance. It is possible for boundary lines to be legally established by an agreement between the owners of adjoining parcels of land.

Boundaries Established by Agreement The well-recognized rule that permits the establishment of a boundary line by agreement on the part of adjoining landowners is sometimes referred to as the "agreed boundary doctrine." For the doctrine to apply in any given situation, certain requirements must be met, namely: (1) there must be uncertainty as to the true location of the boundary line; (2) the parties must agree on a common boundary; (3) the boundary line agreed upon must be clearly marked or identifiable; and (4) there must be acquiescence in the location of the line for a period of time equal to the statute of limitations or under such circumstances that substantial loss would result from a change in position of the boundary.

Uncertainty or Doubt The requirement of uncertainty or doubt as to the true location of a boundary line does not mean that there must be an actual dispute or controversy concerning the line. While the existence of a dispute or controversy is evidence of uncertainty or doubt, the requirement is also met if the parties believe that they are establishing a true boundary because they are not sure of its exact location. It is not required that the uncertainty arise from a faulty description in one of the owners' deeds. Nor is the element of uncertainty lacking if an accurate survey could determine the exact location of the boundary line. What is required is that, irrespective of the property descriptions in the deeds, the parties are uncertain as to the physical location of the boundary line on the land.

Oral or Written Agreement The agreement between adjoining owners regarding the location of the boundary line may be oral or written, express or implied.[15] An oral boundary line agreement is not in contravention of the statute of frauds because such an agreement does not pass title to real estate. The theory underlying the doctrine is that the parties are arriving at an agreement as to the boundary between land that each party already owns.

Line Clearly Marked For a boundary line agreement to be valid, it is essential that the line that is fixed by the agreement be clearly marked and readily identifiable.

Period of Acquiescence Most courts require continuing acquiescence in the location of the boundary line by the parties following execution of the agreement. The best evidence of acceptance and acquiescence in an agreed boundary line is, of course, actual occupation of the land by adjoining owners up to the agreed line.

Some jurisdictions require that acquiescence continue for the full statutory period required for adverse possession,[16] but this does not appear to be the general rule. Just how long a period of acquiescence is required by the majority of states that have not statutorily designated periods cannot be definitely stated. The period will vary depending upon whether circumstances are present that would cause a substantial loss to one of the parties by permitting a change in the location of the boundary line previously agreed upon.

Agreed Line Becomes Boundary Once the required elements for the establishment of a boundary line by agreement have been met, the agreed line becomes the actual boundary between the affected parties. This is the case irrespective of the true location of the line as reflected by deed descriptions and a subsequent survey.

Thereafter not only are the parties to the boundary agreement bound by the new line, but their successors in interest, whether purchasers or heirs, are also similarly bound.

LIABILITY TO PERSONS ENTERING PROPERTY

In the great majority of states, the nature of the duties that an owner or occupier of land owes to persons coming upon his property varies according to the legal status of the entrant. Persons entering upon another's land traditionally have been classified as being either (1) tres-

---

[15] The principle that a boundary line may be permanently and irrevocably established by an oral agreement prevails in a large number of states, including Arkansas, California, Florida, Georgia, Idaho, Illinois, Indiana, Iowa, Kansas, Kentucky, Louisiana, Maine, Massachusetts, Michigan, Mississippi, Missouri, Nebraska, New Hampshire, New York, Tennessee, and Texas.

[16] California, for example, requires acquiescence for the full 5 years of the statute of limitations.

passers, (2) licensees, or (3) invitees. The standard of care by the occupier of land is least in the case of a trespasser and greatest in the case of an invitee, with the duty to the licensee falling somewhere in-between. The occupier's liability for failure to meet the standard of care owed by him extends both to activities conducted on the premises and to the physical condition of the premises in his possession.

Trespassers
Unauthorized Entry upon Land

A **trespasser** is a person who enters upon land in the possession of another without a privilege to do so and without the consent of the possessor. He is a trespasser whether his entry upon the occupier's land is intentional, negligent, or accidental. Generally speaking, no one has the right to enter upon another's land without his consent, and the possessor of the land is free to establish the conditions of his consent.

General Rule Regarding Liability Intruders who enter upon another's property without permission must assume the risk of what they will encounter. The general rule, which is subject to certain exceptions, is that the possessor of land is not liable for injuries suffered by trespassers because of the possessor's failure to carry on his activities in a manner not to endanger them or his failure to exercise reasonable care to put his premises in a safe condition for them. A possessor of land is under no obligation to provide intruders with a safe place to trespass. At the same time, however, the possessor must refrain from intentionally injuring a trespasser.

Exceptions to the General Rule The general rule that an owner or occupier of land is not liable to trespassers is subject to several well-established exceptions. These exceptions have developed in the law because of the growing belief that human safety is of greater social value than an occupier's unrestricted freedom to use his land as he sees fit. Exceptions to the general rule involve three different types of trespassers: (1) discovered trespassers, (2) tolerated intruders, and (3) trespassing children.

Discovered Trespassers Once the presence of a trespasser is known or discovered by an occupier of land, the occupier is under a duty to exercise reasonable care for his safety. The occupier of the land must carry on any activity with the same degree of caution that a reasonable person would exercise for the safety of the discovered trespasser. The occupier's failure to use ordinary care to avoid injuring the trespasser after he has been discovered will render the occupier liable for any harm sustained by the trespasser.

Tolerated Intruders The term **tolerated intruder** is often used to refer to trespassers who, with the knowledge of the occupier of land, are in the habit of entering upon the land in substantial numbers at a particular point or crossing over a small area of the land. Such trespassers are also referred to as "frequent trespassers upon a limited area." The courts of most states have imposed on the occupier of land a duty to use reasonable care to discover the presence of this class of trespassers and to protect them when carrying on activities on the land.

Trespassing Children Because of immaturity and lack of judgment, a child who enters upon another's land without permission may be incapable of appreciating all the risks that he may encounter. At an earlier time, the occupier of land was liable for injuries sustained by trespassing children only if the occupier negligently maintained a condition on his land that enticed or attracted the child onto the land (the so-called **attractive nuisance** doctrine). Modernly, however, the idea of enticing or alluring a child to trespass has largely been discarded. The law with respect to child trespassers is the ordinary law of negligence which imposes upon the occupier the duty to exercise reasonable care for a trespassing child's safety. The fact that an "attraction" exists on the occupier's premises is important only to the extent that it means that a trespass by a child can be anticipated. And the fact that the trespasser is a child is simply one fact to be taken into account in determining the reasonableness of the care exercised by the occupier with respect to the trespasser.

Licensees

A **licensee** is a person who enters upon another's property with the occupier's consent for purposes of his own and which have no relation to the business of the occupier. Only the consent of the owner or occupier to enter the premises distinguishes a licensee from a trespasser. Included among licensees are such persons as social guests, whether expressly invited or not, firemen and police officers on the premises in the performance of a public duty, salesmen canvassing at the door of private homes, solicitors for charity, and those who enter for personal business dealings with employees of occupiers of land.

Duty Regarding Premises In general, a licensee must accept the premises in the condition that an owner or occupier uses them and must assume the risk of whatever he may encounter on the premises when he enters. The granting of permission to enter carries with it no duty on the part of the occupier to make the premises safe for the licensee.

An owner or occupier is under no duty to inspect his premises to discover dangerous conditions which are not known to him. Nor, as to dangerous conditions which are known to him, is the occupier required to correct them for the protection of the licensee. The occupier's duty is satisfied if he warns the licensee of the dangerous condition, but even a warning is not required if the dangerous condition itself is or should be obvious to the licensee. If the occupier has knowledge of a dangerous natural or artificial condition of the premises that is not apparent to a licensee, the occupier is under a duty to exercise reasonable care to see that the licensee is made aware of that danger.

Duty with Respect to Activities As for any activity that an occupier of premises carries on, he is under the duty to exercise reasonable care for the protection of a licensee on the premises. Ordinarily a proper warning given to a licensee will satisfy the occupier's obligation.

Invitees

An **invitee** is one who enters an occupier's premises at the express or implied invitation of the occupier in connection with the occupier's business or for a purpose of advantage to him. A common type of invitee is the business visitor, but the term also includes persons invited to such places as parks and playgrounds where there is no pecuniary benefit to the occupier. It is to be noted that practically all courts agree that a social guest, no matter how cordially he may have been urged to come upon the occupier's premises, is not legally an invitee but a licensee instead.

A typical example of an invitee is a customer in a store or other place of business.

Duty Regarding Premises The occupier of real estate is under a duty to protect invitees against dangers arising from the condition of the premises upon which they enter. The occupier is obligated to protect an invitee's safety not only from dangers of which the occupier has knowledge, but also against those dangers that the occupier might with reasonable care discover. The law imposes on the occupier of real estate a duty to make a reasonable inspection of the premises to discover dangerous conditions. The theory on which the occupier's liability is based is that when he encourages others to enter his premises in furtherance of a purpose of the occupier, he impliedly represents that he has exercised reasonable care to make sure that the premises are safe for them.

The occupier's duty to protect invitees from danger is satisfied when, knowing of or having discovered a dangerous condition, he warns them of the existing danger. The occupier is under no duty to protect invitees from dangers which are known to them or which are so obvious that they may be reasonably expected to discover them. Instead of warning invitees of a dangerous condition, the occupier may of course correct the condition and render it harmless, but he is under no duty to do so.

The occupier's obligation toward invitees exists only while they are in the area of the premises which have been opened to them or in those areas to which they might reasonably be expected to go.

Duty with Respect to Activities The occupier's duty is not limited to protecting invitees from unreasonable risks due to physical condition of the premises. He will be liable for harm sustained by invitees because of unreasonable risks caused by activities which the occupier or others conduct on the premises. The occupier is under a duty to take such measures as may be necessary to restrain the conduct of third persons of which he is aware and which he should realize is dangerous to invitees.

New Approach to Occupier's Liability

The traditional classification of persons entering another's property as trespassers, licensees, or invitees has long been criticized by writers as both unsound in theory and undesirable in practice. Although in most states the traditional classification still essentially controls the nature of the duty of an owner or occupier of premises to one who enters upon them, recent cases have questioned the soundness of the traditional approach.

The California Supreme Court in 1968, in a decision[17] that may well be indicative of a modern trend, abolished the distinctions between the standards of care owed by an occupier to trespassers, licensees, and invitees. In repudiating the trespasser-licensee-invitee approach, the court held that the proper test to be applied with respect to liability of an occupier of land is whether in the management of his property the occupier acted as a reasonable man in view of the probability of injury to others.

[17] *Rowland v. Christian,* 69 Cal. 2d 108, 443 P2d 561 (1968).

DUTY OWED TO PERSONS OUTSIDE THE LAND

Persons to Whom Duty is Owed

The owner or occupier of land is under a legal duty not to endanger persons outside his property. This protection extends to passersby on a public way and to persons on adjoining lands, regardless of whether their presence thereon is lawful or not. An incident of the public's right of passage upon a highway or sidewalk is an obligation placed upon occupiers of abutting properties to use reasonable care to see that the passage is safe and that passersby are not exposed to unreasonable risk. The occupier's obligation to exercise reasonable care extends both to activities that he carries on and the physical condition of his premises.

Duty Distinguished from Nuisance

The duty owed to persons outside the land differs from an occupier's obligation not to commit a nuisance. A nuisance, we have seen, is an interference with the use and enjoyment of land—it is a wrong only to persons who have property rights in land. The protection afforded by the duty under discussion is to an individual's freedom from bodily harm, not his interest in the use and enjoyment of land.

Activities on the Land

An owner or occupier of land is liable for physical harm incurred by persons outside his land that is caused by an activity carried on by him which he realizes or should realize will involve an unreasonable risk of physical harm to them. For example, on a windy day A is burning brush on his farm about 100 feet from a public highway. A high wind blows a thick curtain of smoke across the highway obstructing the view of passing motorists. Because their view is obstructed and despite the fact that they are exercising reasonable care, the automobiles of B and C collide, causing them injuries. A is subject to liability to both B and C.

Natural Condition of the Land

The term "natural condition of the land"

means that the condition of the land has not been changed by any act of man.

In the case of lands not situated in an urban area, an occupier is not liable for any physical harm sustained by persons outside the land that is caused by a natural condition of the land. The occupier of land in an urban area, however, is liable for harm resulting from natural conditions if he fails to exercise reasonable care to prevent that harm—as, for example, where a passerby is injured by branches falling from a dead tree located on the occupier's land near a highway or sidewalk.

Artificial Condition of the Land
Owners and occupiers of land, whether the land is urban or rural, are liable for erecting structures or creating and maintaining other artificial conditions on land which they realize, or should realize, subject persons outside their land to unreasonable risk of harm. For example, an occupier who maintains an excavation so close to a highway that it endangers a person who skids or is forced off the highway may be liable for resulting injuries. An owner or occupant is also liable to persons outside his land for injuries resulting from the disrepair of structures on his premises if such condition of disrepair could have been discovered by a reasonable inspection of the premises by the occupier.

Owners and occupiers of land are not considered to be insurers of the safety of passersby, but are only held liable for injuries resulting from their negligence. If they can establish that they exercised reasonable care, they will not be liable for injuries sustained by passersby.

QUESTIONS
1 Define a trespass. Does a trespass only apply to the surface of land?
2 Comment on the degree of force that a landowner may use to expel a trespasser from his property.
3 Under what circumstances, if any, may a property owner use a deadly weapon against a trespasser?
4 What is the nature of negligence?
5 Does all activity that interferes with an owner's enjoyment of his real property constitute a nuisance?
6 How does the proof required to establish a nuisance per se differ from that required to prove the existence of a nuisance in fact?
7 How does a public nuisance differ from a private nuisance?
8 What is meant by the ordinary sensitivity test in nuisance cases?
9 Why is it important to distinguish between a continuing nuisance and a permanent nuisance?
10 Are fences considered to be fixtures? What difference does it make if they are fixtures or not?
11 What is a party wall?
12 Comment on the remedies available to an owner who is bothered by the overhanging branches of a tree located on his neighbor's property.
13 Distinguish the natural flow doctrine as it relates to surface waters from the common enemy doctrine.
14 How do lateral support and subjacent support for land differ?
15 List the requirements for establishing the location of a boundary line by use of the agreed boundary doctrine.
16 To whom does the term "tolerated intruder" apply?
17 Distinguish a licensee from an invitee.

Chapter 8

Easements, Profits, and Licenses

In the preceding chapter we saw that persons who have neither ownership nor possessory interests in a parcel of land may nevertheless have certain rights with respect to that land. These rights or interests of one person in land owned or possessed by another take a variety of forms and arise either from operation of general rules of law or from legal relations expressly or impliedly created by the parties.

In this chapter we continue our examination of rights that a person may have in property owned or possessed by someone else by looking at the characteristics and operation of interests in real property known as (1) easements, (2) profits, and (3) licenses.

EASEMENTS
General Characteristics
Interest in the Land of Another An **easement** is an interest which one person has in land belonging to or in the possession of another person that entitles the owner of the easement to limited use of the other person's land. An easement is said to constitute a servitude or burden on the land in which the easement is an interest.

Easements and Ownership Interests Compared An easement in land and an estate in land resemble each other in that both the owner of an easement and the owner of an estate are entitled to the *use* of land. They differ, however, in that the owner of an estate has the right to *occupy* the land as well as use it, while the easement owner or holder is only entitled to use, and then only for limited purposes. Because the interest of the owner of an estate in land entitles him to occupy the land, his interest is said to be a *possessory* one. The easement owner's interest, on the other hand, is *nonpos-*

sessory in nature because he has no right of occupancy but only the right of use. The right of occupancy is the significant characteristic that distinguishes a possessory from a nonpossessory interest in land.

Easements Limit a Landowner's Use It should be recognized that when an easement holder acquires rights in land owned by someone else, the landowner's rights in his own land become limited or restricted. The landowner is no longer entitled to the *exclusive* use of his property that he previously enjoyed.

Types of Easements
Easements may be classified in several ways. The more common classifications are in accordance with whether an easement is (1) affirmative or negative, (2) appurtenant or in gross, (3) express or implied, and (4) according to the method by which an easement is created.

Affirmative Easements and Negative Easements All easements are either affirmative or negative, depending upon their basic characteristics. But whether it is affirmative or negative, an easement is a *burden* on the land that is subject to it because the easement interferes with the landowner's otherwise free use and enjoyment of his land. Land that bears the burden or encumbrance of an easement is referred to as a **servient estate** or **servient tenement.**

Classifying easements as affirmative or negative serves to differentiate them as to the kinds of action that an easement owner may take with respect to the servient estate.

Affirmative Easements An **affirmative easement** entitles the easement owner to go upon and perform certain acts on another's land which, were it not for the existence of the easement, would make him a trespasser upon the servient estate. A public utility easement is an example of an affirmative easement, as is a person's right to use a road or driveway on the servient estate, or the right to drain water on it.

Negative Easements A **negative easement** gives the owner of the easement the right to prevent the owner of the servient estate from doing certain things on his land that he would otherwise be entitled to do. The owner of a negative easement does not, however, have any right to enter upon the servient owner's land. Negative easements frequently involve an easement owner's right to the free flow of light and air from across an adjoining servient estate or the right to an unobstructed view. The effect of a negative easement of this type is to prevent the building of structures on the servient estate or to limit the height of them. Negative easements are less common than affirmative easements.

Appurtenant Easements and Easements in Gross An important classification of easements distinguishes between appurtenant easements and easements in gross.

Nature of an Appurtenant Easement An **appurtenant easement** is an easement that was created in one parcel of land for the *benefit* of another parcel. The land that is subject to and burdened by the easement is, we have seen, the servient estate or tenement, and the land that the easement benefits is known as the **dominant estate** or **dominant tenement.** Although the owner of the dominant estate will of course enjoy the use of the easement, the easement attaches to or is appurtenant to the benefited land rather than belonging to the owner personally as an interest that is separate and distinct from the dominant land. The significance of this fact is that the easement cannot be transferred by the easement owner separate from the land that it benefits. Furthermore, the easement will pass with a transfer of the dominant tenement to which it is appurtenant without the need for the easement to be specifically mentioned in the instrument of transfer.

A right of way over servient land to provide the occupants of a dominant estate with access to a street or public road is a common example of an appurtenant easement. Such a right of way is a part of or an appurtenance to the dominant estate, irrespective of who may be in lawful possession of it at any particular time.

Although it is commonly the case, it is not essential that the dominant and servient estates be adjoining properties for an appurtenant easement to exist.

Nature of an Easement in Gross An **easement in gross** belongs to an easement owner personally, independent of any land that he may own or occupy. It is sometimes said that an easement in gross is a "personal" right of the easement holder. With an easement in gross, there is no dominant estate—there is only the servient estate upon which the easement is an encumbrance.

A public utility's right of way across land for lines and poles or underground cables is an example of an easement in gross.

Appurtenant Easements Preferred It is sometimes difficult to determine whether a particular easement that has been created is appurtenant or in gross. The determination depends upon the *intent* of the parties; their intent is ascertained both from the language of the instrument creating the easement and from other evidence as well. Where the courts are called upon to interpret the language of a writing that creates an easement, they prefer to construe the language in favor of finding the easement to be appurtenant rather than in gross.

Creation of Easements

An easement is not a natural incident of ownership or possession of real estate. For an easement to exist, it must somehow be created. Easements, whether appurtenant or in gross, may be created in a number of ways, the more common of which are: (1) by express grant or reservation, (2) by implied grant or reservation, (3) by reason of necessity, (4) by condemnation, and (5) by prescription.

Regardless of how they are created, all easements are the same in that they are burdens or encumbrances on land. There are, however, certain significant characteristics resulting from the method by which easements come into being.

Creation by Express Grant or Reservation
The most common method of creating an easement is by a written instrument, which either expressly grants or transfers an easement to a transferee, or which reserves an easement to a transferor in land which he conveys to another person.

Express Grant A *grant* of an interest in real estate is a transfer or conveyance of that interest from one person to another. An *express* grant is a transfer in which the grantor's intent to convey an interest is revealed by words. Generally speaking, an easement by an express grant is created by a servient owner executing and delivering a deed to a grantee or transferee, who thereby becomes the owner of the easement described in the deed. More rarely, a servient owner's intention is indicated by a provision in a will.

Express Reservation A *reservation* of an interest in real estate occurs when the owner of a parcel transfers less than the entirety of his rights in the parcel. The transferor, in such a case, retains or reserves to himself some interest in land, the legal title to which he conveys to another person. An easement is created by an *express* reservation when the deed that transfers title to a parcel of land contains a provision specifically stating that the right to use the transferee's land for a particular purpose is reserved for the benefit of the transferor. By such a provision, the land that is conveyed is encumbered by the burden of an easement retained by the former owner of the land. The transferred land becomes a servient estate at the very moment that title to the parcel passes.

Importance of Unambiguous Expression
The wording of an express grant or reservation in a deed must be carefully and clearly drafted because ambiguous language can raise a serious question whether it was the fee title to a strip of land or only an easement that was intended to be transferred or reserved. The question be-

comes particularly pertinent when the use to which the strip of land was put by the entitled party is abandoned by him. If merely an easement was created, it will be lost when the authorized use is abandoned. The fee title to a strip of land, on the other hand, is not lost when the owner of it ceases to use it for any particular use.

Creation by Implied Grant or Reservation

Implication Arises from Probable Intent A right is created by implication when, although the parties to a transaction have not expressly provided for it, the circumstances of the transaction are such that the courts conclude that the parties intended to create such a right.

An easement is created by implication when a court infers from the facts before it that the parties to a conveyance of land intended to create an easement even though they did not expressly provide for it. The court's inference arises from the circumstances surrounding the fact of conveyance rather than from any language contained in the instrument that conveys the land. By drawing an inference, the law ascribes an intention to the parties, who not only had not expressed such an intention in words, but who in fact may not have consciously formed any intention with respect to the creation of an easement at the time of their transaction. The implication is based on the probable but unexpressed intention of the parties in light of all of the circumstances surrounding their transaction.

Essential Elements of an Implied Easement Implied easements are created only when the owner of a parcel of land divides his property, transfers part of it to another person, and retains the other portion of the parcel to himself. Before having divided his property and sold part of it, the owner, of course, was free to use all of the land as he saw fit. He may have used or burdened one portion of his land for the benefit of another part as, for example, where A, an owner, constructs and maintains a drainage ditch across the west half of his land to drain the east half of it. Upon separation of A's ownership of the two halves by conveyance of one of them, an easement for the continued use by the owner of the eastern half of the drainage ditch over the former west half of the parcel may arise by implication if the instrument of conveyance contains no express language concerning the use of the ditch.

In order that an easement by implication may arise, certain requirements must be satisfied at the time the division of ownership of land occurs.

The first essential element for the creation of an implied easement is that the use which is to become an easement (the use of the ditch for drainage in the foregoing illustration) must be *apparent* at the time that ownership of the property is divided, which means that the particular use must be discoverable by a careful inspection of the premises. Second, the use must appear to be *permanent* or *continuous* rather than merely temporary or occasional. Finally, the use of the burdened land must be *reasonably* necessary or important for the enjoyment of the land which, after the conveyance, is to become the dominant estate.

Implied Grant An easement arises by an implied *grant* when the owner of a parcel of land transfers the part of the land that benefits from the use of the portion of the property that is retained by him. In the foregoing example, an implied easement in favor of B would be created by grant if A conveyed the east half of his land to B and retained to himself the west half on which the drainage ditch is situated.

Implied Reservation An implied *reservation* of an easement occurs when an owner transfers the burdened portion and retains the benefited part of the land. Thus, a purchaser of land takes the property not only with its obvious benefits but with its obvious burdens as well. In the foregoing example, an easement would be created by an implied reservation if A were to convey the west half of his land upon which the

EASEMENTS, PROFITS, AND LICENSES

drainage ditch is located and retain to himself the east half that benefits from the ditch.

An easement by reservation is less readily implied by the courts than an easement resulting from a grant. The transferor is considered to be more in control of the language and circumstances of a conveyance than is the transferee and, this being the case, his failure clearly to express his intention will work to his disadvantage. Consequently, language and circumstances which might be adequate to imply the grant of an easement in favor of a transferee might not be sufficient to imply the reservation of an easement benefiting the transferor.

Preventing Implied Easements The parties to a transaction may prevent the creation of an easement by implication by using language that clearly negates it. When the negating language used in an instrument of conveyance is sufficiently explicit, no easement will arise by implication regardless of the fact that all essential elements for the creation of an easement by implication may be present.

No Implied Easements for Light and Air The majority of jurisdictions today have adopted the rule that under no circumstances will easements for light and air be implied. Consequently, a transferor may build on his adjoining land even though the structure that he erects will cut off the light and air received by the windows of another building located on land which he sold and transferred.

Easements for light and air may, however, be created by *express* provisions in a document of transfer.

Easement Created by Necessity Implied easements which are created because they are *reasonably* necessary for the use and enjoyment of real property must be distinguished from easements that are created by *strict* necessity.

Benefits Landlocked Land The creation of an easement may be implied by reason of necessity regardless of any prior use to which a divided parcel of land was previously put. An *easement by necessity*, also known as a "way of necessity," is created when a grantor conveys a portion of a larger parcel and by so doing "landlocks" the parcel he transfers. A parcel of land is said to be landlocked when it is entirely surrounded by the land of the transferor and other persons, as a result of which the parcel is shut off from access to any street or road. In such a case, in keeping with the presumed intent of the parties and in accordance with public policy favoring full utilization of land, a right of way across the transferor's land for exit from and access to the transferred parcel is implied.

An easement by necessity would be created, for example, when A, who owns a parcel of land fronting on a road that is adjoined on the sides and rear by lands owned by B, C, and D, divides his lot and sells the rear half of it to E. If A's deed contains no language with regard to an easement for access to E's landlocked parcel, the law implies an easement or way of necessity over A's land to permit E to use and enjoy his parcel, which is entirely surrounded by land owned by other persons.

An easement by necessity may also be created by an implied *reservation* in favor of a transferor where his conveyance to a transferee landlocks the parcel of land that the transferor retains. Such an easement would have been created in the foregoing illustration if A, instead of selling the rear portion of his lot to E had retained that portion to himself and transferred the front half bordering on the road to E. In that case, A would have an easement for access to his landlocked lot across the property that A transferred to E.

Requirement of Strict Necessity A way of necessity or an easement by necessity will be implied only in cases of *strict* or *absolute* necessity and not simply as a matter of convenience to the owner of a parcel of land. If the owner of a transferred or retained parcel of land has any other means of ingress and egress, regardless of the inconvenience such a route may involve, a way or easement of necessity will not be implied. Furthermore, once the absolute need which gave rise to the creation of an easement by necessity no longer exists, the easement itself will terminate.

Contrary Intent of Parties Although the public policy favoring full utilization of land is a substantial one, it nonetheless will give way to the clear manifestation of intent by the parties to a transaction that no easement of any kind is to be created. The transfer and ownership of landlocked land, while not favored, is neither unlawful nor prohibited. Evidence that clearly shows that the parties did not intend for an easement by necessity to be created will prevent such an easement from being implied, regardless of the fact that a parcel of real estate will be landlocked as a result of the transaction.

Easement Created by Condemnation Any government agency or public utility having the power of eminent domain may acquire an easement by means of condemnation proceedings. An easement derived from condemnation will be created despite the wishes of a protesting owner of the servient estate, who will be awarded the "market value" of the easement as compensation for the taking. Although in some instances the fee title to a strip of land may be condemned, where the taking is for purposes of streets, highways, utility lines, etc., the condemnor normally acquires only an easement or right of use.

The acquisition of interests in land by means of condemnation is more fully discussed in Chapter 11.

Easement Created by Prescription
Acquisition of Right of Use by a Wrongdoer
To create an easement by **prescription** is to create it by *adverse use.* As the term is used in connection with **prescriptive easements,** an **adverse user** is one who, as a trespasser, enters upon and uses the land of another and, by continuing his wrongful use of the property for a period of time specified by statute, acquires an easement in the property. The law that permits one to acquire an easement by prescription[1] is in effect a statute of limitations. From the moment an intruder begins his wrongful use of property owned by another person, the landowner has the right to bring a legal action to have the trespasser removed and to prevent his continued use of the property. If, however, the landowner fails to commence his action within the statutorily prescribed period of time, he will forever lose his right to bring an action against the trespasser.

Since a landowner's right to put an end to the wrongful use of his land is lost by the passage of time, the effect of such loss is to create in the wrongdoer the undisturbed right to continue his use of the owner's land. By the process of prescription, the one who wrongfully uses another's property acquires the right to continue that use. The right that the adverse user acquires is called a *prescriptive right.*

The principal objective of the law of prescription is said to be the protection of long-established position of parties so that there may be a relatively prompt termination of controversies involving real estate before witnesses die, memories fade, or evidence is lost.

Requisites for Acquisition of Easement by Prescription For an easement to be acquired by prescription, there must have been (1) an *adverse or wrongful use* of property which was (2) *continuous and uninterrupted* for (3) the *period of time* provided by statute.

The use of land is considered to be adverse to the person whose rights are thereby invaded when the land is used *without permission* of the rightful owner of the land. The use of another's land is adverse only when that use is wrongful and gives rise to a cause of action against the user by the owner or possessor of land. Furthermore, the wrongdoer's use of the land must have been so "open and notorious" that a rea-

---

[1] "Prescription" is defined by the *Restatement of the Law of Property* as "the effect of lapse of time in creating and extinguishing property interests." Ch. 38, Topic A, Intro. Note.

sonable inspection of the premises by the owner would have revealed the wrongful use.

Statutes in some states provide methods whereby landowners may prevent the acquisition of prescriptive easements by granting blanket permission to use their lands and thus prevent the use from being wrongful. One type of statute permits a landowner to record in the county recorder's office a "notice of consent" to use his land for purposes designated in the notice.[2] Such notice can be revoked by the landowner at any time. A second type of statute enables a landowner to grant permission to use his premises by posting signs at entrances and at certain intervals along the boundary stating "Right to pass by permission and subject to the control of owner," or similar language.[3] Use of either or both of these methods successfully insulates a landowner from the danger of persons acquiring prescriptive rights in his property.

If an easement is to be created by prescription, the wrongful use by an adverse user must be "continuous and uninterrupted" for the period of time required by the statute of the state where the land is located.

The continuity requirement does not mean that the property must be used every instant of the day and night, but only with sufficient frequency to give notice of the wrongful use to the landowner. Any change in the location of the wrongdoer's use or his manner of exercising that use will be construed as the abandonment of one use and the commencement of another. Unless either the old or the new use has been continued for the required statutory period, no easement will have been created.

The continuous use of another's land is not interrupted by mere protestations on the part of the landowner. In fact, such protests serve as substantial evidence of the fact that the use of the owner's land is adverse rather than permissive. If, however, the landowner by means of threats or by erecting physical barriers should cause the wrongdoer to discontinue his use of the land, no matter for how brief a time, the continuity of the adverse use will be interrupted and the running of the prescriptive period will stop.

An easement by prescription will be created only if the adverse, continuous, and uninterrupted use of another's land endures for the entire period of time required by statute. Although the statutory periods vary among the states, in each jurisdiction they tend to be of the same duration as is required for the acquisition of title to land by adverse possession.

No Prescriptive Easements for Light and Air The majority of states have adopted the view that prescriptive easements cannot be acquired for the use of light and air coming across another person's property. Under the majority view, such easements can only be created by an express grant or an express reservation.

Exercise of Easement Rights

Extent or Scope of Easement Since an easement gives one person rights in land that belongs to someone else, there is always the likelihood that a conflict will arise between the easement holder and the owner of the servient estate. Conflicts frequently concern the question of the scope or extent of the use to which the easement holder is entitled. As conditions change with the passage of time, the easement holder may desire to change the nature of his use of the servient property or to broaden the scope or the intensity of the existing use. Any

---

[2] For example, California Civil Code, sec. 813 provides: "The holder of record title to land may record in the office of the recorder of any county in which a portion of the land is situated, a description of said land and a notice reading substantially as follows: 'The right of the public or any person to make any use whatsoever of the above described land or any portion thereof . . . is by permission and subject to control, of owner: Section 813, Civil Code.'"

[3] California Civil Code, sec. 1008, for example, provides: "No use by any person or persons, no matter how long continued, of any land, shall ever ripen into an easement by prescription, if the owner of such property posts at each entrance or at intervals of not more than 200 feet along the boundary a sign substantially as follows: 'Right to pass by permission, and subject to control, of owner: Section 1008, Civil Code.'"

increase in the benefit that the holder of the easement derives from it necessarily will result in a corresponding increase in the burden that is suffered by the servient land.

Much of the litigation involving easements arises as a result of changes in conditions since the easement first became an encumbrance. The issue to be resolved by the courts in such cases is whether the original authorized use may change along with the conditions without the express consent of the servient owner. In cases of this type the courts are said to apply the "rule of reason" in determining whether the increased burden on the servient land is more than the land should be expected to bear, given the extent to which conditions have changed.

In deciding controversies involving the scope or extent of the use of easements, the courts are guided by the manner in which the easement was created.

Rights of Easement Owner Ideally, when an easement is *created by a grant,* the document that creates it will be so clearly drafted that it leaves little or no room for judicial interpretation. In determining the rights and obligations of the parties affected by an easement, the language of the instrument granting or reserving the easement is the first and foremost thing to be considered by the courts. If that language is clear and unambiguous, it will be given effect.

Where the terms of an instrument creating an easement are ambiguous, the courts commonly resort to the "rule of reason" as the basis for their interpretation of the language. In so doing, the courts endeavor to place themselves in the position of the parties at the time the document was drafted and to give reasonable meaning to the words as used at that time.

In the absence of express language to the contrary in the granting document, the parties are assumed to have contemplated a normal increase in the intensity of use by the easement holder over the years. In situations involving appurtenant easements, the increase in use generally results from the normal development of the dominant estate. As long as the additional burden placed on the servient property is not unreasonable, the increased intensity of easement use will be permitted.

When determining the scope or extent of an *implied easement,* the court, of course, has no written language of the parties to look to for guidance. In endeavoring to give effect to the unexpressed but apparent intent of the parties, a major factor to be considered by the courts is the scope of the use of the servient land before it was separated from the present dominant estate. The scope of this former use is permitted to be enlarged to accommodate such additional burden as may have been anticipated from reasonably foreseeable changes in the dominant estate.

Few problems ever arise regarding the scope or extent of easements that are created by *necessity.* Because the reason for implying the creation of an easement by necessity is to promote the productive use of land, courts recognize only those rights in an easement holder that are absolutely necessary to achieve that purpose. As previously noted, easements by necessity are created to provide access to land that otherwise would be landlocked.

The scope of an easement acquired by *prescription* is determined by the nature and extent of the use by which the easement was created. As we have seen, the wrongdoer's use must be the same in type and degree throughout the required statutory period. If the intensity of the use is increased at any time during the statutory period, that increased use must be continued for a new statutory period if an easement corresponding to the intensified use is to be created.

Once they have been acquired, however, an easement owner's rights are not narrowly and rigidly limited to the precise use which gave rise to the easement by prescription. The use permitted under a matured prescriptive easement may vary somewhat from the exact use by which it was created. The use of the property that created the prescriptive rights will define the general outline rather than the minute details of the use that the easement holder may make of his easement. As long as the burden that is borne by the servient estate is not unreasonably increased, the holder of an easement obtained by prescription may do such things as are reasonably necessary for his enjoyment of the easement.

Providing he can do so without committing a breach of the peace, an easement owner may remove anything from the easement area that interferes with his use of it. In so doing, the easement owner is, of course, resorting to self-help to abate a nuisance. And, as is true in any exercise of the right of self-help, if the easement holder inflicts unnecessary injury on the servient estate while he is removing the interference, he will be liable in damages to the owner of the servient property.

Under appropriate circumstances, an easement holder may obtain judicial relief, either in the form of a mandatory injunction compelling the servient owner to remove an obstruction or a prohibitory injunction forbidding the servient owner from continuing his objectionable conduct.

Rights of Servient Owner The owner of a servient estate is free to exercise all incidents of ownership that do not interfere with an easement owner's use and enjoyment of his easement. The servient owner may do nothing that would obstruct the easement owner's proper use of his easement. Whether or not a given use by the servient owner is an unlawful interference with the easement owner's rights will depend upon the facts of each case and the terms of the grant or the conditions under which the easement was created.

To the extent that the instrument creating an easement specifies precisely the use that may be made of the easement, it also defines the nature and extent of the limitations that restrict the servient owner's use of the land that he owns. As the descriptive language becomes less and less precise, both the easement holder and the servient owner are more and more governed by the rule of reason when exercising their respective rights.

Unless a contrary intent is clearly apparent, the courts construe all easements as creating "interests in common" rather than exclusive rights. The effect of such an interpretation is to permit the servient owner to share in the easement holder's use of the area subject to the easement, providing that in doing so he does not unreasonably interfere with the easement owner's right of use.

Repair and Maintenance of Easements In the absence of a contrary provision in the document creating an easement, the easement owner is under a duty to repair and maintain the easement.

An easement owner may make such improvements to his easement as may be necessary to accomplish the purpose for which the easement was created, providing the improvements do not unreasonably increase the burden borne by the servient estate.

Every easement is said to include certain secondary or "incidental" easements. These secondary easements give the easement holder the right to enter upon the servient land that adjoins his easement for the purpose of effecting such repairs and maintenance as may be required.

Transfer of Easements

An easement is transferable from one person to another unless the instrument creating it specifically provides otherwise. The method by which an easement may be transferred will depend upon whether the easement is appurtenant or in gross.

Upon Transfer of the Dominant Estate When the dominant estate to which an easement is appurtenant is transferred from one person to another, the easement is a part of that transfer even though it is not mentioned specifically in the instrument conveying the property.

Whether it was created by grant, reservation, necessity, implication, or prescription, an appurtenant easement becomes a part of the dominant estate as of the time of its creation and continues to be a part of it until the easement is terminated by one means or another. We know that when a dominant estate is transferred, unless the deed provides otherwise, the transferee receives exactly the same bundle of rights that the transferor has at the time of the conveyance.

By inserting an express provision in a deed, a transferor can specifically exclude an appurtenant easement from a conveyance of the dominant estate, and the transferee will then take the property without the easement. Where this occurs, the appurtenant easement is not converted into an easement in gross owned by the transferor, but is terminated and the servient estate is forever freed of its burden.

Upon Transfer of the Servient Estate When a servient estate that is encumbered by an appurtenant easement is transferred, the transferee takes the property subject to the burden of the easement. If the transferee of the servient land is a purchaser rather than merely the recipient of a gift, he will take the property subject to the easement only if he had *actual or constructive notice* of the existence of the easement. Constructive notice, as we shall see in Chapter 14, is imparted either by the recordation of the document creating the easement or by the use of the easement by its owner in such a manner as to make the existence of the easement apparent upon a reasonable inspection of the servient premises by a buyer.

Transferability of Easements in Gross Almost without exception, the courts have held easements in gross that are created for such commercial purposes as telephone, telegraph, electric lines, pipelines, etc., to be transferable from one owner to another. Easements in gross which are not predominantly commercial in character are also held to be transferable, providing there is evidence to show that transferability was intended at the time the easement was created. There is a growing tendency to regard all easements in gross as being transferable, except of course for an easement which is obviously intended to benefit only the particular person for whom it was created.

Termination of Easements
The termination of an easement benefits a servient owner by relieving his property from the burden of its servitude. Just as the creation of the easement places a limitation on the landowner's free use of his property, the extinguishment of the easement removes this limitation and restores the owner's right of use of his land.

Methods of Termination Easements, whether appurtenant or in gross may terminate or be terminated in a variety of ways.

Lapse of Time or Fulfillment of Purpose An easement may expire by reason of the period of time set forth in the instrument creating the easement. For example, where an easement was created for the lifetime of the present owner of the dominant tenement, it will expire upon the death of that owner. Similarly, an easement that was created to serve a particular purpose, such as the removal of rock or gravel from a quarry, will end when that purpose has been accomplished. And, as we have previously noted, an easement created by necessity will terminate when the need for which it was created ceases to exist.

Many easements will continue for a potentially unlimited period of time unless some particular act or event occurs to bring them to an end. Chief among the methods by which easements of potentially unlimited duration may be terminated are: (1) release, (2) merger, (3) abandonment, (4) nonuse, (5) estoppel, (6) prescription, and (7) destruction of the servient tenement.

Termination by Release An easement is terminated when the owner of it surrenders all of his rights in the servient estate to the servient owner by means of an express or formal *release*.

EASEMENTS, PROFITS, AND LICENSES

The easement owner normally effects his release by executing a quitclaim deed and delivering it to the servient owner. Upon acceptance of the quitclaim deed by the servient owner, the extinguishment of the easement is complete.

The termination of an easement by a release is a bilateral transaction that requires the intent and consent of both the owner of the easement and the owner of the servient estate. This mutual intent and consent is manifested by the delivery and acceptance of a quitclaim deed identifying the easement.

Termination by Merger A *merger* occurs when an easement owner becomes the owner of the servient estate, or conversely when the owner of the servient estate becomes the owner of the easement.

In the case of an appurtenant easement, one person's ownership of both the dominant and the servient estates, sometimes called "unity of ownership," extinguishes the easement. We have seen that an easement by definition consists of rights of one person in the land of another person, and that for an easement appurtenant to exist, there must be two parcels of land that are separately owned, a dominant estate and a servient estate. When the same owner owns both of the estates, the easement is no longer considered to be an incident of either of them.

An easement in gross terminates by merger when the owner of the easement also becomes the owner of the servient estate. With an easement in gross there is no dominant estate to be merged.

Termination by Abandonment The owner of an easement may relinquish his rights in the servient estate by intentionally abandoning those rights. Unlike the termination of an easement by a release, termination by abandonment does not require an agreement on the part of the servient owner. Whether an abandonment has occurred or not depends entirely on the conduct of the easement owner alone.

Like the termination of an easement by a release, abandonment is the *intentional* relinquishment of the easement by its owner. In the one case, the easement holder's intention to relinquish his claim is manifested by *express words* set forth in a quitclaim deed; in the other case his intention is manifested by his *conduct*. Whether or not an easement owner's conduct in a particular case amounts to an abandonment is a question of fact for jury determination.

While verbal expressions of intention will not alone constitute the necessary manifestation required for abandonment, such expressions by an easement owner coupled with certain acts on his part may be sufficient to indicate his intention to relinquish his rights.

Termination by Nonuse It is necessary to distinguish between nonuse of an easement and an intentional abandonment. Unlike abandonment, mere nonuse by an easement owner will not normally terminate his easement. An easement that was created by a grant, for example, cannot be lost by nonuse *alone,* no matter how long continued. While the fact of nonuse of the easement by the owner may be some evidence of his intent to abandon his rights in the servient estate, nonuse in and of itself is not conclusive of the intention to abandon. Where easements created by grant are concerned, nonuse for any period of time must be considered together with all other circumstances to determine whether or not the nonuser intended to abandon his easement. Nonuse is only one indication of an easement holder's intent to abandon his easement.

As for easements that have been created by prescription, some courts have held that nonuse of the easement for a period of time equal to the prescriptive period establishes a presumption of abandonment, which presumption will prevail unless it is rebutted by evidence to the contrary. Such a view has been criticized as being unwise, however, it being argued that an easement acquired by prescription is just as well established as one created by a grant, and that the rule of nonuse should be the same in both cases. The *Restatement of the Law of Prop-*

erty[4] adopts the view, supported by a number of courts, that nonuse alone is never sufficient to constitute abandonment, but is only evidence to be considered with other facts.

At least one state[5] by statute permits easements acquired by prescription to be lost by nonuse alone if continued for the prescriptive period.

Termination by Estoppel The doctrine of **estoppel** prevents a person from denying the truth of an intentional or careless statement or act by him that leads another person to rely on that statement or act to his detriment. The person who is estopped must have caused the person invoking the benefit of the doctrine of estoppel to believe something to be true which is not in fact true.

As applied to the extinguishment of easements, an estoppel arises from the reasonable belief by the servient owner, based on statements or acts by the easement owner, that the easement owner does not intend to make use of his easement in the future. For example, assume that A owns an easement across land owned by B that gives A access to a public highway. Although A has no intention of abandoning his easement, he does not use it for several years. B, reasonably believing that A intends to abandon the easement, begins to erect a building that covers the entire easement. Although A is at all times aware of the construction work, he makes no complaint to B until the building is nearing completion, at which time he asserts his right to use the easement. Under these facts, A has lost his right to use B's property because his easement was terminated by estoppel.

The termination of easements by estoppel is based on society's desire to free titles to land from encumbrances in the nature of unused easements.

Termination by Prescription An easement will be extinguished by adverse use of the easement by the servient owner for the prescriptive period prescribed by statute.[6] Not only must the servient owner's use of the easement at all times be hostile and adverse to the easement owner, but his wrongful use must also be continuous and uninterrupted for the statutorily prescribed period.

We have previously seen that an owner has the right to use his property that is subject to an easement in any way he desires as long as he does not interfere with the rights of the easement owner. In order to start the running of the period for prescription against the easement, the servient owner's use must clearly be wrongful with respect to the easement holder and be in violation of his rights. The erection by the servient owner of permanent structures such as buildings or walls on the area that is burdened by an easement, or the installation of other obstructions that clearly interfere with an owner's use of his easement, would be sufficiently wrongful to start the running of the statutory period. But unless the servient owner's conduct is such that the easement holder could bring legal action against him, his use cannot extinguish an easement no matter how long it may be continued.

Destruction of Servient Tenement Easements sometimes involve the use of structures on the servient tenement as, for example, in the case of stairs used to reach the upper floors of a dominant owner's building, or the use of walls on the servient estate for the support of a building on the dominant estate. In such situations, there is no easement in the land, but only in the structures. Problems regarding the termination of easements in structures arise particularly when the structures subject to the easements are destroyed. In deciding the issue of termination, the courts have distinguished between the *voluntary* destruction of the servient structures and their *involuntary* destruction.

---

[4] Sec. 504, comment d.
[5] California Civil Code, sec. 811.4.

[6] This period varies from as little as 5 years in California to 10 years in Texas, 15 years in Michigan and New York, 20 years in Illinois and Florida, and 21 years in Ohio.

The rule is well settled that the involuntary destruction of a servient tenement by fire, tornado, or earthquake, for example, terminates any easement in that structure. The rule is based on recognition of the fact that once the servient tenement is destroyed, there is nothing left upon which the easement can be claimed or exercised. To compel the owner of the servient structure to rebuild for the sole purpose of restoring the easement is considered to be unreasonable. Moreover, the general rule is that if the owner of the servient land does decide to rebuild, the easement will not be revived even though the new structure is substantially identical to the one that was destroyed.

When a building becomes obsolete and the income from it is decreasing, a prudent investor will want to demolish it and replace it with a new structure capable of maximizing the income realizable from his land. The existing building, however, may be encumbered by an easement that would be destroyed when the old building is demolished and which would not be replaced in the new one. The problem confronting the owner of the depreciating building is whether he may voluntarily destroy it despite the easement owner's interest in the structure.

The equities of the parties in cases of this type can be persuasive on both sides. To prevent a servient owner from demolishing a depreciating building and replacing it with a highly profitable new one may be patently unfair. On the other hand, to permit destruction of the building and replacement with one that deprives the easement owner of a desperately needed means of access to his dominant estate may be equally unjust.

As might be expected, courts in the various states take divergent views as to the effect of voluntary destruction of servient structures on the rights of easement holders. According to one view, the voluntary demolition or removal of the servient structure does not terminate an easement. The contrary view permits termination of the easement, holding that it was created to last only while the servient structure existed. According to this view, upon demolition of the servient structure the owner of the servient land is under no obligation to provide for continuance of the easement in a new or substituted building.

PROFITS

A **profit**, or more technically speaking, a *profit à prendre*, is the right of one person to enter upon the property of another and take something from the land. That which is taken may be a part of the land itself, such as sand, gravel, or minerals, or it may be a product of the land such as timber or other growing things.

Profits and Easements Not Legally Distinguishable

Although the language of some decisions attempts to distinguish between profits and easements, the legal principles applicable to them are the same. The *Restatement of the Law of Property* does not distinguish between them or treat them separately. The *Restatement* points out[7] that in no decision examined during the preparation of the *Restatement* was there found to be a rule of law applicable to either a profit or an easement that was not also applicable to the other.

LICENSES

Revocable Permission to Use Land

A **license** is a privilege to do an act or a series of acts on land in the possession of another person. It is a personal, nontransferable permission given by a possessor of land, who is the **licensor,** to a *licensee*. The licensee acquires no ownership interest of any kind in the licensor's property, but is merely permitted to do things on the land that would otherwise constitute a trespass.

As a general rule, a license may be revoked or withdrawn by the licensor at any time and for any reason. Revocation may take the form of any manifestation of the licensor's intention

---

[7] Special Note to sec. 450.

to end the license, whether by means of a formal notice of revocation or by acts which obstruct or are otherwise inconsistent with the continued existence of the license.

The licensee, for his part, is free to surrender the privilege extended to him whenever he may desire to do so.

A license will terminate upon the death of either the licensor or the licensee.

License and Easement Distinguished

A license is like an easement in that it authorizes the use of land in the possession of another person. It differs significantly from an easement, however, because the duration of the license is at the will of the licensor or possessor of the land while an easement is not. This ability of the licensor to terminate the license at will is a key factor distinguishing a license from an easement.

License and Lease Distinguished

The test of whether an agreement gives rise to a license or to a lease turns on the right of occupancy of premises. An agreement that gives a person the exclusive right of possession is a lease, while a revocable permission to use premises occupied by the one granting the permission is a license.

Licensor Estopped to Revoke

While a license to enter and use premises is generally said to be revocable by the licensor at any time, there are certain circumstances under which the license cannot be revoked. Where this is the case, the license becomes equivalent to an easement.

Where a licensee, in reliance upon the continuance of a license and with the knowledge of the licensor, makes improvements or expends money on the land, the licensor is said to be estopped from revoking the license.

License Coupled with an Interest

A licensor cannot revoke a license that is "coupled with an interest." A license is said to be coupled with an interest when the license was granted as an incident of a licensee's ownership of personal property which is located on the licensor's land. For example, where the occupier of land has sold personal property to a buyer, that buyer has an irrevocable license to enter and remove his property within a reasonable time period following the purchase. Or, where personal property has been placed on another's land with the landowner's permission, the owner of the personal property has an irrevocable license to enter the land to retrieve his property.

No License by Prescription

A license is never created by prescription or adverse use. Rights to use the land of another that arise from prescription are always easements, never licenses.

QUESTIONS

1. What is an easement? How does it differ from an ownership interest? How is it similar?
2. Why is an easement considered to be a burden or encumbrance on land?
3. How does an affirmative easement differ from a negative easement?
4. How does a servient estate or tenement differ from a dominant estate or tenement?
5. What significant factor distinguishes an easement in gross from an appurtenant easement?
6. Explain how the creation of an easement by an express grant differs from the creation of an easement by an express reservation.
7. List the essential requirements for the creation of an implied easement.
8. Explain how the creation of an implied easement can be prevented.
9. What are the requirements for the creation of an easement by prescription?
10. Describe how statutes in some states enable a landowner to prevent easements by prescription from being acquired in his land.
11. What is a secondary or incidental easement?
12. What happens to an easement that has been properly recorded when the dominant estate or tenement is transferred? The servient estate or tenement?

EASEMENTS, PROFITS, AND LICENSES

13 Explain how an appurtenant easement is terminated by merger.
14 What is the significant difference between nonuse of an easement created by an express grant and abandonment of the easement?
15 What is a profit? How does it differ from an easement?
16 What is a license? How does it differ from an easement?
17 Why can't a license be created by prescription?

Chapter 9

Real Estate Contracts

Every real estate sales transaction involves one or more contracts between the owner of real property and one or more other persons. While contracts relating to real estate have generally been given specific names by real estate practitioners, all of them, however designated, are governed by the general law of contracts.

The objective of the law of contracts is to provide the machinery whereby persons desiring to do so can create legal rights and impose legal duties on themselves by means of an agreement. Once a contractual relationship has been formed between parties, the rights and duties they have created will be enforced by the courts.

Regardless of whether a given real estate agreement has as its purpose the employment of a broker, the sale of a parcel of property, the creation of an option, or the loan of money secured by real estate, for the agreement to be an enforceable contract it must satisfy certain essential requirements. Since all contracts are governed by the same basic rules, it is important that those common rules be understood before the particular characteristics of certain real estate contracts are examined. Consequently, this chapter is divided into two parts, the first of which deals with contracts in general and the second with contracts pertaining to the sale of real estate. Contracts that relate to the use of real estate as security for a debt are discussed elsewhere.

NATURE OF A CONTRACT

In the simplest of terms, a **contract** is an agreement that the law will enforce. More broadly defined, a contract is "a promise or set of promises for the breach of which the law gives a remedy or the performance of which the law in some way recognizes as a duty."[1] As thus defined, it is apparent that the basic feature of a contract is a promise or set of promises that the law will enforce. A **promise** is an expression of intention by a promisor that he will conduct himself in a certain way or bring about a specified result in the future, which is communicated to a promisee.

Not all promises or agreements that people make are legally enforceable. As we have seen, only those agreements that fulfill certain requirements constitute contracts that the law will enforce. Before we examine the essential elements necessary for the formation of a contract, let us look at the various categories into which contracts are classified.

CLASSIFICATION OF CONTRACTS

Unilateral and Bilateral Contracts

Every contract is either unilateral or bilateral in character.

A **unilateral contract** is one in which one of the parties makes a *promise* and the other party performs an *act*. The promise by the promisor is made to induce performance of an act that he requests. The person to whom the promise is made is under no legal obligation to perform the act, but once the requested act has been voluntarily performed by him the promisor becomes obligated to carry out his promise. A common example of a unilateral contract is the promise of one person to pay a reward for the return of a lost article.

In a **bilateral contract,** promises are made by *both* parties to an agreement. There is a mutual exchange of promises between the parties, as where one of them promises to pay a sum of money on a given date in exchange for the other's promise to deliver a certain item on that date. The contract is formed and the parties become bound by its terms as of the moment that the exchange of promises is effected.

[1] *Restatement (2d) of the Law of Contracts,* sec. 1.

Express and Implied Contracts

All contracts are either express or implied. The distinction between them arises from the manner in which the parties indicate their intention to be bound.

An **express contract** is one in which the promises of the parties are revealed in words, either orally or in writing.

A contract is **implied** when no promises are stated, but instead the existence of the contract and its terms are manifested by the acts or conduct of the parties. The intention of the parties to bind themselves by a contract is deduced from the circumstances of their conduct. For example, a person who hails a taxi and simply gives the driver a street address impliedly promises to pay him the metered fare upon arrival at the destination.

Executed and Executory Contracts

A contract is said to be **executed** when all of the contracting parties completely fulfilled the legal obligations imposed on them by their agreement. It is a contract that has been performed in its entirety—nothing more remains to be done.

All other contracts are **executory** in character. Contracts continue to be classified as executory even though one of the parties has fully performed all of his obligations under the contract. As long as anything remains to be done, the contract is said to be executory.

Valid, Unenforceable, Void, and Voidable Contracts

Despite a certain redundancy or contradiction in the use of such terms, contracts are customarily classified as being either valid, unenforceable, void, or voidable.

A contract is **valid** when it is such that the law will enforce it. The use of the term "valid" in connection with a contract is, of course, an obvious redundancy since by definition a contract is enforceable by law. Calling it "valid" makes it no more enforceable than if not so designated. Nonetheless, the expression "valid contract" is commonly used, usually to distinguish it from agreements whose enforceability may be in doubt.

An **unenforceable contract** is an otherwise valid contract that fails to meet the requirements of some particular statute or rule of law and thus is denied a legal remedy for its breach. For example, all states have statutes of limitation which set certain periods of time during which legal actions arising from a breach of contract must be commenced. If the statutory period has expired, a contract, despite the fact that it is otherwise valid, will not be enforced by the courts. Similarly, statutes of frauds in all states require that contracts pertaining to certain subject matter must be in writing to be enforceable. If the parties have not reduced their agreement to writing, it will not be enforced by the courts despite the fact that the agreement meets all requirements for a valid contract.

To say that a contract is **void** is a contradictory use of terms. If an agreement is void, it will not be enforced by a court. In other words, a void contract is not a contract at all—it is a nullity and has no legal effect. Despite this fact, the term "void contract" is commonly used to refer to agreements that cannot be enforced by any of the parties to it.

A **voidable contract** is an agreement that is binding on the parties to it until one of them, exercising rights that arise because of particular circumstances, elects to withdraw from the contract. For example, one who has been induced to enter into a contract through fraudulent representations may, upon discovering the fraud, decide whether to be bound by the contract or to avoid it and be freed from his obligations thereunder.

ELEMENTS OF A CONTRACT

For an agreement to be a contract, the following essential elements must be present: (1) there must be mutual assent to the terms of the agreement by the parties; (2) consideration must have been given by each party; (3) the parties must have legal capacity to contract; (4) the parties' consent to the agreement must be real and freely given; (5) the objective of the agreement must be a lawful one; and (6) when specifically required by statute, the agreement must be in writing.

While there must be at least two parties to a contract, there is no upper limit to the number of contracting parties.

Mutual Assent

To create a contract, the parties must manifest to each other their **mutual assent** to be bound by certain obligations. Ordinarily, before any agreement is reached by the parties there will be a certain amount of negotiating between them. These negotiations will continue until one of the parties makes a definite proposal or promise to do something in the future provided the other party does or promises to do something in return. The proposal or promise of one party is known as an *offer* and the other party's assent to that proposal is called an *acceptance.* In other words, the parties' manifestation of their mutual assent takes the form of an offer made by one of them and an acceptance of that offer by the other.

Offer: A Conditional Promise An **offer** is a promise made by one person, called the *offeror,* to another person, the *offeree,* which by its terms is conditioned on the performance of an act or the giving of a return promise by the offeree. A promise is conditional, for example, when an offeror, R, says to the offeree, E, "I will (I promise to) pay you $15 if (on the condition that) you will mow my lawn." R's promise is similarly subject to a condition when he says to E, "I will (I promise to) pay you $15 if (provided that) you will promise to mow my lawn." In the first instance, R's promise calls for the formation of a unilateral contract and in the second instance, a bilateral one.

How Manifested An offer may be manifested in any manner that communicates to the offeree the intent of the offeror to make a conditional promise. The offer may be expressed orally or in writing or it may be implied from the offeror's conduct. While perfectly permissible legally, the practical shortcoming of an oral offer is the problem of proof when its terms are disputed. For this reason many persons confirm an oral proposal by a written memorandum of their conversation.

As we previously noted, an offeror's promise may be implied from his conduct, as where he hails a taxi and utilizes its services without expressly saying "I promise to pay the amount indicated on the meter upon arrival at my destination."

The use of standard printed forms as a means of making offers is common in many types of business transactions today. We shall have occasion to observe their use in real estate transactions later in this chapter and elsewhere in the book.

Terms Must Be Definite To constitute an offer, a proposal must indicate the essential terms of both the offeror's promise and the promise or the act requested from the offeree with enough certainty to enable the undertakings of the parties to be ascertained. Such things as identification of the subject matter of a promise, the price to be paid, the time of performance, and the work to be done are among the terms considered essential.

The requirement of certainty is complied with if the essential terms, though not expressly indicated in a proposal, can be supplied by implication. For example, an offer to sell designated goods which fails to indicate the time when performance is to be rendered obligates the promisor to deliver the goods within a reasonable period of time following acceptance of the offer. Every offer for the sale of goods contains an implicit promise to deliver them within a reasonable time if no delivery date is indicated.

Distinguished from Other Communications
We have seen that a certain amount of negotiating by the parties will generally precede the formation of a contract. One of the parties must, of course, be the initiator of those negotiations, but that initiator will not necessarily be the offeror. In a sales transaction, for instance, the seller frequently makes statements that manifest his desire to do business without his making a proposal that in law amounts to an offer. Communications of this type by the seller are regarded as being *invitations* or *solicitations* from him that are designed and intended to induce other persons to make offers to him to buy the goods that the seller has indicated are available for sale.

Communications that invite or solicit offers may take a number of different forms.

Although it is possible for an offer to be made by an *advertisement* in a newspaper or magazine, the courts generally hold that advertisements for the sale of goods at a stated price are invitations extended to readers to make offers to buy those goods from the advertiser. Where an advertisement is construed as being an invitation, the language of the advertisement is not such that would lead a reasonable person to believe that the advertiser intended to bind himself without a further expression of assent on his part. However, where the advertisement contains a definite promise by the advertiser to be bound if he receives what is requested in exchange for his promise, the advertisement will be construed as an offer rather than as an invitation for an offer. Advertisements that promise a reward for the return of lost articles or strayed animals are examples of offers made by advertisement.

Neither *catalogues* which set forth descriptions and prices of goods for sale nor published *price lists* are considered to be offers. They are merely invitations to readers to submit offers to buy the goods described or referred to in the publication.

Like advertisements generally, published notices stating that *bids* are sought from builders are not offers. The bids that are submitted in response to the notice constitute offers. The published notice simply serves to solicit or invite offers from interested builders.

Unless it has been announced that an *auction sale* is "without reserve," offers at an auction are made by bidders rather than by the auctioneer. Since he is the offeree, the auctioneer is free to reject any offers in the form of bids by persons interested in buying goods that have been put up for auction. No sale is complete until the fall of the auctioneer's hammer, which indicates his acceptance of the highest bidder's offer.

If an auction has been announced as being "without reserve," once the auctioneer has called for bids on a given article, that article cannot be withdrawn from sale unless no bid is made within a reasonable period of time.

Termination of an Offer By making an offer, the offeror confers upon the offeree a continuing legal power to create a contract simply by accepting the offeror's proposal. The offeree's power to create a contract by acceptance continues until such time as the legal effectiveness of the outstanding offer is terminated.

Any of the following acts or events will terminate an offer: (1) the lapse of time; (2) a revocation by the offeror; (3) a rejection by the offeree; (4) death or insanity of the offeror or offeree; (5) destruction of the subject matter of the offer; or (6) the illegality of the proposed contract as a result of a change in the law.

An offer terminates upon expiration of the period of *time stated in the offer* or, where no time period is stated, after the running of a *reasonable* time period.

When he makes his offer, the offeror is in full control of the terms it will contain and may expressly provide that it will continue only for a stated period of time. With such a provision in the offer, it will terminate automatically when the indicated time period expires. And, of course, with the expiration of the offer, the offeree's power to create a contract by acceptance likewise expires.

An offer containing no express time limitation will expire after the lapse of a reasonable time period. What constitutes a reasonable time period is a question to be answered only after examining the circumstances that surround the making of the offer. Certainly a reasonable time period will be shorter in the case of perishable goods or those whose market price fluctuates rapidly than for nonperishables and goods whose market price is relatively stable.

An offer is terminated by **revocation** when the offeror, prior to acceptance by the offeree, notifies the offeree that the offer is being withdrawn. To be effective, the offeree's revocation must be communicated to the offeree. In most states this means that the revocation is not effective, and hence the offer is not terminated, until the message announcing the withdrawal of the offer is actually received by the offeree, rather than at the time that the offer is dispatched by the offeror. A few states[2] adopt a contrary view.

If the offeree should learn from some third party that the offeror has sold the property described in his offer prior to the offer's expiration date, the offeree cannot thereafter create a contract by notifying the offeror of his acceptance. The offeree's knowledge of the prior sale or disposition, although acquired from a source other than the offeror, terminates the offer just as effectively as an express revocation communicated directly to him by the offeror.

When an offeree rejects an offer his rejection terminates it and the offeree's power to create a contract by acceptance comes to an end. The offeree's attempted acceptance after his rejection amounts to a new offer initiated by him and will result in the creation of a contract only upon acceptance by the original offeror whose status has become that of an offeree.

A **rejection** is a manifestation on the part of an offeree of his intent not to exercise his power

---

[2] For example, California Civil Code, sec. 1587(1) provides that a revocation becomes effective when placed in the course of transmission.

to create a contract on the terms proposed by the offeror. An obvious method of indicating this intent is for the offeree to inform the offeror directly of his refusal to accept the offer. A rejection will also occur if the offeree makes a **counteroffer** to the offeror. Such a counterproposal by the offeree impliedly manifests his unwillingness to assent to the terms of the original offer.

An offer is also rejected when an offeree attempts to make a **conditional acceptance** of an offer. A conditional acceptance is one by the terms of which the offeree indicates his acceptance of an offer providing or on the condition that the offeror do something more or different than he promised to do in his offer. Instead of being an acceptance, a conditional acceptance is a counteroffer which by implication rejects the offer it purports conditionally to accept.

Inquiries, requests, or suggestions by an offeree with respect to terms different from those stated in an offer are not considered to be rejections and hence do not terminate an offer. The problem, of course, is determining whether the offeree's communication is a mere inquiry or is a counteroffer in the form of a conditional acceptance. The resolution of the problem will depend upon the particular facts of a given case.

The *death or insanity* of either an offeror or an offeree prior to acceptance will terminate an offer.

Where the subject matter of an offer is *destroyed* prior to the offeree's acceptance through no fault of the offeror or offeree, the offer is terminated and can no longer serve as the basis for the creation of a contract.

The promised performance of an offeror, which is entirely legal when the offer is made, may become unlawful by a subsequent *change in the law*. Such a change in law will cause the existing offer to terminate. Thereafter, the offeree cannot by his attempted acceptance create a contract the performance of which would be illegal.

Acceptance Until an offer has been accepted by an offeree, the mutual assent required for the formation of a contract is lacking. An **acceptance** of an offer is an expression by an offeree of his assent to the terms set forth in the offer and his willingness to exercise the power to create a contract that the offeror conferred upon him when he made the offer. We have seen that an offer is a promise conditioned upon the offeror receiving something in exchange or return. An acceptance is the fulfillment of that condition—the giving by the offeree of whatever was requested in the offer. Depending upon what is called for by an offer, an acceptance may take the form of either the making of a promise or the doing of an act.

A contract is formed at the point in time that an offeree's acceptance becomes effective.

Who May Accept An offer may be accepted only by the offeree or offerees to whom it is addressed and for whom it is intended. No other person has the power to create a contract by acceptance of the offer.

Even though an offer is not one that calls for the offeree personally to perform, the offeree cannot transfer or assign his power of acceptance to another person.

Acceptance by a Promise Where the return or exchange requested by the terms of an offer is a *promise,* only words which unequivocally manifest a promise by the offeree will constitute an acceptance. The promise made by the offeree must be the exact promise requested by the offeror, free of any changes or qualifications. As we have seen, a communication by an offeree that conditions an offer or changes its terms is not an acceptance but a counteroffer that rejects and terminates the offer.

An offeree's acceptance of an offer by means of a promise gives rise to a bilateral contract.

Acceptance by an Act When an offer calls for the performance of an *act* on the part of the offeree, an acceptance is not effective and no contract is formed until the requested act has been fully performed. There is no requirement that an offeree must notify the offeror that he is accepting the offer and intends to perform the requested act, and such notification if given will not amount to an acceptance. To exercise his power to create a unilateral contract, an offeree must complete the act upon which the offeror's promise is conditioned and not merely promise to do so.

Since an offer calling for the formation of a unilateral contract is not accepted until the requested act has been fully performed, the question arises whether the offeror can revoke his offer *after* the offeree has commenced performance of the act but *before* performance has been completed. Although the older view was otherwise, the majority rule today, based on various theories, regards the offer as becoming irrevocable once the offeree has begun to perform the act called for in the offeror's promise.

Communication of an Acceptance Where a *bilateral* contract is contemplated, an offeree's acceptance is not effective and no contract is formed until the offeree's promise has been communicated to the offeror. Any time prior to communication of an acceptance an offeror may revoke his offer and put an end to the offeree's power to create a contract. Obviously situations will arise in which the question whether an acceptance has been communicated to an offeror will be critical to the existence or nonexistence of a contract.

Where an offer and an acceptance are made orally, a contract is created when the offeree's promise is spoken to the offeror, either face to face or by telephone. In such a case there is no time lag between the offeree's manifestation of his acceptance and its communication to the offeror.

When the parties use the mails or telegraph facilities to transmit their offer and acceptance, there will be a time lag between the dispatching of the acceptance by the offeree and its receipt by the offeror. Not only does the possibility exist that a revocation sent by the offeror and an acceptance dispatched by the offeree might cross in transmission, but there is also the risk that the offeree's acceptance might be lost or misdirected and never be received by the offeror. These possibilities have given rise to the need for certain rules with respect to the point in time that an acceptance is considered to be effective and hence to create a contract.

It should first be recognized that the offeror who is in control of the terms that an offer contains can indicate exactly what is required for an acceptance to be effective. He can, for example, specifically provide that no acceptance will become effective until it has actually been delivered into the hands of the offeror. In these circumstances, the risk of loss or error in transmission of course falls on the offeree.

Being in control of the terms of his offer, an offeror may expressly authorize the method by which an offeree may transmit his acceptance to the offeror. Where a particular means of communication is thus authorized, the offeree's acceptance becomes effective immediately upon being dispatched via the authorized method. Thereafter, the risk of loss or error in transmission will fall on the offeror.

Instead of expressly authorizing a particular means for communicating an acceptance, the offeror may do so by implication. When no method of communication is expressly authorized by an offeror, he is considered to impliedly authorize the offeree to use the same means of communication that the offeror used in transmitting his offer. If the offer, for example, was sent by mail, the mail is the means for communicating an acceptance that is impliedly authorized by the offeror; if the offer is sent by telegraph, acceptance by telegraph is impliedly authorized. As was the case with expressly authorized methods of communication, an acceptance transmitted by an impliedly authorized means becomes effective when it is dispatched or placed in the course of transmission. Under such circumstances, the risk of loss or misdirection of the acceptance in transit falls on the offeror.

If an offeree employs a means of communication for his acceptance that has neither been expressly nor impliedly authorized by the offeror, the acceptance will not be effective and no contract will be formed until the offeror has actually received the acceptance. The risk of loss in transit in such instances rests with the offeree.

When an offer calls for the formation of a *unilateral* contract, the offeree's acceptance will take the form of an act rather than his promise to do something. A difference of opinion exists as to whether an offeree is obligated to inform the offeror when the act has been completed. According to one view, no notice of completion of the act is required to be given by the offeree unless such notice is requested by the offeror in his offer. A second view holds that if the offeree has reason to know that the offeror has no adequate means of learning of the offeree's performance within a reasonable time, the offeree must take appropriate steps to notify him. It has been pointed out, however, that it would be an exceptional situation in which an offeror would have no means of ascertaining that the act requested had been performed.[3]

Consideration

Nature of Consideration Not all promises that people make are legally enforceable. The general rule is that only those promises that are supported by *consideration* will be enforced by the courts—**consideration** being something that a promisor bargains for and receives in exchange for his promise. Consideration for a promise may take the form of an *act*, a *forebearance*, or a *return promise*, depending on what the promisor requested in return for his promise. For an act, forebearance, or promise bargained for by the promisor to constitute consideration, it must result in a legal *benefit* to the promisor or a legal *detriment* to the person from whom the consideration flows.

Benefit or Detriment Although *either* a detriment sustained by the promisee *or* a benefit accruing to the promisor will satisfy the requirement of consideration, it is generally true that when a benefit is present a detriment is also present, and vice versa. In fact, in a bilateral contract where each of the parties is both a promisor and a promisee, each one of them normally acquires a benefit at the same time that he incurs a detriment. For example, where A makes a promise to deliver goods to B at a future date in exchange for B's promise to pay a sum of money on that date, both A and B have simultaneously incurred a legal detriment and acquired a legal benefit. A has given up his right to the goods after a certain date (a detriment) and B has incurred an obligation to pay a sum of money that he was not previously obligated to pay (also a detriment). At the same time, A has acquired the legal right to a sum of money on a certain date (a benefit) and B has a legal right to receive specified goods on that same date (also a benefit). A and B have altered their legal status with respect to each other, both beneficially and detrimentally, by their exchange of promises.

Adequacy of Consideration In the absence of fraud, duress, undue influence, or mistake, the courts do not concern themselves with the economic adequacy of consideration or the question whether an agreed exchange between contracting parties is a fair one. The question whether the benefit and the detriment exchanged by the parties is equivalent in value is for them to decide. For the courts to relieve a competent adult from a bad bargain is regarded as being an unwarranted interference with the freedom of contract. Therefore, if the assent of the parties to a contract is freely given, the fact that one party assumed a burdensome obligation in exchange for a slight benefit will not prevent the contract from being enforced.

Promise, Act, or Forebearance

Promise as Consideration In a bilateral contract, the consideration for a promise is the promisee's return promise that was requested

---

[3] *Restatement (2d) of the Law of Contracts,* sec. 56.

and bargained for by the promisor. However, the promisee's return promise will constitute consideration only if the doing of what he promises to do results in a detriment to him or a benefit to the promisor. If the promisee, for example, is already under a legal obligation to the promisor to do what he now promises to do, the return promise will not constitute consideration—the return promise has not resulted in either a legal detriment or a legal benefit.

Unless both parties' promises in a bilateral contract are binding, the contract is void for lack of consideration. If the language of one of the promises is such that performance of that promise is subject to the whim or desire of the party making the promise, he is not legally obligated to perform, and consequently his promise does not constitute consideration. Such a promise is said to be "illusory" in character.

Act as Consideration In a unilateral contract, the performance of the act that is requested and bargained for by the offeror constitutes consideration. In order for it to amount to consideration for the offeror's promise, however, the act that the offeree performs must be something that he is not already obligated to the offeror to do. For example, the payment of less than the full amount of an existing and undisputed debt in exchange for the creditor's promise to discharge the entire debt is not sufficient consideration to render the creditor's promise binding, and he may thereafter recover the unpaid balance of the debt. In doing what he was already obligated to do, the debtor suffered no detriment, nor did the creditor acquire the benefit of receiving something to which he was not already entitled. If, however, there is some slight benefit or detriment in addition to the partial payment, such as payment before maturity or at a different place than originally agreed upon, the creditor's promise to discharge the debt will be binding.

Forebearance as Consideration Forebearance is the giving up of a right to something that a person is entitled to. Forebearing to exercise a right, or promising to do so, constitutes consideration for a promise if that is what a promisor requested and bargained for. When, for example, one who has a claim that gives him the right to bring a lawsuit forebears or refrains from exercising that right, he clearly sustains a legal detriment. This is true even though the claim may be a doubtful one, providing the claimant honestly and reasonably believes that his claim is valid.

Capacity of Parties

For a contract to be valid, it is essential that the parties to it be legally capable of binding themselves by its terms. As the word is used in law, **capacity** refers to the ability of a person to alter his legal status by incurring liabilities or acquiring legal rights. Not all persons are regarded as having this ability; as a result rules of law have been developed that protect such persons from their own words and acts.

A person's **incapacity** to contract may be due to youthfulness, as in the case of a *minor,* or to some permanent or temporary unsoundness of mind resulting from *insanity* or *intoxication.*

Incapacity Due to Minority The common law rule that a **minor** or "infant" was a person under the age of 21 years has been changed in a number of states, influenced largely by the 1971 federal legislation that extended the right to vote to 18-year-olds. In those states that have altered the common law rule, a minor attains his majority for most if not all purposes at the age of 18. Depending on the statutory provisions in a particular state, a person is a minor if he is under either 18 or 21 years of age, and because of his minority he lacks the legal capacity to alter his legal status and bind himself by contract.

Despite their lack of legal capacity to contract, minors sometimes enter into contracts with adults. Such contracts are normally not *void* in and of themselves but are *voidable* at the election of the minor. Until the minor decides to disaffirm a contract that he has entered into,

REAL ESTATE CONTRACTS

that contract is binding and enforceable. The minor has a reasonable period of time after attaining his majority in which to exercise his right of avoidance. Should he fail to disaffirm his contract within a reasonable time period after attaining his majority, the minor is deemed to have ratified the contract and will be bound by its terms.

The objective of the law with respect to minors is to protect them from their lack of judgment and experience due to their youthfulness and immaturity.

Incapacity Due to Unsound Mind Persons of unsound mind lack the legal capacity or **competency** to enter into contracts. The unsoundness of an individual's mind may be due to insanity, idiocy, senility, or any other mental defect or illness. The important factor with respect to a person's incapacity to contract is that the infirmity from which he suffers renders him incapable of understanding the nature of his contract and its probable consequences.

Contracts by persons of unsound mind are generally *voidable* and may be disaffirmed either by the contracting party, if and when he regains his mental capacity, or by his representative. In a majority of the states, contracts by persons who have been *legally adjudged insane* and for whom a guardian has been appointed are *void*.

Incapacity Due to Intoxication The contract of a person made when he is so intoxicated as to be incapable of understanding the nature and consequences of his act is *voidable* and may be disaffirmed by him after becoming sober. Slight intoxication, however, does not affect a person's legal capacity to contract.

Reality and Freedom of Consent

A person will not be held liable for failure to perform a promise made by him as a result of *mistake, fraud, misrepresentation, undue influence,* or *duress*. All of these factors prevent his *apparent* consent from being *real* consent given by him freely.

Mistake A **mistake** arises when one or both of the parties to a contract make a wrong assumption concerning a material or essential fact relative to the transaction between them. In those circumstances where relief is available, the usual form of that relief is **rescission** of the contract by the courts.

A mistake of fact may be either mutual or unilateral in character.

Mutual Mistake A mistake is *mutual* when both parties enter into a contract under the erroneous belief that certain facts exist which are material to the agreement between them. When one of the parties later seeks to rescind the contract because of mutual mistake, he will be permitted to do so only if he can substantially restore the other party to the legal position he was in before the contract was concluded. If, in reliance on the contract, the other party has so changed his position that he cannot be restored to his former status, no relief will be afforded to the party seeking it.

Unilateral Mistake A mistake is *unilateral* when only one of the parties is under an erroneous assumption on a material fact. Because such mistakes most often result from the mistaken party's negligence, the courts normally will not grant him relief from the contract. However, where one party knows or should know that the other party is mistaken and with that knowledge enters into a contract intending to take advantage of the situation, the courts will grant relief to the mistaken party.

As a general rule, in the absence of fraud, misrepresentation, or other wrongful act by the other contracting party, a person who signs a written contract is conclusively presumed to know its contents and to assent to them. His ignorance of the contents of a written contract does not ordinarily relieve him from liability under the contract, nor does his failure to read a contract before signing it normally affect his liability under it. Every contracting party is under a duty to learn and know a contract's contents before he affixes his signature to it. In the absence of special circumstances excusing his failure to read a contract, a party cannot avoid liability under a contract on the grounds of mistake if he signs it without first reading it.

Fraud and Misrepresentation The misrepresentation of a material fact by one party to a contract may either be *intentional* or *unintentional*. If a misrepresentation is intentional, it is said to be fraudulent; if unintentional, no fraud is present and the misrepresentation is considered to be innocent. Whether a misrepresentation is made fraudulently or innocently, the victim of the misrepresentation may rescind the contract that he entered into as a result of that misrepresentation. Where a misrepresentation is intentionally made and is thus fraudulent, however, the victim is given the alternative remedy of bringing a suit for **damages,** including in some instances punitive damages.

Fraud Fraud is best defined by a statement of its elements. The elements of a fraud are: (1) a false representation of a material fact, (2) made with knowledge of its falsity and (3) with intent to mislead or defraud, that is (4) justifiably relied on by the one to whom it is made and (5) which results in injury to him because of that reliance. To sustain an action for fraud or deceit, the presence of each of these elements must be established.

Innocent Misrepresentation As we have seen, a misrepresentation is innocent rather than fraudulent if it is unintentionally made. An innocent misrepresentation of a material fact that is justifiably relied on by the party to whom it is made renders a contract resulting from such reliance voidable by that party.

Whether a statement is fraudulently or innocently made, a contracting party is not legally justified in relying on that statement if he knows it is erroneous, or if the circumstances are such that he should have investigated and would then have discovered that the statement was false.

Duress and Undue Influence A contracting party whose promise is not voluntarily made may have a contract rescinded. The lack of a party's free will or volition may result either from *duress* or *undue influence,* depending on the circumstances surrounding his making of the promise.

Duress Duress consists of a threat to do, or the actual doing of, a wrongful act that compels another person's assent through fear. The wrongful act that coerces a person to make a promise that he would not otherwise have made may arise from a threat of harm to the promisor's person, a member of his family, or to his property. As a general rule, the courts will grant relief to the coerced promisor if the threatened act is wrongful and deprives the promisor of the exercise of his free will.

Undue Influence Undue influence results from a situation in which one person who is under the domination of another is induced to do something he would not otherwise have done had it not been for the unfair persuasion of the dominant party. It is generally said that undue influence arises from a confidential relationship in which one party mentally dominates the other and uses that position of dominance to benefit himself at the other's expense. The defense of undue influence is intended to protect the elderly and susceptible from unscrupulous persons who gain their confidence and then take unfair advantage of them.

Illegality

For an agreement to constitute a contract and be enforced by the courts, the purpose or objective to be achieved by the agreement must not be an illegal one. An agreement may be illegal either because it violates the provisions of a statute or because it is contrary to public policy. Agreements to commit a criminal act, agreements to defraud third parties, wagering agreements, and agreements in restraint of trade are examples of illegal agreements.

The general rule is that the law will not aid either party to an illegal agreement—it leaves the parties where it finds them. If the agreement is executory, neither party may enforce it. If the agreement has been executed, neither party may rescind it and receive back what he parted with when he performed his side of the agreement.

Statute of Frauds

Except as otherwise provided by statute, a contract need not be in writing to be valid. An oral contract is equally as enforceable as a written one. Today, however, every jurisdiction has enacted statutes that require certain types of contracts to be in writing if they are to be enforceable by the courts. Collectively, these statutes are known as the **statute of frauds.** The objective of such statutes is to remove the possibility of using perjured testimony when proving the existence and terms of certain kinds of contracts.

Included among the various types of contracts that are required to be in writing by the statute of frauds in every jurisdiction are contracts creating or transferring interests in real estate.

PERFORMANCE OF CONTRACTS

Although the great majority of contracts entered into are performed by the parties as agreed, instances do occur in which one of the parties fails to perform at all or performs in an unsatisfactory manner. Unless such conduct is somehow excused, it constitutes a *breach of contract* for which the party who is injured thereby is entitled to a legal remedy. The particular type of remedy available to the injured party—whether it be damages, rescission, or specific performance—will depend on the nature of the contract and the cause of the breach.

When a contract is breached, the breach most commonly occurs at the time that performance is due. When a bilateral contract has been breached, the question of liability frequently turns on the determination of which of the contracting parties had the duty of performing his side of the contract first. The answer to that question depends on the type of condition or conditions that were made a part of the contract by the parties.

Conditions

A **condition** in a contract is an act or event the happening of which either creates or extinguishes a duty on the part of a promisor. If the act or event must occur before a promisor's duty arises, the condition is called a *condition precedent.* If the act or event is such that its occurrence will extinguish a duty already owed by a promisor, the condition is said to be a *condition subsequent.* Conditions which require contracting parties to perform their contractual undertakings at the same time are known as *concurrent conditions.*

With respect to the manner in which they are created, conditions are either *express* or *implied.*

Conditions Precedent A common example of a condition precedent is a provision in an installment contract stating that all period payments must be made by the buyer before the seller is obligated to transfer title to the item purchased. The buyer's act of paying the full contract price is a prerequisite or condition precedent to the seller's duty to pass title as promised. If the buyer fails to make payment of the purchase price in full, the seller may refuse to transfer title and is entitled to sue for damages resulting from the buyer's breach of contract. The seller's refusal to perform before the buyer's fulfillment of the condition precedent does not constitute a breach of contract by him because no performance was yet due from the seller.

Insurance policies commonly contain one or more conditions precedent that must be performed by the insured before the insurance company's obligations under the policy arise. The requirement that the insured must provide written proof of loss within a specified period of time is an example of such a condition.

Conditions Subsequent As we have seen, a condition subsequent is an act or event the occurrence of which extinguishes an obligation that is already owed by one party. Conditions subsequent are unusual in contracts.

Concurrent Conditions Concurrent conditions in a contract call for simultaneous performance by the parties. In the ordinary real estate contract, for example, payment of the purchase price and delivery of the deed to the property are concurrent conditions. Before either party can hold the other liable for default or breach, he must either perform his obligations under the contract or tender performance of them. A **tender** is simply an offer to carry out one's contractual duty.

Breach of Contract

The unjustified or unexcused failure of a party to perform his contractual obligations is known as a **breach of contract.** One party's breach excuses performance by the other contracting party, giving him a choice of remedies in the form of damages, rescission, or, under certain circumstances, specific performance. To avail himself of these remedies, the complaining party must be free from substantial fault. For example, the prevention of hindrance of one party's performance not only excuses him from performing and deprives the hindering party of any remedy, but such conduct also constitutes a breach of contract by the hindering party for which he is liable.

Anticipatory Breach

A breach of contract, we have seen, ordinarily takes place when a party fails to perform his contractual obligation at the time for performance specified in the contract. A breach may occur in advance of the agreed performance date, however, if one party repudiates the contract by making known his intention not to perform when the agreed date arrives. Such an announcement is known as an **anticipatory breach** and may be treated as a present breach of contract by the other party. Instead of waiting until the agreed performance date to see if the contract will in fact be breached, the one to whom the repudiation is made known may proceed at once to pursue his remedy for the breach of the contract.

REAL ESTATE CONTRACTS

Introductory Observations

Contracts Involved in a Typical Sales Transaction From the moment an owner makes the decision to sell his real property until his deed is delivered to the buyer, the typical real estate sales transaction is characterized by a series of contractual relationships. While the details of any given transaction will vary somewhat by geographical area and in accordance with the complexities of the transaction, the contractual steps in a simple real estate sales transaction tend to follow a fairly standardized pattern.

Having made the decision to sell his property and having decided to use the services of a professional to assist him, a seller's initial step is the employment of a real estate broker to act as his agent. The agency relationship between the seller and the broker is created by a contract known as a **listing agreement,** which may take a number of different forms.

Acting in his capacity as an agent of the seller, the broker proceeds to solicit offers to purchase the seller's property from prospective buyers, which offers the broker presents to the seller for possible acceptance. Upon the seller's acceptance of one of the offers made to him, a **contract of purchase and sale** is created between the seller and a buyer.

Thereafter, in order that the executory contract of sale may become an executed one, the buyer and the seller must arrange for **title closing.** Title closing is the process whereby the provisions of the purchase and sale contract are carried out, with the legal title to the property transferred from the former owner to a new one. To facilitate the title closing process, the services of an **escrow agent** or **holder** are commonly used. A transaction is said to be "in escrow" when the buyer and the seller have signed a contract in the form of **escrow instructions** with an escrow holder that they employ.

Since most real estate sales transactions involve some form of financing, one or more contracts providing for a loan to the buyer and security for a lender will be negotiated and executed. The loan or loans may be made by either the seller or some third party lender or both.

This chapter deals only with contracts that lead to and result in the sale of real estate, that is, listing agreements, contracts of purchase and sale, and options. Contracts in the form of *escrow instructions* are discussed in Chapter 13 and contracts involving *financing arrangements* in Chapters 15 and 16.

When examining the various types of real estate contracts, it should be kept in mind that, irrespective of the objective to be attained by a particular agreement, if the agreement is to be enforceable as a contract it must meet all of the criteria discussed earlier in this chapter. The same rules of law that govern the formation of contracts in general control the manner of creation and operation of contracts involving the sale, financing, and transfer of real estate as well.

Contract Distinguished from Deed A contract for the purchase and sale of real estate and a deed are distinctly different types of legal documents. A contract of sale does not transfer legal title to real property. A contract of sale contemplates the subsequent execution and delivery of a deed by the seller to the buyer, which conduct serves to transfer legal title to identified real property.

Whether a particular instrument is a deed to real property or simply an executory contract of sale largely depends on the intentions of the parties. The parties' intentions will be determined from the language and the provisions of the instrument or, where the instrument leaves their intentions in doubt, from the circumstances which surrounded the execution of the instrument.

Adhesion Contracts In simple real estate transactions, the use of so-called standard form contracts is commonplace. These standardized contracts are prepared by skilled attorneys for such organizations as brokers' associations, lending institutions, and title insurance companies. These professionally drafted contracts are reproduced in standard printed forms which contain blanks for the insertion of such information as names, dates, descriptions of property, prices, interest rates, etc., that pertain to particular real estate transactions. Because of the many nonnegotiated provisions ("boiler plate") these contracts contain and the manner in which they are typically used by brokers, lenders, insurers, and others, these standard form contracts are known as **contracts of adhesion.**

The essence of an adhesion contract is that one party to the agreement must accept or "adhere" to the printed provisions because he either lacks the knowledge or the bargaining power to change them. He consents to the terms of the form contract because it is usually presented to him on a take-it-or-leave-it basis, and because most or all competitors in the field use the same or a similar standardized contract. One observer has pointed out that "The consent in these adhesion contracts is a fiction. The party handed a form usually has no time to read it, would not understand it if he took the time, would not be able to find anyone with authority to change it if he wanted to, and very likely would not be able to make the transaction if he insisted upon a change in the standard form."[4]

Where the provisions of an adhesion contract are ambiguous, the general rule is that courts will construe or interpret the ambiguities most strictly against the party who prepared the contract or for whom it was prepared. If, however, the terms of a contract are unambiguous and thus not subject to interpretation, the adhering party is bound by the contract even though he signed it without reading it or understanding its terms, provided of course that his signature was not obtained by means of fraud, duress, or undue influence.

[4] Justin Sweet, "Liquidated Damages in California," 60 *California Law Review* 84, p. 85 (1972).

Listing Agreements

Contracts of Employment A *listing agreement* is a contract of employment between an owner of real property and a real estate broker. The contract creates an agency relationship in which an owner, the *principal,* authorizes a broker, the *agent,* to perform certain services in the owner's behalf.

Although a real estate broker becomes the agent of the owner who employs him, a broker is distinguishable from agents generally by the fact that a broker's authority is special in character and strictly limited in most respects. A broker's authority to act for an owner is limited to the authority that is expressly given to him by the provisions of the listing agreement. His authority ends as soon as the purpose for which he was employed is accomplished.

The provisions of a listing agreement determine the character of the services to be performed by a broker as well as his right to compensation. A broker is ordinarily employed to negotiate a sale, lease, or exchange of real property between his principal and a third party, for which service the broker receives a commission. The listing agreement defines the scope of the broker's authority to act in behalf of his principal, and if he exceeds the authority conferred upon him the broker will be personally liable for any loss resulting from his deviation. With respect to his physical activities, the broker is not an agent of the owner but is an independent contractor who alone is responsible for his acts.

Fiduciary Relationship A broker's relationship with the person who employs him is that of a **fiduciary,** which means that the broker owes his employer a high degree of loyalty. As a fiduciary, the broker's position is one of trust and confidence, requiring him at all times to exercise good faith toward his principal in all matters within the scope of the broker's employment. The broker cannot make a secret profit for himself at his principal's expense, he may not act adversely to his principal's interests, and he is under a duty to disclose all information acquired by him that might affect his principal's negotiating position. The broker must always exert his best efforts to obtain the most advantageous terms for his principal and must disclose to him the highest price that is offered for his property.

A broker may not represent both parties to a real estate transaction without the knowledge and consent of each of them.

Oral or Written Agreement For a broker to be entitled to a commission for his services, there must be a contract between the broker and the person from whom he claims a commission. While it is desirable to have a written listing agreement in all instances so as to avoid misunderstandings, only a minority of the states[5] require that contracts for the employment of brokers must be in writing to be enforceable. In those states where a writing is required, listing agreements tend to be relatively standardized and to follow a form agreed upon by real estate and bar associations.

Provisions of a Written Listing A written listing agreement should include provisions relating to the following matters: (1) the date; (2) the names and addresses of the parties; (3) the purpose of the agreement and the nature of the services required of the broker; (4) whether the broker's authority is exclusive or nonexclusive; (5) the duration of the broker's employment and the manner in which it may be terminated; (6) a description of the property involved; (7) the selling price, including terms and conditions of payment; (8) the obligations of the seller with respect to evidence of title, escrow fees, etc.; (9) the rate or amount of the broker's commission and when payable; and (10) the signatures of the parties.

---

[5] Seventeen states require contracts employing real estate brokers to be in writing: Alaska, Arizona, California, Hawaii, Indiana, Kentucky, Michigan, Montana, Nebraska, New Jersey, New Mexico, Oregon, Rhode Island, Texas, Utah, Washington, and Wisconsin.

Types of Listing Agreements Several basic types of listing agreements are in general use today. Although each creates an agency relationship between an owner and a broker, they differ from each other with respect to the *exclusiveness* accorded to the broker in his pursuit of a commission. In terms of this exclusiveness, listing agreements are of three types: (1) *open* listings, (2) *exclusive agency* listings, and (3) *exclusive right to sell* listings. A variation of the exclusive right to sell listing popular in many areas is the *multiple* listing.

Any of the foregoing listing agreements may also be in **net listing** form. A listing is said to be net when it provides that the broker's commission is to be the difference between the selling price and a stipulated sum demanded by the seller, rather than a fixed percentage of the selling price.

Open Listing By using an **open listing** agreement, an owner employs a broker to find a buyer for his property, but retains the right to sell the property himself as well as the right to hire one or more other brokers to find a buyer for the same property. Under such an arrangement, the broker who first produces a ready, willing, and able buyer is entitled to a commission. If, however, the owner independently finds a buyer and sells his property to him, no commission will be payable to any broker. Obviously such an arrangement can generate disputes where several brokers have been concurrently employed and two or more of them, or a broker and the owner, produce a buyer.

In a suit for a commission, a broker must prove that he produced a buyer who was ready, willing, and able to purchase the seller's property in accordance with the terms set forth in the listing agreement. To establish a buyer's ability to purchase, the broker must show that the buyer had the financial capability to pay for the property. The broker need not prove that the buyer had sufficient cash to complete the transaction, but only that he had adequate funds for the down payment and the ability to obtain the rest of the purchase price by borrowing or otherwise.

Open listings may or may not limit the time period for which a broker is employed. But whether brokers are employed for designated periods of time or not, their open listing agreements will terminate without need for notification from the owner when the property described in the agreements is sold.

Exclusive Agency Listing When an owner uses an **exclusive agency listing** to employ a broker, the owner agrees that for the duration of the listing agreement no other agent will be hired to negotiate a sale of his property. In other words, for the period of time stated in the listing agreement, the broker is the only agent of the owner authorized to procure a buyer. Should the property be sold during the listing period as a result of the efforts of any other broker, the exclusive agent will be entitled to a full commission even though his efforts did not result in the sale. Under such circumstances, the owner could be liable for the payment of two commissions.

An exclusive agency listing does not deprive an owner of his right to sell the property himself during the listing period. By independently procuring a buyer and selling the property to him, the owner defeats the listing broker's right to a commission. The sale of the property by the owner also terminates his agency relationship with the broker. Although a sale by the owner may work a hardship on a broker, who may have incurred expenses in promoting the sale of the property, this is a chance the broker takes unless he otherwise protects himself in his employment contract.

Exclusive Right to Sell Listing An **exclusive right to sell listing** entitles the named broker to receive a commission if the property described in the agreement is sold during the listing period, whether the broker was the procuring cause of the sale or not. By entering into such an agreement, an owner relinquishes his right to sell the property independently during the listing period and thereby defeat the broker's right to a commission.

Exclusive right to sell listing agreements frequently provides that the broker shall be entitled to a commission if, within a specified period *after* the listing agreement expires, the property is sold to a buyer with whom the broker had previously negotiated. To be so entitled, the broker normally is required to submit to the owner upon expiration of the listing period the names of the prospective buyers with whom he had dealings regarding the property.

It should be noted that despite its title, an exclusive right to sell listing does not confer upon a broker the power to transfer title to an owner's property or to enter into a contract in the owner's behalf to do so. Regardless of the type of listing agreement that an owner and a broker may decide to enter into, the broker is merely an agent whose authority is strictly limited to finding a purchaser who is ready, willing, and able to enter into a contract of purchase and sale with the owner.

Some states require that exclusive right to sell listings and exclusive agency listings must indicate a definite time at which the owner-broker agency relationship will terminate. In the states in which such a provision is not statutorily required, an exclusive listing agreement will continue for a reasonable period of time, which will vary depending upon the circumstances of each case.

Multiple Listing By means of a **multiple listing** an owner authorizes any member of an identified group of brokers to act as his agent in procuring a buyer for his property. The authorized brokers normally are members of a local real estate board or a multiple listing service who have agreed to pool and exchange their exclusive right to sell listings. When one member of the board or service receives an exclusive listing from an owner, he submits the listing to a central registry or exchange for processing and distribution to all other members of the multiple listing group. If a buyer is subsequently procured by a member other than the one who obtained the listing from the owner, the commission on the sale is divided between the procuring broker and the listing broker in accordance with regulations adopted by the multiple listing group.

Net Listing As we have seen, a listing agreement whose provisions entitle a broker to receive as his compensation any amount over a stated price is called a net listing. Instead of the broker's earnings being measured as a percentage of the selling price, a net listing permits him to retain the amount by which the sale price exceeds the sum of money demanded by the owner free of all selling costs.

Contracts of Purchase and Sale

If an agreement for the purchase and sale of real estate is to be enforceable, the essential elements of a valid contract must be present. As we have seen, these requirements include the mutual assent, freely given, of legally competent parties, each of whom gives a bargained-for consideration and, where an interest in real property is involved, the agreement must be evidenced by a writing. In keeping with these requirements, the basic real estate sales contract is a written instrument that names the parties to the transaction, identifies the property being sold, sets forth the parties' promises to sell and to buy, indicates the purchase price and the manner in which it shall be paid, and fixes a "closing" or "settlement" time when a deed to the property will be delivered and title will pass.

A real estate sales contract will indicate both the physical condition and the legal condition that the property described in the contract must be in when the contract is to be performed and legal title is transferred. Once a contract has been executed, the seller may not thereafter make physical changes in the premises that would diminish the benefits for which the buyer bargained. And, in the absence of an express contract provision to the contrary, a buyer is entitled to receive a good or marketable title to the property he purchases.

Good or Marketable Title Provided his assent is freely given, a buyer may expressly obligate himself to accept a title that is not a good or marketable one in the eyes of the law. But when a contract contains no such explicit agreement by the buyer, the law *implies* an undertaking on the part of the seller to transfer a good or marketable title to the buyer. Although a distinction is sometimes made between them, the terms "good title" and "marketable title" are generally considered to be synonymous.

A **good or marketable title** is a title that is so free from defects and encumbrances that there can be no reasonable doubt as to its validity nor any reasonable apprehension of danger of litigation with respect to it. It is a title that a reasonable and prudent person who is well informed as to the facts and their consequences would be willing to accept.

Matters which cause a title to be unmarketable include such things as mortgages or other liens, restrictive covenants, leases, and defects in the record chain of title.

Although the law implies an obligation on the part of a seller to furnish a good or marketable title, it does not imply an obligation on his part to furnish a title that is satisfactory to a *particular buyer* or one that he is willing to accept. The mere fact that the seller's title is not satisfactory to his particular buyer does not in and of itself render the seller's title unmarketable.

The situation is different, of course, when a contract of sale *expressly* provides that the title must be satisfactory to the buyer himself or to his attorney. Provisions of this type are generally held to be valid. Similarly, an express provision in a contract requiring a seller to convey a title that a designated title insurance company will insure is an enforceable provision. If the company designated in the sales agreement refuses to insure the title, the buyer is not obligated to accept the policy of some other company that may be willing to insure it.

Requirement of Estate in Fee Simple The general rule is that, in the absence of a contrary provision, a contract for the sale of real estate requires the conveyance of the entire estate in the property sold, that is, an estate in fee simple absolute. A seller's contractual obligation is not satisfied by his tender of an interest less than a fee simple absolute.

Seller's Title at Time of Contracting Unless a seller in some way represents to the buyer that he *presently owns* the property that he is contracting to sell, there is no requirement that the seller have legal title to the property at the time the contract of sale is entered into. In most contracts of sale, a seller's obligation with respect to ownership of the property is that he will convey a good legal title to the buyer on or before a specified date. Notwithstanding his lack of title at the time of contracting, it is not unusual for a seller to agree to transfer legal title by a certain date, and such contracts are held to be valid. Of course in instances of this type, the seller assumes the risk of acquiring title to the property and being able to convey it by the agreed performance date or being liable to the buyer in damages for the buyer's loss of his bargain.

Standardized Contracts of Sale It is the practice in some states to use standard form contracts in simple real estate sales transactions, especially those that involve the purchase and sale of homes. Where these standardized contracts are in common use, they have generally been agreed upon and approved as to form and content by local bar and broker associations, thus reflecting customs and practices prevailing in a particular locality. These forms often contain language that acknowledges receipt by a broker of an "earnest money" deposit, which frequently is demanded of and given by a prospective purchaser. Because of this feature, these standard forms have become known in the trade as "deposit receipts"—a term that is unfortunate because it tends to be misunderstood by unsophisticated buyers.

When it has been completed and signed by a buyer and a seller, a standard form, by whatever name it may be known in the trade, becomes a binding contract of purchase and sale. In a typical transaction the contracting process begins when, as a result of solicitation by the seller's broker, the buyer makes an offer to purchase by completing and signing a standard form furnished to him by the broker. Like offers generally, the buyer's offer empowers the seller, the offeree, to bind the buyer by a contract simply by accepting the offer which the broker transmits to him. If the seller is satisfied with the terms of the buyer's offer, the seller will affix his signature to the standard form, thus manifesting his acceptance and thereby creating a contract of purchase and sale. If he is dissatisfied with the buyer's offer, the seller will either reject it outright or reject it by making a counteroffer. Until his offer has been accepted by the seller, the buyer is free to revoke or withdraw it and in so doing to terminate the seller's power to bind the buyer to a contract.

The validity of a contract created by the completion of a simplified form is judged by the same rules that pertain to contracts generally. If any essential element of a contract is missing, whether by error in the printed material or failure to complete a particular blank, no contract will be created. As is true of contracts generally, the agreement of the parties with respect to all essential matters must be definite and certain. There can be no enforceable contract if an essential element is left for future negotiation.

Deed Discharges Contract Obligations A buyer of real estate is not obliged to accept a deed that fails to conform to the provisions of a contract of sale. The tender of a deed that would convey a title different from that contracted for does not fulfill the seller's contractual undertaking and may be rejected by the buyer. In the absence of fraud or mistake, however, a buyer's acceptance of a deed that is tendered by the seller in full performance of a contract will discharge the seller's obligations under that contract.

When a buyer accepts a seller's deed, the contract of sale is said to have "merged" into the deed and the contract's legal effect comes to an end. Thereafter it is the deed that regulates the rights and liabilities of the parties with respect to the transaction. If any defects develop in the title to the property after the buyer has accepted delivery of the seller's deed, the buyer must look to any covenants in the deed rather than to the provisions of the sales contract when he seeks judicial relief. Evidence of provisions in the antecedent sales contract which vary or contradict the terms of an accepted deed is inadmissible in an action by the buyer involving title to real property.

OPTIONS

In General

An **option** is a contract by the terms of which one party binds himself to hold an offer open for a stated period of time. The party making the offer is called an *optionor* and the one to whom it is made is the *optionee.* The optionor's offer is irrevocable during the stated period because he has in effect sold his right to withdraw the offer by accepting valuable consideration from the optionee.

Real Estate Options

Although there is no requirement that such be the case, options that relate to real estate normally take the form of an offer to sell by an owner of property rather than an offer to purchase by a prospective buyer. In other words, in a typical real estate option, the owner is the optionor-offeror and the buyer is the optionee-offeree. The buyer in such a case is the owner or holder of an option to purchase real estate which gives him the right to buy the property at a stated price within a specified period of time.

A characteristic feature of a real estate option is that one party to the contract, the optionor, is under a legal obligation to sell his property while the optionee who holds the option is not obligated to buy it. As is the case with offerees generally, the optionee is free to accept or reject the seller's offer as he sees fit. As is also true of offerees generally, if and when the optionee accepts the offer by "exercising the option," a contract is formed. By exercising the option, the buyer converts the seller's continuing offer into a contract of purchase and sale.

Option and Contract of Sale Compared

An option and a contract of sale are distinct types of contracts. The distinction arises from the fact that a contract of purchase and sale creates mutual obligations, while an option does not. In a contract of purchase and sale, one party is obligated to sell and the other to buy. In an option, the seller is obligated to sell if the buyer decides to buy, but the buyer is under no obligation to do so.

Rights of Parties

Optionor An optionor's giving of an option to purchase his property does not deprive him of the right to sell that property to a person other than the optionee during the lifetime of the option. When he does sell the property, however, it is sold subject to the rights of the optionee, which are made known to the purchaser by means of actual or constructive notice. If, following the sale of the property, the optionee decides to exercise the option, the new owner of the property must sell it to him and will thereupon be entitled to receive the purchase price from the optionee. If, on the other hand, the option period expires without the option having been exercised, the new owner retains title to the property that he acquired from the optionor and he is thereafter free to deal with the property as he sees fit.

Optionee Until the holder of an option decides to exercise it, he has no ownership or other interest in the property described in the option, nor, without an express authorization from the property owner, does he have any right to possession of the property. The option holder's only right under the option is the right to acquire title to the property—a right that may be and often is of considerable value. Unless the provisions of the option prohibit him from doing so, the holder of an option may sell and assign his rights under the option. When such an assignment occurs, the assignee thereafter stands in the shoes of the optionee and may acquire ownership of the property by exercising the option.

Right of Preemption Distinguished

A **right of preemption** requires that before an owner can sell real property to anyone he must first offer it to a designated person, known as a *preemptioner*. Because of his preferential right to purchase property that is offered for sale, a preemptioner is sometimes said to have a "right of first refusal."

Despite some apparent similarities, a preemptive right differs materially from an option. An option, we have seen, empowers the optionee to compel the optionor to sell his property during a certain period of time even though changed conditions may cause the optionor to be unwilling to do so. Furthermore, the price at which the sale will take place if the optionee decides to buy the property is fixed by the terms of the option. A right of preemption, on the other hand, does not give a holder of such right the power to compel an unwilling owner to sell his property, but merely obligates an owner who does decide to sell to give the preemptioner a prior right to buy. A preemptioner, like an optionee, is under no obligation to buy the offered property. After having received the owner's offer, the possessor of a preemptive right is free to decide whether to accept it or reject it. Should he elect not to purchase the property, the preemptioner will have exercised his "right of first refusal" and the owner is thereafter free to sell the property to someone else.

A right of preemption may provide that an owner who decides to sell his property must offer it to the preemptioner at a stipulated price. But if no selling price has previously been agreed upon, the preemptioner must pay the owner's asking price for it if he wishes to exercise his right to purchase it. An owner may not, however, demand from the holder of a preemptive right a price that is higher than the price at which the owner would be willing to sell the property to some other purchaser.

QUESTIONS

1. What is the objective of the law of contracts?
2. Distinguish between a unilateral contract and a bilateral one.
3. What is the difference between an executed contract and an executory one?
4. How is mutual assent by parties to a contract achieved?
5. Why is an offer said to be a conditional promise?
6. What does it mean when an auction sale is announced as being without reserve?
7. How does the rejection of an offer differ from a revocation? In what respect are they the same?
8. What is an acceptance? Who may accept an offer?
9. What determines whether a promise, an act, or a forebearance can serve as consideration for an offeror's promise?
10. As the term is used with reference to parties to a contract, what is the meaning of "capacity?"
11. List five things that prevent a contracting party's apparent consent to the terms of an agreement from being his real consent.
12. What is the objective of the statute of frauds?
13. Distinguish a purchase and sale contract from a deed as each affects legal title to real estate.
14. Explain what is meant by the terms "adhesion contract" or "contract of adhesion."
15. What is a listing agreement?
16. If you were a broker about to enter into a listing agreement with an owner of real estate, would you prefer an open listing, an exclusive agency listing, or an exclusive right to sell listing? Why?
17. What is a good or marketable title to real estate?
18. In what important respect do an option and a right of preemption differ?

Chapter 10

Deeds, Wills, and Intestate Succession

An important incident of ownership is the right of an owner to transfer his property to another person. When the ownership of real estate is transferred, it is commonly said that it is the "title" to the property that passes. In both common and legal usage, the terms "title" and "ownership" are used interchangeably and treated as being synonymous.

Also used synonymously in connection with real estate transactions are the verbs "transfer" and "convey" and the nouns "transfer" and "conveyance."

A Transfer Creates a New Legal Status

The transfer of ownership or the conveyance of title from one person to another is, as we have seen, a two-part transaction in which (1) the former owner's interest in the property is extinguished and (2) that interest is established in a new owner or transferee. In terms of legal rights and duties between them, the transfer of title from one to the other reverses their former legal positions. The transaction has created a new legal status with a new set of rights and obligations.

Voluntary and Involuntary Transfers

The transfer of ownership of property may be either a *voluntary* act on the part of the transferor or it may be *involuntary* and contrary to the owner's wishes. The sale of real property and the gift of it during the lifetime or upon the death of the owner represent voluntary transfers, while foreclosures, condemnation proceedings, and adverse possession are examples of involuntary transfers.

In this chapter we are concerned with voluntary transfers arising from the sale or gift of real estate. Involuntary transfers are the subject of subsequent chapters.

TRANSFER RESULTING FROM SALE

Contract of Sale

Although it is theoretically possible for real estate to be sold without using a written contract of purchase and sale, the numerous matters incidental to the transfer of title from a seller to a buyer have made a contract an important, if not essential, part of real estate sales transactions. A real estate sales contract may take the form of an elaborately and precisely drafted instrument prepared by a skilled attorney, or it may result from the parties completing the blanks of a relatively simple standard form, with or without the assistance of a broker. In either case, the rules of contract law that regulate the formation and operation of the contracts are the same.

Function of a Deed

The actual transfer of legal title to real property is accomplished by the delivery of a valid deed rather than by the execution of a contract of sale. While the contract for the sale of real estate and the deed conveying title to it are closely related, it is important to recognize that they are separate documents and perform distinct legal functions.

The function of a deed is to transfer legal title to real property, not to bind parties to an agreement for the sale of it. The contract that precedes the execution and delivery of a deed is the instrument that obligates the parties and contains the terms and conditions according to which an exchange of values is to be made. The delivery of the deed from the seller to the buyer is the final fulfillment of the intentions of the parties as those intentions are manifested by their agreement of sale.

A deed is used to transfer title to real estate in both voluntary transfers resulting from contracts of sale and voluntary transfers by means of a gift made during the lifetime of the owner. Except as otherwise indicated in the following discussion, the effect of the delivery of a properly executed deed is the same whether the deed results from a sales transaction or from a gift.

DEEDS

Characteristics of a Deed

A *deed* is a written instrument which, when legally delivered, transfers title to real property from one person to another. An essential characteristic of a deed is that it conveys a *present* ownership interest or estate even though the right to possession and enjoyment of the property may in some instances be deferred until the future.

The owner of an estate in fee simple absolute may transfer all or any portion of his ownership interest by means of a deed. A deed is also an appropriate instrument for transferring subdivided physical parts of an owner's real property.

No Requirement as to Form or Language
Compared with many legal documents, a deed is a simple instrument both as to form and to the relative ease with which it may be executed. There is no requirement that the deed conform to any particular format or that it employ any special language. If the instrument contains the essential elements of a deed and reflects the transferor's intention to transfer his title, it will be effective to do so when properly delivered and accepted by the transferee.

No single form of deed is in universal use throughout the United States. Many states have enacted statutes that permit the transfer of title to real estate by a simple form of deed commonly known as a "statutory short-form deed." For example, the California Civil Code[1] permits the transfer of an estate in real property by means of the following short-form deed:

I, AB, grant to CD all that real property situated in *(insert name of county)* County, State of California, bounded *(or described)* as follows: *(here insert description, or if the land to be conveyed has a descriptive name, as for instance "the Norris Ranch.")* Witness my hand this *(insert day)* of *(insert month)*, 19___.
             AB

Parties to a Deed The person who transfers

---
[1] Sec. 1092.

title to real estate by a deed is known as the **grantor**. The one to whom the ownership interest is transferred is the **grantee**. In any conveyance of real property, there may be more than one grantor or more than one grantee, as where co-owners transfer or receive title to property.

Types of Deeds

There are two basic types of deeds—those that contain personal covenants or warranties by the grantor and those that do not.

Covenants or **warranties** in deeds are promises or assurances by the grantor that certain conditions exist and that something is true. They may be either express or implied. A covenant or warranty is *express* when it is explicitly set forth in the language of a deed. It is said to be *implied* if it is considered by law to be present in the deed even though it is not stated or apparent from the language of the instrument.

Deeds Containing Covenants or Warranties

Warranty Deeds The customary covenants in a **warranty deed** (sometimes referred to as a "full" warranty deed) are covenants of (1) seisin, (2) right to convey, (3) freedom from encumbrances, (4) quiet enjoyment, and (5) warranty. These covenants are commonly referred to as *covenants of title* to distinguish them from *restrictive covenants,* which are discussed in Chapter 19.

In the majority of states a covenant by a grantor that he is "lawfully seised" of the transferred premises constitutes an affirmation by him that he has the whole bundle of rights that constitute ownership. The **covenant of seisin** is breached when the grantor only has an estate which is less in quantity or quality than that which he purports to convey.

For most purposes, a grantor's covenant that he has a *right to convey* the property named in the deed serves the same purpose as the covenant of seisin. Only in a very few special instances does the covenant of right to convey afford protection not also available under a covenant of seisin.

A grantor's covenant that the premises are "free and clear of all encumbrances" refers not only to claims which infringe on the title itself but also to those which involve physical facts concerning the premises. Encumbrances affecting the title itself include such things as outstanding mortgages and deeds of trust, unpaid taxes, an existing lease on the property, and judgment liens. Building restrictions, encroachments, easements, party wall agreements, and fences are types of encumbrances involving physical facts relating to the premises. Where the covenant is breached and the encumbrance is such that it impairs the grantee's beneficial use and enjoyment of the property, he may recover as damages the amount by which the value of his property is diminished.

The covenant of *quiet enjoyment* of the conveyed premises and the covenant for *warranty* are generally treated as being identical in scope and operation by the courts. Under these covenants, the grantor agrees to compensate the grantee for any loss sustained by him by reason of a failure of the title that the deed purports to convey. The covenants are breached when the grantee is evicted from the premises by one who holds a title that is paramount to the grantee's and which was in existence at the time the property was conveyed.

At common law, warranty deeds were created by expressly setting forth the foregoing covenants in full in a deed. In the statutory *short-form warranty deed* authorized in some states today, some or all of the foregoing covenants are implied from the language used. Illinois, for example, authorizes the following short-form warranty deed:[2]

> The grantor *(here insert name or names and place of residence),* for and in consideration of *(here insert consideration)* in hand paid, conveys and warrants to *(here insert the grantee's name or names)* the following described real estate *(here insert description)* situated in the county of _____, in the state of Illinois.
> Dated this ____ day of ____, A.D. 19 ____.   AB

---
[2] Illinois Rev. Stat., ch. 30, sec. 8.

By virtue of this statutory form and the use of the words "conveys and warrants" the grantor impliedly covenants (1) that he has a fee simple title to the premises and the full right to convey them, (2) that the premises are free of all encumbrances, (3) that the grantee and his successors shall enjoy quiet and peaceable possession of the premises, and (4) that he, the grantor, will defend the title to the premises against all persons.

Special Warranty Deeds A *special warranty deed* (also known as a "limited" warranty deed) is one which contains some but not all of the covenants that customarily appear in the "full" warranty deed. Special or limited warranty deeds are usually provided for by statute; the covenants which they contain are implied from the use of such operative words of conveyance as "grant," "bargain," and "sell."

Words of conveyance that are contained in special or limited warranty deeds and the statutorily implied covenants resulting from those words vary somewhat among the states. In some states,[3] the use of the words "grant, bargain, and sell," or some other combination of them implies covenants of seisin, freedom from encumbrances *created by the grantor,* and quiet enjoyment. In other states,[4] the words of conveyance "grant" or "convey" imply that the transfer is free from encumbrances and that the grantor has not previously conveyed the same right, title, or interest to some other person. In still other states,[5] use of the word "grant" alone gives rise to the implied covenant of freedom from encumbrances *created by the grantor* and the grantor's implied covenant that he has not previously conveyed the same estate or any right, title, or interest in the property to another person.

Remedies for Breach of Covenant When the covenants contained in a deed are breached by the grantor, the grantee has a choice of remedies available to him. On the one hand, he may **rescind** the conveyance by returning the property to the grantor and recovering his purchase price or, if he chooses not to rescind the conveyance, the grantee may recover any damages that he has sustained by reason of the breach of covenant. The measure of his damages is the difference between the price that he paid to the grantor and the value of the property as diminished by the breached covenant.

If the grantee received the conveyed property by gift rather than by purchase from the grantor, he has no recourse against the grantor for breach of express or implied covenants.

Deeds without Covenants or Warranties
Quitclaim Deeds A **quitclaim deed** is characterized by the use of the words "remise, release, and quitclaim" or simply the verb "quitclaim." By using a quitclaim deed, a grantor neither expressly nor impliedly affirms that he has any estate or interest in the property described in the deed or that any interest is being transferred to the grantee. The deed is, however, capable of transferring whatever interest the grantor owns at the time of the deed's execution, whether that interest be as little as an easement or as much as a fee simple absolute. If the grantor owns no interest at all in the property described in the deed, no interest is transferred. In modern practice, a quitclaim deed is commonly used to release any claim, real or imagined, of the grantor in order to remove a **cloud** from the title to the property. A quitclaim deed is not used when a grantor knows that he has a title in fee simple and intends to transfer it to a grantee.

A quitclaim deed contains no covenants of any kind, either express or implied, with respect to title to property described in the deed. By accepting a quitclaim deed, a grantee takes the grantor's interest if the grantor has any, and he takes that interest as he finds it. All courts hold that a quitclaim deed passes whatever right, ti-

---
[3] For example, Alabama, Illinois, Mississippi, and Pennsylvania.
[4] For instance, Arizona and Texas.
[5] For example, California and Idaho.

tle, or interest a grantor might have at the time of making the deed, but does nothing more than that.

Elements of a Valid Deed

For a deed to be valid and to effectively transfer title to real property, it must meet certain requirements. In order to be valid a deed must (1) be in writing, (2) identify a grantor, (3) identify a grantee, (4) be signed by the grantor, (5) contain words of conveyance, (6) describe the property, (7) be legally delivered to the grantee, and (8) be accepted by the grantee.

We have seen that there is no requirement that a deed conform to any special form or that it employ any particular language. Any writing that contains the prescribed elements and manifests the grantor's intention to transfer title will be effective to do so when it has been legally delivered to the grantee and accepted by him.

Must Be in Writing All states have statutory provisions requiring that deeds be in writing to be valid. Incidental to the requirement of a writing is the general policy of the law that prevents the use of oral evidence to vary the provisions of the written instrument.

Grantor A deed must indicate the grantor of the property described in the deed in such a manner that he can be identified.

Method of Identification The usual method of identifying the grantor is to designate him by name in the deed. If there has been a change in the grantor's name by reason of marriage or otherwise since the grantor received title to the property, the deed should refer to both the name by which the grantor received his title and the new name by which title is currently being conveyed. Statutes in some states[6] provide that although title passes from the grantor to the grantee even though both of the grantor's names do not appear in the deed, both names are necessary to establish a record **chain of title**

and to put subsequent purchasers and encumbrancers on notice of the grantee's interest.

Must Have Legal Capacity A grantor must have legal capacity to effectuate a valid transfer of title to real estate. Lack of legal capacity to convey title may be the result of youthfulness or mental deficiency.

Although in a few states the deed of a *minor* is *void*,[7] the great majority hold that such deeds are merely *voidable* and subject to disaffirmance by the minor within a reasonable time after becoming an adult.

A person's legal capacity to execute a deed depends upon his *mental ability* to understand the nature of his act and the consequences that result from that act. As long as a grantor is capable of understanding these matters, neither senility nor partial mental impairment is sufficient to affect the validity of his deed.

A grantor who, before his attempted conveyance, has been *judicially declared* to be of unsound mind is totally without legal capacity to transfer an interest in real property. His deed is absolutely *void* and passes no title.

In a majority of the states, if a person who in fact lacks mental capacity executes a deed before he has been judicially declared to be mentally incompetent, his deed will be *voidable* rather than void. A few states have statutes[8] that declare deeds executed by persons who are "entirely without understanding," although not previously declared incompetent judicially, to be *void*.

Grantee A deed must designate and identify an existing legal person as the grantee. Where a grantee is not adequately identified, the deed is void. Similarly, a deed to a person who is dead at the time of execution of the deed is entirely ineffective.

The usual manner in which a grantee is identified is by use of his name, but it is not essen-

---

[6] California Civil Code, sec. 1096 is such a statute.

[7] California Probate Code, sec. 20 makes a minor's deed void.

[8] For example, California Civil Code, sec. 38.

tial that such be the case. If the designation of the grantee is sufficient to identify the person or persons intended to receive the property, the deed will be effective to transfer title. For example, a deed by a grantor to "my wife" or to "my children" identifies the grantee sufficiently.

A deed that is executed to an actual person under an assumed or fictitious name will vest title in that person as long as the grantee's true identity can be established.

Legal Capacity Is Not Required A grantee is legally competent to receive title to real property even though at the time of delivery of the deed he would have been legally incapable of conveying title as a grantor. For example, a minor or a mentally deficient person has the legal capacity to receive and hold title to real property. Under such circumstances, a guardian will normally be appointed to look out for the grantee's interests.

Need Not Be a Natural Person A grantee need not be a natural person for a deed to be valid. Corporations, which are legal but not natural persons, generally are empowered to acquire title to real property as an incident of their corporate existence. And in those states which have adopted the Uniform Partnership Act, partnerships have the power to take and hold title to real property in the partnership name.

Signed by Grantor The signature of the grantor is essential to the validity of a deed. The necessary signature can be affixed by the grantor signing his name on the deed, by the grantor making his mark if he is unable to sign his name, or by a properly authorized agent of the grantor acting in his behalf.

Place of Signature The grantor's signature may appear anywhere in the deed, unless a statute requires that the instrument be "subscribed." In that case, the signature must appear at the end of the deed.

Grantee Does Not Sign The signature of the grantee is not required and normally does not appear on the deed. A grantee is bound by any covenants or restrictions appearing in a deed by his acceptance of the deed rather than by the affixing of his signature to the document.

Words of Conveyance For a deed to be effective to transfer an interest in real property, it must contain what are commonly referred to as "operative words of conveyance." These are words that manifest a grantor's intent to make a present transfer of an interest in the property described in the deed. Such words as "grant," "convey," and "transfer" have been held by the courts to be indicative of a transferor's intent presently to pass title, but it is not required that these particular words or any other technical terms be used. Any words that reflect the grantor's intention to make a *present* conveyance of real property, as distinguished from the intention to make the conveyance at some time in the future, will satisfy the "operative words of conveyance" requirement in a deed. If no such words can be found in a deed, it is void and ineffective to pass title.

For a deed to be valid, it is not required that the real property interest presently being transferred entitle the grantee to present or immediate *possession* of the property. As we have seen, reversions and remainders, which give the right to possession only at some future time, are capable of being transferred before the date of possession.

Description of the Property For a deed to be capable of transferring title to real estate, it must describe or identify the property with reasonable certainty. As we noted in Chapter 3, indefiniteness of description constitutes one of the major reasons for holding attempted transfers of real property to be invalid.

Test of Reasonable Certainty To meet the test of "reasonable certainty," the description must be adequate to enable a qualified surveyor to physically locate the parcel of property on the land mass by using the description contained in the deed.

Usual Methods of Description Various methods of describing or identifying real property have been approved by legislation and by the courts, but no particular method or methods are required. As we have seen, the more usual methods used in deeds to identify real property are description (1) by metes and bounds, (2) by means of the rectangular survey system, or (3) by reference to a recorded subdivision map. These methods are discussed in detail in Chapter 3.

Consideration

Not Essential for Valid Deed Although historically consideration was vital to the validity of a deed, the prevailing view today is that, between a grantor and a grantee and their heirs, consideration is not necessary for a conveyance to be valid. The owner of real estate has the same right to give it away as he has to sell it. A deed which is voluntarily executed and delivered by a grantor is effective to transfer title even though he receives nothing in exchange for it. And, once he has made the gift, the donor cannot thereafter have it set aside because he received no consideration for it. Of course, if the transfer by gift were induced by fraud or undue influence, the grantor may have the conveyance rescinded and receive his property back.

Rights of Grantor's Creditors The lack or inadequacy of consideration for a conveyance of real estate becomes significant when the rights of prior and unpaid creditors of the grantor are affected thereby. Where such creditors stand to lose their claims by reason of the debtor's gift of his assets, they may have the conveyance invalidated.

Recital of Consideration Although not essential to their validity, deeds commonly contain a recital of the fact that consideration was given and an acknowledgment of its receipt, such as the statement "For a valuable consideration, receipt of which is hereby acknowledged." The amount of the consideration acknowledged to have been received by the grantor normally is not set forth in the recital.

Date of Deed An otherwise valid deed is not rendered invalid because the date of its execution is not shown on the instrument. The significant date with respect to the transfer of title to real estate is not the date of which the deed is *executed*, but rather the date on which it is *legally delivered* to the grantee. The date that a deed bears merely raises a rebuttable presumption that the deed was delivered to the grantee on that date.

Attestation by Witnesses Attestation is the act of witnesses signing their names to a deed as a means of assuring its authenticity. In the absence of a statutory requirement, attestation is not essential to the validity of a deed.

While many states do not require attestation, some states[9] by statute make attestation by witnesses essential for a valid transfer of title. Other states'[10] statutes make attestation a method of authenticating a deed so as to entitle it to be recorded in the public records.

Acknowledgment by Public Officer An **acknowledgment** is a certification by a notary public or other public officer of a grantor's statement that he executed the deed. It is in the nature of an attestation by a public officer, but is considered to be more formal than an ordinary attestation.

An acknowledgment is not a part of the deed itself and title will pass from the grantor to the grantee even though the deed has not been acknowledged. Statutes in many states provide

---

[9] For example, Alaska, Connecticut, Florida, Georgia, Louisiana, Michigan, Ohio, Texas, Vermont, and Wisconsin require attestation.
[10] For example, Alabama, Iowa, Kentucky, Mississippi, Nebraska, Nevada, New Jersey, New York, Tennessee, Virginia, Washington, and Wyoming.

that a deed must be acknowledged in order to be eligible for recording. Where so required, the statutes set forth the procedure by which acknowledgment is accomplished.

Seals There was a time when a grantor's private seal was considered to be the very essence of a deed. Later a simple impression on the paper itself was sufficient, and still later the printed word "Seal" or the letters "L.S." were held to constitute a seal.

In most jurisdictions the requirement of a private seal in any form has been dispensed with by statute. Nonetheless, many standard deed forms still bear the printed word "Seal" or letters "L.S." despite their lack of legal significance.

Delivery of a Deed In general, it can be said that a written instrument that identifies a grantor and a grantee and is signed by the grantor, that adequately describes a parcel of real estate and contains words showing an intent to make a present transfer, is a properly executed deed. But proper execution of a deed is not alone enough to divest an owner of his title to real property and to vest that title in another person. A deed does not transfer ownership from a grantor to a grantee until it has been legally delivered.

Legal Delivery Depends on Grantor's Intent The **legal delivery** of a deed may or may not involve the actual handing over of the deed to a grantee. A deed is deemed to be legally delivered when the grantor intends that title shall pass from him to the grantee, irrespective of any *manual* transfer of the document itself. A deed that is legally delivered transfers title at the *moment of delivery*, even though the grantee's right to possession of the transferred property is postponed until some future time. A grantee's right of possession would be deferred, for example, if the property conveyed to him were subject to an unexpired lease.

The legal delivery of a deed is not a formal act but is entirely a matter of the grantor's *intent*. The intent of the grantor to deliver the deed or not to deliver it is a question to be determined from all of the circumstances surrounding the transaction, the acts, and the declarations of the grantor. It is essential to the legal delivery of a deed that the grantor relinquish all dominion and control over the property described in the deed.

Legal delivery of a properly executed deed vests title in the grantee; thereafter, the deed has significance solely as evidence of the grantee's acquisition of title. Each transfer of title to a parcel of land from one owner to another requires the execution of a new deed. Deeds are never endorsed and delivered to successive owners.

Presumptions as to Delivery To assist in the interpretation of circumstances, acts, and declarations to determine whether a deed has been delivered, certain **presumptions** have been developed by the law. These presumptions are subject to being rebutted or overcome by evidence to the contrary, but until they have been rebutted or defeated the presumptions will prevail.

A properly executed deed that is in the possession of the *grantee* is presumed to have been legally delivered to him. Conversely, if the deed is found in the possession of the *grantor,* or if it was in his possession at the time of his death, the presumption arises that the deed was *not* delivered. In either situation, the presumption that arises can be overcome by evidence showing a contrary intent on the part of the grantor. In other words, if it can be established that the grantor had not intended to relinquish dominion and control over the property described in the deed, it is immaterial whether the grantor or the grantee has physical possession of the deed.

A third presumption arises when a deed has been recorded either by the grantor or the grantee. A deed that has been recorded in the public records is presumed to have been delivered.

In those instances where delivery of a deed is

presumed, there is the further presumption that delivery occurred on the date that appears on the deed.

Conditional Delivery of a Deed In the great majority of states, a grantor cannot *conditionally* deliver a deed directly to a grantee. That is to say, if the grantor delivers the deed to the grantee but states that the transfer of title is made dependent upon or subject to the happening of some act or event stipulated by the grantor, the condition upon which the deed was delivered will be totally ineffective and ownership will *unconditionally* pass to the grantee.

If the grantor wishes title to transfer to the grantee only upon the fulfillment of some condition by the grantee, he may deposit the executed deed with a third person as an escrow holder with instructions to deliver the deed to the grantee when the act or event upon which delivery is conditioned occurs. This is the practice that is commonly employed in land transfer transactions in many areas of the country.

Acceptance of a Deed Acceptance of a deed by a grantee is essential to its validity. Even though it has been legally delivered, a deed does not transfer title until it has been accepted. Like delivery, acceptance is a matter of intention and requires some act or declaration by the grantee from which his intent to take title to the property can be inferred. For example, a grantee's intent to accept may be inferred from such conduct as retaining possession of the deed, mortgaging the property, or otherwise exercising rights of ownership. Whether or not the grantee has manifested the required intent is a question of fact in each case.

Where a transfer of ownership is beneficial to the grantee, he is generally presumed to have accepted delivery of the deed. In the absence of evidence to the contrary, the law assumes that every estate is beneficial to the party to whom it is transferred.

Delivery and acceptance of a deed normally are simultaneous and correlative acts, and where delivery has been established acceptance seldom becomes an issue.

Special Clauses in Deeds

In addition to the provisions which are essential to the validity of a deed, there are special clauses which frequently are included in a deed that materially influence the nature of the title that the deed transfers. The special clauses most commonly appearing in deeds refer to (1) reservations, (2) conditions, and (3) covenants.

Reservations A **reservation** in a deed (also referred to as an "exception") is a provision that withholds something from the estate that is being transferred by a grantor. By means of such a provision, the grantor retains some interest in the property that he conveys—he transfers something less than the totality of the rights that he has in the property. Common examples include the reservation of mineral rights in the transferred property, or the retention of an easement that gives the grantor the right to use the grantee's property for a designated purpose.

Conditions A **condition** is a provision in a deed according to the terms of which the estate that is granted may be terminated in case the transferred property is put to a use prohibited by the provisions of the deed, of if an event that is described in the deed should occur. When the grantor exercises his right of power of termination, the grantee's interest in the property comes to an end.

Covenants We have seen that a *covenant* in a deed is a promise by one of the parties to a property transfer that he will do or will refrain from doing a certain act or acts with respect to the property. A covenant differs from a condition primarily in that a breach of covenant gives rise to a suit for injunctive relief or damages, while a breach of a condition will result in the grantee's complete loss of his interest in the property.

Covenants and conditions are discussed in detain in Chapter 19 dealing with restrictions on the use of property.

Void and Voidable Deeds

Although the words "void" and "voidable" are sometimes used interchangeably, there is an important distinction between the two terms.

Void Deed When a deed is **void** it is a nullity and is totally incapable of transferring title to real estate. A void deed is no deed at all.

Voidable Deed A **voidable deed**, on the other hand, transfers a title that is effective until appropriate steps have been taken by the grantor to have the transfer set aside. If appropriate steps are not taken to set a voidable deed aside before the statute of limitations has run, or before the grantee has transferred title to a **bona fide purchaser,** the grantor's right to invalidate the deed is forever lost.

Where a deed to real property is voidable, the conveyance may be rescinded or set aside by the grantor or his representative, with the grantor getting his property back and the grantee having his consideration restored to him.

Types of Void and Voidable Deeds

Deed by Incompetent Grantor We have already seen that a grantor must have legal capacity or competency to transfer title to real estate. An owner may lack the necessary legal capacity, we know, by reason of minority or because of some mental deficiency.

In most states a deed by a *minor* is said to be *voidable* rather than *void;* consequently, such a deed will transfer title to a grantee subject to the possibility of its being set aside by the minor within a reasonable period of time after he attains his majority. The grantor's failure to disaffirm the deed within a reasonable time after becoming an adult forever terminates his right to do so. A few states hold the deed of a minor to be *void* and thus to be totally ineffective to transfer title.

The deed of a person who has been *judicially declared* to be of unsound mind is *void* and passes no title at all.

A majority of the states hold that the deed of a grantor who is in fact mentally incompetent, but who has *not* been judicially so declared, is *voidable* rather than void.

Sometimes a grantor's mental incapacity may be of a temporary nature rather than permanent—that is, the incapacity may have occurred only at the time of his execution of the deed. Such temporary incompetency could result from intoxication, for instance, or from the use of drugs. The deed of a temporarily incompetent person is *voidable* rather than void.

Forged Deed A *forged* deed is absolutely *void* and totally ineffective to transfer title. The owner whose name is forged is not divested of any interest in the property described in the forged deed and, of course, no interest is vested in the grantee. Since the grantee acquires no interest whatsoever in the property, an attempted subsequent transfer of the property by him is wholly ineffective to pass title even to a bona fide purchaser.

Deed Induced by Fraud A deed is *voidable* when the execution of it by the grantor was induced by *fraud.* Upon discovery of the fraud, the grantor may have the deed rescinded and the title that was obtained by the grantee will be restored to the grantor. If, however, the grantee transfers the property to a bona fide purchaser before the fraud is discovered, the grantor's right to rescind is lost and his only recourse is an action against the defrauding party for damages resulting from the fraudulent representation.

Deed Procured by Undue Influence A deed procured by *undue influence* is *voidable* by the grantor. Undue influence occurs when a grantee uses the confidence placed in him by a grantor, or uses some power or authority which the grantor feels the grantee has over him, to obtain an unfair advantage over the grantor. Undue influence is coercion exercised by the

DEEDS, WILLS, AND INTESTATE SUCCESSION

grantee on the grantor which is calculated to hamper or overcome the free will of the grantor. Because the deed procured by undue influence is voidable, the grantor may rescind it and reclaim title providing the title has not passed into the hands of a bona fide purchaser by a transfer from the grantee.

Deed Acquired by Duress A deed that is acquired by *duress* is *voidable* at the election of the grantor. According to modern decisions, duress that will permit a deed to be set aside consists of actual or threatened violence or imprisonment of the grantor, the grantor's husband, wife, parent, or children, inflicted or threatened by the grantee or someone acting in his behalf.

TRANSFER BY *INTER VIVOS* GIFT

Characteristics of a Gift

An **inter vivos** gift is a voluntary transfer of title to property between *living persons* for which the transferor or donor receives *no consideration* or anything of value in return. The owner of real or personal property has the legal right to dispose of his property by gift if he so desires, except where such a transfer would work a fraud on his creditors by depriving them of access to his assets. In order that a gift may be effective and recognized by law, however, certain requirements must be satisfied.

Donor's Intent For an inter vivos gift to be valid, there must be a clear and unequivocal intent on the part of the donor to make a gift of his property. The donor's intent may be manifested by his acts or words, or both, or it may be inferred from the circumstances. His intent must be free from mental incapacity on his part, undue influence, or fraud. Mere weakness of mind or body alone, whether due to sickness, old age, or other infirmity, does not render a person incapable of making a valid gift, providing the donor possesses sufficient understanding to realize the nature and consequences of his act. Fraud or undue influence, of course, prevents the exercise of free will on the part of the donor and thus prevents an attempted gift from becoming effective.

Gift Must Be Fully Executed To be valid, a gift must be fully executed—that is to say, there must have been a *present* delivery or transfer of title of ownership. Depending upon the nature of the property, the delivery may be either actual or symbolic, but a gift is not effective until the donor has relinquished all control over the property. Until control over the subject matter has passed absolutely from a **donor** to a **donee,** a gift is not executed or complete.

The final step in the full execution of a gift is acceptance of it by the donee. Where the gift is beneficial to the donee and would be advantageous for him to receive, his acceptance is presumed.

Promise to Make Gift Distinguished It is important to distinguish between an *executed* gift and a *promise* to make a gift. Where a gift has been completed, the donee's ownership of the transferred property will be protected by the law. But a donor's mere promise to make a gift, which has not yet been performed, is unenforceable for lack of consideration. Until it has been voluntarily carried out by the donor, his promise to make a gift creates no property rights in a donee.

TRANSFER BY WILL

Nature of a Will

A *will* is a declaration by an owner of property according to the provisions of which he makes a disposition of his property to take effect upon his death. A will is also known as a **testamentary disposition.**

No person has an inherent or natural right to dispose of his property by will at the time of his death. The ability to transfer property by will is a statutory *privilege* that is entirely within the control of the legislatures of the various states. Who may make a will, the form in which it must be executed, and related matters are all subject to legislative regulation. Any attempted testamentary disposition is totally ineffective to transfer title to property unless the statutes relating to wills have been properly complied with. The purpose of these regulatory statutes, it has been said, is to prevent secret arrangements that not only are difficult to enforce but which have also been shown by experience to be breeding places for fraud.

The validity of a will disposing of *real* property is determined by the laws of the state in which the property is *physically located*, irrespective of the domicile of the owner of the property at the time of his death. On the other hand, the disposition of *personal* property at death is governed by the laws of the state in which the owner is *domiciled* at the time of his death, irrespective of where the property may be situated.

Right to Change Will

The law recognizes the continuing right of an individual to change or remake his will as long as he lives. A testator's revised disposition of his property may take the form of an entirely new will or it may be an addition or addendum to an existing will, which is known as a **codicil.** Where two or more wills with inconsistent provisions are submitted for **probate,** the terms of the will executed closest to the decedent's death will control.

Will Effective Only at Death

A distinctive feature of a will is that it operates to transfer ownership only upon the death of the person who makes the will. By executing a will, the maker, known as the *testator,* gives up no rights or interest of any kind in the property described in the will, nor do any rights vest in any person named in the will simply by reason of the fact that the testator executed it. A will is said to be "ambulatory" during the lifetime of the testator.

At any time prior to his death, a testator may change his mind with respect to the disposition of his property and revoke his will by destroying it. Or the testator may, after execution of the will and prior to his death, dispose of the property described in the will by sale or by an inter vivos gift and thus have no property on which the will can operate when he dies. But if the will has not been revoked nor the property disposed of during the testator's lifetime, the will ceases to be "ambulatory" at the time of his death and operates as a transfer of ownership of the property described in the will.

Testamentary Capacity

An essential requirement for a valid will is that the testator have **testamentary capacity** or be legally competent to make a will. Statutes in the various states provide that every person above a certain age who is of sound mind is capable of disposing of his property by will.

Minimum Age Most statutes establish the same minimum age for both males and females. The minimum is 21 years in some states[11] and 18 in others,[12] with the latter probably being more common.

Mental Competency Illiteracy, old age, illness, or physical weakness do not affect a testator's testamentary capacity. Mental incapacity of a testator, however, renders his will invalid and ineffective to transfer title to property. The test of a testator's mental capacity is whether he is able (1) to understand the nature of his act when making his will, (2) to recollect the nature and extent of what he owns, and (3) to remember his relationship to persons who would have claims upon his property if he died without leaving a will.

It is important to note that it is the testator's capacity at the *time of making the will,* rather than at the time of his death, that determines the validity of his will.

Fraud and Undue Influence Wills, or particular provisions in wills, that are induced by

---

[11] For example, Arizona, Maine, Oregon, and Washington.

[12] For example, Arkansas, California, Connecticut, Georgia, Florida, and New York.

fraud or undue influence are void and ineffective to transfer title to property. Where only a part of a will is the result of fraud or undue influence, that portion alone is void and the remainder is effective to transfer ownership of the property to which it refers.

Formalities of Execution
In addition to a maker's testamentary capacity, the validity or effectiveness of a will is dependent upon conformance with statutory requirements regarding *formalities of execution.* Each state has fairly comprehensive statutes that prescribe the formalities required for an effective will. Even though the statutory requirements may at times seem arbitrary in nature, they must be complied with if a will is to be valid.

Objectives of Formal Requirements The objectives of statutes providing for formalities in the execution of a will are said to be: (1) to impress upon the testator the importance of his act, (2) to establish a permanent record of the testator's desires which will be available after his death, and (3) to protect the testator at the time of execution of his will against fraud and undue influence.

Regardless of a testator's clearly expressed intention to dispose of his property by will, and the conclusiveness of evidence that no fraud or undue influence was present at the time of its execution, failure on the part of the testator to fulfill the formal statutory requirements will render his attempted testamentary disposition invalid. Instead of his assets being distributed in accordance with his expressed desires, they will be distributed among his heirs upon his death in accordance with the laws of **intestate succession.**

In any given state, the formalities required for a codicil are identical to those required for a will.

Types of Wills
Three distinct types of wills are recognized by the statutes of the various states: (1) witnessed wills, (2) holographic wills, and (3) nuncupative wills.

Witnessed Wills The type of will in most common use is the **witnessed will.** Although the term itself is not expressly used in some statutes, it is widely employed in legal usage. Synonymous with the term "witnessed will," though less frequently used, are the expressions "formal will" and "attested will."

To be an instrument capable of transferring title to property, typical statutes require that a witnessed will (1) be in writing, (2) be signed by the testator, (3) be attested by witnesses, and (4) be "published" by the testator.

Must Be in Writing The statutory requirement that a witnessed will be in writing does not mean that it must be handwritten by the testator. The will may be handwritten or printed by hand by any person in ink or in pencil, may be typewritten, or may be a printed form with blanks completed by handwriting, printing, or typing. It is immaterial whether the will is in English or some other language. The will may be written on both sides of a paper or on several pages that are shown to be complementary and intended by the testator to constitute his entire will.

Signed by Testator The statutory requirement that a will must be signed by the testator is clearly met when the handwritten signature of the testator includes his complete name. Much litigation has involved the question as to the sufficiency of a signature containing only part of the full name of the maker of a will.

It is generally recognized that the testator's mark constitutes a valid substitute for his signature if he affixed his mark to the instrument with the intent of making the instrument his will. Statutes in some states require that the name of the testator be written near his mark by someone who also signs his own name as a witness to the testator's act.

The statutes of many states are silent as to the place where the testator's signature must appear on the will. In those states his signature may appear anywhere in the instrument. Statutes in other states[13] require that the testator's signature appear at the end of the will, on the theory that such a requirement tends to assure that the instrument was complete when the testator signed it.

Attestation by Witnesses The signature of a testator on a witnessed will must be attested to by witnesses. The overwhelming majority of states require two witnesses, while a few demand three. Failure to have the statutorily required number of witnesses renders an otherwise valid will invalid. In a few states a witness is disqualified if he receives anything under the provisions of the will or otherwise has an interest in the decedent's estate. A substantial number of statutes remove a witness's disqualification by invalidating any provision in the will that is in his favor.

Attesting witnesses are normally required to place their signatures on the will as a part of an attestation clause which follows a testator's signature. Some states require that the witnesses actually see the testator sign the will. At least half of the states permit a testator to display his will with his previously affixed signature to the witnesses and acknowledge that the signature is his or declare that the displayed instrument is his will. Witnesses are required to affix their signatures in the presence of the testator. Only a few states require the attesting witnesses to sign their names to the will in the presence of each other.

Publication by Testator The publication of a will is an oral statement or declaration by the testator that the instrument that he executed is intended to be his will. Only a minority of the states[14] today require such a declaration. Requiring a testator to announce that the instrument is his will is said to be one more safeguard against the testator being misled or mistaken as to the nature of the instrument that he signs.

---

[13] For example, California, Connecticut, Kentucky, New York, Ohio, Oklahoma, and Pennsylvania.
[14] Among them California, New Jersey, and New York.

Competent to Transfer Real and Personal Property A witnessed will that fulfills all statutory requirements is a valid document to transfer title to both real and personal property upon the death of the testator. A gift of real property by will is technically known as a **devise** and the gift of personal property as a **bequest.**

Holographic Wills

Handwritten by Testator Statutes in many states[15] permit the transfer of property at death by means of an informal instrument known as a **holographic will.** A holographic will is one that is *entirely in the handwriting of the testator.*

Statutes in some states[16] expressly require that the instrument bear a *date* and specifically provide that the date must be in the testator's own handwriting.

A holographic will is not invalidated by corrections of penmanship errors if the corrections are made in the handwriting of the testator. The same is true of interlineations, cancellations, or changes in the disposing provisions. These corrections or changes may be made at the time of the signing of the will or at a later time, and, being in the testator's handwriting, become a part of the holographic will.

A letter written by a testator can serve as a holographic will if it reflects a **testamentary intent,** even though the major portion of the letter is devoted to nontestamentary matters. A writing is said to reflect a testamentary intent if it reveals that the writer intended to direct the manner in which his property is to be distributed after his death.

Signature of Testator Like the text of a holographic will, the testator's signature must be in his handwriting.

The states are divided with respect to the required place for the testator's signature, some

---

[15] For example, Alaska, Arizona, Arkansas, California, Idaho, Louisiana, Kentucky, Mississippi, Montana, North Dakota, Oklahoma, South Dakota, Texas, Utah, and Virginia.
[16] California, Idaho, Louisiana, Montana, North Dakota, Oklahoma, South Dakota, and Utah.

requiring that it appear at the end of the will, others permitting it to appear anywhere on the instrument.

The testator's handwritten signature satisfies the statutes in most states even though the name that appears on the instrument is not the testator's full legal name. Signatures by initial, nickname, or first name have been held to be sufficient.

The question whether a testator's mark will suffice does not arise because the fact that the text of the will is in his handwriting demonstrates his ability to write.

No Witnesses Required A holographic will need not be witnessed. Instead of requiring that there be witnesses who, if necessary after the testator's death, can attest to his execution of a document intended as his will, it is reasoned that the successful counterfeiting of another's handwriting is exceedingly difficult. Hence the requirement that the instrument be entirely in the testator's handwriting affords the necessary protection against forgery.

Competent to Transfer Real and Personal Property A holographic will that satisfies all statutory requirements is a valid instrument to transfer title to both real and personal property by gift at death.

Nuncupative Wills

Not in Writing A **nuncupative will** is an *oral* will. In some states the privilege of disposing of property by a nuncupative will is denied entirely, while those states that grant the privilege narrowly restrict the scope of its use. Generally speaking, nuncupative wills are not favored because of the high risk of fraud and perjury in the proof of such wills.

A nuncupative will can exist only when a testator declares his will before a witness or witnesses who can testify as to his wishes following his death. In some states[17] a nuncupative will is not valid unless the witness or witnesses to

---

[17] For example, California Probate Code, sec. 325 requires that the testator's words be reduced to writing by a witness within thirty days after they are spoken.

whom it was declared reduce it to writing within a specified period of time.

Expectation of Immediate Death Among the states that recognize nuncupative wills, some restrict the use of them to persons in expectation of immediate death from an injury just received. Other states extend the privilege to persons in their last illness, which is interpreted to mean that the testator must be *in extremis* at the time he makes the will.

Like other testators, the maker of a nuncupative will must have testamentary capacity and testamentary intent at the time he declares his will to witnesses.

Not Competent to Transfer Real Property Statutes that authorize nuncupative wills generally limit their use to the disposition of personal property only. The states differ as to the limits placed on the dollar amount of personal property that may be bequeathed.

TRANSFER BY INTESTATE SUCCESSION

Although the laws of the various states grant individuals the privilege of disposing of their property by will, many people die without having made a will. Such persons are said to have died **intestate.** When an individual dies intestate, his property is distributed among his heirs in accordance with the laws of *succession*. Statutes which regulate the division of a decedent's assets when he dies intestate are also known as laws of *descent and distribution* and sometimes as laws of *inheritance*.

With respect to the *real property* left by a decedent without a will, the laws of the state in which the land is situated will determine how and to whom the property will be distributed. Succession to *personal property*, generally speaking, is regulated by the laws of the state in which the decedent was domiciled at the time of his death.

Purpose of Laws of Succession

The purpose of the laws of succession is to bring about the orderly transition of wealth from generation to generation. They provide for the transfer of title to property upon death and regulate the division of assets among the heirs of a decedent.

By enacting laws of succession, legislatures are in effect making a will for the deceased who did not avail himself of his privilege to do so. The general policy of legislatures is to regulate the devolution of a decedent's property consistent with his probable but unexpressed desires—to distribute his property as the decedent presumably would have done had he made a will.

No Vested Right of Inheritance
All of a decedent's property which is not specifically disposed of by will passes to his heirs in accordance with the laws of succession. Prior to the death of an owner of property, however, his statutory heirs have *no vested rights* of inheritance of any kind in his property. A mere *expectancy* is all they have. But immediately upon the death of the intestate owner, an heir's expectancy becomes a vested right that is constitutionally protected. Because an heir's right accrues immediately upon the decedent's death, it follows that his assets must be distributed among his heirs in accordance with the law as it exists *at the time of death* of the decedent.

Distribution According to Statute
The property of one who dies intestate is distributed in accordance with detailed statutory rules. Unless a person can fit himself strictly within those rules, he cannot inherit by intestate succession. While the statutes vary widely in detail from state to state, they generally indicate the persons who are entitled to inherit, the shares of the estate to which they are entitled, and the order in which they shall take those shares.

Any property, real or personal, in any amount, may be transferred by intestate succession.

ESCHEAT

Escheat is a method of transfer whereby title to private property passes to the state upon the death of a property owner. Property escheats to the state when a person dies without leaving a will naming the recipients of his accumulated wealth and without leaving any heirs at law who would take his property by intestate succession.

The generally recognized rule is that all property, real and personal, is subject to escheat. Real property escheats to the state even though the land was originally obtained by a patent from the federal government.

Statutes in the various states differ as to the conditions under which property shall pass to the state and whether a judicial proceeding is necessary for escheat to be effected. When the state acquires title to property by means of escheat, it becomes vested with all the rights of the person from whom it escheated.

QUESTIONS

1 What is the function of a contract in a real estate sales transaction? The function of a deed?
2 What is a covenant or warranty in a deed? To be legally effective, must it be expressly stated in the deed?
3 What choice of remedies does a grantee who purchased real estate have when the covenants in the deed to the property are breached by the grantor?
4 For what purpose is a quitclaim deed commonly used today? What covenants pertaining to title does it contain?
5 How do an attestation of a deed and an acknowledgment of a deed differ?
6 What is a reservation in a deed? Give an example.
7 What is a condition in a deed?
8 Legal delivery of a deed is said to be a matter of intent. What does that mean?
9 Indicate the three presumptions that have developed with respect to delivery of a deed.
10 Compare the effect of the legal delivery of a void deed and legal delivery of a voidable one.
11 From the standpoint of its effectiveness to transfer title to real estate, what is the difference between a forged deed and a deed induced by fraud?
12 What is a will? A codicil?

13 A will is said to be ambulatory during the lifetime of the testator. What does that mean?
14 Why do statutes in the various states prescribe certain formalities that a will must satisfy to be valid?
15 Under what circumstances can a letter serve as a will?
16 What is the objective of the laws of intestate succession?
17 To what does the word "escheat" refer?

Chapter 11

Eminent Domain

The transfer of ownership of real estate from one person to another may, as we have seen, be either voluntary or involuntary on the part of the owner. An involuntary transfer of title occurs when a change of ownership takes place contrary to the desires of the owner whose title is being divested. Involuntary transfers of real estate are not uncommon; they may occur in a variety of situations and for a number of different reasons.

In this chapter, the involuntary transfer of ownership as the result of the exercise of the power of eminent domain will be examined. In Chapter 12, the involuntary transfer of title by means of adverse possession and accretion is discussed. The transfer of an owner's title against his wishes through the foreclosure of a security interest is considered in Chapter 16, and foreclosures of mechanics' liens and tax liens are part of Chapters 17 and 22, respectively. The involuntary transfer of ownership by a forfeiture resulting from the breach of a condition to which a title is subject is discussed in Chapters 5 and 19.

GENERAL CHARACTERISTICS OF EMINENT DOMAIN

Distinction between Eminent Domain and Condemnation

Eminent Domain Is a Legal Right or Power
Eminent domain has been defined as "the right of the people or Government to take private property for public use"[1] and as the "power of the sovereign to take property for public use without the owner's consent."[2]

---
[1] California Code of Civil Procedure, sec. 1237.
[2] 1 Nichols, *Eminent Domain,*, 3rd ed., sec. 1111.

EMINENT DOMAIN

The right to take private property by eminent domain is a power that is inherent in the sovereign and does not result from any express grant of authority by the Constitution. In fact, the role of the Constitution with respect to eminent domain is to impose limitations on an intrinsic right of the government rather than to bestow any right upon it.

Condemnation Is a Legal Action The government's right of eminent domain is exercised by means of a legal action known as a *condemnation* proceeding. A condemnation proceeding is the consequence suffered by a private owner whose property is needed for a public use who refuses to sell his property at the price offered by a government agency. In order to force the sale of the property, the agency initiates a condemnation action.

In a condemnation action, the condemnor is the plaintiff and the owner whose property is being taken (the condemnee) is the defendant. Although he is made the defendant in the action, the property owner has committed no wrong—refusal to sell property to the government at an offered price is not a wrong.

Condemnation proceedings are sometimes given a certain priority on court calendars. A California statute,[3] for example, provides that "In all actions . . . to enforce the right of eminent domain, all courts wherein such actions are or may hereafter be pending, shall give such actions *preference over all other civil actions* therein, in the matter of setting the same for hearing or trial, and in hearing the same, to the end that all such actions shall be quickly heard and determined." [Emphasis added.]

Depending on the laws of the state in which the proceeding takes place, a condemnation action may be heard either by a court sitting alone or with a jury present. When a jury is present in a condemnation proceeding, its sole function is to determine the amount of compensation to be awarded to an owner for the taking of his property. All other issues raised in the action are resolved by the court.

Inverse Condemnation

Occasionally a court action that ends up as a condemnation proceeding is initiated by a property owner rather than a condemnor. The term **inverse condemnation** is given to this type of suit. "Inverse condemnation results when a public entity engages in an activity amounting to a wrongful taking or damaging of private property without permission of the owner or effort to first compensate him, in consequence of which he has been forced to initiate condemnation proceedings."[4] The rights of the parties to an inverse condemnation action are the same as those in an action that is initiated directly by the condemnor.

Constitutional Limitations

Public Use and Just Compensation Both the United States Constitution and the constitutions of the various states impose limitations on the government's right to take property belonging to a private owner. The limiting provision of the U.S. Constitution appears in the provision of the Fifth Amendment, which says, "nor shall private property be taken for public use, without just compensation." Hence, the government's use of its power of eminent domain is limited to those situations in which private property is taken for a *public use* and for which taking the private owner receives **just compensation.** Except for the constitutional limitations specifically imposed on the exercise of the right, however, the government's power of eminent domain is absolute and free from restriction.

Due Process of Law For a condemnation proceeding to be valid, it must comply with the provisions of the Fourteenth Amendment to the United States Constitution relative to *due process of law.* The requirements of due process are met if the property owner is given notice of

---

[3] Code of Civil Procedure, sec. 1264.

[4] *Heimann v. Los Angeles,* 39 Cal. 2d 746, 753 (1947).

the condemnation proceeding and is afforded a remedy by which he can obtain just compensation without unreasonable delay. The owner is entitled to a judicial hearing in which he is allowed to present evidence and be heard with respect to the propriety of the taking and the determination of the amount of compensation if his property is taken.

Police Power and Eminent Domain Distinguished

The police power, like the right of eminent domain, is an inherent attribute of sovereignty. The *police power* is described as the power of the government to enact laws to promote the safety, health, morals, and general welfare of society. It is commonly exercised by regulations or prohibitions which prevent the use of property in a certain manner. Although the police power is probably the least subject to limitation of all powers of government, it is not without restriction. To be valid, the exercise of the police power must not be arbitrary, unreasonable, or discriminatory, nor may it amount to an improper infringement upon the constitutional rights of individuals.

No Compensation When Police Power Is Exercised Unlike the exercise of the power of eminent domain, there is no constitutional guaranty of just compensation when the police power is exercised. Any damage sustained as a result of the proper exercise of the police power is said to be damage without violation of a legal right. This is an essential distinction between the two attributes of sovereignty.

Police Power Regulates Use of Property It should be clearly recognized that the right of eminent domain is the government's power to *take* private property for a public purpose, while the police power is the right to *regulate the use* of private property in the public interest.

Who May Condemn

The right of eminent domain may be exercised by the federal government and its agencies, the state and its subdivisions, and those entities to which the power is delegated by legislation, such as municipal corporations, public utilities, and certain private corporations that take property for a public purpose.

Estate or Interest That May Be Taken

The general rule is that a condemnor may take by eminent domain only such interest or estate in real property as is reasonably necessary for the accomplishment of the public purpose for which the property is to be used. In the absence of a constitutional prohibition, however, the legislature has the sole power to determine both the quantity and the quality of the interest that a condemnor may take. Consequently, the legislature may authorize the taking of a fee simple or any lesser interest in a parcel of real estate, depending upon the particular public use to which the acquired property is to be put. Where a statute expressly authorizes the acquisition of a fee simple interest, the statute will normally be given effect by the courts even though the proposed public purpose could be accomplished if only an easement were to be taken.

TAKING OF OR DAMAGE TO PROPERTY

When considering a private owner's right to compensation, a distinction is often made between the *taking* of property and the *damaging* of it.

The term "taking" as construed by some courts requires that there be a physical invasion or actual seizure of property, a permanent ouster of the owner from the premises, or such interference with an owner's rights as to deprive him of control over his property. The weight of authority, however, does not subscribe to such a narrow construction of the term.

Early legislatures showed no sympathy with the notion that there was a moral obligation to compensate an owner whose land, though not physically taken, had been damaged by the

EMINENT DOMAIN

construction of a public improvement. Recognizing that serious injuries were occurring to property owners by the construction of public improvements in the rapidly growing city of Chicago, a constitutional amendment was enacted in Illinois in 1870 providing that private property should neither be *taken nor damaged* for a public purpose without payment of just compensation. A number of states followed the example of Illinois, and today similar provisions are contained in many state constitutions.[5]

Consequential Damages

The term **consequential damages** is generally used to refer to damage or injury sustained by a parcel of land when no physical part of it has been taken for a public project or improvement.

Under those constitutions which refer only to the *taking* of property, consequential damages sustained by a property owner generally are not compensable.

On the other hand, where a state's constitutional provisions require payment of compensation for *damage* to property, consequential damages are recoverable by a property owner. Under such provisions, property is considered to have been damaged—irrespective of whether there was an actual taking of any physical part of the property—when it is rendered less valuable, useful, or desirable either as a result of the construction of a public project or its maintenance. For an owner to be entitled to compensation, the diminution in the value of his property must result from damage either to the land itself or to the property rights in the land. Personal inconvenience, discomfort to the owner of the land, or interference with a business conducted thereon are not themselves compensable

---

[5] Similar provisions appear in the constitutions of Alabama, Arizona, Arkansas, California, Colorado, Georgia, Kentucky, Louisiana, Minnesota, Mississippi, Missouri, Montana, Nebraska, New Mexico, North Dakota, Oklahoma, Pennsylvania, South Dakota, Texas, Utah, Virginia, Washington, West Virginia, and Wyoming.

matters, although they may constitute evidence of conditions which adversely affect the land's value.

For an owner to recover consequential damages when no physical part of his property is taken, he must establish that the damage he complains of is peculiar to this land and is not of a kind that is suffered in common with the public in general.

PUBLIC USE

The rule has been universally established that privately owned property can only be taken for a public use.

Meaning of Public Use

It is generally recognized that the term "public use" is not susceptible to precise definition. Nevertheless, from the many attempts to define it, two opposing views as to the meaning of the term have emerged, each with staunch supporters.

Narrower View—Use by the Public According to the narrower view, the expression "public use" literally means *use by the public*—that is to say, the public must as a matter of right be entitled to the use and enjoyment of the property that is taken. This requirement is satisfied even though the property is used primarily by the inhabitants of a small locality, providing the use is for their common good and not for the benefit of a particular individual.

Broader View—Public Advantage or Benefit Under the broader concept of "public use," the term refers to *public advantage* or *public benefit*. According to this view, anything that tends to enlarge the resources and promote the productive power of a considerable number of inhabitants clearly contributes to the general welfare and prosperity of the community and thus constitutes a public use. It is not essential that an entire community directly enjoy or participate in any particular improvement in order that it may be a public use of the property taken. If the project is conceived and carried out in the public interest and for the public's protection, it is considered to be a benefit to the public and hence a public use.

Judicially Recognized Public Uses

Despite the difficulty of precisely defining the term "public use," the weight of judicial authority would appear to use the term to include takings of property that (1) enable the federal or state governments or their agencies or subdivisions to carry on their public functions and to conserve the health, safety, and comfort of the public, whether or not individual members of the public make use of the property taken, and takings that (2) enable municipal or private corporations to supply the public with some necessity or convenience that cannot readily be furnished without some governmental assistance, provided the public is entitled to the use of such necessity or convenience as a matter of legal right.

The mere fact that the public improvement will give an incidental advantage to neighboring privately owned lands does not detract from the public nature of the improvement and the public use of the lands that were taken. Highways almost always benefit the owners of lands through which they are laid out, but the taking of land for highway purposes has never been held to be invalid on that account.

Presumption of Public Use

Generally speaking, it is the province of the legislature to determine what shall constitute a public use. In most states there is the presumption that a use is in fact a public one if it has been declared to be such by the legislature. Although the legislature's declaration in such instances must be given due consideration by the courts, the legislative declaration is not binding on them. If a court finds that the purpose for which the taking of property has been authorized is clearly arbitrary and unreasonable and has no substantial relation to the public use, the legislation authorizing the taking will be declared to be unconstitutional.

In a few states there is no presumption that a taking that is authorized by the legislature is in fact a taking for a public use. Constitutions in these states[6] provide that the issue whether a given use is a public use is purely a judicial question to be determined by the courts without regard to any legislative declaration.

NECESSITY

Political rather than Judicial Question

It is a well-settled and widely accepted rule that, absent a constitutional provision to the contrary, the question of the *necessity* for a taking by eminent domain is a matter exclusively within the discretion of the legislative body and is not subject to judicial review. Once the legislative body has authorized the taking of a particular parcel of land, the landowner has no constitutional right to have a judicial review or hearing on the issue of public need for the proposed improvement for which the land is to be used or the necessity of taking that particular owner's land for the construction of the improvement.

In exercising the right of eminent domain, the state is not required to debate its needs with any property owner. The state, through legislative action, determines for itself whether the exercise of the power of eminent domain is necessary in a given case. The question is said to be *political* in nature rather than *judicial*. Generally speaking, the courts have no power to interfere with the legislative determination of need by substituting their views for those of the representatives of the people.

Exceptions to the General Rule The constitutions of a few states[7] contain express provisions requiring that the question of the necessity of a taking by eminent domain be determined by a jury. Statutes in other states[8]

---

[6] For example, Arizona, Colorado, Mississippi, Missouri, and Washington.

[7] For example, Minnesota and Wisconsin.

[8] For example, Mississippi, Ohio, Virginia, Washington, and West Virginia.

EMINENT DOMAIN

make it the responsibility of the court or court commissioners to determine the necessity of a taking.

Delegation of Power of Determination

A state legislature has the power to delegate to an administrative body its authority to determine what public improvements are to be constructed and the necessity of taking a particular parcel or parcels of property for those improvements. Since the delegated authority involves legislative rather than judicial questions, the administrative body is not required to hold hearings on the issue of necessity.

Those to whom the power of eminent domain has been delegated are vested with broad discretion in determining what property is needed for the public use and where the proposed public work or improvement is to be located. If land that is taken is of some use in carrying out the proposed project, the question of the necessity for taking that particular land is entirely one for those to whom the power of eminent domain was delegated to decide, provided only that they act reasonably and in good faith.

Abuse of Power

The general rule is that the courts will not disturb the action of legislatures and their delegatees in the absence of bad faith, fraud, or gross abuse of discretion. One who seeks to establish that a given taking of property is arbitrary or in bad faith assumes the heavy burden of proof of attempting to persuade a court to overrule a condemnor's determination.

The owner of land that has been taken for a public improvement is not entitled to object merely because an equally available site is already owned by the public or because other suitable land could be acquired elsewhere at less than the market value of his property.

EXCESS CONDEMNATION

In the absence of statutory limitations, the amount of land that may be taken for a particular public improvement is a matter of discretion on the part of the condemnor. Under appropriate circumstances, the taking of more land than is required for a particular public improvement is not considered to be an abuse of discretion.

Excess condemnation of private property is commonly justified on any of three theories: (1) the remnant theory, (2) the protective theory, or (3) the recoupment theory.

Remnant Theory

Under the **remnant theory,** the taking of land in excess of the requirements of a public improvement is permitted only when the land that remains after the necessary portion of a parcel has been taken is of such a size and shape as to be of no practical value to the landowner. Statutes in a number of states[9] authorize a condemnor to take an entire parcel, including an excess remnant, instead of paying severance or consequential damages, since the payment of such damages by the condemnor would in effect be paying for the entire parcel anyway. The public use requirement for the taking is satisfied and the public interest served when the condemnor takes the remnant of land to avoid paying excessive **severance damages**.

Protective Theory

Under the **protective theory,** adjacent lands in excess of the amount needed for a particular public improvement are taken to insure protection of the improvement from undesirable surroundings. This theory is predicated on the notion that the public purpose of the improvement cannot be fully realized when the use of adjoining property is not in harmony with the improvement project. This theory finds expression particularly in the case of highway development or urban renewal.

Recoupment Theory

The **recoupment theory** of excess condemnation permits a condemnor to finance the cost of

---

[9] Alabama, Arizona, California, Colorado, Florida, Georgia, Hawaii, Idaho, Indiana, Kansas, Kentucky, Louisiana, Maine, Maryland, Massachusetts, Montana, Nevada, North Dakota, Utah, and Wisconsin.

public improvements by taking more land than is needed for a project. Thereafter, by selling the excess at a price that is enhanced by the improvement, the condemnor can recoup all or part of the cost of the improvement.

Taking for Future Requirements

In the absence of an express statutory provision, there is no requirement that the taking of land for a public improvement must be limited to the quantity of land that is *presently* needed for construction of that improvement. Condemning authorities may take into consideration any expansion of a project that the probable growth in population will require, and they may acquire such additional land for that later use that, at the time of the taking, appears will be needed. When land is taken for a highway, for example, a much wider strip than is used for the original roadway is almost always taken to accommodate anticipated future needs.

JUST COMPENSATION

Damages Measured by Market Value

Both the United States Constitution and the constitutions of the various states make a sovereign power's right to take property by eminent domain conditional upon the payment of *just compensation* to the owner whose property is taken. The adjective "just" simply means that the compensation to be paid for the taking must be fair and reasonable under the particular circumstances of each case. The payment of just compensation in a condemnation proceeding is in the nature of an award of *damages* to a property owner who suffers an injury when his property is taken. The amount of the damages awarded in any particular case is measured by the *market value* of the property that is taken.

In the majority of condemnation cases, the principal issue is the determination of the market value of the property being taken. The court's award of damages must be just and fair to all parties to the proceeding so that neither the property owner nor the public is permitted to benefit at the expense of the other.

Who Determines Market Value

Constitutions in the majority of states do not expressly require that damages for the taking of land by eminent domain be determined by a jury. The majority of state constitutions simply provide that the right to a trial by jury shall continue as that right existed at common law before the state's constitution was adopted. Since in most states it had never been the common law custom to utilize a jury to assess condemnation damages, in those states a trial by jury on the issue of compensation is not required.

In contrast to the majority view, a substantial minority of states[10] have specific constitutional provisions requiring that the market value of property taken by eminent domain be determined by a jury, either in all or in certain types of takings.

How Market Value is Determined

The amount of a condemnee's compensation is measured by the market value of the property interest taken as of the *time of the taking*. The market value is determined by the court or the jury on the basis of their evaluation of the varying **appraisals** of the market value of the property given by appraisers who act as expert witnesses at the trial. In arriving at their estimates or opinions of market value, appraisers employ standardized valuation techniques. Despite their use of relatively uniform appraising techniques, however, appraisers' estimates of the market value of a given parcel of real estate at any point in time may and often do vary widely. If the appraisers for the condemnor and those for the condemnee were in agreement with respect to the market value of the property taken, there would be no need for a condemnation proceeding to be instituted.

[10] Alabama, Arizona, Arkansas, California, Colorado, Florida, Illinois, Kentucky, Maine, Maryland, Massachusetts, Michigan, Missouri, Montana, New Hampshire, New York, North Dakota, Ohio, Oklahoma, Pennsylvania, South Carolina, South Dakota, Washington, and West Virginia.

Appraisal Techniques In arriving at his opinion of the market value of real estate, an appraiser employs one or more of three traditional approaches to the estimation of value. The standard approaches to estimating value are (1) the cost of reproduction approach, (2) the market or sales comparison approach, and (3) the capitalization of income approach.

Cost of Reproduction Approach The technique of the *cost of reproduction approach,* or simply the **cost approach,** requires the separate valuation of land and the building or buildings on the land. The sum of the two value figures, of course, represents the appraiser's estimate of the market value of the improved property.

The appraiser estimates the value of the land component of the property by using either the market comparison approach or the income capitalization approach. In so doing, he regards the land as if it were vacant and available for development for its highest and best use. After having estimated the value of the land as if vacant, the appraiser then computes the value of the existing building on the land.

To arrive at his estimate of the value of a building by means of the cost approach, the appraiser first ascertains what it would cost at current prices to reproduce the building new today. To do so, the appraiser obtains from some engineering service or other market source the present cost per square or cubic foot to erect a building of the same construction as the building that is being appraised. After measuring the building to determine its dimensions, the appraiser multiplies the total number of square or cubic feet in the building by the present cost of construction per square or cubic foot and arrives at what it would cost to reproduce the existing building new in today's market.

Thereafter, the appraiser is faced with the difficult job of estimating the dollar amount of depreciation that the existing building has incurred since it was built. He then deducts that estimated figure from the cost of reproducing the building new to arrive at its depreciated value. The older the building, the more difficult it is to calculate its depreciation and the more likely it is that the estimate of the building's value will be inaccurate.

The depreciated value of the existing building plus the separately estimated value of the land as if vacant are then added together to reflect the appraiser's estimate of the present value of the entire property.

There are many instances, such as in the case of special-purpose properties that are infrequently sold, when the cost approach with all its limitations is the only approach applicable and available to the appraiser.

Market or Sales Comparison Approach The technique of the *market or sales comparison approach,* or simply the **market approach,** calls for the appraiser to go into the marketplace and observe the actual behavior of buyers and sellers. The appraiser searches the marketplace for properties comparable to the one he is appraising that have recently been sold or offered for sale. Using not only actual sales figures, but also offers to sell and bids to buy comparable properties, and considering such factors as terms of sale, market conditions at time of sale, and the degree of comparability between properties, the appraiser makes whatever adjustments he deems necessary and arrives at his estimate of the market value of the property being appraised.

The reliability of the market approach is largely dependent upon the appraiser's ability to find sales of properties sufficiently similar to the property he is appraising to permit reasonable comparisons, and his ability to make accurate price adjustments for differences in the properties being compared. Where no data on sales of comparable properties are available, the market approach cannot be used.

The market approach is theoretically sound because it reflects the behavior of real-life buyers and sellers in completed sales transactions. The approach is favored by many appraisers because it is easily understood by their clients and other users of their reports.

Capitalization of Income Approach Estimating the value of real estate by means of the *capitalization of income approach,* or simply the **income approach,** involves dividing the annual net income earned by the property under appraisal by a capitalization rate which includes both a certain return on the money invested in the property and a return of the investment to offset the property's depreciation. Although the capitalization process is simple in concept, it can be complicated in use because of the many mathematical formulas that have been developed for use with the approach. And it is these mathematical formulas that tend to give the income approach a greater appearance of accuracy than it in fact warrants.

Underlying the income approach are several significant assumptions: (1) that the property will generate a stream of net income during the future; (2) that this net income will either remain the same, will increase, or will decrease each year; (3) that the stream of income will include both a return *on* the capital that the owner invests as well as a return *of* his capital as the value of the property declines; (4) that any income to be received in the future is worth less than income to be received immediately and hence should be discounted; and (5) that the returns on and of the investment are stated in terms of percentages of the value of the property, which percentages are combined into a single capitalization rate that, when divided into the annual net income from the property, represents the value of the property.

While the capitalization of income approach is a usual method for appraising income-producing properties, it is of limited value where owner-occupied dwellings are concerned. The method is particularly useful where property has been leased for a long term to a highly credit-worthy tenant who, by the terms of the lease, agrees to pay all taxes, insurance, and expenses of maintaining the leased premises.

Verdict within the Range of Evidence A jury's verdict or a court's opinion as to the amount of compensation to be awarded to a condemnee will not be disturbed on appeal as long as the amount awarded is within the range of the evidence introduced at the trial. If the award is within the range of the high and low opinions of the expert witnesses concerning the property's market value, reversal of the award on grounds of excessiveness or inadequacy is very unlikely.

Just Compensation Is Not Indemnification

The meaning of the term "compensation" in condemnation awards differs somewhat from its meaning elsewhere in the law of damages. For other types of legal actions, the term "compensation" connotes **indemnity.** In the law of torts, for example, the general objective of compensation is to award the injured party a sum of money that will as nearly as possible restore him to the position he would have been in had the wrong not been committed. And in cases involving the breach of a contract, the goal of compensation is to place the nonbreaching party in the same position he would have been in had the contract been properly performed. If this indemnity approach were employed in condemnation cases, the award given to a condemnee would be sufficient to restore him to substantially the same position that he occupied prior to the taking of his property. This is not the case, however, because in many jurisdictions there are items of cost or damage incurred by a condemnee for which he receives no compensation at all.

Noncompensable Items

To the extent that certain damages sustained by an owner are noncompensable, the constitutional provision requiring payment of *just* compensation means something less than *full* compensation for losses resulting from condemnation actions. Principal among these noncompensable items of expense or damage, in the absence of legislation expressly providing

EMINENT DOMAIN

otherwise, are attorney and expert witness fees and loss of goodwill of a business.[11]

Attorney and Expert Witness Fees Although a condemnor is required to compensate a property owner for his legal costs in a condemnation proceeding, not all of a condemnee's expenses of litigation are included. Reimbursement is normally limited to the costs incurred for ordinary witnesses, the costs of certification of documents and notary fees, the cost of filing an answer, and the costs of necessary depositions. The condemnee's expenses for his attorney's fees and payments made to appraisers acting as expert witnesses, both of which are substantial expenses, are not a part of the condemnee's award for the taking of his property. Commentators have observed that just compensation minus a property owner's costs of litigation is no longer *just* compensation.

Loss of Goodwill When a site that is condemned was formerly used for the carrying on of a business activity, the forced relocation of that business could result in the loss of customers and **goodwill**. But in most jurisdictions the displaced businessman receives no compensation for such loss, it being argued that it was his real property rather than his business that was condemned.

TAKING LESS THAN AN ENTIRE PARCEL

The amount of damage that a property owner incurs by reason of condemnation depends in part on the *quantity* of his real property that is taken. The requirements of a public improvement may necessitate the taking of an owner's entire parcel of land, which is called a "total taking," or only a portion of his land may be needed for the project, in which case a "partial taking" will suffice.

The taking of an entire parcel of land causes no special valuation problems in arriving at the measure of the landowner's damages. A partial taking of a parcel of land, on the other hand, gives rise to the special problem of estimating not only the value of the portion of the land taken by the condemnor, but also the effect of that taking on the value of the part of the parcel remaining to the owner.

The rule is well settled that when only a part of a single unit of land is taken by eminent domain, the compensation to which an owner is entitled includes whatever damages are sustained by the remnant of the parcel that is left to him as well as the market value of the portion of his land that is taken. The landowner bears the burden of proving that the taking of part of his property did in fact result in injury to the remainder of the parcel. Failure on his part to establish that fact will limit the owner's compensation to the market value of the land that the condemnor actually takes.

Compensation for Partial Taking

When only part of a parcel of land is taken, the public improvement for which the taken land is used frequently benefits the remainder of the parcel that is left to the owner. In such circumstances, the question arises whether the benefit should be taken into consideration when determining the amount of the condemnee's compensation and, if so, to what extent. A difference of opinion with respect to this issue has caused the measure of compensation for partial takings of property to vary among the states.

Treatment of Benefits Benefits that accrue to property from public improvements are distinguished as being either general or special in character. *General benefits* result from the completion of an improvement for which property was taken and are enjoyed by the public at large. *Special benefits*, on the other hand, accrue only to a specific parcel of land and arise from

---

[11] California Code of Civil Procedure, sec. 1263.510, effective July 1, 1976, permits businesses that are forced to move to be compensated for loss of goodwill to the extent that the loss could not reasonably have been prevented by relocation or other efforts by the owner to mitigate the loss.

the particular relation of that parcel to the public improvement. Special benefits differ in *kind* rather than in *degree* from benefits enjoyed by the public at large.

When the amount of damages suffered by a landowner because of a partial taking of his property are being calculated, only the *special* benefits that accrue to his remaining land are taken into consideration. His land's participation in the *general* benefits that result from the public improvement are ignored.

In the absence of constitutional provisions to the contrary, the almost universally accepted rule is that when computing compensation for a partial taking, special benefits should be charged against and deducted as an offset from the estimated amount of damages suffered by the part of the land that is not taken.

TAKING LESS THAN FEE INTEREST

Just as a condemnor may take less than all of an owner's physical property, so too may the *interest* that is condemned be less than an owner's fee simple estate. While the typical example of such a taking involves the condemnation of an easement, the taking of less than a fee interest also occurs when restrictive covenants benefiting a parcel of land are terminated because neighboring property is taken by eminent domain.

Easements

Problems concerning the valuation of easements arise in two situations: (1) where an easement to be used for a public purpose is acquired in an owner's land, thus rendering his land a servient tenement, and (2) where an easement belonging to the owner of a dominant tenement is lost because the property that is subject to the easement is taken. In both instances there will be a diminution in the value of an owner's land as a result of the taking of the easement by a condemnor.

Easements Created for Public Use In a large number of takings by eminent domain, the interest that is taken for a public use is not the fee simple title to land but an easement in land for a particular use. In such cases, the landowner's continued right to prevent any use of his land other than that for which the easement is created is well recognized and enforced.

The normal measure of damages sustained by an owner whose land has become a servient tenement for a public easement is the difference in the market value of the land without the easement and its market value as burdened by the easement that has been imposed on it. The measure of damages is simply an application of the so-called before and after rule.

Where the use for which an easement is taken requires a permanent and substantially exclusive use of land, as for purposes of a highway or railroad, the distinction between the taking of a fee or an easement is in practice meaningless. Under such circumstances, the owner's damages are determined as if title to the strip of land had in fact been taken.

Taking of an Existing Easement A very large proportion of easements are appurtenant to dominant tenements which they benefit at the expense of the servient tenements that bear the burden of them. Under normal circumstances, a dominant tenement is worth more with the easement that is appurtenant to it than it is without it. Consequently, when the appurtenant easement is terminated or destroyed by the taking of the servient tenement for a public use, the owner of the dominant tenement to which the easement belongs is damaged.

The measure of damages sustained by the dominant owner whose easement has been taken from him is the difference between the market value of his property with the appurtenant easement and the property's value without it. Again, the so-called before and after rule is employed in calculating the condemnee's compensation.

Restrictive Covenants

Restrictive covenants impose limitations on the use or uses to which an owner may put his property. Such controls over the use of property are designed to benefit adjoining or neighboring parcels of land. Restrictive covenants are commonly referred to as "building restrictions" because their purpose frequently is to limit the area of a lot that may be covered by a building, the permissible height of buildings, or other characteristics of structures to be erected on land.

Restrictive covenants may be applicable only to a single parcel of land or they may be part of a general plan of development and apply to all lots in a tract or subdivision. In the latter case, they are said to be "mutual" in that each lot is not only burdened by the applicable restrictions upon it, but the lot also benefits from similar restrictions imposed on all other lots in the tract as well.

A problem arises when land that bears the burden of restrictive covenants is taken for a public use because, since the restrictions do not continue to apply to the condemnor, the adjacent property owners are deprived of the benefits that previously accrued to them. There is a conflict of opinion as to whether a property owner in whose favor restrictions operate is entitled to compensation in situations of this type.

Majority View The majority view[12] holds that restrictions imposed on land for the benefit of neighboring land constitute property in the constitutional sense. Therefore, when the land that is burdened by such restrictions is taken for a public use and the restrictions are thereby terminated, there is a compensable taking of property belonging to owners of lands that the terminated restrictions were designed to benefit.

The measure of damages sustained by landowners who are deprived of the benefits afforded by the restrictions is the amount of the diminution in market value of their lands as a result of the termination of the restrictive covenants.

[12] Adopted, for example, by the courts of California, Connecticut, Florida, Massachusetts, Michigan, Minnesota, Missouri, Nebraska, Nevada, New Jersey, New York, North Carolina, Pennsylvania, South Carolina, Tennessee, Virginia, and Wisconsin.

Minority View Courts in a minority of jurisdictions[13] refuse to award damages to property owners who lose the benefits of restrictive covenants because land that is burdened by such restrictions is taken for a public use. Denial of compensation is usually based either on the argument that restrictive covenants were never intended to be applicable to public improvements or that condemnors are impliedly excepted from the operation of restrictive covenants.

TAKING LEASED PROPERTY

When the fee simple owner of real property leases that property for a period of time, the relationship of landlord and tenant or lessor and lessee is created. By reason of the rental agreement between them, the landlord and the tenant become owners of separate and concurrent interests in the leased premises.

Leasehold and "Leased Fee" Interests

A tenant's interest in leased property is known as a *leasehold* and, absent provisions in a rental agreement to the contrary, he may use and deal with that interest as he sees fit. The tenant's leasehold entitles him to the present possession, use, and enjoyment of the leased premises to the exclusion of all other persons, including the landlord. The tenant's interest in the property continues for the period of time agreed upon by the parties in their rental agreement.

A landlord's interest in leased property is known as a *reversion.* The nature of this interest is such that upon expiration of the lease the right to possess, use, and enjoy the premises returns to the landlord, freed of any interest of the tenant. In addition to his reversionary interest, the landlord has the right to receive rent in the amount stated in the lease for the duration of the lease period. In appraising practice, the combination of the landlord's reversionary interest and his right to receive rental payments is referred to as a **leased fee.**

It is well established that the interests of both

[13] For example, Arkansas, Colorado, Florida, Georgia, Louisiana, and Ohio.

a landlord and a tenant are property in the constitutional sense and that, under appropriate circumstances, each is entitled to compensation when leased property is taken by eminent domain. However, where the terms of a lease provide that it will terminate upon the total or partial taking of the leased premises for a public purpose, the tenant generally is not entitled to compensation when a taking occurs. Such so-called condemnation clauses commonly appear in leases of valuable urban properties.

The period of a lease may run from month to month, year to year, or for a fixed number of years. Unlike tenants whose leases run from year to year or for a fixed period, a tenant under a lease that runs from month to month is not considered to have the type of interest that entitles him to compensation. It is reasoned that upon taking the leased premises the condemnor succeeds to the landlord's title and, like the landlord, has the right to terminate the tenant's leasehold interest by the giving of appropriate notice.

Compensation for Total Taking

Since both the landlord and the tenant have property interests in leased property, when that property is taken for a public purpose each of them is entitled to compensation for damages to his interest that results from the taking.

In most jurisdictions, when the entire leased property is taken, the compensation that is payable to the parties is computed in two stages.

First, the value of the *entire* property is determined by treating the property as if it were not encumbered by the existing lease. The value estimate is based on an appraiser's assumption that the property at the time of valuation is available for leasing at the current market rental, which may be either higher or lower than the contract rent provided for in the existing lease.

In the second stage of computations, the value figure arrived at in the first stage is apportioned and paid to the landlord and the tenant in accordance with the estimated value of their respective interests in the property. It is sometimes said that the award of compensation stands in place of the property that was taken and that the landlord and the tenant may recover out of the award the same proportionate shares that they held in the property that was condemned.

Value of Landlord's Interest The value of the landlord's interest in the property that he has leased is the present worth or value of the rental payments to be received over the term of the lease plus the present worth of the property at the end of the lease period. The present worth (as of the time of condemnation) of the future value figures is arrived at by applying a discount factor to those figures.

Value of Tenant's Interest The value of the tenant's interest in the leased premises is the difference between the **contract rent** that the tenant is obligated to pay under the rental agreement and the amount that the premises would currently rent for if they were available for lease, which amount is called the **economic rent.** In those instances where the contract rent is equal to or exceeds the economic rent, the tenant's leasehold interest has no market value and consequently he is not entitled to compensation for the taking of his leasehold interest. To the extent, however, that the economic rent exceeds the contract rent, the tenant is entitled to compensation because the difference between them represents the amount that he could receive as a "bonus" if he were to sell his leasehold in the market or if he subleased the premises.

Compensation for Partial Taking

In the absence of lease provisions to the contrary, there is no pro rata diminution in a tenant's obligation to pay the full agreed rental when only a portion of the leased premises is taken by eminent domain. In the majority of jurisdictions, the tenant remains under a continuing obligation to pay the rent in full for the remainder of the lease term even though he has been deprived of the use of part of the leased premises.

This majority view is based on the notion that the court before which a condemnation proceeding is brought has no authority to change the parties' rental agreement and to provide for a pro rata reduction in rent. Instead of a rent deduction, the tenant is entitled to receive from the total compensation award a sum of money that represents the present value of the estimated future rent attributable to that portion of the leased premises that was taken.

UNIFORM RELOCATION ASSISTANCE ACT

The most significant legislation in the field of eminent domain to be enacted by the Congress in recent years is the **Uniform Relocation Assistance and Real Property Acquisition Policies Act** of 1970.[14] Relocation assistance provided for by the act is entirely independent of the condemnation procedure itself and provides for additional payments that have no effect on the amount of condemnation award for the property that is taken.

Purpose of the Act

The legislation was enacted to establish a uniform policy for the fair and equitable treatment of persons who are displaced from their homes, businesses, or farms, or who have their property taken for federal or federally assisted programs.[15]

The act defines a "displaced person" as any person who moves from real property, or moves his personal property from real property, as a result of a written notice from an acquiring agency to vacate such property for a program or project undertaken by a federal agency or by a state agency with federal financial assistance. The term "federal financial assistance" means any grant, loan, or contribution provided by the United States, except a federal guarantee or insurance.[16]

Need for the Legislation

The need for the legislation is said to arise from the increasing impact of federal and federally assisted programs as those programs have evolved to meet the needs of a growing urban population. At any earlier time, federal and federally assisted public works projects seldom involved major displacements of people. With the growth and development of an economy that is increasingly urban and metropolitan, the demand for public facilities and services has increasingly centered on such urban areas. A major public project such as a highway or urban renewal inevitably involves the acquisition and clearance of sites which provide residential, commercial, or other services. The Congress found that as federal and federally assisted programs increasingly involved urban areas,

> . . . it became increasingly apparent that the application of traditional concepts of valuation and eminent domain resulted in inequitable treatment for large numbers of people displaced by public action. When applied to densely populated areas, with already limited housing, the result can be catastrophic for those whose homes or businesses must give way to public needs. The result far too often has been that a few citizens have been called upon to bear the burden of meeting public needs.[17]

The legislation recognizes that

> . . . relocation is a serious and growing problem in the United States and that the pace of displacement will accelerate in the years immediately ahead. It recognizes that advisory assistance is of special importance in the relocation process especially for the poor, the nonwhite, the elderly, and people engaged in small business. It recognizes the need for more equitable land acquisition policies in connection with the acquisition of real property

---

[14] P.L.91-646, secs. 101-306; 42 U.S.C., secs. 4601-4655.
[15] House Report (Public Works Committee) No. 91-1656, 3 U.S. Code Congressional and Administrative News, 91st Cong., 2nd Sess., 1970, p. 5850.

[16] 42 U.S.C., sec. 4601.
[17] House Report (Public Works Committee) No. 91-1656, 3 U.S. Code Congressional and Administrative News, 91st Cong., 2nd Sess., 1970, p. 5850.

for these programs. In short, the legislation recognizes that the Federal Government has a primary responsibility to provide uniform treatment for those forced to relocate by federal and federally aided public improvement programs and to ease the impact of such forced moves.[18]

Commenting on the act, the House Public Works Committee stated that it was

. . . especially concerned that the public have adequate knowledge of the relocation program and that persons to be displaced be fully informed at the earliest time of such matters as relocation payments and assistance available; the specific plans and procedures for assuring that suitable replacement housing will be available for homeowners and tenants, in advance of displacement; the eligibility requirements and procedures for obtaining payments and assistance; and the right to appeal to the head of the agency concerned, and the procedure for appealing.[19]

In providing for relocation assistance, the legislation draws a distinction between (1) persons displaced from dwellings and (2) persons displaced from businesses or farming operations.

Persons Displaced from Dwellings

Moving Expenses Any person who is displaced from a dwelling may receive his *actual* moving expenses or he may elect to receive an optional payment of a *fixed amount*. The amount of the optional moving expense allowance is determined according to a schedule and may not exceed $300 plus a dislocation allowance of $200.[20]

Optional payments are "designed to facilitate agreements, accelerate the delivery of funds to displaced persons, simplify administration, and minimize red tape. Generally, optional payments will be advantageous to displaced persons and to administrative agencies, and the use of such payments should be encouraged."[21]

Moving expense allowances, both actual and optional, are available to displaced owners of dwellings and to tenants alike.

Replacement Housing for Owners Section 203 of the act[22] is based on the principle that, at least within limits, a displaced homeowner should not be left worse off economically than he was before displacement, and that he should be able to relocate in a comparable dwelling which is decent, safe, sanitary, and adequate to accommodate him. The section authorizes a supplemental payment, not to exceed $5,000, which is allowed *in addition* to the payment of the market value of the property that is taken. This supplemental payment is intended to assist displaced persons in locations where comparable and decent replacement housing is available but at somewhat higher prices than the market value payments made for the dwellings that were taken. In such locations, the supplemental payment is often sufficient to cover the housing cost differential and, if broadly administered, it could cover closing costs and to some degree, the loss of favorable financing.

In those instances where an adequate supply of housing is not available and cannot be developed to sell at prices displaced persons can afford, even the full $5,000 supplemental payment may not be sufficient to resolve relocation problems. The act[23] therefore authorizes an additional payment, not to exceed $15,000, to be made to a displaced person to compensate him for the following:

1 The difference, if any, between the *acquisition payment* of the market value of the dwelling taken and the *actual and reasonable cost* to a displaced homeowner of a comparable dwelling, which is decent, safe, sanitary, and adequate to accommodate him, in an area not generally less desirable with regard to public utilities and public and commercial facilities and services, and reasonably accessible to places of employment. Replacement housing

---

[18] Id., p. 5852.
[19] Id., p. 5863.
[20] 42 U.S.C., sec. 4602(a) and (b).
[21] House Report (Public Works Committee) No. 91-1656, 3 U.S. Code Congressional and Administrative News, 91st Cong., 2nd Sess., 1970, p. 5855.

[22] 42 U.S.C., sec. 4623.
[23] Id., secs. 4623 and 4630.

satisfying these requirements must be available to the homeowner before displacement at terms he can afford and which do not worsen his economic condition.

2 An amount that will compensate the displaced homeowner for the present worth of any *loss of favorable financing.* The displaced person should not have to spend more for interest on a mortgage for the comparable replacement housing.

An example[24] of the way in which an increase in interest cost payments is computed is as follows:

and occupied the dwelling from which he is displaced for a period of not less than 180 days prior to commencement of the negotiations for the acquisition of the property.

The dwelling from which a person is displaced may be a single-family building, a one-family unit in a multifamily building, a unit of a condominium or cooperative housing project, or any other residential unit, including a mobile home, which is considered to be real property under state law and which cannot be moved

Dwelling To Be Acquired

Acquisition price	$12,000.00
Existing mortgage:	
Interest rate (percent)	6
Remaining term (years)	10
Remaining principal balance	$ 7,295.93
Monthly principal and interest payment	$81.82
Owner's equity	$ 4,704.07

Available Comparable Decent, Safe, And Sanitary Dwelling

Price	$15,000.00
Prevailing interest rate (percent)	8
Supplemental payment for replacement housing cost differential	$ 3,000.00
Payment for increased interest cost	$ 700.00

Computation Of Payment For Increased Interest Cost

Monthly principal and interest cost for new mortgage of $7,295.93 for 10 years at 8 percent interest	$ 88.57
Monthly principal and interest cost for existing mortgage of $7,295.93 for 10 years at 6 percent interest	$ 81.02
Monthly interest difference	$ 7.55
Present worth of $7.55 monthly interest for 10 years, discounted at the assumed interest rate paid on savings deposits, at 5 percent	$700.00
Increased interest cost payment due to property owner	$700.00

3 An amount to compensate the homeowner for reasonable costs of evidence of title, recording fees, and other closing costs incidental to the purchase of the replacement dwelling.

To qualify for any of the foregoing payments, a displaced person must have owned

without substantial damage or at unreasonable cost.

The supplemental payment is available only if a displaced person purchases and occupies a decent, safe, and sanitary replacement dwelling within *one year* from the date that he receives final payment for his acquired dwelling or the date on which he moves from the acquired dwelling, whichever is the later date.

---

[24] Taken from House Report (Public Works Committee) No. 91-1656, 3 U.S. Code Congressional and Administrative News, 91st Cong., 2nd Sess., 1970, p. 5859.

Replacement Housing for Tenants In addition to moving allowances, tenants who are displaced from their dwellings are entitled to *rental assistance payments.*[25]

To be entitled to such payments, a displaced tenant must have occupied the acquired dwelling for a period of at least 90 days prior to the initiation of negotiations for acquisition of the property. A displaced tenant will receive payment of a sum, not to exceed $4,000, that is necessary to enable him to lease or rent a comparable dwelling for a period not to exceed four years.

In order to encourage home ownership, the act[26] provides that a displaced tenant may receive a sum of money to enable him to make a *down payment* and to cover his *reasonable expenses* for evidence of title, recording fees, and other closing costs for the *purchase* of a decent, safe, and sanitary dwelling. The maximum payment to the displaced tenant for the purchase of a home is $4,000. However, if more than $2,000 is required for the down payment, the tenant is required to match any amount in excess of $2,000 by an equal amount from his own funds.

Persons Displaced from Business or Farm

Moving Expenses Persons whose businesses or farming operations are displaced by acquisition of property by eminent domain may receive the *actual* reasonable expenses of moving their operations to a new location.

Actual Direct Losses of Personal Property Payments for direct losses of personal property are allowed where a person who is displaced from his place of business or farming operation is entitled to relocate his personal property but decides not to do so. Typical items of business property include equipment, machinery, or fixtures which are no longer required because the business or farming operation is to be discontinued or the property is not suitable for use at the new location. The relocation of old trade fixtures, machinery, or equipment frequently is impractical or uneconomical, and could be a deterrent to the establishment of a business.[27]

A person displaced from a business or farming operation may be compensated for actual direct personal property losses whether he discontinues or reestablishes his operation. However, the maximum amount of any payment to which he is entitled may not exceed the reasonable expenses that would have been required to relocate the property and, in the case of heavy machinery, equipment, or other property involving substantial sums, also should not exceed the in-place value of the property.

Loss of Net Earnings A person who is displaced from his business or farm may receive in lieu of moving and related expenses a fixed relocation payment equal to the average annual net earnings[28] of the business or farm operation, except that such payment shall not be less than $2,500 nor more than $10,000. A fixed payment can be made, in the case of a business, only if the federal agency head determines that the business cannot be relocated without a substantial loss of its existing patronage and is not a part of a chain store operation.[29]

The minimum $2,500 fixed payment provision was included to assist owners of "mom-pop" businesses and owner-occupants of multifamily dwellings, many of whom might lose their sole or primary source of livelihood as the result of the displacement. Any displaced owner-occupant of a multifamily dwelling who

---

[25] 42 U.S.C., sec. 4624.
[26] Id., sec. 4624(2).

[27] House Report (Public Works Committee) No. 91-1656, 3 U.S. Code Congressional and Administrative News, 91st Cong., 2nd Sess., 1970, p. 5856.
[28] HUD Handbook. *Relocation Policies and Procedures,* paragraph 6-37 states: "Average annual net earnings means one-half of any net earnings of the business or farm operation, before Federal, State, and local income taxes, during the two taxable years preceding the taxable year in which displacement takes place. Annual average net earnings include salaries, wages, or other compensation paid by the business or farm operation to the owner, his spouse, or his dependents."
[29] 42 U.S.C., sec. 4622(c).

earns income from such a dwelling is regarded as being displaced from his business as well as having been displaced from his dwelling.[30]

Expenses in Searching for Replacement Business or Farm The act[31] authorizes payment for actual reasonable expenses incurred by a displaced person in searching for a replacement business or farm. These expenses include transportation, meals, and lodging away from home and, within limits, the reasonable value of the person's time actually spent in the search.

The act does not provide such payments for displaced persons required to move from dwellings, since the optional moving expenses payment and fixed dislocation allowance available to such persons is considered to achieve the same objective without the substantial administrative effort that would be required if such provisions were made applicable to dwellings.[32]

Relocation Assistance Advisory Services

The act[33] provides for a relocation assistance advisory program to be made available to persons displaced by federal or federally assisted projects. When a federal agency head determines that any person occupying property *adjacent* to the project area is caused economic injury because of the project, such advisory services may also be made available to him.

Each relocation assistance program includes measures, facilities, and services that may be necessary or appropriate to:

  1 determine the needs, if any, of displaced persons for relocation assistance;
  2 provide current and continuing information on the availability, prices, and rentals of comparable, safe, and sanitary housing and of comparable commercial properties and locations for displaced businesses;
  3 assure that within a reasonable period of time prior to displacement there will be available, to the extent that such can reasonably be accomplished, in areas not generally less desirable in regard to public utilities and commercial facilities and at rents or prices within the financial means of families and individuals displaced, decent, safe, and sanitary dwellings;
  4 assist a person displaced from his business or farming operation in obtaining and becoming established in a suitable replacement location;
  5 supply information concerning federal and state housing programs, disaster loan programs, and other federal or state programs offering assistance to displaced persons; and
  6 provide other advisory services to displaced persons in order to minimize hardships to such persons in adjusting to relocation.

The foregoing advisory assistance and coordination activities are considered to be key elements of any successful relocation effort and are to be given positive support by all who are concerned with the implementation of the act.[34]

Payments Not Considered Income

The act[35] provides that no payment or assistance received under the provisions of the act shall be considered as income of the displaced person for purposes of the Internal Revenue Code. The act further provides that such payment or assistance shall not be regarded as income for purposes of determining eligibility of any person for assistance under the Social Security Act or any other federal law.

UNIFORM REAL PROPERTY ACQUISITION POLICY

Subchapter III of the Uniform Relocation Assistance and Real Property Acquisition Policies

---

[30] House Report (Public Works Committee) No. 91-1656, 3 U.S. Code Congressional and Administrative News, 91st Cong., 2nd Sess., 1970, p. 5857.

[31] 42 U.S.C., sec. 4622(a).

[32] House Report (Public Works Committee) No. 91-1656, 3 U.S. Code Congressional and Administrative News, 91st Cong., 2nd Sess., 1970, p. 5856.

[33] 42 U.S.C., sec. 4625.

[34] House Report (Public Works Committee) No. 91-1656, 3 U.S. Code Congressional and Administrative News, 91st Cong., 2nd Sess., 1970, p. 5863.

[35] 42 U.S.C., sec. 4636.

Act of 1970 establishes a uniform policy for the acquisition of real property "in order to encourage and expedite acquisition by agreements with owners, to avoid litigation and relieve congestion in the courts, to assure consistent treatment for owners in the many Federal programs, and to promote public confidence in Federal land acquisition policies."[36]

Policy Provisions

In order to guide federal agencies to the greatest possible extent in their acquisition of real property, certain policy provisions have been enacted.[37]

Acquisition by Negotiation The act requires that federal agency heads shall make every reasonable effort to acquire real property expeditiously through negotiation.[38]

Appraisal before Negotiation It is the policy that real property shall be appraised before the initiation of negotiations, and that the owner be given an opportunity to accompany the appraiser during the inspection of the property.[39]

Offer Must Be for Full Market Value Before negotiations have been initiated, the appropriate agency head shall establish an amount that he believes to represent just compensation for the property to be acquired. Promptly thereafter, he shall attempt to acquire the property for the *full amount* of the compensation so established.[40]

The head of the federal agency acquiring real property is required to provide the property owner with a written statement summarizing the basis on which the just compensation was established. Where appropriate, the just compensation for the property acquired and for damages to remaining real property shall be separately stated.[41]

The House committee report on the act points out that the foregoing policy requirements "seek to assure that government agencies will deal fairly with owners of real property needed for Federal programs."[42] After pointing out that a number of federal agencies have followed a policy of making an initial offer and often acquiring property at an amount below the approved appraisal value of the property, the report states that "Any policy which does not entitle the property owner to an offer of the full amount of the agency's approved value estimate, where the owner must sell, is unfair. It is fundamental that all citizens be dealt with fairly by their government."[43]

Notice to Vacate Dwelling The construction or development of a public improvement shall be so scheduled that, to the greatest extent practicable, no person lawfully occupying real property shall be required to move from a dwelling, or to move his business or farming operation without *at least 90 days' written notice* from the head of the federal agency concerned.[44]

Avoidance of Inverse Condemnation If any interest in real property is to be acquired by the exercise of the right of eminent domain, the head of the federal agency concerned shall institute formal condemnation proceedings. No federal agency shall intentionally make it necessary for an owner to institute legal proceedings to prove the fact of the taking of his real property.[45]

Taking of Uneconomic Remnants The act establishes the policy that if the acquisition of

---

[36] House Report (Public Works Committee) No. 91-1656, 3 U.S. Code Congressional and Administrative News, 91st Cong., 2nd Sess., 1970, p. 5871.
[37] 42 U.S.C., secs. 4651-4655.
[38] 42 U.S.C., sec. 4651(1).
[39] Id., sec. 4651(2).
[40] Id., sec. 4651(3).

[41] Id.
[42] House Report (Public Works Committee) No. 91-1656, 3 U.S. Code Congressional and Administrative News, 91st Cong., 2nd Sess., 1970, p. 5871.
[43] Id., pp. 5872–73.
[44] 42 U.S.C., sec. 4651(5).
[45] Id., sec. 4651(8).

only part of a parcel of real estate would leave its owner with an uneconomic remnant, the head of the federal agency concerned shall offer to acquire the entire parcel.[46] The House committee report states that "No property owner should be forced into the position of retaining an uneconomic remnant in any case. Moreover, when this does occur, the acquiring agency frequently pays most if not all of the value of such remnant as severance damages, but the public does not get the benefit of the property."[47]

Expenses Incidental to Title Transfer The Uniform Act provides[48] for an owner to be reimbursed for the following expenses as soon as possible after real property has been purchased or compensation has been awarded:

1 recording fees, transfer taxes, and similar expenses incidental to conveying real estate to the United States;

2 penalty costs for prepayment of a preexisting recorded mortgage encumbering the acquired property;

3 the pro rata portion of any real property taxes that have been paid which is allocable to a period of time subsequent to the date of the vesting of title in the United States, or the effective date of possession of such property by the United States, whichever is the earlier.

Litigation Expense The act authorizes[49] reimbursement to an owner of any right or interest in real estate for reasonable litigation expenses, including legal, appraisal, and engineering fees actually incurred because of the taking of property by federal agencies where either: (1) the court determines that a condemnation was *unauthorized*, (2) the federal government *abandons* a condemnation, or (3) an owner brings an action in the nature of *inverse condemnation* and obtains an award of compensation.

The House committee report notes that "Ordinarily the Government should not be required to pay expenses incurred by property owners in connection with condemnation proceedings. The invitation to increased litigation is evident."[50]

Policies Applicable to State Agencies The act provides[51] that state agencies that administer programs receiving federal financial assistance must make payments for expenses that are incidental to the transfer of title and litigation expenses in the same manner as federal agencies. In addition, to the greatest extent practicable under state law, state agencies must be guided by the other land acquisition policies as a condition to receipt of federal financial assistance.

UNIFORM EMINENT DOMAIN CODE

The **Uniform Eminent Domain Code** was approved by the National Conference of Commissioners on Uniform State Laws in 1974 and recommended for enactment by all states. The code "is a response to widely felt concern for the potential injustices that may result from the diversities of eminent domain procedures in the several states."[52] The code "provides for the acquisition of property by condemnors, the conduct of condemnation actions, and the determination of just compensation. It does not confer the power of eminent domain, and does not prescribe or restrict the purposes for which or the persons by whom that power may be exercised."[53]

---

[46] Id., sec. 4651(9).

[47] House Report (Public Works Committee) No. 91-1656, 3 U.S. Code Congressional and Administrative News, 91st Cong., 2nd Sess., 1970, p. 5873.

[48] 42 U.S.C., sec. 4653.

[49] Id., sec. 4654.

[50] House Report (Public Works Committee) No. 91-1656, 3 U.S. Code Congressional and Admininstrative News, 91st Cong., 2nd Sess., 1970, p. 5875.

[51] 42 U.S.C., sec. 5655.

[52] Uniform Eminent Domain Code (hereafter cited as UEDC), Prefatory Note.

[53] UEDC, sec. 102(a).

Acquisition of Real Property

Article II of the code, entitled "Policies Governing Land Acquisition," was drafted with the intention of assuring that state laws with respect to the acquisition of land by eminent domain are in accord with requirements prescribed by the federal Uniform Relocation Assistance and Real Property Acquisition Policies Act. While the acquisition policies of the federal act apply to state and local governments only when their improvement projects receive federal financial assistance, Article II of the Uniform Eminent Domain Code extends the same acquisition policies to projects that are not federally funded.[54]

Like the federal act, the uniform code requires that reasonable and diligent efforts be made by a condemnor to acquire property by negotiation,[55] that the property be appraised before negotiations begin[56] and a written appraisal be provided to the owner,[57] and that the condemnor's offer to an owner not be less than the condemnor's approved appraisal.[58] Also like the federal act, the uniform code provides that a condemnor must, except in an emergency, give an occupant at least 90 days' written notice to vacate premises,[59] must offer to acquire any uneconomic remnant[60] that a partial taking would leave,[61] and must, as soon as practicable after payment of the purchase price, reimburse the owner for recording fees, transfer taxes, prepayment penalties, and other expenses incidental to the transfer of title.[62]

The uniform code incorporates the provision of the federal act that prohibits a condemnor from intentionally making it necessary for an owner to commence an inverse condemnation action to prove the fact of the taking of his property.[63]

Relocation Assistance

Article XIV of the uniform code, entitled "Relocation Assistance," was included in the code "to satisfy the provisions of Title II of the Federal Uniform Relocation Assistance and Real Property Acquisition Act. . . . While the Federal Act is limited in scope to federally assisted projects and programs, this Article is intended to extend the same benefits and requirements to all projects and programs conducted or directed by both public and private condemnors, whether or not federal financial assistance is being provided."[64]

With one exception, the provisions of the Uniform Eminent Domain Code relative to relocation assistance[65] are counterparts of the provisions of the federal act. The uniform code contains an express provision for judicial review of administrative decisions regarding relocation assistance which the federal act does not. The code provides that "After exhaustion of administrative remedies, a determination by a condemnor as to eligibility or lack of eligibility for, or as to the extent of, any relocation assistance service or payment authorized by this Article, may be reviewed by a court of competent jurisdiction and modified or set aside, if it is found to be arbitrary, unreasonable, or an abuse of discretion."[66]

Compensation Standards

Article X of the Uniform Eminent Domain Code sets forth general standards concerning

---

[54] UEDC, Article II, Prefatory Comment.
[55] UEDC, sec. 202(a).
[56] Id., sec. 202(b).
[57] Id., sec. 203(c).
[58] Id., sec. 203(a). The UEDC defines an "appraisal" as "an opinion as to the value of or compensation payable for property, prepared under the direction of an individual qualified by knowledge, skill, experience, training, or education to express an opinion as to the value of property." UEDC, sec. 103(2).
[59] Id., sec. 205.
[60] The UEDC states that "'Uneconomic remnant' . . . means a remainder following a partial taking of property, of such size, shape, or condition as to be of little value or that gives rise to a substantial risk that the condemnor will be required to pay in compensation for the part taken an amount substantially equivalent to the amount that would be required to be paid if it and the remainder were taken as a whole." UEDC, sec. 208(b).
[61] UEDC, sec. 208(a).
[62] Id., sec. 211.
[63] Id., sec. 213.
[64] Id., Article XIV, Preliminary Comment.
[65] Id., secs. 1401–12.
[66] Id., sec. 1412.

the determination of the amount of compensation to which an owner is entitled for the taking of his property. The objective of the article is the formulation of uniform principles governing the major elements of just compensation because, as the draftsmen of the code point out, "the features of eminent domain law chiefly responsible for disparities of results, with attendant inequities for both condemnors and condemnees, relate to compensation standards."[67]

Compensation for Taking *Total Taking* The measure of compensation for the taking of property is its fair market value.[68] The fair market value of property "for which there is a relevant market is the price which would be agreed to by an informed seller who is willing but not obligated to buy."[69] The fair market value of property "for which there is no relevant market value is its value as determined by any method of valuation that is just and equitable."[70]

Partial Taking Where there is a partial taking of property, the uniform code provides that the measure of compensation will be either the value of the property that is taken or "the amount by which the fair market value of the entire property immediately before the taking exceeds the fair market value of the remainder immediately after the taking"—whichever is the greater.[71] The latter alternative is the so-called before and after rule for measuring compensation and is presently followed in a minority of states and in federal condemnation practice.

Loss of Goodwill The uniform code provides that the owner of a business conducted on property taken by eminent domain shall be compensated, in addition to the fair value of property taken, for the loss of goodwill. The code defines "goodwill" as consisting of "the benefits that accrue to a business as a result of its location, reputation for dependability, skill, or quality, and other circumstances resulting in probable retention of old or acquisition of new patronage."[72]

To receive compensation for the loss of goodwill under the uniform code, the owner of a business must prove that the loss (1) is caused by the taking of property, (2) cannot reasonably be prevented by a relocation of the business or by taking steps and adopting procedures that a reasonably prudent person would take and adopt to preserve the goodwill, (3) is not included in relocation payments received by the owner, and (4) is not duplicated in the compensation awarded to the owner.[73]

QUESTIONS

1 While the terms "eminent domain" and "condemnation" are related, there is an important distinction between them. What is it?
2 What is necessary to satisfy the requirement of due process of law when private property is taken for a public use?
3 Indicate two ways in which the police power differs from the right of eminent domain.
4 What are consequential damages? Under what circumstances is a landowner entitled to compensation for such damages?
5 When land is taken by eminent domain, what is meant by the statement that the question of necessity is political in nature rather than judicial?
6 What is meant by excess condemnation? Distinguish the three theories that are used to justify such condemnation.
7 What is "just compensation" as that term is used in connection with the taking of property by eminent domain?
8 Describe briefly the cost approach to estimating the value of real property.
9 Describe briefly the market approach to estimating the value of real property.
10 Describe briefly the income approach to estimating the value of real property.

---

[67] Id., sec. 1001, Comment.
[68] Id., sec. 1002.
[69] Id., sec. 1004(a)(1).
[70] Id., sec. 1004(a)(2).
[71] Id., sec. 1002(b)(2).
[72] Id., sec. 1016(b).
[73] Id., sec. 1016(a).

Chapter 12

Adverse Possession and Accretion

Ownership of real estate may be involuntarily transferred from one person to another by a process known as **adverse possession.** Title is acquired by adverse possession when a parcel of real estate is wrongfully occupied for a statutorily prescribed period of time in such a manner that the owner's title is lost and that title is vested in the occupant. Once the occupant has met all legally required conditions, the title to the occupied premises is transferred to him by operation of law without the consent of the property owner and despite his vigorous protests.

Laws relating to adverse possession vary from one state to another not only because of differing statutory provisions but also because of local judicial attitudes as to what constitutes "possession" and the particular circumstances under which possession is deemed to be "adverse."

The great majority of controversies involving adverse possession have their origins in the attempted conveyance of title by an owner who fails to make an effective transfer because his deed was invalid for any of the reasons discussed in Chapter 10. The grantee named in such a deed, believing that he in fact received title from the grantor, thereafter enters into possession of the property, occupying and using it as any owner normally would do. After having occupied the property for the required statutory period of time, the title that the grantee failed to obtain by deed from his grantor is acquired by adverse possession.

Adverse possession cases also arise because of mistaken boundary lines, and a few instances still occur in which a wrongdoer willfully enters upon and occupies another person's property with the preconceived intention of acquiring title to it by adverse possession.

GENERAL CHARACTERISTICS OF ADVERSE POSSESSION

Operates as a Statute of Limitations

Statutes that provide for acquisition of title by adverse possession are in the nature of statutes of limitations in that they prescribe a period of time within which an owner whose property is wrongfully occupied may commence a legal action to remove the occupant and regain possession of his property. If the owner fails to initiate a legal action within the period of time prescribed by the statute, his right to recover possession of his property is forever lost.

Objective of the Law

The objective of the law with respect to adverse possession is to bring about a relatively prompt termination of controversies involving the right to possession of land. As one observer has noted:

> The statute has not for its object to reward the diligent trespasser for his wrong nor yet to penalize the negligent and dormant owner for sleeping on his rights; the great purpose is automatically to quiet all titles which are openly and consistently asserted, to provide proof of meritorious titles, and correct errors in conveyancing.[1]

No Adverse Possession of Public Property

While *private* owners in every state can be deprived of their properties by adverse possession, statutes in many states[2] prohibit acquisition of title by adverse possession from *government entities* and *public utilities.* In states which have no such statutory provisions, the courts frequently adopt the same attitude by holding that, in the absence of legislation to the contrary, the statute of limitations does not run against the government and hence the government may bring an action to remove a wrongful possessor at any time.

No Adverse Possession of Future Interests

The interest of a reversioner, a remainderman, or an owner of some other type of real estate interest that postpones the right of possession until a future time cannot be acquired by adverse possession. This rule arises from the fact that the owner of a future interest has no right to bring a legal action against an adverse possessor until such time as the future interest becomes a *possessory* one. As soon as the owner of the future interest is entitled to possess and occupy the premises, his cause of action against a wrongful occupant commences and the statute of limitations begins to run.

For example, the acquisition by A of O's life estate in Blackacre through adverse possession has no effect on R's remainder interest until the death of O. Upon O's death, the life estate terminates, R's interest becomes a present possessory one, and A's continued occupancy of the premises is subject to an action by R to remove him—an action which was not available to R while O lived. Thereafter, if A satisfies the necessary requirements, A can acquire R's interest in Blackacre by adverse possession.

ESSENTIAL ELEMENTS OF ADVERSE POSSESSION

In order that title to real estate may be acquired by adverse possession, the one who claims title must be able to establish that he satisfied *each* of the following requirements: (1) the possessor's occupation of the premises must have been *open, notorious, and visible;* (2) occupation by the possessor must have been *hostile and adverse;* (3) the possession of the premises must have been under either a *claim of right* or *color of title;* (4) the possessor's occupancy must have been *uninterrupted and continuous* for the statutorily prescribed number of years; and, in a minority of the states, (5) the adverse possessor must have *paid all taxes* assessed and levied against the premises during the statutory period.

OPEN, NOTORIOUS, AND VISIBLE OCCUPATION

Sufficient to Be Apparent to Owner

Although an adverse possessor is not required actually to give notice of his occupancy to an

---

[1] Henry W. Ballantine, *Titles by Adverse Possession,* 32 Harvard L.R.135 (1918).

[2] For example, Alabama, Arizona, California, Florida, Georgia, Illinois, Indiana, Louisiana, Massachusetts, Mississippi, Missouri, Nevada, Oregon, South Dakota, Texas, Virginia, Vermont, and Washington.

owner by mail or other communication, his presence on the owner's property must be sufficiently obvious to be apparent to a reasonably alert owner. The fact that the owner does not reside in the vicinity where his property is situated or that he is not in fact aware of the possessor's presence on his property is of no significance. The law requires only that the claimant's occupancy be such that if the owner had made a reasonable inspection of his premises he would have become aware of the occupant's presence and his wrongful use of the property. Whether occupancy by an adverse possessor is sufficiently open and notorious to impart the notice required by law is a question of fact in each case.

The requirement that occupancy be open, notorious, and visible is based on the notion that rights in real property should not be lost without the owner having had an opportunity to prevent the loss by taking appropriate action. Such action, of course, cannot be commenced until an owner is aware of the fact that his rights are being violated. The requirement that a possessor's occupancy be open, notorious, and visible becomes particularly significant with respect to land on which a possessor's acts normally occur only infrequently, as in the case of range or timber lands.

Failure on the part of a wrongful possessor to satisfy the requirement of open, notorious, and visible occupancy means that no title can be acquired by him regardless of the fact that all other requirements of adverse possession have been met. The question whether the occupancy requirement has been satisfactorily met becomes an important issue in cases where surface rights and subsurface rights to a parcel of land are *separately owned*. In such circumstances, unquestioned fulfillment of all requirements for obtaining title to the surface by adverse possession is not sufficient to establish open, notorious, and visible possession of underground minerals and thus extinguish the separate ownership of the mineral rights. Of course, if the one who adversely possesses the surface also openly, notoriously, and visibly exploits the property's mineral resources, it is possible for him to become the owner of the mineral rights as well as the surface.

Proof of Possession

The burden of proving that possession was open, notorious, and visible rests with the adverse possessor who claims title to a parcel of land. The nature of the proof required of him will depend on the characteristics of the land that he occupied. Evidence of having done those things with or on the land that an owner of that particular type of land would naturally and normally do will satisfy the occupancy requirements. It would, for example, be sufficient to show that a building lot was enclosed and built upon, that agricultural land had been cultivated in season, or that pasture and grazing land had been used for grazing.

An adverse possessor's use of the land that he occupies must be so evident and observable that neither his neighbors nor the public at large would entertain any doubts as to the exclusive character of the occupant's possession. Proof of an adverse possessor's acts may be established by the testimony of witnesses who have observed his conduct.

Occupancy by Tenant of Claimant

The person claiming title by adverse possession is not required personally to occupy the premises throughout the entire statutory period. The requirement is satisfied if the premises are occupied by a tenant of the adverse possessor, providing only that such occupancy by a tenant be open, notorious, and visible.

HOSTILE AND ADVERSE OCCUPANCY

To acquire title to real property, a possessor's open, notorious, and visible occupancy of the property must also be hostile and adverse.

Without Express or Implied Permission

A possessor is said to occupy another person's property hostilely and adversely when he occupies it without the express or implied permission of the owner of the property. To be hostile and adverse, the occupant's possession must be either *intentionally* wrongful or *innocently* wrongful, thus giving rise to a cause of action by the owner to remove the possessor from the premises. If the claimant's occupancy is in any way permissive, the requirement of hostile and adverse occupancy is not met and title cannot be acquired by the possessor.

The term "hostile" does not require animosity or belligerency on the part of an occupant. It is a word of art meaning simply that a claimant's occupancy of the premises is in no way subordinate to or derived from the owner's title.

Hostility Is a Question of Fact

The presence or absence of hostility on the part of an adverse possessor is a question of fact to be determined in each case. In general, the same acts or declarations by a possessor that serve to establish his open, notorious, and visible possession are held to be sufficient to show hostility and adverseness toward the owner of the land and the rest of the world.

CLAIM OF RIGHT OR COLOR OF TITLE

For title to be acquired by adverse possession, a possessor's open and notorious, hostile and adverse occupancy of another's property must either be based upon (1) a *claim of right* or (2) *color of title.* The requirements that an adverse possessor must satisfy when he occupies land under a claim of right vary slightly from what is required when occupancy is based on color of title.

Claim of Right

Statutes and court decisions frequently use the terms **claim of** *right* and **claim of** *title* synonymously and occasionally employ the inclusive expression "claim of *right or title.*" These terms have been defined as meaning that the adverse claimant, without any semblance of actual right or title, entered upon another's property with the intent to appropriate it and use it as his own to the exclusion of all other persons.

The essence of a possessor's occupancy under a claim of right is that he is in possession of property without either the permission of the owner or any document or writing that he believes gives him title to the property. The requirement of occupancy under a claim of right is very close to being simply a restatement of the requirement that a possessor's occupancy must be *hostile.* In fact, the adverse possessor can ordinarily establish his claim of right or title by the same evidence that he uses to establish the hostile and adverse character of his possession. Because of this fact, it has been said that "claim of right" means nothing more than "hostile," and if an occupant's possession is established as being hostile, his possession is therefore under a claim of right.

To emphasize the distinction between the "claim of right" requirement and the "color of title" requirement, statutes in some states[3] refer to the former as a "claim of title exclusive of any other right," a "claim of title not founded upon a written instrument, judgment, or decree," or substantially similar language.

In a minority of states,[4] an adverse possessor occupying property under a claim of right must establish that he "protected by a substantial enclosure" the land to which he claims to have acquired title.

Color of Title

A possessor is said to occupy a parcel of real estate under **color of title** when he occupies the premises under the authority of an instrument or judicial decree that appears to give him title to the property but which in fact does not do so. Color of title, as distinct from *true* title, arises when the instrument or decree under which the occupant claims title describes the occupied premises and appears on its face to have conveyed title to him but, due to some invalidity in the document or decree of which the occupant

---

[3] For example, California, Florida, Georgia, Mississippi, New York, Utah, Texas, and Wisconsin.

[4] California, Florida, Idaho, Montana, Nevada, New York, North Dakota, South Carolina, Utah, and Wisconsin.

is not aware, actually transfers no title at all. The writing that constitutes a possessor's color of title may, for example, be a deed to which a grantor's name has been forged, a deed executed by a grantor whose title was imperfect, a tax deed or sheriff's deed which, despite its apparent validity, is void because of defective foreclosure procedures, or a faulty decree of partition or distribution of a court. To amount to color of title, the writing or instrument upon which an adverse possessor relies must not be so obviously imperfect that one not skilled in the law would be aware of its invalidity. As some courts put it, the instrument must be such that it creates the "appearance of title."

Possession of real property based on color of title is sometimes referred to as occupancy under "a claim of right having a written basis."

Statutes in some states[5] provide that an occupant who meets the requirements of adverse possession based on color of title acquires title to *all the land described* in his faulty document, even though he actually occupied only a portion of the described premises. In such circumstances, the claimant is said to have *constructively* possessed or occupied the entire area described in the instrument by which he claims title.

CONTINUOUS AND UNINTERRUPTED POSSESSION

Period Required by Statute

To acquire title by adverse possession, a claimant's notorious and hostile occupancy under either claim of right or color of title must have been *continuous and uninterrupted* for the period of time required by the statutes or the courts of the state in which the occupied property is situated. A few states[6] have adverse possession statutes containing provisions that expressly limit the period within which an owner may bring an action to recover possession of his property from an adverse possessor. Although adverse possession statutes in general do not contain such express provisions, the statutes are uniformly construed by the courts as limiting the period of time during which an action by the owner may be brought to recover his land. The period of time used by the courts in such instances is the period provided by the statute of limitations of the state in which the property is located. The effect of an owner's right to recover his property being barred by the running of the statute of limitations is to destroy all of his right, title, and interest in the occupied property.

The statutory periods for acquiring title by adverse possession vary considerably among the states,[7] with the time ranging from as little as 5 years to as much as 30.

Statutes of limitation do not run against a person who is under a legal disability. Many circumstances can give rise to such a disability, the more common causes being the fact that the person against whom the statute could otherwise run is below a certain age, is insane, or is imprisoned. A property owner's disability may exist at the time the statute would otherwise have commenced to run, that is, when the adverse possessor originally entered the property, or it may arise at any time during the statutory period and thus stop the running of the statute. If an owner's disability does not occur until after the statute of limitations has run, it would of course have no effect on the title already acquired by the adverse possessor.

---

[5] Among them are California, Florida, Idaho, New York, and Wisconsin.

[6] California, Colorado, Kentucky, Mississippi, New Jersey, Oklahoma, Pennsylvania, and Texas.

[7] The required periods in the various states are: 5 years—California, Idaho, Montana, and Nevada; 7 years—Alaska, Arkansas, Florida, Tennessee, and Utah; 10 years—Alabama, Arizona, Hawaii, Iowa, Mississippi, Missouri, Nebraska, New Mexico, New York, Oregon, Rhode Island, South Carolina, Texas, Washington, West Virginia, and Wyoming; 15 years—Connecticut, District of Columbia, Indiana, Kansas, Kentucky, Michigan, Minnesota, Oklahoma, Vermont, and Virginia; 18 years—Colorado; 20 years—Delaware, Georgia, Illinois, Maine, Maryland, Massachusetts, New Hampshire, New Jersey, North Carolina, North Dakota, South Dakota, and Wisconsin; 21 years—Ohio; 30 years—Louisiana.

Constant Occupancy Not Required

The requirement of continuous and uninterrupted possession does not mean that the adverse possessor must constantly occupy the premises. To fulfill the requirement, the possessor's occupancy need only be consistent with the character of the land claimed and the purpose for which the land is suitable and would customarily be used. In appropriate circumstances, the continuous and uninterrupted requirement may be satisfied by daily, weekend, or seasonal occupancy.

Controversies concerning the continuity of a claimant's possession most often focus on the adequacy of his acts to indicate a continuing assertion of his claim to the property. A claimant must consistently act as if he were the owner by doing those things that an owner would normally do, given the character of the land and the uses to which it would ordinarily be put.

Abandonment of possession of the premises during the statutory period clearly constitutes a fatal break in continuity. But once the claimant has acquired title by proper occupancy for the statutory period, his subsequent abandonment of possession will not cause his title to be lost.

Tacking of Successive Occupancies

It is not necessary for the *same* person to adversely occupy the premises throughout the entire statutory period in order that the requirement of continuous and uninterrupted possession be met. At any time after the original occupant's entry upon the premises he may transfer, by deed or otherwise, the rights that have accrued to him as a result of his hostile and notorious occupancy. In this manner, successive occupancies by two or more claimants may be "tacked" or added together to make up the total required statutory period. Of course there can be no time break between any of the successive occupancies.

The tacking together of successive periods of occupancy is permissible only if what the law calls "privity" exists between the successive claimants. Privity arises from a relationship such as that of a grantor and grantee, decedent and heir, devisor and devisee, or by the intentional surrender of possession by one claimant to another.

PAYMENT OF PROPERTY TAXES

Statutes in a minority of states require that an adverse possessor must pay all annual property taxes that are assessed and levied against the property occupied by him if he is to acquire title to it. While statutes in some states[8] limit the tax payment requirement to vacant or unoccupied land and other states[9] to land claimed under color of title, statutes in most of the states[10] that require taxes to be paid are general in their application.

Where payment of taxes is a requirement, the period for adverse possession begins to run when the occupant enters the property and begins his physical acts of possession rather than on the date when the first tax payment is made by the occupant.

The payment of taxes *alone* for the statutory period will never give rise to title by adverse possession. Where expressly required by statute, the payment of taxes is only one of the essential requirements for the acquisition of title by adverse possession.

NATURE OF ADVERSE POSSESSOR'S TITLE

New and Original Title

After having satisfied all statutory requirements, an adverse possessor becomes the owner of the physical property that he occupied. The title that he acquires to that property, however, is not the identical title that was previously held by the former owner. The adverse possessor's title is said to be a *new and original* title rather than one that is derived from the previous own-

---

[8] Colorado, Illinois, and Washington.
[9] Arizona and Texas.
[10] These states are California, Florida, Idaho, Indiana, Maine, Minnesota, Montana, Nevada, New Mexico, North Dakota, and Utah.

er. It is a title created by operation of law and is independent of any former or recorded title to the property.

If it is hostile and adverse at all, an adverse possessor's occupancy during the statutory period is hostile and adverse not only to the owner of the property himself, but also to every person who has any *present* interest in the occupied property. Once the occupant's adverse possession has ripened into title to the property, the statute of limitations cuts off the rights of all persons claiming present interests in the property to regain their interests.

Future Interests Not Terminated
We have seen that occupancy in fulfillment of the statutory requirements does not defeat the rights of owners of *future interests* in the occupied property. This is due, we observed, to the fact that the statute of limitations does not begin to run until the owner of a property interest has a legal cause of action against the adverse possessor for wrongful occupancy.

When Claimant's Title Vests
An adverse possessor's title to the property that he occupied vests in him by operation of law at the moment that all statutory requirements have been met. Proof of having fulfilled those requirements will defeat all attacks on his ownership. Title will be vested in the adverse possessor even though the public records continue to show the former owner to be the owner of record. There is no requirement that the adverse possessor, once he has acquired title, publicly proclaim it by recording his title in order to protect himself against the claims of purchasers from the former owner.

Claimant's Title Is Not Marketable
Although the title acquired by an adverse possessor is a new and original one, it is not a marketable title. The question as to the title's marketability usually arises when the adverse possessor contracts to sell the property that he acquired. We have seen that for a title to be marketable it must be so free from defects and encumbrances that there can be no doubt as to its validity, and it must be in such a condition that an informed and reasonable buyer, willing to buy and exercising the prudence ordinarily exercised by businessmen, would and should accept. The adverse possessor's title does not meet these criteria. No informed and reasonable purchaser would be willing to buy property from an adverse possessor when the public records reflect that the property is owned by a person other than the seller.

Rendered Marketable by Quiet Title Action To render the title that he acquired by adverse possession a marketable one, the adverse possessor must bring a court action to quiet title to the property. When the action is being heard by a court, the adverse possessor will be required to show that he has satisfied all the requirements for the acquisition of title by adverse possession. Upon proof of fulfillment of these requirements, a judgment will be rendered in his favor. As a result of that judgment the adverse possessor's title becomes a marketable one.

By recording an abstract or summary of his judgment with the county recorder or other appropriate official in the county in which the land is situated, the adverse possessor establishes his title as a **title of record.**

MISTAKEN BOUNDARIES AND ADVERSE POSSESSION

Controversies frequently arise because a landowner who is mistaken as to the true location of the boundary line between his property and an adjoining owner's land erects a fence or other boundary marker beyond the true boundary on the other owner's land. The question raised by such controversies is whether the mistaken landowner, after having occupied the land up to the mistaken boundary for the statutory period, will acquire title to the land between the true boundary and the mistaken boundary.

Visible and Exclusive Possession
The basic issue in mistaken boundary cases is whether the occupancy of land by *mistake* satis-

fies the requirement that an occupant's possession must be *hostile and adverse* if he is to acquire title to the disputed strip of land by adverse possession.

A growing number of states[11] have adopted the view that it is immaterial whether occupancy results from an honest mistake as to the location of a boundary line or from a deliberately wrongful entry on another's land. According to this view, an occupant's possession is regarded as being adverse despite the fact that he occupied the land under the mistaken belief that he owned it. What these states require is that his occupancy of the land that belongs to another person should be *visible and exclusive,* which means that the mistaken boundary line that encloses the claimed land must be clearly marked by a hedge, fence, wall, or other type of structure.

While visible and exclusive occupancy up to a readily discernible boundary line is an important factor in determining the hostile character of a claimant's possession, the controlling factor in mistaken boundary cases generally is held to be the *intent* with which the claimant took possession of the land he now claims.

Intention of the Mistaken Claimant
The rule is widely accepted that where a landowner who is mistaken as to his actual boundary line occupies land up to a clearly marked line that is beyond the limits of his property, believing that line to be the true boundary, and with the *intention* of claiming title up to the *mistaken line,* his possession will ripen into title if continued for the statutory period.[12]

It is the occupant's visible possession coupled with his intention to occupy the land to the mistaken boundary under the honest belief that the land is his that gives the hostile and adverse character to his possession. Being visible and exclusive, the occupant's possession imparts notice to all interested parties that he is adversely claiming the land as his own. His intention to occupy the land adversely to all others is evidenced by the acts of ownership that he performs while occupying the land.

ACCRETION

Accretion is the process by which the area of a parcel of land bounded by a river, lake, or tidal waters is gradually increased by soil deposited by the natural action of the water. The solid material that is deposited by current, wave, or tidal action is called **alluvion** and it belongs to the owner upon whose land it has been deposited.

A prime requisite for the acquisition of title by accretion is that the deposit of the alluvial soil must be *gradual and imperceptible* in its progress. According to some courts, the test of a gradual and imperceptible increase in land is met when, despite the fact that persons who view the land from time to time might be aware that accretion is taking place, they could not perceive it occurring from day to day.

Avulsion Distinguished
Accretion must be distinguished from what is known as avulsion. **Avulsion** is a *sudden and perceptible* separation of land resulting from floods, channel breakthroughs, or sudden changes in the course of a river or stream. Although such an abrupt or violent action might cause a former boundary line to be altered, title to the land remains with the owner of the parcel from which it was separated.

Reliction Compared
Reliction is a process somewhat similar to accretion, but differs in that reliction applies to the recession of waters which leaves additional dry land exposed. Like accretion, reliction changes the boundary of an owner's land. Where reliction has taken place, the land that has been exposed by the withdrawal of waters belongs to the owner of the land that is riparian to the receding waters.

---

[11] Alabama, Arkansas, California, Connecticut, Kansas, Maine, Michigan, Minnesota, Mississippi, Montana, New York, Oklahoma, Oregon, and Wisconsin.

[12] This view has been adopted, for example, by the courts in Alabama, Arkansas, California, Iowa, Kentucky, Missouri, Montana, Oklahoma, and Texas.

For the acquisition of title by reliction to occur, the recession of the waters that expose land must be gradual and imperceptible.

Boundary Lines Formed by Rivers or Streams
When the location of the margin or the bed of a river or stream that serves as a boundary of a parcel of land is gradually and imperceptibly changed by accretion or reliction, the general rule is that the margin or the bed as thus changed continues to be the boundary line of the affected property. The justification for permitting a boundary line to continue to follow the changing bank of a stream is the desirability of having land that was riparian under previous conditions remain riparian, thus assuring its owner continuing access to the water.

Waters to Which Law Applies
The law of accretion and reliction applies both to waters whose bed is owned by the state and waters where riparian owners' titles extend to the center of a stream. Largely because each state has been free to determine its own policy, there has been much diversity of opinion as to ownership of land under waters. Some states have followed common law rules and presumptions, while others have modified or abrogated those rules and established their own regulations.

Rules with respect to ownership of land under streams or bodies of water also vary depending upon whether the waters in question are navigable or nonnavigable.

Navigable Waters The federal test of navigability, which is followed by most state courts, turns on the question of whether a stream or body of water in its *natural state* is such that it affords a channel or highway for useful commerce and travel. If a stream or body of water in its natural state is capable of being used for purposes of commerce, those waters are navigable, notwithstanding the fact that they are not actually used for those purposes.

The question as to whether the title to riparian land that borders on a navigable river extends to the margin of the water or to the center of the stream is determined by the laws of the state in which the riparian land is situated. The rule prevailing in most states is that the state owns the beds of navigable waters located within the state.

Nonnavigable Waters The general rule with regard to nonnavigable waters is that the land under them is owned by the adjoining riparian owners, each of whom owns to the center of the stream. Consequently, when lands for which a nonnavigable stream serves as a boundary are conveyed, a rebuttable presumption arises that the grantor intends that the lands transferred will extend to the middle of the watercourse.

QUESTIONS

1 Describe briefly the process by which title to real estate is acquired by adverse possession.
2 What is the objective of the law that permits ownership of real estate to be obtained by adverse possession?
3 Compare the terms "claim of right" and "color of title" as they are used in connection with adverse possession.
4 An adverse possessor who satisfies all statutory requirements is said to obtain a new and original title to the property he occupied. What does that mean?
5 Why is the title that is acquired by an adverse possessor not a marketable title? How can it be made marketable?
6 With respect to the manner in which they occur, how does accretion differ from avulsion? Compare them as to their effects on title to land.
7 What is reliction? How does it affect title to land?

Chapter 13

Title Closing and Settlement Procedures

As used in connection with real estate sales transactions, **title closing** refers to the process by which the obligations assumed by the parties to a contract of purchase and sale are satisfied. Recent federal legislation[1] calls the process a **settlement** rather than title closing, and describes it as being the time when title to real property is transferred from a seller to a buyer.

In the title-closing or settlement process, the legal title that the seller promised to transfer is actually transferred and the purchase price that the buyer promised to pay is paid. Performance of the sales contract has a profound effect on the legal relations of the parties in that their previous legal status with respect to each other is reversed. When title is "closed" or "settlement" occurs, the former owner is divested of his title to the property in question and, at the moment of that divestment, the title is vested in the new owner. With this change in ownership, the former rights and obligations of the parties to the transaction become redefined.

In all but the most unusual situations, the closing of a real estate sales transaction involves more than simply the execution and delivery of a deed and the payment of the purchase price. Ordinarily there are many ancillary or incidental charges known as **closing costs** or **settlement costs** that need to be allocated and adjusted between the parties. Included in these settlement or closing costs are various selling costs, financing costs, and costs of establishing and recording title—all of which are discussed in appropriate chapters.

In rural communities where a seller and a buyer know and trust each other and where settlement matters tend to be less complex, title

---

[1] The Real Estate Settlement Procedures Act of 1974, as amended in 1975.

closing or settlement without using the services of an impartial third party is not uncommon. In urban areas, however, the services of a third party are commonly used to conclude a sales transaction. Depending upon the area of the country, the third party may be a professional escrow company or agent,[2] an attorney,[3] or a lending institution.

In terms of the total number of title closings that occur, those involving the purchase and sale of family residences far exceed all other types of closings. Not infrequently, buyers who have borrowed money to purchase homes are astounded at the amount of money they are called upon to pay at the time of title closing. To make these buyer-borrowers more fully aware of the costs of completing or closing a home purchase transaction, the Congress in 1974 passed and in 1975 significantly amended the federal **Real Estate Settlement Procedures Act.**[4] This act is examined later in the chapter, but before we do so it will be useful to understand the nature and the function of real estate escrows and the process by which real estate sales transactions are settled or closed.

REAL ESTATE ESCROWS

Nature of an Escrow

In the narrow meaning of the term, an *escrow* is a written instrument or thing of value deposited by a grantor, promisor, or obligor with a third party as a holder or depositary to be delivered by him to a grantee, promisee, or obligee upon the fulfillment of a condition or the happening of an event. In modern real estate practice, however, the term **escrow** has been broadened to refer to the general arrangement for the closing or completion of a real estate transaction and the transfer of title from a seller to a buyer. As used in this chapter, a *real estate escrow* is an arrangement whereby one party to a sales transaction deposits written instruments or money with a depositary, known as an escrow agent or escrow holder, to be held by him until a certain condition has been performed or an event has occurred, and thereafter to be delivered to the other party to the transaction.

According to usage in some areas of the country, when the title-closing process has been initiated the parties to a real estate transaction are said to have "opened an escrow" or to have "gone into escrow." A transaction is said to be "in escrow" while the terms and conditions of a sales contract are being fulfilled by the parties. When all the terms and conditions of the agreement of sale have been fully performed, the escrow is said to have "closed," at which time the buyer becomes the owner of the property that was formerly owned by the seller. The "closing" results in a concurrent exchange of purchase money and documents which brings about the transfer of title.

Escrow Accounts Distinguished In the process of title closing, the parties to a sales transaction are required to pay to the person conducting the settlement whatever sums of money are needed to satisfy the parties' contractual obligations. Funds deposited or paid into escrow for purposes of closing a real estate transaction must be distinguished from payments made into an "escrow account."

Escrow accounts, which are also called "impound accounts," "trust accounts," and "reserves," are funds held by lenders which are derived from monthly payments made by borrowers to be accumulated for the payment of estimated annual property taxes, hazard insurance premiums, and other recurring charges. Monthly installments to be accumulated are, of course, in addition to a borrower's monthly payment for the retirement of his loan and interest charges.

---

[2] Title closing by escrow agents is predominant in Arizona, California, Idaho, Mississippi, Nevada, New Mexico, Oregon, Texas, and Washington. See *U.S. Department of Housing and Urban Development Report on Mortgage Settlement Costs*, pp. 74–75 (Jan. 1972).

[3] Closings are conducted by attorneys in most eastern and southern states. Id., pp. 59, 66–67.

[4] 12 U.S.C., secs. 2601–2617.

Payments that are made to an escrow account continue for the entire duration of a borrower's debt; withdrawals are made regularly to pay annual taxes and insurance premiums. On the other hand, payments made in escrow when title is being closed are paid but once, at the time of title closing, and are entirely disbursed upon close of escrow or settlement of a real estate sales transaction.

Why Escrows Are Used

The principal reason for utilizing a real estate escrow is the desire of the parties to a real estate transaction to have their conflicting interests handled in such a manner as to adequately protect them during the period between the date that the parties agree to transfer title to property and the date that title is actually transferred. While protecting the parties' mutual interests, the third-person depositary also performs important clerical and clearing-house functions by collecting, safeguarding, and distributing documents, reports, and funds.

Although a sale of real property can be completed by a seller and a buyer themselves, the nature of completing a real estate sales transaction is often such that the services of a professional are desirable. There are many risks incident to the closing of the transaction that the contracting parties clearly want to avoid. A buyer, for example, does not want to risk handing his money to the seller until he is satisfied that the title to the property is free and clear as agreed upon in the contract of sale. The seller, on the other hand, does not want to risk transferring title to the property until he has been paid. Furthermore, the seller may need the proceeds of the sale to pay off existing encumbrances against the property so as to be able to deliver a free and clear title to the buyer. And the buyer may need a free and clear title to the property to pledge as security for a loan which is to be used to make up part of the purchase price. In such circumstances, instead of the transaction being merely a two-party one between the seller and the buyer, it is a four-party arrangement involving the seller, the buyer, the seller's lender, and the buyer's lender.

Requirements for a Valid Escrow

For an escrow to be valid and capable of accomplishing the objectives of the parties, certain requirements must be met.

Contract of Purchase and Sale To be binding on the parties, a real estate sales escrow must be based on an enforceable contract of purchase and sale. An agreement for the purchase and sale of real estate will constitute an enforceable contract only if it satisfies all of the requirements discussed in Chapter 9. While in most instances a sales contract will have been concluded prior to the opening of escrow, it is possible for negotiating parties to enter simultaneously into a sales contract and to open an escrow simply by executing an escrow agreement.

Escrow Agreement An **escrow agreement** is a contract between the parties to a real estate sales transaction and a third person employed by them to conduct a settlement. The escrow agreement serves not only to open an escrow but also to hire the services of the escrow holder and to instruct him as to the manner in which he shall act in behalf of the parties to the transaction. An escrow agreement commonly takes the form of written **escrow instructions** which the parties give to the escrow holder. Where this is the case, the escrow holder must accept the parties' instructions and agree to their provisions before a valid escrow will be created. Generally speaking, the escrow holder's acceptance of the parties' instructions is a foregone conclusion since he commonly prepares the instructions himself for the signatures of the parties.

The function of the escrow instructions is to define the duties which the escrow holder is employed to perform in order that the transfer of an interest in real property may be completed.

Third Person as Escrow Holder It is essential to the validity of a real estate escrow that the escrow holder be a third person who is not a party to the transaction for which the escrow was created. In a valid escrow, the escrow holder or depositary is a mere stakeholder of the documents and moneys entrusted to him and has no legal interest in them. His sole function in a real estate sales transaction is to carry out the instructions of the seller and the buyer in exchange for a fee paid to him. Other than receiving compensation for the closing services he performs, an escrow holder is totally disinterested in the outcome of the escrow.

Who May Serve as Escrow Holder In the absence of statutory provisions to the contrary, any third person who is a stranger to the transaction he is employed to close may serve as an escrow holder. Some states require that individuals or firms engaging in the escrow business must be licensed and meet certain financial responsibilities.[5] Often exempted from such requirements, however, are the escrow departments of banks, trust companies, savings and loan associations, insurance companies, attorneys, and real estate brokers performing escrow functions which are incidental to their brokerage business.[6]

Conditional and Irrevocable Deposit It is essential to a valid escrow that the documents and moneys be *actually deposited* with an escrow holder and that the deposits be both *conditional* and *irrevocable*.

Nature of a Conditional Deposit In a real estate sales escrow, documents or moneys are *deposited* with the escrow holder by one party for *delivery* by the holder to the other party when conditions set forth in the escrow instructions have been satisfied. For example, S, a seller, may deposit an executed deed with E, an escrow holder, with express instructions that it is to be delivered to the buyer, B, when B has placed the agreed purchase price in the escrow holder's hands. In such a case, E's authorization to deliver S's deed to B and thus transfer title is conditioned upon B's depositing the purchase price with E. By making a conditional deposit of his deed to the property, seller S eliminates the risk of title passing to buyer B before the property has been paid for.

The effect of depositing an item in escrow subject to the performance of a condition is, of course, to postpone delivery of the deposited item until the designated condition has been met. The nature or terms of a condition to which an escrow deposit is subject can be altered or eliminated only if the parties to the transaction mutually agree to such change.

Delivery of a deposited item by the escrow holder *before* performance of the condition stated in the escrow instructions is ineffective to transfer title to the item.

Nature of Irrevocable Deposit For a valid escrow to be created, items that are deposited with an escrow holder must pass beyond the control of the parties who deposit them. An item cannot be "in escrow" if the escrow holder's possession of the item continues to be subject to the control of the person who has deposited it.

Once a valid deposit has been made, the depositor cannot revoke or withdraw his deposit unless the other party to the escrow defaults on his promise and fails to perform the conditions to which he agreed. Upon failure of performance of the condition upon which a deposit was made, the depositor is entitled to withdraw his deposit and the escrow terminates. For example, where seller S deposits his deed with escrow holder E for delivery to buyer B when B has deposited the agreed purchase price with E, and thereafter B advises S and E that he, B, is unable to raise the necessary funds, perfor-

---

[5] The California Financial Code, sec. 17200, for example, provides that no firm or individual may engage in the escrow business except as a corporation licensed by the corporations commissioner in accordance with provisions of the Financial Code.

[6] Id.

mance of the condition on which S deposited his deed fails, S becomes entitled to the return of his deed, and the escrow terminates without title passing from S to B.

Despite the fact that items deposited in escrow are no longer within the possession and control of the depositor and cannot be withdrawn from escrow, *title* to those items remains with the one who deposited them until the conditions set forth in the escrow agreement have been performed. Title to real estate as evidenced by a deed deposited in escrow by seller S, for example, remains with S until B, the buyer, has deposited the purchase money with the escrow holder. Conversely, title to moneys deposited by B remains with him until S has deposited his deed and such other documents as the escrow agreement calls for.

In the absence of a waiver, the performance of all conditions must occur within the time period specified in the escrow agreement if title is to pass. If the time period expires without all conditions having been met, and the buyer and seller do not agree to an extension of the period, the escrow "fails to close" and the parties are entitled to the return of their deposits.

Escrow Holder as Agent
An escrow holder becomes the agent of the parties to a real estate transaction when he accepts the instructions that the parties have signed. The escrow holder is considered to be the agent of both parties with respect to the handling of all instruments and moneys until the time that the conditions of the escrow are satisfied. When the escrow conditions have been performed, the dual agency ceases and the escrow holder becomes the agent of the buyer with respect to the deed and the agent of the seller with respect to the moneys in his possession. At that point, possession by the escrow holder of the things held by him in escrow is equivalent to possession by the party who is entitled to receive those things from him.

An escrow holder is a very limited or special type of agent whose authority to act is narrowly limited to the specific provisions contained in the instructions that he receives from the parties. By defining the escrow holder's duties, the instructions also serve to describe and limit the scope of his agency relationship with the parties to the escrow. An escrow holder is charged with strict compliance with the escrow instructions and may perform no acts with respect to the items deposited with him that are not authorized by the instructions. Like any other agent, an escrow holder is liable to the person for whom he acts for any damages that result from his exceeding the authority granted him, or for failure to do those things for which the agency was created.

Escrow Not Terminated by Death
The rule is well established that once an escrow agreement has been entered into and an escrow has been opened, neither the death of the seller nor that of the buyer before performance of the escrow conditions will in any way affect or terminate the escrow. Should death of one of the parties occur, the conditions to which the decedent was subject will be performed by his executor or administrator.

Similarly, the death of the escrow holder during the pendency of an escrow will not invalidate or terminate the escrow. The buyer and seller may substitute another escrow holder, who will be bound by the terms of the original escrow agreement.

Rights and Duties of Parties during Escrow
   Seller   In the absence of an agreement with the buyer to the contrary, the seller in escrow, like any owner of real property, is entitled to possession of the property until title passes. Being entitled to possession of the premises prior to the closing of title, the seller may either occupy the property himself or lease it to a tenant. As long as title continues to be held by the seller, he is entitled to all of the benefits the property produces.

As the holder of legal title to the property during the pendency of an escrow, a seller is subject to the burdens of ownership as well as being entitled to the benefits. He is, for example, liable for all taxes and assessments that are levied against the property prior to the close of escrow. Once the conditions of the escrow have been met, however, and the title passes to the buyer, the burden of paying taxes and assessments also passes to the buyer.

Buyer The buyer has no right to occupy property he has contracted to purchase until such time as he secures legal title to it. Of course, by agreement between the buyer and seller, the seller can be given the right to possession of the premises prior to the passage of title. In that event, the agreement should contain provisions with respect to whether taxes and other charges are to be paid by the buyer. Generally speaking, a seller is reluctant to give the buyer the right of possession before title passes because there is always the possibility that, for one reason or another, all of the conditions of the escrow will not be met before the agreed escrow period expires. In that case, of course, the sales transaction is not completed, no title passes, and the seller as owner of the property is entitled to possession—but he may have to sue to obtain it.

It is not uncommon, either in the sales contract or the escrow agreement, for the buyer to agree to permit the seller to continue in possession of the premises for a stated number of days *after* title has passed to the buyer. The purpose of such an agreement is to give the seller time to pack his effects and move them from the premises after all conditions of the escrow have been performed and title has passed to the buyer.

Escrow Holder As a limited agent of the buyer and the seller, an escrow holder is restricted to doing only those things that are necessary to carry out the escrow instructions he has received. Documents and funds that have been deposited with the escrow holder can be delivered by him only upon performance of the conditions of the escrow.

As an agent, the escrow holder's responsibilities to the buyer and the seller are *fiduciary* in character; for that reason he must deal with both of them in absolute good faith. The escrow holder is required to exercise reasonable skill, care, diligence, and objectivity in conducting the escrow. All funds entrusted to him must be deposited in a bank account that is separate and distinct from his own funds.

If the seller and buyer should disagree as to the interpretation of certain provisions of the escrow agreement and make conflicting demands with respect to the items deposited in escrow, the escrow holder is under no obligation to attempt to settle or resolve their dispute himself. If he acts in accordance with one party's interpretation, he does so at his peril and will be liable in damages if he delivers something to one who is not legally entitled to receive it. Instead of attempting to resolve the conflicting claims himself, the escrow holder may bring an **interpleader** action in court against the claimants, compelling them to litigate their claims and have the dispute resolved by the court.

When Title Passes

In the ordinary escrow, a deed deposited by the seller transfers title to the buyer *automatically* when the buyer deposits the purchase money with the escrow holder. This passage of title is effected by operation of law and requires no physical delivery of the deed or money by the escrow holder. In the eyes of the law the deed is considered to be *legally* delivered to the buyer when the conditions upon which the deed was deposited in escrow have been met, and at that point in time the title to the property is said to have "closed." Whether or not the required escrow conditions have been fully performed in a given case is a question of fact.

A buyer and a seller can, of course, specifically provide in an escrow agreement that the passage of title shall be conditioned upon *recordation* of the deed from the seller to the buyer after the purchase money has been paid into

TITLE CLOSING AND SETTLEMENT PROCEDURES

escrow. In that case, the transfer of title is delayed until the deed has in fact been recorded.

Risk of Loss Pending Close of Escrow The effect of the seller and the buyer retaining legal title to their respective deposits is that any loss or damage to them before the close of escrow is borne by the title holder. If the real estate is damaged or destroyed by fire or other casualty before the conditions of the escrow have been met, the loss falls upon the seller. Conversely, if the moneys deposited by the buyer are embezzled by the escrow holder before the buyer acquires title to the real estate, the loss falls on the buyer.

Operation of an Escrow

Although escrow procedures differ from one area of the country to another, the following examples will serve to illustrate the manner in which escrows operate in general. The mechanics of an escrow will vary depending upon whether the sale that is being settled is for cash or involves the loan of money.

Escrow Involving a Cash Sale The simplest illustration of an escrow is one involving the cash sale of a parcel of real estate which is not at the time of sale subject to the lien of a mortgage or deed of trust.

Let us assume that an owner who now resides in another state is renting his former home to a tenant. Through an exchange of correspondence, the owner agrees to sell the premises to the tenant for a certain cash sum. The seller and buyer also agree that the transaction will be completed or closed at a named bank in the city where the property is situated.

The seller then forwards his deed executed in favor of the buyer to the bank with instructions to deliver the deed to the buyer when the purchase price has been paid to the bank for the account of the seller. When the buyer pays the agreed purchase price to the bank, he thereby performs the condition to which the legal delivery of the deed is subject and title passes to the buyer.

Frequently this basic type of escrow will include particular conditions with respect to the status of title to the property being sold. For example, the buyer's instructions may provide that the purchase money is to be delivered to the seller by the bank only when an abstract of title furnished by the seller has been approved by the buyer's attorney.

In other instances, the buyer may authorize the bank to record the seller's deed to him at the time the purchase money is paid but before a title examination has been made by the buyer's attorney. In such a case, at the same time that he deposits the purchase money the buyer will also deposit a quitclaim deed executed by him in favor of the seller. After the deed from the seller to the buyer has been recorded, the title to the property is examined up to the date of recording and, if the title is approved, the bank will deliver the purchase money to the seller and return the unused quitclaim deed to the buyer for destruction. If, however, the title to the property is not approved by the buyer's attorney, the bank will record the buyer's quitclaim deed to offset the prior recorded deed of the seller and will return the purchase money to the buyer. In those circumstances, the escrow will not have closed and the sales transaction will not have been completed because the conditions of the escrow were not met.

Escrow Involving a Mortgage If in the foregoing illustration the seller's property had been subject to an existing mortgage that needed to be paid off in order to clear the title, the escrow instructions would normally authorize the bank to use part of the purchase price that the buyer paid in escrow to accomplish that purpose.

On the other hand, if the seller's title were clear but the buyer did not have sufficient cash to pay the full purchase price, the buyer would likely borrow funds and give a mortgage on the purchased property to the lender as security for the loan. In that event, the buyer would deposit a promissory note and a mortgage executed by him with instructions to the bank to deliver them to the lender upon receipt of the loan funds from the lender. Following receipt of the funds from the lender, the bank would deliver them to the seller when he had satisfied the escrow conditions to which he had agreed.

Escrow Involving an Installment Contract

When a buyer is unable to pay cash for the purchase of real estate, a seller will sometimes agree to sell his property under a credit arrangement in the form of an **installment contract.** Normally in such an arrangement the buyer is not entitled to a deed to the property until the purchase price has been paid in full at the end of an agreed period of years. To assure that legal title will be transferred to him when all installments have been paid, the buyer may require as a condition of the purchase that the seller deposit an executed deed with a bank or other third party to be held in escrow for delivery to the buyer when all installment payments have been made.

Escrow Practices

The role played by escrow holders in the preparation of documents necessary for title closing, including deeds and mortgages, differs from one part of the country to another. The preparation of such documents traditionally has been, and perhaps in most areas still is, the work of lawyers. In some areas, however, participation by lawyers in routine escrow transactions rarely if ever occurs. In California, for example, escrow holders prepare documents for buyers' and sellers' signatures that elsewhere are prepared only by lawyers. An agreement between the State Bar of California and the Escrow Institute of California permits holders to complete legal forms in general use that are necessary to consummate an escrow transaction without fear of prosecution for practicing law without a license.

REAL ESTATE SETTLEMENT PROCEDURES ACT

The federal Real Estate Settlement Procedures Act of 1974, as amended in 1975[7] (referred to by the acronym "RESPA"), seeks to regulate certain aspects of real estate transactions involving the purchase of homes by buyers who borrow part of the purchase price and mortgage their newly acquired homes as security for the borrowed funds. Before the buyer acquires title to his new home, the sales transaction, as we have seen, must be settled or closed. As the term is used in RESPA, a real estate "settlement" or "closing" is the process whereby the terms and conditions of a real estate sales contract are fulfilled, the buyer receives his loan funds and becomes obligated to repay them, and all charges incident to the transfer of title are paid by the parties to the real estate transaction. These charges are called "settlement costs" and constitute payment for settlement services that have been provided to the buyer and the seller.

The act provides that the term **settlement services** refers to any service that is provided in connection with a real estate settlement and includes, but is not limited to, the following: (1) title searches, (2) title examinations, (3) the providing of title certificates, (4) title insurance, (5) services rendered by an attorney, (6) the preparation of documents, (7) property surveys, (8) the rendering of credit reports, (9) appraisals, (10) pest and fungus inspections, (11) services rendered by a real estate agent or broker, and (12) the handling of the processing and closing of a sales transaction.[8]

Necessity for the Act

Passage of RESPA resulted from findings by Congress that "significant reforms in the real estate settlement process are needed to insure that consumers throughout the Nation are provided with greater and more timely information on the nature and costs of the settlement process and are protected from unnecessarily high settlement charges caused by certain abusive

---

[7] 12 U.S.C., secs. 2601–2617, P.L.93-533 as amended by P.L.94-205.
[8] 12 U.S.C., sec. 2602(3).

TITLE CLOSING AND SETTLEMENT PROCEDURES

practices that have developed in some areas of the country."[9]

These findings were the result of hearings held by the Banking, Housing and Urban Affairs Committee of the Senate, which ascertained that there were "three major problem areas that must be dealt with if settlement costs are to be kept within reasonable bounds":

    1 Abusive and unreasonable practices within the real estate settlement process that increase settlement costs to homebuyers without providing any real benefits to them;

    2 The lack of understanding on the part of most home buyers about the settlement process and its costs, which lack of understanding makes it difficult for a free market for settlement services to function at maximum efficiency; and

    3 The basic complexities and inefficiencies in the present system for the recording of land titles on the public records, which has been identified as the single most important barrier to reduce significantly the present level of settlement costs.[10]

Purpose of the Act

The stated purpose of the act is "to effect certain changes in the settlement process for residential real estate that will result":

    1 in more effective advance disclosure to home buyers and sellers of settlement costs;

    2 in the elimination of kickbacks or referral fees that tend to increase unnecessarily the costs of certain settlement services;

    3 in a reduction in the amounts home buyers are required to place in escrow accounts to insure the payment of taxes and insurance; and

    4 in significant reform and modernization of local record-keeping and land title information.[11]

Commenting on the 1975 amendments to the act, the House Banking, Currency and Housing Committee said that "The objective of this legislation is to amend the Real Estate Settlement Procedures Act of 1974, to repeal or amend those provisions of that Act which have been found unworkable or defective."[12]

When enacting the Real Estate Settlement Procedures Act last year, your committee was attempting to provide the prospective homebuyer with adequate protection against unscrupulous practices that were causing homebuyers to pay unconscionable fees in closing costs, and to provide homebuyers with adequate advance disclosure of what the costs of settlement would be.

Real estate settlement procedures are different in each of the 50 states and each state differs extensively within the numerous governmental subdivisions. The attempt to legislate nationally with the Real Estate Settlement Procedures Act on problems that had risen with regard to real estate practices in a number of jurisdictions has proved in many areas of the country to be unworkable, overly rigid in a number of other areas, and too inflexible to be administered adequately in those jurisdictions where real estate settlement practices needed the attention of Federal regulations. Your committee still believes that Federal attention should remain directed at real estate settlement practices around the country but not within the framework of the 1974 Act.[13]

Implementation of the Act

The Secretary of the Department of Housing and Urban Development (HUD) is charged with the responsibility of implementing the provisions of RESPA. In carrying out this responsibility, the Secretary "is authorized to prescribe such rules and regulations, to make such interpretations, and to grant reasonable exemptions for classes of transactions, as may be necessary to achieve the purposes of this Act."[14] The rules and regulations which the Secretary of HUD has issued[15] pursuant to the directives of the act are collectively referred to as **Regulation X**.

---

[9] 12 U.S.C., sec. 2601(a).
[10] Senate Report (Banking, Housing and Urban Affairs Committee) No. 93-866, Legislative History P.L.93-533, 3 U.S. Code Congressional and Administrative News, 93rd Cong., 2nd Sess., 1974, p. 6547.
[11] 12 U.S.C., sec. 2601(b).

[12] House Report (Banking, Currency and Housing Committee) No. 94-667, Legislative History P.L.94-205, 2 U.S. Code Congressional and Administrative News, 94th Cong., 1st Sess., 1975, p. 2455.
[13] Id., pp. 2448–49.
[14] 12 U.S.C., sec. 2617(a).
[15] See 24 C.F.R., secs. 3500.1–3500.14.

Scope of the Act

Restricted to Residential Property The provisions of RESPA apply only to *residential real property*, which is defined to mean dwellings for occupancy by one to four families. Included within the meaning of residential properties are individual units in condominiums and cooperatives as well as mobile homes.[16]

Restricted to Purchase Money First Liens The act is limited to real estate transactions in which a borrower obtains a loan and uses the borrowed money in whole or in part to finance the purchase of residential property and secures the loan by a *first lien or mortgage* on the purchased property.[17]

Exempt Transactions Specifically exempted from the provisions of RESPA are the following:[18]

1 A loan to finance the purchase of a parcel of property comprising 25 acres or more.

2 A home improvement loan, refinancing loan, or other loan where the proceeds are not used to acquire title to real property.

3 A loan to finance the purchase of a vacant lot when none of the proceeds will be used to build a one- to four-family residential structure or to purchase a mobile home to be placed on the lot.

4 An assumption, novation, or sale subject to a preexisting loan.

5 A construction loan, except where the construction loan is converted to a permanent loan to finance a purchase by a first user.

6 A permanent loan, the proceeds of which will be used to finance the construction of a one- to four-family structure, where the lot is already owned by the borrower.

7 A loan to finance the purchase of a property where the primary purpose of the purchase is for resale.

8 Execution of a land sales contract where legal title is not transferred to the purchaser at the time of execution.

[16] 12 U.S.C., sec. 2602(1); HUD Regulation X, sec. 3500.5(2)(i–v).
[17] HUD Regulation X, sec. 3500.5(b)(1)(2).
[18] Id., sec. 3500.5(d)(1)–(8).

Lenders Covered by the Act A lender who makes a first mortgage loan secured by residential property as described above is subject to the provisions of the act if

1 the lender's deposits or accounts are insured by the Federal Savings and Loan Insurance Corporation (FSLIC), the Federal Deposit Insurance Corporation (FDIC), or any other agency of the federal government;

2 the lender is regulated by the Federal Home Loan Bank Board or any other agency of the federal government;

3 the loan is made in whole or in part, or is insured, guaranteed, supplemented, or assisted in any way, by the Secretary of HUD or any other officer or agency of the federal government;

4 the loan is made in connection with a housing or urban development program administered by the Secretary of HUD or other agency of the federal government; or

5 the loan is intended to be sold by the originating lender to the Federal National Mortgage Association (FNMA), the Government National Mortgage Association (GNMA), the Federal Home Loan Mortgage Association (FHLMA), or to a financial institution which intends to sell to FHLMA.

A first mortgage loan on residential property by a lender that is covered by RESPA is designated in the act as a "federally related mortgage loan."[19]

Solving the Problem of Settlement Costs

The Senate Banking, Housing and Urban Affairs Committee observed that "there are two basic approaches that can be taken in solving the problems of costs."[20] One approach, the committee noted, was to regulate closing costs directly by establishing maximum charges that may be made for real estate settlement services.

[19] 12 U.S.C., sec. 2602(1).
[20] Senate Report (Banking, Housing and Urban Affairs Committee) No. 93-866, Legislative History P.L.93-533, 3 U.S. Code Congressional and Administrative News, 93rd Cong., 2nd Sess., 1974, p. 6548.

The other approach would "regulate the underlying business relationships and procedures of which the costs are a function."[21]

The committee was of the opinion that "Federal rate regulation is not the preferred solution at this time"[22] and the latter approach to settlement problems was adopted by RESPA.

According to the committee, RESPA would correct the major problem areas indicated earlier in the chapter in three basic ways.

First, by prohibiting or regulating abusive practices, such as kickbacks, unearned fees, and unreasonable escrow account requirements, RESPA seeks to "ensure that the costs to the American homebuying public will not be unreasonably or unnecessarily inflated by abusive practices."[23]

Second, by requiring that homebuyers be provided "both with greater information on the nature of the settlement process and with an itemized statement of all settlement charges well in advance of settlement," the committee "expected that many unnecessary or unreasonably high settlement charges will be reduced or eliminated." The committee noted that "Home buyers who would otherwise shop around for settlement services, and thereby reduce their total settlement costs, are presently prevented from doing so because frequently they are not apprised of the costs of these services until the settlement date or are not aware of the nature of settlement services that will be provided."[24]

Third, by taking steps toward the simplification of the land recordation process that are calculated to facilitate and simplify land transfers and mortgage transactions, the committee hoped "to reduce the time and effort presently involved in the searching of real estate titles." The committee observed that a substantial portion of the fees charged for title examination and related services "can be eliminated if the work that must be done under the present chaotic recording systems can be significantly reduced by the institution of modern computerized recordation systems."[25]

Kickbacks and Unearned Fees Prohibited

The report of the Senate committee points out that "In a number of areas of the country, competitive forces in the conveyancing industry have led to the payment of referral fees, kickbacks, rebates and unearned commissions as inducements to those who are in a position to refer settlement business."[26] Such payments, the committee noted, may take various forms.

For example, a title insurance company may give 10 percent or more of a title insurance premium to an attorney who performs no services for the title insurance company other than placing a telephone call to the company or filling out a simple application form. A discount or allowance for the prompt payment of a title insurance premium or other charge for a settlement service may be given to real estate agents or lenders as a rebate for the placement of business with the individual company giving the discount. Another example pointed out by the committee involves an attorney who gives a portion of his fee to another attorney, lender, or real estate agent who simply refers a prospective client to him. And, in some instances, a "commission" may be paid by a title insurance company to a corporation that is wholly owned by one or more savings and loan associations, even though that corporation performs no substantial services in behalf of the title insurance company. "In all these circumstances, the payment or thing of value furnished by the person to whom the settlement business is referred tends to increase the cost of settlement without providing any benefits to the homebuyer."[27]

RESPA prohibits all kickbacks and fee arrangements whereby a payment is made simply for the referral of real estate settlement business. The act also prohibits any person or com-

[21] Id.
[22] Id., p. 6549.
[23] Id., p. 6548.
[24] Id.

[25] Id., pp. 6548–49.
[26] Id., p. 6551.
[27] Id.

pany that renders a settlement service from giving or rebating any portion of a settlement charge except in return for services actually performed.[28]

Cooperative Brokerage Arrangements Exempted Because the language of the original act was obscure on the subject, the 1975 amendment "makes it clear that cooperative brokerage and referral agreements between real estate agents and brokers relating to real estate commissions are not considered kickbacks."[29]

Penalty for Violation Violations of the prohibition against kickbacks and unearned fees are subject to both criminal and civil penalties.

The criminal penalty for violation of the provisions is a fine of not more than $10,000 or imprisonment for not more than one year, or both.

In addition, a violator is liable to the person whose business has been referred for an amount three times the prohibited payment, kickback, or referral fee, plus reasonable attorney fees.[30]

Escrow Accounts Regulated

We have seen that lenders frequently require borrowers to maintain escrow or impound accounts with them so that funds may be accumulated for the payment of property taxes and hazard insurance premiums when they fall due. The funds accumulate by reason of monthly payments made by borrowers, which include payment of approximately one-twelfth of the estimated annual property taxes and insurance premiums together with a payment on the principal amount of the mortgage debt and interest charges.

Size of Escrow Account Limited RESPA limits the size of escrow or impound accounts that a lender may require a borrower to maintain. The act provides[31] that the maximum amount lenders can require borrowers to maintain in an escrow account at any time is the accumulation of the monthly payments to date plus an additional amount not to exceed one-sixth of the estimated annual charges. The inclusion of the additional sum equal to two months' payments was deemed to be "necessary since monthly mortgage payments are often due before a tax payment should be made, and such mortgage payments are often made late."[32]

The following example illustrates the manner in which the maximum amount of an escrow account is calculated. Assume that the annual property taxes on borrower B's property are $720 ($60 per month) and his annual hazard insurance premium is $120 ($10 a month). In addition to making payments on his debt and interest charges, B's monthly payment to his lender, L, would include one-twelfth of his annual $840 ($720 + $120) taxes and insurance premiums, or $70 per month. If annual payments of both property taxes and hazard insurance fall due on January 1 each year, the maximum amount that L could require B to have in his escrow account on July 1 would be $560, which represents six months' (January through June) accumulation of $70 per month ($420) plus a permissible "cushion" equal to two monthly payments of $140 ($70 × 2).

Special Information Booklet

Prepared by HUD The Real Estate Settlement Procedures Act requires the Secretary of HUD to prepare and distribute to all lenders that make federally related mortgage loans a special information booklet "to help persons borrowing money to finance the purchase of residential real estate to better understand the nature and costs of real estate settlement services."[33] In accordance with this directive, the

---

[28] 12 U.S.C., sec. 2607(a) and (b).
[29] House Report (Banking, Currency and Housing Committee) No. 94-667, Legislative History P.L.94-205, 2 U.S. Code Congressional and Administrative News, 94th Cong., 1st Sess., 1975, p. 2448; 12 U.S.C., sec. 2607(a)(3).
[30] 12 U.S.C., sec. 2607(d).
[31] 12 U.S.C., sec. 2609.
[32] House Report (Banking, Currency and Housing Committee) No. 94-667, Legislative History P.L.94-667; 2 U.S. Code Congressional and Administrative News, 94th Cong., 1st Sess., 1975, p. 2448.
[33] 12 U.S.C., sec. 2604(a).

Secretary of HUD has prepared and distributed to lenders a booklet bearing the title *Settlement Costs—A HUD Guide*.[34]

Distributed by Lenders Lenders are required to give a copy of the special information booklet to every person from whom they receive or for whom they prepare a written application to borrow money to finance the purchase of residential real estate. A copy of the booklet is to be given or mailed to a prospective borrower not later than three days after receipt or preparation of a written loan application.[35]

Lenders are permitted to print or reproduce the special information booklet with their names, addresses, pictures, and artwork on the cover provided no changes, deletions, or additons are made to the text as prescribed by HUD. No discussion of matters contained in the booklet may appear on the cover.[36]

Contents of the Booklet The special information booklet as prepared and prescribed by HUD is in two parts.

Part I describes the nature of the settlement process and the nature of settlement charges. It suggests questions that a prospective borrower might ask of lenders, attorneys, and others to make clear what services will be provided for the charges they quote. It also sets forth information relative to the rights and remedies available to prospective borrowers under RESPA and alerts them to unfair and illegal practices.[37]

Under the heading "Negotiating a Sales Contract"[38] the booklet sets forth some valuable suggestions for prospective buyers. Unfortunately for a large number of buyers, however, the suggestions come too late, because a buyer commonly will have signed a sales contract with the seller before he applies for a loan and receives the booklet from a lender.

Part II of the special information booklet contains an item by item explanation of settlement services and costs with sample forms and worksheets designed to assist a prospective borrower in making cost comparisons.[39]

A Settlement Costs Worksheet as set forth in the special information booklet[40] for use by a prospective borrower when shopping for a loan and settlement services appears at Figure 13-1.

Good-Faith Estimates of Settlement Charges

Along with a copy of the special information booklet, lenders are required to furnish a prospective borrower a good-faith estimate of each charge for a settlement service which the borrower is likely to incur.[41] Like the special information booklet, the good-faith estimate of settlement service charges must be given or mailed to a prospective borrower not later than three days after receipt or preparation of a written loan application by a lender.[42]

A lender is required to give a loan applicant a good-faith estimate of each settlement charge that the applicant is likely to incur, except the items at line 903 and lines 1001 through 1008 appearing in Schedule L of the form entitled "Settlement Statement" (Figure 13-2).[43] The estimate may be stated either as a dollar amount or as a range and is based upon the lender's experience with real estate settlements in the particular locality where the property to be purchased is located. Lenders are not required to give good-faith estimates for reserves deposited with them (line items 1001-1008) or the prepaid hazard insurance premium (line item 903) because these charges require information that normally is not known to the lender at the time of the loan application.

The special information booklet contains the following comments with respect to estimated settlement costs:

---

[34] The booklet as presently prescribed by HUD appears in the *Federal Register*, Vol. 41, No. 113, June 10, 1976, at pages 23621–23661.
[35] HUD Regulation X, sec. 3500.6(a).
[36] Id., sec. 3500.6(b) and (c).
[37] 41 *Federal Register*, p. 23623.
[38] Id., p. 23625.
[39] Id., p. 23623.
[40] Id., p. 23640.
[41] 12 U.S.C., sec. 2604(c).
[42] HUD Regulation X, sec. 3500.7(a).
[43] Id., sec. 3500.7(c).

CHAPTER 13

SETTLEMENT COSTS WORK SHEET *(Use this worksheet to compare the charges of various lenders and providers of settlement services.)*	PROVIDER 1	PROVIDER 2	PROVIDER 3
800. ITEMS PAYABLE IN CONNECTION WITH LOAN:			
801. Loan Origination Free %			
802. Loan Discount %			
803. Appraisal Fee to			
804. Credit Report to			
805. Lender's Inspection Fee			
806. Mortgage Insurance Application Fee to			
807. Assumption Fee			
808.			
809.			
810.			
811.			
900. ITEMS REQUIRED BY LENDER TO BE PAID IN ADVANCE:			
901. Interest from to @ $ per day			
902. Mortgage Insurance Premium for months to			
903. Hazard Insurance Premium for years to			
904. years to			
905.			
1000. RESERVES DEPOSITED WITH LENDER:			
1001. Hazard Insurance months @ $ per month			
1002. Mortgage Insurance months @ $ per month			
1003. City property taxes months @ $ per month			
1004. County property taxes months @ $ per month			
1005. Annual assessments months @ $ per month			
1006. months @ $ per month			
1007. months @ $ per month			
1008. months @ $ per month			
1100. TITLE CHARGES:			
1101. Settlement or closing fee to			
1102. Abstract or title search to			
1103. Title examination to			
1104. Title insurance binder to			
1105. Document preparation to			
1106. Notary fees to			
1107. Attorney's fees to			
(includes above items numbers:)			
1108. Title insurance to			
(includes above items numbers:)			
1109. Lender's coverage $			
1110. Owner's coverage $			
1111.			
1112.			
1113.			
1200. GOVERNMENT RECORDING AND TRANSFER CHARGES:			
1201. Recording fees: Deed $: Mortgage $: Releases $			
1202. City/country tax/stamps Deed $: Mortgage $			
1203. State tax/stamps: Deed $: Mortgage $			
1204.			
1205.			
1300. ADDITIONAL SETTLEMENT CHARGES:			
1301. Survey to			
1302. Pest Inspection to			
1303.			
1304.			
1305.			
1400. TOTAL SETTLEMENT CHARGES			

Figure 13-1 *Source:* HUD booklet, "Settlement Costs— A HUD Guide," 41 Fed. Reg. 23640.

TITLE CLOSING AND SETTLEMENT PROCEDURES

A.	B. TYPE OF LOAN	
U.S. DEPARTMENT OF HOUSING AND URBAN DEVELOPMENT **SETTLEMENT STATEMENT**	1. ☐ FHA 2. ☐ FmHA 3. ☐ CONV. UNINS. 4. ☐ VA 5. ☐ CONV. INS.	
	6. File Number:	7. Loan Number:
	8. Mortgage Insurance Case Number:	

C. NOTE: *This form is furnished to give you a statement of actual settlement costs. Amounts paid to and by the settlement agent are shown. Items marked "(p.o.c.)" were paid outside the closing; they are shown here for informational purposes and are not included in the totals.*

D. NAME OF BORROWER:	E. NAME OF SELLER:	F. NAME OF LENDER:

G. PROPERTY LOCATION:	H. SETTLEMENT AGENT:	I. SETTLEMENT DATE:
	PLACE OF SETTLEMENT:	

J. SUMMARY OF BORROWER'S TRANSACTION		K. SUMMARY OF SELLER'S TRANSACTION	
100. GROSS AMOUNT DUE FROM BORROWER:		**400. GROSS AMOUNT DUE TO SELLER:**	
101. Contract sales price		401. Contract sales price	
102. Personal property		402. Personal property	
103. Settlement charges to borrower *(line 1400)*		403.	
104.		404.	
105.		405.	
Adjustments for items paid by seller in advance		*Adjustments for items paid by seller in advance*	
106. City/town taxes to		406. City/town taxes to	
107. County taxes to		407. County taxes to	
108. Assessments to		408. Assessments to	
109.		409.	
110.		410.	
111.		411.	
112.		412.	
120. GROSS AMOUNT DUE FROM BORROWER		**420. GROSS AMOUNT DUE TO SELLER**	
200. AMOUNTS PAID BY OR IN BEHALF OF BORROWER:		**500. REDUCTIONS IN AMOUNT DUE TO SELLER:**	
201. Deposit or earnest money		501. Excess deposit *(see instructions)*	
202. Principal amount of new loan(s)		502. Settlement charges to seller *(lines 1400)*	
203. Existing loan(s) taken subject to		503. Existing loan(s) taken subject to	
204.		504. Payoff of first mortgage loan	
205.		505. Payoff of second mortgage loan	
206.		506.	
207.		507.	
208.		508.	
209.		509.	
Adjustments for items unpaid by seller		*Adjustments for items unpaid by seller*	
210. City/town taxes to		510. City/town taxes to	
211. County taxes to		511. County taxes to	
212. Assessments to		512. Assessments to	
213.		513.	
214.		514.	
215.		515.	
216.		516.	
217.		517.	
218.		518.	
219.		519.	
220. TOTAL PAID BY/FOR BORROWER		**520. TOTAL REDUCTION AMOUNT DUE SELLER**	
300. CASH AT SETTLEMENT FROM/TO BORROWER		**600. CASH AT SETTLEMENT TO/FROM SELLER**	
301. Gross amount due from borrower *(line 120)*		601. Gross amount due to seller *(line 420)*	
302. Less amounts paid by/for borrower *(line 220)*	( )	602. Less reductions in amts. due seller *(line 520)*	( )
303. CASH (☐ FROM (☐ TO) BORROWER		603. CASH (☐ TO) (☐ FROM) SELLER	

–2–

L. SETTLEMENT CHARGES			
700. TOTAL SALES/BROKER'S COMMISION based on price $ @ % = Division of Commission (line 700) as follows:		PAID FROM BORROWER'S FUNDS AT SETTLEMENT	PAID FROM SELLER'S FUNDS AT SETTLEMENT
701. $	to		
702. $	to		
703. Commission paid at Settlement			
704.			
800. ITEMS PAYABLE IN CONNECTION WITH LOAN			
801. Loan Origination Fee	%		
802. Loan Discount	%		
803. Appraisal Fee	to		
804. Credit Report	to		
805. Lender's Inspection Fee			
806. Mortgage Insurance Application Fee to			
807. Assumption Fee			
808.			
809.			
810.			
811.			
900. ITEMS REQUIRED BY LENDER TO BE PAID IN ADVANCE			
901. Interest from to @ $ /day			
902. Mortgage Insurance Premium for months to			
903. Hazard Insurance Premium for years to			
904. years to			
905.			
1000. RESERVES DEPOSITED WITH LENDER			
1001. Hazard insurance	months @ $	per month	
1002. Mortgage insurance	months @ $	per month	
1003. City property taxes	months @ $	per month	
1004. County property taxes	months @ $	per month	
1005. Annual assessments	months @ $	per month	
1006.	months @ $	per month	
1007.	months @ $	per month	
1008.	months @ $	per month	
1100. TITLE CHARGES			
1101. Settlement or closing fee	to		
1102. Abstract or title search	to		
1103. Title examination	to		
1104. Title insurance binder	to		
1105. Document preparation	to		
1106. Notary fees	to		
1107. Attorney's fees	to		
(includes above items numbers:)			
1108. Title insurance	to		
(includes above items numbers:)			
1109. Lender's coverage	$		
1110. Owner's coverage	$		
1111.			
1112.			
1113.			
1200. GOVERNMENT RECORDING AND TRANSFER CHARGES			
1201. Recording fees: Deed $: Mortgage $: Releases $			
1202. City/county tax/stamps: Deed $: Mortgage $			
1203. State tax/stamps: Deed $: Mortgage $			
1204.			
1205.			
1300. ADDITIONAL SETTLEMENT CHARGES			
1301. Survey to			
1302. Pest inspection to			
1303.			
1304.			
1305.			
1400. TOTAL SETTLEMENT CHARGES (enter on lines 103, Section J and 502, Section K)			

Figure 13-2 *Source:* HUD booklet, "Settlement Costs— A HUD Guide," 41 Fed. Reg. 23638-39.

Once you have obtained these estimates from the lender be aware that they are only estimates. The final costs may not be the same. Estimates are subject to changing market conditions, and fees may change. Changes in the date of settlement may result in changes in escrow and proration requirements. In certain cases, it may not be possible for the lender to anticipate exactly the pricing policies of settlement firms. Moreover, your own careful choice of settlement firms might result in lower costs, just as hasty decisions might result in higher costs. Remember that the lender's estimate is not a guarantee.[44]

Uniform Settlement Statement

In accordance with the provisions of RESPA,[45] the Secretary of HUD has developed and prescribed a standard "Settlement Statement" form which, with such variations as may be necessary to reflect differences in legal and administrative practices in different areas of the country, must be used in all transactions involving federally related mortgage loans. This standard form for the statement of real estate settlement costs is referred to as "HUD-1" (Figure 13-2).

The uniform Settlement Statement must be completed to itemize all charges paid by the buyer-borrower and the seller in connection with the settlement, except for those charges which were not required by the lender and which the buyer-borrower or seller contracted to pay for separately outside of the settlement.[46]

Who Prepares the Statement The uniform Settlement Statement must be completed by every person who performs real estate settlement activities in federally related mortgage loan transactions whether that person is the lender or not. In addition to giving copies of the uniform Settlement Statement to both the buyer-borrower and the seller, if the person conducting the settlement is not the lender he must give a copy of both the buyer-borrower's statement and the seller's statement to the lender, who must retain such copies for a period of two years.[47]

Advance Inspection of Statement If the borrower so requests, the person conducting the settlement must permit him to inspect the completed uniform Settlement Statement during the business day preceding the date on which the settlement is to occur. However, if the settlement is the type at which neither the borrower nor his agent is present, or if the person conducting the settlement does not require a meeting of the parties at the time of settlement, the borrower has no right to inspect the statement in advance of settlement.[48]

Delivery of Statement The completed uniform Settlement Statement must be delivered or mailed to both the buyer-borrower and the seller or their agents at or before the time of settlement. The borrower may, however, waive the right to have delivery of the statement at or before the time of delivery by executing a written waiver. In that event, the completed statement must be mailed or delivered to the buyer-borrower and the seller as soon as practicable after settlement.[49]

Delivery of the statement at or before the time of settlement is also excused if neither the buyer-borrower nor his agent attends the settlement, or if the person conducting the settlement does not require a meeting of the parties at the settlement. Where delivery at or before settlement is excused, the completed uniform Settlement Statement must be mailed or delivered to the buyer-borrower and seller or their agents as soon as practicable after the settlement has taken place.[50]

When Statement Is Not Required There are two situations in which the uniform Settlement Statement need not be completed and delivered

---

[44] 41 *Federal Register,* p. 23632.
[45] 12 U.S.C., sec. 2603(a).
[46] HUD Regulation X, sec. 3500.8(b).
[47] Id., sec. 3500.8(a)(b)(c).
[48] Id., sec. 3500.10(a) and (d).
[49] Id., sec. 3500.10(b) and (c).
[50] Id., sec. 3500.10(d).

by the person who conducts a settlement. One situation involves transactions in which the borrower is not required to pay any settlement charges or adjustments. The other involves transactions in which the total amount the borrower is required to pay at settlement is a fixed amount for all charges, and the borrower is informed of that amount at the time he makes his loan application.[51]

Land Parcel Recordation System

It will be recalled that one of the three real estate settlement problem areas that the Senate Banking, Housing and Urban Affairs Committee felt must be dealt with resulted from "The basic complexities and inefficiencies in the present system for the recording of land titles on the public records, which has been identified as the single most important barrier to reduce significantly the present level of settlement costs."[52] The committee was of the opinion that a substantial portion of the fees charged for title examination and related services "can be eliminated if the work that must be done under the present chaotic recording systems can be significantly reduced by the institution of modern computerized systems."[53]

In furtherance of the objective of simplifying the recording of land titles, RESPA requires[54] that the Secretary of HUD establish in representative political subdivisions in various areas of the country on a demonstration basis a model system for the recordation of land title information. The model system must be designed to facilitate and simplify land transfers and mortgage transactions and to reduce the cost of them. It is anticipated that experience gained from model systems might lead to the development of a nationally uniform system of land parcel recordation.

The Senate Committee hazarded the guess that "in the long run" this aspect of RESPA "may be the single most important feature of the legislation from the standpoint of making significant reductions in the present level of settlement charges."[55]

QUESTIONS

1 Explain what happens in the title-closing or settlement process.
2 Why are escrows commonly used by parties to real estate sales transactions?
3 What is an escrow agreement? What form does such an agreement commonly take?
4 With respect to real estate sales escrows, what is the nature of an irrevocable deposit?
5 Discuss the nature of the agency relationship between an escrow holder and the parties to a real estate sales escrow.
6 What are the rights and duties of a seller and a buyer prior to the closing of a real estate sales escrow to which they are parties? How are the risks of loss during escrow borne?
7 Why did Congress consider it necessary to enact the Real Estate Settlement Procedures Act?
8 As the term is used in the Real Estate Settlement Procedures Act, what do "settlement services" include?
9 Describe the manner in which the Real Estate Settlement Procedures Act regulates escrow accounts.
10 Describe the contents of the two parts of the booklet entitled *Settlement Costs—A HUD Guide*.

---

[51] Id., sec. 3500.8(d).
[52] Senate Report (Banking, Housing and Urban Affairs Committee) No. 93-866, Legislative History P.L.93-533, 3 U.S. Code Congressional and Administrative News, 93rd Cong., 2nd Sess., 1974, p. 6547.
[53] Id., pp. 6548–49.
[54] 12 U.S.C., sec. 2611.

[55] Senate Report (Banking, Housing and Urban Affairs Committee) No. 93-866, Legislative History P.L.93-533, 3 U.S. Code Congressional and Administrative News, 93rd Cong., 2nd Sess., 1974, p. 6549.

Chapter 14

Recording and Other Methods of Title Protection

When a buyer purchases a parcel of real estate, he is concerned with more than merely receiving a properly executed deed from the seller. Before parting with his purchase money, the buyer will want to be assured that the seller actually has title to the property described in the deed and that the title is in the condition agreed upon by the parties in their contract of purchase and sale. The protection or assurance that the buyer seeks may take any of several different forms, all of which are derived from information obtainable from a search (**title search**) of public records and an inspection of the premises described in the sales contract. Although the buyer may search and examine the records and inspect the premises himself, it is more likely that he will use the services of someone who is skilled in performing those tasks.

Depending on the customs and practices in the locality in which a real estate transaction takes place, evidence reflecting the condition of title to real property may take the form of either (1) an abstract of title as shown by the public records, (2) an abstract of title together with an attorney's opinion as to the condition of the title, (3) a Torrens registration certificate, or (4) a policy of title insurance.

THE RECORDING SYSTEM

Nature of Recording

Recording is the process by which documents relating to the transfer of interests in real property are reproduced in official records that are freely available to any member of the public who may wish to consult them. The recording of a document places on file in a public place written evidence of the transfer of an interest in an identified parcel of real estate. The official who maintains the public records is variously known as the county recorder, the recorder of deeds, the registrar of deeds, or some similar designation, depending upon the area of the country. Before a recorder or registrar will accept a document for copying in the public records, certain statutory requirements must be satisfied.

Recording Not Essential for a Valid Transfer In our discussion of deeds we saw that the *recording* of a deed is *not* an essential requirement for the deed to be effective to transfer title from a grantor to a grantee. The same is true when a real estate security interest is transferred from a debtor to a creditor. Between the immediate parties to a real estate transaction, whether written evidence of that transaction is recorded or not has no bearing on the validity or invalidity of the transfer of an interest in real property. For example, if owner O properly executes and delivers to B a deed to Blackacre which B neglects to record, O cannot legally claim that title to Blackacre remains with him until the evidence of the transfer of title is made a matter of public record. When O *legally delivered* his deed to B, O divested himself of title to Blackacre and vested that title in B. B's subsequent failure to record his evidence of ownership does not operate to restore that ownership to O. As between O and B, who are the immediate parties to the transaction, recording of the deed is not necessary to effect a valid transfer of title.

Just as a valid deed is not rendered invalid by a failure to record it, a deed that for some reason is void will not be validated by the act of recording it. We know, for example, that a forged deed is totally void and ineffective to transfer title. Despite its legal invalidity, it is quite possible for such a deed to be accepted by a recorder and reproduced by him in the public records. The mere fact that the deed has become a part of the public records does not make it a valid document.

When Recording Is Significant The recording or lack of recording of a real estate document becomes a matter of significance when the interests or claims of persons other than those whose names appear in a real estate document are concerned. This situation is due to the fact that an owner of real property has the power or ability, but not the legal right, to transfer an identical interest in the same parcel of land to two or more persons. For example, a deed which is clearly effective to *transfer* title from owner O to buyer B may prove to be ineffective to *preserve* B's title against the claim of C who received a later deed to the same property from O, unless B recorded his deed before O made the second transfer.

An important function of a state's recording laws is to define the respective rights of parties when an owner has wrongfully exercised his power to convey the same interest in real property to more than one person.

Recording Laws

Objective of Recording Laws Because recording laws are fundamental to the protection of titles to real estate, all states have enacted them. Although they differ to some extent in phraseology and detail, the statutes of the various states are basically very similar. Underlying the recording laws is the policy that public records should disclose all matters affecting title to real estate, and that every property owner should have the right to have his evidence of ownership appear in those records. Even the very earliest recording acts reflect a desire on the part of enacting bodies to establish a permanent record of transactions that have a bearing on the condition of title to real estate.

Parties Protected by Recording Laws Recording systems of the various states are designed to protect both those persons who have already acquired an interest in a parcel of real estate and those who are in the process of doing so.

A person who has just acquired an interest in real property can preserve and protect that interest by recording the document by which the interest was acquired. Where buyer B, for example, acquires title to Blackacre by owner O's legal delivery of a deed to him, B's timely recording of that document will preserve to him the title that he acquired. We have seen, however, that if B fails promptly to record his deed, O could wrongfully exercise his power to transfer the same title to buyer C, who was ignorant of the prior sale, and thereby expose B to the risk of losing his unrecorded title to C.

A person contemplating the acquisition of an interest in real property must assure himself that the party who purports to have title to the property in question actually has it. The recording laws enable such a prospective purchaser or creditor to obtain this assurance by checking the public records to determine the condition of title to the property before concluding any transaction relating to it. In the foregoing example, when C, prior to purchase, checked the public records they showed that O was the owner of the property and, under the recording laws, C was justified in relying on that record. Although B had previously acquired title to the property by his deed from O, B failed to protect his title by recording his deed so that C might find it.

Recording laws normally extend their protection to both purchasers and creditors. Included in the term "purchaser" is any person whose interest in real property is acquired in exchange for a consideration. Although consideration may consist of anything of value, such as an exchange of property or the performance of services, consideration commonly takes the form of the payment of money or a promise to do so. The requirement of consideration under the recording laws is not satisfied by the payment of only a nominal sum of money or the mere recital in a document that value has been received by the one transferring an interest. For a payment to constitute consideration, the sum paid must have some substantial relation to the market value of the interest acquired by a purchaser.

Although a creditor is not a purchaser as the latter term is used in recording laws, recording statutes in a large number of states expressly provide that their protection shall also be accorded to persons who have loaned money or extended credit. Statutes in some states specifically designate the particular categories of creditors that are granted protection, and without exception mortgagee-lenders are among those protected.

Place of Recording As a general rule, recording acts provide that public records pertaining to land shall be maintained by a designated public official in the county in which the *land is situated*. If a parcel of land is located in two or more counties, all documents affecting the title to that parcel should be recorded in *each* of the counties.

Eligibility for Recording Recording statutes normally specify the kinds of documents that are entitled to be included in the public records. Generally speaking, any instrument that pertains to the transfer of an interest in real property is eligible for recording under the laws of the various states.

Chain of Title

The expression **chain of title** refers to the recorded history of all transactions involving the title to a given parcel of land beginning with the patent or deed from the government or other original owner to the present time. The "links" that form the chain of title are created by the succession of deeds, wills, and other instruments by which the title to real property can be traced back to its original source. Every instrument relating to a particular parcel of land that is filed for record adds yet another link to the ever-lengthening chain, because once a document has been recorded it thereafter remains a permanent part of the public record.

Record Title An unbroken chain of recorded documents in which each transferee in turn became the next transferor until title is finally acquired by the present owner gives rise to what is known as a **record title** or **title of record,** with the present owner (who is the last transferee in the chain) being the holder of that title. A prime requisite of a *good* record title to land is that the various instruments in the chain of title show a direct connection between each of the successive owners—there must be no gap in the sequence of ownership.

If the public records show, for example, that F is the present owner of Blackacre, for his title to be a good record title it must be possible to trace the evolution of his title back to the first owner of Blackacre. The link in the chain of title that shows that F, the apparent present owner, acquired his title by deed from E must interlock with the previous link by which E in turn acquired title from D, D from C, C from B, and B from A, who was the original owner of Blackacre. If the link by which D acquired his title from C, for instance, is missing, the chain is broken and F, the apparent present owner, will not have a good record title.

Record Title Is Not Always a Clear Title It does not follow that the holder of a flawless record title necessarily has a title that is free and clear of claims of other persons. The great diversity of interests in real property that our legal system recognizes has caused some parcels to have a highly complex legal history. In some instances the termination of older interests may be in doubt, with the result that more than one person may presently have rights in the property. Furthermore, there may be matters which are not shown by the public records that prevent the holder of a perfect *record* title from having a perfect title *in fact.*

Mechanics of Recording
Prerequisites to Recording

Eligibility The basic prerequisite to the recording of any instrument is that the instrument must meet the eligibility requirements of the recording laws of the state in which it is to be recorded. As we have seen, all documents that relate to the transfer of real property interests are made eligible for recording by the laws of every state.

Acknowledgment Recording statutes commonly require that instruments which create or transfer real property interests must be *acknowledged* before a notary public or other designated official before they will be accepted for recording. The purpose in requiring the acknowledgment of an instrument is to minimize the possibility of forged documents being entered in the public records.

To acknowledge an instrument, the person who signed it appears before a notary and declares that he is the person who executed the document and whose signature appears on it. After having satisfied himself as to the declarant's identity, the notary completes an acknowledgment form (Figure 14-1) which commonly appears on the face of the instrument, and in so doing the notary certifies that the person whose signature appears on the instrument acknowledged having executed it.

It is important to note that a certificate of acknowledgment appearing on the face of a deed or other real estate instrument is not a substantive part of the instrument itself, but is merely formal proof of the instrument's execution.

A notary does not verify the fact that the person who acknowledges an instrument that purports to convey an interest in real property actually has any interest to convey. In other words, the notary is not a guarantor of that person's interest in the property described in the instrument. His responsiblity is limited simply to identifying the person whose signature appears on the acknowledged instrument.

Figure 14-1

```
┌─────────────────────────────────────────────────────────────┐
│                    ACKNOWLEDGMENT                           │
│                    ───────────────                          │
│                                                             │
│   State of _____                                  │
│                                  SS                         │
│   County of _____                                 │
│                                                             │
│        On _____, 19__, before me (name and title of       │
│   officer) personally appeared (name or names of persons    │
│   acknowledging) known to me to be the person(s) whose      │
│   name(s) is (are) subscribed to the foregoing instrument,  │
│   and acknowledged that (he, she, or they) executed the     │
│   same as (his, her, or their) free and voluntary act.      │
│                                                             │
│                                    (signature of notary)    │
│                                 _____ │
│   (Notarial Seal)                _____ County, State of __│
│                                 My commission expires __(date)│
└─────────────────────────────────────────────────────────────┘
```

Payment of Fees Despite the fact that an instrument may satisfy all eligibility tests and be properly acknowledged, it will not be accepted for recording until the statutorily prescribed fees have been paid. Recording fees vary from state to state but tend to be nominal in amount.

Documentary Transfer Tax A number of states[1] require that a documentary transfer tax be paid at the time a deed is submitted for recording. The most common rate at which this tax is levied is 55 cents per $500 of consideration. The tax generally is paid by the grantor.

Submission and Reproduction

Submitted by Recipient of Property Interest It is the recipient of an interest in real property, or someone acting in his behalf, who submits an instrument to the appropriate public official for recording. A deed, for instance, would be offered for recording by the named grantee and a mortgage by the lender of money, because it is their respective interests in the property that recording of the document will serve to protect.

Time for Recording Although most statutes do not place a time limit on the period during which an instrument may be recorded, as a practical matter the one who receives delivery of a real property document should record that document just as soon as it comes into his or his agent's possession.

Recorder's Notation on Document When a document is presented to an appropriate official for recording, that official endorses on the instrument (1) a chronological filing number, (2) the date and the exact time that the instrument is received, (3) the amount of the recording fee, (4) the amount of any transfer tax

---

[1] Including, for example, California, Colorado, Florida, Illinois, Kentucky, Massachusetts, Michigan, Nebraska, North Carolina, Ohio, and Pennsylvania.

that the local law requires to be paid, and (5) the book and page number where the instrument will be recorded.

Reproduction by the Recorder After making his notations on the document, the recording official reproduces it in permanently bound books by means of some photographic process. The instrument may also be copied on microfilm, a copy of which is made available for the viewing public. After it has been copied in the public records, the recorder returns the original document to the person whose interest is protected by the recording.

Indexing Recording laws universally require that instruments which have been accepted for reproduction in the public records must be indexed by the county recorder or registrar. Statutes in the various states authorize two basic types of indexing systems: (1) the *grantor-grantee index* system, which is the more prevalent type, and (2) the *tract index* system.

Grantor-Grantee Index System In the grantor-grantee system of indexing, the recording official maintains two separate indexes, a general index of *grantors* and a general index of *grantees*. When an instrument affecting an interest in real estate is recorded, the names of the parties appearing in the instrument are listed in the appropriate index.

The indexes of grantors and grantees are alphabetically arranged and generally are maintained on a calendar-year basis.

Although called a "grantor" index, the index includes the names of all parties who, as shown by instruments offered for recording, transfer or relinquish interests in real property. Therefore, in addition to actual grantors, whose names appear in deeds, the grantor index also includes the names of lessors, mortgagors, trustors in deeds of trust, and other transferors of real estate interests.

The "grantee" index includes, in addition to actual grantees named in deeds, all persons such as lessees, mortgagees, beneficiaries in deeds of trust, and others who are recipients of interest in real property.

Tract Index System Instead of using the names of persons that appear in real estate documents, the tract index system is established on the basis of identified parcels of land. In the tract index system, each parcel of land is assigned a separate page in the index and every transaction affecting that parcel is noted on that page. As the term is used in the tract index system, a "parcel of land" is any unit of land that has been surveyed and platted, such as sections, blocks, and lots. Besides describing a parcel of land, the tract index system discloses the nature of every instrument affecting title to the parcel, the date the instrument was executed, the date it was filed for record, and the names of the parties to the transaction giving rise to the execution of the instrument. All documents affecting the title to a given parcel of property appear on one page of the tract index. By locating that page, a researcher will find reference to all recorded instruments that have a bearing on the condition of the title that he is researching.

From the standpoint of efficiency and expense of title searches, the tract index system is considered to be much superior to the grantor-grantee system.

Effects of Recording

The recording of an instrument pertaining to real property serves three principal functions: (1) it imparts *constructive notice* of the existence of the recorded document and its contents, (2) it establishes the *order of priority* of the interest evidenced by the document in relation to other interests in the land, and (3) it provides a *depository* for the safekeeping of valuable evedence.

Constructive Notice

Actual versus Constructive Notice To have "notice" of something is to have *knowledge* of it. The law recognizes notice or knowledge as being either actual or constructive. Notice or knowledge of a fact is *actual* when it is acquired by a person who is expressly told of the fact, who overhears it being discussed by others, or who personally observes the fact. **Constructive notice,** on the other hand, is knowledge of a fact that is attributed to an individual by operation of law, even though he has no actual knowledge whatsoever of the fact.

Theory Underlying Constructive Notice As it functions within the recording system, the concept of constructive notice is based on the theory that purchasers, lenders, and others concerned with a parcel of real estate are considered to know the contents of any recorded instrument that could have been discovered by a diligent search of the public records. It is immaterial that the parties may not in fact have searched the records. They are charged with knowledge of what they *would have learned* had they consulted the public records and examined the language of the instruments found there.

Order of Priorities

Early Common Law Rules At early common law, the order of priority of claims made by two or more persons to interests in the same parcel of real property was based on the principle of "first in time, first in right." In other words, each claimant was assigned a priority or preferential status based exclusively on the date or time at which his claim of interest in the property was acquired. For example, if O, the owner of Blackacre, mortgaged his property to lender A on a given day and on a later date mortgaged the same property to lender B, lender A was considered to have a security interest that had a priority or preferential status over that of lender B. This meant that if at some later date the two mortgages were foreclosed and the proceeds from the foreclosure sale were only sufficient to pay the debt of lender A in full, lender B would receive nothing. Similarly, if owner O first sold his property to buyer A and later sold the same property to buyer B, A would hold title to the property and B would have no interest in it. Instead, B would have a cause of action against O for fraud arising from the double sale.

While the "first in time, first in right" notion of priorities is a logical arrangement, it is no longer a practical one. Under such an arrangement, purchasers and lenders in today's complex society would have no reliable way of checking on the status of title to a parcel of land.

Modern Statutory Rules Recording laws have replaced the common law with systems of statutory priorities that have as their objectives the orderly protection of successive purchasers and mortgagee-lenders of land. While the statutes of the various states all serve the same basic purpose of protecting subsequent parties, they differ somewhat in the manner in which this protection is provided.

With respect to the manner in which priorities among claimants operate, the recording laws in the various states can be divided into three categories: (1) the *race*-type statutes, (2) the *notice*-type statutes, and (3) the *race-notice*-type statutes.

Race-Type Statutes The earliest statutes for the protection of persons dealing with real property were the so-called race-type statutes. Such statutes still exist in only a very few states.[2] These statutes derive their name from the fact that, according to their provisions, priority among successive grantees depends on who records first—who wins the race to the recording office. Under this type of statute, it is entirely immaterial that a subsequent purchaser *actually* knew of an earlier *unrecorded* conveyance at the time he purchased the property, because the test of priority between an earlier and a later recipient of the same property interest is not what notice or knowledge the second purchaser or mortgagee may have had, but who recorded his document first.

Assume, for example, that O, the owner of Blackacre, in performance of a contract of sale delivered a deed to the property to buyer A, who neglected to record the deed. Shortly thereafter, O sold the same property to buyer B,

---

[2] In Arkansas the statutes apply only to mortgages, in North Carolina both to deeds and mortgages, in Ohio to mortgages and oil and gas leases, and in Pennsylvania to mortgages other than purchase money mortgages.

who immediately recorded the deed that O delivered to him. As a result of having recorded first, B holds title to Blackacre that cannot be divested by A. This is true even if B knew of A's unrecorded deed at the time B purchased the property from O. A has a cause of action against O for damages resulting from O's wrongful double sale.

Notice-Type Statutes Under a second type of recording statute, the notice-type statute, priority is granted to a later purchaser or mortgagee-lender if at the time he purchased the property or loaned money he had no notice or knowledge of a prior conveyance by the owner. If a purchaser at the time of acquiring his interest had no *actual* knowledge of a prior conveyance by the seller, and if the earlier purchaser had *not recorded* his deed, according to notice-type statutes the former unrecorded conveyance is totally ineffective as far as the subsequent purchaser is concerned. While it is advisable for the subsequent purchaser to promptly record his deed to protect himself against purchasers subsequent to him, under the notice-type statutes he need not record to be protected against *prior* unrecorded interests of which he had no actual knowledge.

In the foregoing example, B would not acquire title to Blackacre in a state with a notice-type statute because B had actual knowledge of A's unrecorded deed. If, however, B did not know of A's unrecorded deed, B would acquire title even if A thereafter recorded his deed before B did.

A substantial number of states[3] have enacted notice-type statutes.

Race-Notice-Type Statutes Nearly half of the states[4] have enacted a third type of statute known as race-notice-type statutes. Under these statutes, in order that a purchaser or mortgagee may have priority over a previous *unrecorded* conveyance, not only must he have *no actual notice* or knowledge of the previous conveyance but he must also *record* his document *before* the holder of the earlier interest records his. The term "race-notice" is given to this type of statute because both the race to the recorder's office to record first and the lack of notice of previous unrecorded interests are necessary for establishing the priority of the subsequent purchaser's interest.

In the foregoing example, if B, in a state with a race-notice-type statute, were to acquire title to Blackacre, not only must he have purchased the property from O without actual knowledge of A's unrecorded deed, but B must also have recorded his deed before A recorded his.

Recording Provides a Safe Repository Once a document has been properly recorded, its subsequent loss or destruction does not jeopardize an owner's or mortgagee's interest in real property. Public records that are maintained in accordance with recording statutes have evidentiary value in judicial proceedings. Statutes in many states provide that certified copies of recorded instruments constitute primary evidence without the need to account for the reason why the original document cannot be produced in court. In other states it is necessary to explain why the original document cannot be produced before the contents of an instrument may be proved by a recorded copy. In either case, it is apparent that the public records provide a secure place for the safekeeping of documents that relate to valuable interests in real property.

---

[3] Alabama, Arizona, Arkansas (except for mortgages), Colorado, Connecticut, Delaware, Florida, Illinois, Iowa, Kansas, Kentucky, Maine, Massachusetts, Missouri, New Hampshire, New Mexico, Ohio (except for mortgages and oil and gas leases), Oklahoma, Rhode Island, South Carolina, Tennessee, Texas, Vermont, Virginia, and West Virginia.

[4] Alaska, California, District of Columbia, Georgia, Hawaii, Idaho, Indiana, Maryland, Michigan, Minnesota, Mississippi, Montana, Nebraska, Nevada, New Jersey, New York, North Dakota, Oregon, Pennsylvania (except for most types of mortgages), South Dakota, Utah, Washington, Wisconsin, and Wyoming.

CONSTRUCTIVE NOTICE OTHER THAN FROM RECORDING

In addition to all matters that are revealed by the public records, a prospective purchaser or creditor is charged with notice or knowledge of what he would have learned from a reasonable inspection of the real property with which he is concerned. Therefore, a prospective purchaser or lender should inspect real estate not only to determine the possible existence of such physical conditions as easements that are apparent on the ground and mechanics' liens that can be anticipated as a result of construction in progress on the premises, but also to ascertain the rights of any occupants whose interests in the property might be inconsistent with the record title. Occupancy of the premises by a person whose right to possession is not apparent from the public records puts a prospective purchaser or creditor on inquiry as to the nature of the occupant's interest in the property, and the law charges him with constructive notice of all facts that a reasonable investigation and inquiry would have disclosed. But his duty to investigate is not satisfied by merely making inquiries of the owner of the property. The prospective purchaser or creditor is charged with knowledge of what a full and diligent investigation of the occupant's rights would have revealed.

The rights of persons in possession arising from the mere fact of possession are just as effective against persons dealing with real estate as are rights of individuals that are revealed by the public records. In other words, possession of property imparts constructive notice of any and all rights that an occupant of property may have, just as the public records do.

TORRENS SYSTEM OF TITLE REGISTRATION

Sir Robert Torrens, an Australian, originated a system for the registration of title to land which, though popular in many areas of the world, has not been widely adopted in the United States. The so-called **Torrens system** of land title registration is provided for by the statutes of only twelve states[5] today, and in none of them is the registration of land titles compulsory. Enthusiasm for the Torrens system was greatest in this country during the early part of this century, but interest waned and eight states[6] that had previously passed title registration statutes either have repealed them or have let them expire. The most extensive use of the Torrens system today is in the Honolulu area, in Cook County (Chicago), Illinois, on Cape Cod and in Boston, Massachusetts, in St. Paul and Minneapolis, Minnesota, on Long Island and the Buffalo area of New York, and in the area around Cleveland, Ohio.

While the Torrens system presently is little used outside the foregoing areas, renewed interest in it or some similar system of title registration or recordation appears to be a real possibility in view of the recent passage of the Real Estate Settlement Procedures Act by the U.S. Congress. Among other things, the act provides that the Secretary of the Department of Housing and Urban Development "shall establish and place in operation on a demonstration basis, in representative political subdivisions (selected by him) in various areas of the United States, a model system or systems for the recordation of land title information in a manner and form calculated to facilitate and simplify land transfers and mortgage transactions and reduce the cost thereof, with a view to the possible development (utilizing the information and experience gained under this section) of a nationally uniform system of land parcel recordation."[7]

In its comments on the Real Estate Settlement Procedures Act, the Senate Banking, Housing and Urban Affairs Committee noted that "By assisting in the establishment of simplified land recordation systems, the Commit-

---

[5] Colorado, Georgia, Hawaii, Illinois, Massachusetts, Minnesota, New York, North Carolina, Ohio, Oregon, Virginia, and Washington.

[6] California, Mississippi, Nebraska, North Dakota, South Carolina, South Dakota, Tennessee, and Utah.

[7] 12 U.S.C., sec. 2611.

tee hopes to reduce the time and effort presently involved in the searching of real estate titles. A substantial portion of the fees presently charged for title examination and related services can be eliminated if the work that must be done under the present chaotic recording systems can be significantly reduced by the institution of modern computerized recordation systems. In the long run, this aspect [of the act] may be the single most important feature of the legislation from the standpoint of making significant reductions in the present level of settlement charges."[8]

Objective of the Torrens System

The objective of the Torrens system of title registration is to make the status of title to land ascertainable from a certificate issued by a public official known as a *registrar*. A familiar personal property analogy to a land certificate is the certificate of title to an automobile issued by motor vehicle licensing officials which shows ownership of the vehicle and whether it is subject to liens of any sort.

Method of Registration

The initial registration of title to land under the Torrens system requires a judicial proceeding. In such a proceeding, the party who claims to be the fee simple owner files an application with the court in which he names all known claimants to rights or interests of any kind in an identified parcel of land. The persons indicated by the owner as being claimants to interests in the property are made parties to the judicial proceedings by means of notice sent to them and by notice published in a newspaper. The owner's application is referred by the court to official title examiners who, after having made their examination, report the condition of the applicant's title to the court. If the examiners have approved the owner's title and if no meritorious claims have been established by persons receiving notice of the judicial proceeding, the court will confirm the applicant's title and order the registrar to issue a certificate of title.

The registrar issues the certificate of title in duplicate; one copy is given to the registered owner and the other is retained in the registrar's office. The certificate states that the applicant has a fee simple title to the property described in it, subject to whatever interests or encumbrances the court has confirmed. Aside from certain statutory exceptions, such as liens for taxes, public highways, etc., which vary somewhat from state to state, the certificate issued by the registrar becomes the exclusive determinant of the condition of title.

Transfer after Registration

After the title to land has been registered, all subsequent transfers of ownership to it involve the certificate of title. An owner conveying real property delivers his certificate of title along with his deed to the purchaser, who in turn files them with the registrar. The old certificate is then cancelled by the registrar and a new one is issued in the name of the purchaser and given to him. The old certificate in the possession of the registrar is likewise replaced by a new certificate.

If an owner should want to transfer only a part of the property described in his certificate of title, his existing certificate is cancelled and two new ones are issued. One certificate is issued to the owner of the retained property and describes the part of the parcel that is still owned by him. The other certificate is issued to the purchaser and describes the portion of the divided parcel to which he acquired title.

Notation of Subsequent Liens

All subsequent liens and encumbrances created on property for which a certificate of title has been issued are noted on the registrar's copy of the certificate when the lienor or encumbrancer files with him a copy of the document that evidences the lien or encumbrance.

---

[8] Senate Report (Banking, Housing and Urban Affairs Committee) No. 93-866, 3 U.S. Code Congressional and Administrative News, 93rd Cong., 2nd Sess., 1974, pp. 6548–49.

ABSTRACTS OF TITLE AND LAWYER'S OPINIONS

Since he is charged with constructive notice of everything that appears in the public records, a purchaser or mortgagee of real estate would be foolish to buy real estate or lend money secured by it without having first carefully checked the relevant records in the appropriate public offices.

The constructive notice with which a purchaser or lender is charged is not limited solely to the records maintained by the county recorder or recorder of deeds. Constructive notice is also imparted by court records that may contain judgments which may affect title, by tax and special assessment records, by probate records for testate and intestate matters, and by other records kept by public officials. Before a purchaser or mortgagee can safely invest his money in a parcel of real estate, all of these records must first be searched and evaluated.

Since all records pertaining to interests in real estate are open and available to the public, any purchaser or mortgagee desiring to do so may search the records and make copies of them. As a practical matter, however, very few purchasers or mortgagees have the ability to make a proper and thorough search of the various public records. And even though a purchaser or mortgagee was able to locate all pertinent documents, he would normally have considerable difficulty in interpreting them to determine their legal effect on the title to the property to which they relate. Consequently, most record searches and title examinations are made by professionals hired by a buyer, seller, or lender for that purpose. The professional who conducts a search of the public records prepares a report of his findings known as an *abstract of title*, which is thereafter examined and interpreted by a second professional who renders an *opinion* as to the status of title to the property described in the abstract of title.

Abstract of Title

Nature of an Abstract An **abstract of title** is a summary, usually arranged in chronological order, of the essential features of every recorded document that pertains to the title to a particular parcel of land. An abstract provides a title examiner with the necessary evidence from which he can arrive at an opinion as to the condition of an owner's title at a particular point in time. In some states, the records are searched and an abstract prepared by the same attorney who examines the title and renders an opinion as to its condition. More commonly, however, skilled professionals known as **abstracters** search the records and prepare abstracts for clients who employ them for that purpose for a fee. An abstracter expresses no opinion as to the legal significance of any particular instrument that is referred to in the abstract, nor does he comment on the combined effect of all instruments on the title to the property to which they relate. For him to do so would constitute the unauthorized practice of law in most states. The abstracter's sole function is to locate all recorded documents relating to title and to summarize them for use by an examining attorney who will judge their legal significance.

Normally it is the seller or the mortgagor-borrower of real estate who employs an abstracter. Although a seller or mortgagor is under no obligation to furnish a buyer or mortgagee-lender with an abstract of title unless he binds himself to do so by contract, in those areas where abstracts of title are in common use it is customary for the contract between the parties expressly to provide that the seller or mortgagor will do so. Such a provision in a contract is a condition which the seller or mortgagor must satisfy before the buyer or mortgagee will be obligated to perform his side of the contract.

Contents of an Abstract In addition to the main body of an abstract in which all instruments having a bearing on a seller's or mortgagor's title are summarized, an abstract normally will include a definite caption and a comprehensive certificate.

Caption Besides stating that the document

is an abstract of title, the *caption* of an abstract sets forth the full legal description of the property to which it relates.

Certificate An abstracter's *certificate* appears at the end of the document and usually defines the extent of the abstracter's search and indicates the records that were searched. Only the records of the county in which the land is situated are normally examined by an abstracter.

Period Covered The period covered by an abstract may be indicated either in the caption or in the certificate. Once an abstract that traces title back to the original patent has been prepared, it is a fairly simple matter to keep that abstract up-to-date by adding to it each time the land to which it relates is transferred or encumbered. In those cases where an abstract has been updated from time to time, it is important for a buyer or mortgagee to check the beginning and ending dates to make sure that no time gaps exist.

Abstracter's Title Plant Individual abstracters and abstract companies that have been active in a given area for some time will have accumulated files called *title plants* in which past transactions involving properties in the area are collected and indexed. As new transactions involving these properties occur, information concerning them is added to the materials contained in the title plants. By preserving copies of abstracts previously prepared by him, an abstracter needs only to update them when a new abstract for a particular parcel of land is requested by a client.

Abstracter's Liability An abstracter is liable for any loss that results from his negligence in searching records pertaining to a title or in the preparation of an abstract of that search. Although an earlier view held that an abstracter was liable only to the party who employed him, the more modern view extends his liability to any person who sustains a loss in reliance on an abstract prepared by him. Thus, in those instances where a sales contract requires a seller to furnish an abstract of title to a buyer and the buyer suffers a loss by relying on the abstract, the buyer can recover from the negligent abstracter despite the fact that there is no direct contractual relationship between the buyer and the abstracter.

Since he does not pass judgment on the validity of the title to property described in an abstract, an abstracter is not liable if the title to the property proves to be defective.

Lawyer's Opinion

We have seen that in areas where abstracts of title are commonly used it is customary for a real estate sales contract to require the seller to furnish the buyer with an abstract of title. We have also seen that an abstract of title expresses no opinion as to the validity or the condition of the seller's title. Consequently, it is necessary for a prudent buyer, before parting with his purchase money, to obtain a professional opinion relative to the condition of the title that the seller proposes to transfer to him. That professional opinion necessarily will be given by an attorney, because the rendering of opinions concerning the validity of title to land has been held to constitute the practice of law.

Attorney as Title Examiner In his role as *title examiner,* an attorney scrutinizes and evaluates all evidence, as revealed by an abstract of title, by means of which the seller's title to his property can be proved. The attorney will make certain that the abstracter's search was sufficiently comprehensive to include all records which have a bearing on the title to be acquired by his client. The attorney, however, assumes no responsibility for the correctness of the abstract he examines. His opinion is limited to the condition of the title as that title is disclosed by the summary of the records contained in the abstract of title examined by him.

Attorney's Liability

Limited to Negligence An attorney who undertakes to examine the title to a parcel of real property is required to exercise reasonable care and skill when conducting his examination. His failure to exercise the requisite care and skill constitutes negligence for which he will be liable if it causes injury to his client. An attorney, however, is not a guarantor of the title that he approves. His liability arises only from negligence in the examination of the title and is limited to errors and oversights that a competent and diligent attorney would not make. If the attorney's opinion is arrived at nonnegligently but it nonetheless proves to be erroneous either as to the law itself or the application of the law to the facts, he will not be liable for any resulting damages.

From a practical point of view, an attorney's liability is also limited to the extent of his financial ability to pay for losses sustained by his client that result from the attorney's negligence.

Not Liable for Hidden Defects Attorneys who examine titles are not liable for losses resulting from defects that are not apparent from the public records. Hidden defects in deeds, we have seen, include such matters as fraud, forgery, identity of parties, competency of parties, lack of delivery, and failure to comply with a particular law. Even the most diligent examination of an abstract of title will not reveal defects of this type.

Where a buyer's loss results from hidden defects in a title acquired by him, his cause of action for damages, if any, is against the seller of the property and not the attorney who examined the abstract. Recovery in such cases, of course, is dependent upon the seller's ability to pay the amount of the judgment entered against him and, consequently, even where a buyer wins his suit, he could end up with a hollow victory and an out-of-pocket loss.

TITLE INSURANCE

Title insurance has become a predominant method of title protection in many metropolitan areas and is likely to expand to other areas as land title records become increasingly more voluminous and difficult to search. The growth in the prevalence of title insurance since the mid-1940s has been phenomenal and has displaced many other forms of title protection, particularly title searches and examinations traditionally performed by attorneys in private practice. In a number of principal cities[9] throughout the country and in smaller cities in the Far West, title search and examination has been entirely eliminated from the private practice of law. In New England and much of the South and Midwest outside the urban centers, however, the private practice of law continues to include a great deal of title examination work and, in some communities, the searching of the public records as well.

Reasons for Increased Use of Title Insurance

The remarkable growth in the incidence of title insurance in recent years is attributable to three factors.

Probably the single most important reason for the increased use of title insurance has been the demand for such protection by life insurance companies, whose role as mortgage lenders has today become very significant. The relatively standardized risk coverage that title policies afford appeals to these large national lenders.

A second reason for growth in the use of title insurance arises from the fact that public records in metropolitan areas have become so voluminous and difficult to search that title searches of those records have become increasingly inefficient and costly. To overcome these difficulties, title insurance companies have extracted copies of the public records and arranged them in a manner that is considerably more efficient than most public record systems.

Finally, the increased use of title insurance results from aggressive promotion and solicitation of new business by title insurance companies.

---

[9] Such as Chicago, Cleveland, Los Angeles, New York, and San Francisco, for example.

Regulation of Title Insurance Companies

Although title insurance companies, generally speaking, are subject to less rigorous regulation than most other types of insurers, certain restrictions have been imposed on them by state statutes and regulations. For example, title insurers are required to meet certain financial standards in the form of capital and reserves[10] and are limited as to the amount of any single risk that they may assume.[11] In addition, title insurers are sometimes required to file their rate schedules with a state agency that has the power to disapprove proposed charges.[12]

Operation of Title Insurance Companies

Title insurance companies operate in two different ways. Under one method of operation, the company simply performs an insurance function and issues its policy in reliance on a private attorney's opinion as to the condition of title, which opinion is based on a title search made by the attorney himself or by a private abstracter. Under the other method, the title insurance company performs all of the functions itself, utilizing its own title searchers and attorney-examiners and issuing the policy of title insurance in reliance on their services and judgment.

Nature of a Title Insurance Policy

Policy Is a Contract   A policy of title insurance is a contract according to the terms of which a title insurance company (the insurer) obligates itself to indemnify an owner or a lender (the insured) against losses resulting from imperfections in the title to a designated parcel of real estate. Unlike other kinds of insurance, title insurance does not insure against future risks but only against those risks that are in existence at the time the policy is issued. Title insurance, in other words, protects the insured against the day when it is discovered that the title to real property was faulty on the date that his contract of title insurance went into effect.

Single Premium Policy   Only a single premium is paid for a policy of title insurance, and that premium is payable at the time the insurance contract becomes effective. Customs throughout the country vary as to which party to a real estate transaction pays the premium. In some areas, contracts of purchase and sale commonly provide that the seller shall pay all or part of the cost of a policy that insures the buyer's title. In other areas, if the buyer wants his title insured, the full cost of the insurance coverage is his responsibility.

The usual practice with respect to title policies that name lenders as beneficiaries is for the mortgagor-borrower to pay the premium.

Not Written for a Fixed Period   A title insurance policy is not written for a fixed or specific period of time. It continues in effect as long as the insured is subject to the risks that the policy covers. A mortgagee-lender's insurance coverage terminates when the mortgagor-borrower's debt is paid and the mortgage that secures the debt is released by the lender. An owner's policy of title insurance comes to an end when the owner divests himself of title.

Transferability of Title Policies

Owner's Policy   An owner's title policy is not transferable from an insured seller to a buyer. If the buyer wants title insurance coverage on the property he purchases, a new policy naming him as the beneficiary must be issued by a title insurance company.

Lender's Policy   Although an owner cannot transfer his title insurance policy to a grantee, lenders' policies generally can be transferred to assignees who purchase mortgage-secured loans from lenders in the secondary mortgage market.

Title Plants

Nature of a Title Plant   In order that title searches may be facilitated and expeditiously

---

[10] See, for example, California Insurance Code, secs. 1238–1288.
[11] See, for example, Pennsylvania Stat. tit. 40, secs. 910–919.
[12] Id., secs. 919–940.

concluded, the major title insurance companies maintain their own title plants. An insurance company's title plant is made up of copies of the public records relating to real estate with the materials organized in such a manner as to permit both speedy and accurate searches of titles. The basic information in a title plant is identical to that appearing in the public records. The significant difference between the two is the manner in which the information that they contain is organized and indexed.

Like the public records, a title plant is never complete. It continues to grow and change with every newly recorded instrument involving an interest in real estate.

Data Contained in Title Plants Land title information contained in title plants is derived from sources other than merely the records that are maintained by a county recorder or recorder of deeds. Title plants also include data gathered from the clerks of the various municipal, county, state, and federal courts in the area where a parcel of land is situated and from the county clerk, county treasurer, county assessor, or other public official who is charged with maintaining records pertaining to general property taxes or special assessments.

Recorded data is gathered from the various public offices by title company employees, who either reproduce the recorded documents by some photocopying technique or prepare typewritten or longhand abstracts ("daily slips") of each document.

Indexes of Title Data Critical to the efficient operation of a title plant is the *indexing* of the title data that has been gathered from the public records. Instead of using the cumbersome grantor-grantee indexes adopted by most public recording systems, the method of indexing most commonly used in title plants is the *tract book* system. We have seen that under this system a set of books is maintained in which each tract or parcel of land appears in accordance with its legal description. Every transaction involving the title to a particular parcel of land is posted to the page assigned to that parcel in the tract index as soon as the data is obtained from the public records. Consequently, the complete title history of an identified parcel of land is readily available from the page or pages that have been allotted to that parcel.

Not all recorded instruments lend themselves to being indexed in accordance with land descriptions. Some instruments that appear in the public records do not refer to any particular parcel of land. Included among instruments of this type are such things as powers of attorney, declarations of trust, court decrees affecting the status of parties such as bankruptcy, divorce and incompetency decrees, and judgments that create liens on all of a debtor's property. Since abstracts of such matters cannot be posted to any particular parcel of land in a tract book, title plants have another set of books in which the names of persons appearing in the foregoing types of records are arranged alphabetically. This set of books is known as the *general index*.

A title search of a title plant's records would, of course, include a search of both its tract books and its general index.

Guaranty of Title

A title insurance policy guarantees that title to an identified parcel of real property is in the condition indicated by the policy. The contractual undertaking of a title insurance company is more than a mere assurance that the company conducted a careful title search and made a skillful analysis of all pertinent documents. By the terms of its contract, a title insurance company promises to indemnify an insured for any damage or loss sustained by him should any risk embraced by the policy become a reality.

The potential risks against which an insured is protected by title insurance arise from (1) the possibility of an error having been made in the searching of the public records, (2) the likelihood of mistaken interpretation of the legal effect of instruments appearing in the records, and (3) certain facts that are not discoverable by a proper search of the public records, which are known as "off-record risks."

Title insurance affords protection both against any errors or omissions in the conveyancing process and against hidden defects which escape discovery even by the most proficient of record searches.

Title Insurance versus Attorney's Opinion

Title insurance increases an owner's or a lender's protection over that afforded by an attorney's opinion based on his examination of an abstract of title in three principal ways.

First, if an insured buyer or lender suffers a loss because of a defect in title to real estate, he can be sure of indemnification for his loss up to the face amount of his title policy. His recovery is not dependent upon a showing of negligence in the making of a title search or the interpretation of documents by the insurer. On the other hand, as we have seen, negligence on the part of an attorney must be established if an injured party is to recover for errors committed by him.

Second, the insured is protected against hidden defects or off-record risks that are not revealed by the public records. An attorney's opinion, however, often is specifically limited by an express statement that his opinion is based only upon facts that are revealed by the public records.

Finally, and perhaps most significantly, is the fact that a title insurance company assumes the responsibility for defending the insured's title against all claims made by third parties. By virtue of his policy of title insurance, an insured owner or lender has in effect retained a highly competent defender of his title against possible adverse claims to interests in the property. Even if the title that is defended by the title insurance company proves to be perfect, the company will have borne the costs of the litigation establishing that fact. In the case of most title insurance policies, the expense of defending a title in court can easily and substantially exceed the entire amount of the premium on the policy.

Coverage

A title insurance policy protects an insured owner or lender against all losses resulting from title defects and deficiencies except those that are specifically excluded by the provisions of the policy.

Standardization of Coverage Although certain variations in the coverage afforded by title insurance policies occur because of requirements imposed by some state insurance departments and because of differences in local laws, title insurance policies tend to be highly standardized.

Standardization of title insurance policies results in part from the growth in the number of companies operating on a nationwide basis, but more so because of the use of standardized policy forms that have been developed by the American Land Title Association (ALTA), a national association of title insurance companies, abstracters, and title attorneys. The standard policy forms approved by the American Land Title Association, and especially its lender's policy, have been widely adopted and are obtainable in all states except New York and Texas.[13]

Risks Commonly Excluded Risks not usually covered by title insurance policies include in the first instance those title risks which are disclosed by a search of the public records and an examination of title documents. Such risks are specifically listed as exclusions or exceptions to the coverage by a policy. In addition, the general insurance principles that exclude losses re-

---

[13] New York requires the use of policy forms approved by the New York Board of Title Underwriters; in Texas policy forms that have been promulgated by the State Board of Insurance are required. With respect to substantive restrictions and enforcement efforts generally, New York and Texas have regulated title insurers more strictly than other states. See New York Insurance Law, secs. 430–442 and Texas Insurance Code Ann., art. 9.01 et seq.

sulting from misrepresentation and concealment of facts by the insured are also applicable to title insurance.

Lender's Policy Provides Broader Coverage

Included in the coverage of the lender's policy but excluded from the usual owner's policy are risks that arise from rights, claims, or interests of parties that would be revealed by an inspection of the premises or by a correct survey. Among the risks or title defects that an inspection or survey would disclose are the claims of adverse possessors, easements acquired by prescription, unrecorded leases, encroachments, incorrect boundary lines, and setback violations. Because of its broader coverage, the lender's policy commands a higher premium than the owner's policy does.

The purchaser of property who does not feel competent to make a proper inspection of the premises himself may, instead of purchasing an owner's policy of title insurance, pay the higher premium and obtain the coverage afforded by the lender's policy.

It is not uncommon for a title company to issue two separate policies at the time real property is sold, one policy insuring the interests of the mortgagee-lender and the other the interest of the new owner. In some areas[14] the two policies are combined in a single joint-protection policy which provides for coverage of the changing values of the interests of the owner and the lender as the mortgage debt is gradually paid off.

ADJUDICATION OF TITLE TO REAL PROPERTY

While title to land can be adjudicated in several different kinds of legal proceedings, the most common type of proceeding is the action or suit to quiet title. An **action to quiet title** is a proceeding to determine the condition of the title to real property by adjudicating the validity of all adverse claims to the title or to interests in the property.

It is frequently necessary for an owner to bring a quiet title action when he desires to sell his property but a record search reveals that defects exist which render his title unmarketable. In such a situation, the objective of the owner's suit is to restore salability to his property.

In some jurisdictions, a quiet title action is called "an action to remove a cloud upon a title." A **cloud on the title** to a parcel of real estate is an adverse claim which appears from the public records to be good, but which in fact is invalid or barred for reasons which must be proved by evidence available from sources outside the public records. A recorded real estate mortgage that was not released by a mortgagee-lender when the borrower paid his secured debt in full is an example of a cloud on the title to real property.

QUESTIONS

1 Indicate the various forms that evidence of the condition of title to real estate may take.
2 What is the meaning of "recording" as that term is used in connection with real estate transactions?
3 What is the objective of recording laws? Whom do they protect?
4 Explain what is meant by the expression "chain of title."
5 What is a record title? Is a record title always a clear or perfect one?
6 Explain what happens when a real estate document is acknowledged. What is the purpose of requiring an acknowledgment prior to recording an instrument?
7 Distinguish between actual notice and constructive notice.
8 What is the Torrens system of title registration designed to do that the recording system does not do?
9 Describe an abstract of title. What is the function of an abstracter? What is the nature of his liability?

---

[14] In California, for example.

10 What does an attorney do in his role as a title examiner? What is the nature of his liability?
11 Explain why the use of title insurance has grown so much since the mid-1940s.
12 Describe the nature of a title insurance policy. What is the primary difference between title insurance and other types of insurance?
13 Explain how title insurance affords a landowner greater protection than does an attorney's opinion based on his examination of an abstract of title.
14 What is an action to quiet title to real property?

Chapter 15

Mortgages, Deeds of Trust, and Installment Contracts—Part I

Like any other valuable asset, real estate can be and commonly is used as security for the performance of an obligation. In most cases, the obligation that is secured is a promise to pay a certain sum of money. The pledging of real estate as security for a debt is accomplished by the owner of the property executing a legal instrument that creates a security interest in favor of the person to whom the obligation is owed. The instrument that creates the security interest in real estate may take the form of such legal devices as mortgages, deeds of trust, and installment sales contracts.

Basic to most real estate sales transactions is the fact that a buyer seeks to finance his purchase on the most favorable terms that prevailing market conditions and the buyer's financial situation will permit. For many buyers, such as those buying their first homes, the obtaining of financing is critical to their ability to purchase. For others, such as investors seeking to maximize their returns, tax sheltering and leverage provide the incentive for financing their real estate purchases.

THE MORTGAGE MARKET

As the term **mortgage market** is generally used, it refers to the availability of loan funds for financing the acquisition, construction, or improvement of real property, but the term also applies to the availability of funds to be used for consumer purposes quite unrelated to the real estate that secures the loan. The availability of real estate loans is subject to substantial variation ranging from conditions of "easy money" when the supply of funds is ample to "tight money" situations when the supply has been exhausted.

Although it is common to speak of *the* mortgage market, the market actually is a conglomerate in which separate markets or "submarkets" exist for single-family dwellings, multiple dwellings, commercial and industrial properties, and for unimproved land. There are also separate mortgage markets for old buildings and new ones, for short-term construction loans, and for long-term "permanent" loans.

PRIMARY AND SECONDARY MARKETS

The mortgage market is broadly organized into what are known as a primary market and a secondary market.

The **primary mortgage market** is the market where loans secured by real estate mortgages are *originated* between a borrower and a lender. It is the market in which lending transactions are negotiated and consummated.

The **secondary mortgage market** is the market in which an originating lender sells loans secured by real estate mortgages to an investor. The funds derived by the originating lender from the sale of a mortgage-secured loan become available for additional new loans in the primary market.

INSURED, GUARANTEED, AND CONVENTIONAL LOANS

FHA-insured Mortgages

The FHA-insured mortgage was designed and created by Congress in 1934.[1] Despite popular belief to the contrary, a prospective home buyer does not borrow money directly from the Federal Housing Administration.[2] The borrower obtains his money from a lending institution that makes the loan on the basis of a commitment from FHA to *insure* the lender against losses resulting from the borrower's default. An insurance premium amounting to ½ of 1 percent of the loan outstanding is paid by the borrower as a part of his monthly payment.

VA-guaranteed Morgages

The Servicemen's Readjustment Act of 1944,[3] popularly referred to as the "GI Bill of Rights," authorized the federal government, through the Veterans Administration, to guarantee or underwrite mortgage-secured loans made to veterans. Like FHA loans, VA loans are made by private lending institutions and not by the federal government. Unlike FHA loans, there is no insurance premium required for VA loans.

Conventional Mortgages

A mortgage is said to be *conventional* when it has no federal government backing either by way of insurance or guarantee. The loan which such a mortgage secures is made by private lenders and the risks of loss due to default are borne exclusively by them. In recent years, however, private mortgage insurers have appeared on the scene so that today even conventional mortgages may be insured against risks of loss arising from defaults by borrowers.

HOME MORTGAGE DISCLOSURE ACT

The Concept of Redlining

The federal **Home Mortgage Disclosure Act** of 1975[4] "establishes a home mortgage disclosure system for the purpose of providing information to citizens, financial institutions and public officials at all levels, both Federal and State."[5] In its report on the legislation, the House Committee on Banking, Currency and Housing observed that the withdrawal of private investment capital for home mortgage loans and rehabilitation loans from an increasing number of geographic areas located primarily in metropolitan centers "exacerbates the problem of providing public sector investments to stabilize and rehabilitate essentially older neighborhoods within our cities and adds to the frustration of millions of Americans denied access to credit at reasonable rates of interest for the sale, improvement and rehabilitation of residential housing."[6] This process, the report states, has led to the use of the word **redlining,**

---

[1] By enactment of 12 U.S.C., secs. 1701 et seq.
[2] An agency of the Department of Housing and Urban Development (HUD).
[3] 38 U.S.C., secs. 1801 et seq.
[4] P.L. 94-200, Title III; 12 U.S.C., secs. 2801 et seq.
[5] House Report (Committee on Banking, Currency and Housing) No. 94-561, 2 U.S. Code Congressional and Administrative News, 94th Cong., 1st Sess., 1975, p. 2305.
[6] Id.

"which increasingly has served to polarize elements of our society in a manner wherein the dialogue has become entirely destructive rather than constructive. As polarization intensifies neighborhood decline accelerates.'"[7]

The report continues, "The words 'redlining' or 'mortgage disinvestment' have come to symbolize the 'facts of failure' in this nation, despite a decade—and even longer—of good faith efforts by both parties under three Presidents to insure the realization of the American dream: 'a decent home and a suitable living environment for every American family.' "[8]

What Constitutes Redlining

A mortgage lender is said to redline when, in a specific geographic area located within a larger geographic area that is normally serviced by that lender, the lender (1) refuses to accept any applications for loans secured by real estate within the specific area; (2) refuses to make any loans secured by real estate in the area; (3) refuses to make loans secured by real estate within the specific area unless the loans are guaranteed by some form of mortgage insurance, either public or private; or (4) will grant loans secured by real estate in the area but only on terms more onerous than accorded such loans outside of the specific area, such as lower loan to value ratios requiring larger down payments, higher rates of interest, larger loan fees, and shorter loan periods.[9]

The House Committee observed that "Today, communities populated by the backbone of our cities and nation—the blue-collar worker—are being deprived of adequate credit—the credit necessary to purchase a home or make improvements to existing property simply because of the location of the property. . . . The refusal of local lenders, throughout the country, to make loans, not on the basis of the credit worthiness of the individual applicant or the soundness of the particular house, but on the very subjective judgment on the part of the lender that the neighborhood may be 'declining' has accelerated the process of neighborhood deterioration and discouraged revitalization of cities."[10]

Purpose of the Act

The Home Mortgage Disclosure Act observes that some depository institutions[11] have sometimes contributed to the decline of certain geographic areas by "their failure pursuant to their chartering responsibilities" to provide home financing to qualified applicants on reasonable terms and conditions.[12] The stated purpose of the act is to provide both citizens and public officials with sufficient information "to enable them to determine whether depository institutions are filling their obligations to serve the housing needs of the communities and neighborhoods in which they are located and to assist public officials in their determination of the distribution of public sector investments in a manner designed to improve the private investment environment."[13]

To accomplish this purpose, the act requires every depository institution with a home office or branch in a Standard Metropolitan Statistical Area (SMSA), as defined by the Bureau of the Census, to compile and make available for public inspection and copying at the home office and at least one branch in the area, the following information:[14]

1 The number and total dollar amount of mortgage loans[15] originated or purchased during each fiscal year, itemized by census tract if

---

[7] Id.
[8] Id., p. 2311.
[9] See State of California Business and Transportation Agency, *Special Hearings on Redlining* (1975).
[10] House Report (Committee on Banking, Currency and Housing) No. 94-561, 2 U.S. Code Congressional and Administrative News, 94th Cong., 1st Sess., 1975, p. 2313.
[11] Defined as meaning any commercial bank, savings bank, savings and loan association, building and loan association, or credit that makes federally related mortgage loans. 12 U.S.C., sec. 2802(2).
[12] Id., sec. 2801(a).
[13] Id., sec. 2801(b).
[14] Id., sec. 2803(a)(1).
[15] As the term "mortgage loan" is used in the act it means a loan which is secured by *residential* real estate or a loan for *home improvements*. 12 U.S.C., sec. 2802(1).

readily available at reasonable cost or, if not, by postal zip code.[16]

2 The number and total dollar amount of mortgage loans secured by real estate located outside the Standard Metropolitan Statistical Area.[17]

3 The number and dollar amount of mortgage loans within the census tract that are FHA-insured or VA-guaranteed.[18]

4 The number and dollar amount of mortgage loans made to borrowers who, at the time of executing the mortgage, did not intend to reside in the mortgaged property.[19]

5 The number and dollar amount of home improvement loans.[20]

Use of Disclosed Information

The House Committee on Banking, Currency and Housing while recognizing that "arbitrary disinvestment by lending institutions" is only one of the many causes of urban decline, expressed the belief that the information required to be disclosed by the act is a vital and essential step in the process of reversing and preventing neighborhood decline. "Disclosure," the committee stated, "will help people exercise their right to inform about lending practices and patterns in their neighborhoods and assist public officials at all levels in their determination of the distribution of public sector investments in a manner designed to improve the private investment environment."[21]

The committee also expressed the belief that the disclosure of the information required by the act will "identify the beginning stages of redlining, the point at which a neighborhood can be saved."[22] "It will also provide a vehicle for neighborhood residents, public officials and financial institutions to enter into partnerships with each other in joint efforts to plan reinvestment strategies for a declining neighborhood."[23]

UNIFORM LAND TRANSACTIONS ACT

The **Uniform Land Transactions Act,** referred to as the "ULTA," is a proposed law drafted by the National Conference of Commissioners on Uniform State Laws and submitted to the various states for adoption.[24] The act consists of three articles: (1) Article 1 which contains definitions and general provisions applicable both to sales and security transactions; (2) Article 2 which deals with sales of real estate, including lease transactions; and (3) Article 3 which is concerned with secured transactions and contains provisions relative to contract formation, extent of security interests including provisions as to future advances and after-acquired property, rights of the debtor and secured creditor as to the real estate, and provisions with respect to foreclosure.

Although no state has yet adopted the ULTA in its entirety, it is reasonable to assume that at one time or another the entire act or its separate articles will be considered by the legislatures of most states and, with modifications to conform to local customs and preferences, be adopted in whole or in part by a significant number. Because of this likelihood, when considering the rights and obligations of mortgagor-debtors and mortgagee-creditors as created by operation of law, it seems desirable to examine the manner in which those rights and obligations are treated in the uniform act.

Objectives of the ULTA

The declared purposes of the ULTA are

1 to simplify, clarify, and modernize the law governing real estate transactions;

2 to promote the interstate flow of funds for real estate transactions;

---

[16] Id., sec. 2803(a)(1) and (2)(A).
[17] Id., sec. 2803(a)(2)(B).
[18] Id., sec. 2803(b)(1).
[19] Id., sec. 2803(b)(2).
[20] Id., sec. 2803(b)(3).
[21] House Report (Committee on Banking, Currency and Housing) No. 94-561, 2 U.S. Code Congressional and Administrative News, 94th Cong., 1st Sess., 1975, p. 2315.
[22] Id.
[23] Id., p. 2316.
[24] The final draft of the act was approved for submission to the states by the National Conference of Commissioners on Uniform State Laws at their annual conference Aug. 2–8, 1975. The act was extensively amended in 1977.

3 to protect consumer buyers and borrowers against practices which may cause unreasonable risk of harm to them; and

4 to make uniform the law with respect to the subject of the Act among the states enacting it.[25]

Uniformity in land transactions, according to the commissioners,[26] is needed not so much because land is fixed and hence does not move from state to state, but rather because individuals and business entities do move from state to state and frequently conduct land transactions involving land in many states. This is the case particularly with respect to national lenders and dealers in the secondary mortgage market.

One observer has pointed out that "Although the enumerated goals of the Act will not invoke much support from real estate interest groups, the objective of promoting money flow will engender considerable enthusiasm. It is possible, therefore, that state legislatures will adopt only that portion of the Act, article 3, that promotes real estate financing."[27] The same observer noted that the ULTA has received little support from the legal community and that this is unfortunate, at least as far as Article 3 is concerned, because an overhaul of mortgage law is long overdue. And while the act's attempted reform of mortgage law is "subject to criticism on several counts, it is a thoughtful and progressive answer to many deep-rooted real estate financing problems."[28]

Need for Uniformity in Security Transactions

The Introductory Comment to Article 3 of the ULTA states that the article sets out a comprehensive scheme for the supervision of consensual transactions creating security interest in real estate. The comment also notes that "this Article covers the portion of real estate law where the need and desirability of uniformity is most pressing."

In a federal proposal to establish a uniform foreclosure system for government underwritten or owned mortgages, there is a congressional finding[29] that a uniform foreclosure system would correct the lack of free flow of mortgage money to home owners at reasonabe rates, the delays in completing real estate foreclosures that have resulted in vandalism, depreciation, and waste, and the fact of excessive foreclosure costs in many parts of the country.

Introduction of the Term "Protected Party"

The ULTA introduces the new and significant concept of the "protected party." As the term is used in Article 3 of the act, a *protected party* is one who contracts to give a real estate security interest in residential real estate, all or part of which he occupies or intends to occupy as his residence.[30] As compared to other persons who contract to give real estate security interests, the ULTA accords special treatment and a privileged status to a protected party.

The act defines "residential real estate" as it relates to a protected party to be real estate, improved or to be improved. "containing not more than [3] acres, not more than 4 dwelling units, and no non-residential uses for which the protected party is a lessor."[31] A condominium unit that otherwise qualifies as residential real estate does not lose that status even though the common elements of the condominium include more than the act's 3 acres or the fact that the condominium contains units used for nonresidential purposes.[32]

According to the act's draftsmen, the foregoing definition of a protected party, "which confines the protection to owner-occupied residential real estate, should be compared with many of the consumer credit protection laws in

---

[25] Uniform Land Transactions Act (hereinafter cited as "ULTA"), sec. 1-102.

[26] Id., sec. 1-102, Comment.

[27] Jon W. Bruce, "Mortgage Law Reform under the Uniform Land Transactions Act," 64 *Georgetown Law Journal* 1245 (1976), pp. 1246–1247.

[28] Id., p. 1288.

[29] Federal Mortgage Foreclosure Act of 1973, H.R.10688 and S.2507, 93rd Cong., 1st Sess., sec. 402.

[30] ULTA, sec. 1-203(a)(1).

[31] Id., sec. 1-203(b).

[32] Id.

which protection is given to the individual regardless of the character of the real estate if the purpose of the credit is a consumer purpose."[33]

THE UNDERLYING OBLIGATION

The sole function of a mortgage is to provide security for an obligation that is owed by the person who creates the security. In the case of real estate mortgages, the secured obligation normally arises from the loan of money. The existence of a debt or obligation is absolutely essential to the existence of a mortgage and the validity of the mortgage is itself dependent upon the validity of the obligation that the mortgage secures. Because a mortgage is incidental to the underlying obligation, any benefit to be derived by a lender from a mortgage is conditioned upon the failure of the debtor to repay his loan in accordance with the terms of the loan agreement. The rights of the lender in the borrower's real estate *after* the borrower defaults on his obligation are the essence of a real estate mortgage. The existence of these rights is what distinguishes a secured lender or creditor from an unsecured one.

Although the obligation that is secured by a real estate mortgage may be evidenced by a promise contained in the mortgage instrument itself, more commonly the promise is in a writing that is separate and distinct from the mortgage. Where, as is commonly the case, the mortgagor-debtor's obligation is a promise to pay a sum of money, the obligation will be evidenced by a written instrument known as a promissory note.

Promissory Note

General Characteristics A **promissory note** is a written promise of one person, technically known as the *maker*, to pay a specified sum of money to another person called the *payee*, in accordance with the terms and conditions agreed upon by the parties.

A promissory note may be either negotiable or nonnegotiable in form, but most if not all notes used in real estate transactions are made negotiable by the parties. The effect of a note being negotiable is that it may be passed from one person to another almost in the same manner as money itself. Technically, it is said that if a note is *negotiable* it may be transferred to a holder in due course free from certain types of defenses that the maker of the note might have asserted against the original payee when he endeavored to collect on the note. A *nonnegotiable* instrument does not possess these attributes and for that reason is much less commonly used by institutional lenders.

Whether a note is negotiable or not is merely a question of whether it satisfies certain statutory requirements as to form. The Uniform Commercial Code[34] requires that for a note to be negotiable it (1) must be in writing and be signed by the maker, (2) must contain an unconditional promise to pay a certain sum in money, (3) must be payable on demand or at a determinable future time, and (4) must be payable to the order of a named person or to the bearer of the note.

Types of Promissory Notes Two types of promissory notes are in general use in real estate financing transactions: (1) the straight note and (2) the installment note. Either type may be negotiable or nonnegotiable but, as indicated above, the note most commonly will be negotiable.

Straight Note A **straight note** is one which provides that during the term of the note only interest on the debt need be paid. Interest at the rate agreed on by the contracting parties is payable at intervals stated in the note with the full amount of the principal becoming payable in a lump sum at the end of the term. Figure 15-1 is an example of a straight note in negotiable form.

---

[33] Id., sec. 1-203, Comment 2.

[34] Article 3, secs. 3-104 through 3-111. The UCC has been adopted by all states except Louisiana.

Figure 15-1

```
                    PROMISSORY NOTE—STRAIGHT

$  (amount)                           (place of making)         ,
                                      (date)           , 19

    On  (date) , 19   , for value received, the undersigned promises to pay
to  (name of payee) , or order, at  (street address) , City of          ,
State of       the sum of  (written amount)  Dollars ($       ), with interest
from  (date) , 19   , until the principal is paid, at the rate of  (amount)  per
annum, interest payable  (indicate the method for payment of interest)  .

    Should interest not be paid as herein provided it shall bear interest at the
same rate as the principal. If there should be a default in the payment of interest
when due, the whole sum of principal and interest shall become immediately due
at the option of the holder of this note, without notice.

    Principal and interest are payable in lawful money of the United States.

    In the event a suit to enforce payment of this note be commenced, the
undersigned agrees to pay all costs of collection including reasonable attorney's
fees.

    This note is secured by a Mortgage (or Deed of Trust) of even date herewith,
executed in favor of the above-named payee.

                                            (signature of maker)
```

Installment Note An **installment note** is one that provides for equal or constant periodic payments throughout the term of the note. Each periodic payment includes both interest on the outstanding debt and sums to retire or amortize the principal over the term of the note. Figure 15-2 is an example of a negotiable installment note.

By agreement of the parties and provisions to that effect in the note, the periodic installment payments may be designed to pay all interest currently due and an amount calculated to amortize the entire amount of the principal by the end of the term of the note. On the other hand, in order to keep the payments smaller, the periodic installments may cover all interest currently due but not be large enough to fully retire the debt at the end of the term of the note. In such a case, the note will provide for the debtor to pay a lump sum at the end of the term when the note falls due. This lump sum payment that becomes due and payable upon maturity of the note is called a *balloon* payment.

Although interest-only notes and notes providing for balloon payments are not uncommon in real estate investment financing, they are not generally used in the financing of pur-

Figure 15-2

PROMISSORY NOTE—INSTALLMENT

$ __(amount)__   __(place of making)__ ,
                                                  __(date)__ , 19 __ .

    In installments as herein stated, for value received, the undersigned promises to pay to __(name of payee)__ , or order, at __(street address)__ , City of _____ , State of _____ the sum of __(written amount)__ Dollars ($ _____), with interest from __(date)__ , 19 __ , on the unpaid principal at the rate of __(amount)__ percent per annum. Principal and interest shall be payable in equal installments of $ __(amount)__ on the _____ day of each month, beginning on __(date)__ , 19 __ , and continuing until __(date)__ , 19 __ , on which date the entire unpaid principal with unpaid interest due thereon shall be due and payable.

    Each installment payment shall first be credited to interest then due with the remainder credited to the principal. If there should be a default in the payment of any installment when due, the whole sum of principal and interest shall become immediately due at the option of the holder of this note, without notice.

    Principal and interest are payable in lawful money of the United States.

    In the event a suit to enforce payment of this note be commenced, the undersigned agrees to pay all costs of collection including reasonable attorney's fees.

    This note is secured by a Mortgage (or Deed of Trust) of even date herewith, executed in favor of the above-named payee.

                                                __(signature of maker)__

---

chases of single-family homes. Obligations resulting from the loan of funds for the purchase of homes by borrowers almost always provide for equal monthly payments that not only pay the interest on the outstanding debt but also fully amortize the debt by the end of the period for which the loan was made.

Common Provisions in Promissory Notes

Since a promissory note results from negotiations and an agreement between a lender and a borrower or a creditor and a debtor, the note may contain any provisions that the parties are legally competent to agree upon. Despite the wide range of possible provisions, there are certain ones that tend to be more or less standard in promissory notes secured by real estate mortgages. These relatively common provisions include the following.

It should be noted that it is not uncommon for some of the same provisions to appear in both the note and the mortgage that secures it, but this is not necessary. In real estate security transactions, the note and the mortgage taken together make up the contract between the parties. In those relatively rare instances where the provisions of the note and the mortgage are in conflict, the provisions in the promissory note will control.

Provisions Pertaining to Interest Within relatively narrow limits fixed by market conditions and competition, the rate of interest applicable to a loan is a matter for negotiation by the parties and agreement between them.

Contract Rate and Market Rate of Interest The rate of interest agreed upon by the parties and which is stated in the promissory note is referred to as the **contract rate.** Except in unusual cases, the contract rate that appears in the note will reflect the rate of interest prevailing in the money market at the time the loan agreement was concluded. The **market rate** of interest for loans secured by mortgages fluctuates in accordance with the demand for such loans and the supply of funds available for mortgage lending.

In most notes today the stated or contract rate of interest is a fixed or invariable rate that does not change during the term of the note. This is, of course, in sharp contrast to the market rate of interest which is subject to considerable fluctuation during the period that a long-term loan is outstanding. Consequently, whenever during the term of the loan the market rate of interest is higher than the contract rate appearing in the note, the borrower has the economic advantage. Conversely, when the market rate falls below the stated contract rate, the economic advantage shifts to the lender who holds the note.

Variable Interest Rate To overcome or minimize the shifting of economic advantage between the borrower and the lender during the term of the loan, promissory notes in recent years have begun to include provisions for what is known as a "variable interest rate." A **variable interest rate** is a device that permits the interest rate that is payable on a loan to fluctuate up and down in accordance with changes in economic conditions. The interest rate is pegged to some index or other fixed standard agreed to by the borrower or provided by statute.[35] Pegged as it is to a standard subject to economic conditions, a provision for variable interest of course can cause the rate of interest on a loan to fluctuate and tend to equal the market rate of interest at any given point in time.

Statutes authorizing the use of variable interest rates typically contain provisions designed to protect the interests of one who buys a home with borrowed funds and secures his variable interest loan with a mortgage on his home. The California statute,[36] for example, provides that (1) the rate may not change more often than once during any half-year period, (2) the change in rate may not exceed ¼ of 1 percent during any such period nor exceed 2½ percent over the period of the loan, (3) the borrower must be permitted to prepay any amount of his loan without charge or penalty within 90 days of notification of a rate increase, and (4) the provision for variable interest in a loan must be clearly and prominently disclosed in writing prior to the time the loan is made, and that provision must be set forth both in the promissory note and in the security document.

In some states, usury laws make the use of variable interest rates difficult or impossible.

Maximum Interest Rates and Usury **Usury** is the charging of a rate of interest that exceeds the maximum rate permitted by statute. Because of the diversity of statutory provisions, maximum rates and penalties for exceeding them vary considerably among the states.

Maximum interest rates in any given state commonly vary according to type of lender and

---

[35] For example, in California the standard for savings and loan associations is "the last published weighted average cost of savings, borrowings and Federal Home Loan Bank advances to members of the Federal Home Loan Bank of San Francisco as computed from statistics tabulated by the Federal Home Loan Bank of San Francisco." 10 California Administrative Code, sec. 240.2(a).

[36] California Civil Code, sec. 1916.5.

type of transaction that is financed. Revolving credit extended by retailers and personal loans by small-loan companies typically are permitted to charge a higher rate of interest than are loans that are secured by real estate mortgages, particularly when that real estate is the residence of the borrower. The maximum rate of interest permissible for loans secured by real estate tends to be in the 8 to 12 percent range on the average, but state usury laws are often subject to a number of complicated exceptions. Ceilings on interest rates for home mortgage loans have created problems in some states as rates of interest have continued to rise. Constitutions and statutes in a few states[37] specifically exempt savings and loan associations, the largest lenders of funds for the purchase of homes, from ceilings imposed by their usury laws.

Penalties for exceeding maximum interest rates vary from the mere loss of excess interest by the usurer[38] to the loss of the unpaid principal and interest,[39] with many forfeiture variations in between. The usury laws in some states[40] provide that anyone charging interest on a loan in excess of the maximum rate is guilty of a felony or a misdemeanor.

ULTA Position Because many state usury laws that set maximum rates for obligations secured by real estate mortgages have caused financing problems, the ULTA, except where protected parties are involved, eliminates interest ceilings altogether. Regardless of the identity of the lender or the priority of his lien, all real estate loans not involving protected parties may be made at any rate.[41]

Without recommending a particular rate, the act provides that loans to borrowers who are protected parties may not exceed a fixed rate which is to be determined and set on a local basis by each adopting legislature.[42]

In addition to requiring restitution of any excess charges paid, the ULTA requires a lender who exceeds the maximum rate to pay a protected party penalty damages in the amount of three times the excess amount received by the lender, but not more than $5,000 total damages. In addition, the protected party may receive attorney's fees and court costs.[43] Lenders do not lose their loan or their real estate security interest, however. They continue to exist unimpaired, except to the extent that the interest rate on the loan and the amount of the monthly payments are recalculated.[44]

Acceleration Clauses Promissory notes secured by real estate mortgages commonly contain provisions known as acceleration clauses. An **acceleration clause** is a provision that enables lenders, if they so choose, to declare the entire outstanding debt immediately due and payable if the borrower fails to perform a specified obligation and, if the borrower fails to pay the debt in its entirety, to foreclose on the security. Before a provision for acceleration can become operative, there must be a breach by the mortgagor-borrower of the condition on which the lender's right of acceleration is dependent. According to the general rule, the outstanding debt does not automatically mature upon the default or breach by the borrower. Instead, the default gives rise to an option or election on the part of the lender to accelerate the due date and declare the whole debt due and payble. The prevailing view is that under the ordinary acceleration clause the lender has a reasonable time after the borrower's default in which to elect to declare the debt to be due. If lenders do not exercise their option to accelerate within a reasonable period after the borrower's default, they will be deemed to have waived their right of acceleration. Their waiver,

---

[37] Among them are California, Colorado, Connecticut, and Illinois.
[38] As in Missouri and Ohio, for example.
[39] As in Arkansas and Connecticut, for example.
[40] For example, California, Florida, New Mexico, South Dakota, Texas, Vermont, and West Virginia.
[41] ULTA, sec. 3-403(a).
[42] Id., sec. 3-403(b).
[43] Id., sec. 3-405(a) and (b).
[44] Id., sec. 3-405(b).

however, applies only to the present default and does not preclude lenders from exercising their option with respect to any future default or breach by the debtor.

The prevailing view holds that an acceleration clause neither provides for a forfeiture nor a penalty on the part of the mortgagor-debtor but is simply a contractual provision that determines when the secured debt is payable. In the absence of fraud or bad faith on the part of the mortgagee-creditor, an acceleration clause as a general rule will be enforced against a mortgagor-debtor even though his default is not willful but results instead from his negligence, mistake, or by accident. Some courts protect a mortgagor-debtor from defaults that result from unusual circumstances that are beyond the mortgagor's control.

While the provisions of acceleration clauses may vary considerably with respect to the acts or events that will trigger a lender's right to accelerate the maturity of the debt, such clauses can be roughly classified in three general categories: (1) clauses providing for acceleration upon default of a promise or obligation of the debtor, (2) clauses permitting acceleration upon sale of the mortgaged premises by the debtor, and (3) clauses providing that the lender shall have the right to accelerate if the debtor further encumbers the mortgaged premises. It should be recognized that the three types of clauses may be, and in practice frequently are, combined in a single all-inclusive acceleration clause.

Acceleration Because of Default One type of acceleration clause gives the lender the right to call the entire outstanding debt due and payable upon the debtor's failure to pay any installment when due, to pay real property taxes or assessments, or to pay premiums on hazard insurance on the property that secures the debt. The following is typical of acceleration clauses pertaining to such matters.

> If any default should occur in the payment of any installment of the principal of the indebtedness secured, or any interest thereon, the lender shall have the right to elect to have the entire secured indebtedness become immediately due, and the lender may thereupon commence legal proceedings for the foreclosure of the mortgage securing this indebtedness and for the sale of the mortgaged premises, and from the net proceeds of such sale the lender shall receive all indebtedness secured by the mortgaged premises, together with attorney fees and costs.
>
> The entire amount of the principal sum of the indebtedness shall, at the option of the lender, become due and payable upon default by the debtor in the payment of any tax or assessment for a period of (state number) days or after the default in keeping the buildings on the mortgaged premises insured against loss by fire or other casualty for the benefit and to the satisfaction of the lender.

Acceleration clauses of this type rarely, if ever, encounter any difficulty in the courts.

As an alternative to this kind of clause, or sometimes in addition to it, a note will contain a provision expressly authorizing the lender to pay taxes, assessments, or insurance premiums in behalf of the buyer and to add those expenditures to the amount of the loan and the security.

Sometimes the foregoing type of acceleration clause will also contain a provision requiring the mortgagor-borrower to keep the mortgaged property in good repair—in other words, not to commit waste. Waste, as we have seen, is commonly defined as conduct done or permitted by one in lawful possession of property that causes physical damage to or destruction of the property. Waste, it will be recalled, may be either voluntary, as where structures or ornamental trees or shrubbery are removed, or permissive, as where the property is allowed to fall into disrepair. It is accepted without dispute that where either type of waste occurs, the lender's right to accelerate arises and if the debt is not paid in full the lender may foreclose. If future waste is threatened before foreclosure can take place, the lender may obtain an injunction to protect his security interest.

Acceleration Because of Sale A common type of acceleration provision appearing in notes secured by real estate mortgages is the **due-on-sale clause.** In such clauses, the event that triggers the lender's right to call the borrower's entire debt immediately due and payable is the sale of the mortgaged property by the mortgagor-borrower without first having obtained the lender's approval to do so. A typical due-on-sale clause would be similar to the following.

> If the borrower shall sell, transfer, or dispose of the mortgaged property, or any part thereof, without the prior written consent of the lender, then the lender shall have the right, at his option, to declare all sums secured by the mortgaged property to be immediately due and payable.

The traditional purpose of due-on-sale clauses has been to protect a lender's security interest by reducing the risk of waste and depreciation of mortgaged property that might result from a conveyance by the borrower to a person with a poor reputation for maintenance and repair. Because protection of his security is a valid and prudent objective of a lender, all states permit the enforcement of due-on-sale clauses when a sale jeopardizes the lender's security position.

To the extent that sales of mortgaged properties do occur, the enforceability of due-on-sale clauses enables a lender to keep his loan portfolio at or near current interest rates by accelerating the maturity of existing loans with interest rates below the market and freeing funds for new loans. In the words of the National Conference of Commissioners on Uniform State Laws, "One reason for the due-on-sale clause is that of empowering the security creditor to get rid of an old security agreement of long duration which has an interest rate substantially below market. The clause restricts the power of a debtor to sell his favorable interest rate."[45]

[45] Id., sec. 3-208, Comment 1.

Acceleration Because of Encumbrance Promissory notes commonly contain an acceleration provision in the form of a **due-on-encumbrance clause.** The effect of such a clause is clearly distinguishable from that of a due-on-sale clause. In a due-on-encumbrance clause, as contrasted with a due-on-sale clause, the event that triggers a lender's option to call the debt due and payable is not the sale of the mortgaged property but the giving of a second or junior mortgage on the mortgaged property without the consent of the lender. In practice, a provision giving a lender the option to accelerate the outstanding debt upon further encumbrance of the property is often combined with one giving him the right to accelerate on sale. The following is an example of such a combined "due-on" clause.

> If the borrower shall sell, convey, alienate, or further encumber the mortgaged property without the prior written consent of the lender, the lender may at his option declare all sums secured by the mortgaged property immediately due and payable.

While the majority rule recognizes a lender's right of automatic enforceability of a due-on-sale clause because of the need to protect his security, the prevailing view does not accord automatic enforceability to due-on-encumbrance clauses. Before a due-on-encumbrance clause will be enforced, the lender seeking to call the outstanding debt due and payable must show that the borrower's new encumbrance on the mortgaged property impairs or endangers the lender's security. If the security is not endangered by the borrower's execution of a second lien, the due-on-encumbrance clause will not be enforced but will instead be construed as being an unreasonable restraint on alienation.

Federal Home Loan Bank Board Regulations In its regulation of federally chartered savings and loan associations, the Federal Home Loan Bank Board, using the term "due-on-sale" clause to include acceleration options arising both from sales and encumbrances, limits the powers of federal associations with respect to loans secured by homes occupied by the borrower. The FHLBB regulations provide that where the security for a loan is a borrower-occupied home a federal association may not exercise a due-on-sale clause that is based on (1) the "creation of a lien or other encumbrance subordinate to the association's security instrument," (2) the "creation of a purchase money security interest for household appliances," or (3) the "transfer by devise, descent, or by operation of law upon the death of a joint tenant." The regulations further provide that in those situations where acceleration is permissible no association "shall impose a prepayment charge or equivalent fee in connection with the accleration of the loan pursuant to a due-on-sale clause."[46]

ULTA Position The Uniform Land Transaction Act provides that a debtor has the *power* to transfer his interest in mortgaged real estate even though the mortgage or deed of trust attempts to prohibit that power.[47] Despite the fact that the debtor has this power to convey, the act specifically permits the mortgage or deed of trust to contain a due-on-sale clause in which the parties agree that the mortgagor's debt becomes subject to acceleration by the secured creditor and thus becomes due and payable in full if a sale is made without the creditor's consent.[48]

The act accords special treatment to a person who sells his or her *dwelling* that is subject to a mortgage or deed of trust containing a due-on-sale clause that provides for acceleration of the outstanding debt in the event of a sale. If the creditor consents to the sale without accelerating the debt but demands as a condition to that consent a rate of interest higher than that applicable to the existing mortgage, the demand may be refused and the outstanding debt be prepaid.

If the outstanding debt is paid within 3 months following the rejection of the demand for a higher interest rate, no prepayment penalty may be charged by the creditor.[49]

Prepayment Clauses Unless the provisions of a promissory note expressly permit it, the maker-borrower may not pay off his debt until the agreed maturity date. Just as lenders may insist on not being paid late, they also have the right to refuse to accept payment of a loan early. Financial institutions are in the business of loaning money at interest to credit-worthy borrowers and as long as the contract rate of interest on a well-secured loan remains equal to or higher than the market rate, it is generally to their interest to have the loan continue to maturity. On the other hand, when the contract rate of interest becomes higher than the existing market rate, there is an incentive for the borrower to refinance the loan at the lower market rate and pay off the existing loan with the proceeds of the new loan. Unless the note evidencing the existing loan provides that it may be paid in full before maturity, the borrower may prepay his loan only if the lender agrees to permit him to do so. When the borrower's inducement to refinance and prepay his loan is a decline in the market rate of interest, he is apt to find himself in a weak bargaining position when he seeks to obtain the right to prepay from the creditor. The time for the borrower to bargain for the privilege to prepay his debt is at the time the loan is originated.

While some lenders may be reluctant to do so, competition often requires them to agree to the inclusion of a **prepayment clause** in loan contracts, which grants the borrower a limited or qualified right to prepay his debt. A restriction commonly imposed by lenders permits prepayment only if a fee or penalty is paid, with the amount of the fee generally decreasing as the loan grows older, until no fee is charged at all. For example, a loan may not be prepayable

---

[46] 12 C.F.R., sec. 545.6-11(g). These provisions apply to loans made after July 31, 1976.
[47] ULTA, sec. 3-208(a).
[48] Id.

[49] Id., sec. 3-208(b).

at all during the first year of its existence, or it may be subject to a prepayment fee equal to 6 months' advance interest on any amount prepaid during the first 3 years, 3 months' interest on the amount prepaid during the fourth and fifth years, and no fee if prepaid after 5 years.

In addition to prepayment privileges being granted by lenders at the time loans are originated, the prepayment of certain types of loans is authorized by federal and state statutes. Federal law provides that VA-guaranteed loans may be prepaid, in whole or in part, together with accrued interest, at any time without penalty[50] and that FHA-insured loans secured by mortgages on single-family residences may be prepaid subject to a formula that limits the fee to not more than 1 percent of the loan balance.[51] Federally chartered savings and loan associations must permit the prepayment of conventional loans on owner-occupied homes with penalties being limited to "6 months' advance interest on that part of the aggregate amount of all prepayments made on such loan in any 12-month period which exceed 20 percent of the original principal amount of the loan."[52]

A California statute[53] provides that

> the principal and accrued interest on any loan secured by a mortgage or deed of trust on real property containing a *single-family, owner-occupied dwelling* may be prepaid in whole or in part at any time but only a prepayment made within five years of the date of execution of such mortgage or deed of trust may be subject to a prepayment charge and then solely as herein set forth. An amount not exceeding 20 percent of the original principal amount may be paid within any 12-month period without penalty. A prepayment charge may be imposed on any amount paid in any 12-month period in excess of 20 percent of the original principal amount of the loan which charge shall not exceed an amount equal to the payment of six months' advance interest on the amount prepaid in excess of 20 percent of the original principal amount. [Emphasis added.]

Prepayment and Usury Prepayment fees have been attacked on the grounds that when the interest rate on a loan is at the legal maximum rate, the imposition of a prepayment penalty renders the transaction usurious. The standard judicial response to such an allegation is that the prepayment is not interest but is consideration for the exercise of a privilege. The courts have emphasized that it is the borrower who controls the time and the fact of prepayment and have reasoned that the borrower should not have it within his power to render an otherwise proper loan usurious by exercising his privilege to prepay.

Maintenance of Escrow Accounts

Nature of an Escrow Account Promissory notes often provide that the borrower's monthly mortgage payments shall include, in addition to sums for retirement of the principal of the debt and interest, certain amounts for the payment of such recurring items as real estate taxes and hazard insurance premiums. These funds are set aside by the lender each month in **escrow accounts** (also known as "impound" or "trust" accounts) and accumulated for the payment of tax bills and insurance premiums as they fall due. A lender's purpose in requiring advance payments into these accounts is the desire to protect its security from the priority of tax liens and the possibility of loss of security due to fire and other hazards.

It is important to distinguish an escrow account that is accumulated for the payment of taxes and insurance premiums from the term "escrow" as it is used in connection with the closing of real estate sales transactions. Payments that are made into an escrow account continue on a regular basis throughout the entire period of the loan, while the payment of purchase money into escrow at the time of title closing is made only once.

---

[50] 38 C.F.R., sec. 36.4113 (1968).
[51] 24 C.F.R., secs. 203.22, 285 (1968).
[52] 12 C.F.R., sec. 545.6-12(b).
[53] California Civil Code, sec. 2954.9(b).

Escrow Accounts Frequently Required The requirement that escrow accounts be maintained for loans secured by mortgages on homes is relatively widespread, in large part because such accounts are mandatory for FHA-insured loans.

The Federal Housing Administration's regulations[54] provide that: "The mortgage shall provide for such equal monthly payments by the mortgagor to the mortgagee as will amortize (1) the ground rents, if any; (2) the estimated amount of all taxes; (3) special assessments, if any; (4) flood insurance premiums, if flood insurance is required by the [Federal Housing] Commissioner; and (5) fire and other hazard insurance premiums, if any, within a period ending one month prior to the dates on which the same become delinquent."

Although the Veterans Administration requires that escrow accounts be maintained under its *direct* loan program, such accounts are not required under the more common *VA-guaranteed* home loan program.[55]

The Farmers Home Administration, which makes both direct and insured loans in rural areas, does not require that escrow accounts be maintained.

The Federal Home Loan Bank Board which supervises all federally chartered savings and loan associations provides that such associations "may require that any or all portions of the estimated annual taxes, assessments, insurance premiums, and other charges on any loan to be paid in advance in addition to interest and principal payments on such loan, to enable the association to pay such charges as they become due from the funds so received."[56]

Many lenders making conventional loans, that is, loans that are not underwritten by a federal government agency, require that escrow accounts be maintained, particularly when the loan-to-value ratio is high. A high loan-to-value ratio results when a mortgagor-borrower supplies only a small percentage of the sales price as a cash down payment for the purchase of real estate. Maximum permissible loan-to-value ratios are usually established by state legislation or by state and federal agencies' banking and lending regulations.

Dispute Relative to Payment of Interest According to the prevailing practice, borrowers are not paid interest on the funds accumulated in their escrow accounts. Because of this, many borrowers view such accounts as being in the nature of interest-free, short-term loans or lines of credit extended by them which yield an income to lenders when those funds are invested by them. Borrowers argue that the denial of interest on these accounts is in effect a hidden charge for the loan of money that is not reflected in the loan agreement.[57]

Lenders reply that they do not make extra profit and that the income earned from investing funds from escrow accounts fails to offset the costs of handling these accounts. The argument is also made that lenders provide a service to the homeowner by making his property tax and insurance payments for him.

Over the past several years borrowers have brought a number of unsuccessful lawsuits to recoup lost interest. Also, for a number of years borrowers have sought state and federal legislation that would require lenders to pay interest on escrow accounts. Recently a few states have responded to borrowers' demands and have enacted legislation requiring the payment of interest on escrow accounts. For example, Califor-

---

[54] 24 C.F.R., sec. 23(a).
[55] 38 C.F.R., sec. 4512.
[56] 12 C.F.R., sec. 545.6-11(b).

[57] The General Accounting Office has estimated that homeowners collectively lose over $235 million a year in possible interest income. The $235 million figure is based on the GAO estimate that escrow account collections nation-wide amount to $9.4 billion annually. The interest loss estimate assumes that escrow payments are collected monthly and disbursed annually, and that the homeowners would earn the passbook rate of 5 percent interest. See General Accounting Office, "Study of the Feasibility of Escrow Accounts on Residential Mortgages Becoming Interest Bearing" (1973), pp. 6–7.

nia[58] and Connecticut[59] have laws requiring the payment of 2 percent interest on such accounts, a New Hampshire statute[60] requires interest at a rate not less than 2 percent below that paid on savings accounts, and a Massachusetts law[61] requires interest to be paid on escrow accounts but leaves the interest rate to the discretion of the lender.

Some commentators point out that any increased costs imposed by legislation on lenders will undoubtedly be passed on to borrowers in the form of increased interest rates and service charges on loans. Others insist that if additional charges are necessary to pay the lenders' costs of servicing escrow accounts, they should be openly reflected in mortgage loan rates and not disguised or hidden.

RESPA Position Concerning Escrow Accounts Section 10 of the Real Estate Settlement Procedures Act[62] places limits on the amount of advance payments that a lender may require a borrower to pay into escrow or impound accounts, which the act calls "reserve accounts."

RESPA provides that the amount paid into escrow or reserve accounts at the *time of settlement*[63] may not exceed "a sum that will be sufficient to pay such taxes, insurance premiums and other charges attributable to the period beginning on the last date on which each such charge would have been paid under the normal lending practice of the lender and local custom . . . and ending on the due date of its first full installment payment under the mortgage, plus one-sixth of the estimated total amount of such taxes, insurance premiums and other charges to be paid on dates, as provided above, during the ensuing twelve-month period."[64]

The act also limits the amount of any deposit paid into an escrow or reserve account that a lender may require *after the date of settlement* to not more than one-twelfth of the annual taxes and other charges each month. A lender's demand for a larger payment, however, is permissible under the act if the larger amount is needed to make up a deficit in the borrower's escrow account or to maintain the cushion of one-sixth of annual charges paid at the time of settlement.[65] A deficit in the borrower's account would occur, for example, if real estate taxes or hazard insurance premiums should be increased.

MORTGAGE AS A SECURITY DEVICE

Difference between Secured and Unsecured Obligations

The function of a real estate mortgage is to provide security for the performance of an obligation—the obligation usually being in the form of a promissory note by which one person promises to repay borrowed funds to another. As we have seen, the presence of an underlying obligation is absolutely essential to the existence of a mortgage. The validity of an otherwise enforceable mortgage is entirely dependent on the validity of the obligation that the mortgage secures.

A debt that is secured by a real estate mortgage differs markedly from an unsecured obligation. A mortgage gives to a lender-creditor certain rights in a designated parcel of real estate belonging to a borrower-debtor in the event of the latter's default on his debt. These rights of the creditor are what distinguishes a secured obligation from an unsecured one. For example, if an unsecured debt is defaulted on, the creditor must, after having obtained a judg-

---

[58] California Civil Code, sec. 2954.8.
[59] Connecticut Public Act, No. 73-607 (1973).
[60] New Hampshire Rev. Stat. Ann., sec. 384.1c.
[61] Act of May 21, 1973, ch. 299, Massachusetts Acts and Resolves, 1975.
[62] 12 U.S.C., sec. 2609.
[63] "Settlement" is defined as "the formal process by which ownership of real property passes from seller to buyer. It is the end of the home buying process, the time when title to the property is transferred from the seller to the buyer." HUD Special Information Booklet entitled "Settlement Costs—A HUD Guide," 41 Fed. Reg. 23623 (June 10, 1976), p. 1.

[64] RESPA, sec. 10(1), 12 U.S.C., sec. 2609(1).
[65] RESPA, sec. 10(2), 12 U.S.C., sec. 2609(2).

ment from a court, search for assets of the debtor that may be seized and sold by an officer of the court in satisfaction of the creditor's judgment. The unsecured creditor may either find that the debtor's assets are statutorily exempt from seizure and sale or that other creditors have preferred claims in those assets. A secured creditor, on the other hand, by virtue of his mortgage or similar security device, acquires a security interest in a specific asset of the debtor which gives the creditor, in the event of a default by the debtor, a preferential claim against the proceeds of the sale of the asset up to the full amount of the unpaid debt.

Parties to a Mortgage

A borrower or debtor who executes a mortgage is known as a **mortgagor** and the lender or creditor for whose benefit the security is created is called a **mortgagee**.

Two Theories of Mortgages

Traditionally, two distinct theories concerning the nature of a real estate mortgage have existed among the various states—the *title theory* and the *lien theory*. The essential difference between the two theories arises from divergent views as to who holds title to the mortgaged property after a security transaction has been concluded.

Title Theory A minority of states[66] adopted the title theory of real estate mortgages as a part of their inherited common law and, with certain modifications, have retained that concept today. According to the title theory, a mortgage transfers legal title to the mortgaged property from the mortgagor-borrower to the mortgagee-lender as security from the former to the latter. While this conveyance of title carries with it the incidents of ownership and hence entitles the mortgagee to possession of the mortgaged real estate, mortgages in "title states" generally contain provisions that permit the mortgagor to remain in possession of the premises as long as he does not default on the secured obligation. Absent a stipulation or agreement to the contrary, however, the general rule at common law is that, because of his legal title, the mortgagee-lender is entitled to possession of the mortgaged premises immediately upon execution of the mortgage.

Lien Theory A majority of the states have adopted the lien theory of real estate mortgages. Under this theory, the mortgagor-borrower is regarded as retaining the legal title to the mortgaged property and as transferring only a security interest in the form of a lien to the mortgagee-lender. Being a security interest rather than legal title, the lien acquired by the mortgagee does not entitle him to possession of the mortgaged property. The right of possession, which is an incident of the mortgagor's retained title, remains with him until such time as he defaults on his obligation and he is divested of his title when the mortgaged property is sold at foreclosure.

ULTA Position The Uniform Land Transactions Act adopts neither the title theory nor the lien theory of mortgages. Article 3 of the act, which deals with secured transactions, makes no determination as to whether the title to the mortgaged property is with the mortgagor or the mortgagee. The Introductory Comment to Article 3 states that "Rights, obligations and remedies under this Article do not depend on location of title. If under other law the location of title is important, for example the incidence of taxation, the parties are left free to contract as they will."

Requirements for a Valid Mortgage

Although no precise words or form are generally necessary to create a mortgage, in view of the fact that both title and lien theory states consider a mortgage to be the transfer of an inter-

---

[66] Alabama, Arkansas, Connecticut, Illinois, Maine, Maryland, Massachusetts, New Hampshire, New Jersey, North Carolina, Ohio, Pennsylvania, Rhode Island, Tennessee, Vermont, Virginia, and West Virginia.

est in real estate, certain requirements must be met. The execution of a real estate mortgage is ordinarily regulated by statute and the statutory formalities vary considerably among the states. Generally speaking, however, the requirements and formalities for a mortgage are essentially the same as those prescribed for the execution of deeds. The minimum requirements for the creation of a valid mortgage call for (1) a written instrument, (2) signed by the mortgagor, (3) that names the mortgagor and the mortgagee, (4) describes the mortgaged property sufficiently to identify it, (5) indicates the nature of the transaction, and (6) must be delivered to the mortgagee.

As a practical matter, the question whether a given mortgage satisfies a particular state's minimum requirements seldom arises because in most instances lenders, lawyers, and others execute mortgages either by completing standard printed forms or by using standardized or sterotyped models when drafting individual mortgages.

Termination of Mortgage

The mortgagee's security interest in mortgaged property is extinguished when the secured debt is paid in full. Upon termination of the mortgagee's security interest, full legal ownership is restored to the mortgagor in both title and lien states without the need for a release, reconveyance, or any other instrument being executed by the mortgagee. As we previously observed, a mortgage as a security device has legal existence only if there is an underlying obligation for it to secure. When the obligation ceases to exist because of payment in full, the mortgage is also extinguished.

DEED OF TRUST

Three-Party Security Device

A number of states,[67] including both those subscribing to the title theory and those adopting the lien theory, recognize a security device known variously as a **deed of trust,** a **trust deed,** or a **trust deed mortgage.** Unlike the "ordinary" mortgage which involves only two parties, the mortgagor-borrower and the mortgagee-lender, a deed of trust is a three-party security transaction. By executing a deed of trust, a borrower, known as the *trustor,* transfers title to real estate to a *trustee* who holds it in trust for the lender, called the *beneficiary,* to secure performance of an obligation owing from the trustor-borrower to the beneficiary-lender. Under the terms of a deed of trust, when the trustor-borrower has paid the secured loan, title will be reconveyed to him by the trustee. A deed of trust also contains a provision by which the trustor grants a power of sale to the trustee that enables him, upon the trustor's default on his obligation, to sell the real estate and apply the proceeds of the sale to the unpaid debt owing to the beneficiary. By virtue of his power of sale, when the trustee sells the property he transfers to the purchaser all the right, title, and interest that the trustor had in the property at the time he executed the deed of trust.

Functionally Similar to Mortgage

Although the differences between deeds of trust and ordinary form mortgages may have been significant at one time, there is a tendency for courts and legislatures to recognize the functional similarities between the two forms of security devices and to abolish any difference between them. For example, in a lien theory state a trustor-borrower retains the right to possession of the securing real estate despite the fact that he parts with legal title when he executes the deed of trust.

Because they are functionally so similar to real estate mortgages, deeds of trust do not warrant discussion separate and apart from mortgages. To the extent that the law governing deeds of trust differs significantly from the ordinary form of mortgage, the difference will be noted and examined. Otherwise, for convenience sake, the term "mortgage" as used here-

---

[67] Among them are Alabama, Alaska, California, Colorado, District of Columbia, Illinois, Mississippi, Missouri, Montana, Nebraska, Nevada, New Mexico, Oregon, Tennessee, Texas, Virginia, and West Virginia.

after includes deeds of trust, trust deeds, and trust deed mortgages.

ULTA Position

The ULTA uses neither the term "mortgage" nor "deed of trust" in Article 3 dealing with security transactions. "In place of such terms as 'mortgage,' 'contract for deed,' 'trust deed,' etc. this Article substitutes the general term 'security agreement.' "[68] **Security agreement** as defined by the act "means a writing that creates or provides for a security interest in real estate."[69] "Security interest," in turn, "means an interest in real estate which secures payment or performance of an obligation."[70]

PRIORITIES

Governed by Recording Laws

The relative priority of a mortgage with respect to other liens and claims against a particular parcel of real estate is governed by the recording laws of the state in which the mortgaged property is situated. Under most of these laws, in the absence of an agreement to the contrary or the mortgagee's actual knowledge of a previously existing mortgage, priorities between two or more mortgages on the same parcel of land are determined by the order in which the mortgages were recorded, rather than in accordance with the time sequence in which they were executed. In disputes between mortgagee-lenders as to the priority of their liens on the mortgagor's property, the critical date is the date of recordation of each of the mortgages.

Purchase Money Mortgage

Nature of a Purchase Money Mortgage A **purchase money mortgage** is a mortgage executed by a borrower to secure a loan which the borrower uses to purchase the property described in the mortgage and which constitutes the security for the money loaned. While it is said that a purchase money mortgage must be executed by a mortgagor contemporaneously with his acquisition of title to the property that serves as security, the two events need not occur at the same moment or even on the same day. A borrower's acquisition of title and his execution of a mortgage as security for a purchase money loan are deemed to be contemporaneous if they are parts of one continuous transaction.

A mortgage is a purchase money mortgage whether it names as mortgagee the seller of the mortgaged property or a third party lender who supplied funds for the purchase.

Priority of a Purchase Money Mortgage A purchase money mortgage has priority over all other liens or claims arising through the purchaser-mortgagor even though those liens and claims are prior in time or attach when the purchaser-mortgagor acquires title. The most frequent and important application of this rule occurs in connection with liens arising from judgments obtained against the purchaser-mortgagor before he executed the purchase money obligation.

In the absence of an agreement to the contrary, where purchase money mortgages are executed contemporaneously to the seller of the mortgaged property as part of the purchase price and to the lender of funds for the purchase of the property, the seller's mortgage will have priority over that of the lender.

The rationale most frequently advanced for the rule giving preference to purchase money mortgages over outstanding liens or claims previously acquired through the mortgagor is that the delivery of the deed giving title to the buyer and his execution of the mortgage are simultaneous acts and consequently no lien or claim arising through the mortgagor can attach to his title before the purchase money mortgage does.

To retain priority against subsequent liens or claims arising through the purchaser-mortgagor, purchase money mortgages must be recorded. For example, assume that S sold Blackacre to B, executed and delivered a deed to him, and took back a note secured by a mortgage on the property as part of the purchase

---

[68] ULTA, sec. 3-103.
[69] Id., sec. 3-10-(a)(6).
[70] Id., sec. 3-103(a)(7).

price. Assume also that the deed received by B was recorded but for some reason S's mortgage was not. Thereafter B borrowed money from L to make an investment in the stock market and gave L a mortgage on his premises which L promptly recorded. Assume that at the time of making the loan and recording his mortgage L had no actual knowledge of B's prior mortgage to S. Under these circumstances, although subsequent in time, L's mortgage has priority over S's purchase money mortgage.

Effect of Subordination Agreements

The order of priority that would otherwise arise from the recording of two or more mortgages on the same parcel of real estate may be changed by a mortgagee agreeing that the lien of his mortgage shall be inferior to another or others. An arrangement of this type is known as a **subordination agreement** and may exist between the subordinating mortgagee and the mortgagor or between the subordinating mortgagee and another mortgagee. By means of such an agreement, the subordinating mortgagee relinquishes the priority position he would otherwise have had with respect to the mortgaged property.

A situation in which an earlier recorded mortgage is subordinated to a later one typically occurs when unimproved land is sold to a developer who intends to build improvements on the land. For example, suppose that D, a developer, purchases raw land from seller S, makes a small down payment in cash, and gives S a promissory note secured by a purchase money mortgage for the remainder of the purchase price. D intends to finance the cost of construction of a building on the land by obtaining a loan from L, a bank or savings and loan association, giving a mortgage on the land as security. Assuming that S's and L's mortgages were recorded in the order in which they were executed, L's construction loan would be junior to S's purchase money mortgage. Because of state or federal regulations or due to internal operating policies, however, institutional lenders generally cannot or will not loan funds secured by junior mortgages. Therefore, in order for D to be able to obtain construction funds and give L the first priority L demands, D must induce S at the time of the sale of the land to accept a clause in his mortgage that expressly subordinates S's lien on the mortgaged property to the lien acquired later by L when the construction loan is made. To induce S to agree to the subordination of his mortgage, D would likely be required to pay a somewhat higher price for the land he purchased.

Agreements for Future Advances

Nature of Such Agreements In addition to serving as security for funds given to a borrower by a lender at the time a mortgage is executed, that same mortgage may, if the parties so provide, constitute security for additional sums to be advanced by the lender in the future. Although not limited to such transactions, mortgages to secure future advances are probably most common in construction loan arrangements in which borrowed funds are advanced or disbursed in installments as work on a building or another improvement progresses. In such arrangements, the secured loan or obligation does not consist of a series of separate and independent promises by the borrower-mortgagor, each requiring its own consideration, but consists instead of a single promise by him, made at the time the transaction is first entered into, undertaking to repay all advances made then and later that fall within the scope of the agreement between the borrower and lender. Similarly, the security interest that is transferred by the mortgagor-borrower to the mortgagee-lender by the mortgage executed at the time the transaction is originally entered into is intended by the parties to serve as security for advances made against the borrower's single promise and the obligations that flow from it.

Obligatory versus Optional Advances In determining the relative priority of a mortgage for future advances among other mortgages and liens on the same property, a distinction is made between security agreements by which a mortgagee-lender is obligated to advance funds in the future, known as *obligatory future advances,* and those agreements in which he is not so bound, known as *optional future advances.* Construction loans in which a lender commits himself to advance sums of money as certain stages of the work are completed are typical of agreements for obligatory future advances. An agreement for optional future advances, on the other hand, would provide that the mortgage that was executed when the security transaction was first entered into "shall be security for any sums that may hereinafter be advances" or some similar language.

Priority of Mortgages Securing Future Advances

As to Previously Recorded Liens As between regular mortgages on a given parcel of real estate that have been executed and recorded before either a mortgage for obligatory future advances or one for optional advances is executed and recorded, the earlier recorded mortgages will have priority.

Mortgages Securing Obligatory Advances Recorded mortgages securing obligatory future advances have priority, up to the amount of the funds that the lender has committed himself to loan, over all subsequently recorded mortgages even though a later mortgagee-lender pays loan funds to the borrower before some of the loan installments are paid by the lender who is obligated to make the future advances. For example, assume that construction lender, CL, is obligated by the terms of a loan contract to loan $100,000 to builder, B, payable in equal installments of $20,000, each installment being made payable upon completion of a certain stage of construction. Assume also that after CL had recorded his mortgage and advanced $40,000 to B, B borrowed and received $25,000 from another lender, L, who promptly recorded B's mortgage to him. Thereafter, with knowledge of L's loan to B, CL advanced the remaining $60,000 of his loan to B in accordance with his construction loan contract. Upon conclusion of these transactions, CL has a prior or preferred security interest in the mortgaged property in the amount of $100,000 with L's mortgage being inferior to that entire amount, rather than just to the $40,000 that had been advanced by CL before L loaned his funds and recorded his mortgage. Under the facts of this supposed situation, there was nothing that L could have done, short of getting CL to subordinate, that would have accorded his $25,000 mortgage priority over CL's security for the $60,000 later advanced by him to B.

Mortgages Securing Optional Advances Priority of mortgages arising from future advances differs when a mortgage secures optional future advances rather than obligatory advances of funds. The general rule is that where a loan agreement provides for optional advances, and hence a lender is not committed to loaning any fixed sum, future advances of funds by him will be superior to other mortgaged-secured loans that intervene between the original lender's mortgage and his later advances of funds, unless his subsequent optional advances were made with *actual knowledge* of another lender's intervening mortgage. Except in a minority of states,[71] intervening lenders who hope to obtain priority for their claims over subsequent optional future advances made by the original mortgagee-lender must do more than just record their mortgages in the public records. To establish their priorities, intervening mortgagees must do more than merely give constructive notice to the lender whose mortgage secures future advances. They have the responsibility of making sure that he has *actual* knowledge of their intervening loans and mortgages. While actual notice may take a number of forms, an effective means of giving such notice to the original lender would be for a subsequent lender to advise him in writing of the subsequent loan and mortgage.

---

[71] For example, Illinois, Michigan, and Pennsylvania.

Unless the original lender has actual knowledge of a subsequent secured loan made by another lender before the original lender makes an optional advance of funds, the priority of the security for his optional advance relates back to the date that the mortgage arising from his original loan agreement was recorded. If, however, the optional lender advances funds after he has obtained actual knowledge of another lender's loan and mortgage, the lien securing the optional advance will be inferior to the intervening loan.

Suppose, for example, that lender L-1 loaned B the sum of $20,000 secured by a mortgage on B's home. The mortgage provided that B's home "shall be security for any sums that may hereafter be advanced by L-1 to B." The mortgage was promptly recorded by L-1. Thereafter B borrows $20,000 from L-2 which is secured by a mortgage on B's home. L-2 promptly records his mortgage. Sometime later, L-1 loans B an additional $20,000 and shortly thereafter B becomes insolvent and defaults on all of his obligations. A foreclosure sale of B's home yields net proceeds of $40,000, half of which is claimed by L-2 in satisfaction of the loan he made to B before L-1 made his second loan. Despite the fact that L-2 recorded his mortgage before L-1 made his second loan to B, L-2's claim will fail because L-1's original mortgage securing future advances gave him priority over all loans of which he did not have actual knowledge at the time he advanced additional funds to B.

ULTA Position

Among Unrecorded Security Interests The Uniform Land Transactions Act takes the position that as between conflicting security interests in the same parcel of real property which have *not been recorded*, the first security interest to attach has priority.[72] According to the act, a security interest *attaches* to real estate when (1) the debtor has signed a security agreement containing a description of the property, (2) value has been given by the creditor, and (3) the debtor owns an interest in the real estate serving as security.[73] With respect to all future advances made by a lender, value is deemed to have been given at the time the first payment was made by him to the borrower.[74]

Among Recorded Security Interests Except where future advances are concerned, the uniform act leaves the question of priorities among *recorded* security interests to the individual legislatures to resolve.

Future Advances of Funds In keeping with prevailing law, the uniform act expressly provides that a security agreement may secure not only funds given to a borrower at the time the agreement is entered into but may also secure advances of funds made thereafter, whether those advances are optional or obligatory on the part of the lender.[75] The act provides that if a future advance of funds by a lender is to be secured by the original security agreement, the funds that are later advanced must not exceed the maximum amount stated in the agreement.[76] "Thus in an amortized mortgage the security agreement may provide that the debtor may borrow again up to the initial amount of the debt. It may also provide that the debtor may borrow any sum unrelated to the initial obligation up to an amount stated in the security agreement. If the debtor becomes obligated to the secured creditor for a sum in excess of these stated limits, the obligation is not secured by the real estate."[77]

There are two situations under the ULTA in which future advances are secured even though the security agreement makes no provision for the future advances. In one situation, payments which are made by a lender for the protection of his security, such as payments for real estate

---

[72] ULTA, sec. 3-301(a).
[73] Id., sec. 3-203(a).
[74] Id., sec. 3-203(c).
[75] Id., sec. 3-205.
[76] Id., sec. 3-205(c).
[77] Id., sec. 3-205, Comment 3.

taxes, premiums on hazard insurance, and maintenance charges imposed by condominium declarations, are secured despite no mention of them in the security agreement.[78] In the other situation, sums of money that are advanced under a construction security agreement to enable completion of contemplated buildings or improvements are secured even though such advances are not specifically provided for in the security agreement.[79] In both these situations, the sums advanced are secured even though the amount of such payments, when added to the other advances exceeds the maximum amount stated in the security agreement.[80]

The ULTA adopts the prevailing view that, with respect to security agreements involving *obligatory* advances, a recorded security interest takes its priority as of the time of recording if the secured party advances funds pursuant to a commitment made by him.[81] The act also adopts the majority view relative to *optional* future advances and gives the lender of a recorded interest who advances funds priority over all intervening interests of which he did not have knowledge at the time of making his advances.[82]

RIGHTS OF THE MORTGAGOR

In both lien theory and title theory states, the mortgagor is the owner of the property with all rights and privileges of ownership, subject only to the mortgagee's security interest created by the security agreement between the parties. With a few exceptions, title theory states have taken away from the legal title acquired by the mortgagee-lender most of the incidents of his legal title that are considered by the courts to be unnecessary for security purposes. It can be said, as a generalization, that the courts in varying degrees recognize the true function of a mortgage as a security device and accord to it only those incidents deemed desirable for security purposes.

Possession of Mortgaged Property

Where, as in the case of the majority of states today, a mortgage is regarded as creating a lien and not as conveying title, the right of possession of mortgaged property remains with the mortgagor-borrower until he is deprived of it by foreclosure. And in most title theory states, despite the fact that legal title passes to the mortgagee-lender by a mortgage, mortgages normally provide that possession of the premises will remain with the mortgagor-borrower.

Use of Property by Mortgagor A mortgagor, whether in possession of mortgaged property by virtue of his own right or by permission of the mortgagee, may enjoy all the ordinary benefits of ownership as long as his use of the property does not unreasonably prejudice the security interest of the mortgagee. The mortgagor is free to use the mortgaged property in the same manner in which an owner would ordinarily use his property, except he may not commit acts of waste which impair the sufficiency of the mortgagee's security.

There are two views as to what constitutes an impairment of a mortgagee's security interest. According to one view, if the value of the mortgaged property is less after the mortgagor's act than before, there has been an impairment. The other view holds that an impairment of security does not occur until the value of the mortgaged property has been reduced to an amount that is less than the secured debt.

Where the commission of waste is threatened by a mortgagor, the mortgagee may obtain an injunction forbidding the mortgagor to perform the acts that threaten injury to the property. Before an injunction will be granted, however, most courts require that the threatened injury be such that it will decrease the value of the mortgaged premises to the point where it is barely equal to the amount of the secured debt.

---

[78] Id., sec. 3-205(e)(1).
[79] Id., sec. 3-205(e)(2). Most security agreements, it is true, will have provided for such a contingency.
[80] Id., sec. 3-205(e).
[81] Id., sec. 3-301(b)(1).
[82] Id., sec. 3-301(b)(2).

Lease of Mortgaged Property

In the absence of an agreement between the mortgagor and the mortgagee to the contrary, a mortgagor may lease the mortgaged premises and receive the rents therefrom. If the lease is executed after a mortgage on the premises has been recorded, the tenant's leasehold interest is inferior to the mortgagee's security interest. This means, of course, that if the mortgagor-landlord defaults on his debt to the mortgagee, all rights of the tenant under his lease will be fully terminated by a foreclosure sale of the premises.

Where real estate that is already leased is mortgaged by the landlord, the security interest of the mortgagee will be inferior to the tenant's lease, unless the tenant's lease contains a subordination provision.

Sale of Mortgaged Property

Unless the security agreement between a mortgagor-borrower and a mortgagee-lender provides otherwise, the mortgagor is free to sell the mortgaged property without first obtaining the consent of the mortgagee. The transfer of ownership of the property by sale, however, neither terminates the mortgagor-seller's responsibility for the obligation arising from the note he signed nor does it have any affect on the lien on the property resulting from the mortgage that secures the debt.

When purchasing the mortgaged property from the mortgagor-borrower-seller, the buyer may either (1) take title "subject to" the existing mortgage, (2) "assume" the debt secured by the mortgage, or (3) pay the full purchase price in cash.

Taking Title Subject to the Mortgage The contract of sale between the mortgagor-seller and a buyer may provide that the buyer will pay the seller in cash the difference between the agreed selling price and the amount of the outstanding mortgage and will accept title to the property subject to the existing mortgage. Thereafter, if the buyer wishes to keep the purchased property he must make payments on the secured debt to the mortgagee to prevent a default and foreclosure. While the buyer of the mortgaged property is under no legal obligation to prevent a default, his failure to do so will cause him to lose the property when the unpaid mortgagee-lender forecloses. However, if the proceeds of the foreclosure sale are insufficient to pay the amount of the outstanding mortgage debt in full, the buyer-owner of the foreclosed property will have no personal liability for the unpaid balance. It is the mortgagor-seller who, having signed the note that the mortgage secures, remains liable for any deficit resulting from the failure of the proceeds received at the foreclosure sale to fully satisfy the unpaid balance due on the note. It is sometimes said that in a sale of property subject to a mortgage the real estate bears primary liability for the mortgage debt and the mortgagor-seller is in the position of a surety or one secondarily liable. As far as the one who purchased the property from the mortgagor is concerned, his loss from his default is the amount that he has invested in the property.

By way of illustration of a "subject to" sale of mortgaged property, suppose that S owns a house with an existing mortgage debt of $35,000 against it. S sells the house to buyer B for $42,000. B pays $7,000 to S in cash and by deed receives title to the property subject to the mortgage that secures S's outstanding $35,000 debt. Because of unavoidable circumstances, B is unable to make the payments on the mortgage debt and the mortgagee-lender forecloses. Due to unfavorable market conditions, the net proceeds from the foreclosure amount to $33,000—$2,000 short of satisfying the outstanding mortgage debt. In the absence of an antideficiency statute, the mortgagee-lender can obtain a judgment against S for the $2,000 deficiency but no judgment may be had against B. Nor can S, after having paid the $2,000 judgment, look to B for recovery. B's loss is limited to the $7,000 investment he had in the foreclosed property.

Assuming the Secured Obligation By the provisions of a contract of purchase and sale, a purchaser of mortgaged property may promise the seller that he, the buyer, will pay off the seller's mortgage debt. Such a promise by a buyer is commonly referred to as an "assumption" and the language used in the parties' contract generally says that the buyer "assumes the mortgage" on the property. More accurately, however, it is the mortgagor-seller's secured debt owing to the mortgagee that the buyer assumes by his promise. Since the debt that the buyer assumes is secured by the property he purchases, his failure to pay the seller's debt as agreed will result in the buyer's loss of the mortgaged property when the mortgagee forecloses.

Besides losing his property when the assumed debt is defaulted on, the buyer, because of his promise of assumption, will be personally liable to the mortgagee-lender if the proceeds of a foreclosure sale of the mortgaged property are insufficient to satisfy the entire balance of the defaulted mortgage debt. The prevailing view with respect to the buyer's personal liability is that the mortgagee-lender is a third party beneficiary of the contract between the buyer and the seller. The mortgagee-lender, however, who was not a party to the assumption agreement, is not required to look only to the buyer, who may be insolvent, for the unpaid balance of the mortgage debt. The buyer's promise to the mortgagor-seller in no way relieves the latter of his continuing obligation to pay his debt to the mortgagee. In an assumption situation, the mortgagee-lender has three sources to look to for satisfaction of the mortgage debt: (1) the mortgaged property, (2) the mortgagor-borrower who signed the secured note, and (3) the buyer who by contract promised to pay the mortgagor's indebtedness.

Where the proceeds of a foreclosure sale are inadequate to pay off the outstanding debt and recovery of the deficit is obtained by the mortgagee-lender from the mortgagor who sold the property, the mortgagor-seller is entitled to recover the amount he paid from the buyer who promised he would pay the mortgage debt.

In the example given above, if when B purchased the mortgaged property from S for $42,000 he had promised to assume S's $35,000 mortgage debt, B would have been subject to a personal judgment for $2,000 for the deficit resulting from the foreclosure sale. The mortgagee-lender could obtain a personal judgment from both S, the mortgagor-seller, and B, but could of course only recover a total of $2,000 either entirely from one of them or partly from each, depending upon their financial conditions. If S pays all or part of the $2,000 to the mortgagee-lender, S is entitled to a judgment against B for the amount S paid and may recover on the judgment if and when B is financially able to pay.

Payment of Purchase Price in Cash Instead of agreeing to take title to the purchased property subject to an existing mortgage or promising to assume the mortgagor-seller's mortgage debt, the buyer may wish to pay the seller cash for the property. In such a case, the sales contract will provide that title to the property will be delivered to the buyer free and clear of the existing mortgage, and the mortgage debt will be paid by the seller from the sales proceeds and the mortgage released during the escrow or title closing process. The cash paid to the seller may have been derived from the buyer's savings or his sale of assets, or the buyer may have acquired a new loan from a new lender and secured that loan by a mortgage on the newly purchased property.

Whether the seller will be able to pay off his outstanding debt prior to its maturity will depend upon whether the security agreement with his lender, or a statute, provides for the privilege of prepayment. If such a privilege does exist, the premature retirement of the debt by the mortgagor-seller may be conditioned on the payment of a prepayment penalty or fee. If the mortgagor-seller has no prepayment privilege, before he can pay off the debt prior to its scheduled maturity he will have to negotiate with the mortgagee-lender to obtain the right to prepay. The mortgagor in such circumstances may find that he is in a disadvantageous bargaining position.

Operation of Due-on-Sale Clause We have seen that promissory notes secured by real estate mortgages typically contain acceleration provisions in the form of due-on-sale clauses which give a mortgagee-lender the option of calling the entire amount of a mortgage debt immediately due and payable if the mortgagor sells the mortgaged property without first having obtained the mortgagee's consent to the sale. We have also seen that due-on-sale clauses are valid and enforceable provisions of security agreements.

Where a sale by a mortgagor-borrower is for cash, the mortgagee-lender's election to call the mortgage debt immediately due and payable has no effect on the right of the mortgagor to sell the mortgaged property other than to require him to pay a prepayment penalty in those instances where the security agreement provides that such a penalty is payable whether prepayment by the mortgagor is voluntary or involuntary. On the other hand, where the buyer wants to assume the existing mortgage debt or to purchase the property subject to the present mortgage, the due-on-sale clause places the buyer and the mortgagor-seller in a position where they must negotiate with the mortgagee-lender to prevent his calling the entire mortgage debt due and payable and conceivably frustrating the sale.

Assumption Fees and Points If the prospective buyer of mortgaged property is a good credit risk, a lender will generally permit him to "assume the mortgage" then existing on the property rather than exercise his option under a due-on-sale clause. In such a case, the lender will normally charge the assuming buyer an assumption fee of one or more "points" as consideration for forgoing the right to accelerate the debt. One point is 1 percent of the amount of the mortgage-secured debt that is assumed by the purchaser. If the loan that is assumed is $40,000 and the assumption fee is one point, for example, the charge to the buyer will be $400; if the fee is one and one-half points, the assumption fee will be $600.

It frequently happens that where the mortgage debt to be assumed by the purchaser is several years old, the contract rate of interest stated in the secured note is less than the market rate of interest at the time of the sale. It is inconceivable that a prudent lender, having the power to prevent it, would continue to loan money at an interest rate that is less than the market rate, except in unusual circumstances. As a condition of his agreeing to the assumption, a lender either rewrites the loan agreement to reflect the high market rate or, alternatively, he continues the contract rate of interest as written and charges the assuming buyer sufficient points to bring the contract rate of interest up to the desired rate. In the latter method, the payment of points by the assuming buyer amounts to a lump sum prepayment of interest.

Further Encumbrance of Mortgaged Property

To the extent that a mortgagor has an equity in mortgaged property and to the extent that a lender is willing to accept a mortgage on that equity as security for a loan, the mortgagor may further encumber his property with additional mortgages, deeds of trust, or similar liens. On the assumption that the original mortgage had been properly recorded by the mortgagee, any subsequent mortgage on the same property would be junior to it or what is popularly called a "second." This means, as we have seen, that upon foreclosure for default of the secured debts, the debt secured by a first priority mortgage is entitled to be paid in full before any of the foreclosure sale proceeds are available to the junior or second mortgagee-lender.

Promissory notes secured by mortgages and

deeds of trust, as we know, commonly contain an accleration provision in the form of a due-on-encumbrance clause which, according to the language of the clause, entitles a mortgagee-lender to call the entire debt due and payable if the mortgagor further encumbers the property with an additional mortgage. We have seen, however, that according to the prevailing view such clauses are not automatically enforced by the courts but will be enforced only if the mortgagee-lender can establish that the mortgagor's additional encumbrance of the mortgaged property impairs or endangers the original mortgagee-lender's security.

Mortgagor Has an Insurable Interest

To be able to ensure something against risk of possible loss or destruction, the one seeking insurance must have an insurable interest in the thing subject to risk. If such an interest is lacking, a contract to indemnify when a loss occurs is a wagering agreement and not a contract of insurance. A person has an insurable interest in real estate if its destruction or damage would directly affect him financially.

In both title theory and lien theory states, a mortgagor, as owner of the mortgaged property, has an insurable interest in it. His insurable interest is the full value of the mortgaged property.

Release of Mortgage When Debt Paid

Payment of the debt secured by a mortgage releases the mortgaged premises from the mortgagee's security interest in the property. A mortgagor-debtor who has paid his secured debt is entitled to have the public record cleared of the mortgagee-creditor's interest in the mortgaged property. To clear the record, it is customary for the mortgagee to execute, in form proper for recording, an instrument releasing the mortgagor's property from the security interest. Recording of the releasing instrument serves to offset the prior recorded mortgage and thus clears the mortgagor's title of the encumbrance of the mortgagee's security interest.

RIGHTS OF THE MORTGAGEE
No Right of Possession

We have seen that even in the title theory states the courts and statutes recognize the true function of a mortgage as an instrument creating a security interest rather than as a device for transferring ownership and that, as a consequence, the incidents of the mortgagee's title are limited to those features that are considered necessary for security purposes. A significant result of this recognition is that, with minor exceptions, in both title and lien theory states the execution of a real estate mortgage gives the mortgagee no right to posesion of the mortgaged premises as long as the mortgagor does not default on his contractual obligations. A mortgagor and a mortgagee can, of course, provide in their security agreement for the shifting of the right of possession upon the happening of designated acts or events.

Prevention of Impairment of Security

The general rule is that the mortgagee has the right to prevent impairment of his security by acts of the mortgagor that constitute waste. As we have seen, waste to the mortgaged property occurs when the mortgagor does or permits to be done acts which damage or destroy the property thus causing a diminution in its value. Although security agreements frequently contain due-on clauses giving the mortgagee the right to accelerate the mortgage debt when waste is committed, even in the absence of such a clause he may obtain an injunction prohibiting future waste in order to protect the adequacy of his security interest in the property.

In order that he may determine whether his security is being impaired by the commission of waste, a mortgagee may, in both title states and lien states, enter the mortgaged premises at reasonable times and under reasonable circumstances to inspect them.

Transfer of Debt and Security Interest

Debt and Security Are Incidents of Each Other A mortgagee of real estate, as we know, has two things: (1) the debt or obligation owed to him, which commonly is in the form of a promissory note, and (2) a security interest in mortgaged property, which is evidenced by a real estate mortgage. Both the obligation and the security interest arise out of the same transaction or agreement and one is the incident of the other. Recognition of this interrelationship of the debt and the security is particularly important in those instances where the mortgagee, as he has the unqualified right to do, transfers or assigns the mortgage debt to another person.

Neither Debt nor Security Transferable Separately A mortgagee can neither transfer the underlying debt without the mortgage nor the mortgage without the underlying debt. It is a fundamental principle that the only function of a mortgage is to serve as security for the obligation to which it relates and is inseparable from it. If the mortgagee attempts to transfer the mortgage alone, the transaction is a nullity and the transferee, not having received the debt that the mortgage secures, has a worthless piece of paper. On the other hand, if the mortgagee transfers or assigns only the underlying debt, the transfer carries with it the right to the mortgage that secures the debt, even though the transferee does not know of the existence of the mortgage. The principle of inseparability of the debt and its security is explicitly stated by statute in some states.[83]

Transfer of Negotiable Debt In lending transactions involving real estate mortgages the secured obligation commonly takes the form of a negotiable promissory note. By the great weight of authority, the negotiation of a negotiable instrument to a holder in due course[84] transfers to him the mortgagor-borrower's promise free from personal defenses which the mortgagor-borrower could have asserted against the mortgagee-lender had he continued to hold the note. Personal defenses include such things as fraud in the inducement, failure of consideration, etc., which are available to a promisor when sued on a simple contract. A promisor's right to assert such defenses when sued for nonpayment of a negotiable note is lost when the note is transferred to a holder in due course by negotiation.

Transfer of Nonnegotiable Debt A promissory note that is not negotiable in form cannot be transferred by negotiation but only by assignment. Like any other simple contract, when a nonnegotiable note is assigned by a mortgagee-lender-assignor it passes to the assignee subject to all the defenses that the mortgagor-borrower could have asserted against the mortgagee-lender had he continued to hold the note. Because of this fact, it is common practice for the assignee of a nonnegotiable mortgage note to demand an estoppel certificate from the mortgagor-borrower before the assignee will accept the note. An *estoppel certificate* is a written statement signed by the mortgagor-borrower which states the amount due on a nonnegotiable mortgage note and which indicates whether the note is subject to any offsets or defenses. The effect of his execution of such a certificate is to estop or bar the mortgagor-borrower from setting up defenses against the assignee of the note which the mortgagor signed.

Mortgagee Has an Insurable Interest

A mortgagee-lender has an insurable interest in the real estate that serves as security for the

---

[83] For example, California Civil Code, sec. 2936 states: "The assignment of a debt secured by a mortgage carries with it the security."

[84] A holder in due course is one who takes a negotiable instrument (1) that is complete and regular on its face, (2) before it was overdue and without notice that it has been dishonored, (3) in good faith and for value, and (4) without knowledge of any infirmity in the instrument or defect in the title of the person from whom it is received.

mortgagor-borrower's debt. The extent of his insurable interest is measured by the amount of the secured debt outstanding at any point in time. Because of his insurable interest, the mortgagee-lender may enter into a separate contract of insurance to protect himself against fire or other hazards that might impair or destroy his security. More commonly, however, it is customary to include in security agreements a provision that requires the mortgagor-borrower to obtain casualty or hazard insurance for the benefit of both himself and the mortgagee-lender "as their respective interests may appear." In addition to calling for the mortgagor to pay the total premium on the policy, the agreement will normally provide that if the mortgagor fails to make any such premium payment when due, the mortgagee may at his option accelerate the entire principal sum of the secured debt then outstanding. As an alternative, the mortgagee may make the premium payments in behalf of the mortgagor and add the amount paid to the mortgagor's debt to him.

Security agreements, we have seen, frequently require a mortgagor-borrower to include a pro rata amount in his monthly installment payments which the lender holds in an escrow or impound account for the payment of insurance premiums when they fall due.

QUESTIONS

1 Distinguish between the primary mortgage market and the secondary mortgage market.
2 What is a conventional mortgage?
3 Explain what is meant by the term "redlining" as that term is used in connection with mortgage lending.
4 What is the purpose for which the Home Mortgage Disclosure Act was enacted?
5 What are the objectives of the Uniform Land Transactions Act? What is a "protected party"?
6 How does a straight promissory note differ from an installment note?
7 What is a variable interest rate in a promissory note? What purpose is it designed to serve?
8 Describe the manner in which an acceleration clause in a promissory note operates. What are the three events that commonly give rise to the right to accelerate?
9 What is a prepayment clause in a promissory note?
10 What is an escrow or impound account? Why do some lenders require borrowers to maintain such accounts?
11 Explain why it is desirable for a lender to have his loan secured by a real estate mortgage rather than being unsecured.
12 Despite their formal differences, what is the functional similarity between a deed of trust and a mortgage?
13 What is the effect of a subordination agreement between lenders whose loans are secured by mortgages on the same real estate?
14 How does the liability of a purchaser of mortgaged property who takes title to the property "subject to the mortgage" differ from the liability of a purchaser who "assumes the obligation" owed by his seller?
15 What is an estoppel certificate? What effect does it have?

Chapter 16

Mortgages, Deeds of Trust, and Installment Contracts—Part II

FORECLOSURE

Nature of Foreclosure

Foreclosure is a process or proceeding by which property serving as security for an obligation is sold when a default occurs. The most important single feature of the mortgagor-mortgagee relationship is the power of the mortgagee to compel the sale of the mortgaged property in order to minimize or eliminate any loss to him because of the mortgagor's default on his debt.

When Right to Foreclose Arises A mortgagee-creditor's right to initiate foreclosure proceedings does not arise until the mortgagor-debtor fails to perform an undertaking he has assumed by the terms of the security agreement, which failure of performance the parties have agreed shall constitute a default. Default in the performance of an obligation that a mortgage is given to secure is a fundamental condition precedent to the mortgagee's right to foreclose. In the majority of real estate security transactions, the default that causes foreclosure procedures to be commenced is the mortgagor-debtor's failure to make installment payments on the mortgaged debt when they fall due.

Mortgagee's Remedies Defined by Law Once the mortgagor-debtor has failed to perform in accordance with the security agreement, the mortgagee-creditor may pursue whatever remedies are made available to him by the laws of the state in which the mortgaged real estate is located. The rights that the law gives to a mortgagee in the mortgaged real estate after there has been a default by the mortgagor are the essence of a real estate security transaction. It is the presence of these rights that distinguish a secured lender or creditor from an unsecured one.

Types of Foreclosure

In the United States today there are two methods by which mortgaged real estate is sold in satisfaction of a defaulted obligation: (1) foreclosure by judicial sale and (2) foreclosure by power of sale.

In a very limited number of states, a form of foreclosure not involving the sale of mortgaged property, known as "strict foreclosure," is permitted.

Foreclosure by Judicial Sale

Conduct and Confirmation of Sale The successful prosecution of a foreclosure suit by a mortgagee-creditor following a default by the debtor culminates in a court decree stating that if the debt is not paid within a specified number of days the mortgaged property will be sold by an officer of the court. All requirements for advertising the sale, the giving of notice to appropriate parties, the place where the sale shall be held, and the manner of conducting the sale are established by the statutes of each state. Such statutes generally require that the sale be at public auction under the direction of the sheriff or other officer designated by the court.

After the sale has been concluded, a report of the sale is made back to the court that ordered it for the court's confirmation of the sale. Following confirmation by the court, an officer of the court executes and delivers a deed to the successful bidder which vests title in him but which contains no warranties as to the character of that title.

Figure 16-1 sets forth an example of a deed executed by an officer of the court following a foreclosure sale.

Proceeds of Foreclosure Sales The proceeds of the foreclosure sale, after payment of costs and expenses, may be either more or less than the sum needed to satisfy the debt secured by the foreclosed mortgage.

If there is a surplus it will be disbursed among junior mortgagees, if any, in accordance with the relative priorities of their claims. Where a sale yields surplus funds, the foreclosure of a mortgage has the effect of accelerating all security interests that are subordinate to it, such as second mortgages, and these are paid out of the surplus even though by their provisions they are not yet due.

If there are no junior liens against the foreclosed property, the surplus represents the mortgagor-debtor's equity in the property and will be paid to him.

The Uniform Land Transactions Act provides that the proceeds from a judicial sale shall be applied in the following order: (1) the expenses of the sale, (2) the reasonable expenses of securing possession before sale and holding, maintaining, and preparing the real estate for sale, (3) satisfaction of the secured indebtedness, (4) satisfaction in the order of priority of any security interest of record, and (5) remittance of any excess to the debtor.[1]

If the proceeds of the foreclosure sale are less than the amount needed to pay the costs and expenses of the foreclosure action and to satisfy the debt secured by the foreclosed mortage in full, there will be a "deficiency." In the absence of a statute prohibiting it, a "deficiency judgment" will be entered against the mortgagor-debtor which judgment may be satisfied from other assets of the debtor.

Nature of Purchaser's Title By virtue of his deed from an officer of the court, the purchaser takes title to the foreclosed property free of all interests of the mortgagor and mortgagee and all persons whose claims in the property are junior to the foreclosed mortgage, if the latter were made parties to the foreclosure action. It is well established, however, that if a junior mortgagee is not made a party defendant in the foreclosure action, his claim against the foreclosed property is not affected and the purchaser will take title subject to them. As a general rule, such a junior mortgagee has all the same rights after the foreclosure sale as he had be-

---

[1] ULTA, sec. 3-510(a).

This Deed made __(date)__ , 19___ , by ___(name)___ , (Sheriff of the the County of _____ , State of _____), and ___(name)___ of __(address)__ _____ , herein called the grantee.

RECITALS

1. In an action in the __(name of the court)__ , County of _____ , State of _____ , between ___(name)___ , plaintiff, and ___(name)___ , defendant, a judgment was rendered and filed on __(date)__ , 19___ , for the foreclosure of a mortgage on the real estate described in the mortgage and the judgment, as well as in this deed, the mortgage having been executed by ___(name)___ , mortgagor, to ___(name)___ , mortgagee, on __(date)__ , 19___ . The mortgage was recorded in Book __(number)__ of Mortgages at page __(number)__ on __(date)__, 19___ , in the office of the County Recorder of _____ County, State of _____ .

2. After having given due notice of the time and place of such sale as ordered by the court, ___(name)___ , Sheriff, sold the described property at public auction as ordered by the court to the grantee for the sum of __(amount)__ dollars, ($_____), which was the highest sum bid for the property. Pursuant to such sale, ___(name)___ , Sheriff, issued to the grantee a Certificate of Sale dated __(date)__ , 19___, which was recorded in Book __(number)__ of Mortgages at page __(number)__ on __(date)__ , 19___ in the office of the County Recorder of _____ County, State of _____ .

3. The time for redemption of the property expired without the property having been redeemed and the grantee is the owner and holder of the Certificate of Sale.

By reason of the foregoing and in consideration of the payment of the purchase price, receipt of which is hereby acknowledged, __(name and title of sheriff)__ , pursuant to the judgment of the court and applicable statutes, grants and conveys to the grantee, his heirs and assigns forever, the following described real property situated in the County of _____ , State of _____ : (set forth the legal description of the property conveyed) , together with all improvements and appurtenances.

To have and to hold the real property above described and herewith conveyed to the grantee, his heirs and assigns forever.

In witness whereof, __(name and title of sheriff)__ has affixed his signature hereto on the date indicated above.

(Acknowledgment)

_____
(signature of sheriff)

Figure 16-1 Deed by Officer of Court Following Foreclosure Sale.

fore, including the right to bring an action to foreclose his own mortgage.

If the mortgagor-debtor remains on the foreclosed premises and refuses to yield possession to the purchaser, summary remedies are available in all states to remove him.

Universally Available as a Remedy Judicial foreclosure is available in all of the states today and is either the only method or the one most frequently used in a substantial majority of them.

Despite the fact that judicial foreclosure is the best method of foreclosure for producing solidly marketable titles, it is often criticized and sometimes shunned because it is complicated, costly, and time-consuming.

Foreclosure by Power of Sale

Use of Method Regulated by Statute In those states in which such a method is permitted,[2] a foreclosure sale may be had without a judicial decree if by the terms of the mortgage the mortgagor confers on the mortgagee the power to sell the mortgaged property in the event of a default by the mortgagor. Statutes in the states that permit the use of this method invariably require that the sale be held at public auction and contain provisions concerning the giving of notice and the manner of conducting the sale. While state laws vary with respect to whether a mortgagee-creditor may bid at the sale, he is generally allowed to do so if the provisions of the mortgage give him that right or if the sale is conducted by a public officer.

Proceeds of Foreclosure Sale A foreclosure sale conducted under the authority of a power of sale granted by a mortgagor may yield a surplus after satisfaction of the mortgage debt and the payment of expenses of the sale. Such excess or surplus, of course, represents the mortgagor's equity in the foreclosed property and is payable to him.

The Uniform Land Transactions Act provides that the proceeds from a nonjudicial sale shall be applied in the following order: (1) the reasonable expenses of securing possession of the property before the sale, holding, maintaining, and preparing it for sale, together with the reasonable expense of making the sale, (2) satisfaction of the secured indebtedness, (3) satisfaction of claims of holders of subordinate interests *but only* those claims for which the creditor received written demands for satisfaction before the date of sale, and (4) remittance of any excess to the debtor.[3]

Where a foreclosure by power of sale yields a surplus, a question arises as to how the mortgagee-creditor who conducted the sale should distribute that surplus when there are junior lienors with claims against it. The safest course is for the mortgagee, by bringing an interpleader action, to invoke the assistance of the court instead of distributing the funds on his own. If he makes the distribution without the aid of a court, it is clear that to the extent that he has actual notice or knowledge of junior encumbrances he must pay the surplus to them in the order of their priorities. The courts are in disagreement as to whether the mortgagee must also make a search of the public records to discover claimants who are entitled to participate in the surplus. Some states[4] have statutes that prescribe the mortgagee's responsibilities.

If the proceeds of a foreclosure by power of sale are insufficient to satisfy the secured debt and expenses of the sale, the foregoing mortgagee must commence a court action to obtain a deficiency judgment, except where such judgments are denied by statute.[5]

---

[2] Nonjudicial foreclosure by power of sale is permitted in Alabama, Arkansas, California, District of Columbia, Georgia, Hawaii, Iowa, Kentucky, Massachusetts, Michigan, Mississippi, New Hampshire, New York, North Carolina, Oklahoma, Pennsylvania, Rhode Island, Texas, Virginia, Wisconsin, and Wyoming.

[3] ULTA, sec. 3-510(a).

[4] For example, California, Maryland, Michigan, New York, North Dakota, Wisconsin, and Wyoming.

[5] The California Code of Civil Procedure, sec. 580(d), for example, specifically denies a deficiency judgment where foreclosure is by power of sale.

Nature of Purchaser's Title In theory the purchaser at a nonjudicial foreclosure sale obtains the same rights as he would have acquired at a judicial one, because what is being sold is the title as it existed at the time the mortgage containing the power of sale was given. Despite this fact, however, the more costly and cumbersome judicial sale is often preferred because it creates a permanent court record of matters leading to the transfer of the mortgagor's interest, whereas the purchaser at a nonjudicial sale commonly has only the statements contained in his deed to show how his title was acquired.

Method Not Widely Used In none of the states where foreclosure by power of sale is permitted do the statutes exclude judicial sale as a method of foreclosure. The foreclosing mortgagee is entitled to choose one method or the other as he deems advisable. Foreclosure by power of sale, in other words, is in all cases a cumulative and not an exclusive remedy.

Although as compared with foreclosure by judicial sale, foreclosure by power of sale is both speedy and inexpensive, the foreclosing mortgagee often finds his conduct of the foreclosure sale challenged in court and the foreclosure delayed even longer than it would have been had he resorted to judicial foreclosure in the first instance. Because the requirements of the power of sale statutes are highly technical and the risk of noncompliance with the letter of them is a constant danger, the power of sale foreclosure is used very little today in many of the states where it is permitted. The most frequent use of foreclosure by power of sale appears to be in connection with defaults involving deeds of trust.

In all states that permit the method, a foreclosure by power of sale is always subject to judicial review.

Strict Foreclosure Strict foreclosure is a proceeding in which the court orders a defaulting mortgagor-debtor to pay his obligation within a stated period of time or be forever barred from asserting any rights in the title to the mortgaged property held as security by the mortgagee-creditor. In bringing an action for strict foreclosure, the mortgagee-creditor in a title theory state seeks to perfect the title he holds rather than to have the mortgaged property sold and apply the proceeds to his secured debt. Strict foreclosure is regarded as eliminating all of the mortgagor's interest in the property, leaving the mortgagee's title free and clear. It is analogous to an action to quiet title. In those instances where the mortgaged property is clearly inadequate to satisfy the secured debt and the mortgagee-creditor has little confidence in the value of a deficiency judgment, strict foreclosure is a more expedient and less expensive procedure than foreclosure by judicial sale.

For various reasons, strict foreclosure traditionally has been viewed in a negative way and today in only three of the title theory states[6] is it of any importance as a method of foreclosure.

ULTA Position

Methods of Foreclosure The uniform act makes three remedies available to a creditor after the debtor has defaulted on his obligation: (1) the creditor may enter into an agreement with the debtor that terminates the debtor's interest in the property; (2) the creditor may institute proceedings leading to a judicial sale; or (3) the creditor may exercise a power of sale if such a power is authorized by the security agreement.

Notice of Intention to Foreclose The ULTA requires that before a creditor can commence proceedings for a judicial sale or exercise his power of sale, he must give the debtor notice of his intention to foreclose.[7] Except where the debtor is a protected party, notice of intention to foreclose must be given a reasonable period of time before the creditor begins to foreclose.[8] "If at the time of default a dwelling unit in the real estate is occupied by a protected party or an individual related to him, the notice to fore-

---

[6] Connecticut, Illinois, and Vermont.
[7] ULTA sec. 3-505(b) and (c).
[8] Id., sec. 3-505, Comment 2.

close may not be given until a payment of money has not been made when due and remains unpaid for 5 or more weeks . . ."[9] This provision is designed to permit the protected party to take steps to protect his equity.[10]

For both protected-party and nonprotected-party debtors, the creditor's notice of intention to foreclose must be in writing, sent to the debtor both by registered or certified mail and by ordinary first class mail and must contain the following information: (1) the identity of the security interest to be foreclosed; (2) the nature of the default claimed; (3) the fact that the creditor has accelerated maturity of the debt, if that is the case; (4) the manner in which the debtor may cure the default; (5) the methods by which the debtor's ownership of the real estate may be terminated; (6) any right the debtor has to transfer the real estate to another person subject to the security interest or to refinance the obligation; (7) the circumstances under which the debtor's right to possession will be terminated and that on termination he may be evicted by judicial process; (8) the debtor's right to any surplus from the sale and whether the debtor will be liable for any deficiency; (9) the method of foreclosure the creditor intends to use; and (10) the debtor's right to apply for a court order controlling the foreclosure.[11]

Agreement to Terminate Debtor's Interest As provided in the uniform act, a debtor's interest in mortgaged property may be terminated without resorting to a foreclosure sale by an agreement between the debtor and the creditor. Such an agreement would normally result in the debtor's executing a "deed in lieu of foreclosure" in favor of the creditor. The debtor's motivation for giving a deed in lieu of foreclosure and the possible pitfalls for the creditor in accepting it are discussed below.

Foreclosure by Judicial Sale The uniform act provides that any security interest may be foreclosed in a judicial proceeding but makes certain changes in the traditional procedure.[12] Once a judgment has been entered for the amount determined to be due, the court may order the sale of the mortgaged property in satisfaction of the judgment debt. Unlike much existing law, the act permits the court to select any person to conduct the sale that the court feels will be the person best suited under the circumstances. This may be the secured creditor, the debtor, or any other person whether he is an official of the court or not.[13]

When the sale has been completed, the person conducting it must obtain the court's confirmation.[14] If the conduct of the sale did not comply with the provisions of the act, the court can refuse to confirm it.[15] If the sale is confirmed by the court, the person who conducted it executes a deed conveying the property to the purchaser which gives him a title free from the interests of the debtor and all junior claimants.[16] If possession of the property which was sold is wrongfully withheld from the purchaser after acquiring title, the court may direct the appropriate official to evict the withholding occupant.[17]

Foreclosure by Power of Sale Although foreclosure by power of sale has been adopted in only a limited number of states, the uniform act authorizes the power of sale as a method of foreclosure in all cases where parties to a security agreement provide for it.[18]

The act requires a creditor who decides to foreclose by power of sale to comply with notice requirements which are generally different from and stricter than many existing state statutory procedures. The notice requirements of the uniform act are designed to perform two functions: (1) the giving of notice to the debtor and junior lienholders that their interests are about to be cut off and (2) the giving of notice

---

[9] Id. sec. 3-5-5(d).
[10] Id., sec. 3-505, Comment 1.
[11] Id., sec. 3-506.
[12] Id., sec. 3-509.
[13] Id., sec. 3-509(c) and Comment 3.
[14] Id., sec. 3-509(e).
[15] Id., sec. 3-513(a).
[16] Id., sec. 3-511(b).
[17] Id., sec. 3-509(g).
[18] Id., sec. 3-505(c).

to potential purchasers that the mortgaged real estate is available for sale.[19] Existing statutes generally provide that notice of the sale by an advertisement in a legal publication performs both functions.

The uniform act requires that the creditor notify the debtor 5 weeks before the sale of the mortgaged property. The notice must reasonably apprise the recipients of the time and the place of a public sale of the property and the fact that the creditor may bid and purchase at such sale.[20] Instead of a public sale, the property may be sold at a private sale and may be purchased by the creditor if the sale is conducted by a fiduciary or other person not related to the creditor.[21] A debtor who believes that he has a defense to the default claim by the creditor or who contends that the creditor did not comply with the provisions of the act may initiate a judicial proceeding to stop the sale of the mortgaged property, whether the proposed sale is to be public or private.[22]

The act requires that the sale of the property be conducted in a reasonable manner, which is interpreted to mean that the person conducting the sale should use the ordinary methods of making prospective buyers aware of it that are used by an owner when he voluntarily sells his property. This could be accomplished by employing a professional real estate agent or by placing an advertisement in that part of a daily newspaper where such advertisements regularly appear.[23]

The act provides that the purchaser under a power of sale foreclosure takes the property free of the interests of the debtor and all subordinate or junior claimants, even though the person conducting the sale has not met all of the procedural requirements.[24] "The purpose of freeing the purchaser from the risk of faulty foreclosure is to further assure that the sale price at the foreclosure sale will be more closely related to the real market value of the property thus liquidating the debt for the best interest of the lender and the borrower."[25] The provision also serves to remove the traditional objection that a power of sale foreclosure does not provide a title that is as marketable as a title obtained at a judicial foreclosure.

EQUITY OF REDEMPTION

Nature of Redemption

In all states a mortgagor who defaults on his obligation may prevent foreclosure and have the encumbrance of the mortgage removed from his title by paying the full amount of the outstanding debt plus interest and any expenses incurred by the mortgagee. This right of the mortgagor is called an **equity of redemption.** If the mortgage was recorded by the mortgagee-creditor, as it normally would be, the redeeming mortgagor is entitled to receive a recordable release to clear his record title, although he may have to sue to get it.

Who May Redeem

In addition to the mortgagor-debtor, all persons having an interest in the property that would be prejudiced by foreclosure of the mortgage may redeem. Included among these persons are those who purchase the equity of redemption from the mortgagor, heirs and devisees of the mortgagor, and junior lienors. Where there are successive mortgages on the property, the mortgagee who seeks to redeem must pay off all encumbrances on the property that are senior to his own, but may ignore those that are junior. Every redeeming party is liable to be redeemed in turn by those junior to him and these latter persons are liable to be redeemed by the mortgagor or a purchaser from him.

When the Equity Terminates

The equity of redemption is terminated by the foreclosure of the mortgaged property, which is essentially a process for the extinguishment of

---

[19] Id., sec. 3-508, Comment 1.
[20] Id., sec. 3-508(a).
[21] Id., sec. 3-508(a).
[22] Id., sec. 3-513(a).
[23] Id., sec. 3-508, Comment 1.
[24] Id., sec. 3-511.

[25] Id., sec. 3-511, Comment 1.

the equity. In some states, extinguishment of the equity of redemption gives rise to another right known as a statutory right of redemption.

ULTA Position

The Uniform Land Transaction Act provides that any time before the creditor has disposed of or contracted to dispose of mortgaged real estate under power of sale, or before the time specified in a decree of judicial foreclosure, the debtor or the holder of any subordinate interest in the property may cure the debtor's default by tendering the payments due, including any amounts due because of a mortgagee's right to accelerate, plus reasonable expenses incurred by the creditor and reasonable attorney fees.[26] For a creditor to exercise his right to accelerate against a debtor, the creditor must give him written notice that if the default is not cured within 15 days from the date of the notice, the debt will be accelerated and the entire outstanding balance will become due and payable. This requirement may be waived by a debtor other than a protected party.[27] A protected party may cure his default by paying the past due installments, late charges, the creditor's reasonable costs, and reasonable attorney fees at any time before foreclosure.[28] The uniform act limits a protected party's right to cure defaults to once every 12 months.[29]

The act permits a debtor, after default, to make certain agreements with respect to redemption that he is not permitted to make before default. He may, for example, assign or sell his equity of redemption.[30] If it is a protected party who assigns or sells and the assignee or buyer attempts to cure the debtor's default by paying past-due installments rather than pay the entire accelerated debt, the creditor is permitted to refuse to accept payment until he receives adequate assurance of the ability of the buyer or assignee to perform under the original debt.[31]

[26] Id., sec. 3-512(a).
[27] Id., sec. 3-512(b).
[28] Id., sec. 3-512(c).
[29] Id., sec. 3-512(d).
[30] Id., sec. 3-512(e).

The act also permits a debtor who pays an accelerated debt in full with funds obtained from refinancing to demand that the secured creditor who is paid off assign the secured debt to the refinancing lender so that he may acquire the same priority position that the original creditor enjoyed.[32]

STATUTORY RIGHT OF REDEMPTION

Nature of the Right

A **statutory right of redemption** is a right given to a mortgagor-debtor in about half of the states[33] that enables him to regain the property he lost through a foreclosure sale. In other words, the statutory right enables a defaulting mortgagor to cure his default even after foreclosure has occurred.

The statutory right of redemption is clearly distinguishable from a mortgagor's equity of redemption which arises upon default and ends with foreclosure. The statutory right of redemption comes into operation only after the equity of redemption has been extinguished and entitles the mortgagor to buy back his property from the one who purchased it at the foreclosure sale. In the one case the period for redemption precedes the foreclosure sale, in the other it follows it.

General Statutory Provisions

The right to redeem real estate after foreclosure is a special statutory privilege that may be exercised only in those states that specifically authorize it. While the details of these statutes vary, they commonly designate the persons who are entitled to the right, fix the time period within which the right may be exercised, indicate the amount that must be paid to redeem the property, and contain provisions as to the effect of redemption.

[31] Id., sec. 3-512, Comment 3.
[32] Id., sec. 3-512(f).
[33] Alabama, Alaska, Arizona, Arkansas, California, Colorado, Hawaii, Idaho, Illinois, Iowa, Kansas, Kentucky, Maine, Michigan, Minnesota, Missouri, Montana, Nevada, New Mexico, North Dakota, Oregon, South Dakota, Tennessee, Utah, Vermont, Washington, and Wyoming.

Who May Redeem The statutes usually confer the right of redemption on the mortgagor, judgment creditors, junior mortgagees, and other encumbrancers whose claims are subordinate to the foreclosed mortage.

The statutes generally make the right of redemption transferable.

Period for Redeeming The statutory period during which the right of redemption may be exercised typically is either 6 months[34] or 1 year.[35] Redemption periods differ in some states in accordance with whether foreclosure is by judicial proceedings or power of sale[36] and sometimes with regard to whether the foreclosed property is agricultural or not.[37]

Cost to Redeem The cost to redeem foreclosed real estate usually is the price paid by the purchaser at the foreclosure sale plus expenses and interest. Unlike equitable redemption which requires payment of the amount of the outstanding mortgage debt plus interest at the rate fixed by the secured debt, statutory redemption is effected by the payment of the foreclosure sale price, whether more or less than the debt, plus interest at the rate specified in the redemption statute.

Buyer's Interest during Redemption Period
Divergent views exist as to the nature of the purchaser's interest in the foreclosed property during the interval between the sale of the property and the end of the statutory period for redemption. One view holds that the purchaser does not acquire title to the property until the statutory period expires without the property having been redeemed, at which time he receives a deed. If redemption occurs during the period, of course, the purchaser receives the redemption money. Another view regards the purchaser as having acquired a defeasible title at the foreclosure sale which either terminates upon redemption or becomes absolute upon expiration of the redemption period without the property having been redeemed.

Positive and Negative Features of the Right
The statutory right of redemption has been both praised and condemned.

The most important objection is that the availability of redemption renders the title or interest obtained by the purchaser at the foreclosure sale defeasible for the period of redemption and that this discourages bidding by investors who are not attracted to conditional titles. It is also pointed out that a period of redemption allows speculation by those entitled to redeem since they may elect to exercise their right only if the value of the property rises during the redemption period.

On the other hand, it is argued that the period of redemption allows the mortgagor time to refinance and save his property and, more importantly, that the right of redemption serves as a strong inducement to those who bid at the foreclosure sale to bid a price that is more in keeping with the value of the property. Furthermore, by permitting junior lienors to bid at the foreclosure sale, the statutes enable them to protect the security they might otherwise lose.

ULTA Position
The Uniform Land Transactions Act makes no provision for a right of redemption either after a judicial or a nonjudicial foreclosure sale.

DEFICIENCY JUDGMENTS

A **deficiency judgment,** we have seen, is a personal judgment against a mortgagor-debtor for an amount by which the net proceeds of a foreclosure sale fail to satisfy his defaulted debt.

---

[34] As in Arizona, Illinois, Michigan, Minnesota, Utah, and Vermont.

[35] As in Alabama, Alaska, California, Hawaii, Iowa, Kansas, Kentucky, Maine, Missouri, Montana, Nevada, North Dakota, Oregon, South Dakota, and Washington.

[36] For example, there is no statutory redemption in California, Colorado, Hawaii, or New Mexico in power of sale foreclosures; in Arkansas statutory redemption is available only when foreclosure is by power of sale; and in Michigan the period of redemption is shorter for nonjudicial foreclosure sales than it is for judicial sales.

[37] In Colorado and Wyoming, for example, the period is longer if agricultural lands are foreclosed.

The mortgagee-creditor in whose favor a deficiency judgment operates may cause other assets of the judgment debtor to be seized and sold by an officer of the court in satisfaction of the deficiency.

Obtainable in Most States
Regardless of the method of foreclosure a mortgagee-creditor may pursue, he can in most states obtain a deficiency judgment. Where, as is usually the case, foreclosure is by a judicial sale, the net proceeds from the sale are applied against the defaulted debt and, except where statutes provide otherwise, the court in the same proceeding awards a judgment for the unpaid balance of the debt. Where foreclosure is by power of sale instead of judicial sale, the mortgagee-creditor may, in the absence of a statute prohibiting it, bring a lawsuit after the sale to obtain a judgment from a court for any deficiency.

Antideficiency Legislation

Conditions Prompting Such Legislation Largely as a result of experience during the Depression of the 1930s, some states enacted **antideficiency legislation** that prohibits deficiency judgments in certain instances. Often, at a time when real estate values were declining, the successful if not the only bidder at a foreclosure sale was the mortgagee-creditor and his bid was generally less than the amount of the outstanding debt. In such a case, the mortgagee ended up not only with the mortgagor's property but with a personal judgment against him as well—a situation considered by some legislatures to be unreasonably oppressive for the debtor. As might be expected in view of the policy considerations involved, antideficiency statutes vary among those states which have enacted such legislation.

Purchase Money Security Interests Some states[38] abolish deficiency judgments whenever purchase-money security interests are involved regardless of whether foreclosure is by judicial or nonjudicial sale. In these states, a purchase money security is generally defined to include both transactions in which a seller of property takes back a mortgage or other security and transactions in which the money that is used for the purchase is obtained from a source other than the seller.

Limitation Rather Than Abolition Instead of abolishing deficiency judgments, statutes in some states[39] regulate the method by which the amount of a deficiency judgment is determined. According to such statutes, a deficiency judgment is limited to the difference between the amount of the unpaid obligation and the fair market value of the mortgaged property at the time of the foreclosure sale, the fair value being determined by the court. It is generally agreed that even in normal times the amount received at a forced foreclosure sale does not usually reflect the market value of the property that would be realized at a negotiated sale. In times of depression the difference can be very substantial.

The validity of a New York fair value statute was upheld by the U.S. Supreme Court[40] on the grounds that the intent of the parties to a mortgage was to permit the mortgagee to collect his debt from sale of the mortgaged property but not to enrich him at the expense of the mortgagor-debtor. Unjust enrichment would occur, the court held, if instead of the actual market value of the mortgaged property, the price realized at a public sale in a depressed market were applied to the mortgage debt.

Mortgagor's Right May Not Be Waived
Statutes that give a mortgagor-debtor the right either to be free from deficiency judgments or to be protected as to the size of them sometimes

---

[38] For example, California, Montana, North Carolina, and North Dakota.

[39] For example, California, New Jersey, New York, and Pennsylvania.

[40] *Honeyman v. Jacobs,* 306 U.S. 539, 59 Sup. Ct. 702, (1939).

include provisions against the mortgagor waiving of this right. Such provisions are said to protect the mortgagor against waiver clauses that are included in mortgages as a matter of practice and which the mortgagor's typically weak bargaining position would cause him to accept.

ULTA Position

The Uniform Land Transactions Act imposes certain limitations on a creditor's right to a deficiency judgment for the difference between the outstanding debt and the net proceeds of a foreclosure sale.[41]

Except where the borrower is a protected party, the borrower is liable for a deficiency judgment whether the lender has foreclosed by a judicial sale or has exercised his power of sale. A deficiency judgment cannot be obtained against a borrower who is a protected party if the debt is secured by a purchase money security interest.[42] The act adopts the majority view that a purchase money interest includes both a mortgage in which the seller of property is the mortgagor-creditor and a mortgage that secures a loan obtained from a third party lender the proceeds of which the borrower used to purchase the real estate.[43] The drafters of the act observed that "If the policy of eliminating deficiency judgments is sound at all it would seem to be equally sound whether the mortgagee is a seller or a cash lender furnishing the cash to pay the seller."[44]

DEED IN LIEU OF FORECLOSURE

Before commencing to foreclose a mortgage, it is not uncommon for the mortgagee-creditor to contact the mortgagor to determine whether there is any possibility of refinancing the debt or otherwise curing the mortgagor's default. During these discussions, if it appears that the mortgagor's financial condition is such that foreclosure is inevitable, the parties may agree that instead of the creditor proceeding to foreclosure, the debtor will give him a deed to the mortgaged property in satisfaction of the unpaid debt. Such a deed is referred to as a **deed in lieu of foreclosure** and like other deeds cuts off or terminates any rights that the transferor has in the property.

Factors Prompting Use of the Deed

A mortgagor-debtor may be motivated to give the mortgagee-creditor a deed in lieu of foreclosure by the fact that he has an aversion to the real or imagined publicity arising from a foreclosure proceeding or, in states that do not have antideficiency statutes, the debtor may feel that the net proceeds of a foreclosure sale will not be sufficient to pay his debt and he will therefore be subject to a personal judgment for the unsatisfied balance.

A mortgagee-creditor, by agreeing to accept a deed in lieu of foreclosure, obviously believes that even though he could have obtained a deficiency judgment in a foreclosure proceeding, the judgment would not be worth the effort.

Pitfalls for the Mortgagee-Grantee

While there is a popular belief that the mortgagee-creditor should be willing to take a deed in lieu of foreclosure in almost any case, there are certain pitfalls of which he should be aware. Unlike a foreclosure sale, a deed in lieu of foreclosure does not terminate liens that are junior to the creditor's and hence he should not agree to such a deed unless he is willing to take title to the property subject to the junior liens. Moreover, there is the potential problem regarding the adequacy of consideration given by the creditor in exchange for the property when the debtor has other creditors and is insolvent. The problem can arise both under the federal Bankruptcy Act and state statutes dealing with conveyances in fraud of creditors.

ULTA Position

The Uniform Land Transactions Act provides that after a default, the secured creditor and the

---

[41] ULTA, sec. 3-510(b).
[42] Id., sec. 3-510(b).
[43] Id., sec. 30510, Comment 2.
[44] Id., sec. 3-510, Comment 3.

debtor may agree to terminate the debtor's interest in the real estate without proceeding to foreclosure.[45] The most common method of accomplishing this end is by the debtor executing a deed in lieu of foreclosure in favor of the creditor.

INSTALLMENT SALE CONTRACT

Nature of the Security Agreement

When a seller of real estate is willing to finance a buyer's purchase of it, the parties may agree that instead of using a note secured by a purchase money mortgage or deed of trust, the transaction will take the form of an installment sale contract, which is also known as a **land contract,** an **agreement for deed,** or a **contract for deed.** An **installment sale contract** is an agreement between a seller and a buyer in which an owner-seller of real estate promises to deliver a deed to the buyer at some time in the future when the buyer, after making an agreed number of installment payments, will have paid the purchase price in full. The contract remains executory until all installments have been paid and the deed is delivered to the buyer.

Distinguished from Ordinary Sales Agreements

An installment sale contract differs appreciably from the more common agreement to purchase real estate contained in a "deposit receipt" or similar contract of sale.

Long-Term versus Short-Term One important difference between the two types of contracts is the length of time each contract is to remain executory. The deposit receipt sales contract is a short-term arrangement calling for the simultaneous payment of the purchase price in full and the delivery of the deed to the property at the time of title closing. The installment sale contract, on the other hand, is a long-term arrangement in which the deed is delivered after a relatively extended series of payments have been made. The time at which the seller must deliver the deed to the buyer is set by the schedule of payments to be made by the buyer.

Dependent versus Independent Promises The distinction between real estate installment sales contracts and ordinary real estate contracts of purchase and sale can also be explained in terms of dependent and independent promises. If the law will not compel one party to perform his promise until the other party to a contract has performed his, the promise of the one who must perform first is said to be an *independent* promise and the other a *dependent* one.

The promises contained in an ordinary contract for the sale of real estate are *mutually dependent,* which means that the promise of the buyer to pay is dependent upon the seller's promise to transfer a marketable title and vice versa. The two promises are performed simultaneously at the time the sales transaction is closed. Neither of the parties must perform first and then trust the other to perform.

The promises of the parties to an installment sale contract are *not* mutually dependent and consequently simultaneous performance is not required. The buyer's promise to pay the periodic installment payments is not dependent upon any performance on the part of the seller. Until the buyer has fully performed his promise to pay the purchase price, the seller is not obligated to perform his promise to transfer title.

Risk Assumed by Installment Purchaser In an installment sale arrangement, the buyer assumes the risk that, after having made all payments as agreed, the seller will not or cannot convey title to him. If the seller has title to the property but simply refuses to transfer it, the seller, after having established the fact of his performance, may go to court and obtain specific performance of the seller's promise, thus receiving title to the property. If, however, the seller is unable to perform because he does not have title to the property, all the buyer can obtain is a judgment for damages which may or may not be collectible.

---

[45] Id., sec. 3-505(a).

In the absence of fraud, the seller under an installment sale contract is not required to have title, marketable or otherwise, to the property at the time the contract is entered into. The promise of the seller is to deliver title to the buyer after all installments have been paid and not before. As a general rule, in the absence of fraud or a contrary provision in the installment contract, the buyer cannot be heard to complain because of defects in the seller's title prior to the time set for conveyance.

Possession of Premises by Buyer A second important difference between an installment sales contract and a deposit receipt sales contract is that in the former the buyer is normally given possession of the property prior to his receiving title to it, while in the latter he normally is not.

Installment Sale Contract Is a Financing Device Finally, an installment sale contract is a real estate financing device while a deposit receipt sales contract is not. In the latter the buyer arranges for the financing of his purchase quite independent from his acquisition of title from the seller. To be sure, in some cases the seller may accept a note secured by a mortgage or deed of trust as part of the purchase price, but the transfer of title to the buyer is not conditioned upon his payment of the note in full.

Alternative to Purchase Money Mortgage

The installment sale contract is an alternative security device frequently used by a seller of real estate instead of a purchase money mortgage arrangement. The installment contract may be used for the sale of either improved or unimproved real estate and the popularity of the device depends both upon the locale and the condition of the real estate market at a given time. In some areas its use is confined almost exclusively to sales of undeveloped lots and unimproved property, thus accounting for the use of the term "land contract." In other areas, and particularly at times when the supply of low-cost housing exceeds the normal down payment capabilities of purchasers, the device is used for improved real estate and is then frequently referred to as an "agreement for deed" or "contract for deed." But whether it is used for the purchase and sale of improved property or unimproved property, the objective in using an installment sale contract is to serve both as a merchandising and a financing device.

Typically, the installment sale contract is used by a seller, whether a developer or individual property owner, when real estate is sold to buyers whose down payments are often no larger than one of the monthly installment payments. The cost of foreclosing a purchase money mortgage during the early years when the mortgagor's equity is small causes the seller to want to avoid the necessity for foreclosure when the buyer defaults. To avoid the necessity of a costly foreclosure suit, the seller uses an installment sale contract with a provision that permits him to declare a forfeiture of the buyer's rights in the property without resorting to foreclosure proceedings. The effectiveness of such a provision, however, as we shall see, may be illusory.

Seller Retains Legal Title

When real estate is sold under an installment sale contract, the legal title to the property is not transferred to the buyer until he has paid the purchase price in accordance with the terms of the agreement, despite the fact that the buyer is usually given immediate possession of the property. As long as the contract remains executory, no legal title passes. The seller retains the legal title as security against the possibility that the buyer will default on his installment payments. In accordance with the doctrine of equitable conversion, however, despite the fact that the buyer under an executory contract for the sale of real estate does not have legal title to the property, he is considered to be the beneficial owner of it subject to liability for the unpaid purchase price. The seller holds the legal title subject to an equitable obligation to convey it to the buyer upon receipt of the purchase price.

Risk of Damage or Destruction

From the notion that the buyer is the beneficial owner of the property to which the seller holds legal title as security there developed the idea that any damage to the property prior to delivery of the deed, without the fault of either party, falls on the buyer. Some states, however, have rejected the idea in whole or in part while others[46] by adopting the Uniform Vendor and Purchaser Risk Act make the *right to possession* rather than beneficial ownership the controlling determinant as to who shall bear losses due to damage or destruction. That act provides as follows:

> Any contract hereafter made in this State for the purchase and sale of realty shall be interpreted as including an agreement that the parties shall have the following rights and duties, unless the contract expressly provides otherwise:
> (a) If, when neither the legal title nor the possession of the subject matter of the contract has been transferred, all or a material part thereof is destroyed without fault of the purchaser or is taken by eminent domain, the vendor cannot enforce the contract, and the purchaser is entitled to recover any portion of the price that he has paid;
> (b) If, when either the legal title or the possession of the subject matter of the contract has been transferred, all or any part thereof is destroyed without fault of the vendor or is taken by eminent domain, the purchaser is not thereby relieved from a duty to pay the price, nor is he entitled to recover any portion thereof that he has paid.

The question as to who bears the risk of loss is particularly important where improved property is concerned and should be clearly provided for in an installment sale contract.

Common Contract Provisions

Except as prohibited by statute or public policy, the parties to a real estate installment sale contract are free to contract as they see fit.

[46] California, Hawaii, Illinois, Michigan, New York, North Carolina, Oklahoma, Oregon, South Dakota, and Wisconsin.

Some of the more common provisions of such agreements relate to the following matters.

Possession by Buyer Although the buyer under an installment sale contract is considered to be the beneficial owner of the property, he is not entitled to possession of the premises unless he is specifically given that right by the terms of the contract. The seller retains all the rights incident to his legal title that he does not agree to part with. Where the property sold is a dwelling unit, the contract obviously would provide for possession by the buyer during the term of the contract.

Taxes, Insurance, and Repairs Installment sale contracts commonly contain undertakings by the buyer to pay all taxes and assessments when due, to acquire hazard insurance payable to the seller and the buyer in accordance with their interests, and to keep the property in good repair. In some instances the contract will provide for monthly payments of pro rata sums for taxes and insurance to be held by the seller who pays those charges as they fall due.

Acceleration Clause In the absence of a statutory prohibition, the contract may provide for acceleration of the contract debt upon the buyer's failure to make any payment when due or upon his assignment of the contract without the seller's consent.

Prepayment Privilege Except as that privilege may be granted by statute, a buyer under an installment sale contract has no right to prepay the purchase price unless the right is expressly given to him by the terms of the contract.

A California statute provides that "A buyer shall be entitled to pay all or any amount of the balance due on any real property sales contract with respect to the sale of land which has been subdivided into a *residential lot or lots which contain a dwelling for not more than four families.*" [Emphasis added.][47]

[47] California Civil Code, sec. 2985.6.

Enforceability of Forfeiture Provisions We have seen that where real estate is sold for a very small down payment, many sellers prefer to use an installment sale contract instead of a purchase money mortgage because the inclusion of a forfeiture clause in the contract enables him to avoid the burdens of foreclosure proceedings in the event of a default by the buyer. The following is typical of a forfeiture clause.

> If the buyer fails to make any payment when due or fails to perform any other undertaking on his part, and fails to cure such default within 30 days after receiving a written notice thereof from the seller, the seller may thereupon terminate this agreement by giving the buyer a notice of termination. In that event, the seller shall retain all payments made by the buyer in full satisfaction and liquidation of all damages sustained and shall have the right to re-enter and take possession of the property to be conveyed by this agreement and to expel the buyer and all persons who may be in possession.

The question of enforceability of such a provision will in most instances depend upon whether it is construed by the court as providing for the payment of liquidated damages as it states or whether it is in fact a provision for a penalty.

Liquidated Damages versus Penalty In general contract law the distinction between **liquidated damages** and a penalty is that the former bears a reasonable relationship to actual damages occasioned by a breach and is essentially compensatory in character, while the latter is a form of punishment for the breach which has no relation to actual damages and may easily result in the unjust enrichment of the party enforcing the contract provision. If a clause in a contract provides for a penalty it is unenforceable and the defaulting party will be liable for actual damages sustained by the other party. If, on the other hand, the provision is found to be one for the payment of liquidated damages it is valid and enforceable and the sum specified will be recoverable by the injured party upon breach of the agreement.

Although the majority view does not hold the distinction between liquidated damages and a penalty to be applicable in determining whether a buyer defaulting on an installment contract containing a forfeiture clause can recover any part of his payments, there are instances where the rights of the defaulting buyer are made to turn on the distinction. Courts of equity will intercede to prevent a forfeiture where they determine that strict enforcement of a forfeiture clause would lead to unconscionable results.

There is no single rule for determining whether a provision in an installment sale contract is enforceable as a bona fide liquidated damage clause or is a penalty and therefore unenforceable. Each case will depend upon its own facts and equities. If a court feels that the result of finding a particular provision to be one for liquidated damages rather than a penalty would not be in accord with the general equities of the case, the chances are good that the clause will be construed as a penalty, and vice versa. For example, where the contract equates liquidated damages with the installments paid and thus increases the buyer's forfeiture inversely to the actual damage sustained by the seller, such a provision is likely to be construed as a penalty and not as a liquidated damage clause.

The mere use of the words "liquidated damages" in a forfeiture clause is not controlling as to whether the provision is one for liquidated damages or a penalty. The courts will construe the clause for what it is in fact rather than what the language says it is.

ULTA Position The Uniform Land Transactions Act takes the position that "Damages for breach by either party may be liquidated in the agreement, but only in an amount that is not unreasonable in the light of the anticipated or actual harm caused by the breach, the time the real estate is withheld from the market, the difficulties of proof of loss, and the inconvenience or nonfeasibility of otherwise obtaining an adequate remedy. A provision for unreasonably large liquidated damages is void."[48]

The act permits a buyer who breaches the contract to recover the amount by which the payments made by him exceed either the actual damages sustained by the seller or the value of the benefits received by the buyer, whichever is the larger.[49] The buyer's right to recover the excess is not dependent upon the nature of his breach or whether he acted in good or bad faith in breaching the contract.[50]

TRUTH IN LENDING LAW

Objective of the Act

The declared purpose of the federal **Truth in Lending Law**[51] is "to assure a meaningful disclosure of credit terms so that the consumer will be able to compare more readily the various credit terms available to him and avoid the uninformed use of credit."[52]

The stimulus for passage of the act was the congressional opinion that consumers were not fully aware of the various charges they assumed in credit transactions and that some clarification by creditors of the costs of credit was needed.[53] It was recognized that while some borrowers understood the rate of interest they paid on their loans, many were confused by the terminology used by lenders and were sometimes led into error by the complexities of a lending transaction. To correct this situation, the act requires "truth-in-lending" in the form of disclosure of certain kinds of information in consumer credit transactions.

Act Implemented by Regulation Z

The Truth in Lending Law provides[54] that the Board of Governors of the Federal Reserve System "shall prescribe regulations to carry out the purposes" of the act. In accordance with that charge, the Board of Governors issued Regulation Z[55] which sets forth detailed explanations and regulations of the law.

Regulation Z states that, in implementing the act, its purpose is "to assure that every customer who has need for consumer credit is given meaningful information with respect to the cost of that credit which, in most cases, must be expressed in the dollar amount of finance charge, and as an annual percentage rate computed on the basis of the amount to be financed."[56] In addition, Regulation Z states, it is necessary that other relevant credit information be disclosed "so that the customer may readily compare the various credit terms available to him from different sources and avoid the uninformed use of credit."[57]

Regulation Z makes clear that neither it nor the act is intended to control charges made for consumer credit or to interfere with trade practices, except to the extent that such practices may be inconsistent with the purpose of the act.

Regulation of Real Property Transactions

As the term is used in Regulation Z, a "real property transaction" is an "extension of credit in connection with which a security interest in real property is or will be retained or acquired."[58] A "security interest" in turn is defined as being "any interest in property which secures payment or performance of an obligation" and includes real property mortgages, deeds of trust, and the interest of a seller in a contract for the sale of real property.[59] Regulation Z governs all real estate credit transactions

---

[48] ULTA, sec. 2-516(a).
[49] Id., sec. 2-516(c) and (d).
[50] Id., sec. 2-516, Comment 3.
[51] This is Title I of the federal Consumer Credit Protection Act which became effective on July 1, 1969, and is codified as 15 U.S.C., secs. 1601–1655.
[52] 15 U.S.C., sec. 1601.
[53] See House Report (Banking and Currency Committee) No. 1040, 2 U.S. Code Congressional and Administrative News, 90th Cong., 2d Sess., 1968, pp. 1962 et seq.

[54] 15 U.S.C., sec. 1604.
[55] 12 C.F.R., sec. 226 et seq.
[56] Id., sec. 226.1(a)(2).
[57] Id.
[58] Id., sec. 226.2(x).
[59] Id., sec. 226.2(z).

in any amount when credit is extended to an individual other than for business purposes, unless the business is agricultural.[60]

Regulation Z applies only to a person or organization that "in the ordinary course of business regularly extends or arranges for the extension of credit."[61] It does not apply to the private seller of a home who takes back a note secured by a mortgage as part of the purchase price.

Like other lenders and creditors, a lender whose loan is secured by a real estate security interest must disclose the annual percentage rate which a borrower must pay on his secured loan, but in certain situations involving real estate he is not required to disclose the total dollar amount of the finance charge over the period of the loan.

In some instances, the borrower will have the right to cancel his loan agreement with the lender.

Finance Charge for Loan

Nature of a Finance Charge The cost of money to a borrower is more than simply the contract rate of interest that he pays on his loan. This larger cost that the borrower bears for the use of a lender's money is called a **finance charge** and is defined in Regulation Z as being the sum of all charges that are payable directly or indirectly by the borrower and which are imposed directly or indirectly by the lender as an incident to the granting of the loan.[62]

Costs Included in Finance Charge Costs which are part of the finance charge and must be disclosed to the borrower include:[63]

1 Interest, time price differential, and any amount payable under a discount or other system of additional charges.

2 Service, transaction, activity, or carrying charge.

3 Loan fee, points, finder's fee, or similar charge.

4 Charges or premiums for life, accident, health, or loss of income insurance written in connection with any credit transaction unless the creditor clearly states in writing that such insurance coverage is not required.

5 Charges or premiums for insurance, written in connection with any credit transaction, against loss of or damage to property unless the creditor clearly states in writing the cost of the insurance if obtained through the creditor or if the writing states that the debtor may choose the person from whom the insurance is to be obtained.

6 Premiums or other charges for any guarantee or insurance that protects the creditor against the debtor's default.

Costs Excluded from Finance Charge Specifically excluded from determination of the finance charge in a real property transaction are the following items:[64]

1 Fees or premiums for title examination, abstract of title, title insurance, or similar purposes and for required related property surveys.

2 Fees for the preparation of deeds, settlement statements, or other documents.

3 Amounts required to be placed or paid into an escrow or trustee account for future payment of taxes, insurance, and water, sewer, and land rents.

4 Fees for notarizing deeds and other documents.

5 Appraisal fees.

6 Credit reports.

Once the finance charge has been determined, it must be disclosed to the borrower as an *annual percentage rate*. The calculation of the finance charge and its statement as an annual percentage rate will appear in a disclosure statement similar to that appearing at Figure 16-2.

Annual Percentage Rate

As the term is used in connection with real estate loans, the **annual percentage rate** indicates

---

[60] Id., sec. 226.3(a).
[61] Id., 226.2(m).
[62] Id., sec. 226.4(a).
[63] Id., sec. 226.4(a) (1)–(8).

[64] Id., sec. 226.4(e)(1)–(6).

MORTGAGES, DEEDS OF TRUST, AND INSTALLMENT CONTRACTS—PART II

I. A. Cash price (contract sales price) $ _____
       1. Less any cash downpayment $ _____
       2. Less any trade-in $ _____
       3. Total downpayment $ _____
    B. Equals unpaid balance of cash price $ _____
    C. Plus any other amounts financed:
       1. Property insurance premiums $ _____
       2. _____ $ _____
       3. Total other amounts financed $ _____
    D. Equals unpaid balance $ _____
    E. Less any prepaid finance charges:
       1. Origination fee or points
          paid by borrower $ _____
       2. Loan discount or points
          paid by seller $ _____
       3. Interest from (specify date)
          to (specify date) $ _____
       4. Mortgage quaranty insturance $ _____
       5. _____ $ _____
       6. Total prepaid finance charge $ _____
    F. Equals amount financed $ _____
II. The **FINANCE CHARGE** consists of
    A. Interest (simple annual rate
       of ___ %) $ _____
    B. Total prepaid finance charge
       (I. E. 6.) $ _____
    C. _____ $ _____
    D. Total **FINANCE CHARGE** $ _____
III. A. The **ANNUAL PERCENTAGE RATE** on the amount financed is ___ %
    B. If the contract includes a provision for variation in the interest rate, describe _____
_____

Figure 16-2 Truth-in-Lending Disclosure Statement.

```
  IV. The repayment terms are: _____
      _____

   V. The finance charge begins to accrue on  (specify date)
  VI. In the event of late payments, charges may be assessed as follows:
      _____

 VII. (Use either A or B as appropriate)
      A. Conditions and penalties for prepaying this obligation are _____
         _____

      B. Identification of method of rebate of unearned finance charge is
         _____

VIII. Insurance taken in connection with this obligation: _____

  IX. The security for this obligation is _____
      _____

*Indicates a date, rate or amount that is estimated and may be subject to change.
```

Figure 16-2 (Continued)

the cost of money to the borrower on an annual basis and is a function of the amount of the loan and the finance charge. In virtually all instances where real estate loans are involved, the annual percentage rate will be higher than the contract rate appearing in the loan agreement because the latter rate includes only interest while the annual percentage rate includes all items which comprise the finance charge for the use of the borrowed money.

Regulation Z requires that the annual percentage rate be disclosed with an accuracy at least to the nearest quarter of 1 percent and prescribes methods for calculating the rate.[65] Because calculation of the rate may be difficult for some lenders, the Federal Reserve Board has published the Regulation Z Annual Percentage Rate Tables which may be used to determine the annual percentage rate on a loan and any rate determined from such tables will comply with the requirements of the regulations.[66]

Statement of Total Finance Charge

In most credit transactions, Regulation Z requires that the total dollar amount of the finance charge over the credit period be disclosed. This requirement does *not* apply, however, in the case of a loan on a *dwelling* that was used to purchase the dwelling and was secured by a *first* mortgage or lien on it.[67]

Right to Rescind Certain Transactions

Nature of the Right   The Truth in Lending Law grants an individual the right to rescind "any consumer credit transaction in which a security interest is retained or acquired in any real property which is expected to be used as the residence of the person to whom credit is extended."[68]

[65] Id., sec. 226.5(b).
[66] Id., sec. 226.5(c).
[67] Id., sec. 226.8(d)(3).
[68] 15 U.S.C., sec. 1635(a).

MORTGAGES, DEEDS OF TRUST, AND INSTALLMENT CONTRACTS—PART II

(Identification of Transaction)

Notice To Customer Required By Federal Law:

You have entered into a transaction on __(date)__ which may result in a lien, mortgage, or other security interest in your home. You have a legal right under federal law to cancel this transaction, if you desire to do so, without any penalty or obligation within three business days from the above date or any later date on which all material disclosures required under the Truth in Lending Act have been given to you. If you so cancel this transaction, any lien, mortgage, or other security on your home arising from this transaction is automatically void. Your are also entitled to receive a refund of any downpayment or other consideration if you cancel. If you decide to cancel this transaction, you may do so by notifying

_____(name of creditor)_____

at _____(address of creditor's place of business)_____

by mail or telegram sent not later than midnight of __(date)__ . You may also use any other form of written notice identifying the transaction if it is delivered to the above address not later than that time. This notice may be used for that purpose by dating and signing below.

I hereby cancel this transaction

__(date)__   __(customer's signature)__

Figure 16-3 Notice of Right of Rescission
Source: Regulation Z, 12 C.F.R., sec. 226, Appendix B.

An agreement is **rescinded** when one of the parties to an agreement exercises his right to terminate it. The result of a rescission is to return the parties to the legal status or relationship that existed between them before they entered into the agreement. If either party received a consideration or thing of value from the other party as a result of their agreement, that consideration must be returned if the rescission is to be effective.

Exception to Right of Rescission The right of a borrower to rescind a loan agreement secured by real estate is subject to a very significant exception. Regulation Z provides that rescission is *not* available in a transaction that involves the "creation, retention, or assumption of a *first lien* to finance the *acquisition of a dwelling* in which the customer *resides or expects to reside.*" [Emphasis added.][69] This means, of course, that a borrower's right to rescind does not apply to the usual first purchase money mortgage transaction in which the loan is used to buy a home for the borrower. Rescission is available to a borrower, however, where he seeks a loan to refinance an existing first mortgage or where a second mortgage on the home he presently owns and occupies is given to secure a loan.

[69] 12 C.F.R., sec. 226.9(g). Regulation Z defines a "dwelling" as "a residential-type structure which is real property and contains one or more family housing units. or a residential condominium unit wherever situated." Id., sec. 226.2(p).

Notice by Lender and Borrower In those transactions in which the right to rescind is available, the lender must give the borrower notice of that fact by furnishing him with two copies of the notice appearing at Figure 16-3, one copy of which may be used by the borrower to cancel the loan transaction.[70] The borrower may exercise his right of rescission any time within three business days after consummation of the loan transaction or the date of delivery of the notice of the right to rescind, whichever is later.[71] Notification of rescission may be either by mail, using the form provided by the lender if desired, or by telegram. Notification by mail is effective at the time it is mailed by telegram when filed for transmission.

Effect of Rescission by Borrower When the borrower exercises his right to rescind, he is not liable for any finance or other charge and any security interest given by him becomes void. Within 10 days following receipt of notice of the borrower's rescission, the lender must return to the borrower "any money or property given as earnest money, downpayment, or otherwise, and shall take any action necessary or appropriate to reflect the termination of any security interest created under the transaction."[72] Regulation Z requires that the paragraph shown in Figure 16-4 concerning the effect of rescission must either appear on the face of the notice to the borrower or on the reverse side of it. If it appears on the reverse side of the notice of the right to rescind, the face of the notice must say, "See reverse side for important information about your right of rescission."[73]

---

[70] Id., 226.9(b).
[71] Id., sec. 226.9(a).
[72] Id., sec. 226.9(d).
[73] 12 C.F.R., sec. 226, Appendix B.

EFFECT OF RESCISSION. When a customer exercises his right to rescind under paragraph (a) this section, he is not liable for any finance or other charge, and any security interest becomes void upon such a rescission. Within 10 days after receipt of a notice of rescission, the creditor shall return to the customer any money or property given as earnest money, downpayment, or otherwise, and shall take any action necessary or appropriate to reflect the termination of any security interest created under the transaction. If the creditor has delivered any property to the customer, the customer may retain possession of it. Upon the performance of the creditor's obligations under this section, the customer shall tender the property to the creditor, except that if the return of the property in kind would be impracticable or inequitable, the customer shall tender its reasonable value. Tender shall be made at the location of the property or at the residence of the customer, at the option of the customer. If the creditor does not take possession of the property within 10 days after tender by the customer, ownership of the property vests in the customer without obligation on his part to pay for it.

Figure 16-4 Reverse Side of Notice of Right of Rescission
Source: Regulation Z, 12 C.F.R., sec. 226, Appendix B.

Civil and Criminal Penalties

Failure on the part of a lender to comply with the requirements of the Truth in Lending Law and Regulation Z may subject him to both civil[74] and criminal[75] liability.

EQUAL CREDIT OPPORTUNITY ACT

After hearings conducted by the House of Representatives revealed that credit applicants were being discriminated against because of sex and marital status, Congress enacted the **Equal Credit Opportunity Act** of 1974.[76] Two years later the act was amended[77] to enlarge the prohibitions against discrimination in credit transactions to include such factors as an applicant's age, race, color, religion, national origin and the fact that the applicant receives public assistance benefits, in addition to sex and marital status.[78]

Purpose of the Act

According to the Senate Committee on Banking, Housing and Urban Affairs, the amended legislation "is intended to prevent the kinds of credit discrimination which have occurred in the past, and to anticipate and prevent discriminatory practices in the future."[79] The committee expressed the belief that the act will accomplish this end without infringing on the freedom of creditors to make informed credit judgments and to avoid unsound credit practices. The committee further believed that the legislation should result in "a more informed and competitive marketplace, where credit applicants can be assured of evenhanded treatment in their quest for what has become a virtual necessity of life."[80] And because "credit has ceased to be a luxury item," the committee was of the opinion that it must be established as a clear public policy that "no credit applicant shall be denied the credit he or she needs or wants on the basis of characteristics that have nothing to do with his or her creditworthiness."[81]

Implementation of the Act

The amended act provides that the Board of Governors of the Federal Reserve System "shall prescribe regulations to carry out the purposes of the act."[82] Pursuant to this provision, the Board issued Regulation B.[83]

Denial or Revocation of Credit

The act requires that creditors must notify credit applicants of action taken on their applications within 30 days following receipt of a completed application.[84]

If the action taken by a creditor is adverse,[85] credit applicants must be advised of the reasons for such action.[86] The Senate committee was of the opinion that such a requirement is "a strong and necessary adjunct to the antidiscriminatory purpose of the legislation" because, the committee reasoned, "only if creditors know they must explain their decisions will they effectively be discouraged from discriminatory practices."[87] The committee also expressed the view that the requirement "fulfills a broader need" because rejected credit applicants will be able to know why their credit standing is deficient

---

[74] 15 U.S.C., sec. 1640.
[75] Id., sec. 1611.
[76] The act is Title VII of the Consumer Credit Protection Act, 15 U.S.C., secs. 1691 et seq.
[77] Equal Credit Opportunity Act Amendments of 1976, P.L.94-239, 15 U.S.C., secs. 1691–1691f.
[78] 15 U.S.C., sec. 1691(a)(1)–(3).
[79] Senate Report (Committee on Banking, Housing and Urban Affairs) No. 94-589, 2 U.S. Code Congressional and Administrative News, 94th Cong., 2nd Sess., 1976, p. 406.
[80] Id.
[81] Id., p. 405.
[82] 15 U.S.C., sec. 1691b(a).
[83] 12 C.F.R., secs. 202.1–202.13.
[84] 15 U.S.C., sec. 1691(d)(1).
[85] The act says that "the term 'adverse action' means a denial or revocation of credit, a change in the terms of an existing credit arrangement, or a refusal to grant credit in substantially the amount and on substantially the terms requested. Such term does not include a refusal to extend additional credit under an existing credit arrangement where the applicant is delinquent or otherwise in default, or where such additional credit would exceed a previously established credit limit." 15 U.S.C., sec. 1691(d)(6).
[86] 15 U.S.C., sec. 1691(d)(1)–(3).
[87] Senate Report (Committee on Banking, Housing and Urgan Affairs) No. 94-589, 2 U.S. Code Congressional and Administrative News, 94th Cong., 2nd Sess., 1976, p. 406.

"and this information should have a pervasive and valuable educational benefit. Instead of being told only that they do not meet a particular creditor's standards, consumers particularly should benefit from knowing, for example, that the reason for the denial is their short residence in the area, or their recent change of employment, or their already over-extended financial situation. In those cases where the creditor may have acted on misinformation, the statement of reasons gives the applicant a chance to rectify the mistake."[88]

In referring to the provision entitling credit applicants to receive a statement of reasons for rejection as being one of the most important parts of the act, the committee noted that, with but few exceptions, creditors have normally done no more than notify unsuccessful applicants of the fact that their applications have been rejected without giving even a cursory explanation for it. "The creditors' apparent rationale," the committee observed, "has been that since they had no legal obligation to explain their action they would not venture the effort or the potential embarrassment of doing so." This attitude is not only considered to be shortsighted by the committee but it also deprives rejected credit applicants of needed and useful information. Disclosure of reasons for rejection of credit "is essential to achieve the antidiscrimination goals of this legislation, for a creditor who knows he may have to explain his decision is much less likely to rest it upon improper grounds. In addition," the committee stated, "we believe that knowing the reasons for adverse action will, over time, have a very beneficial competitive effect on the credit marketplace."[89]

A creditor's statement of the reasons for his adverse action is deemed to be sufficient if it is specific and indicates the principal reason for the action taken. A creditor may formulate his own statement of reasons in a checklist or letter form or he may use all or parts of a sample form prepared by the Federal Reserve Board, which if properly completed meets the requirements of the act. (See Figure 16-5.)[90]

Enforcement of the Act

Administrative enforcement of the requirements imposed by the act and Regulation B is assigned to various government agencies for particular classes of creditors.[91]

In addition to assigning administrative enforcement responsibilities, the act authorizes the United States Attorney General to bring enforcement actions, either on the referral of cases from the administrative agencies or on his own initiative for practices that are in violation of the act.[92]

"The chief enforcement tool, however, will continue to be private actions for actual and punitive damages."[93] The act makes any creditor who fails to comply with a requirement of the act liable to the aggrieved applicant for actual damages sustained by him acting either in an individual capacity or as a member of a class.[94] In addition to actual damages, any

---

[88] Id.

[89] Id., p. 409.

[90] 12 C.F.R., sec. 202.9(b)(2).

[91] Administrative enforcement of (1) national banks is assigned to the Comptroller of the Currency, (2) state member banks of the Federal Reserve System to the Federal Reserve Board, (3) nonmember banks insured by the Federal Deposit Insurance Corporation to the Board of Directors of that corporation, (4) savings institutions insured by the Federal Savings and Loan Insurance Corporation to the Federal Home Loan Bank Board, (5) federal credit unions to the Administrator of the National Credit Union Administration, (6) creditors subject to the Civil Aeronautics Board to that board, (7) creditors subject to the Interstate Commerce Commission to that commission, (8) creditors subject to the Packers and Stockyards Act to the Secretary of Agriculture, (9) small business investment companies to the Small Business Administration, (10) brokers and dealers to the Securities and Exchange Commission, (11) Federal Land Banks and production credit associations to the Farm Credit Administration, and (12) retail and department stores, consumer finance companies, all nonbank credit card issuers, and all other creditors to the Federal Trade Commission. 15 U.S.C., sec. 1691c(a).

[92] Id., sec. 1691e(h).

[93] Senate Report (Committee on Banking, Housing and Urban Affairs) No. 94-589, 2 U.S. Code Congressional and Administrative News, 94th Cong., 2nd Sess., 1976, p. 406.

[94] 15 U.S.C., sec. 1691e(a).

MORTGAGES, DEEDS OF TRUST, AND INSTALLMENT CONTRACTS—PART II

STATEMENT OF CREDIT DENIAL, TERMINATION, OR CHANGE

Date _____

Applicant's Name: _____

Applicant's Address: _____
_____

Description of Account, Transaction, or Requested Credit: _____
_____
_____

Description of Adverse Action Taken: _____
_____
_____

PRINCIPAL REASON(S) FOR ADVERSE
ACTION CONCERNING CREDIT

___ Credit application incomplete
___ Insufficient credit references
___ Unable to verify credit references
___ Temporary or irregular employment
___ Unable to verify employment
___ Length of employment
___ Insufficient income
___ Excessive obligations
___ Unable to verify income
___ Inadequate collateral
___ Too short a period of residence
___ Temporary residence
___ Unable to verify residence
___ No credit file
___ Insufficient credit file
___ Delinquent credit obligations
___ Garnishment, attachment, foreclosure, repossession, or suit
___ Bankruptcy
___ We do not grant credit to any applicant on the terms and conditions you request
___ Other, specify: _____
_____

Figure 16-5 *Source:* Regulation B, 12 C.F.R., sec. 202.9(b)(2).

**DISCLOSURE OF USE OF INFORMATION
OBTAINED FROM AN OUTSIDE SOURCE**

___ Disclosure inapplicable

___ Information obtained in a report from a consumer reporting agency

Name: _____

Street address: _____

Telephone number: _____

___ Information obtained from an outside source other than a consumer reporting agency. Under the Fair Credit Reporting Act, you have the right to make a written request, within 60 days of receipt of this notice, for disclosure of the nature of the adverse information.

Creditor's name: _____

Creditor's address: _____

Creditor's telephone number: _____

The Federal Equal Credit Opportunity Act prohibits creditors from discriminating against credit applicants on the basis of race, color, religion, national origin, sex, marital status, age (provided that the applicant has the capacity to enter into a binding contract); because all or part of the applicant's income derives from any public assistance program; or because the applicant has in good faith exercised any right under the Consumer Credit Protection Act. The federal agency that administers compliance with this law concerning this creditor is (name and address as specified by the appropriate agency).

Figure 16-5 (Continued)

creditor other than a government, governmental subdivision, or governmental agency is liable to the aggrieved applicant for punitive damages up to $10,000. "In determining the amount of such damages in any action, the court shall consider, among other relevant factors, the amount of any actual damages awarded, the frequency and persistence of failure of compliance by the creditor, the resources of the creditor, the number of persons adversely affected, and the extent to which the creditor's failure of compliance was intentional."[95]

An aggrieved credit applicant who successfully prosecutes his action against a creditor is also entitled to be awarded reasonable attorney fees as determined by the court.[96]

[95] Id., sec. 1691e(b).
[96] Id., sec. 1691e(d).

Relation to State Laws

The Senate committee was of the opinion that "practices of discrimination are so abhorrent that federal law ought not foreclose the states from initiating their own laws unless those laws are incompatible with this legislation."[97] As a consequence of this view, the act provides that it does not exempt any creditor from complying with the laws of any state with respect to credit discrimination unless those laws are inconsistent with the act. State laws that afford greater protection to a credit applicant are not considered to be inconsistent with the federal act.[98]

QUESTIONS

1 What is the nature of a foreclosure? When does the right to foreclose arise?

2 Describe how an equity of redemption operates. How does it differ from a statutory right of redemption?

3 What is a deficiency judgment?

4 What would motivate a mortgagor to give a mortgagee a deed in lieu of foreclosure?

5 Distinguish an installment sale contract from an ordinary contract for the purchase and sale of real estate.

6 What is the objective of the Truth in Lending Law? What was the stimulus for its passage?

7 What is a "finance charge" as that term is used in the Federal Reserve Board's Regulation Z? What costs does the charge include?

8 What is the relationship between the interest rate and the annual percentage rate on a real estate loan?

9 Briefly describe the right of rescission that the Truth in Lending Law extends to certain borrowers? In what important instance is the right not available to the resident of a dwelling?

---

[97] Senate Report (Committee on Banking, Housing and Urban Affairs) No. 94-589, 2 U.S. Code Congressional and Administrative News, 94th Cong., 2nd Sess., 1976, p. 414.

[98] 15 U.S.C., sec. 1691d(f).

Chapter 17

Mechanics' Liens

A **mechanic's lien** is a claim against real property created by law for the purpose of securing payment for work or services performed or materials furnished in the erection or repair of buildings or the making of other improvements to real property. The lien operates in favor of all persons to whom a debt is owed for labor and services performed or materials furnished for the improvement of real estate. The obtaining of a mechanic's lien is a statutory right which an entitled person may exercise or not as he sees fit. Once the right has been exercised by a claimant, however, a mechanic's lien becomes an encumbrance on real estate in the form of security for an unpaid debt. If the debt is not paid, the mechanic's lien may be foreclosed by causing the encumbered property to be sold at public auction and using the proceeds of the sale to satisfy the debt.

A mechanic's lien is a statutory lien and the right to acquire and enforce such a lien exists solely by reason of legislative enactment. Every state in the union has statutes on the subject and in a few states[1] such legislation is specifically required to be enacted by provisions in their constitutions. Although the statutes of the several states vary in many details, a general policy pervades all mechanic's lien statutes and most of them contain the same basic elements.

Mechanic's lien laws are founded on the equitable principle that one whose services or materials have enhanced the value of a parcel of real estate should be entitled to follow his contribution and be able to enforce payment for that contribution by proceeding against the benefited property.

[1] For example, California, Florida, and Texas have such constitutional provisions.

Because a mechanic's lien is an encumbrance on real estate that can lead to a foreclosure sale, it is important for property owners, purchasers, and lenders to be aware of the existence of such liens, the way in which they are created, and the manner of their discharge or termination.

PERSONS ENTITLED TO MECHANICS' LIENS

The right to a mechanic's lien is limited to those persons who fall within the class of persons designated by statute as being "mechanics." Mechanic's lien laws are generally quite comprehensive as to what persons are entitled to liens and embrace practically any person whose labor, services, or materials enhance the value of real property. Some states' statutes do not designate particular types of entitled persons but instead include all persons whose work or materials improve real property. More commonly, however, the statutes designate or describe the specific classes of persons who are entitled to mechanics' liens.

Major Classes of Entitled Persons

While the statutes of the various states are often quite detailed as to what particular persons may acquire a mechanic's lien,[2] persons entitled to liens can be classified in four major categories: (1) contractors, (2) subcontractors, (3) laborers, and (4) materialmen.

Contractors As the term is used in mechanic's lien laws, a *contractor* is a person who has a direct contractual relationship with the owner of real estate. In the construction industry, one whose contract is directly with the owner is commonly referred to as being the "prime" or "general" contractor on a job. While it is possible to have more than one person on a job who qualifies as a contractor because of a direct contract with the owner, more often there will be a single prime or general contractor who will perform most if not all of the work contracted for through subcontractors whose direct contracts are with the contractor rather than with the owner.

Requirement of a Contractor's License For the protection of persons using contractors' services, a number of states have statutes requiring that any person engaging in the business or acting in the capacity of a contractor must be licensed by the appropriate state office. For purposes of such licensing statutes, the term "contractor" includes any person who submits a bid or undertakes to construct, improve, or demolish an improvement to real property.

Licensing laws commonly provide that one who acts in the capacity of a contractor without being properly licensed to do so cannot bring an action for compensation when he is not paid.[3] Since an unlicensed person cannot recover for having rendered services of the type for which a license is required, it follows that he is not entitled to a mechanic's lien.

Subcontractors A *subcontractor* is a person whose contract to perform certain work is directly with the prime or general contractor rather than with the owner of real property. A subcontractor agrees with the general or principal contractor to perform part of the work that the contractor is obligated to the owner to do. A subcontractor's relation to the prime contractor is substantially the same as the prime contractor's relation to the owner. There may be and usually is more than one subcontractor performing work on any given construction project.

---

[2] For example, California Civil Code, sec. 3110 states: "Mechanics, materialmen, contractors, subcontractors, lessors of equipment, artisans, architects, registered engineers, licensed land surveyors, machinists, builders, teamsters and draymen, and all persons and laborers of every class performing labor or bestowing skill or other necessary services on, or furnishing materials or leasing equipment to be used or consumed in or furnishing appliances, teams, or power contribution to a work of improvement shall have a lien upon the property . . ."

[3] Statutes in Alaska, Arizona, Arkansas, California, Michigan, Nevada, New Mexico, North Carolina, and Washington so provide.

The owner-contractor-subcontractor relationship arises, for example, when owner O contracts with contractor G for the construction of a building on O's land in accordance with certain plans and specifications. G, who has no work crews of his own, thereafter enters into a series of contracts with a series of subcontractors who agree to complete certain aspects of the construction job. Subcontractor S-1, for instance, may agree with G to lay the foundation of the building, S-2 to do the framing, S-3 to perform the electrical and plumbing work, and so forth. Each subcontractor owes a duty of performance to G who in turn is obligated to O.

Included in the term "subcontractors" are those persons who agree with subcontractors to perform part of the work that the subcontractors are obligated to do. In the foregoing example, subcontractor S-3, who is obligated to G to do the electrical and the plumbing work, might himself enter into an agreement with S-4 for completion of the electrical work. While persons in the position of S-4 are sometimes referred to as "sub-subcontractors" or "subcontractors in the second degree," under the mechanic's lien laws their status is the same as subcontractors.

Laborers As the term is used in connection with mechanic's lien laws, a *laborer* is a person who, acting as an employee, performs work or uses skill for the purpose of improving real property. A laborer's services are no less "work" or "labor" because they are performed with the use of machinery rather than hand tools.

A laborer is entitled to a mechanic's lien under the various statutes whether he is an employee of the owner of real property or of a contractor, subcontractor, or sub-subcontractor. Employees of materialmen are *not* laborers for purposes of the mechanic's lien laws.

Materialmen A *materialman* is a person who furnishes materials or supplies to be used for the improvement of real property. Statutes generally extend the right to a mechanic's lien to persons who supply materials but who have no other connection with the work being done to improve real estate. To be so entitled, however, materialmen must be specifically referred to in a statute because persons who merely furnish materials are not normally regarded as being included within the terms "contractor" and "subcontractor." To be considered a contractor or subcontractor, a person must do something more than simply supply materials to be used in an improvement.

A materialman is entitled to a mechanic's lien whether he supplies materials for an improvement to the owner of real estate, the general contractor, or any subcontractor or sub-subcontractor. Some states[4] require that a materialman, in order to obtain a mechanic's lien, must prove that the materials he delivered to a construction site were actually used in the improvement of the site. Other states hold that the delivery of materials to a building site creates a presumption of their use in the improvement of the site. In these states, an owner seeking to refute the validity of a materialman's claim to a lien would have the burden of establishing that although the materials were delivered to his property they were in fact used to improve other property.

Entitled Persons Must Have Contract Directly or Indirectly with Owner To be entitled to a mechanic's lien, a person who furnishes labor, services, or materials must have a valid contract with the owner of the property improved or with someone acting in his behalf. The general rule is that, for purposes of mechanic's liens, architects, contractors, subcontractors, or sub-subcontractors are agents of the owner in the contracting for labor, services, or materials. It is just as essential for a subcontractor, sub-subcontractor, materialman, or la-

---

[4] For example, Alabama, California, Georgia, Nebraska, and Washington.

borer to have a contract with the owner as it is for the prime or general contractor. The only difference is that a prime contractor's contract is *directly* with the owner while the contract of a subcontractor, sub-subcontractor, or laborer is made *directly* with the prime contractor and only *indirectly* with the owner.

May Be Express or Implied The contract that underlies a mechanic's lien may be one in which the terms are expressly stated or an agreement that is implied from the conduct of the parties or the circumstances that surround the furnishing of labor, services, or materials. In the absence of a statute that requires it, the contract need not be in writing.

Must Be Substantially Performed For one who furnishes labor, services, or materials to be entitled to a mechanic's lien, he must have substantially performed his direct or indirect contract with the owner of the improved premises. Substantial performance is a question of fact in any given case. Generally speaking, minor deficiencies which can be satisfied by compensation in money will not prevent a claimant from obtaining a lien.

NATURE OF SERVICES FOR WHICH A LIEN MAY BE HAD

The nature of the services for which a mechanic's lien may be obtained depends upon the provisions of the statutes in a given state. While the statutes are, generally speaking, quite diverse and very detailed as to the matters they cover, there are certain features that are common to all of them.

Under all mechanic's lien laws, the unpaid supplier of labor, services, or materials for the construction of buildings or other new improvements to real estate is entitled to a lien. While under early statutes a mechanic's lien could not be acquired for repairs made to real property, the right to a lien for repairs is generally conferred by all mechanic's lien laws today. Statutes in most, if not all, states also extend the right to a lien to those who provide labor, services, or materials for the alteration or renovation of buildings as well.

Some states' statutes expressly provide for a mechanic's lien in favor of one who performs labor or supplies materials for the demolition or removal of buildings or other structures. In the absence of an express statutory provision, however, the prevailing view is that no mechanic's lien can be had for demolition or removal.

PROPERTY INTEREST SUBJECT TO LIEN

Estate in Fee Simple

The property interest against which a mechanic's lien is most often sought is the estate in fee simple absolute. Where this is the case, the lien claimant is required to show that the owner of the fee expressly or impliedly contracted for the labor, services, or materials upon which the claim of lien is founded.

Interest Less Than a Fee

Sometimes the property interest of the person who contracts for improvements to real estate is less than a fee simple—for example, a life estate or an estate for years. Like the fee simple, these less than fee interests are subject to mechanic's liens when owners of such interests fail to pay for the labor, services, or materials they contracted for. Except where statutes provide otherwise, only the less than fee interest in the improved property is subject to foreclosure sale to satisfy an unpaid claimant's lien.

Improvements By Tenant A tenant who contracts for improvements to leased property generally cannot subject the landlord's property interest to mechanics' liens even though the improvements permanently enhance the value of the property. A tenant is not considered to be an agent of the landlord under mechanic's lien laws merely by reason of their landlord-tenant relationship. Consequently, a tenant who contracts for improvements to his leased premises does not bind the landlord by that contract. And since there is no contractual relationship between the improver and the landlord, the landlord's property is not subject to a mechanic's lien in the event the improver is not paid for his services or materials.

Statutes in a number of states provide that where a landlord has knowledge that improvements are being made to his property, his interest in the property will be subject to a mechanic's lien unless he takes certain steps to protect his interest.

Protection for Noncontracting Landlord
Landlord with Knowledge of Improvement
To protect his property interest from a lien, the statutes require that a landlord who knows of the improvements contracted for by the tenant must give notice to improvers that he, the landlord, will not be responsible for those improvements.

The landlord's **notice of nonresponsibility** must be in the form required by statute and must, within a stipulated number of days after the landlord acquired knowledge of the improvement, be posted in a conspicuous place on the premises and/or recorded in the office of the county recorder. Some statutes require the landlord to give written notice to the persons whose labor, services, or materials contribute to the improvement. An example of a notice of nonresponsibility to be posted on an owner's property and to be recorded as well appears at Figure 17-1.

If the landlord fails to comply with the statutory requirements after having learned of the improvements being made, his interest in the property will be subject to mechanics' liens for debts arising out of the tenant's contracts with improvers. The landlord's noncompliance with statutory requirements does not, however, make him personally liable for the tenant's debts to the improvers of the property.

Landlord without Knowledge of Improvement Most statutes provide that the interest of a landlord who has no knowledge of the work a tenant is having done on the landlord's property is not subject to a mechanic's lien. Whether or not a landlord had knowledge in a given case is a question of fact to be determined by a court or a jury.

PHYSICAL PROPERTY SUBJECT TO A LIEN

Statutes commonly use the term "improvement" to describe the work for which a mechanic's lien may be available. Where so used, an improvement is generally defined in the broad sense to mean anything that enhances the value of land, whether it be the erection of a new building or other structure, repairing or renovating existing structures, the installation of articles or equipment, the grading of land, landscaping, or the supplying of materials.

Both Improvement and the Improved Property
A mechanic's lien attaches to both an improvement to property and to the improved property itself. Where an improvement takes the form of a newly constructed building on an owner's land, for example, liens of unpaid claimants will attach to the land as well as to the building.

Installed Items Must Become Fixtures
Where articles or equipment are installed in an owner's building, the supplier and the installer will be entitled to a mechanic's lien only if the installation is such that the installed articles have become fixtures. Once they qualify as being fixtures, the installed articles or equipment are, of course, a part of the owner's real property and any mechanic's lien arising because of them attaches not only to the building in which they have been installed but also to the land on which the building is situated.

No Liens on Public Property
The prevailing view is that a mechanic's lien does not attach to and cannot be enforced against public property. Public policy is opposed to the forced sale of public property which of course is the end result of acquiring a mechanic's lien.

MECHANICS' LIENS

NOTICE OF NONRESPONSIBILITY

To whom it may concern:

 Notice is hereby given that the undersigned (name of owner) of (address of owner) is the (sole or co-owner) of real property located at (street address) and more particularly described as follows:

(description of property)

 Other persons having an ownership interest in such property, and the interests of such persons therein are as follows: (set forth names and interests).

 On _____, 19__, the undersigned first learned of (indicate the nature of the construction, alteration, or repair work) on such property.

 (The statutory number) days have not elapsed since the undersigned first obtained such knowledge.

 The undersigned will not be responsible for such (construction, alteration, or repair work) nor will he be responsible for any labor, services, or materials that have been, are being, or may in the future be furnished to the above-described premises with respect to such (construction, alteration, or repair work).

 This notice is given pursuant to (citation to appropriate statute).

Dated _____, 19__, and posted _____, 19__.

(signature of owner)

State of _____
County of _____

 (Name of owner) being duly sworn, deposes and says that:

 The above notice of nonresponsibility is a true copy of a notice posted at (street address of property) on _____, 19__.

 He has read the above notice and knows the contents thereof and that the facts stated therein are true to the best of his knowledge.

(signature of notary public   (signature of owner)
or other appropriate official,
date, and seal)

Figure 17-1

PROCEDURE FOR OBTAINING A LIEN

Before a mechanic's lien claimant can acquire a lien, he must satisfy certain procedural requirements imposed by statutes in the various states. Mechanics' liens, it will be recalled, are strictly creatures of statute, and compliance with prescribed statutory procedures is a condition precedent to obtaining or perfecting a lien. While the statutory requirements vary considerably from state to state, the basic procedures for perfecting a mechanic's lien have many features in common.

A supplier of labor, services, or materials who fails to satisfy the necessary procedural steps cannot obtain a mechanic's lien. This does not mean, of course, that the property owner's debt to him comes to an end. The debt arising from the contract for improvements will continue to obligate the owner but, in the absence of a mechanic's lien, the debt will be an unsecured one. And, as is true of unsecured debts generally, the remedies available to the unpaid improver are those of a general creditor rather than one having a security interest in a specific asset of the debtor.

Preliminary Notice

In many states, as a preliminary step to acquiring a mechanic's lien, a lien claimant must give written notice to the property owner or his agent before a claim of lien is filed or recorded. Some statutes require that the preliminary notice be given before or at the time the labor, services, or materials are furnished, while others do not require the giving of notice until a given period after the furnishing of labor, services, or materials has begun or been completed. The period of time within which such a notice must be given varies among the states, but the period normally is short.[5] The usual methods of serving written notice are (1) by delivering the writing personally to the owner or his agent, (2) by leaving it at his residence or place of business, or (3) by sending it by registered or certified mail to his residence or place of business.

Where the giving of preliminary notice is required, a mechanic's lien will be denied to a claimant who does not give notice in the required manner and within the period prescribed by statute.

Who Must Give Notice Most statutes provide that preliminary notice is required to be given only by lien claimants who have no direct contractual relationship with the property owner. Such a requirement would apply to subcontractors, materialmen, and laborers who deal with the general contractor or subcontractors and whose identity may be unknown to the owner, but not to laborers who work for the owner or materialmen who supply materials on the owner's order. Prime or general contractors are exempt from the requirement, of course, because their contracts are directly with owners of property.

Purpose of Notice The purpose in requiring that preliminary notice be given to an owner is to inform him of a potential lien claimant's identity and the nature and the amount of the claim. With this information the owner can protect himself in his future dealings with the person with whom the claimant contracted by withholding funds or otherwise.

An example of a preliminary notice appears at Figure 17-2.

Recording the Claim of Lien

Statutes in practically all states require that a *claim of lien*[6] in an appropriate form be filed for record with a designated official, such as the county recorder or registrar of deeds. Recording a claim of lien is a requirement separate and distinct from the giving of preliminary notice. Recording is the act that brings into being a claimant's security interest in the property he improved. The preliminary notice creates no security interest but serves instead to inform a property owner of an improver's intention to acquire such an interest in his property if payment for his labor, services, or materials should not be forthcoming.

In addition to creating a security interest in favor of the lien claimant, the recording of a claim of lien imparts constructive notice to the

---

[5] For example, California Civil Code, sec. 3097(a) requires that written notice be given within 20 days after the claimant has begun to furnish his labor, services, or materials to the job site.

[6] Sometimes called a "statement of lien," a "notice of lien," or a "certificate of lien."

MECHANICS' LIENS

PRELIMINARY NOTICE

To: (name of owner)
(address of owner)

Notice is hereby given that the undersigned, (name of improver) of (address of improver), by a contract dated _____, 19___, contracted to provide (indicate type of labor, services, or materials) to (name and address of general contractor or subcontractor, as appropriate) to assist (the general contractor or subcontractor) in the (indicate type of improvement being made) on your property at (address of owner's property), which property is more particularly described as follows:

(description of the property)

For the supplying of the above (labor, services, or materials) there will become due from (name of general contractor or subcontractor) to the undersigned (amount in writing) dollars ($_____). Pursuant to the provisions of (citation to appropriate statute) the undersigned will claim a lien on the above-described property should (name of general contractor or subcontractor) fail to make payment as agreed.

Dated _____, 19___. (signature of improver)

State of _____
County of _____

(Name of improver), being first duly sworn, deposes and says that he is the (type of improver) named in the foregoing preliminary notice; that he has read the foregoing preliminary notice and knows the contents therof; and that to his knowledge the statements contained therein are true.

(signature of notary public (signature of improver)
or other appropriate official,
date, and seal)

Figure 17-2

owner, prospective purchasers, lenders, and all the world of the claimant's encumbrance on the property.

Mechanic's lien laws prescribe the form and content of claims of lien and the period within which they must be recorded. Failure on the part of an improver to record his claim within the statutory period denies him his right to a lien.

It is generally required that a separate claim

CLAIM OF LIEN

Notice is hereby given by (name and other appropriate identification of the contractor), hereafter referred to as the lien claimant, as follows:

The lien claimant is properly licensed by the laws of the State of _____ to carry on business as (a general contractor).

On _____, 19___, the lien claimant entered into a contract with (named and address of owner) according to which the lien claimant agreed to (furnish all labor and materials for and generally supervise the construction of a house) on the property described as follows:

(description of property)

The owner of the above-described property is (name and address of owner).

Performance under the contract commenced on _____, 19___, and all work under the contract was completed on _____, 19___. (Statutory number) days have not elapsed since such completion.

In the course of performing the contract, the lien claimant furnished labor, services, and materials as follows:

Date	Description	Value
_____	_____	_____
_____	_____	_____
_____	_____	_____

All materials listed above were delivered to (the building site) and were used in performance of the contract.

The agreed price and reasonable value of the services rendered by the lien claimant is (amount in writing) ($_____). Payment in full was due on _____, 19___, but has not been received by the lien claimant despite his repeated demands. After deduction of (amount in writing) ($_____) for all credits and offsets (if any), the sum of (amount in writing) ($_____) remains owing to the lien claimant.

Pursuant to (citation of appropriate statute), the lien claimant hereby claims a lien on the above-described property for (amount in writing)($_____).

Dated _____, 19___   (signature of general contractor)

State of _____
County of _____

Figure 17-3

MECHANICS' LIENS

> (Name of general contractor), being duly sworn, deposes and says that he is the lien claimant named in the foregoing claim of lien; that he has read the foregoing claim of lien and knows the contents thereof; and that to his knowledge the statements contained therein are true.
>
> (signature of notary public or other appropriate official, date, and seal)   (signature of general contractor)

Figure 17-3 (Continued)

of lien must be recorded for each separate contract under which an improver claims.

Contents of Claim of Lien Mechanic's lien laws usually specify what information a claim of lien must contain if it is to be sufficient to create a security interest in behalf of the recording claimant. A claim of lien will satisfy the requirements of most statutes if it (1) names the owner of the improved property, (2) describes the premises sufficiently for identification, (3) contains a general statement of the kind of labor, services, or materials furnished, (4) states the amount due the claimant, from whom and for what, (5) sets forth the name and address of the lien claimant, and (6) is properly verified.[7]

The detailed statements in a claim of lien are intended to apprise the owner of property and the public of the nature and amount of the improver's claim against the identified property. Since a claim of lien must be recorded for a lien to be created, the contents of the claim constructively become a matter of public knowledge.

Substantial compliance with the statutory requirements concerning the contents of a claim of lien is, generally speaking, sufficient to create a lien. But a claim of lien that falls short of substantial compliance is defective and will not impose a lien on improved property.

[7] A verification is an affidavit in a form prescribed by statute.

An example of a claim of lien form that satisfies the foregoing requirements appears at Figure 17-3.

Time for Recording Practically all mechanic's lien laws require a claim of lien to be recorded within a certain period of time if a lien is to be created. The usual period provided by statute is 30, 60, or 90 days after an improvement has been completed or work on it has otherwise ceased. The period for recording is commonly longer for a general contractor than it is for other classes of lien claimants.

The time when an improvement is deemed to have been completed or work to have ceased is to be ascertained from the language of mechanic's lien statutes, the provisions of the parties' contract, and the surrounding circumstances. Consequently, a question of fact may arise that requires determination by a court or jury.

Notice of Completion of Work Statutes in some states provide that a property owner may record a notice stating that a contract or project has been completed and, where such a notice is recorded, that notice is the equivalent of completion. As an inducement to an owner to record a notice of completion, mechanic's lien laws commonly shorten the period during which an improver may record his claim of lien following the recordation of the owner's notice. For example, lien claimants may have 90 days following completion of a contract or work of

---

NOTICE OF COMPLETION

Pursuant to the provisions of (citation to appropriate statute), notice is given of the completion on ____, 19___, of (indicate type of construction or improvement) on the property of the undersigned, (name of owner) of (address of owner), which property is described as follows:

(description of property)

The (indicate type of construction or improvement) was undertaken in accordance with a contract between the undersigned and (name of general contractor) of (address of general contractor), dated ____, 19___, under the terms of which (name of general contractor) was to provide (indicate what the general contractor undertook to do).

The undersigned is the (sole owner or co-owner, as the case may be) of the above-described property. (Where applicable add: The names and addresses of all other co-owners of the above-described property are _____).

Dated ____, 19___   (signature of owner)

State of _____
County of _____

(Name of owner) being first duly sworn, deposes and says that he is the (sole or co-owner) named in the foregoing notice of completion; that he has read the foregoing notice of completion and knows the contents thereof; and that to his knowledge the statements contained therein are true.

(signature of notary public   (signature of owner)
or other appropriate official,
date, and seal.)

Figure 17-4

improvement in which to record their claims if no notice has been recorded, but only 30 or 60 days when a notice is recorded.

A notice of completion similar to Figure 17-4 would meet the requirements of most statutes.

Notice of Cessation of Work For any number of reasons, work on an improvement may stop before the project has been completed. Statutes in general permit unpaid improvers who have not willfully breached their contract to record claims of lien within a designated period of time following cessation of work. These same statutes commonly permit an owner to shorten the period during which claims of lien may be recorded by his recording of a notice of cessation. Lien claimants who might otherwise have 90 days following cessation of work in which to record their claims could find them-

MECHANICS' LIENS

NOTICE OF CESSATION

Pursuant to the provisions of (citation to appropriate statute), notice is given that on _____ , 19___ , all work ceased and that such cessation has continued from that date to the date of this notice on (indicate the type of construction or improvement) on the property of the undersigned (name of owner) of (address of owner) described as follows:

(description of property)

The (indicate type of work or improvement) was begun on _____ , 19___ , in accordance with a contract between the undersigned and (name of general contractor) of (address of general contractor) under the terms of which (name of general contractor) was to provide (indicate what general contractor undertook to do).

The undersigned is the (sole or co-owner, as the case may be) of the above-described property. (Where applicable add: The names and addresses of all other co-owners of the above-described property are _____).

Dated _____ , 19___ (signature of owner)

State of _____

County of _____

(Name of owner) being first duly sworn, deposes and says that he is the (sole or co-owner) named in the foregoing notice of cessation; that he has read the foregoing notice of cessation and knows the contents thereof; and that to his knowledge the statements contained therein are true.

(signature of notary public (signature of owner)
or other appropriate official,
date, and seal)

Figure 17-5

selves limited to 30 or 60 days if the owner were to record a notice of cessation of work.

A notice of cessation similar to Figure 17-5 would meet the requirements of most statutes.

OPERATION AND EFFECT OF A LIEN
Amount Secured by Lien

Since a mechanic's lien is a security, the amount of the lien is the amount of the debt that it secures. We have seen that the debt owing to a lien claimant arises out of his having performed a direct or indirect, express or implied, contract with the owner whose property the lien claimant has improved.

When Lien Attaches

Statutes vary considerably as to the time that a mechanic's lien attaches to an owner's property. Some statutes provide that a lien attaches at the time the one who furnished labor, services, or materials becomes bound by contract. In a few states, a lien does not attach until the date on which an improver's claim of lien has been recorded. A majority of states take an intermediate position and provide that a mechanic's lien attaches as of the time that work on the improvement was first begun.

Under the majority view, until an improver records a claim of lien he has no lien on the improved property but only a *right to* a lien. Once the claim of lien is recorded as required by statute, a lien is created and that lien relates back and attaches as of the date that work on the improvement was commenced. Statutes differ as to whether the lien attaches as of the date that the lien claimant commenced performance of *his* contract or the date on which the *first work* was begun or the *first materials* were furnished to the project or improvement. In those states in which a claimant's lien attaches at the time a project or improvement is first begun, work is considered to have commenced when it is obvious on the premises that a work of improvement is under way. This is sometimes referred to as the "visible to the eye" test.

The date on which a mechanic's lien attaches is of particular significance where priorities among several claimants to security interests in the same real property come into play.

Duration of Lien

Once a claim of lien has been recorded and a mechanic's lien has been created, the lien continues for the period of time prescribed by statute. The statutory periods vary from as little as a few months in some states to as much as a year in others.

If an improver who has acquired a lien does not take steps to enforce it during the period for which it endures, his lien will be lost and the debt owing to him will become an unsecured debt rather than a secured one.

PREVENTION AND EXTINCTION OF A LIEN

Mechanics' liens can be prevented from arising or be extinguished after creation by several different methods.

By Contract against Lien

At the time a contract for the furnishing of labor, services, or materials for a work of improvement is entered into, an improver can bind himself by an agreement not to encumber the improved property with a mechanic's lien should circumstances otherwise entitling him to do so arise. Such a contract is sometimes referred to as a "no lien" contract and, where the language of the agreement clearly expresses the improver's intent, it will effectively prevent a mechanic's lien from arising.

By Waiver of Statutory Right

The statutory right to a mechanic's lien can be waived by the person entitled to exercise that right. A **waiver** is the voluntary and intentional relinquishment of a known right, claim, or privilege. A waiver may take the form of an express agreement or it may be inferred from the conduct of the party whose right is relinquished. To prevent a mechanic's lien from being created, an improver's waiver, like other contracts, must be supported by a valid consideration.

An example of an express waiver of a mechanic's lien appears at Figure 17-6.

By Release of Lien

Although the terms "waiver" and "release" are sometimes used synonymously, a waiver generally refers to an anticipatory disclaimer of a lien that subsequent events might otherwise create, while a release commonly refers to the relinquishment of an existing lien.

Where a claim of lien has been recorded and the debt that it secures is paid before the lien is foreclosed by the lien claimant, the owner of the improved property must obtain a release of lien from the claimant and record that release in order to offset the encumbrance of the lien on the public record and clear his title.

MECHANICS' LIENS

WAIVER OF LIEN

On _____, 19__, (name of potential lien claimant) contracted with (name of person with whom potential lien claimant contracted) to furnish (indicate type of labor, services, or materials) for the (indicate type of construction or improvement) on property owned by (name of owner), which property is described as follows:

(description of property)

In consideration of (amount in writing) dollars ($ _____), receipt of which is hereby acknowledged, (name of potential lien claimant) waives the right that he now has or may have in the future to claim a mechanic's lien against the above-described property to secure payment for (indicate type of labor, services, or materials) furnished by him under the contract referred to above.

(Name of potential lien claimant) has executed this waiver voluntarily and with full knowledge of his rights under the laws of the State of _____.

Dated _____, 19__.   (signature of potential lien claimant)

State of _____
County of _____

On _____, 19__, before me (name and title of officer) personally appeared (name of potential lien claimant) known to me to be the person whose name is subscribed to the foregoing instrument and acknowledged that he executed the same as his free and voluntary act.

(Notarial Seal)

(signature of notary)
_____ County, State of _____
My commission expires (date)

Figure 17-6

An example of a release of lien appears at Figure 17-7.

Bond to Release Lien Disputes sometimes arise as to the amount of the debt that a recorded claim of lien secures. Until a dispute has been resolved by a court, which may take some time, the lien constitutes an encumbrance on the owner's title which may make it difficult if not impossible for him to sell his property or to borrow on it.

To enable an owner to free his property from the encumbrance of a mechanic's lien, the statutes of some states provide that the property may be released from the lien by the recording of a surety bond in a prescribed amount. Where this is done, the owner's bond is substi-

> **RELEASE OF LIEN**
>
> On _____, 19__, (name of lien claimant) contracted with (name of person with whom lien claimant contracted) to furnish (indicate type of labor, services, or materials) for the (indicate type of construction or improvement) on property owned by (name of owner) described as follows:
>
> (description of property)
>
> On _____, 19__, (name of lien claimant) filed for record a claim of lien against the above-described property in the office of the (recorder of deeds, registrar of deeds, or other appropriate officer) of _____ County, State of _____, which claim of lien was recorded in (book or volume number) at page _____ of the (type of records) of such county.
>
> In consideration of (amount in writing) dollars ($ _____), receipt of which is hereby acknowledged, (name of lien claimant) releases the above-described property and (name of owner) personally from all liability arising from the furnishing of (indicate type of labor, services, or materials) by (name of lien claimant) under the provisions of the above-mentioned contract, and authorizes and directs that the above-mentioned lien be discharged of record.
>
> Dated _____, 19__.   (signature of lien claimant) _____
>
> State of _____
> County of _____
>
> On _____, 19__, before me (name and title of officer) personally appeared (name of lien claimant) known to me to be the person whose name is subscribed to the foregoing instrument and acknowledged that he executed the same as his free and voluntary act.
>
> (Notarial Seal)   (signature of notary) _____
>   _____ County, State of _____
>   My commission expires (date)

Figure 17-7

tuted for the owner's property as security for the improver's unpaid but unproved debt.

By Payment of the Debt

Since a mechanic's lien exists only for the purpose of securing an unpaid debt, when the debt is discharged the lien, of course, is extinguished.

By Expiration of Time

We have seen that once a mechanic's lien has been perfected by the recording of a claim of lien, a lawsuit to enforce the lien must be commenced within a statutorily prescribed period of time. If the lien claimant permits the time period to expire without initiating his suit, his lien will automatically be extinguished.

ENFORCEMENT OF A MECHANIC'S LIEN

A lien claimant's final step in the process of obtaining payment for his labor, services, or materials is to bring a court action to enforce his mechanic's lien.

Limited Period for Enforcement

The statutes of the various states regulate the period of time within which an action to enforce a mechanic's lien must be commenced. The statutory period normally is quite short and is generally counted from the date a claim of lien is recorded and the security interest created. If the lawsuit is not commenced within the statutorily prescribed period, the claimant's lien is extinguished and his debt becomes an unsecured one. If the improver does not thereafter, within the period of his state's statute of limitations, bring suit for breach of the contract that resulted in the debt owing to him, his right to recover on the debt will be forever barred.

Burden of Proof Is on Claimant

A lien claimant's suit to enforce his mechanic's lien terminates in a foreclosure sale of the property that is subject to the lien. Before a court will order the sale of the improved property the lien claimant must prove the following: (1) that he had a direct or indirect contract with the owner of the property to provide labor, services, or materials in exchange for an agreed consideration; (2) that, where required by statute, he gave the owner preliminary notice in the proper manner and within the statutorily prescribed time of his intention to claim a lien if the agreed consideration were not paid; (3) that he in fact furnished labor, services, or materials to the owner's property as agreed; (4) that the owner or his agent failed to pay the claimant in accordance with the terms of the contract; (5) that the claimant recorded a claim of lien in the manner and within the period prescribed by statute and thus acquired a mechanic's lien; and (6) that the present suit to enforce the lien was commenced within the statutorily required period.

When the claimant has established his case by proving the foregoing, the court will enter a judgment for the amount of the claimant's unpaid debt and will order the owner's improved property to be sold in satisfaction of that debt. Whether the lien claimant will be paid in full, in part, or at all from the proceeds of the foreclosure sale will depend upon the relative priority of his claim as compared with the claims of other persons who have interests in the same property.

PRIORITY OF MECHANICS' LIENS

It is not uncommon for a parcel of improved land to be subject to more than one lien at the same time. These liens may be all of the same type—all mechanics' liens, for example—or they may be different kinds, such as mechanics' liens, mortgages, tax liens, and so forth. In the event these liens should be foreclosed, the question arises as to the order of priority among them. The priority order is important because a debt that is secured by a lien with a high priority will be paid in full from the proceeds of a foreclosure sale before claimants whose liens have a lesser priority receive anything.

Mechanics' Liens among Themselves

The relative priority of mechanics' liens among themselves is a matter established by statute in each state. As we previously observed, the statutes of the several states vary considerably as to the time that a mechanic's lien attaches to an owner's property. In a few states[8] the lien attaches on the date that the improver becomes bound by contract, in a few other states[9] the lien attaches at the time the claim of lien is recorded, and in still other states[10] a claimant's lien attaches at the time he begins his improve-

---

[8] Illinois is such a state.
[9] Iowa and North Carolina, for example.
[10] Washington, for example.

ment to the property. In the majority of states,[11] however, all mechanics' liens on the same construction job or work of improvement attach as of the date that the first labor, services, or materials were furnished to the improved site. Some states[12] establish priorities among various classes of lien claimants and provide that the liens of laborers for daily wages be satisfied first and liens of subcontractors and materialmen take procedure over those of general contractors.

Under the majority view, all improvers whose claims of lien arise out of the same construction job or improvement project are equal in rank. If a construction job, for example, begins with subcontractor A bulldozing and grading the site and progresses through a series of steps in which subcontractor B builds the foundation and flooring, subcontractor C does the framing and roofing, subcontractor D encloses the building with walls, and so forth through the final painting and landscaping, the priority date for the lien of each subcontractor is the date that subcontractor A first broke ground with his bulldozer. If the proceeds of a foreclosure sale of the improved premises are insufficient to satisfy the debts of all mechanic's lien claimants in full, the proceeds will be distributed among them pro rata because no improver has a preferential claim over another.

Mechanics' Liens and Other Liens

The order of priorities between mechanics' liens and other types of liens such as those created by mortgages or deeds of trust is, like the relative priorities among mechanics' liens themselves, a matter that is regulated by statute. In the absence of contrary statutory provisions, the priority between mechanics' liens and other liens depends upon the time when the different liens attach to the encumbered property. Mechanics' liens, we have just seen, may attach either when the first work is done on a project, when an improver becomes bound by a contract, when an improver commences his particular work, or when an improver records his claim of lien. Liens created by mortgages or deeds of trust become effective when the instruments that evidence those liens are recorded. Depending upon the mechanic's lien statutes in his state, a lender must be vigilant if he wants to be assured that the security for his loan has a first priority status.

Statutes in a number of states[13] declare that mechanics' liens have priority over all other encumbrances that attach after the first work was commenced or the first materials were furnished to a construction job or work of improvement. In this type of situation, construction lenders, instead of relying solely on the public records, must inspect an owner's premises before extending a loan to him because work could have been commenced on the site but no claim of lien have yet been recorded.

For example, if construction lender L were to check the public records, find no existing liens against borrower B's property, then make a loan to B and promptly record B's mortgage, lender L could not be sure that his security has a first priority claim against B's property. If B had previously entered into a construction contract with general contractor G who in turn contracted with subcontractor A for grading the site, and S had commenced work on the site which was "visible to the eye" before L recorded his mortgage, claims of liens subsequently recorded by G, S, and all other improvers employed directly or indirectly by G would have priority over the mortgage recorded by L.

If, in the foregoing example, the statutes in L's state had provided that a mechanic's lien does not attach until a claim of lien has been

---

[11] Alabama, Arkansas, California, Louisiana, Minnesota, Nevada, New Mexico, Pennsylvania, Tennessee, Utah, Virginia, and Wisconsin are among the states adopting this view.

[12] For example, Florida, Georgia, Michigan, New Jersey, New York, Ohio, and Oklahoma.

[13] Alabama, Arizona, Arkansas, California, Colorado, Connecticut, Kansas, Michigan, Missouri, Montana, Ohio, Oklahoma, Washington, Wisconsin, and Wyoming.

recorded, B's mortgage to L would have priority over all subsequently recorded mechanics' liens irrespective of when work on the project was commenced.

QUESTIONS

1 What is a mechanic's lien? What is the principle upon which mechanics' lien laws are founded?
2 Identify and describe the four classes of persons entitled to mechanics' liens.
3 How can a landlord who knows that someone under contract with his tenant is improving the leased property protect that property from mechanics' liens?
4 What is the purpose of requiring a supplier of labor, services, or materials to give a preliminary notice to a property owner in order to be entitled to a mechanic's lien?
5 What is a notice of completion? Who prepares and records it? What is gained by recording it?
6 Describe the manner in which a mechanic's lien is enforced.
7 What is the order of priorities among several mechanics' liens on the same property?
8 What is the order of priority between a mechanic's lien and other types of liens on the same property?

Chapter 18

Homesteads

Unless a debtor's assets are specifically exempted by law, all of them, including his home, are subject to being sold to satisfy his obligations. Although no such exemption exists at common law, drafters of constitutions and legislatures of the various states early recognized the desirability of protecting the home from forced sale and in furtherance of that policy enacted homestead exemption laws. Today all but a half dozen states[1] have laws pertaining to homesteads.

As the term is used in connection with immunity from the claims of creditors, a **homestead** is the dwelling in which a family resides, together with the land on which it is situated and the appurtenances belonging to that land. In preventing the seizure and sale of an owner's residence for unpaid debts, the homestead exemption laws have created a right that is independent of and additional to the ordinary rights of ownership. In furtherance of the rights they create, homestead laws, generally speaking, are liberally construed in favor of a debtor and his family.

A state's homestead exemption statutes apply only to property situated within the territorial boundaries of that state. The laws of that state that are in effect at the time a home owner contracts his debt define the owner's homestead rights.

The term "homestead" as used in this chapter is distinct from and entirely unrelated to the system for acquiring title to public lands as provided by federal homestead laws.

OBJECTIVE OF HOMESTEAD LAWS

The principal objective of homestead laws is to secure to a householder a home for himself and

---

[1] Connecticut, Delaware, Maryland, New Jersey, Pennsylvania, and Rhode Island.

his family and, in the event of his death, for the surviving members of his family, that is beyond the reach of creditors. The right of the householder to have the family home exempt from liability is deemed to be superior to the right of creditors to have the property applied to the payment of debts owing to them. Homestead rights, it is said, have been created to shelter the family and to provide it with a refuge from the stresses and strains of financial misfortune and the improvidence of the head of the family.

Homestead laws are founded on considerations of public policy which seek to prevent disruption of the home and family. And while the benefit of homestead laws inures directly to the family, their ultimate value accrues to the general welfare of the state. The preservation of the home is considered to be of paramount importance, even at the sacrifice of the just claims of creditors.

Despite their common purpose, the constitutional and statutory provisions in the several states vary widely in form and content. The discussion that follows summarizes the more important features of this legislation.

TYPES OF HOMESTEADS

Based upon the time and the manner in which they are established, homesteads can be classified into two distinguishable categories: (1) homesteads that are created during the lifetime of a householder by reason of his fulfilling certain statutory requirements and (2) homesteads that are created by a probate court after a householder's death in favor of a surviving spouse and minor children. The latter type of homestead is commonly called a *probate homestead* to distinguish it from the former.

PERSONS ENTITLED TO HOMESTEADS

Only those persons who are designated by statute are entitled to the benefits of a homestead exemption. Although statutes in general restrict homestead rights to persons who qualify as the "head of a family," legislation in a few states[2] extends the right to persons other than heads of families.

Head of Family

For homestead exemption purposes, a person is considered to be the "head of a family" if he has residing with him another person or persons whom he is under a legal or moral obligation to support. A claimant who is unable to show that he is the head of a family as required by statute is not entitled to a homestead exemption.

Married Persons According to most homestead statutes, it is the husband, not the wife, who is the head of the family. Ordinarily, a wife who is living with her husband, with or without other family members, is not entitled to claim a homestead.

Unmarried Persons Although in a few states only married persons can claim homesteads, the general rule is that a claimant need not be married to be entitled to a homestead. Thus a single person who has residing with him or her a person that he or she is legally or morally obligated to support has the right to claim a homestead. Statutes which identify these supported persons commonly include the claimant's minor children and grandchildren, minor brothers and sisters, the father, mother, grandfather, and grandmother of the claimant or the claimant's deceased spouse, and any of the foregoing who, although having reached the age of majority, are unable to support themselves.

[2] For instance, California Civil Code, sec. 1260 provides that *any person* may claim a homestead, but classifies claimants as to the dollar value of their exemptions with heads of family receiving a $30,000 exemption and persons other than heads of family $15,000. Texas Revised Statutes, art. 3833 extends the right to single adults not constituents of a family. Rural homesteads for single adults in Texas are limited to 100 acres while the heads of family are entitled to 200 acres.

PROPERTY SUBJECT TO HOMESTEAD

Permanent Residence Owned by Claimant

To be exempt from the claims of creditors, homestead property must be owned by the claimant and be occupied by him as his permanent residence at the time the homestead is claimed or declared. A part-time residence cannot serve as a homestead. For example, a married couple living in a rented apartment near their work in the central city cannot claim their lakeside cottage or mountain cabin as a homestead.

Not Limited to Single-Family Dwellings

Modern statutes do not limit homesteads to single-family dwellings but extend them to family residences in duplexes, condominiums, cooperative apartment buildings, or other multiple unit structures. The rule is also very well settled that a homestead may be claimed in a building that is used for the production of income, such as a building in which the first floor is used for the owner's business and the second floor for his residence, or an apartment house in which the owner occupies one unit as his permanent residence. A homestead cannot, of course, be claimed in a building that is owned solely for the production of income.

Not Confined to Fee Simple Interest

Although a claimant must own an interest in the dwelling that he occupies to be entitled to a homestead, that interest need not be an estate in fee simple. Where there is the requisite occupancy, the nature or extent of the homestead claimant's estate or interest in the property frequently is regarded as being immaterial. Courts in the various states have held that homestead rights attach to life estates,[3] to leasehold estates,[4] and to the equitable estate of one who occupies a dwelling under a contract of purchase and sale.[5] Of course, if a homestead claimant only has an estate for life or for years, the homestead will terminate at the time of his death or upon the expiration of the term for years.

Limits on Size and Value

Constitutional and statutory provisions in the various states limit homesteads as to size or value or both. In limiting the size or value of homesteads, homestead laws define the respective rights of homestead claimants and their creditors. A majority of the states[6] impose only a dollar value ceiling on homesteads with the limits ranging from as little as $500 in Iowa to as much as $40,000 in North Dakota. A number of states[7] limit homesteads with respect to both value and area. As concerns area, these states commonly distinguish between homesteads located in towns or cities and rural homesteads. Permissible urban homesteads range in size from a single lot in Michigan, for example, to one city block in Oregon and rural homesteads[8] from as little as 40 acres in Iowa to as much as 320 acres in Montana. Where both a value and an area ceiling apply, the lesser of the two normally sets the limits for a homestead.

A few states[9] impose no value ceilings on rural homesteads but limit the permissible acreage instead.

---

[3] For example, the courts in Alabama, Arkansas, California, Illinois, Kentucky, Michigan, Missouri, Nebraska, Oregon, Tennessee, and Texas have so held.

[4] For example, Illinois, Iowa, Michigan, Minnesota, Texas, Washington, and Wisconsin.

[5] For example, California, Illinois, Iowa, Michigan, Minnesota, Texas, Vermont, and Wisconsin adopt this view.

[6] Arizona, California, Colorado, Georgia, Idaho, Illinois, Indiana, Kentucky, Maine, Massachusetts, Nevada, New Hampshire, New Mexico, New York, North Carolina, Ohio, Oregon, South Carolina, Tennessee, Utah, Vermont, Virginia, Washington, West Virginia, and Wyoming.

[7] Alabama, Alaska, Arkansas, Hawaii, Iowa, Louisiana, Michigan, Mississippi, Missouri, Montana, Nebraska, North Dakota, Oklahoma, South Dakota, Texas, and Wisconsin.

[8] A rural homestead consists of a tract of land which is used in part for a residence and the remainder for the support of the family.

[9] Florida, Kansas, Minnesota, North Dakota, and Texas.

Property Value in Excess of Exemption The fact that the size or value of homestead property exceeds the statutory exemption does not invalidate the homestead. Where the homestead property exceeds the maximum statutory exemption in size or value, the statutes of most states[10] make the excess subject to the claims of creditors. In many of these states, creditors may institute proceedings to have the debtor's property appraised and divided in order that the nonexempt part may be sold in satisfaction of the claims of creditors. But unless it is determined that an excess does in fact exist, there can be no sale of the debtor's property.

If the debtor's property cannot be physically divided into exempt and nonexempt portions without substantial prejudice, the entire property may be sold with the debtor being paid the amount of his exemption from the proceeds and the creditor receiving whatever part of the remainder may be necessary to satisfy his claim.

Proceeds of Sale of Homestead Property

Voluntary Sale In some jurisdictions,[11] in the absence of constitutional or statutory provisions to the contrary, the voluntary sale of homestead property by the owner totally extinguishes the homestead exemption and the proceeds of the sale are subject to the claims of creditors. In other states,[12] the proceeds of a voluntary sale of a homestead are exempt from the claims of creditors for a "reasonable period of time" pending their reinvestment in another homestead. Still other states[13] have statutes that exempt the proceeds of the sale of homestead property from claims of creditors for a statutorily specified period of time, providing the funds are held in good faith for the purchase of another homestead.

Forced Sale Statutes authorizing the forced sale of homestead property to make the excess value of the property available to creditors uniformly provide that the homestead owner shall first receive an amount equal to his homestead exemption from the proceeds of the sale. These funds commonly remain exempt from the claims of creditors in the hands of the owner for periods of time ranging from 6 months to 1 year pending investment by the owner in a new homestead.

Where exempt proceeds are used to purchase another residence, the new dwelling will be exempt from the claims of creditors providing it meets the statutory requirements and, in most states, the owner takes appropriate steps to claim an exemption.

ACQUISITION OF HOMESTEAD EXEMPTION

By Occupancy Alone

In a majority of states,[14] if a debtor is the head of a family or is otherwise entitled to a homestead, his mere occupancy of a dwelling as his home is sufficient to impress the premises with a homestead exemption. Where this is the case, the time at which the owner commenced occupation of the property is the time when the exemption becomes effective.

The statutes of the various states are not in agreement as to whether a homestead, once acquired, is a positive right under all circumstances or whether the exemption arises only if the debtor takes affirmative steps to claim it. In some states[15] the debtor loses his homestead exemption unless he notifies and makes his

---

[10] This is the case, for example, in Arizona, California, Illinois, Michigan, Missouri, Montana, Nebraska, North Carolina, Oklahoma, South Carolina, South Dakota, Tennessee, Utah, Virginia, Vermont, and Wyoming.

[11] Arizona, Arkansas, Iowa, North Carolina, and Texas, for example.

[12] Such as Kansas, Kentucky, Oregon, and Washington.

[13] For example, California, Iowa, Minnesota, Nebraska, Vermont, and Wisconsin.

[14] Alaska, Arkansas, Georgia, Hawaii, Illinois, Indiana, Kansas, Kentucky, Louisiana (if not in a city), Michigan, Minnesota, Mississippi, Missouri, Nebraska, New Hampshire, New Mexico, North Carolina, Ohio, Oklahoma, South Carolina, South Dakota, Tennessee, Texas, Vermont, Virginia, West Virginia, Wisconsin, and Wyoming.

[15] For example, Arizona, Arkansas, Florida, Georgia, Indiana, Louisiana, Minnesota, Nebraska, New York, North Dakota, Oregon, and Texas.

claim of exemption on an officer of the court before that officer concludes the judicial sale of the debtor's property in satisfaction of creditors' claims. In other states[16] the homestead exemption is not lost by a debtor's failure to claim it. The statutes in these states impose on the officer who seizes the debtor's property the duty of setting off the exemption. In some jurisdictions[17] the homestead exemption is not lost because the debtor fails to claim it before the property is sold. In these states if the homestead property is sold by judicial sale, the debtor is permitted to assert his exemption at the time the buyer sues him to obtain possession of the homestead property.

By Occupancy and Declaration

Statutes in a sizable number of states[18] require that if a home owner is to acquire homestead rights and be entitled to the statutory exemption, he must, in addition to occupying the premises, execute and record a formal declaration of his intention to claim a homestead. Under such statutes, there can be no homestead rights in any specific property until the homestead declaration has been recorded. The constitutional or statutory provisions that prescribe what a declaration of homestead shall contain must be substantially complied with if a claimant is to be entitled to an exemption. The form appearing at Figure 18-1 would satisfy most statutory requirements.

In states that require the recording of homestead declarations to make the exemption operative, the mere failure to record a declaration at the time a home is acquired, or a reasonable time thereafter, will not cause the right to a homestead to be lost. There is no time limit set for recording a declaration but any delay in recording after acquiring property will diminish the protection of the homestead laws.

OPERATION OF HOMESTEAD EXEMPTION

The effect of a homestead exemption on the claim of a creditor depends essentially on two things: (1) whether the creditor has a lien on the debtor's homestead and, if so, (2) whether that lien has priority over the debtor's homestead exemption. A homestead exemption affords no protection against liens of creditors that attached to the debtor's residence before his homestead exemption became effective. Therefore, whenever a creditor seeks to foreclose his lien on a debtor's home, it is necessary for him to ascertain the order of priority between his lien and the debtor's homestead exemption.

Priority of Homestead Exemption

Since homesteads are entirely creatures of statute, the order of priority between homestead exemptions and the various kinds of claims of creditors is likewise a matter for legislative determination. As we observed when discussing the recording laws, legislatures have the power to accord preferential status to certain competing claims irrespective of the time sequence in which those claims were created or arose.

Existing Debts versus Homestead Exemption In some states[19] a homestead exemption may not be asserted against a home owner's unsecured debts that were contracted before the debtor commenced to use the homestead premises as his residence or before he recorded a homestead declaration where such a declaration is required.

Other states[20] take the view that a homestead exemption has priority over an unsecured debt that was in existence at the time the exemption

---

[16] Alabama, Colorado, Kansas, Massachusetts, Michigan, Missouri, and Ohio, for example.

[17] For example, Kentucky, Michigan, Minnesota, Missouri, New Hampshire, Washington, and Wisconsin.

[18] Alabama, Arizona, California, Colorado, Florida, Idaho, Iowa, Louisiana (if not in a city), Maine, Massachusetts, Montana, Nevada, New York, North Dakota, Oregon, Utah, Virginia, and Washington.

[19] For example, Iowa, Minnesota, Montana, and Vermont.

[20] Such as California, Colorado, Louisiana, Nebraska, and Tennessee.

HOMESTEADS

DECLARATION OF HOMESTEAD

We, (name of husband) and (name of wife), hereby declare that:
We are husband and wife.

I, (name of husband), am the head of a family consisting of myself and my wife (name of wife) and (number of) children.

At the time of making this declaration we actually reside on the premises hereinafter described and we claim and declare the premises, with the dwelling house (and outbuildings) on it, together with its appurtenances, as a homestead for our joint benefit and for the benefit of our family.

The premises on which we reside and claim as a homestead are described as follows:

(description of property)

No former declaration of homestead has been made by either of us, jointly or severally (or A former declaration of homestead was made by (name of husband or wife or both), but it was abandoned before the execution of this declaration.)

The actual cash value of the above-mentioned premises is estimated to be (amount in writing) dollars ($_____).

Dated _____, 19___   (signature of husband)
                            (signature of wife)

State of _____
County of _____

On _____, 19___, before me (name and title of officer) appeared (names of husband and wife), known to me to be the persons whose names are subscribed to the foregoing instrument and acknowledged that they executed the same as their free and voluntary act.

(Notarial Seal)   (signature of notary)
                              _____ County, State of _____
                              My commission expires (date)

Figure 18-1

was acquired, whether the exemption was acquired by occupancy and use alone or by recording a declaration of homestead. According to this view, a creditor's order of priority is determined as of the date that his claim is reduced to a judgment lien rather than the time when the unsecured debt was incurred.

Creditors' Liens versus Homestead Exemptions The prevailing view[21] is that if a debtor's homestead exemption was acquired prior to the time a creditor's lien attached to the debtor's property, the homestead exemption will have priority over the creditor's lien.

A few states[22] hold that where a creditor's lien has attached to property belonging to a debtor and the debtor subsequently devotes that property to homestead purposes, the debtor's subsequent occupation relegates the creditor's lien to a position inferior to the homestead exemption.

Existing Mortgage or Deed of Trust The rule that an existing mortgage or deed of trust is not subordinated to a subsequently acquired homestead exemption is recognized in many states.[23] This means, of course, that the homestead exemption applies only to the owner's equity in the mortgaged property.

Purchase Money Mortgage or Deed of Trust The priority of a homestead exemption is inferior to a mortgage or deed of trust given by a homestead claimant to secure payment of the purchase price of his residence.[24] Even in those states where a homestead is acquired simply by ownership and occupancy, the homestead exemption is subordinated to a purchase money mortgage or deed of trust. If needed, the entire proceeds of a foreclosure sale of the debtor's residence will be used to satisfy the unpaid purchase money obligation and none will apply to the homestead exemption.

Purchase money transactions are not limited simply to those situations in which a seller takes a promissory note secured by a mortgage or deed of trust as part of the purchase price. A majority of the courts hold that money borrowed by a buyer from a bank, savings and loan, or other third party lender and paid to the seller either by the lender or the buyer is purchase money and the mortgage or deed of trust received by the lender is a purchase money security that is superior to a homestead exemption.

Subsequent Mortgage or Deed of Trust In the absence of a contrary constitutional or statutory provision, an owner who gives a mortgage or deed of trust on his property after having acquired a homestead, subordinates his homestead to the mortgage or deed of trust. Therefore, in the event of a foreclosure sale, the proceeds will be applied first to the mortgage or deed of trust before anything is applicable to the homestead exemption.

Mechanics' Liens Statutes in some states[25] subordinate homestead exemptions to all claims of mechanics' liens arising from the construction or improvement of debtors' residences. Where this is the case, prescribed statutory formalities for perfecting a mechanic's lien must of course be satisfied.

In the absence of a statute subordinating homestead exemptions to claims of mechanics' liens, a homestead exemption will prevail if the homestead claimant can establish that the homestead right existed at the time the work was done or materials were furnished for the repair or improvement of his residence.

---

[21] Arkansas, California, Colorado, Florida, Illinois, Kansas, Missouri, Nebraska, North Dakota, Oklahoma, and Texas, for example, adopt this view.

[22] For example, Mississippi, Nevada, Tennessee, and Virginia.

[23] Among them being Alabama, Arkansas, California, Florida, Illinois, Texas, and Vermont.

[24] Alabama, Arkansas, California, Florida, Georgia, Illinois, Iowa, Kansas, Massachusetts, Minnesota, Nebraska, North Carolina, North Dakota, Oklahoma, Texas, and Wyoming are among the states adopting this view.

[25] For example, California, Florida, Kansas, Louisiana, Minnesota, Montana, Texas, and Virginia.

Real Property Taxes and Assessments In most states, liens for real property taxes and assessments have priority over homestead exemptions even though the date on which the taxes became a lien is subsequent to the time the homestead exemption was acquired. Tax authorities normally can proceed against a delinquent taxpayer's homestead property as though no exemption were in existence.

Debts Arising from Tort Claims

Statutes frequently exempt a homestead only from judgments "for debts" or "debts founded on contract" and make no mention of judgments arising from tort actions. These statutes have usually been construed as not protecting the homestead from debts arising out of tort claims.[26]

Statutes in some states leave no room for judicial interpretation and expressly provide that homesteads are exempt from tort judgments as well as contract debts.

From the standpoint of policy, it is difficult to determine whether the interest of a tortiously injured person or the interest of the tortfeasor's family should be accorded greater protection.

TRANSFER OR ENCUMBRANCE OF HOMESTEAD PROPERTY

The fact that a parcel of property is subject to a homestead exemption does not operate to prevent the owner from voluntarily transferring title to the property or encumbering it with a mortgage or deed of trust. Where the homestead claimants are husband and wife, however, the constitutional or statutory provisions of most states require that both spouses must join in the conveyance or encumbrance of homestead property. An attempted conveyance or encumbrance by one spouse only, even though that spouse is the sole owner of the property, is ineffective to pass title or to create a lien.

RIGHTS OF SURVIVORS OF HEAD OF FAMILY

In nearly all states, on the death of the head of a family the homestead which was acquired during his lifetime continues for the benefit of his surviving family member.

It is reasoned that although the homestead property belonged to the deceased who had title to it, the surviving family members, while not owners, have an interest in the property that the owner cannot divest them of by will. It is considered that the family's need for protection is as great if not greater after the death of the head of the family, particularly if the deceased was the husband and father. If the homestead should cease at the death of the head of the family, the objective of the homestead statutes would be defeated. Consequently, where the deceased is survived by a spouse or minor children, the survivor or survivors are entitled to occupy the homestead premises not only free from the claims of the decedent's creditors but from the claims of the survivors' creditors as well.

Many states[27] limit a surviving widow's homestead interest to a life estate and upon her death, if there are no minor children, the property becomes liable for the decedent's debts. Some statutes[28] require that a widow occupy the homestead premises and her failure to do so causes the homestead exemption to be lost. In some jurisdictions,[29] a widow's homestead rights terminate upon her remarriage while in other states[30] that is not the case.

TERMINATION OF HOMESTEADS

Once a parcel of real property has acquired the status of a homestead, that status will continue

---

[26] Courts in Alabama, Georgia, Kentucky, and Oklahoma have so held, while those in Michigan, North Carolina, and Wisconsin have held to the contrary.

[27] For example, Alabama, Arkansas, Georgia, Iowa, Kentucky, Massachusetts, Minnesota, Missouri, Nebraska, New Hampshire, South Carolina, South Dakota, Tennessee, Texas, Utah, and Virginia.

[28] Alabama, Arkansas, Illinois, Iowa, Kansas, Kentucky, Massachusetts, North Dakota, Oklahoma, Tennessee, and Wyoming.

[29] California, Georgia, Kansas, Michigan, Mississippi, Utah, and Wisconsin, for instance.

[30] For example, Illinois, Iowa, Missouri, New Hampshire, North Dakota, and Texas.

until the homestead is terminated in some legally recognized way. Generally speaking, a homestead will come to an end (1) when it is abandoned by the person or persons entitled to the homestead, (2) when the homestead property is conveyed by the owner, (3) when the owner dies without leaving survivors who are entitled to the continuance of the homestead, and (4) when the estate or interest that is subject to the homestead expires.

By Abandonment of Homestead
A homestead is considered to have been abandoned when the owner of the homestead property vacates the premises with the intention of no longer using them as his home. Whether there has been an abandonment in a given case is essentially a question of intention. The temporary nonuse of a homestead resulting from military service, illness, business, or other reasons does not constitute an abandonment. Nor does renting the homestead premises during a prolonged absence itself indicate an intent not to return. But where a homestead owner and his family move from homestead property to a newly acquired home, it is presumed that the homestead was abandoned.

The burden of proving the existence of a homestead is on the person claiming the exemption, but once its existence has been established the homestead is presumed to continue. Thereafter, the burden of proving that abandonment has occurred falls upon the person attempting to defeat the exemption and evidence that the homestead was abandoned must be positive and clear.

By Conveyance of Homestead
A homestead terminates when the owner of homestead property transfers title to it and relinquishes possession of the premises to a buyer or a donee. If the homestead property is co-owned by a husband and a wife, or if the wife acquired homestead rights in the property being sold, both the husband and the wife must sign the deed in order that title to the property may be transferred and all homestead interests in it be extinguished.

We have seen that in a number of states the proceeds of the voluntary sale of homestead property are exempt from claims of creditors either for a specified or reasonable period of time following the sale or until the seller reinvests them in another home. We also saw that a few states take the position that the voluntary sale of homestead property extinguishes all homestead rights and, until they have been invested in other exempt property, the proceeds are subject to the claims of the seller's creditors.

Although a conveyance of title to homestead property terminates a homestead exemption, mortgaging the property or otherwise making it security for a debt does not. Instead of extinguishing the exemption, a mortgage or deed of trust executed by all persons having homestead rights in property subordinates the homestead exemption to the debt secured by the mortgage or deed of trust and subjects the homestead property to foreclosure sale in satisfaction of the secured debt.

By Death without Surviving Family
When the owner of homestead property dies without leaving surviving family members who might have taken the property, the homestead exemption terminates. If the property is thereafter to be exempt from the claims of creditors, the person receiving the property by will or intestate succession would have to acquire a homestead exemption in his own right, not by derivation from the decedent.

By Expiration of a Limited Estate
We have seen that it is not necessary for a householder to own a fee simple interest in the premises he occupies to be entitled to a homestead. A homestead exemption can be acquired by the owner of a life estate or leasehold interest as well. Like the limited estates to which they attach, homestead rights in a life estate or a leasehold terminate when the life tenant dies or the period of the lease expires.

PROBATE HOMESTEADS

Like homesteads acquired merely by occupying a dwelling as a home and those acquired by recording a declaration of homestead, probate homesteads are exclusively creatures of statute and have as their purpose the exempting of a home from the claims of creditors. But unlike homesteads that are acquired by an act of the claimant during his lifetime, a probate homestead is created by a court setting aside from a decedent's assets a home for the surviving spouse and minor children that is beyond the reach of creditors. Statutes that authorize the setting aside of probate homesteads do so only in those cases where no homestead exemption existed during the lifetime of a decedent which would continue in his surviving family. Consequently, probate homesteads, as distinct from what might be called "survivors' homesteads," would appear to be confined to those states[31] in which a homestead can be acquired during a claimant's lifetime only by recording a declaration of homestead. In such states, if no declaration is recorded there is no homestead to continue in a decedent's survivors and hence there is need to set aside a probate homestead to protect them from the claims of creditors. If a declaration was recorded during the decedent's lifetime, the homestead created by the declaration will continue in favor of the decedent's surviving family and no probate homestead will be necessary.

Statutes which provide for probate homesteads generally make it compulsory for a court to set such a homestead aside when a decedent's surviving family has no other homestead. In a few states, unless the surviving family members specifically apply to the court to have certain property set aside for them, they will receive no homestead rights.

---

[31] That is, Alabama, Arizona, California, Colorado, Florida, Idaho, Iowa, Louisiana (if in a city), Maine, Massachusetts, Montana, Nevada, New York, North Dakota, Oregon, Utah, Virginia, and Washington.

Property Selected as Homestead

As a general rule, a decedent's property which a court may set aside from his estate as a probate homestead must be suitable for residential purposes and be of such a character that the decedent could have acquired homestead rights in it prior to his death. Normally the court is not restricted by value or area limitations in its selection of a probate homestead.

Duration of Probate Homestead

Life Estate or Fee Simple Interest Although statutes commonly limit the probate homestead of a surviving spouse to a life estate for the spouse's lifetime, some statutes give the courts discretionary power to set aside a fee simple interest where circumstances warrant such action.

During Minority of Children If a probate homestead is created for the benefit of minor children rather than for a surviving spouse, the homestead will continue until the last child achieves adulthood. Thereafter, the court will distribute the property to the decedent's heirs in accordance with his will, if he left one, or according to the laws of intestate succession.

Termination of Probate Homestead

Probate homesteads are terminated (1) by abandonment of the homestead property by the claimant, (2) by conveyance of the homestead property by the claimant, (3) by death of the life tenant where the homestead claimant's interest is a life estate, or (4) by the coming of age of all minor children for whom the homestead was set aside.

QUESTIONS

1 What is the meaning of "homestead" as that term is used in a state's homestead exemption law?
2 What is the primary objective of homestead exemption laws? What are the public policy considerations on which such laws are founded?

3 Under modern statutes, what types of dwellings are eligible for homestead exemptions?
4 Describe the manner in which a homestead exemption is acquired in a majority of the states. What additional factor is required by a sizable minority of states?
5 What is the general rule with respect to the relative priorities between real property tax liens and homestead exemptions?
6 Indicate the ways in which a homestead exemption is terminated.
7 Under what circumstances will a probate homestead be created?
8 How are probate homesteads terminated?

Chapter 19

Restrictive Covenants and Conditions

While an owner's right to use his land is an incident of ownership that is carefully protected by the law and vigorously affirmed by the courts, it is not a right without limitation. Restraints that limit an owner's use of his land may result either from actions of private individuals or public authorities. And although all controls have the effect of restricting or limiting the use to be made of land regardless of who imposes them, private and public controls differ in the manner in which they are created and the way in which they are enforced.

This chapter is concerned with the characteristics of privately imposed controls on land use in the form of restrictive covenants and conditions. In the real estate trade such limitations are often referred to as "CC and Rs," an abbreviation for "covenants, conditions, and restrictions," which is a redundant expression because the restrictions to which it refers are the covenants and conditions already contained in the expression.

The most common method of regulating the use of land by public authorities is by means of zoning, which is the subject of the following chapter. A later chapter considers the manner in which environmental laws also limit the use of land. In Chapter 7 we examined other non-private limitations on the use of land resulting from the law of nuisance and lateral support for adjoining lands.

The law of nuisance, restrictive covenants, zoning, and environmental regulations—all methods of controlling the use of land—testify to the fact that a landowner cannot enjoy the use of his land without limitation on the manner of its use.

PRIVATE RESTRICTIONS ON LAND USE

Restrictions imposed on the use of land by private persons may either be covenants or conditions. A **covenant** is a promise in a deed or an agreement concerning the manner in which land will be used. A **condition** is a provision in an instrument of conveyance that will cause ownership of an interest to terminate if the property is put to a prohibited use.

Covenants and conditions are similar in that either can be used to control the use that an owner may make of his own land. They differ importantly, however, in the consequences that result from their breach. As we observed previously when discussing defeasible estates, the consequence of the breach of a condition is a drastic one resulting in the loss or forfeiture of the breaching owner's title. The consequence of a breach of a covenant, on the other hand, is merely a suit for damages or an injunction with the owner retaining title to the land. Because of this significant difference, restrictive covenants are more commonly used for controlling the use of land than are conditions.

It should be clearly understood that privately imposed restrictions are limitations on the use of land that are voluntarily assumed by the purchaser of land that is subject to them. In theory, at least, the effect of the restrictions is a factor that is reflected in the purchase price of the land. Once a person has acquired title to a parcel of land, use restrictions cannot thereafter be imposed on that land by private persons without the owner's consent. We shall see, however, that the same is not true of use restrictions imposed by public authorities through zoning ordinances.

Enforceable and Unenforceable Restrictions

For any of a number of reasons, owners of real estate often wish to control the future use of property after it has passed from their ownership and control. As long as they do not violate existing laws or act contrary to public policy, owners may transfer real property subject to whatever use limitations they may choose to impose. Their motives for restricting the use of transferred property ordinarily is immaterial. The courts, however, do not favor restrictions on the use of land that is transferred in fee simple and, generally speaking, will resolve any doubt concerning a restriction against its enforcement.

Restrictions imposed on real property are invalid if they contravene some constitutional or statutory provision or if they are of no benefit to anyone and their enforcement might seriously interfere with the proper development of a community. Subject to these limitations, the courts will enforce restrictions on the use of land to the same extent that they would enforce any other valid contractual relationship.

Typical Enforceable Restrictions Restrictions in deeds which limit a grantee's use of his property to a single purpose, such as for a church, a school, or public park, are held to be valid and enforceable use limitations. Conversely, restrictions in deeds that prohibit a grantee from using land for a particular purpose are normally upheld. For example, restrictions that prohibit the use of property for commercial purposes are valid and enforceable.

Provisions in deeds that require buildings and other structures to be set back certain distances from the front and side lines of a lot, provisions that prescribe minimum or maximum square footage of buildings, or limit the height of walls, fences, or hedges are examples of land use restrictions that the courts will enforce. A frequent restriction in residential subdivisions concerns the minimum price or cost of houses erected on lots therein. Such restrictions have generally been held to be valid and the erection of a house below the established minimum gives rise to a cause of action by other owners in the subdivision.

So-called building restrictions are probably the most common kind of land use limitations created by restrictive covenants.

Typical Unenforceable Restrictions Deed restrictions that deny the use of land to members of particular racial, ethnic, or religious groups and restrictions that have as their objective the creation of a monopoly are typical examples of land use limitations that the courts will not enforce.

It is now clearly established[1] that enforcement of race restrictions by state courts is prohibited as constituting state action in violation of the equal protection clause of the Fourteenth Amendment. Enforcement of race restrictions is also precluded by the federal Civil Rights Act[2] which declares that all citizens in every state and territory shall have the same right to inherit, purchase, lease, hold, and convey real property as is enjoyed by white citizens.

The fact that a race restriction in a deed is void does not render the deed ineffective to transfer title nor does it render other building and use restrictions in the deed void unless, of course, they are not severable from the race restriction.

Benefit-Burden Effect of Restrictions

The likely effect of imposing restrictions on the use of real property is to change the value of parcels of land that are affected by those restrictions. The change in the value results from the fact that the regulation of land use is capable of conferring benefits as well as imposing burdens on lands that were previously unaffected by land use limitations.

The Benefit-Burden Relationship Restrictive covenants are commonly designed to benefit one or more parcels of land by conferring on the land an advantage it would not otherwise have enjoyed. This advantage or benefit, however, accrues at the expense of other land that is made to bear the burden of a use limitation to which it previously was not subject. Because the use of land and the value of land are so intimately related, a parcel of land whose potential use has been limited would tend to be of less value than a similarly situated but unrestricted parcel. Similarly, a parcel of land enjoying a benefit to which it previously was not entitled would tend to increase in value.

Although the nature of the benefit-burden relationship between parcels of land may be as varied as there are reasons for imposing restrictions, a simple example will serve to illustrate the important distinction between the benefit and the burden resulting from a restrictive covenant.

Suppose that owner A who owns two adjoining lots sells one of them to B. Suppose also that the deed conveying the property to B contains a covenant providing that no building higher than one story nor located closer than 10 feet from the side boundary lines may be erected. B's lot is now burdened by a restriction that prevents B from building a multistory structure covering the entire area of the lot that B would be entitled to build in the absence of the restriction. It can be presumed that the price that B paid A for the lot reflected the burden of the use limitation that the property bears. The lot that A retained will benefit from the fact that there will be no structures on B's adjoining lot cutting off the light, air, and view enjoyed by A.

In the foregoing example, involving as it does a single parcel of land, there are no reciprocal benefits and burdens enjoyed and suffered by the two adjoining properties. The benefits of the restriction accrued to A's property and the burdens were sustained by B's. If, instead of the facts being as stated in the example, the situation had involved lots in a subdivision and the restrictions applied equally to all lots in the tract, both A's and B's properties would have been burdened by the use limitations and both would also have benefits from them.

---

[1] *Shelley v. Kraemer*, 334 U.S. 1 (1948).
[2] 12 U.S.C., sec. 1982 et seq.

Burden But No Direct Benefit Some types of restrictions are burdens on a particular parcel of land but do not directly benefit any other parcel. For example, if an owner transfers land subject to a condition that the land be used only for the erection of a church, the transferred property is burdened by a use limitation but no other particular parcel or parcels of land sustain a direct benefit from it.

METHODS OF CREATING RESTRICTIONS

Privately imposed restrictions on the use of land may be created by (1) a contract, (2) a deed to a single parcel of land, or (3) a general plan or scheme of land development.

By Contract between Parties

Restrictive Covenants As we have seen, a covenant is a promise. A **restrictive covenant** is a promise made by a covenantor (promisor) to a covenantee (promisee) by the terms of which the covenantor agrees to refrain from using his land in a certain manner or for a certain purpose. While the limitation on the covenantor's use of his land commonly arises in connection with the transfer of land, a restrictive covenant may also be created by a contract between adjoining property owners without any property being conveyed.

Suppose, for example, that A and B own adjoining parcels of land on which they contemplate building their respective homes. Assuming there are no zoning ordinances prohibiting such action, either A or B can erect outbuildings or other structures right up to their common boundary line and thus conceivably interfere with the other party's access to light, air, view, and general feeling of openness. To prevent this eventuality, A and B can enter into an agreement in which they mutually promise not to build any structure closer than a specified number of feet from the common boundary. Despite the fact that no transfer of property took place, the agreement will be enforceable.

Considering the number of restrictive covenants that are created during any given period of time, covenants that arise without the conveyance of land being involved are relatively uncommon.

Conditions Land use restrictions in the form of conditions are never created by a separate contract but result only from provisions in deeds conveying real property to which the use restrictions apply. An example of such a restriction is a provision in a deed by which A conveys Blackacre to B stating that the conveyance is made "upon the express condition that the premises shall be used for a place of worship and for no other purpose whatsoever."

Deed to Single Parcel

Both restrictive covenants and conditions can be created by the provisions of a deed that conveys title to a single parcel of land. An essential difference between the two forms of restrictions is the manner in which they are enforced and the consequences of their breach. In modern conveyancing, restrictive covenants are preferred over conditions as limitations on land use because a breach of the latter subjects the breaching owner to loss of his title through forfeiture. Furthermore, because of the law's abhorrence of forfeitures, unless the language of a restriction clearly indicates that the creation of a condition was intended by the parties, the courts will construe the provision to be a restrictive covenant.

Ordinarily, a restrictive covenant that is created by a deed to a single parcel of land imposes a burden on the land that is conveyed, but this is not always the case. The covenant may be such that it burdens a parcel of land retained by a transferor in favor of the land that is conveyed. For example, A may own two adjoining lots, Lot 1 on which A has built a residence, and Lot 2 which is vacant. To induce B to purchase Lot 1 with its dwelling, A may agree not to build a house on Lot 2 higher than one story and no closer than 15 feet to the common boundary between the two lots. A's deed to Lot

1 will set forth the promise or covenant to B and upon delivery of the deed the covenant simultaneously becomes a burden on A's retained lot and a benefit to the lot acquired by B.

Where the grantee of a parcel of land is the covenantor, the general rule is that his acceptance of the deed containing the covenant is equivalent to a promise made by him.

General Plan of Development

Privately imposed land use controls play an important role in the development of modern subdivisions. Regulation of the use of land in a general plan of development is accomplished by means of restrictive covenants rather than conditions, with the covenants being imposed on every lot in the subdivided tract.

Subdivision restrictions are either set forth in their entirety in each deed to every lot or they appear separately in a recorded "declaration of restrictions" which is incorporated in each deed by reference. The purpose of incorporating a recorded declaration of restrictions by reference is to minimize recording costs when the list of restrictions applicable to a development is extensive.

RESTRICTIVE COVENANTS

General Characteristics

No technical terms or particular forms of expression are required to create a restrictive covenant. Since a restrictive covenant is a promise, the requirements for creating a valid and enforceable covenant are no different than the requisites for the creation of any promise or contractual undertaking. The courts, in construing or interpreting a covenant, are guided by the intention of the parties as determined from the express language of the promise and reasonable inferences drawn from it. In interpreting the language of restrictive covenants, the courts resolve any doubt or ambiguity in favor of the unrestricted use of property and adopt the interpretation that least restricts an owner's free use of his land. But the courts will not apply rules of construction in such a way as to defeat the plain and obvious purpose of a restrictive covenant.

While the courts have manifested some disfavor with covenants that restrict the use of land, they have generally enforced them where they are not contrary to law or public policy and are not in restraint of trade. At an earlier time, covenants were viewed primarily as encumbrances on the title to land and of little social value, but today they are recognized as being beneficial to the proper development of land.

Affirmative and Negative Covenants Although covenants may be either affirmative or negative in character, only negative covenants limit the covenantor in the use of his land and are referred to as restrictions. Most covenants concerning land use are restrictive.

An **affirmative covenant** is a promise by a covenantor to do something on his land that he was not previously required to do. A promise to build or maintain a party wall is an example of an affirmative covenant.

A **negative covenant** is a promise by a covenantor to refrain from doing something on or with his land. For example, a promise by an owner to erect no structure on his property other than a single-family residence is a negative covenant. As a result of the covenant, the owner's use of his land is restricted.

Similarity to Negative Easement In Chapter 8 we saw that a negative easement was one that, while not permitting the easement holder to go upon the servient property and use it, prevented the owner of the servient estate from doing certain things with his property. For example, a negative easement might prevent a servient owner from erecting any structure above a certain height so as not to interfere with a dominant estate owner's easement for light, air, and view. The similarity between a negative easement and a restrictive covenant is apparent; both burden an owner's land with a limitation on its use and both serve to benefit the land of another.

Covenant Is an Interest in Land A majority of states that have considered the matter[3] hold that restrictive covenants are property rights for purposes of condemnation proceedings and that a condemnor must compensate a landowner who is damaged when a condemnor takes land subject to a restrictive covenant that benefits him.

A promise concerning the use of burdened land that may be enforced by an injunction creates an equitable interest in that land in behalf of the owner of benefited land. Condemnation of the burdened land for a public purpose that violates the promise also condemns the rights that make up the equitable interest and the owner of that equitable interest is entitled to compensation for its taking. For example, when a condemnor takes A's property which is burdened by a building restriction for the benefit of B's property, the condemnor must compensate B for the damage sustained from the taking of A's property and putting it to a use that is inconsistent with the restriction. The building restriction that benefited B's property is a compensable property interest.

A majority of the courts hold that a covenant is an interest in land and must meet the requirements of the statute of frauds and be in writing if it is to be enforceable.[4] If a restrictive covenant is regarded as a property interest in the burdened land that is appurtenant to the benefited land, it logically follows that the statute of frauds is applicable and must be satisfied. A few courts take a contrary position and hold that a covenant does not relate to an interest in land but merely to its use and consequently those courts will enforce oral covenants.

Enforcement of Covenants

Breach Has No Effect on Title The breach of a restrictive covenant has no effect on the breaching owner's title to his land. If a restriction is in the form of a covenant rather than a condition, the burdened land is not subject to forfeiture when the restricted act is performed. Nor is the owner's right to possession of the burdened land affected by his violation of a restrictive covenant.

Remedies for Breach of Covenant The remedies available to a covenantee for breach of a restrictive covenant are an action for damages suffered by reason of the breach or for injunctive relief or both. Although historically an action for money damages was the only remedy available for a breach of covenant, the usual method of enforcing restrictive covenants today is by an injunction. An injunction is an order of a court that prohibits the continuation of conduct by a covenantor that violates the terms of a restrictive covenant. An award of money damages compensates the covenantee for injuries he can show to have resulted from the breach of the covenant.

For example, suppose that a deed from A to B contains a covenant by the terms of which B agrees not to use the transferred premises for commercial purposes. Assume that the covenantor, B, begins to conduct commercial activities on his property that directly compete with the business for which A uses his premises. Because of this breach, A may bring an action to have the court order B to cease from carrying on his commercial activities and, if A can establish that he suffered a monetary loss as a result of those activities, he will be entitled to receive compensation from B.

When a covenant containing a building restriction is breached, the remedy most commonly sought by a covenantee is an order of the court directing the covenantor or the

---

[3] California, Connecticut, Kentucky, Louisiana, Maine, Maryland, Massachusetts, Michigan, Minnesota, Missouri, Nebraska, Nevada, New Jersey, New York, North Carolina, Pennsylvania, South Carolina, Tennessee, and Virginia.

[4] For example, the courts in Florida, Illinois, Missouri, New York, North Carolina, Ohio, Pennsylvania, Texas, and Vermont have so held.

covenantor's successor to comply with the building restrictions.

Who May Enforce against Whom One who seeks to enforce restrictions must be able to show that he or she has been legally injured by the breach of them.

Like any party to a valid contract, a covenantee may bring an action against a covenantor who fails to abide by his promise. Unless he is somehow excused from doing so, a covenantor is bound to perform his promise to a covenantee and will be liable for his failure to do so. While a covenantee's right to sue a covenantor for the breach of a promise made directly to him is unquestioned, problems of enforcement arise when the land of either the covenantor or the covenantee is transferred to a third person who was not a party to the agreement creating the covenant, and thereafter a breach occurs.

The issue involved in situations of this type has two aspects: (1) whether a new landowner can enforce a covenant which is a benefit to his land despite the fact that the promise was made to the former owner and not to him, and (2) whether the owner of land that is burdened by a previously made covenant can be held liable for its violation.

Whether a third person to whom benefited or burdened land has been transferred may sue or be sued for the breach of a covenant that was not made by or to him or her turns on the question whether the promise that was not performed was a covenant running with the land.

Covenants Running with the Land Restrictive covenants are of two types: (1) personal covenants and (2) covenants that run with the land. A personal covenant affects only the covenantor and the covenantee as original parties to an agreement. A covenant that runs with the land affects all successive owners of land benefited or burdened by the covenant.

A covenant is said to "run with the land" when both the benefit and the burden created by it attach to or become appurtenant to the lands of the covenantor and the covenantee. When a covenant runs with the land, the benefit and the burden of the covenant continue as rights and duties incident to the ownership of it even though the land is no longer owned by the covenantor or the covenantee. Transferees of the lands of the covenantor and covenantee are bound in the same manner as if they had been original parties to the covenants, whereas if the covenant did not run with the land it would affect the use and enjoyment of the properties only while they were owned by the covenantor and the covenantee.

The question as to whether a covenant runs with the land or not arises when there is a transfer of land by the covenantor or the covenantee to a third person. After the land is transferred by the covenantor, his transferee becomes liable on the covenant and the covenantor is relieved of any further obligation. Similarly, where the covenantee transfers his land, the transferee becomes entitled to enforce the covenant and the covenantee is no longer entitled to do so.

For a covenant to run with the land it must relate to the use of the land. A primary test of whether a covenant does or does not run is whether it is so related to land as to confer a benefit on it and enhance its value. Among other covenants that have been held to run with the land are covenants that limit property to residential use, provide setback distances, provide that a building plan will be submitted for approval, that the property will not be used for a particular business for a period of time, and that it will be used for a single purpose.

Courts traditionally have been freer in permitting a covenant to run with the benefited land than with the burdened land. The courts' reluctance to enforce covenants that impose a burden on a covenantor's transferee has largely been the result of the policy of the law favoring the free transferability and use of land and the view that restrictions on use impair its transferability. Restrictive covenants were regarded primarily as constituting encumbrances on land that had very little social value. In order that a covenantee might have a remedy for breach of covenant in those instances where a remedy was not available in an action at law, courts of equity enforced restrictions as equitable servitudes. Courts of equity have been less reluctant to regard restrictions as equitable servitudes and enforce them as such than the law courts have been in allowing covenants to run with the land.

Enforced as Equitable Servitudes In cases in which a covenant does not run with the land because an essential requirement is lacking, a court of equity will sometimes enforce the burden of the covenant against the successors of the covenantor by issuing an injunction against its breach. This has given rise to the burden of the covenant becoming known as an **equitable servitude** in the land burdened by a restrictive covenant. In the great majority of states, equitable servitudes are considered to be equitable property interests in the burdened land that belong to or are appurtenant to the benefited land. The similarity between an equitable servitude and a negative easement is apparent.

The modern law of restrictive covenants is based on an equitable theory that originated in the landmark case of *Tulk v. Moxhay*.[5] That case initiated the equitable notion that restrictive covenants are enforceable by or against successors to the interests of the covenantor and the covenantee if (1) they intended that their successors be so bound or entitled and if (2) the party against whom the covenant is to be enforced had actual or constructive notice of the covenant. An equitable servitude exists only when the successor to the covenantor acquired his interest in the burdened property with notice of the promise made by the covenantor. Normally this will be constructive notice resulting from the recordation of the deed by which the covenantor acquired his title.

[5] 2 Phillips 774, 41 Eng. Rep. 1143 (1848).

The doctrine of equitable servitudes is founded on the principle that it would be inequitable to allow a property owner to violate a restriction of which he had actual or constructive notice when he purchased the burdened property.

Termination of Covenants

Because restrictive covenants limit the use to which land may be put, their termination frequently becomes a question of major importance to owners of lands that are burdened by them. Restrictive covenants may be terminated or rendered unenforceable in a number of ways, including (1) by the lapse of time, (2) by merger, (3) by release, (4) by waiver, (5) by acquiescence, (6) by laches, (7) by agreement, (8) by changed neighborhood conditions, and (9) by condemnation.

By Lapse of Time Restrictive covenants are sometimes written so that by their own terms they will expire after a specified period of time, such as 25 or 30 years. At the end of such a period, the covenant terminates automatically. It is considered desirable for covenants to provide for their automatic termination at a certain date or after a stated number of years because covenants tend to outlive their usefulness.

In the majority of cases, however, covenants contain no provision for automatic termination and consequently have a potentially infinite duration. In the absence of a stated time limitation, the mere lapse of time is not itself a sufficient basis for concluding that a restrictive covenant is no longer enforceable.

By Merger Restrictive covenants are terminated by merger. A *merger* occurs when title to the property that is benefited by a covenant and title to property burdened by the covenant are acquired by the same person. If that owner subsequently sells either the burdened parcel or the benefited parcel. the restrictive covenant is not revived. Of course, as is true of any owner, he is free to impose new restrictions on either the property he sells or the property he retains.

By Release A person who is entitled to enforce the benefit of a restrictive covenant may extinguish that right by means of a release. A *release* is the giving up of a right or claim to the person against whom it might have been enforced. To be effective to relinquish a claim or a right, a release must be supported by a sufficient consideration and, in the case of a release of a property right, must be in writing to satisfy the requirements of the statute of frauds.

By Waiver A *waiver* is the voluntary relinquishment of a right or the intentional refraining from enforcing a right. If a person who has the right to enforce a restrictive covenant waives that right, the covenant for all practical purposes comes to an end.

By Acquiescence A restrictive covenant is terminated by *acquiescence* when a covenantee who failed to enforce a breach against a covenantor or covenantors in the past now seeks to enforce the covenant against another covenantor who breaches it. Acquiescence is based on the notion that tolerated violations of a restrictive covenant in time tend to defeat the objective of the covenant. Where landowners in a tract or subdivision have ignored or failed to enforce continuous violation of general plan setback restrictions, for example, their right to prevent owner A from similarly violating the setback restrictions will be lost because of their having acquiesced in previous violations. Violations of restrictions may be so general in a tract or subdivision as to indicate an intention on the part of the residents of the community to abandon the general plan or scheme of restrictions.

Whether there has been such acquiescence in prior violations as to defeat the enforcement of a restrictive covenant depends upon the circumstances of each case and the character and seriousness of the permitted breaches.

By Laches The right to enforce a restrictive covenant may be lost by *laches,* which is a delay in bringing an action to enforce the covenant by one having a right to do so. But the mere lapse of time in bringing an action is not alone enough to terminate the covenantee's right. In order for the right to enforce a covenant to be lost or barred because of laches, the covenantor seeking to prevent the enforcement must show that the delay caused him such prejudice that it would now be inequitable to permit enforcement.

Termination of the right of enforcement by laches differs from termination of the right by the running of the statute of limitations in that in the case of the statute of limitations there need be nothing more than the mere lapse of time to bar an action to enforce.

By Agreement Covenants which create restrictions on all lots in a tract or subdivision frequently provide that they can be eliminated or changed by written agreement of a stated percentage of property owners in the tract. The agreement by the required percentage of owners is binding on dissenting lot owners as well, and they are thereafter barred from seeking to enforce the original covenants.

Even though subdivision restrictions contain no provisions for the manner of terminating or changing them, they may be terminated or amended by agreement of *all* the owners of lots in the tract. Such action is simply the exercise of the owners' right of contract.

By Changed Neighborhood Conditions If the character of a neighborhood has so changed that it is no longer possible to accomplish the original purpose intended by restrictive covenants, the courts will refuse to enforce them on equitable grounds. When the benefits intended to flow from restrictive covenants can no longer be obtained, the restrictions will have outlived their usefulness and enforcement will be denied. The extent of the change in a neighborhood that will prevent enforcement of a restrictive covenant presents a question of fact that cannot be answered in a categorical manner. When considering the question of change in a neighborhood's character, the courts look at such matters as the purpose for which the restrictions were originally imposed, the location of the property subject to the restrictions in relation to the area that has changed, and the period of time during which the restrictions have been in effect.

In most jurisdictions, changed neighborhood conditions can be used both defensively and affirmatively by the owner of land burdened by a restrictive covenant. For example, an owner who has breached a covenant may assert the defense of changed conditions in an action brought against him for an injunction or, before doing anything that would violate the restriction, the owner may bring an action seeking a judicial declaration that the covenant is no longer enforceable because of change in the character of the neighborhood.

By Condemnation Restrictive covenants are extinguished when the land burdened by them is taken by condemnation for a public use that is inconsistent with the restrictions contained in the covenants. Condemnation of property burdened by restrictions gives rise to the question as to whether someone whose land is benefited by the covenants is entitled to compensation from the condemning authority. As we previously observed, a majority of the states confronted with the problem have held that the benefit of a restrictive covenant is an interest in land for which compensation may be had when that interest is taken by condemnation.

Effect of Zoning Laws Zoning ordinances do not extinguish restrictive covenants on land nor do they enlarge the force and effect of such restrictions. If a covenant to which a parcel of land is subject is more restrictive than a zoning law, the covenant will control the use of the land. Conversely, if the zoning ordinance is more restrictive, it will control. Thus, an ordinance which zones or rezones property in a given area for commercial purposes will not nullify restrictive covenants limiting parcels of real estate in that area to residential use.

While a newly enacted zoning ordinance will neither extinguish nor enlarge existing restrictive covenants, the ordinance will serve as a circumstance tending to show that in the opinion of zoning authorities the character of the neighborhood within the zoned area had changed since the time the restrictive covenants were originally imposed.

CONDITIONS

Conditions relating to the transfer of estates in real property are of two types: (1) conditions subsequent which serve to restrict the use to which land may be put and (2) conditions precedent which do not.

Conditions Precedent and Conditions Subsequent Distinguished

A **condition precedent** requires the performance of some act before title will vest in a grantee; the passage of title from a grantor to a grantee must be preceded by the performance of a stated condition. When the condition precedent has been satisfied, the title to real property passes to the grantee and his use of the property thereafter is free from any restriction or control by the grantor. A common example of a condition precedent is the requirement by a grantor who deposited an executed deed in escrow that the grantee must deposit the purchase money with the escrow holder before he is authorized to deliver the deed to the grantee.

A **condition subsequent,** on the other hand, becomes effective only after a deed has been delivered and title has passed to a grantee. A condition subsequent appears as a provision in a deed that limits the use to which property transferred by the deed may be put, and in so providing renders the estate that is transferred a *defeasible* one.

When the term "condition" is used alone when discussing limitations on the use of land, it always refers to a condition subsequent.

RESTRICTIVE COVENANTS AND CONDITIONS

Consequence of Breach of Condition

The consequence of the breach of a restriction in the form of a condition is far more drastic than that resulting from the breach of a restrictive covenant. As we have seen, an owner who breaches a covenant continues to retain his title but will be subject to an injunction and liability for damages, while the title of one who breaches a condition will be forfeited or lost. Upon forfeiture, title to the property reverts to the grantor whose deed created the condition or to his successor in interest. The owner who breached the condition and forfeited his title receives no compensation either for the land or any improvements made by him to the land. This is the nature of a forfeiture.

We have seen that because of the law's abhorrence of forfeitures, limitations on the use of land in the form of conditions are not favored by the courts. As a consequence, where the language of a provision in a deed does not clearly reflect the parties' intention to create a condition, the courts will construe the language as being a covenant. Even though the language of an instrument limiting the use of land refers to the restriction as being a condition, the courts generally will not construe the restriction as being a technical condition unless it clearly appears that the parties intended it to be such.

Persons Affected by Conditions

A condition is like a covenant that runs with the land in that it limits the use which all successive owners of the land may make of it. The defeasible estate that is created by a condition remains subject to being terminated or forfeited if the property should be used for a purpose prohibited by the condition whether so used by the original grantee or some subsequent owner of the property. A grantee who receives title to an estate in real property that is defeasible because its use is restricted by a condition cannot transfer that estate free from the condition even though the deed by which he transfers title omits any mention of the condition. He can convey no greater interest in the property than he owns and that interest is a defeasible rather than an absolute fee.

Suppose, for example, that A who owns Blackacre in fee simple absolute conveys Blackacre to B subject to an express condition in the deed that the property be used only for a place of worship. In so doing, A conveyed a lesser estate (a defeasible fee) than he owned (a fee simple absolute) and retained to himself an interest known as a power of termination or right of entry. A or any successor to his interest may terminate B's estate if B uses Blackacre for any purpose other than a place of worship. Assuming A's deed to B was recorded, the condition which limits the use of the land does not terminate when B conveys the land to C by a deed that does not mention the condition. If C thereafter devotes the property to a commercial purpose, A or any successor to his power of termination may bring an action that will result in C's forfeiting his ownership of Blackacre.

Termination of Conditions

Restrictions on the use of land in the form of conditions may be terminated by the same conduct and events that terminate restrictive covenants. Because of the courts' dislike of forfeitures and their desire to avoid them when they can reasonably do so, conditions in deeds that have become obsolete because of the passage of time and changed neighborhood situations are seldom enforced.

QUESTIONS

1 Why is the expression "covenants, conditions, and restrictions" as used in connection with real estate a redundant expression?
2 In what respect are covenants and conditions in deeds similar? How do they differ?
3 Describe the benefit-burden relationship brought about by restrictive covenants in deeds.
4 Distinguish between an affirmative covenant and a negative covenant. Give an example of each.

5 What is the significance of the fact that restrictive covenants are property rights for purposes of condemnation proceedings?
6 What remedies are available to one who is injured by a breach of a restrictive covenant?
7 Distinguish between a personal covenant and a covenant that runs with the land.
8 Explain how a restrictive covenant is terminated by merger.
9 What happens when restrictive covenants and zoning laws applicable to a particular parcel of land are in conflict?
10 Distinguish between a condition precedent and a condition subsequent.

Chapter 20

Zoning

Of the various methods of regulating the use of land, the one most widely employed today is zoning. The word **zoning** derives from the fact that a community is divided into districts or zones with land use controls varying from one zone to another. Zoning controls the activities that are permitted on a parcel of land, regulates the size of buildings that may be situated on it, and controls the location of buildings and other structures on the land in relation to its boundary lines.

In virtually every urban area in the country and in a growing number of rural communities, before an owner can commence to use or improve his real estate he must examine the applicable zoning regulations to determine whether it is permissible to use his parcel of land for a proposed purpose.

Unlike restrictive covenants which are privately imposed land use controls, zoning regulations are imposed by governmental authority. By means of enabling acts passed by state legislatures, local legislative bodies have been empowered to regulate the use of land situated within the areas over which they exercise authority. Unlike restrictive covenants which are voluntarily agreed to and accepted by landowners, zoning ordinances may impose controls on the use of land even though the owner opposes the purpose and the nature of the use limitations.

By means of zoning ordinances, uses of land which do not amount to nuisances can be prohibited. Thus zoning goes beyond the scope of nuisance law. However, while the growth of zoning has lessened the need to resort to nuisance actions to prevent incompatible land uses, landowners still bring nuisance suits for protection when existing zoning laws fail to deal with a particularly troublesome use of land.

DEVELOPMENT PLANNING AND ZONING

Land use control through zoning is only one aspect of the much broader field of planning for community development. State enabling acts commonly require that a general or master plan for the physical development of a municipality or county be prepared before zoning ordinances can become effective. Although the two functions are closely related, planning and zoning clearly are not the same and it is important to note the significant legal distinction between them.

General Plan of Development

A general or master plan is a statement of policies for the future development of a community. It sets forth an outline of the major uses to be made of land and indicates the location of districts to be used for residential, commercial, and industrial purposes as well as the location of such public facilities as schools, parks, civic centers, streets, highways, and sewage disposal plants. A master plan is never complete; it must continually be revised to meet the needs of changing conditions.

A general plan of development is prepared by a planning commission which holds public hearings and submits its findings to a city or town council, county board of supervisors, or similar local legislative body. There is no assurance that the commission's recommended plan will be accepted by the legislative body or, if accepted, that it will be carried out as proposed or intended.

A general plan, even though accepted by the local legislative body has no legal effect of its own. If it is to achieve its purpose of encouraging the most efficient use of land throughout the community, a general plan must be implemented by the imposition of legal controls on the use of land.

Plan Implemented by Zoning

A general or master plan of development is rendered legally effective by means of zoning regulations enacted by the local legislative body. Zoning is the most important legal device for the implementation of a general plan for development of a community. It is also the method of land use control with which most people are familiar.

Although a general plan serves as the basis for comprehensive zoning of the community, planning for the use of land may precede the actual adoption of the plan and enactment of zoning. Where that occurs and where a land use map showing the pattern of urban growth and indicating the type and location of permissible zones has been prepared, development planning may exert a considerable influence on the level of property values in the community.

PURPOSES OF ZONING

In the 1920s the **Standard State Zoning Enabling Act** was drafted and distributed to each state by the U.S. Department of Commerce.[1] The enabling acts of most states are based substantially on that act.

The standard act authorizes local legislative bodies to enact zoning regulations and states that

> Such regulations shall be made in accordance with a comprehensive plan and designed to lessen congestion in the streets; to secure safety from fire, panic, and other dangers; to promote health and the general welfare; to provide adequate light and air; to prevent the overcrowding of land; to avoid undue concentration of population; to facilitate the adequate provision of transportation, water, sewerage, schools, parks, and other public requirements. Such regulations shall be made with reasonable consideration among other things, to the character of the district and its peculiar suita-

---

[1] The act was drafted by an Advisory Committee on Building Codes and Zoning which was appointed by the then Secretary of Commerce, Herbert Hoover. The act was revised in 1926.

bility for particular uses, and with a view to conserving the value of buildings and encouraging the most appropriate use of land throughout the municipality.[2]

SOURCE OF ZONING POWER

The regulation of land use through zoning is an exercise of the police power and can be exercised only by the state legislature and those to whom the legislature delegates the power. In a few states[3] the people's use of the initiative for zoning has been authorized by statute.

The Police Power

Governments exist for the services they render for the promotion of the health, safety, morals, and general welfare of the people that are governed. The authority by which the government does those things for which it exists is called the **police power.** The police power is described as being the inherent power of the state to subject the rights of individuals to reasonable regulation.

Limitations on Police Power

While the courts have repeatedly said that individual rights are subject to regulation by the exercise of the police power, they have also repeatedly stated that the power of government over the rights of individuals is not unlimited. Limitations imposed on the rights of individuals must, to be valid, be promotive of the public health, safety, morals, and welfare, and be neither arbitrary nor discriminatory in character. The principal limitation on the exercise of the police power is the *due process clause* of the Fourteenth Amendment of the United States Constitution which makes any unreasonable or arbitrary exercise of the police power a violation of substantive due process. Also limiting the exercise of the police power is the *equal protection clause* of the Fourteenth Amendment. That clause prohibits the discriminatory selection and classification of rights or activities to be regulated by the police power.

Scope of Police Power

Given the essential characteristics of the police power, it is apparent that it is not a static power but instead is one that changes both in scope and content with society's changing notion as to what are the proper functions of government. The scope of the power to regulate individuals' rights may be temporarily and appreciably enlarged during times of emergency or crisis. At any point in time, the extent of the police power is a function of prevailing legislative and judicial philosophies concerning the balance between individual rights and those of society.

With respect to the function of government in controlling the use of land, the history of the United States reflects a steadily broadening influence. From the earlier notion that a landowner may do as he pleases with what he owns, the scope of the police power has been consistently extended to give effect to a recognition of the increasing social interest in the utilization of land.

Loss of Use Not Compensable

From the standpoint of the owner of real property, limiting the use of his land by the exercise of the police power and the taking of it by eminent domain are markedly different. We saw in Chapter 11 that when an owner's property is taken through condemnation he is constitutionally entitled to payment of its market value. We also saw that when the owner is deprived of property rights relating to the use of his land under the police power, no such constitutional entitlement exists and no compensation is paid to him for any loss in the value of his land because of his being deprived of certain rights of use. "Damage caused by the proper exercise of the police power is merely one of the prices an individual must pay as a member of society."[4]

---

[2] Standard State Zoning Enabling Act, sec. 3.
[3] See, for example, Arizona Rev. Stat. Ann., sec. 11-826; Michigan Comp. Laws Ann., sec. 125.271; Ohio Rev. Code Ann., sec. 303.25.

[4] *Los Angeles v. Gage,* 127 CA2d 442, 453 (1954).

The assertion is often made that implicit in the zoning of land is the conservation of land values. To the extent that this assertion is correct, the question of compensation will not arise. The assertion, however, is not always true. The immediate impact of newly enacted zoning regulations may well be the diminution in the market value of regulated land. Courts that find the decrease in property value to be greater than what a landowner's contribution to the social welfare ought to be, hold the particular regulation to be arbitrary and unreasonable and hence invalid.

ZONING AUTHORITY OF LOCAL GOVERNMENTS

Being derived from the police power, zoning authority, we have seen, resides initially in the legislatures of the various states. Because the power to zone can most effectively be exercised by the government closest to the people, state governments have chosen to delegate their zoning authority to local legislative bodies through enabling acts. State enabling acts, therefore, are the basis of local zoning authority and local ordinances which exceed the grant of delegated power are void.

The Standard State Zoning Enabling Act, which we have seen serves as the basis for most state enabling acts, delegates the zoning power to "the legislative bodies of cities and incorporated villages."[5] Like the standard act, the enabling statutes of all states today delegate the zoning power to municipalities and a substantial majority of them[6] extend the authority to counties and townships as well. The legislative bodies of municipalities and counties in turn commonly delegate certain aspects of their zoning authority to appropriate administrative agencies.

CONSTITUTIONALITY OF ZONING

The Fifth Amendment to the United States Constitution provides that "No person shall . . . be deprived of . . . property, without due process of law; nor shall private property be taken for a public use without just compensation." While the Fifth Amendment applies to the federal government and its agencies, the Fourteenth Amendment has been judicially interpreted as imposing the same requirement on the states.[7]

Early ordinances that regulated the use of land through building codes, fire laws, and the like were clearly enough related to the public health and safety to be enforced by the courts as reasonable and proper exercises of the police power and hence not violative of due process of law. Not so clearly related to the police power, however, were ordinances that excluded certain types of uses from designated areas of the community. A diversity of judicial opinion existed among the states as to the constitutionality of such zoning ordinances until the year 1926 when the U.S. Supreme Court in the now historic case of *Village of Euclid v. Ambler Realty Company*[8] declared that comprehensive zoning was a constitutional exercise of the police power.

The facts of *Euclid v. Ambler* are as follows. The village of Euclid, an Ohio municipal corporation adjoining the city of Cleveland, by ordinance adopted a comprehensive zoning plan. The objective of the plan was to regulate and restrict the location of commercial and industrial activities in relation to residences. The

---

[5] Standard State Zoning Enabling Act, sec. 1.

[6] Alabama, Alaska, Arizona, Arkansas, California, Colorado, Connecticut, Delaware, Florida, Georgia, Hawaii, Idaho, Illinois, Indiana, Iowa, Kansas, Kentucky, Louisiana, Maine, Maryland, Massachusetts, Michigan, Minnesota, Mississippi, Missouri, Montana, Nebraska, Nevada, New Hampshire, New Jersey, New Mexico, New York, North Carolina, North Dakota, Ohio, Oklahoma, Oregon, Pennsylvania, Rhode Island, South Carolina, South Dakota, Tennessee, Texas, Utah, Vermont, Virginia, Washington, West Virginia, and Wyoming.

[7] *Chicago, B & Q Railroad v. Chicago,* 166 U.S. 266 (1897).

[8] 272 U.S. 365 (1926).

plan divided the entire area of the village into districts or zones and classified them as to permissible uses. The Ambler Realty Company owned a 68-acre tract of land, a substantial portion of which was limited to residential use by the zoning ordinance. The company attacked the constitutionality of the ordinance on the ground that it deprived the company of property without due process of law as guaranteed by the Fourteenth Amendment. In support of its contention, the company pointed out that the tract lay in the path of Cleveland's industrial development and that the land was worth $10,000 an acre for industrial use but not more than $2,500 for residential purposes.

The U.S. Supreme Court upheld the validity of the village ordinance and in so doing firmly established the constitutionality of comprehensive zoning. The court found that the division of the community into districts and the exclusion of certain uses from particular districts was a valid exercise of the police power.

Following the Supreme Court's approval of comprehensive zoning as an exercise of the police power, municipal zoning was approved by the courts in all states. State courts took the position that the Fourteenth Amendment guarantees of just compensation and due process did not exempt private property from reasonable regulations adopted pursuant to the police power for the protection of the public health, safety, morals, and general welfare. Private property was said to be held subject to the authority of the state to regulate the use of it in the interest of the public health, safety, or welfare without compensation for economic loss resulting from reasonable regulation.[9]

The general legality of zoning has been clearly established. However, a zoning ordinance may be valid on its face but be unconstitutional as applied to a specific parcel of land. The effect of zoning regulations on specific parcels of land is examined by the courts on a case-by-case basis. The courts today are receptive to cases brought by individual landowners to test the constitutionality of zoning regulations as they apply to a single parcel of land. Challenges by landowners are not based on the municipality's right to zone, but on the basis of the application of the zoning ordinance to their particular parcel of land. Furthermore, litigation generally arises from the fact that a zoning ordinance as applied to a specific parcel of land at a given point in time may become invalid later when circumstances have significantly changed.

NATURE OF COMPREHENSIVE ZONING

Division and Classification of Land by Use

Comprehensive zoning involves the division of an area over which a municipality has jurisdiction into districts or zones and the classifying of each of them in accordance with land use restrictions applicable to each zone. The two basic classifications of restrictions on the use of land employed in comprehensive zoning relate to (1) the *type* of use that is permitted in a designated zone and (2) the *intensity* with which land within a zone may be used for a permissible purpose.

The Standard State Zoning Enabling Act upon which most state enabling acts are based provides that "the local legislative body may divide the municipality into districts of such number, shape, and area as may be deemed best suited to carry out the purpose of the act."[10] The standard act also provides that while land use regulations may be different in one zone from those in other districts, all such regulations must be uniform within each zone.[11] Uniformity here means that similar situations must be regulated in the same manner.

---

[9] See, for example, *Gilbert v. Stockton Port District,* 1 Cal.2d 384, 60 P2d 847 (1936); *Ellis v. West University Place,* 141 Tex. 608, 175 SW2d 396 (1943); *Robinson v. Town Council of Narragansett,* 60 R.I. 422, 199 A 308 (1938).

[10] Standard State Zoning Enabling Act, sec. 2.
[11] Id.

Regulation of Type of Use

No Limit on Use Categories The types of uses for which land is zoned traditionally have fallen into four principal categories: (1) residential use; (2) commercial or business use; (3) industrial use; and (4) agricultural use. Zoning authorities, however, are not restricted to these traditional classifications because, generally speaking, enabling acts do not limit the particular types of uses for which land may be zoned. The Standard State Zoning Enabling Act empowers local legislative bodies to regulate and restrict land "for trade, industry, residence, *or other purposes.*"[12] [Emphasis added.]

New categories of use zones are created to meet changing community conditions and needs as they arise and as a result the types of use zones in a typical comprehensive plan have increased considerably in recent years. In addition, within each category of use zones subcategories have been developed that classify such uses as industrial, for example, according to light, medium, and heavy industry and residential with respect to single- or multiple-family dwellings. Like zoning actions generally, the creation of new types of use zones must meet all police power requirements.

Relative Restrictiveness of Uses Zoning theory classifies different types of land uses according to the extent or degree of their restrictiveness. Zoning theory holds that the limiting of land to residential use is more restrictive than limiting it to commercial use. Commercial use, in turn, is considered to be more restrictive than industrial use. Stated another way, residential use is the "highest" use of land with commercial use and industrial use each in turn being a progressively "lower" use of land. Within the principal categories of land use, the various subcategories are also assigned their relative degrees of restrictiveness. In the residential use category, for example, land limited to single-family use is "higher" or more restricted than land on which multiple-family dwellings are permitted. The single-family use zone is the "highest" or most restrictive of all zones.

Cumulative or Noncumulative Zoning Zoning is either cumulative or noncumulative in character. This feature results from the fact that for zoning purposes some land uses are ranked as higher or lower than others or that different types of uses vary in the extent to which they restrict the use of land.

Cumulative Zoning Zoning is **cumulative** when all higher or more restrictive uses are permitted in an area that is zoned for a lower or less restrictive use. For example, we have seen that residential use is a higher or more restrictive use of land than is industrial use. Consequently, cumulative zoning permits land in a district that is zoned for industrial use to be used for residential purposes as well. But the reverse is not true. Cumulative zoning does not permit industrial or any other lower use of land in a residential zone.

Noncumulative Zoning When the use of land in an area is regulated by **noncumulative** zoning, only the type of use specifically authorized by the zoning ordinance is permitted in the area. In noncumulative zoning there is no need to be concerned with higher and lower uses of land because all uses other than those expressly designated by the zoning law are excluded from the regulated area. If a district is zoned for industrial use, for example, and if the zoning is noncumulative, neither residential nor commercial nor any other use may be made of the land within the district. The exclusion of residential uses from an industrial district serves to minimize or eliminate the likelihood of private nuisance actions arising from industrial activities.

Regulation of Intensity of Use

Zoning ordinances that classify land areas according to the *intensity* of use regulate the extent to which land in a given district may be used for the type of use that is permitted in that

---

[12] Id., sec. 1.

district. The intensity with which land is used can be regulated in several ways, such as by building height limitations, setback requirements, minimum lot size, and limitations on the number of units per parcel. Controls on the intensity of land use are, of course, equally applicable to any type of use to which land may be put, whether that use be residential, commercial, industrial, or some other use.

Height and Bulk Limitations A common method of limiting the intensity with which land is used is by ordinances that restrict the height and bulk of buildings that may be erected on a parcel of land. *Height* is usually regulated either in terms of maximum allowable feet or permissible number of stories or both. *Bulk* regulation, on the other hand, generally deals with the horizontal measurements of buildings rather than vertical measurements and is controlled by such devices as minimum lot size and limitations on the percentage of the area of a lot that may be occupied by buildings. Both height regulations and bulk regulations serve the same function of controlling the *volume* of a structure on a parcel of land, which in turn regulates the intensity of the use of the parcel.

Floor Area Ratio Instead of setting maximum heights for buildings and limiting land coverage through setback, side-line, and other area restrictions, zoning ordinances often provide for what is known as a *floor area ratio* (FAR) to control the intensity of land use. The ratio involved in such a regulation is the relationship between the total floor area of a building and the total land area of a lot. A permissible ratio of 5 to 1, for example, would allow a 5-story building to occupy the entire area of a lot, while a 10-story building would be permitted to occupy only half of the lot's surface area.

Minimum Lot Size Zoning ordinances also regulate the intensity of land use by prescribing the minimum size for lots in a given district. Minimums are commonly stated in terms of width and depth dimensions or in square footage of area.

Exclusionary Zoning

Zoning that prohibits the use of land in a municipality for certain types of purposes is known as "exclusionary zoning." Manufacturing activities, junkyards, drive-in theaters, and mobile parks are examples of land uses that are frequently excluded. Exclusionary zoning that seeks to keep a municipality purely residential is usually sustained by the courts when such restrictions are part of a comprehensive regional plan that makes provision for the excluded uses elsewhere in the region.

Zoning that sets minimum lot sizes, minimum floor areas of buildings, and that regulates the percentage of the area of a lot that may be occupied by buildings is also exclusionary in character. Zoning for these purposes is sometimes called "snob" zoning because its effect is to exclude lower income groups from the regulated area because such zoning regulations increase the cost of construction dramatically.

Aesthetic Zoning

Aesthetic controls on the use of land seek to preserve or improve the beauty of a regulated area. The traditional view which still prevails in a majority of the states[13] is that zoning which is *solely* for aesthetic purposes is not a proper exercise of the police power. A principal objection stated by the courts is that aesthetic zoning is subjective in nature and beyond the capabilities of legislative bodies since what is beautiful in the eyes of one person may be an abomination to another.

Zoning ordinances in which aesthetic considerations are *incidental* to the main purpose for

---

[13] California, Colorado, Connecticut, Delaware, Illinois, Iowa, Kansas, Kentucky, Louisiana, Maine, Maryland, Massachusetts, Michigan, Minnesota, Mississippi, Missouri, Nebraska, New Jersey, New York, North Carolina, Ohio, Pennsylvania, Rhode Island, Tennessee, Texas, Virginia, and Wisconsin.

which the ordinances were enacted are generally upheld by the courts. Aesthetics are, to a greater or lesser degree, inherent in all zoning. The courts are more and more recognizing that considerations of beauty are an objective of zoning, especially since the U.S. Supreme Court in 1954 said that it is "within the power of the legislature to determine that a community should be beautiful as well as healthy."[14]

Among the various forms of **aesthetic zoning** are ordinances that impose architectural controls on a designated area. The validity of zoning ordinances that regulate the architectural style or design of structures has been upheld in most instances and especially when used as a means for the preservation of historical areas.

For example, a city ordinance that prescribed detailed regulations concerning the maintenance, alteration, and construction of buildings and signs in the historical Vieux Carré section of New Orleans was held to be a valid exercise of the police power by the Louisiana Supreme Court.[15] The court held that the preservation of the Vieux Carré in its original state was not only a benefit to the inhabitants of New Orleans for its sentimental value, but also for its commercial value as a tourist attraction. In a similar case, the New Mexico Supreme Court[16] upheld a Santa Fe city ordinance that created a historical district and regulated in detail the design of buildings constructed or altered in order to preserve the old Santa Fe style of architecture. The court noted that the announced purpose of the ordinance was to preserve the historic sections of the city and their old architectural style for the cultural and economic advantage of the people. It further noted that the tourist trade was a vital factor in the state's economy and that Santa Fe was known throughout the country for its historic features and culture. The court concluded

[14] *Berman v. Parker,* 348 U.S. 26 (1954).
[15] *New Orleans v. Pergament,* 198 La 852, 5 S2d 129 (1941).
[16] *Santa Fe v. Gamble-Skogmo Inc.,* 73 N.M. 410, 389 P2d 13 (1964).

that the general welfare of both the community and the state was enhanced by the ordinance.

Interim or Hold Zoning

When zoning authorities are studying an area either for original zoning or for rezoning, a long period of time may elapse between the beginning of the study and the enactment of zoning ordinances. In the meantime, land developers can frustrate the proposed land use controls by developing land in the area in a way that would be inconsistent with the objectives of ordinances ultimately passed. To prevent this from occurring, local legislative bodies adopt what is known as **interim or hold zoning** which protects the area from development until the study is concluded and implementing zoning regulations are enacted.

Boundary Lines between Zones

When zones with differing land uses are established in a community, boundary lines that demarcate them must be drawn. Local legislative bodies, whose function it is to establish boundaries, endeavor to do so in a manner that minimizes harm to all landowners. Admittedly, however, those owners whose lands are situated at the boundary of a zone will find the enjoyment of their properties more affected by uses in an adjacent zone than property owners farther removed from the boundary. The enjoyment of a single-family residence, for example, that is directly across a boundary line street from a commercial district will be interfered with more by noise and traffic than will a home located several blocks away in the middle of a residential zone. This inequality of interference is not itself sufficiently discriminatory for a court to order the boundary line changed. In the absence of a clear abuse of discretion, the courts will not disturb the local legislative body's determination as to where a boundary line should be located.

ZONING PROCEDURES

The Standard State Zoning Enabling Act charges local legislative bodies with the responsibility of establishing procedures by which zoning ordinances are enacted and amended.[17]

To assure that due process of law requirements are met, the act provides that no zoning regulation "shall become effective until after a public hearing in relation thereto, at which parties in interest and citizens shall have an opportunity to be heard."[18] In a comment on this provision, the draftsmen of the act say that the phrase "and citizens" was included because "This permits any person to be heard, and not merely property owners whose property interests may be adversely affected by the proposed ordinance. It is right that every citizen should be able to make his voice heard and protest against any ordinance that might be detrimental to the best interests of the city."[19]

The standard act provides that before a public hearing on a proposed zoning is held, at least 15 days notice of the time and place of the hearing must be published in an official newspaper or a newspaper of general circulation.[20]

RELIEF FROM ZONING REGULATIONS

An owner of land sometimes wishes to use or improve his property in a way that existing zoning regulations do not permit. Every landowner has available to him three alternative methods by which he may seek relief from zoning laws that affect his property. Depending upon the particular situation in which he finds himself, a landowner may either seek (1) legislative, (2) administrative, or (3) judicial relief. Of course, regardless of which of the alternatives an owner pursues, he has no assurance or guaranty that the relief he seeks will be forthcoming.

Legislative Relief

A property owner who hopes to obtain relief from existing zoning regulations by legislative means will take his case to the city council, the county commissioners or board of supervisors,

---

[17] Standard State Zoning Enabling Act, sec. 4.
[18] Id.
[19] Id., sec. 4, Note 28.
[20] Id., sec. 4.

or other appropriate local body possessing the power to enact zoning ordinances.

Amendment of Existing Ordinance An owner seeking legislative relief has the task of inducing the legislative body of the local government to pass a new ordinance that amends the existing law in such a way as to permit the type of use that the owner wishes to make of his property. To be upheld by the courts, an amendment to a zoning ordinance ordinarily must be applicable to all properties within the regulated zone and not merely to the lot or parcel owned by the person seeking relief. Amendments which accord a different use to one or a few parcels of land within a zone give rise to invalid "spot zoning."

The effect of a valid zoning amendment is to rezone the entire district or zone to which it is applicable. Frequent amendments can have a significant effect on a comprehensive zoning plan and unless prudently controlled can result in the gradual deterioration of a master plan for the development of a given area.

Justification for Amendment The usual justification for rezoning by means of amendment is that conditions have changed in the regulated area since the original ordinance was passed. An owner who can establish that fact should have a relatively easy time in obtaining legislative relief. Generally speaking, local legislative bodies are sensitive to the influence of changed conditions on land use and view planning and zoning as a continuing process.

Administrative Relief

Instead of endeavoring to have the entire zone in which his property is located rezoned by legislative action, a landowner desiring relief from strict compliance with existing ordinances may petition for administrative relief. Enabling acts and zoning ordinances generally authorize zoning authorities to grant two different types of administrative relief: (1) variances and (2) conditional or special use permits. Variances and conditional use permits are designed to give zoning ordinances sufficient flexibility to meet instances where a hardship would otherwise result.

Zoning relief in the form of variances and conditional use permits is granted by a local administrative body known variously as the board of adjustment, zoning appeals board, or some similar designation. In granting relief to a property owner, the board is guided by standards set forth in the applicable zoning ordinance. When facts and conditions as detailed in the ordinance are found to exist with respect to the petitioning owner's property, the board may grant the requested relief.

The administrative board has no power to amend the ordinance from which a petitioner seeks relief because that is a function of the legislative body.

Variance Practically all zoning ordinances authorize designated administrative bodies to grant landowners relief in the form of variances. A **variance** is permission to use a parcel of land in a manner that a zoning law on its face prohibits. Authority to grant variances is a means of preventing unwanted rigidity in zoning ordinances.

The authority to grant variances is not without limitations. Enabling acts and ordinances commonly require that for a variance to be granted the petitioner must show (1) that he would sustain a substantial hardship peculiar to his land if the ordinance as written were enforced and (2) that the use he proposes to make of his property will not be unduly disruptive of the general zoning scheme for the area.

There are two kinds of variances: (1) those having to do with bulk, including the height of a building and the area of a lot covered by it, and (2) variances with respect to the type of use to which a parcel is put. Some enabling statutes[21] do not authorize the granting of *use* variances because they are much more disruptive of a comprehensive zoning plan than are variances relating to bulk. For example, a variance permitting commercial activity in a residential area has a more destructive influence on a comprehensive plan than does a variance granting relief from a setback restriction for a single-family home in an area zoned for single-family residences.

Even where the granting of variances is authorized by enabling acts or zoning ordinances, many administrative bodies are reluctant to grant them for large parcels of land on the ground that rezoning by amendment is the proper form of relief.

While the standards that must be met before a variance will be granted differ somewhat among enabling acts and local ordinances, administrative bodies are typically concerned with such questions as: (1) whether the variance would adversely affect neighboring properties; (2) whether it would be adverse or beneficial to the public interest; (3) whether the property differs in size, shape, and topography from neighboring lands in the same zone; (4) whether the denial of a variance would result in a hardship to the petitioner; and (5) whether granting the variance would be unduly disruptive to the general plan.

Special Permit Most enabling acts and zoning ordinances vest local administrative bodies with authority to grant landowners permission to put their land to a use different from that for which an area is zoned provided certain conditions are met. If an administrative body determines that the conditions set forth in an ordinance are met, it will issue a special permit—sometimes called a conditional use permit, a special use permit, or a special exception. The Standard State Zoning Enabling Act empowers the local "board of adjustment" to "hear and decide special exceptions to the terms of the ordinance upon which such board is required to pass under such ordinance."[22]

---

[21] For example, California Government Code, sec. 95906 states: "A variance shall not be granted for a parcel of property which authorizes a use or activity which is not otherwise expressly authorized by the zone regulation governing the parcel of property."

[22] Standard State Zoning Enabling Act, sec. 7.

The special uses for which permits may be granted by administrative boards usually are listed in the ordinance that authorizes their issuance. The uses for which special permits may be issued customarily include but are not limited to such things as churches, schools, and recreational facilities in otherwise residential districts. Unlike variances, special use permits refer primarily to type of use of land rather than to the physical characteristics or uniqueness of property. Like variances, however, special permits will not be issued if either neighboring property owners or the public are adversely affected.

An administrative board is authorized to issue a special permit only when the conditions detailed in the ordinance are found to be present.

The issuance of a special permit does not, of course, change the basic classification of a zone. In that respect the granting of a special permit differs appreciably from rezoning by the amendment of an existing ordinance.

Judicial Relief

A property owner may seek judicial relief from burdensome zoning either because he believes a zoning ordinance improperly restricts the use of his land or because he disagrees with a decision made by an administrative body. In the first situation, the owner's judicial attack is against an ordinance as originally passed or amended; in the second, he attacks a determination to grant or deny a variance or a special permit.

Relief from Legislative Action Legal attacks on zoning ordinances or amendments are based on constitutional grounds. Since zoning is the exercise of the police power, it is only reasonable for the courts to require that zoning regulations have a substantial relation to the general welfare and not be arbitrary, unreasonable, or discriminatory in character. Attacks on the validity of an entire ordinance or scheme of zoning have been very few since the U.S. Supreme Court in the *Euclid* case[23] sustained the validity of comprehensive zoning. On the other hand, there have been numerous cases in which a zoning ordinance is alleged to be unconstitutional as that ordinance is applied to the specific property of a complaining party. This means, of course, that a zoning ordinance may be held to be invalid as to one parcel of land but remain valid as to all other parcels in the same district or zone.

An example of a case in which the constitutionality of an ordinance as applied to a particular parcel of land was challenged involved an ordinance which set a zone boundary line so that it included a 100-foot strip of an owner's land in a residential zone. The strip of land, however, was so situated that its use for residential purposes was impractical. In an action brought by the owner, he urged that the ordinance was unconstitutional as applied to his property. The court found that the facts of the case showed that the ordinance rendered the owner's land of "comparatively little value" and that the ordinance did not bear a substantial relation to the public health, safety, or general welfare. Therefore, the ordinance was held to be unconstitutional as it applied to the property of the complaining owner.[24]

Relief from Administrative Action The action of an administrative body, such as a board of adjustment, in denying or granting a variance or special permit is subject to attack in the courts. The Standard State Zoning Enabling Act provides[25] that "Any person or persons, jointly or severally, aggrieved by any decision of the board of adjustment, or any taxpayer, or any officer, department, board, or bureau of the municipality, may present to a court of record a petition, duly verified, setting forth that such decision is illegal, in whole or in part,

---

[23] *Village of Euclid v. Ambler Realty Co.,* 272 U.S. 365 (1926).
[24] *Nectow v. City of Cambridge,* 277 U.S. 183, 48 Sup. Ct. 447 (1928).
[25] Standard State Zoning Enabling Act, sec. 7.

specifying the grounds of the illegality. . . . The court may reverse or affirm, wholly or partly, or may modify, the decision brought up for review."

Having been denied a request for a variance or special permit, a property owner may attack the administrative body's decision as an arbitrary, unreasonable, or capricious exercise of power that deprives him of property without due process of law. The burden of establishing such an allegation, of course, rests with the complaining owner, but more so because of a judicial attitude that favors decisions reached by administrative bodies in zoning cases. The courts have repeatedly declared their reluctance to substitute their judgment for conclusions reached by boards of adjustment or other administrative bodies except in the face of a clear abuse of power.

As the foregoing quote from the standard act indicates, one who opposes the action of an administrative body in granting a variance or special permit to someone may take his grievance to the courts. A situation of this type might arise, for example, when the granting of a special permit for a given parcel will unreasonably affect the use and value of neighboring properties.

NONCONFORMING USE

Nature of Nonconforming Use

A **nonconforming use** is a use of land that lawfully existed before a zoning ordinance was enacted and which is continued after the effective date of the ordinance even though the use no longer complies with the new zoning regulations applicable to the district in which the land so used is located. A neighborhood grocery store lawfully operating in a residential area, for example, would become a nonconforming use following the passage of a new or amended zoning regulation restricting the area to single-family dwellings.

Practically all zoning ordinances provide for the continuation of lawfully existing uses after passage of an ordinance even though such a use could not thereafter be newly begun in the regulated zone. Not only does permission to continue the existing use make implementation of the new regulation easier but, more significantly, it makes it less likely that the ordinance will be found to be unconstitutional by the courts. There has been considerable uncertainty as to whether an ordinance that requires the immediate termination of a use of land that is not a nuisance constitutes a deprivation of property without due process of law. The courts have, however, consistently upheld zoning ordinances which permit the continuation of existing uses while prohibiting any such new uses in the future.

Zoning ordinances generally do not identify the particular parcels of land that may continue their existing uses but make the permission applicable to all parcels on which such uses existed prior to a certain date. The burden is on the nonconforming user to prove that his use existed prior to the designated date.

Types of Nonconforming Uses The term "nonconforming use" is a general one that refers to both nonconforming buildings and nonconforming activities. The term includes the following different types of nonconforming use situations: (1) the nonconforming use of a nonconforming building, (2) the nonconforming use of a conforming building, (3) the conforming use of a nonconforming building, and (4) the nonconforming use of land without a building.

A building that is built up to the boundaries of a lot becomes nonconforming, for example, after an ordinance requiring setback from the lot line has been enacted. A single-family residence used for a cottage industry in a newly created single-family residential zone constitutes a nonconforming use of a conforming building. And the use of a lot for the storage of machinery and equipment in an area zoned exclusively for residential purposes amounts to a

ZONING

nonconforming use of land that does not involve a building.

Recognition of the different types of nonconforming uses is important when considering the problem of terminating them. It is apparent that nonconforming uses impede the realization of the goals of community planning and comprehensive zoning. Consequently, public policy demands that nonconforming uses be firmly regulated with a view to their eventual elimination without violation of landowners' constitutional rights. In general, nonconforming uses are looked upon as necessary evils that should be eliminated as soon as it is conveniently and legally possible to do so.

Must Be an Existing Use In order that it may be entitled to continue as a nonconforming use, the use to which an owner's property is put must have been lawfully established or existing at the time a newly enacted ordinance becomes effective. The question frequently arises as to whether a given use of land was sufficiently advanced when the restricting ordinance went into effect for the use to be considered an established and existing one.

A landowner's mere intent to put his land to a particular use clearly is not sufficient to establish it as an existing use. Nor is the fact that the owner's land has the potential for such use sufficient. Mere preliminary planning, clearing the land, arranging for financing, or receiving a building permit have been held to be insufficient to bring a use into sufficient existence to qualify as a nonconforming use.

Ordinarily the making of substantial expenditures other than for the purchase of the land itself or the incurring of substantial contractual obligations will be adequate to establish a use as a nonconforming use.

Existing Use Cannot Be Enlarged In the absence of a provision in an ordinance specifically authorizing it, a nonconforming use cannot be expanded or enlarged. The use must continue substantially the same as it was prior to the enactment of the statute that rendered the use nonconforming. The making of repairs or minor physical changes to property is generally permitted but major alterations, replacement of buildings, or increasing the number of buildings devoted to a nonconforming use are commonly prohibited either by ordinances or by the courts.

Termination of Nonconforming Uses

Zoning ordinances generally provide several different methods by which nonconforming uses are brought to an end. These methods include termination because of destruction of a nonconforming building, abandonment of the nonconforming use, and the phasing out of the use over a period of years. Ordinances providing for these and other methods of terminating nonconforming uses are valid as long as they are neither arbitrary nor unreasonable or do not otherwise deny nonconforming users their due process of law guarantees.

Destruction and Abandonment Zoning ordinances commonly provide that if a nonconforming building is substantially destroyed by fire, windstorm, or other act of God it cannot be rebuilt. What amounts to *substantial* destruction is usually measured in terms of assessed, replacement, or market value or as a percentage of the physical structure. Where an ordinance is silent with respect to the matter, a court may hold that a building that is substantially destroyed by an act of God can be rebuilt by the owner.

The right to continue a nonconforming use may be lost by abandonment. Ordinances which contain provisions relating to abandonment often specify a period of time after which nonuse will be presumed to constitute abandonment. Where no time period is stated, nonuse for a reasonable period of time will terminate a nonconforming use.

The essential characteristic of a nonconforming use precludes changing the use from what it was on the effective date of the ordinance or amendment. Therefore, a nonconforming use must be a continuance of substantially the same use that existed prior to the ordinance. What has been referred to as the "natural expansion" of nonconforming businesses is permitted in many jurisdictions.

Amortization As long as nonconforming uses continue in an area, the objectives of the ordinance or amendment that caused those uses to become nonconforming cannot be fully realized. During the continuance of commercial activities in a newly classified single-family residential zone, for example, the quiet and comfortable living conditions visualized for the area will fall short of achievement. Consequently, the timely elimination of nonconforming uses is of prime concern to planners and zoning authorities.

Nature of Amortization In recent years local governments have adopted the technique of **amortization** as a means of terminating nonconforming uses. Amortization provisions in ordinances establish time periods during which nonconforming uses must be phased out. After expiration of the amortization or phasing out period, buildings and activities on land located within the regulated zone must comply with the requirements of the regulating ordinance. Nonconforming uses are not entitled to be continued perpetually and ordinances that require their elimination within a specified time have been sustained as a reasonable exercise of the police power.

Amortization Periods May Vary Zoning ordinances that contain amortization provisions commonly establish time periods of differing length for the phasing out of the different types of nonconforming uses. Typically, because such activities presumably can be moved elsewhere at relatively little loss, the amortization period is shortest for nonconforming uses of land on which there are no buildings. Because of the investment involved, the time for amortization is longest where nonconforming buildings are concerned. Where conforming buildings are put to nonconforming uses the periods for their phasing out are relatively short because such buildings can be devoted to uses that conform to the classification of the zone. Amortization periods may also vary in accordance with different types of buildings.

The Los Angeles Municipal Code is an example of zoning regulations that vary amortization periods for different kinds of nonconforming uses. The code provides that nonconforming uses of land without buildings in residential zones must be terminated within 5 years of the date the uses become nonconforming.[26] Similarly, if the use of a conforming building in a residential zone is nonconforming, the use must be discontinued within a 5-year period.[27] And, depending upon the type of building, a nonconforming building located in a residential zone must either be made to conform to the code or be removed when the building becomes 20, 30, or 40 years old.[28]

Rather than indicating specific periods of time for amortization of nonconforming uses, some ordinances simply provide for phasing out within a reasonable period of time. What constitutes a reasonable period of time, of course, is a question of fact that depends upon the particular circumstances of each case in which it is an issue. And it should be noted that even the specific periods set forth in an ordinance are always subject to the test of reasonableness as well. A time period for amortizing a nonconforming use that is found to be unreasonable or arbitrary will be an invalid deprivation of an owner's property without due process of law.

Nonconforming Use as a Nuisance A nonconforming use that constitutes a public nuisance may be terminated immediately by public authorities. Zoning ordinances sometimes

---

[26] Los Angeles Municipal Code, sec. 12.23.C.1(a).
[27] Id., sec. 12.23.B.1(a).
[28] Id., sec. 12.23.A.6.

declare that a use which is in violation of the ordinance constitutes a nuisance. If the courts agree that such a legislatively declared nuisance is in fact a nuisance, the offending use may be terminated. Courts generally are inclined to regard the question as to whether a use is a nuisance to be more of a legislative than a judicial matter and tend to uphold the ordinance without serious examination.

ENFORCEMENT OF ZONING LAWS

Many Violations Go Undetected
Although the power to enforce zoning regulations is both real and extensive, many violations go undetected and consequently the regulations are unenforced. Zoning authorities seldom have any effective regularized system for checking on and discovering zoning violations. Because of limited personnel, authorities responsible for zoning law enforcement must to a large extent rely on neighboring landowners and other government agencies to apprise them of the existence of violations. As a result of these shortcomings, the chance that a violation will be discovered is an improbable one.

Requirement for Zoning Report
Both as a consumer protection device and a means of discovering zoning violations, some states[29] have passed laws empowering local governments to enact ordinances requiring sellers to obtain a zoning report from designated authorities prior to the sale of residential buildings. The report will indicate the zoning classification of the property being sold and its authorized occupancy and use and must be delivered to the buyer prior to the consummation of the sale.

In jurisdictions where zoning reports are not required a buyer may have a cause of action for fraud or misrepresentation against a seller who knows his property violates zoning regulations. Situations giving rise to a buyer's cause of action range from one in which a seller who knows of a violation deliberately assures the buyer that none exists to the situation where the seller simply fails to disclose a known zoning violation which the buyer could not have discovered through ordinary diligence.

Notice of Violation
When zoning authorities learn of a zoning violation, they send a notice of the violation to the property owner together with a demand that he do whatever is necessary to bring the property into conformity with applicable regulations. Where the demand is ignored or improperly satisfied, several remedies are available to local authorities.

Abatement and Injunction
Zoning violations that constitute public nuisances may be terminated by abatement actions brought by appropriate public officers or authorities. Not all zoning violations, of course, amount to public nuisances, nor is there any requirement that they must do so in order to be terminated. Zoning regulations quite properly can prohibit uses of land that do not amount to nuisances.

Zoning violations which are not public nuisances and hence cannot be abated may nonetheless be terminated by an injunction obtained by public authorities. Injunctions are widely used to enforce compliance with zoning regulations.

Penalties for Violation
The Standard State Zoning Enabling Act, setting the pattern for a large number of state enabling acts, empowers local legislative bodies to provide for enforcement of the act and any ordinance or regulation made in accordance with it. The standard act also provides that "A violation of this act or such ordinance or regulation is hereby declared to be a misdemeanor, and such local legislative body may provide for the punishment thereof by fine or imprisonment or both."[30]

---

[29] For example, California Government Code, secs. 38780 et seq.

[30] Standard State Zoning Enabling Act, sec. 8.

In addition to the foregoing criminal penalties, the standard act also empowers local legislative bodies to impose civil penalties on zoning violators.[31]

BUILDING CODES

In addition to being required to conform to zoning ordinances that regulate the use of his property, an owner desirous of erecting a building on his land must comply with the applicable building codes.

Nature of Building Codes

Building codes, which are part of the land use controls of most communities, establish detailed standards for the construction of new buildings and the alteration of existing ones. Like zoning regulations, building codes restrict an owner's freedom to use his land as he sees fit. The regulating of land use by establishment of building standards is a proper exercise of the police power, provided, of course, the standards imposed are necessary for the general welfare and are neither arbitrary nor unreasonable. Building regulations which are entirely reasonable and proper in a densely populated urban center may be unreasonable and oppressive in a small and sparsely populated town. The determination as to whether a building regulation is reasonably necessary is a matter of judgment and discretion of the local legislative body and unless the regulation is clearly arbitrary and unreasonable with no substantial relation to the public welfare, the courts will uphold it.

Objective of Building Codes

A principal objective of building codes is the protection and preservation of the health and safety of a community. Building regulations are commonly in the nature of fire laws that require buildings to meet minimum requirements with respect to entrances and exits and the use of fire resistance materials. Building code provisions also regulate the quality, strength, or safety of construction or structural safeguards. Code regulations designed to promote a decent and sanitary mode of living are, when reasonable in scope and effect, justified under the police power.

As with zoning, the courts generally refuse to regard building regulations that are based solely on aesthetic considerations as being a proper exercise of the police power.

Local legislative bodies may require reasonable changes in existing buildings in order for them to comply with new standards and requirements for the protection of the public health and safety, notwithstanding the fact that at the time such buildings were erected they complied with regulations then in effect. The question to be considered in such cases is whether the public welfare requires retroactive application of the new code regulations or whether such application is unreasonable as applied to the properties affected by them.

Compelling Removal of Building

In accordance with their power to abate nuisances, local authorities may compel the removal or demolition of a building which has become a public nuisance. Removal or demolition can be ordered, however, only if danger arises from the building itself and not simply from the use to which it is put, or provided the danger cannot be remedied by some means other than destruction.

Local legislative bodies can declare buildings which constitute a menace to the health and safety of the public to be a nuisance. But such a legislative declaration does not make a building a nuisance when in fact it is not. Where the declaration is challenged, only a court of competent jurisdiction can determine whether a nuisance actually exists or not.

Building Permits

Local legislative bodies have the authority to enact legislation requiring persons who desire to construct, alter, or substantially repair build-

---

[31] Id.

ings to apply to some official or board for permission to do so. The conditions which an applicant for a building permit must meet must be reasonable ones and refusals to grant a permit are subject to judicial review to determine whether the applicant's constitutional rights have been impaired. Applications for building permits are examined by officials or boards for compliance both with applicable building codes and zoning ordinances.

Although there is some difference of opinion among the states, the more common view is that once a building permit has properly been issued to an applicant, it cannot be arbitrarily revoked by local authorities, especially where the applicant has incurred substantial expense on the basis of it. However, if the holder of a building permit fails to comply with the terms and conditions contained in the permit or to conform to the building plans submitted with his application, the permit may be revoked.

The validity of regulations which require such safeguards as roofed passageways, sidewalk enclosures, etc., during the process of constructing a building has generally been upheld.

QUESTIONS

1 In what respect are zoning regulations and restrictive covenants similar? How do they differ?
2 According to the Standard State Zoning Enabling Act, what are some of the purposes served by zoning regulations?
3 What is the nature of the police power? How is it limited?
4 What does comprehensive zoning of an area do to it?
5 Explain how zoning theory classifies different types of uses of land in accordance with their relative restrictiveness.
6 Indicate three ways in which the intensity of land use can be regulated by zoning ordinances.
7 Distinguish between cumulative and noncumulative zoning.
8 What is aesthetic zoning? Why do courts in a majority of states object to it?
9 What does a landowner do when he seeks legislative relief from existing zoning regulations? Upon what does he generally base his request for relief?
10 What is a variance? Describe the two kinds of variances?
11 What is a nonconforming use of land? What are the different forms that nonconforming uses take?
12 Indicate some of the problems that can arise in connection with amortization provisions in zoning ordinances.
13 How are zoning laws enforced?
14 What are building codes? What is their principal objective?

Chapter 21

Pollution Control and Environmental Protection

The word **environment** has been defined as meaning "the physical conditions which will be affected by a proposed action, including land, air, water, minerals, flora, fauna, noise, objects of historic or aesthetic significance, existing patterns of population, distribution, or growth, and existing community or neighborhood character."[1]

Man's environment has been described as consisting of the totality of his surroundings—the natural and man-made physical, biological, and cultural factors that affect his health, senses, and intellect. The principal *physical* features of his environment are land, water, air, climate, sound, odor, and structures erected by man. *Biological* environmental factors include both wild and domestic plants and animals, whether natural or introduced, and of course man himself. Architectural styles, human activities, and the available services and amenities that are characteristic of a given stage of civilization are features of man's *cultural* environment.[2]

In commenting on the use of the word "environment" in an important federal statute,[3] the Department of Housing and Urban Development (HUD) has said that "the term is meant to be interpreted broadly to include physical, social, cultural, and aesthetic dimen-

---

[1] Proposed State Environmental Policy Act, sec. 4(4), Council of State Governments, 33 *Suggested State Legislation* p. 6 (1974).

[2] See the report, "Environmental Bill of Rights," California Assembly Select Committee on Environmental Quality, p. 14, Mar. 16, 1970.

[3] National Environmental Policy Act, 42 U.S.C., sec. 4321 et seq.; Public Law 91-90, Jan. 1, 1970.

332

sions. Examples of environmental considerations are: air and water quality, erosion control, natural hazards, land use planning, site selection and design, subdivision development, conservation of flora and fauna, urban congestion, overcrowding, displacement and relocation resulting from public and private action or natural disaster, noise pollution, urban blight, preservation of cultural resources, including properties on the National Register of Historic Places, urban design and the quality of the built environment, the impact of the environment on people and their activities."[4]

DEVELOPMENT OF ENVIRONMENTAL LAW

Although the control of environmental pollution is not a new concern of the law, it was not until the decade of the 1960s that the quality of the environment became a major social issue. Prior to the 1960s, the doctrines of nuisance and trespass and the police power served to protect an owner's enjoyment of his property and the health of the public from activities that threatened the environment with contamination and deterioration. But these control measures, while adequate to regulate particular instances when pollution was alleged and found, were unsuited to cope with the broader problem of environmental degradation and the growing social awareness of the need to do something about it. Increasing industrialization has raised questions as to whether environmental pollution is the necessary price of progress, has caused misgivings as to the continuing capacity of the physical environment to absorb wastes, and has sharpened the awareness of the fact that the earth's resources are not inexhaustible.

As a result of these factors, by the latter part of the 1960s a new set of controls for the prevention and containment of environmental pollution and the conservation of resources had begun to develop. Conservation laws of the past became environmental laws and the conservationists of an earlier era became today's environmentalists.

We previously noted that it is by means of our legal system that organized society adopts rules and regulations designed to achieve certain socially desirable objectives. At any point in time, the particular goals sought and the means of achieving them are reflections of the attitudes and philosophies of whatever segment of society may be instrumental in having appropriate legislation enacted. Until relatively recently, no one particular social philosophy regarding the environment was dominant enough to serve as the foundation for a body of environmental law. Since society is composed of some who desire to exploit the natural environment, others who want to preserve it at all costs, and still others who are indifferent to environmental factors, a consensus with respect to environmental goals was slow in developing.

The creation and development of a body of environmental law has given rise to a new set of legal rights and duties. The objective of environmental law is to define and protect the environmental rights of both individuals and society. If a complaining party is to prevail in a court action based on environmental issues, he is charged with establishing three things: (1) that the law has accorded him a certain right or rights with respect to his surroundings, (2) that his right or rights have been violated by the party against whom he complains, and (3) that the law has provided him with a legal remedy that is capable of redressing the injury which the complainant sustained.

Because it is a relatively new field of law, environmental law is still in the process of defining the respective rights of the public and individuals and assigning relative priorities to them. Every law designed to protect the environment implicitly defines and assigns private

---

[4] "Departmental Policies, Responsibilities and Procedures for Protection and Enforcement of Environmental Quality" (also known as HUD Handbook 1390.1), Department of Housing and Urban Development, 38 Federal Register 19182, July 18, 1973.

and public legal rights and duties. A law which asserts that the public has a right to reasonably clean air and water, for example, implies that industry and others do not have the right to use air and water in such a way as to interfere with the public's right. And laws that impose rigid pollution control standards on industry imply that the cost of such controls in the first instance must be borne by industry but may thereafter be passed on to the ultimate consumers of industry's product.

The adoption of environmental laws, both at the federal and state levels, has engendered a greater public interest and encouraged a broader public participation in environmental matters, especially where the physical environment is concerned. The publicity surrounding the debates and passage of environmental legislation has quickened the awareness of a growing segment of society that the environment does not have an infinite capacity to absorb an increasing volume of waste and has stimulated the realization that our natural resources are not without limit.

There are private injuries caused by environmental pollution for which the injured party ought to be compensated and litigation involving such injuries is not much different from other controversies involving torts. There are also violations of legally established environmental standards that result in wide-ranging injuries that involve the public interest in a more general way. In the latter case, environmental pollution controls are enforced by public agencies to which such a task has been delegated by legislative directives.

Rather than penalizing polluters by means of fines and payment of damages, environmental laws today tend more toward the types of sanctions that compel compliance in a more direct fashion. The assessment of damages against polluters that are less than the amount of the economic benefits derived by the offender in failing to comply with environmental regulations obviously does little to compel compliance and hence to improve the quality of the environment. Remedies in the form of injunctions and abatement orders are the principal sanctions of modern environmental laws. Ideally, injunctions would be issued in a form that compels compliance with environmental laws at the least economic cost.

Property damage and personal injuries sustained by individuals as a consequence of air and water pollution are not new phenomena. While the term "air pollution," for example, may be a relatively modern one, private actions for nuisance due to the emission of smoke, dust, noxious gases, and noisome odors have been brought for a long time. While nuisance was the earliest theory on which such private actions were brought, more recently private air pollution litigation has been based on the tort of trespass—the unlawful invasion of a possessory interest in land. While nuisance and trespass actions may serve to protect an individual or a class of persons from activities that interfere with the quality of life and the enjoyment of property, the growing awareness of degradation of the larger environment has resulted in legislation authorizing and requiring regulation and control of the environment by public authorities.

FEDERAL ENVIRONMENTAL LEGISLATION

At the federal level, Congress has enacted laws designed to prevent or control the pollution of particular aspects of the physical environment as well as broader legislation intended to protect the physical environment in all of its aspects. Significant among the federal laws directed toward the control of specific types of pollution are the federal acts concerned with the quality of air and water, the control of noise, and the regulation of disposal of solid waste. In addition to the regulation of particular areas of man's environment, the Congress has enacted a broad environmental act intended to protect all aspects of the physical environment from preventable contamination and degradation.

Control of Air Pollution

Air becomes polluted or contaminated when its capacity to dilute pollutants emitted into it is overburdened or exceeded. Air pollution is primarily an urban problem that results from population concentration and growth, from industry, and from modern society's substantial dependence on internal combustion engines. The serious adverse effects that result from air pollution are numerous. Besides the soiling of homes and buildings by causing exterior paint to crack and peel, the prevalence of offensive odors, and the harmful effects on plant life and crops, the primary impact of air pollution is on human health.

The **Air Quality Act**,[5] which was passed by Congress in 1967, established a program for the control of air pollution throughout the United States. While the primary responsibility for developing and enforcing air pollution standards was left to the individual states, the federal government assumed the leadership role in the fight against contamination of the air. The Air Quality Act, as amended by the Clean Air Amendments of 1970,[6] requires the federal Environmental Protection Agency to establish primary and secondary air quality standards.[7]

Primary air quality standards, according to the act, are those that are necessary to protect the *public health*, while *secondary* standards are needed to guard the *public welfare*. The notion underlying the establishment of air quality standards on a national basis is that all regions of the country should be free from air pollution above a certain tolerable level.

Control of Water Pollution

Water pollution is of two types: (1) *biological* pollution which results from the discharge of sewage and other biological wastes into water and (2) *chemical* pollution which stems from the release of significant amounts of toxic chemicals into rivers and lakes.

The "poisoning" of a watercourse was early recognized by the law as grounds for a cause of action. Private users who had rights to reasonably clean water were clearly the first to combat water pollution by those who used waterways as open sewers and cheap means for the transportation and disposal of waste. But the problem of water pollution was and is too general to be resolved by private suits brought to protect private interests.

Federal Water Pollution Control Act The principal national legislation for the prevention of water pollution is the **Federal Water Pollution Control Act**[8] as substantially amended in 1972. The amended act declares that it is the objective of the legislation "to restore and maintain the chemical, physical, and biological integrity of the Nation's waters."[9] The act further states that it is "the national goal that the discharge of pollutants into the navigable waters be eliminated by 1985"[10] and that "wherever attainable, an interim goal of water quality which provides for the protection and propagation of fish, shellfish, and wildlife and provides for recreation in and on the water be achieved by July 1, 1983."[11] The act also declares it to be a national policy to prohibit "the discharge of toxic pollutants in toxic amounts."[12]

The Federal Water Pollution Control Act is administered by the Environmental Protection Agency.

Federal Ocean Dumping Act In addition to amending the Federal Water Pollution Control Act, Congress passed the Marine Protection, Research and Sanctuaries Act[13] in 1972 which

---

[5] 42 U.S.C., sec. 1857 et seq.
[6] 42 U.S.C., secs. 1857–1858a.
[7] Id., sec. 1857c-4.
[8] 33 U.S.C., secs. 1251 et seq.
[9] Id., sec. 1251(a).
[10] Id.
[11] Id., sec. 1251(a)(2).
[12] Id., sec. 1251(a)(3).
[13] 33 U.S.C. secs. 1401 et seq.

is more commonly referred to as the **"Federal Ocean Dumping Act."** In a manner similar to the Federal Water Pollution Control Act's protection of inland waters, the Federal Ocean Dumping Act regulates the discharge and dumping of waste in the offshore areas of the ocean over which the United States has control.

Safe Drinking Water Act In 1974 Congress amended the Public Health Service Act by enacting the **Safe Drinking Water Act.**[14] A report by a committee of the House of Representatives[15] states that "The purpose of the legislation is to assure that water supply systems serving the public meet minimum national standards for the protection of the public health. At present, the Environmental Protection Agency is authorized to prescribe Federal drinking water standards only for water supplies used by interstate carriers. Furthermore," the report continues, "these standards may only be enforced with respect to contaminants capable of causing communicable disease."[16] The report points out that in contrast to existing legislation the Safe Drinking Water Act "would (1) authorize the Environmental Protection Agency to establish Federal standards for protection from *all harmful contaminants,* which standards would be applicable to *all public water systems,* and (2) establish a joint Federal-State system for assuring compliance with these standards and for protecting underground sources of drinking water."[17] [Emphasis added.]

Based on evidence presented at hearings, the House committee was of the opinion that legislation in effect at the time the Safe Drinking Water Act was passed was inadequate to assure that the water supplied to the public was safe to drink[18] and that "recent investigations demonstrate that the public confidence in the safety of drinking water supplies may, in many instances, be misplaced."[19] A representative sampling of 969 water systems by the Department of Health, Education, and Welfare in 1970 reflected among other things: (1) that 36 percent of 2,600 water tap samples contained one or more bacteriological or chemical elements exceeding limits set by the Public Health Service Drinking Water Standards; (2) that 56 percent of the water systems had physical deficiencies such as poorly protected groundwater sources, inadequate disinfection capacity, and inadequate clarification capacity; (3) that 77 percent of the water plant operators were inadequately trained in fundamental water microbiology and 46 percent of them were deficient in chemistry relating to water plant operation; (4) that an insufficient number of bacteriological samples were analyzed for 85 percent of the water systems, 69 percent not even analyzing half the number of samples required by the Public Health Service Drinking Water Standards; and (5) that in 50 percent of the water systems the plant officials could not recall when, if ever, a state or local health department had last surveyed the system and the water supply.[20]

Formulation of regulations and administration of the Safe Drinking Water Act is entrusted to the Environmental Protection Agency.

Noise Pollution and Control

Nature and Effect of Noise Pollution A committee of the U.S. Senate observed that "Noise—unwanted sound—is increasing in urban areas at a rate which may double the average person's exposure to it within 10 years."[21] Noise pollution, the committee said, like other forms of pollution is man-made and occurs as a

---

[14] 42 U.S.C., secs. 300f–300j-9.
[15] House Report (Interstate and Foreign Commerce Committee) No. 93-1185, 4 U.S. Code Congressional and Administrative News, 93d Cong., 2d Sess., 1974, pp. 6454 et seq.
[16] Id., p. 6454.
[17] Id., pp. 6454–6455.

[18] Id., p. 6456.
[19] Id., p. 6457.
[20] Id., pp. 6457–6458.
[21] Senate Report (Public Works Committee) No. 92-1160, 3 U.S. Code Congressional and Administrative News, 92d Cong., 2d Sess., 1972, p. 4655.

by-product of an enormous number of commercial and domestic machines. The acoustic vibrations which make up noise pollution are invisible, they leave no residue, and they disappear almost instantly when the noise is turned off.[22]

The Senate committee noted that testimony "indicates clearly that the impact of noise goes well beyond mere unpleasantness, stress, and other psychic effects. It may in fact cause serious physiological effects on the human body ranging from deafness to enhanced risk of cardiovascular disease to alteration of fetal nervous systems."[23] "According to the Environmental Protection Agency," the committee added, "noise has a significant impact on more than 80 million Americans. Of those, about 40 million persons are literally listening to a health hazard, risking hearing impairment and other physiological effects."[24] Because noisemakers abound in urban environments, it is almost impossible for an individual to find even short unbroken periods of rest or retreat from noise.

Private Actions for Excessive Noise The right to bring a lawsuit for the consequences of excessive and unreasonable noise has long been recognized at common law. While such actions have traditionally been based on the law of nuisance, claims for protection against noise have also been founded on negligence and, where overflights by aircraft are involved, theories of trespass and inverse condemnation have been invoked. While noise itself is not normally considered to be a trespassory invasion of land, overflights by aircraft may constitute a trespass and the resulting injury be caused by excessive and unreasonable noise.

The law of private nuisance is particularly suited to actions resulting from noise because, as we observed in Chapter 7, a private nuisance action is based on interference with one's quiet enjoyment of his property and the consequences of another person's acts rather than his intent.

Noise Control Act Federal regulation aimed at creating a quieter environment in which to live is a relatively new development. Until recently, noise pollution has largely been regarded as a local problem to be controlled by local authorities. The first federal regulatory legislation dealing directly with noise pollution concerned the problem of aircraft noise. By a 1968 amendment to the Federal Aviation Act,[25] the Congress directed the Federal Aviation Administration to consider aircraft noise as a factor when certifying aircraft.

General noise pollution was not given specialized attention by the federal government until the **Noise Control Act** of 1972[26] was enacted. The act is similar in many of its features to the earlier federal legislation regulating the areas of air and water pollution.

Objective of the Act The federal Noise Control Act of 1972 declares it to be the national policy to promote an environment free from noise that jeopardizes the public health and welfare.[27] Commenting on the act, the Senate Public Works Committee stated that the act was based on the theory that, while primary responsibility for noise control rests with state and local governments, federal action is required to deal effectively with noise problems created by vehicles, construction equipment, and other machinery which commonly move in interstate commerce. The committee pointed out that the major regulatory objective of the legislation was to require the EPA administrator to establish emission standards for newly manufactured products which he identifies as being major sources of noise.[28]

---

[22] Id.
[23] Id.
[24] Id.
[25] 49 U.S.C., sec. 1431 et seq.
[26] 42 U.S.C., sec. 4901 et seq.
[27] Id., sec. 4901(b).
[28] Senate Report (Public Works Committee) No. 92-1160, 3 U.S. Code Congressional and Administrative News,

The term "product" as used in the act specifically excludes aircraft and related components but "Noise emission standards must be established for any major source which falls into the categories of construction equipment, transportation equipment, motors or engines, turbines and compressors, percussion and explosive equipment, or electrical and electronic equipment (other than sound reproduction equipment)."[29]

Noise Emission Standards The EPA administrator is required to set limits on noise emissions which in his judgment reflect the degree of noise reduction achievable through the application of the best available technology, taking into account the cost of compliance. The committee pointed out that "While the intention of the whole bill is to protect public health and welfare from environmental noise, the Committee expects that the application of the best available technology will just begin to realize that goal in the foreseeable future."[30]

After the date on which noise emission standards for a given product become effective, "the manufacturer of that product must warrant to the purchaser and subsequent owners of that product that it conforms with the standards at the time of sale and that it is free from defects in materials and workmanship which cause the product, under normal use, operation, and maintenance to fail to conform during its useful life."[31]

Control of Solid Waste Disposal

The federal **Solid Waste Disposal Act** has twice been amended and while it now appears as Title II of the Resource Conservation and Recovery Act of 1976, it continues to be referred to and cited as the Solid Waste Disposal Act.[32]

Although the title of the act continues to use the term "solid waste," the House committee to which the pending legislation was referred recognized "that Solid Waste, the traditional term for trash or refuse is inappropriate. The words solid waste are laden with false connotations. . . . The words *discarded materials* more accurately reflect the Committee's interest." [Emphasis added.] The committee pointed out that "Not only solid wastes, but also liquid and contained gaseous wastes, semi-solid wastes and sludges are the subject of this legislation."[33] The committee stated that it was concerned not only with the waste by-products of manufacturing but also with the products themselves once they have served their purposes and are no longer wanted by the consumer. "For these reasons," the committee said, "the term discarded materials is used to identify collectively those substances often referred to as industrial, municipal or post-consumer waste; refuse, trash, garbage, and sludge."[34]

---

[29] 92d Cong., 2d Sess., 1972, p. 4657. For the EPA administrator's list of noise sources, see Environmental Protection Agency, "Identification of Products as Major Sources of Noise," 39 Federal Register p. 22297 (1974).

[29] Senate Report (Public Works Committee) No. 92-1160, 3 U.S. Code Congressional and Administrative News, 92d Cong., 2d Sess., 1972, pp. 4658–4659.

[30] Id., p. 4659.

[31] Id.

[32] Originally enacted as the Solid Waste Disposal Act of 1965, Public Law 89-272 (1965), it was first amended by the Resource Recovery Act of 1970, Public Law 91-512 (1970), and later by the Resource Conservation and Recovery Act of 1976, Public Law 94-580 (1976). As Title II of the 1976 act, it appears at 42 U.S.C., secs. 6901 et seq.

[33] House Report (Interstate and Foreign Commerce Committee) No. 94-1491, 5 U.S. Code Congressional and Administrative News, 94th Cong., 2d Sess., 1976, p. 6240.

As defined by the Resource Conservation and Recovery Act, "The term 'solid waste' means any garbage, refuse, sludge from a waste treatment plant, water supply treatment plant, or air pollution control facility and other discarded material, including solid, liquid, semisolid, or contained gaseous material resulting from industrial, commercial, mining, and agricultural operations, and from community activities, but does not include solid or dissolved material in domestic sewage, or solid and dissolved materials in irrigation return flows or industrial discharges subject to permits under section 402 of the Federal Water Control Act, as amended (89 Stat. 880), or source, special nuclear, or byproduct material as defined by the Atomic Energy Act of 1954, as amended (68 Stat.)." 42 U.S.C., sec. 6903(27).

[34] House Report (Interstate and Foreign Commerce Committee) No. 94-1491, 5 U.S. Code Congressional and Administrative News, 94th Cong., 2d Sess., 1976, p. 6240.

Resource Conservation and Recovery Act

"The Resource Conservation and Recovery Act of 1976 is a multi-faceted approach toward solving problems associated with the 3–4 billion tons of discarded materials generated each year, and the problems resulting from the anticipated 8% annual increase in the volume of such waste."[35]

Congressional Findings The act contains a long list of Congressional findings with respect to (1) solid waste, (2) environment and health, (3) materials, and (4) energy.[36]

With respect to *solid waste,* the Congress found

1 that technological progress and improved methods of manufacture, packaging, and marketing of consumer products have "resulted in an ever-mounting increase, and a change in the characteristics, of the mass of material discarded by the purchaser of such products";

2 that national economic and population growth and an improved standard of living have required increased industrial production which, together with commercial and agricultural operations, have resulted in "a rising tide of scrap, discarded, and wasted materials";

3 that the continuing concentration of population in urban areas has created serious financial, management, and technical problems "in the disposal of wastes resulting from the industrial, commercial, domestic, and other activities carried on in such areas";

4 that while the collection and disposal of solid waste should continue to be primarily the function of state, regional, and local agencies, the problems of waste disposal have become a matter that is national in scope and in concern and require federal action "through financial and technical assistance and leadership in the development, demonstration, and application of new and improved methods and processes to reduce the amount of waste and unsalvageable materials and to provide for proper and economical solid waste disposal practices."[37]

As concerns the *environment and health,* the Congress found

1 that "although land is too valuable a national resource to be needlessly polluted by discarded materials, most solid waste is disposed of in open dumps[38] and sanitary landfills";

2 that the disposal of solid and hazardous waste in or on land without careful management "can present a danger to human health and the environment";

3 that "as a result of the Clean Air Act, the Water Pollution Control Act, and other Federal and State laws respecting public health and the environment, greater amounts of solid waste (in the form of sludge[39] and other pollution treatment residues) have been created." Also, inadequate and unsound solid waste disposal practices have created greater amounts of air and water pollution and other environmental health problems;

4 that "open dumping is particularly harmful to health, contaminates drinking water from underground and surface supplies, and pollutes the air and the land";

---

[35] Id., p. 6239.
[36] 42 U.S.C., sec. 6901 (a)–(d).
[37] 42 U.S.C., sec. 6901(a)(1)–(4).
[38] As defined by the act, "The term 'open dump' means a site for the disposal of solid waste which is not a sanitary landfill within the meaning of section 4004." 42 U.S.C., 6903(14).
Section 4004 of Public Law 94-580 provides: "Not later than one year after October 21, 1976, after consultation with the States, and after notice and public hearings, the Administrator [of EPA] shall promulgate regulations containing criteria for determining which facilities shall be classified as sanitary landfills and which shall be classified as open dumps within the meaning of this chapter. At a minimum, such criteria shall provide that a facility may be classified as a sanitary landfill and not as an open dump only if there is no reasonable probability of adverse effects on health or the environment from disposal of solid waste at such facility. Such regulations may provide for the classification of types of sanitary landfills." 42 U.S.C., sec. 6944.
[39] "The term 'sludge' means any solid, semisolid or liquid waste generated from a municipal, commercial, or industrial wastewater treatment plant, water supply treatment plant, or air pollution control facility or any other such waste having similar characteristics and effects." 42 U.S.C., sec. 6903(26A).

5 that hazardous waste[40] presents special dangers to health and requires a greater degree of regulation than nonhazardous solid waste; and

6 that, because many cities will be running out of suitable solid waste disposal sites within 5 years unless immediate action is taken, alternative methods of disposal must be developed.[41]

The House Interstate and Foreign Commerce Committee's report on the act states that the "overriding concern" of the committee was "the effect on the population and the environment of the disposal of discarded hazardous wastes—those which by virtue of their composition or longevity are harmful, toxic, or lethal. Unless neutralized or otherwise properly managed in their disposal, hazardous wastes present a clear danger to the health and safety of the population and to the quality of the environment."[42]

Hazardous wastes, the committee pointed out, typically have little, if any, economic value, often are not susceptible to neutralization, present serious danger to human life and the environment, and can only be safely stored, treated, or disposed of at considerable cost to the one who generates such wastes. Because of these factors, a regulatory approach is necessary to solve the problem that hazardous wastes present. "Without a regulatory framework, such hazardous waste will continue to be disposed of in ponds or lagoons or on the ground in such a manner that results in substantial and sometimes irreversible pollution of the environment."[43]

With respect to *materials,* the Congress found

1 that "millions of tons of recoverable materials which could be used are needlessly buried each year";

2 that there are methods available for separating usable materials from solid waste; and

3 that the recovery of such materials can reduce our dependence on foreign resources and reduce the balance of payments deficit.[44]

With regard to *energy,* the Congress found

1 that "solid waste represents a potential source of solid fuel, oil, or gas that can be converted into energy";

2 that there is a present need to develop alternative energy sources "to reduce our dependence on such sources as petroleum products, natural gas, nuclear and hydroelectric generation"; and

3 that the technology exists today to produce usable energy from solid waste.[45]

The House committee reported that it had determined that discarded materials have value because energy and usable materials can be recovered from them. The committee observed that "In the recovery of such energy or materials, a number of environmental dangers can be avoided. Scarce land supply can be protected. The balance of trade deficit can be reduced. The nation's reliance on foreign energy and materials can be reduced and useful employment can be generated by the construction of needed waste management facilities."[46]

Objectives of the Act The stated objectives of the Resource Conservation and Recovery

---

[40] "The term 'hazardous waste' means a solid waste, or a combination of solid wastes, which because of its quantity, concentration, or physical, chemical or infectious characteristics may—

"(A) cause, or significantly contribute to an increase in mortality or an increase in serious irreversible, or incapacitating reversible, illness; or

"(B) pose a substantial present or potential hazard to human health or the environment when improperly treated, stored, transported, or disposed of, or otherwise managed." 42 U.S.C., sec. 6903(5).

[41] 42 U.S.C., sec. 6901(b)(1)–(6).

[42] House Report (Interstate and Foreign Commerce Committee) No. 94-1491, 5 U.S. Code Congressional and Administrative News, 94th Cong., 2d Sess., 1976, p. 6241.

[43] Id.

[44] 42 U.S.C., sec. 6901(c)(1)–(3).

[45] 42 U.S.C., sec. 6901(d)(1)–(3).

[46] House Report (Interstate and Foreign Commerce Committee) No. 94-1491, 5 U.S. Code Congressional and Administrative News, 94th Cong., 2d Sess., 1976, p. 6241.

Act of 1976 are "to promote the protection of health and the environment and to conserve valuable material and energy resources."[47] According to the act, these objectives are to be attained by

1 providing technical and financial assistance to state and local governments and interstate agencies for the development of solid waste management plans that will promote improved management techniques, new and improved methods of collection, separation, and recovery of solid waste, and the environmentally safe disposal of nonrecoverable wastes;
2 providing grants for training in occupations that involve the design, operation, and maintenance of solid waste disposal systems;
3 prohibiting future open dumping on land and requiring that existing open dumps be converted to facilities which do not pose a danger to the environment or to health;
4 regulating the treatment, storage, transportation, and disposal of hazardous wastes which have adverse effects on health and the environment;
5 providing for the preparation and issuance of guidelines for the collection, transport, separation, and recovery of solid waste, and disposal practices and systems;
6 promoting a national research and development program for improved waste management and resource conservation techniques, and better methods of collection, separation, recovery, and recycling of solid wastes;
7 promoting the demonstration of solid waste management, resource recovery, and resource conservation systems that preserve and enhance the quality of air, water, and land resources; and
8 establishing a cooperative effort among federal, state, and local governments and private enterprise in order that valuable materials and energy may be recovered from solid waste.[48]

The House committee expressed the belief that the Resource Conservation and Recovery Act of 1976 "eliminates the last remaining loophole in environmental law"—that loophole being the unregulated disposal of discarded materials and hazardous wastes. The committee believed that the legislation was necessary if other environmental laws were to be effective. "At present the federal government is spending billions of dollars to remove pollutants from air and water, only to dispose of such pollutants in an environmentally unsound manner.... This legislation will eliminate this problem and permit the environmental laws to function in a coordinated and effective way."[49]

Separation of Functions of the Act According to the House committee's report, the provisions of the act recognize that regulatory functions and strictly promotional functions relating to the management of discarded materials are separate and conflicting functions. As a consequence, the two types of functions are assigned to separate agencies so that each can better carry out the Congressional directives contained in the act. "The justification for this separation of functions," the committee points out, "is so that one agency does not promote solely the technology it has developed or to develop markets solely for the products recovered by a process developed by the agency."[50]

The act provides that "The Administrator [of EPA] shall establish within the Environmental Protection Agency an Office of Solid Waste"[51] and that office is responsible for carrying out the regulatory, technical, and planning functions of the act. A primary function of the Office of Solid Waste is "to develop reasonably flexible guidelines for State and regional discarded materials management plans. Such plans will prohibit open dumping and promote

---

[47] 42 U.S.C., sec. 6902.
[48] 42 U.S.C., sec. 6902(1)–(8).
[49] House Report (Interstate and Foreign Commerce Committee) No. 94-1491, 5 U.S. Code Congressional and Administrative News, 94th Cong., 2d Sess., 1976, pp. 6241–6242.
[50] Id., p. 6242.
[51] 42 U.S.C., sec. 6911.

rehabilitation of existing open dumps."[52] In addition, the Administrator is given authority to make financial grants to state and local governments for developing and enforcing their discarded materials plans and hazardous waste management programs and also to make technical assistance available to them.

Promotional functions that relate to resource recovery technology, the development of markets for recovered materials, and the development of an index which shows the characteristics of recovered materials that can be substituted for virgin materials[53] with similar performance characteristics are placed in the Department of Commerce.[54] "The Department of Commerce is directed to promote proven resource recovery technology; to help identify and stimulate markets for materials recovered; to develop specifications for recovered materials so they can be substituted for virgin materials; and to promote the transfer of resource recovery technology within the industry so as to encourage the improvement of such technology."[55]

Federal Procurement of Recovered Materials When using federally appropriated funds, federal agencies are required to procure recovered materials when those materials are available at reasonable prices.[56] By way of assisting federal agencies in determining whether a recovered material has the performance characteristics of a virgin material, the National Bureau of Standards is required to establish a substitutibility index. The index will show when recovered materials can be substituted for virgin materials.

COASTAL ZONE CONSERVATION AND MANAGEMENT

The significance of the coastal zone of the United States and the need for conservation and prudent management of it has been the subject of critical examination and comment by an important committee of the U.S. Senate.[57]

Problem Created by Population Concentration
In its comments the Senate committee pointed out that

> The problems of the coastal zone are characterized by burgeoning populations congregating in ever larger urban systems, creating growing demands for commercial, residential, recreational, and other development, often at the expense of natural values that include some of the most productive areas found anywhere on earth. Already 53% of the population of the United States, some 106,000,000 people, live within those cities and counties within 50 miles of the coasts of the Atlantic and Pacific Oceans, the Gulf of Mexico, and the Great Lakes. Some estimates project that by the year 2000, 80% of our population may live in that same area, perhaps 225,000,000 people.
>
> The space available for that increased population will not change significantly in the next thirty years. The demand for that limited space will increase dramatically. . . . [58]

Need to Expand State Control of Coastal Zone
The Senate committee noted that while local governments until recently have exercised most of the states' powers to regulate land and water uses, in the last few years a change has been taking place, particularly as the states have recognized the need for better management of the coastal zone. Despite recognition of this fact, however, the state and local governments have

---

[52] House Report (Interstate and Foreign Commerce Committee) No. 94-1491, 5 U.S. Code Congressional and Administrative News, 94th Cong., 2d Sess., 1976, p. 6242.

[53] The act states that "The term 'virgin material' means a raw material, including previously unused copper, aluminum, lead, zinc, iron, or other metal or metal ore, any undeveloped resource that is, or with new technology will become, a source of raw materials." 42 U.S.C., sec. 6903(35).

[54] 42 U.S.C., secs. 6951–6954.

[55] House Report (Interstate and Foreign Commerce Committee) No. 94-1491, 5 U.S. Code Congressional and Administrative News, 94th Cong., 2d Sess., 1976, p. 6243.

[56] 42 U.S.C., sec. 6962.

[57] Senate Report (Commerce Committee) No. 92-753, 3 U.S. Code Congressional and Administrative News, 92d Cong., 2d Sess., 1972, pp. 4776 et seq.

[58] Id., p. 4777.

failed to deal adequately with pressures calling for economic development which has resulted in "numerous examples of commercial development within the coastal zone taking precedence over protection of the land and waters in the coastal zone."[59] The committee pointed to "the need for expanding state participation in the control of land and water use in the coastal zone,"[60] and expressed the belief that the states presently possess "the resources, administrative machinery and enforcement powers, and constitutional authority on which to build a sound coastal zone management program."[61] But, the committee noted, the coastal states require assistance in assuming the responsibility for management of the coastal zone and stated that the "key to more effective use of the coastal zone in the future is the introduction of management systems permitting conscious and informed choices among various alternatives."[62]

To assist in achieving the goal of better management and conservation of the land and water resources within the coastal zone, the Congress in 1972 enacted the **Coastal Zone Management Act.**[63]

Coastal Zone Management Act

Definition of Coastal Zone The act defines the *coastal zone* as including "the non-Federal coastal waters and the land beneath the coastal waters, and the adjacent non-Federal shore lands including the waters therein and thereunder." The offshore limit of the coastal zone is "the outer limit of the territorial sea, beyond which the States have no clear authority to act."[64] The inner boundary of the coastal zone "is somewhat flexible. It extends inland only to the extent necessary to allow the management program to control shorelands whose use have a direct and significant impact upon the coastal water."[65]

Purpose of the Act The main purpose of the Coastal Zone Management Act is to encourage and assist the states in "preparing and implementing management programs to preserve, protect, develop and whenever possible restore the resources of the coastal zone of the United States."[66] The act authorizes the making of federal grants-in-aid to coastal states for development of coastal zone management programs and to help in the implementation of such programs once they have been approved. "Through the system of providing grants-in-aid, the States are provided financial incentives to undertake the responsibility for setting up management programs in the coastal zone. There is no attempt to diminish state authority through federal preemption. The intent of this legislation is to enhance state authority by encouraging and assisting the states to assume planning and regulatory powers over their coastal zones."[67]

Federal Grants to States Federal grants-in-aid to states to assist in the development of management programs for the land and water resources of a state's coastal zone are limited to two-thirds of the cost of the program in any one year[68] and are conditioned upon a state meeting certain program requirements.

In addition to identifying the boundaries of

---

[59] Id., p. 4779.
[60] Id., p. 4780.
[61] Id.
[62] Id., p. 4781.
[63] P.L. 92-583 (1972), 16 U.S.C., secs. 1451 et seq.
[64] In 1953 Congress passed the Submerged Lands Act (43 U.S.C., secs. 1301–1343) which vested in the states title to land and natural resources beneath the navigable waters within their boundaries. The act limits the offshore or seaward boundaries of the states to three geographical miles in the Atlantic and Pacific Oceans and to three marine leagues in the Gulf of Mexico. The U.S. Supreme Court has held that only Florida and Texas have offshore boundaries extending three marine leagues, the other Gulf states being limited to three geographical miles. *U.S. v. Louisiana,* 363 U.S. 1 (1960) and *U.S. v. Florida,* 363 U.S. 121 (1960).
[65] Senate Report (Commerce Committee) No. 92-753, 3 U.S. Code Congressional and Administrative News, 92d Cong., 2d Sess., 1972, p. 4783, 16 U.S.C., sec. 1453(a).
[66] Id., p. 4776.
[67] Id.
[68] 16 U.S.C., sec. 1454(c).

the coastal zone and designating areas of particular concern within the zone, a management program must include a definition of permissible land and water uses within the coastal zone and set forth guidelines as to the priority of uses in particular areas.[69] A state's coastal management program must also include a description of the organizational structure proposed to implement the management program, "including the responsibilities and interrelationships of local, areawide, state, regional, and interstate agencies in the management process."[70]

Before a state's coastal management program is approved, the Secretary of Commerce must find that the state has complied with all rules and regulations promulgated by him and that the state has established an effective mechanism for continuing consultation and coordination between the different levels of government and various agencies involved in carrying out the purposes of the Coastal Zone Management Act.[71] A state's program will not be approved unless the state can show that it has adequate authority to administer land and water use regulations and control development to assure compliance with the management program and to resolve conflicts that may arise between competing users.[72]

NATIONAL ENVIRONMENTAL POLICY ACT (NEPA)

The **National Environmental Policy Act** of 1969,[73] hereinafter referred to as "NEPA," was Congress' response to demands for the creation of an agency to coordinate the many programs aimed at environmental protection or to oversee conservation and environmental efforts generally.

Purposes of the Act

The stated purposes of the act are the following: (1) to declare a national policy which will encourage productive and enjoyable harmony between man and his environment; (2) to promote efforts which will prevent or eliminate damage to the environment and biosphere and stimulate the health and welfare of man; (3) to enrich the understanding of the ecological system and natural resources important to the nation; and (4) to establish a Council on Environmental Quality.[74]

Consistent with the act's statement of purposes, NEPA is divided into two parts or titles. Title I consists of a "Declaration of National Environmental Policy" while Title II creates the Council on Environmental Quality and charges the President with submitting to Congress an annual environmental report prepared with the advice and assistance of the council.

Declaration of National Policy

Recognizing "the profound impact of man's activity on the interrelationships of all components of the natural environment" and "the critical importance of maintaining environmental quality to the overall welfare of man," Congress declared it to be "the continuing policy of the Federal Government . . . to create and maintain conditions under which man and nature can exist in productive harmony, and fulfill the social, economic, and other requirements of present and future generations of Americans."[75]

Congress asserted that "each person should enjoy a healthful environment and that each person has a responsibility to contribute to the preservation and enhancement of the environment."[76]

NEPA states that it is the continuing responsibility of the federal government to improve and coordinate federal plans, functions, programs, and resources, in order that the nation may

    1 fulfill the responsibilities of each generation as trustee of the environment for succeeding generations;

---

[69] Id., sec. 1454(b).
[70] Id., sec. 1454(b)(6).
[71] Id., sec. 1455(c)(1)(2).
[72] Id., sec. 1455(d)(1).
[73] P.L. 91-190, 42 U.S.C., secs. 4321–4347.

[74] 42 U.S.C., sec. 4321.
[75] Id., sec. 4331(a).
[76] Id., sec. 4331(c).

2 assure for all Americans safe, healthful, productive and aesthetically and culturally pleasing surroundings;

3 attain the widest range of beneficial uses of the environment without degradation, risk to health or safety, or other undesirable and unintended consequences;

4 preserve historic, cultural, and natural aspects of our national heritage, and maintain, wherever possible, an environment which supports diversity and variety of individual choice;

5 achieve a balance between population and resource use which will permit high standards of living and a wide sharing of life's amenities; and

6 enhance the quality of renewable resources and approach the maximum attainable recycling of depletable resources.[77]

The act sets forth the congressional directive that to the fullest extent possible the "policies, regulations and public laws of the United States shall be interpreted and administered in accordance with the policies set forth in this Act"[78] and that "all agencies of the Federal Government shall utilize a systematic, interdisciplinary approach which will insure the integrated use of the natural and social sciences and the environmental design arts in planning and decision making which may have an impact on man's environment."[79]

Procedures to Implement Policy

To implement the national environmental policy announced by NEPA, the act sets forth certain procedures which all federal agencies are required to follow. For every recommendation or proposal for legislation and other federal action that significantly affects the quality of the environment, the responsible agency official is required to prepare a detailed statement indicating:

(i) the environmental impact of the proposed action,

(ii) any adverse environmental effects which cannot be avoided should the proposal be implemented,

(iii) alternatives to the proposed action,

(iv) the relationship between local short-term uses of man's environment and the maintenance and enhancement of long-term productivity, and

(v) any irreversible and irretrievable commitments of resources which would be involved in the proposed action should it be implemented.[80]

The detailed statement containing the foregoing information is known as an **environmental impact statement** (EIS).

Enforcing Compliance with the Act

NEPA contains no provisions with respect to remedies available or sanctions to be applied when an agency fails to comply with the act's requirements. The act is totally devoid of procedures for its enforcement. This apparent shortcoming, however, has presented no problem to parties complaining of noncompliance.

The remedy generally sought and frequently granted is an injunction prohibiting an agency from going ahead with a program or project until an environmental impact statement that meets the requirements of the act has been made available to the appropriate parties.[81] When action by a federal agency constitutes a major federal action having a significant impact on the human environment and no environmental impact statement or an inadequate one has been filed, an injunction will normally be issued. An injunction is the only remedy suitable to prevent a possible irreversible effect on the environment before the consequences of the proposed action can be fully examined.

Act Applies to Certain Private Activities

Although the language of NEPA refers only to major *federal actions* that significantly affect the human environment,[82] guidelines prepared by the Council on Environmental Quality make

---

[77] Id., sec. 4331(b).
[78] Id., sec. 4332(1).
[79] Id., sec. 4332(2)(A).

[80] Id., sec. 4332(2)(C).
[81] Courts of Appeal in every circuit have upheld the courts' authority under the Administrative Procedures Act (5 U.S.C., sec. 701–706) to grant injunctions to enforce compliance with the provisions of NEPA.
[82] Id., sec. 4332(2)(C).

it clear that the act extends to private activity when the guidelines say that the term "actions" includes "New and continuing projects and program activities: directly undertaken by Federal agencies; or supported in whole or in part through Federal contracts, grants, subsidies, loans, or other forms of funding assistance . . . ; or involving a Federal lease, permit, license certificate or other entitlement for use."[83] But where neither federal funding nor federal permits are involved, private citizens owe no duties under NEPA. The same is true of states and municipalities.

COUNCIL ON ENVIRONMENTAL QUALITY (CEQ)

Title II of NEPA establishes a three-member **Council on Environmental Quality,** known as the "CEQ" for short, in the Executive Office of the President and defines the scope of its duties and responsibilities.[84] Besides being required to assist and advise the President in preparing his annual Environmental Quality Report to the Congress[85] and to review and appraise the programs and activities to determine the extent to which they contribute to the achievement of the national environmental policy,[86] the Council on Environmental Quality is required by Executive Order to issue "guidelines to Federal agencies for the preparation of detailed statements on proposals for legislation and other Federal actions affecting the environment, as required by section 102(2)(c) of the Act" and to oversee compliance with the act by federal agencies.[87] Revised guidelines prepared by the Council on Environmental Quality appear in the Code of Federal Regulations, Title 40, Chapter V, at Part 1500.[88]

---

[83] 40 C.F.R., sec. 1500.5(a)(2), 38 Federal Register p. 20551, Aug. 1, 1973.
[84] 42 U.S.C., secs. 4341–4347.
[85] Id., secs. 4341, 4344(1).
[86] Id., sec. 4344(3).
[87] Executive Order 11514, *Protection and Enhancement of Environmental Quality,* 35 Federal Register p. 4247, Mar. 7, 1970.
[88] They also appear in 38 Federal Register pp. 20550 et seq., Aug. 1, 1973.

NEPA does not give the Council on Environmental Quality either the power to direct the specific actions of any federal agency or the power to compel an agency to file an environmental impact statement if it should fail to do so. Nor has the act given the council the right to reject inadequate statements filed by any agency.

To provide the professional and administrative staff needed by the three-member Council on Environmental Quality, the Congress passed the Environmental Quality Improvement Act of 1970[89] establishing in the Executive Office of the President an office known as the Office of Environmental Quality.

ENVIRONMENTAL PROTECTION AGENCY (EPA)

The **Environmental Protection Agency,** hereafter referred to as "EPA," was created by Executive Reorganization Plan No. 3 of 1970[90] and is the first federal government agency established exclusively for the purpose of environmental protection.

In transmitting the reorganization plan to the Congress on July 9, 1970,[91] the President observed that prior to that date the federal government was "not structured to make a coordinated attack on the pollutants which debase the air we breathe, the water we drink, and the land that grows our food. Indeed," the President's message continued, "the present governmental structure for dealing with environmental pollution often defies effective and concerted action." The message made the point that "Despite its complexity, for pollution control purposes the environment must be perceived as a single, interrelated system" and went on to observe that the "Present assignments of departmental responsibilities do not reflect this

---

[89] 42 U.S.C., secs. 4371–4374.
[90] See 38 Federal Register p. 15623, July 1970.
[91] While 5 U.S.C., ch. 9, secs. 901–913, entitled "Executive Reorganizations," gives the President the authority to reorganize federal agencies, any reorganization plan can be vetoed by a majority of either house of Congress.

interrelatedness." It was the intention of Reorganization Plan No. 3 to assign much of the responsibility for establishing and enforcing environmental standards that was formerly scattered among various federal agencies to a single agency, the Environmental Protection Agency.[92]

Functions of the Environmental Protection Agency

The principal functions of the EPA as defined by the President's message transmitting Reorganization Plan No. 3 to Congress include:

> The establishment and enforcement of environmental protection standards consistent with national environmental goals.
>
> The conduct of research on the adverse effects of pollution and on methods and equipment for controlling it, the gathering of information on pollution, and the use of this information in strengthening environmental protection programs and recommending policy changes. Assisting others, through grants, technical assistance and other means in arresting pollution of the environment.
>
> Assisting the Council on Environmental Quality in developing and recommending to the President new policies for the protection of the environment.[93]

Differing Roles of EPA and Council

In his reorganization plan message to Congress, the President pointed out that it was his intention that the EPA and the Council on Environmental Quality would work in close harmony, with each agency reinforcing the other's mission in the environmental field.

The Council on Environmental Quality, the message states, is considered to be a "top-level group (which might be compared with the Council of Economic Advisers), while the EPA would be an operating, 'line' organization. . . . In short, the Council focuses on what our broad policies in the environmental field should be; the EPA would focus on setting and enforcing pollution control standards. The two are not competing, but complementary—and taken together, they should give us for the first time, the means to mount an effectively coordinated campaign against environmental degradation in all of its many forms."[94]

GUIDELINES FOR PREPARATION OF ENVIRONMENTAL IMPACT STATEMENTS

We have seen that an important responsibility imposed on the Council on Environmental Quality by executive order[95] is the issuance of guidelines to federal agencies for the preparation of statements concerning what impact actions by them would have on the environment. An "environmental impact" has been defined as being "any alteration of environmental conditions or creation of a new set of environmental conditions, adverse or beneficial, caused or induced by the action or set of actions under consideration. Assessment of the significance of the environmental impact generally involves two major elements: A quantitative measure of the magnitude and a qualitative measure of the importance. Such a determination is a matter of agency judgment and consensus. . . ."[96]

By requiring that federal agencies prepare environmental impact statements, the Congress hoped to ensure that the agencies would consider the environmental effects of actions taken by them. NEPA does not require an environmental impact statement (an "EIS") in every instance of federal action, but only when an agency's proposal involves a *major* action that will have a *significant effect* on the quality of the human environment.[97] Generally speaking, a major action will nearly always have a signifi-

---

[92] The text of the President's message to Congress appears at 6 Weekly Compilation of Presidential Documents pp. 908 et seq., July 13, 1970, compiled by the Office of the Federal Register, General Services Administration.

[93] Id., p. 912.

[94] Id.

[95] Executive Order 11514, *Protection and Enhancement of Environmental Quality,* 35 Federal Register p. 4247, Mar. 7, 1970.

[96] "Department Policies, Responsibilities, and Procedures for the Protection and Enhancement of Environmental Quality," also known as HUD Handbook 1390.1, Department of Housing and Urban Development, 38 Federal Register p. 19192, July 18, 1973.

[97] 42 U.S.C., sec. 4332(2)(C).

cant effect and, conversely, any action that has a significant effect will usually be considered to be a major action. The dividing line between a major action and a not-so-major action has not been clearly defined.

Contents of Environmental Impact Statements

To assist federal agencies in preparing environmental impact statements required by NEPA, the Council on Environmental Quality's guidelines[98] require that all such statements contain the following information.

    1 A description of the proposed action, a statement of its purposes, and a description of the environment affected. . . . Agencies should also take care to identify, as appropriate, population and growth characteristics of the affected area and any population growth assumptions used to justify the project or program or to determine secondary population and growth impacts resulting from the proposed action and its alternatives. . . .[99]

    2 The relationship of the proposed action to land use plans, policies, and controls for the affected area. This requires a discussion of how the proposed action may conform or conflict with the objectives and specific terms of approved or proposed Federal, State, and local land use plans, policies, and controls, if any, for the area affected including those developed in response to the Clean Air Act or the Federal Water Pollution Control Act Amendments of 1972.[100]

    3 The probable impact of the proposed action on the environment. This requires agencies to assess the positive and negative effects of the proposed action as it affects both the national and international environment. . . .[101] Secondary or indirect, as well as primary or direct, consequences for the environment should be included in the analysis. . . . Such secondary effects, through their impacts on existing community facilities and activities, or through changes in natural conditions, may often be even more substantial than the primary effects of the action itself. For example, the effects of the proposed action on population and growth may be among the more significant secondary effects.[102]

    4 Alternatives to the proposed action, including, where relevant, those not within the existing authority of the responsible agency. . . . A rigorous exploration and objective evaluation of the environmental impacts of all reasonable alternative actions, particularly those that might enhance environmental quality or avoid some or all of the adverse environmental effects, is essential.[103]

    5 Any probable adverse effects which cannot be avoided (such as water or air pollution, undesirable land use patterns, damage to life systems, urban congestion, threats to health or other consequences adverse to environmental goals set out in section 101(b) of the Act).[104]

    6 The relationship between local short-term uses of our environment and the maintenance and enhancement of long-term productivity. This section [of an EIS] should contain a brief discussion of the extent to which the proposed action involves tradeoffs between short-term environmental gains at the expense of long-term losses, or vice versa, and a discussion of the extent to which the proposed action forecloses future options.[105]

    7 Any irreversible and irretrievable commitments of resources that would be involved in the proposed action should it be implemented. . . . Agencies should avoid construing the term "resources" to mean only the labor and materials devoted to an action. Resources also means the natural and cultural resources committed to loss or destruction by the action.[106]

    8 An indication of what other interests and considerations of Federal policy are thought to offset the adverse environmental action. . . . The statement should also indicate the extent to which these countervailing benefits could be realized by following reasonable alternatives to the proposed action . . . that would avoid some or all of the adverse environmental effects.[107]

---

[98] 40 C.F.R., sec. 1500.8, 38 Federal Register pp. 20553–20554, Aug. 1, 1973.
[99] 40 C.F.R., sec. 1500.8(a)(1).
[100] Id., sec. 1500.8(a)(2).
[101] Id., sec. 1500.8(a)(3)(i).
[102] Id., sec. 1500.8(a)(3)(ii).
[103] Id., sec. 1500.8(a)(4).
[104] Id., sec. 1500.8(a)(5).
[105] Id., sec. 1500.8(a)(6).
[106] Id., sec. 1500.8(a)(7).
[107] Id., sec. 1500.8(a)(8).

DRAFT EISs, REVIEW OF COMMENTS, AND FINAL EISs

Draft Environmental Impact Statements

The Council on Environmental Quality Guidelines require that federal agencies considering a project or program that requires an environmental impact statement (EIS) shall first prepare a draft EIS and obtain comments on this draft from other federal agencies having expertise in the area of proposed action,[108] from the Environmental Protection Agency,[109] from state and local environmental agencies,[110] and from public and private organizations and individuals.[111]

Comments by agencies and members of the public on draft EISs should place emphasis "on the assessment of the environmental impacts of the proposed action, and the acceptability of those impacts on the quality of the environment, particularly as contrasted with the impact of reasonable alternatives to the action. Commenting entities may recommend modifications to the proposed action and/or new alternatives that will enhance environmental quality and avoid or minimize adverse environmental impacts."[112]

Public Participation and Hearings

The CEQ Guidelines point out that both the NEPA and Executive Order 11514 charge federal agencies with the responsibility of ensuring the fullest practicable provision of timely public information regarding federal plans and programs having an environmental impact in order to obtain the views of interested members of the public. In view of this responsibility, the guidelines require federal agencies to adopt procedures whereby notice is given to the public of an agency's decision to prepare a draft EIS and to solicit comments that may prove helpful in preparing the statement.[113]

The guidelines provide that, whenever appropriate, federal agencies shall hold public hearings to provide the public with relevant information pertaining to proposed major actions. In determining whether a public hearing is appropriate, an agency is told to consider: (1) the magnitude of the proposal in terms of economic costs, the geographic area involved, and the size of the commitment of resources; (2) the degree of interest in the proposal as reflected by requests from federal, state, and local authorities that a hearing be held; (3) the complexity of the issues involved and the likelihood that the information to be presented at the hearing will help the agency in fulfilling its responsibility to inform; and (4) the extent to which public involvement has already been achieved through such means as earlier public hearings, meetings with citizen representatives, and written comments on the proposed action.[114]

Draft environmental impact statements must be made available to the public at least 15 days before public hearings on a federal proposal and copies shall be either provided without cost or at a fee which is not more than the actual cost of reproducing the copies.[115]

The Council on Environmental Quality publishes in the Federal Register on a weekly basis a list of environmental statements that it received during the preceding week and which are available for public comment.

Review of Comments and Final Statement

The CEQ Guidelines provide that "where opposing and professional views and responsible opinion have been overlooked in the draft statement and are brought to the agency's attention through the commenting process, the agency should review the environmental effects of the action in the light of those views and should make meaningful reference in the final statement to the existence of a responsible opposing view not adequately discussed in the

---

[108] Id., sec. 1500.9(a).
[109] Id., sec. 1500.9(b).
[110] Id., sec. 1500.9(c).
[111] Id., sec. 1500.9(d).
[112] Id., sec. 1500.9(e)(1).
[113] Id., sec. 1500.6(e).

[114] Id., sec. 1500.7(d).
[115] Id., sec. 1500.9(d).

draft statement, indicating the agency's response to the issues raised."[116] All substantive comments are required to be attached to the final environmental impact statement, whether or not such comments have been discussed individually in the text of the statement.[117]

Copies of all final EISs with comments attached are sent to all federal, state, and local agencies and private organizations that made substantive comments on the draft EIS. Copies of all final EISs must also be sent to the Environmental Protection Agency and to private individuals who request a copy.

JUDICIAL REVIEW OF FEDERAL AGENCY ACTION

Although NEPA contains no provisions for judicial review of the need for the filing of an environmental impact statement in a given case, or the adequacy of such a statement when one has been filed, the courts have used the authority of the federal Administrative Procedures Act[118] to review federal actions.

If, however, a federal agency has prepared and fully considered an entirely adequate statement and has satisfied all statutory procedures, the agency may proceed with its proposed project even though the environmental statement indicates that the effect on the environment will be adverse. Nothing in NEPA prohibits actions which may have adverse environmental effects from being undertaken. There are those among the environmentalists who would like for NEPA to prohibit proposed agency action if the effects of that action are adverse and cannot be mitigated. That, however, clearly is not the law as NEPA is presently written.

A federal court, without addressing itself directly to the question, has suggested that where the costs to the environment clearly outweigh the benefits to be derived from a project or program, the courts should have the power to prevent it.[119] Where there has been a clear error of judgment on the part of an agency, the courts will ordinarily block the agency's proposed action. But where an agency's decision is only moderately insensitive to environmental effects, the court normally will not impose its policy choice on the agency.

STATE ENVIRONMENTAL LEGISLATION

Except where federal financing or other participation is involved, states, municipalities, and private citizens contemplating projects or programs owe no duties under NEPA. Many states, however, have adopted or are considering adopting legislation relating to the effects of state and local activities. A number of state environmental policy laws that have been adopted are patterned after NEPA,[120] while a few[121] have implemented environmental regulation programs by executive directive.

All of the states' environmental acts and executive orders contain declarations of environmental policy and impose obligations requiring adherence to that policy. While the policies and obligations of some states are more rigorous than others, all states have used NEPA as a point of departure. In one form or another, all states with environmental legislation have adopted the provisions of the federal act requiring the preparation of environmental impact statements. The majority of the state environmental laws do not, however, create a body similar to the federal Council on Environmental Quality, but delegate duties to existing state agencies instead.

Model State Environmental Policy Act

At its Second National Symposium on State Environmental Legislation, held in 1973, the

---

[116] Id., sec. 1500.10(a).
[117] Id.
[118] 5 U.S.C., secs. 701–706.
[119] *Calvert Cliffs' Coordinating Committee v. Atomic Energy Commission,* 146 U.S. App. (D.C.) 33 (1971).
[120] Among those having "little NEPAs" are California, Connecticut, Delaware, Illinois, Indiana, Maryland, Massachusetts, Minnesota, Montana, Nevada, New Mexico, North Carolina, Virginia, Washington, and Wisconsin.
[121] For example, Arizona, Hawaii, Michigan, Texas, and Utah.

Council of State Governments drafted a suggested State Environmental Policy Act for guidance and possible adoption by those states that have not enacted environmental legislation.[122] According to the council, the suggested act which was drafted by workshop participants, draws heavily on the National Environmental Policy Act and the California Environmental Quality Act of 1970.[123] The suggested act adopts the simplicity of NEPA and leaves details to be filled in by administrative guidelines, thus affording states the flexibility needed in adjusting the many minor details to their individual situations.

Purposes of the Act The suggested legislation states that "The purposes of this Act are: to declare a state policy which will encourage productive and enjoyable harmony between man and his environment; to promote efforts which will prevent or eliminate damage to the environment and stimulate the health and welfare of man; and to enrich the understanding of the ecological systems and natural resources important to the people of the State."[124]

Environmental Impact Statements Like the acts from which it draws guidance, the suggested act seeks to achieve its announced purposes through the mechanism of the environmental impact statement.

The workshop participants pointed to certain important issues that states considering a proposed law dealing with environmental impact statements should consider and offered solutions to those issues.

Who Must Prepare Statements The workshop noted that in most existing state statutes examined by it the question as to whether the requirement for environmental impact statements applies to local agencies as well as to state agencies is not clear. The California act, the workshop pointed out, applies to both state and local agencies, but the council refrained from taking a definite position on the issue. The model act offers legislatures a choice of alternative definitions of an "agency" that is required to file an environmental statement, one definition including both state and local agencies and the other being limited to state agencies only.[125]

With regard to the issue whether a state environmental act should apply only to public works construction or should extend to the regulation of private activities as well, the workshop noted that NEPA has always applied both to direct government operations and to regulatory and licensing activities. The workshop also pointed out that the California Environmental Quality Act was amended in 1972 to make it clear that the act applied to regulatory activities and to the granting of discretionary approvals for private activities. The suggested act includes among those "actions" that require an environmental impact statement "the issuance to a person of a lease, permit, license, certificate or other entitlement for use by one or more public agencies."[126] The model legislation also provides that "It is the intent of the Legislature that all agencies which regulate activities of private individuals, corporations, and public agencies which are found to affect the quality of the environment shall regulate such activities so that major consideration shall be given to preventing environmental damage."[127]

Types of Actions Requiring Statements As to whether a state environmental act should apply only to major actions or to all actions which may have a significant effect on the environment, the workshop noted that NEPA applies only to major actions while the California act sets no size limitations and requires statements on all actions which may have a significant effect on the environment. The suggested act leaves the choice to the adopting state by pro-

---

[122] Council of State Governments, 33 *Suggested State Legislation* pp. 3–9 (1974).
[123] California Public Resources Code, secs. 21000–21174.
[124] Model State Environmental Policy Act, sec. 2.
[125] Id., sec. 4(1).
[126] Id., sec. 4(2)(i).
[127] Id. sec. 3(8).

posing language that reads: "All agencies shall prepare, or cause to be prepared by contract, an environmental impact statement on any [major] action they propose or approve which may have a significant effect on the environment."[128] Legislatures which feel that large activities will be the main ones that have significant effects on the environment and that government may become bogged down if it has to prepare or review too many statements will include the bracketed work "major" in their statutes. On the other hand, legislatures that believe that there are many small projects which may have a significant effect on the environment will omit the term.

Balancing of Social and Economic Considerations On the issue as to whether environmental effects should be weighed against both social and economic considerations, the suggested act provides: "It is the intent of the Legislature that the protection and enhancement of the environment shall be given appropriate weight with social and economic considerations in public policy. Social, economic, and environmental factors shall be considered together in reaching decisions on proposed public activities."[129] The council's comments on the suggested act note that this statement of legislative intent "follows the belief that public policy calls for the balancing of many potentially competing factors and that environmental protection does not require the shutting down of the economy."[130]

[128] Id., sec. 5(b).
[129] Id., sec. 3(6).
[130] Council of State Governments, 33 *Suggested State Legislation* p. 4.

QUESTIONS

1 What are the principal features of the human environment? What is meant by pollution of the environment?
2 Distinguish between biological and chemical pollution of water.
3 What is the purpose of the federal Safe Drinking Water Act? Why was passage of the act considered necessary?
4 According to a committee of the U.S. Senate, what impact does noise have on human beings?
5 What is the major regulatory objective of the federal Noise Control Act?
6 As used in the federal Solid Waste Disposal Act, to what does the term "solid waste" refer?
7 According to a committee of the U.S. Senate, what characterizes the problems of the coastal zone of the United States?
8 What is the main purpose of the federal Coastal Zone Conservation and Management Act? How is that purpose to be accomplished?
9 What are the declared purposes of the National Environmental Policy Act?
10 What are the duties and responsibilities of the Council on Environmental Quality?
11 What are the principal functions of the Environmental Protection Agency?
12 According to the National Environmental Policy Act, what kinds of federal actions require the preparation of environmental impact statements? What was the Congressional intention in requiring such statements?
13 What are the stated purposes of the model State Environmental Policy Act that was drafted by the Council of State Governments?
14 According to the model State Environmental Policy Act, what types of actions require the preparation of environmental impact statements.

Chapter 22

Real Property Taxes

A tax is a charge or involuntary contribution levied by public authorities to raise revenue necessary for carrying on the functions of government. The power to determine what shall be subject to taxation and what shall be immune is vested in the legislatures of the various states. The obligation of the citizen to pay taxes is purely a statutory creation and taxes can be levied, assessed, and collected only in the method provided by statute. Each of the 50 states, without exception, has made real estate a significant source of tax revenue. And although policy implications of the real property tax may vary considerably from one state to another because of exemptions, preferences, and administrative differences, the structure of real estate tax systems, with only relatively minor variations, is similar in all the states.

Power to Tax Is a Sovereign Right
The power to tax is an attribute of sovereignty and the exercise of that power through the levying and collecting of taxes is vested exclusively in the legislature. As an attribute of sovereignty that inheres in the state, the power to tax is not dependent upon any grant of authority by its constitution. Instead of being a grant of power, constitutional provisions that relate to taxation impose limitations on the exercise of that inherent power. Except as restricted by the provisions of its constitution, a state's power to levy and collect taxes is unlimited.

Delegation of Power to Tax
The right to raise revenue is one of the most essential powers of government. But unless that power has been specifically granted to them by

constitutional or statutory provision, local government subdivisions such as counties, townships, cities, towns, and school districts have no power to tax. In all states, however, the power of taxation has been delegated to local government by express grants. It is today firmly established that the state may confer upon local governments the power to tax property within their jurisdictions to raise revenue for local governmental purposes. Significant among the taxing powers delegated to local governments is the power to tax real estate situated within their territorial boundaries.

Any power to tax that is conferred on local governments always operates prospectively, never retrospectively.

Major Source of Local Tax Revenue
While its proportionate contribution to total local government revenue may vary from one state to another, the real property tax clearly is a major source of local tax revenue. It has been estimated that the real property tax provides about 87 percent of all taxes collected by local governments.[1] As a principal source of income for local governments, taxation of real estate finances such services as education, welfare, law enforcement, fire protection, streets, and roads. Despite the existence of potential alternate sources of local government revenue, real estate taxes have been rising in many areas of the country.

Unpopularity of the Tax
The real property tax may well be the most unpopular of all major taxes levied by government at all levels. It is under attack from all quarters. Welfare economists denounce it as being the most regressive major tax, businessmen complain of its inflexibility, the elderly condemn it as being a tax least related to ability to pay, while taxpayers generally criticize it as being the most dishonestly assessed and ineptly administered of all major taxes.

And yet, probably for want of politically acceptable alternatives, no one predicts the early demise of the real property tax. That is not to say, however, that exemptions resulting from political pressures on legislatures and direct initiatives by the people will not erode the significance of the tax as a source of local revenue and alter the incidence of the tax.

NATURE OF THE REAL PROPERTY TAX

The real property tax is a charge that is levied on the assessed value of real estate. It is, in other words, an **ad valorem** tax.

Real estate or real property, as we have seen, is composed of land, the improvements to land, and those things which are appurtenant or belong to the land. It is the assessed value of these combined components of real estate that constitutes the basis against which a tax rate is applied to calculate the dollar amount of a taxpayer's bill.

Not Based on Benefits Received
The amount of a given property owner's tax bill is entirely a function of the value of his taxable property. The amount is neither calculated nor measurable in terms of the total benefits received by the property or enjoyed by its occupants that are derived from the public services made possible by tax revenues. A home owner with a number of children attending the local public school pays the same amount of real estate taxes as does his neighbor who owns a home of equal value but who has no children in school. Similarly, the property owner in a high fire risk area who frequently requires the services of the local fire department to extinguish grass or brush fires pays no higher taxes than an owner of property of equal value who never uses such services.

The real property tax is levied to raise revenue for the general public good and there is no requirement in the law that the burden of the

---
[1] L. L. Ecker-Racz, *The Politics and Economics of State-Local Finance,* Prentice-Hall, Englewood Cliffs, N.J., 1970, p. 76.

dered that property by the taxing district, the burden imposed on other taxpayers by the federal exemption can range from negligible to very substantial.

In partial recognition at least of the potential hardship resulting from loss of tax revenue, federal laws provide for the making of certain payments in lieu of taxes to local taxing districts. These payments include, for example, a percentage of the receipts of royalties and rentals derived from development of mineral resources on federal lands,[5] 25 percent of the revenues received from national forests,[6] and 10 percent of the rents received from federally financed low-rent housing projects.[7] It is not unlikely, however, that these in lieu payments bear little or no relation to the cost of services rendered by the taxing district or the tax revenue that the property would have yielded had it been subject to taxation.

State and Local Government Property Like federally owned real estate, property owned by both state and local governments is generally exempt from the real property tax. While the amount of land owned by state and local governments is not as great as that owned by the federal government, state and local government exemptions can nonetheless cause taxing problems for many local taxing districts.

Institutional Exemptions Constitutions and statutes in the various states commonly exempt from taxation property that is used for religious, educational, charitable, and similar purposes not intended to yield a profit. The precise exemptions will vary from state to state as will the impact of those exemptions on the revenue raising capabilities of the local government involved.

Veterans' and Home Owners' Exemptions
As a reward for service in the armed forces, veterans and their widows are sometimes granted limited exemptions from real property taxes. The California Constitution,[8] for example, extends to qualified veterans an exemption of $1,000 from the assessed value of their taxable real property.

All states have enacted some form of tax relief legislation to ease the burden of the real estate tax on home owners. These relief measures commonly exempt a portion of the value of the taxpayer's home from taxation or provide for tax cuts or rebates to home owners whose property tax liability exceeds a specified percentage of their total gross income.

A few states[9] have extended real property tax relief to tenants of dwelling units and other states have adopted programs for providing additional tax relief to elderly home owners.

Preferential Taxation for New Industries
Some states, most of which are located in New England and the South, endeavor to stimulate industrial development by granting tax concessions to new industries. The period during which an industry is either taxed at a preferential rate or exempted entirely from the payment of real property taxes varies from state to state but usually runs from 5 to 10 years.

The effect of affording preferential tax treatment to any significant amount of property within a taxing district is, of course, to increase the tax rate and hence the tax burden for those properties that are not accorded the same treatment.

Appraising or Estimating Market Value
Since the real property tax is an ad valorem tax, before a property owner's tax bill can be calcu-

---

Land Review Commission, *One Third of the Nation's Land,* Appendix F (June 1970). The title of the commission's report is derived from the fact that 33.3 percent of the land mass of the United States is owned by the federal government.

[5] 30 U.S.C., secs. 191, 285.
[6] 16 U.S.C., sec 500.
[7] 42 U.S.C., sec. 1410(h).

[8] Article XIII, sec 1¼.
[9] For example, Arizona, California, Minnesota, Oregon, and Wisconsin.

tax be proportionate to the benefit derived from public services by a particular property or taxpayer.

Not a Personal Obligation

In the absence of a specific statutory provision to the contrary, a tax on real property is a charge upon the property itself and, if unpaid, does not become a personal obligation of the owner of the property. As we shall see later, the tax becomes a lien on the property against which it is levied and foreclosure of that lien will result if delinquent taxes continue unpaid. If, however, the foreclosure sale of the tax-delinquent property fails to generate sufficient revenue to satisfy all of the unpaid taxes, the owner of the property is not personally liable for the resulting deficit. This means, of course, that none of the property owner's other assets can be seized and sold in satisfaction of the unpaid balance of the tax debt.

Requirement That Tax Be Uniform

It is a fundamental principle of taxation that the various types of taxes be uniform in their operation. As applied to the taxation of real estate, the principle of uniformity means that all property of the same class within a given taxing district be assessed in the same manner and taxed at the same rate. The U.S. Supreme Court has recognized the right of a state to classify property for purposes of taxation[2] and has upheld a system of classification if it can be shown to have a rational basis.[3]

Most state constitutions contain provisions requiring uniformity in the taxation of real property. Over the years, however, the strict application of the principle of uniformity has been relaxed by the granting of exemptions and the classification of properties in categories subject to different rates or assessed at differing percentages of value. The power to determine what classes of properties shall be immune or exempt from taxation, as we have seen, has traditionally been the province of the legislature. With respect to this legislative function, the statement has been made that the courts do not pass judgment on the legislature's wisdom, but only on its power.

THE ASSESSMENT PROCESS

As the word **assessment** is commonly used in connection with the real property tax, it refers to (1) the preparation of a roll or list of all properties subject to the tax and (2) the valuation of such taxable properties. An assessment is the act of an elected or appointed public officer, which act is a matter of public record so that a property owner may ascertain the fact that his property has been assessed and the amount of the assessment.

Assessments are presumed to be correct and assessing officers are presumed to have acted validly and in good faith. As a consequence of this presumption, when the correctness of an assessment is attacked by a complaining taxpayer, the burden of proving that the assessment is faulty falls upon him.

Exemptions and Preferential Taxation

Not all real estate situated within a taxing district's territorial boundaries is subject to the real property tax. By the provisions of both federal and state laws, certain properties are exempt from taxation.

Federally Owned Property It has been long established that real estate owned by the federal government is not subject to taxation by the state in which it is located unless Congress has consented to it being taxed. Depending on the amount of federally owned property in a given tax district[4] and the amount of services ren-

---

[2] *Nashville, V. and St. L. Ry. v. Browning,* 310 U.S. 362 (1940).

[3] *New York Rapid Transit Corp. v. New York,* 303 U.S. 573 (1938).

[4] For example, the federal government owns as much as 95.4 percent of the land in Alaska, 44.3 percent of California, 63.9 percent of Idaho, 86.4 percent of Nevada, and 66.5 percent of Utah but as little as .3 percent of Connecticut, .7 percent of Maine, and .8 percent of New York. U.S. Public

REAL PROPERTY TAXES

lated it is first necessary that the value of his taxable property be determined. The value figure that is used for real property tax purposes is the **market value** of the property that is subject to taxation.[10] A commonly accepted definition of market value defines it as being the price at which a property would sell in the open market if exposed for sale for a reasonable period of time with both the buyer and the seller being fully informed of the uses to which the property may be put, both seeking to maximize their gains, and neither of them being under pressure to buy or to sell.

The Traditional Approaches to Estimating Value. In Chapter 11 we examined the methodology of the three traditional approaches to estimating value that are employed by real estate appraisers, namely (1) the cost of reproduction approach, (2) the market or sales comparison approach, and (3) the capitalization of income approach. These three classic approaches are normally used by appraisers whether the objective of a given appraisal is to estimate value for purposes of taxation, condemnation, purchase and sale, mortgage lending, or other type of transaction where the value figure is needed.

While theoretically each of the appraisal approaches would yield an identical value figure for the same parcel of real estate at any given point in time, it is not the case in practice. The lack of available data to be processed by any particular approach and the consequent need for the appraiser to make numerous assumptions may result in a value figure that is both unreal and unreliable.

Preferred Approach for Tax Purposes With respect to the appraisal of real property for tax purposes, at least one state[11] has established a system of preferences in the use of the three standard approaches to estimating value. Those preferences, couched in terms of availability of data, are as follows:

> When reliable market data are available with respect to a given property, the preferred method of valuation is by reference to sales prices.[12]
>
> The income approach to value is used in conjunction with other approaches when the property under appraisal is typically purchased in anticipation of money income and either has an established income stream or can be attributed to a real or hypothetical income stream by comparison with other properties. It is the preferred approach for the appraisal of land when sales data for comparable properties are not available. It is the preferred approach for improved real properties . . . when reliable sales data are not available and the cost approaches are unreliable. . . . [13]
>
> The reproduction . . . cost approach to value is used in conjunction with other approaches and is preferred when neither reliable sales data (including sales of fractional interests) nor reliable income data are available. . . . [14]

The Concept of Highest and Best Use It is an accepted principle of appraising that the appraiser seeks to find the market value of a parcel of land when that property is devoted to its highest and best use. The highest and best use of a parcel of land, generally speaking, is the use that would maximize the return from the land, which return is reflected in the market value of the land. It is probably safe to say that the actual use to which most properties are being put is their highest and best use, but there are important exceptions when this is not the case. For example, agricultural and open lands are sometimes valued as being suitable for subdividing several years before the area is actually needed or desired for that purpose. The effect

---

[10] Despite the fact that tax statutes provide that property be assessed at its "full cash value" in California, its "true and actual value" in Connecticut, its "fair cash value" in Illinois, its "full value" in New York, or its "actual value" in Pennsylvania, all such expressions have been held to mean assessment at market value.

[11] California.
[12] 18 California Administrative Code, sec. 4.
[13] Id., sec. 8(a).
[14] Id., sec. 6(a).

of such a practice is to increase the owner's tax burden substantially, which burden often forces subdividing simply to pay taxes when both the owner and the local planning agency may have desired to retain the area in its open or agricultural state. Some states have enacted legislation aimed at correcting this situation. A Florida statute, for example, provides that "All lands being used for agricultural purposes shall be assessed as agricultural land...."[15]

Cyclical Reappraisals and Fluctuating Market Values Tax assessors are plagued by the problem of keeping their appraised values current with market prices of taxable properties. Because of personnel limitations, tax assessors have been forced to adopt what has been called a cyclical reappraisal policy in which the assessor concentrates his reappraisal efforts in one part of the taxing district one year and another part the next year, covering the whole district every 4 or 5 years or more and then repeating the cycle all over again. The problem with cyclical appraisals, of course, is that the assessor's appraised values throughout the taxing district are not kept current with fluctuating market values. The use of old appraisals for some properties and new appraised values for others results in a lack of uniformity and inequality of the tax burden. Recognizing the inequalities in tax burdens arising from cyclical reappraisals as well as the tax revenue that is lost in times of rapidly rising property values, taxing districts that can afford to do so have increasingly turned to computerized appraisals for a solution, particularly where single-family residences are concerned.

All Interests Appraised as a Unit In most jurisdictions it is not the policy to assess the different estates or interests that might exist in a single parcel of land separately to the respective owners, but to assess the property as a unit representing the sum of those interests. For example, the interests of a mortgagor and a mortgagee, those of a landlord and a tenant, and the interests of an easement holder and the owner of the servient property typically are not separately appraised and taxed. Mineral rights, however, that are owned separately from the surface are commonly assessed separately. In the case of oil and gas leases, for instance, the land is usually assessed to the lessor and the mineral rights either to the lessee alone or to both the lessor and the lessee in accordance with their proportionate interests in the mineral rights.

While it is generally required that real estate held in cotenancy be assessed in the names of all co-owners, the assessor is not required to ascertain the particular share or interest of each co-owner.

Assessed Value of Real Property Although the terms "appraised value" and "assessed value" are often used synonymously and in those instances refer to an identical value figure, there are other occasions when the terms refer to two quite different value figures.

Meaning of "Assessed Value" The **assessed value** of real property is the value figure to which a tax rate is applied to arrive at a property owner's tax bill for a given tax year. In a majority of states, the market value of real estate as determined by an appraisal is also the assessed value of the property. In those states, the tax rate for the current tax year as computed and fixed by the local legislative body is applied to a property's market value as estimated by an appraiser from the tax assessor's office.

Fractional Assessment A substantial minority of states have statutes that provide for what is sometimes termed **fractional assessment.** Those statutes require that real property will be assessed for tax purposes at some stated fraction or percentage of its market value.[16] Where

---

[15] Florida Stat. Ann., sec 193.11(3).

[16] Alabama assesses agricultural, forest, and residential property at 15 percent of market value, utilities at 30 per-

all taxable property within the same class is assessed at the same percentage of market value, fractional assessment does not violate the fundamental taxing principle of uniformity and, as reflected in the footnote, a few states do assess different classifications of properties at different percentages.

In those states where taxable properties are not classified into categories, it really matters little whether property is fractionally assessed or assessed at 100 percent of its appraised market value. Since the tax rate which is applied against assessed value is calculated by dividing the amount of the tax revenue to be raised by the total assessed value of all taxable property, fractional assessment would simply yield a higher tax rate than assessment at full market value. Given the same amount of tax revenue to be raised and the same market values of taxable properties, a property owner's tax bill would be the same whether a higher tax rate is applied to a lower assessed value or a lower rate to a higher value.

Assessed to Owner of Record

Tax statutes generally require that real property taxes be assessed to the person who appears in the public records to be the owner on a specified date preceding the tax year. Consequently, one who holds an unrecorded deed of which the assessor has no knowledge cannot complain when his taxes become delinquent that he did not receive a tax bill. Unless his property is specifically exempted by statute, a property owner is presumed to know that his property is subject to taxes and must take appropriate steps to learn the amount of his tax bill and pay it.

Assessment Review

The manner in which a taxpayer may have his tax assessment reviewed and the extent of the authority of administrative officers or agencies charged with the function of equalizing taxes are matters regulated entirely by statute.

Protests Generally Concern Value Almost without exception, protests by taxpayers and demands for assessment review relate to the assessor's appraisal of the market value of property subject to taxation or, in jurisdictions where fractional assessment is practiced, to the ratio at which property is assessed. Whichever reason may be the basis of his protest or appeal, the taxpayer bears the burden of demonstrating that his property is excessively assessed as compared with other properties similar in character and location.

When hearing a taxpayer's protest, an administrative body operates similar to a court in that it listens to evidence presented by both the taxpayer and the assessor and is then required to arrive at a decision as to the property's value that is supported by the evidence.

The Due Process Requirement Due process of law requires that at some point before a tax becomes an irrevocable charge against property, a property owner must be given notice of an opportunity to be heard concerning the correctness of the assessed value of his property. The due process of law requirement is satisfied when the assessor, at the time he informs a taxpayer of the assessor's estimated value of his property, notifies the taxpayer of the time and the place for filing a protest and the time when protest hearings will be held. The precise

---

cent, and all other properties at 25 percent. California assesses at 25 percent, Colorado at 30 percent, and Connecticut at 60 percent. In Hawaii the Department of Taxation may set the percentage, which currently is 60 percent. Idaho assesses at 20 percent of market value, Illinois at 33 1/3 percent, except in counties larger than 200,000 where the county board may fix the percentage, and Indiana assesses at one-third. Louisiana assesses land at 10 percent, residential improvements at 10 percent, and all other property at 15 percent. Michigan assesses at 50 percent and Minnesota up to 43 percent, depending upon classification of properties. Missouri assesses at 33 1/3 percent, and Montana according to classification, which for most properties is 30 percent. Both Nebraska and Nevada assess 35 percent, while New Jersey's percentage may be fixed by the county board of taxation at not less than 20 percent or more than 100 percent of true value. North Dakota assesses at 50 percent, South Dakota at 60 percent, and Tennessee assesses public utilities at 55 percent, residential and commercial properties at 40 percent, and farm properties at 25 percent. In Utah, real property is assessed at 40 percent.

method of notification and the conduct of hearings varies somewhat from one state to another.

The right to a hearing, as required by due process, implies that the one being heard shall have the right to support his protest and allegations by argument and evidence. A taxpayer's due process right to a hearing does not, however, entitle him to an opportunity for judicial review of his complaint prior to paying his taxes. To prevent the tax on his property from becoming delinquent, a taxpayer may, after an unsuccessful hearing before an adminstrative agency, pay his taxes under protest and proceed with his request for judicial review.

Judicial Review of Administrative Action

The nature and extent of judicial review of administrative decisions concerning the reduction or abatement of real property taxes are matters that are exclusively within the control of the legislature.

THE TAX LEVY

As the term is normally used in real property taxation, a *levy* refers to the official action of a legislative body in determining and declaring that a tax of a certain rate or amount shall be imposed on all taxable real estate within its jurisdiction.

Setting the Rate

Annually, after having reviewed its budget of expenditures for the coming fiscal year, a local legislative body determines the amount of revenue that must be raised from real property taxes. The legislative body then divides the amount of the real property tax revenue needed by the total assessed value of all taxable property and arrives at a tax rate that will generate the desired revenue. This rate is commonly expressed in terms of so many dollars and cents for each $100 or $1,000 of assessed value of taxable property.

The real property tax rate varies widely, of course, from one taxing jurisdiction to another, partly because of differing needs for revenue, partly because of differences in the size of the tax base, and partly because of differences in the ratio of assessed value to market value among the various jurisdictions.

For purposes of comparing the impact of the real property tax from one jurisdiction to another, the "effective tax rate," that is, the percentage that the tax bill represents of the market value, is often used. For example, using such a basis of comparison, it has been reported that the mean tax rate for the United States in 1962 was 1.4 percent.[17]

PAYMENT AND COLLECTION OF TAXES

Because a continuing flow of revenue is essential to the existence of government, public policy requires that taxes be paid promptly when they fall due and it is the obligation of every citizen to make his tax payments on time.

Due Dates, Delinquencies, and Penalties

Statutes in the various states set the dates when real property taxes become due and payable. By way of lessening the burden of tax payments, many jurisdictions permit annual property taxes to be paid in installments. Statutes also commonly provide that unpaid taxes become delinquent a certain period of time following the date they first become due.[18]

---

[17] Dick Netzer, *Economic Impact of the Real Property Tax*, The Brookings Institution, Washington, 1965, p. 103.

[18] For instance, in Arizona one-half of the tax is due Sept. 1 and delinquent Nov. 1, the second half is due Mar. 1 and delinquent May 1; in California one-half is due Nov. 1 and delinquent Dec. 10, the second half is due Feb. 1 and delinquent Apr. 10; in Florida the tax is due Nov. 1 and delinquent Apr. 1 with discounts for early payment of 4 percent if paid in Nov., 3 percent in Dec., 2 percent in Jan., and 1 percent in Feb.; in Hawaii one-half is due Aug. 20 and the second half on Feb. 20 and are delinquent if not paid on those dates; in Illinois, except in counties over 1 million, the first half is due and becomes delinquent on June 1, the second half on Sept. 1; in New Jersey taxes are payable in four installments on Feb. 1, May 1, Aug. 1, and Nov. 1, and are delinquent after each installment date; in Ohio half is due Dec. 20 and the second half on June 20 and both are delinquent if not paid on those dates; in Texas half is payable before Nov. 30 and the second half before June 30 and the taxes are delinquent after those dates; in

A property owner can only discharge his tax obligation by the payment of his tax bill. Most taxpayers pay their taxes when they are due and before they become delinquent, but there are always a few who do not. Because local governments cannot tolerate delays in the payment of needed revenue and as a means of inducing property owners to pay their taxes when they fall due, statutes generally impose penalties on taxpayers who fail to pay their taxes within a specified period after the due date.[19] The imposition of penalties is within the constitutional power of the legislature and the amount of the penalty is a matter of discretion.

Method of Collection

It is within the power of the legislature to adopt any reasonable method for the collection of taxes. Once the method has been legislatively adopted, the act of collecting taxes is a purely ministerial function that may be performed by a public official, who is usually known as a tax collector.

REAL PROPERTY TAX LIENS

As security against the possibility that an owner may default on his obligation to pay his real property tax, many states have enacted statutes that impose liens on taxable properties.[20] As we have seen, a lien is a charge or legal claim against property that makes it security for an obligation and which permits the property to be sold if the secured obligation or debt is not paid.

Real property taxes do not become liens on property against which they are assessed unless so declared by statute. The existence of tax liens, their duration, operation, and priority are matters for legislative determination and enactment. Where tax liens are created by statute, the lien attaches to property automatically without the filing or recording of any notice of its existence or extent and it is immaterial whether any attempt has yet been made to collect the tax.

Priority of Tax Lien

Most statutes that create tax liens give to those liens a priority over all other liens on the property, whether those liens were created before or after the assessment of the property.[21] The effect of such a provision, of course, is to subordinate mortgages or deeds of trust executed and recorded even years earlier to a position that is junior or inferior to a tax lien.

Freeing Property from Lien

Once a tax lien has attached to a parcel of real estate, that property is not relieved of its encumbrance until the tax bill that the lien secures is paid by the taxpayer or the obligation is satisfied from the proceeds of a lien foreclosure sale of the property. Tax liens can only be foreclosed in accordance with procedures authorized by the legislature of the state in which the encumbered property is located.

As we observed previously, in the absence of a contrary statutory declaration, the real prop-

---

Washington half is payable by Apr. 30 and the second half by Oct. 31 and are thereafter delinquent; and in Wisconsin half is payable Jan. 31 and the second half on July 31, but if the first installment is not paid when due, all taxes are payable on Feb. 28.

[19] For example, in Alabama delinquent taxes bear 6 percent interest plus certain statutory fees; in Arizona the interest is 10 percent on delinquent taxes; in California there is a one-time 6 percent penalty plus 1 percent per month interest; in Colorado interest is 2/3 of 1 percent on delinquent taxes; in Georgia the interest rate is 7 percent on delinquent taxes; Hawaii imposes a one-time penalty of up to 10 percent and interest at the rate of 2/3 of 1 percent thereafter; in Illinois the interest rate is 1 percent per month on delinquent taxes; in Mississippi the rate is 1/2 of 1 percent per month; Ohio imposes a delinquent penalty of 10 percent; Virginia imposes a 5 percent penalty plus interest at the rate of 8 percent; in Washington interest on tax delinquencies is 8 percent annually; and in Wisconsin the delinquency interest rate is 1 percent per month.

[20] For example, California Revenue and Taxation Code, sec. 2187 provides that "Every tax on real property is a lien against the property assessed."

[21] For example, California Revenue and Taxation Code, sec. 2192.1 provides that real property tax liens "have priority over all other liens, regardless of the time of their creation."

erty tax is an obligation against the assessed property only and is not a personal obligation of the owner of the property. Consequently, the owner has no personal liability for any tax deficit that remains after the property has been sold at foreclosure.

SALE OF TAX-DELINQUENT PROPERTY

The sale of tax-delinquent property by public authorities to enforce payment of taxes assessed against it is conceded to be within the taxing power of the states. The procedure for conducting such "tax sales" is entirely statutory and, although details of the methods employed by the various states differ, the basic procedure is generally similar in all states.

Tax Judgment Not Required

There is no constitutional requirement that a judicial proceeding must precede the sale of real property for unpaid taxes. No judgment for the tax debt is necessary before the property can be sold. A tax sale is an act of the tax collector or comparable officer that is administrative rather than judicial in character. However, as is always the case where property rights are involved, the procedure that results in the sale of the tax-delinquent property must meet the requirements of due process of law.

Sale Must Satisfy Due Process

In order that the sale of real estate for nonpayment of taxes may satisfy due process of law requirements, a legislature that authorizes such sales will prescribe certain steps in a procedure that ultimately leads to a sale foreclosing the tax lien on the delinquent premises. Any sale to foreclose a tax lien that is made without notice, either actual or constructive, to the owner of the land is a denial of due process of law.

Proceeds of Tax Sale

The proceeds of a sale to foreclose a tax lien on real estate are used to pay the delinquent property taxes, interest on the tax debt, whatever penalties may be imposed by statute, and costs of conducting the sale. Any surplus proceeds that might remain after these payments have been made are paid to the property owner.

Who May Purchase at Sale

Generally speaking, any person who is legally competent to contract may be a purchaser at a tax sale.

The purchaser at a tax sale buys strictly under the rule of **caveat emptor.** Unless otherwise provided by statute, the state or other public body selling the tax-delinquent property makes no warranties with respect to it.

REDEMPTION FROM TAX SALE

According to many statutes that provide for the collection of taxes by the sale of real property, the tax sale itself does not finally and irrevocably divest the taxpayer of his title to the tax-delinquent property. These statutes provide that the sale merely operates to vest in the purchaser an inchoate or incipient interest in the sold property. The inchoate interest that is acquired by the purchaser at the tax sale may, after the passage of a certain period of time following the sale, ripen into title to the property, providing the property is not "redeemed" by someone authorized to do so.

Nature of Right of Redemption

The usual statutory **right of redemption** empowers the former owner, his successors in interest, or any person having a legal or equitable interest in the premises to defeat the tax sale and thus vest title in himself by paying the purchaser the amount that he paid for the property together with interest and costs. All statutes that create the right of redemption provide a period of time following the tax sale within which the right to redeem may be exercised.[22] If not exer-

---

[22] For example, the redemption period in Alabama is 1 year; Alaska, 1 year; Arizona, 3 years; Arkansas, 2 years; Colorado, any time prior to execution and delivery of a treasurer's deed; Florida, any time before a deed is issued; Illinois, 2 years; New Jersey, 2 years; Ohio, before entry of confirmation of the sale; Texas, 2 years; and Wisconsin, 3 years.

REAL PROPERTY TAXES

cised within the designated time period, the right of redemption is lost.

Operation of Right of Redemption

The manner in which the right of redemption operates is entirely statutory and consequently the details of the exercise of the right vary among the states. Despite these variations in detail, however, the methods by which property sold at a tax sale may be redeemed fall into two general classes, both of which accomplish the same objective by different routes.

Deed Conveying Defeasible Title According to one method that prevails in many states, within a few days after the sale of tax-delinquent property a deed is delivered to the purchaser which passes to him a title that is subject to **defeasance** by redemption during the statutory period. If the owner fails to exercise his right of redemption within the specified period, the purchaser's title becomes absolute without the need for any further proceedings to establish that title.

Certificate of Sale By the second method, the purchaser's title, at the time of the tax sale, is merely inchoate and he receives no deed to the property until the statutory period of redemption has expired. Instead of a deed, the purchaser's right or interest acquired at the tax sale is evidenced by a *certificate of sale* issued by the official who conducts the sale. Before expiration of the redemption period the purchaser must give the owner notice of the time when the right of redemption will expire and the amount that must be paid to redeem the property. Until this notice is given, the purchaser receives no deed to the property and no title passes to him.

Payment of Redemption Money

Because it is often difficult for the taxpayer or his successor in interest to locate the person who purchased the property at the tax sale in order to tender payment of the redemption money to him, most redemption statutes provide that payment may be made to the county treasurer or some other designated public officer.

Unless otherwise provided by statute, if the recipient insists, the redemption payment must be made in cash rather than by check.

TAX DEED

Divests Former Owner's Interest

The transfer of title to property sold for nonpayment of taxes is normally evidenced by a deed to the premises which is executed by the tax collector and delivered by him to the successful purchaser at the tax sale. As we have seen, in some jurisdictions the deed is delivered at the time of the tax sale, while in others a certificate of sale is issued at that time and later, when the redemption period has expired, the certificate is exchanged for a deed. We have also seen that, if the property is not redeemed from the tax sale, a valid tax deed is delivered to the purchaser which serves to terminate the former owner's estate and vests all of his right, title, and interest in the property in the grantee named in the deed. But a tax deed does more than merely convey the former owner's title to the named grantee.

Grantee Receives a New Title

As a general rule, a tax deed conveys to the grantee-purchaser a new and complete title to the property in fee simple absolute, which title is created by a grant from the sovereign and which extinguishes all rights, interests, and encumbrances of private persons that were in existence at the time of the tax sale. It follows, therefore, that all persons who have an interest in real estate, such as a mortgage lender's interest, for example, must at their peril make sure that real property taxes are paid on the premises.

Statements Contained in Tax Deeds

To be valid, a tax deed must contain a statement indicating that the tax authorities performed all statutory acts essential to the legal right to sell the described property for delinquent taxes. The law requires strict compliance with all essential steps prescribed by statute that regulate the sale of real property for unpaid taxes. A tax deed, as we have seen, contains no warranties of any kind and the rights of the purchaser at a tax sale are governed strictly by the doctrine of caveat emptor.

QUESTIONS

1. Do all states have the power to tax real property? What is the source of the power to tax in those states that have it? Is it an unlimited power?
2. What types of local government services are financed by real estate taxes? What is the source of the power of local governments to impose such taxes?
3. What is an ad valorem tax? What is the significance of the fact that the real property tax is an ad valorem tax?
4. What are the consequences of the presumption that assessments by public officers are correct?
5. What is the market value of a parcel of real estate? How can it be estimated?
6. What is the problem that is created by cyclical reappraisal of real estate for tax purposes?
7. What is fractional assessment of real estate?
8. Explain how the due process of law requirement operates with respect to the assessment of real estate for tax purposes.
9. Explain how a local taxing body arrives at a real property tax rate.
10. What is a real property tax lien? How does it attach? How is it removed?
11. If the proceeds of the foreclosure of a property tax lien are more than enough to pay delinquent taxes, what happens to the surplus? What happens when the proceeds are not sufficient to pay the taxes?
12. What is the nature of the right of redemption given by statute to delinquent taxpayers?

Chapter 23

Landlord and Tenant—Part I

One of the more significant attributes of ownership of real property is the right of the owner to possess his property and, within certain limitations, to use that property as he sees fit. The law not only permits an owner to occupy and use the property himself but, if he so desires, also permits him to confer the right of possession on another person for an agreed period of time. When an owner of real estate, while continuing to own it, relinquishes his right of possession and use of the property to another person for a specified period of time in exchange for a consideration, the legal relationship of *landlord and tenant* is created.

The law of landlord and tenant has undergone many changes over the years. Traditionally, the relationship of landlord and tenant was considered to result primarily from the conveyance of an interest in land from the landlord to the tenant. In recent years, however, the law of landlord-tenant relations has changed significantly in that the lease which was previously considered to be primarily a conveyance of real property has come to be regarded as a contract. This change in legal perspective has had important consequences for the landlord-tenant relationship.

Recently the law of landlord and tenant has also taken a turn toward consumerism, especially in those instances where the leasing of dwelling units is concerned.

LANDLORD-TENANT RELATIONSHIP

Created by Contract
The relationship of landlord and tenant is created by means of a contract between the owner of real property, *the landlord,* and one who is

permitted to occupy and use that property, the *tenant*. In both legal and ordinary usage, the term "lessor" usually has the same meaning as "landlord" and the word "lessee" the same as "tenant"; the terms are commonly used interchangeably. The contract that gives rise to the landlord-tenant relationship is known as **lease** or a **rental agreement,** depending on local custom, and, except where otherwise provided by statute, may be either oral or in writing.

When Written Contract Required All states have statutes known as **statutes of frauds** that require certain types of contracts to be in writing if they are to be enforced by the court. These statutes are intended to prevent the giving of false testimony in court and the fraud that would result from such testimony. Although the provisions of statutes of frauds vary somewhat from state to state, all of them require that contracts which involve the transfer of interests in real property must be in writing if the contracts are to be enforceable by the courts. Practically all states exempt short-term leases or rental agreements from statute of frauds requirements and will enforce such contracts even though oral. While exempt oral agreements are just as valid and legally enforceable as written ones, there are obvious evidentiary advantages to written agreements when controversies arise with respect to the terms and conditions agreed upon by the contracting parties. A written lease that has been signed by both the landlord and the tenant constitutes good documentary evidence which eliminates the need for oral testimony which may be derived from mistaken impressions or faulty recollections of witnesses.

Nature of Parties' Interests

Leasehold and Reversion The execution of a lease by a landlord does not divest him of his ownership of the fee simple interest in the leased property but simply deprives him of his right presently to occupy and use the leased premises. By executing a lease, the landlord sells and transfers his right to present possession of the premises to the tenant in exchange for a consideration in the form of rent. In the popular sense of the term, the landlord continues to *own* the leased property but his right to occupy and enjoy it is suspended until some future time when the tenant's right of possession terminates. The landlord's right to occupy and use the leased property at some time in the future is a property interest known as a reversion. The interest that the tenant acquired in the leased premises that entitles him to immediate possession is called a **leasehold.**

A landlord and a tenant have separate estates in the same parcel of real estate. Where a wrongful act by a third person injures the interests of both the landlord and the tenant, each of them has a cause of action against that person for injuries resulting from his act. The landlord is entitled to damages for injury to his reversionary interest and the tenant for harm done to his leasehold interest. This rule does not compel the wrongdoer to respond in damages twice for the same injury, but simply to compensate each owner of an interest in the property for injuries sustained by his particular interest.

Other Relationships Distinguished
The relationship of landlord and tenant is always created by a contract, either express or implied; the relationship cannot exist without such an agreement. The landlord-tenant relation will not be implied, however, where the parties have expressly agreed that such a relationship is not contemplated. In all instances, the guiding principle for determining the nature of the relationship is the intention of the parties.

Tenant Compared with Licensee The rights of tenants and licensees in real property are clearly distinguishable. The critical factor in determining whether an agreement creates a landlord-tenant relationship or a licensor-licensee relationship is the presence or absence of the right of *exclusive possession* of real property. By means of a licensing arrangement, an owner of real estate, who is the licensor, authorizes another person, the licensee, to use the owner's property for a specified purpose. The licensee acquires no estate or interest in the owner's land, but merely has the privilege of using the land in a manner which would otherwise be a trespass. With limited exceptions, a license may be revoked and terminated by the licensor at any time without the consent of the licensee.

In the landlord-tenant relationship, on the other hand, a tenant acquires an interest or estate in the landlord's real property which interest entitles the tenant to the exclusive possession of designated premises for a specified period of time. Unlike a license, a lease is not revocable at the whim of the landlord. During the agreed period of a lease, the landlord can terminate the relationship only for causes stated in the rental agreement or for reasons provided by law.

It is sometimes difficult to determine whether a particular agreement is a lease or a license. In making their determinations, the courts look to the intent of the parties as reflected by the language used in their agreement. The question can arise, for example, with regard to an agreement by the terms of which A is authorized to operate a concession in B's department store, a contract that permits A to install coin-operated washing machines in B's apartment building, or an agreement that authorizes A to install signs on the roof of B's building. The mere fact that A pays for the privilege of use does not make A's relationship with B one of landlord and tenant rather than licensor and licensee.

Tenant Compared with Lodger The distinction between a tenant and a lodger in a hotel, motel, or rooming house, like that of a tenant and a licensee, depends primarily on the question of the occupant's right of exclusive possession of designated areas or premises. Like the licensee, a lodger merely has the right to use the premises he occupies with the owner of the lodging house retaining control over the occupied premises and being responsible for their care and condition. While in the absence of a statute to the contrary it is the tenant who is responsible for the condition of the premises he occupies, a lodger is not expected to keep the premises in repair. A lodger may recover for injuries sustained by him as a result of the owner's negligently permitting the space the lodger occupies to fall into disrepair.

Tenant Compared with Purchaser There is a clear and substantial difference between a sale and the leasing of real property. The seller-buyer relationship that is created by an executory contract of purchase and sale terminates upon the legal delivery of a deed to the premises, while the landlord-tenant relationship created by the execution of a lease is a continuing contract for the duration of the lease period regardless of the fact that the lease has been delivered to the tenant. As owner of the property, a purchaser's right of exclusive possession is of potentially infinite duration, while a tenant's possessory right endures only for the agreed term of his lease.

CHARACTERISTICS OF A LEASE
Conveyance and Contract
Historically, the law has regarded a lease or rental agreement primarily as being the conveyance of an interest in real property rather than a contract between a landlord and a tenant. A significant consequence of this view has been the application of the doctrine of caveat emptor which placed the burden on the tenant to determine the initial fitness of the leased premises and to maintain them during the period of his tenancy. However, as it became increasingly apparent that viewing a lease primarily as a conveyance was impractical and unrealistic in modern urban society, the courts have recognized and, particularly with respect to dwelling units, have stressed the contractual aspects of a lease.

Today, a lease of real property is considered not only to be a conveyance of an interest or estate in real property but also as constituting a contract between a landlord and a tenant which expressly or impliedly defines the conditions that regulate their legal relations.

Form and Contents of a Lease

Essential Requirements If a lease is to be valid it must (1) identify the landlord and the tenant, both of whom must be capable of contracting, (2) describe the leased premises with sufficient certainty to enable them to be identified, (3) specify the amount of rent to be paid and the method of payment, and (4) indicate the term or period of time during which the tenant shall be entitled to possession and use of the premises.

Signing Written Leases If a written lease is to be enforceable, it must be signed by the landlord. But, while the tenant's signature also customarily appears on the lease, signing by the tenant is not essential to the validity of a written lease. The tenant binds himself to the provisions of a lease when he accepts it. A tenant's intention to accept a lease is generally manifested by his taking possession of the leased premises or by paying rent.

No Particular Form or Terminology Required No particular terminology is required to make a lease a valid legal document. All that is required is that the language used by the parties reflect their intent to create a landlord-tenant relationship with regard to a certain designated parcel of real estate. The prevailing rule in nearly all jurisdictions is that where the provisions of a lease are ambiguous, they will be construed more strictly against the landlord than against the tenant, especially when the lease has been prepared by the landlord or his agent. This rule is in accord with the principle of construction applicable to contracts generally.

Except where the statute of frauds requires that a lease be in writing to be enforceable, a lease is valid whether it is oral or written. Although printed lease forms are commonly used in many localities, the use of standardized forms is a matter of custom rather than a legal requirement.

The law presumes that a lease which has been reduced to writing contains the entire agreement between a landlord and a tenant. Consequently, the general rule is that oral evidence (legally known as "parol" evidence) is not admissible to vary or contradict the provisions of a written lease, except where it can be shown that because of fraud or mistake the writing fails to express the agreement of the parties. In the absence of fraud or mistake, all negotiations concerning a lease of real property become merged into a written lease and it is the controlling evidence of the terms and conditions on which the property is leased.

A well-drafted lease will, of course, contain all the essential elements of a valid contract and will set them forth in clear and unambiguous language. In addition to the basic requirements, a thoughtfully prepared lease will explicitly indicate the particular undertakings of the parties rather than leave them to implication. The objective of a written lease is to expressly state the mutual undertakings of the landlord and the tenant with respect to the preservation of the premises for the benefit of the landlord and the use and enjoyment of them by the tenant.

The rule that, except where an agreement discloses a contrary intent, statutes and settled law existing at the time a contract is made become a part of that contract, is commonly applied to leases.

Appurtenances Included by Implication

In the absence of any language or express provision to the contrary, a lease of real property transfers by implication everything that is appurtenant to the leased premises. Easements and facilities that are reasonably necessary to the beneficial use and full enjoyment of the rented premises, such as stairways, elevators, hallways, and means of access to the street, pass by a lease of real estate without the need for any express lease provision. However, nothing impliedly passes as an appurtenance to the leased premises other than those easements and facilities which are reasonably necessary to the proper enjoyment of the premises. Mere convenience to the tenant is not sufficient to create an easement or impose a burden on other property of the landlord as an appurtenance for the benefit of the leased property.

TYPES OF LEASEHOLD INTERESTS

We have seen that when the owner of real estate executes a lease he carves two separate estates out of his ownership interest, one of which, known as a reversion, is retained by the owner as landlord, while the other estate, a leasehold interest, is transferred by him to a tenant. The leasehold estate or interest that is acquired by a tenant is commonly also referred to as a *tenancy*.

All jurisdictions recognize four different kinds of leasehold interests or tenancies: (1) a tenancy for years, (2) a periodic tenancy, (3) a tenancy at will, and (4) a tenancy at sufferance. These tenancies are distinguishable from one another primarily with respect to the period of time they will endure and the manner in which they expire.

The particular type of tenancy that is created in any given case depends upon the intent of the parties as reflected by the language of the lease or rental agreement they have executed.

Tenancy for Years

Despite its common usage, the term **tenancy for years** is misleading because the leasehold interest to which it refers can be one that endures for any *fixed period* of time, whether it be for 2 or more years, 1 year, 6 months, 4 weeks, or any other definite period. An expression that is more descriptive of the nature of the leasehold interest which it identifies would be "tenancy for a fixed term" or "tenancy for a definite period" because it is *definiteness of duration* that characterizes a tenancy for years.

A tenancy for years is a leasehold interest created by an express agreement between a landlord and a tenant that has a fixed beginning and a fixed end, regardless of the length of the period for which the period endures. In the absence of a contrary provision in the lease, a tenancy for years cannot be terminated before the expiration of its term by the giving of notice by either the landlord or the tenant. When the term fixed by the lease expires, however, the tenancy terminates automatically without the need for notice by either party. Upon termination of the tenancy, of course, the tenant's right to possession of the premises likewise comes to an end.

As a general rule, a tenancy for years is not terminated by the death of either the landlord or the tenant before expiration of the designated period. The interest of the deceased landlord or tenant passes to his executor or administrator.

Periodic Tenancy

A **periodic tenancy** is a leasehold interest that continues for successive periods of time—from year to year, month to month, week to week—unless it is terminated by either party to the rental agreement. The most important characteristic of a periodic tenancy is its continuity. Unlike the tenancy for years which ends upon the expiration of a definite term, a periodic tenancy is automatically renewed for another period unless the landlord or tenant takes appropriate steps to terminate it. The length of time for which the tenancy is renewed is determined by the period for which the rent is paid, which in the case of dwellings commonly is 1 month.

A large number of urban tenants occupy dwelling units under leasing arrangements that give rise to periodic tenancies. Periodic tenants in lower and middle-income groups frequently do not occupy their dwellings under written leases. They rent their living quarters by orally trol as he chooses the use to which the leased premises may be put and it is not for the tenant to say that the landlord's restrictions are unreasonable.

Covenant to Repair Except where the provisions of a lease or a statute provide otherwise, or where the lease of a *dwelling* is involved, a landlord is under no obligation to repair the rented premises during the period they are occupied by the tenant. The landlord can, of course, by an express covenant in a lease, impose upon himself the responsibility of maintaining the premises in good repair after the tenant has taken possession of them. When a lease contains an express covenant of this type, the courts view the landlord's obligation as applying to repairs that are required in the future and not the need for repairs existing at the time the premises are leased.

After receiving notice from the tenant that certain repairs to the premises are needed, the landlord has a reasonable period of time, determined by the circumstances and apparent need for prompt action, within which to make the repairs before he will be considered to have breached his covenant. The rule that requires a tenant to notify the landlord of the need for repairs is based on the fact that the landlord, who ordinarily has no right to enter the leased premises, has no way of knowing the condition of the premises unless he is informed by the tenant.

Common Express Covenants by Tenant Like a landlord, a tenant may obligate himself by an express covenant in a rental agreement to do certain things with respect to the leased premises that he would not otherwise be required to do. Express covenants by tenants that frequently appear in leases include (1) a covenant to pay a stipulated rent, (2) a covenant to pay property taxes and assessments, and (3) a convenant to repair or rebuild.

Covenant to Pay Rent Rent is the compensation or price paid for the right to occupy and use real estate. It is a normal incident of the landlord-tenant relationship. In the rare or unlikely situation where a rental agreement fails to specify the amount of rent to be paid, a landlord is entitled to receive the reasonable rental value of the leased premises.

Rental agreements, almost without exception, contain express covenants by which tenants agree to pay a specified amount of rent and which also provide the time and place for making payments. In the absence of a provision in the lease, the rule is that rent is not due and payable until the end of a lease period and is payable at the leased premises. An express agreement by a tenant to pay rent in advance is both enforceable and common, as is an agreement to make payment elsewhere than at the leased premises. Failure on the part of a tenant to make rent payments in accordance with his promise is, of course, a breach of his agreement for which the landlord has certain legal remedies available to him.

While rent is most commonly made payable in dollars, this need not be the case. Where a rental agreement so provides, the compensation given in exchange for the use and occupancy of real estate may be in the form of services, chattels, provisions, or anything else other than money.

Leases of buildings to be used for retail businesses sometimes provide that the rent to be paid shall be a percentage of the gross income generated by the business. The rental to be paid may be a flat percentage of gross receipts, but more commonly will be a fixed minimum amount plus a percentage of the gross income. The theory of the percentage lease is that, since a favorable location is the key to success for many retail businesses, when a site proves to be a successful one for the tenant, the owner of the site should be compensated commensurate with the locational value of the site.

Covenant to Pay Taxes and Assessments A tenant is under no obligation merely by reason of the landlord-tenant relationship to pay real estate taxes and special assessments levied upon the leased premises. Commercial and industrial leases, and particularly long-term ones, often contain provisions by the terms of which the tenant expressly covenants to pay all real property taxes and assessments levied on the premises during the period of the lease. In some areas, the term "net" lease is used to refer to rental agreements containing covenants of this type.

Covenant to Repair or Rebuild An agreement or covenant by a tenant to repair the leased premises during the term of his lease or to rebuild in the event of destruction of all or part of the premises is valid and enforceable.

Reservation of Easement by Landlord A landlord may impose an easement or servitude on the leased premises for the benefit of other property owned and retained by him. According to the prevailing view, if a landlord intends to reserve an easement on the leased premises he must do so by an express provision in the lease because, except where strictly necessary to the use of the property retained by the landlord, easements on the leased premises cannot be reserved merely by implication.

Security Deposits by Tenants

Amount and Use Regulated by Statute
Leases commonly require the tenant to deposit a sum of money with the landlord as security against the tenant's failure to pay rent, injury to the premises that exceeds normal wear and tear, or the breach of any of the covenants in a lease. These security deposits are entirely for the benefit of the landlord and, while serving a legitimate purpose, they are subject to certain abuses. To protect tenants against possible abuses by landlords, many states[2] have enacted legislation limiting the amount of security deposits and restricting the use of them by the landlord.

All statutes require that any deductions from the security deposit by the landlord be fairly made and be reasonable in amount. Any surplus remaining after proper deductions have been made by the landlord must be returned to the tenant in a timely manner following termination of the tenancy.[3] Many statutes provide that a mandatory written statement be given to the tenant by the landlord indicating the purposes for which any money was deducted from the tenant's deposit.

Following receipt of a security deposit, the landlord is assured that the deposited funds will remain in his hands until the lease expires because any premature termination of the lease by the tenant will ordinarily result in permanent retention of the deposit by the landlord. If the landlord invests the deposited funds during the period of the lease, the question arises as to whether the income derived from the invested funds belongs to the landlord or to the tenant. The answer to the question depends upon how the courts regard the relationship that is created between the landlord and the tenant as a result of the deposit. Most often, in the absence of a contrary statute, the landlord is regarded as being a debtor of the tenant with respect to the deposit and is permitted to use the funds as he desires with no obligation to pay the tenant any part of the interest or profits derived from the investment.

A growing minority of states[4] have enacted legislation providing for the payment of interest on deposits made by a tenant. Interest rates

---

[2] Alaska, Arizona, California, Colorado, Connecticut, Delaware, District of Columbia, Florida, Hawaii, Illinois, Iowa, Kentucky, Louisiana, Maryland, Massachusetts, Michigan, Minnesota, Montana, New Jersey, New York, Ohio, Oklahoma, Oregon, Pennsylvania, Texas, and Washington.

[3] For example, Arizona, California, and Hawaii require that refunds be made to the tenant within 14 days after termination of the lease; Florida, 15 days; Louisiana, 1 month; Massachusetts, New Jersey, and Pennsylvania, 30 days; and Maryland, 45 days.

[4] Among them being Florida, Illinois, Maryland, Massachusetts, New Jersey, New York, and Pennsylvania.

and methods for the payment of interest vary among the states.[5]

A deposit by a tenant which, according to the terms of the lease, is applicable to the rent payable for the last part of the lease period has no effect on the landlord's right to terminate the lease for nonpayment of currently accruing rent.

Security Deposits as Liquidated Damages
We previously noted that contracting parties sometimes agree upon the amount of money to be paid for a loss or injury that would result in the event one of them defaults on his promise. It will be recalled that in determining whether or not such a provision is enforceable, the basic question before the courts is whether the provision is one for the payment of damages or whether it provides for the payment of a penalty by the one who breaches the agreement. If determined to be a provision for the payment of a penalty rather than damages, the courts refuse to enforce it.

The courts tend to regard provisions in contracts that fix in advance the amount to be paid in case of a breach as providing for the payment of penalties rather than damages. If a provision for the forfeiture of a stipulated sum of money is to be held to be an enforceable agreement to pay liquidated damages, it is essential that the actual contemplated damages, at the time of the agreement, be difficult to ascertain and that the stipulated damages represent a reasonable estimate of the probable damages to be sustained.

In deciding whether a security deposit shall serve as liquidated damages for the breach of a covenant by the tenant, the courts look to the apparent intent of the landlord and the tenant as reflected by the language of the lease, determine whether the damages sustained by the landlord would be difficult to measure if a breach occurred, and decide whether the amount of the security deposit represents a good faith estimate of the probable and foreseeable loss that the landlord would suffer because of the tenant's breach. Unless all of the foregoing criteria are satisfied, a provision in the lease for the retention of the deposit by the landlord will not be regarded as liquidated damages which the landlord may retain, but rather as an unenforceable provision for the forfeiture of funds imposed upon the tenant as a penalty for his breach. Where such a determination is made by the court, the landlord will be allowed to retain only as much of the security deposit as is necessary to indemnify him for injuries actually resulting from the tenant's breach of his agreement.

Landlord's Lien on Tenant's Property In the absence of an agreement by the tenant giving a lien or a statute creating one, a landlord has no lien on a tenant's personal property as security for rent.

The parties to a lease may stipulate that the landlord is to have a lien on crops or the personal property of the tenant brought upon the leased premises and such a provision will be enforced by the courts. Most authorities consider such a stipulation in a lease to be a chattel mortgage in legal effect. The courts are divided as to whether the tenant may, by provision in the lease, waive his right of exemption for certain types of property from seizure for unpaid debts.

---

[5] Florida requires the payment of 5 percent interest if the deposit is not kept in trust or 75 percent of the interest earned if the deposit is kept in an interest-bearing trust; Illinois requires 4 percent interest to be paid to the tenant; Maryland, 3 percent; Massachusetts 5 percent; New Jersey, New York, and Pennsylvania require the landlord to place the deposited funds in accounts which draw the currently prevailing rate of interest and permit the landlord to withhold 1 percent as an administrative fee.

As to the time when interest payments must be made, Florida requires that accumulated interest be paid when the deposit is returned; Illinois requires payment or credit to the tenant within 30 days after the expiration of each 12-month period; Maryland, at the end of each year; New Jersey requires the interest to be credited toward the rental that is due for each term; New York, payment annually or held and paid or credited toward rentals at the end of the lease term; and Pennsylvania, paid annually on the anniversary of the lease after it has run for 2 years.

Statutes in some states[6] give landlords a lien for rent on the personal property of their tenants and, where agricultural lands are leased, on crops raised on the leased premises. A landlord's statutory lien attaches when the personal property is brought upon the premises, or when the crops commence their growth, regardless of whether rent is due. Where statutory liens exist, the legal title and right of possession of the personal property remain with the tenant, subject simply to the charge of the landlord's lien. The landlord has no right forcibly to seize and sell the property to satisfy his claim for unpaid rent; his lien must be enforced by judicial proceedings.

Option to Purchase the Leased Premises
Leases sometimes contain provisions that give a tenant an option to purchase the leased premises. The option, which is an offer by the landlord to sell the premises at a stated price, cannot be withdrawn by him during the period specified in the option because the tenant's payment or promise to pay rent constitutes the consideration that makes the landlord's offer irrevocable. As long as the tenant's option remains dormant or unexercised, the lease continues in full force and effect with all the incidents and obligations resulting from the landlord-tenant relationship being fully operative. When the option is exercised by the tenant accepting the landlord's offer, the landlord-tenant relationship comes to an end and the relationship of seller and buyer is created.

An option in a lease may give the tenant an absolute right to purchase the leased property at a stated price at any time or it may merely give him a prior right to purchase the property (a "right of first refusal") should the landlord decide to sell.

Option Terminates with Expiration of Lease The expiration of a lease containing an option to purchase the leased premises terminates the option as well.

If the lease provides for an extension or renewal at the tenant's election and the tenant chooses to extend or renew it, the period of time within which the option may be exercised is likewise extended.

Transferability of Option Unless the terms of an option in a lease clearly and unmistakably restrict it to the tenant, an *assignment* of the lease will transfer the right to purchase the leased property to an assignee. On the other hand, if instead of assigning the lease, the tenant *sublets* the premises to a sublessee, the option to purchase is not transferred to the sublessee merely by virtue of the sublease. To transfer the option to the sublessee, the language of the instrument that creates the sublease must clearly and expressly indicate an intention also to transfer the option to the sublessee.

The distinction between an assignment and a sublease is examined later in the chapter.

Option Unaffected by Sale of Reversion
The right of a tenant to enforce an option to purchase leased property is not affected by the landlord's sale of his reversionary interest in the property. The general rule is that an option to purchase contained in a lease is a covenant which runs with the land and is binding upon anyone who purchases the landlord's reversion.

Option Unaffected by Death of Parties A tenant's right to exercise an option to purchase leased premises is not affected by the death of the landlord before the period of the lease has expired. Nor does the death of the tenant terminate the option. In the absence of a provision in the option to the contrary, the administrator or executor of the deceased tenant's estate may exercise the option and purchase the property.

Exercising the Option To exercise an option a tenant needs only to notify the landlord of the tenant's acceptance of the landlord's offer to sell the leased property. The tenant's acceptance, of course, is valid only if made within the validity period of the landlord's offer, which

---

[6] For example, Alabama, Arkansas, Georgia, Iowa, Mississippi, New Mexico, North Carolina, South Carolina, Texas, and Washington.

period normally will coincide with the period of the lease. When the tenant accepts the landlord's offer to sell, an executory contract of purchase and sale is formed between them. Unless required by the provisions of the option, payment of the purchase price by the tenant is not necessary for his acceptance to become effective. However, title to the leased premises does not pass to the tenant until the agreed purchase price has been paid, and at that time and by that act the parties' executory contract becomes an executed one. Until the title has closed, the landlord-tenant relationship continues and the parties are of course governed by the terms of the lease under which the tenant took possession of the rented premises.

Whether all or any part of the rental payments made by the tenant to the landlord are applicable to the purchase price of the leased premises when the tenant exercises his option depends on the provisions of the option itself. In the absence of any provision, no part of the tenant's payments apply toward the purchase price of the property.

Rights and Obligations Implied by Operation of Law

When the respective rights and duties of a landlord and a tenant are not spelled out by the provisions of a rental agreement, those rights and obligations are created and defined by implication or operation of law. The law that operates to regulate the landlord and tenant relationship is an amalgam of the common law as reflected by decisions of the courts and statutes passed by legislatures.

Rights and Duties at Common Law At common law, in the absence of a specific agreement in a lease to the contrary, landlords owe their tenants very few obligations. The early common law viewed a lease as being the conveyance of an interest in real property and from this notion three basic rules governing the landlord-tenant relationship developed.

The first of these early common law rules was that the *doctrine of caveat emptor* prevailed with respect to the relation of landlord and tenant. According to this rule, the landlord was absolved of any obligation to deliver premises to the tenant that were suitable to the tenant's use. A prospective tenant was charged with inspecting the premises to determine their fitness and the tenant who neglected to make such an inspection before executing a lease did so at his peril. The tenant could only recover damages for injuries resulting from unfit premises if he obtained an *express* warranty of fitness from the landlord.

A second early common law rule, related to the principle of caveat emptor, held that in the absence of an express undertaking the landlord owed no duty to maintain the leased premises or to make repairs during the term of the lease. As a part of his duty not to commit waste, it was the tenant who was obliged to maintain the premises during the period of his tenancy.

The third rule of the early common law, also founded on the notion that a lease was a conveyance rather than a contract, held that covenants in a lease were mutually independent unless expressly made dependent by the provisions of the lease. In accordance with this view, the breach of an express or implied covenant by the landlord neither suspended nor discharged the tenant's obligation to perform his covenants. While the tenant could ultimately recover damages resulting from the landlord's breach, he had to continue to make rent payments to the landlord.

Because the application of the early common law rules frequently yielded unduly harsh results, exceptions developed and the rules were softened or substantially altered by the decisions of the courts and by legislative enactments. Both the common law and the statutory law relating to landlord and tenant have been the subject of considerable change in recent years to meet the needs of a changing society as perceived by the courts and legislatures.

Although the early common law did not do

so, the modern trend in the law of landlord and tenant is to differentiate between residential tenants and all other types of tenants. In no other aspect of landlord and tenant law has change been as pronounced as in the area that involves the leasing of premises for residential purposes. Most of the recent legal reforms relating to the rights and obligations between residential landlords and tenants have been incorporated in the Uniform Residential Landlord and Tenant Act.

Uniform Residential Landlord and Tenant Act The **Uniform Residential Landlord and Tenant Act,** referred to as the "URLTA," is a proposed law drafted by the National Conference of Commissioners on Uniform State Laws and submitted to the various states for adoption.[7] In addition to making the law uniform among the states, the stated purposes of the act are (1) "to simplify, clarify, modernize, and revise the law governing the rental of dwelling units and the rights and obligations of landlords and tenants" and (2) "to encourage landlords and tenants to maintain and improve the quality of housing."[8] As the title of the act indicates, the proposed uniform law applies only to landlord-tenant relationships arising from rental agreements for dwelling units used for residential purposes;[9] it does not extend to leases for commercial, industrial, agricultural, or any other nonresidential purpose.[10] The act, therefore, is a special one rather than an act of general application to all tenancies.

With certain variations the URLTA has been adopted in some 13 states[11] and has been introduced in the legislatures of at least 10 others.[12] It is reasonable to assume that at one time or another the act will be considered by the legislatures of most of the states and, with modifications to conform with local customs and preferences, be adopted by a significant number. Because of this likelihood, when considering the rights and obligations of tenants that are created by operation of law, it seems desirable to examine the manner in which those rights and obligations are treated by the uniform act.

Significant Implied Rights and Obligations Among the more significant rights and obligations of landlords and tenants that are implied by operation of law when the lease contains no contrary provisions are the following: (1) the right of a landlord to receive rent and a tenant's obligation to pay, (2) the tenant's right to possession and quiet enjoyment of the leased premises, (3) the landlord's obligations with respect to the condition of the leased premises, (4) the liability of the landlord and the tenant for personal injuries resulting from use of both the leased and the retained premises, and (5) where dwellings are concerned, the rights and duties of the parties with respect to habitability of the leased premises. The nature of the extent of these and other implied rights and obligations are examined in the materials immediately following.

Rights and Obligations Regarding Rent As we have seen, rent is the price paid for the use of real estate and is a normal incident of the landlord-tenant relationship. Although rental agreements rarely fail to specify the amount of rent to be paid, where the oversight does occur it is held that the landlord is entitled to a rea-

---

[7] The final draft of the act was approved for submission to the states at the annual meeting of the National Conference of Commissioners on Uniform State Laws on Aug. 10, 1972.

[8] Uniform Residential Landlord and Tenant Act (hereafter cited as URLTA), sec. 1.102(b).

[9] URLTA, sec. 1.301(3) states that a "'Dwelling unit' means a structure or the part of a structure that is used as a home, residence, or sleeping place by one person who maintains a household or by 2 or more persons who maintain a common household."

[10] URLTA, sec. 1.201 and sec. 1.101, Comment.

[11] Alaska, Arizona, Delaware, Florida, Hawaii, Kansas, Kentucky, Nebraska, New Mexico, Ohio, Oregon, Virginia, and Washington.

[12] California, Connecticut, Idaho, Illinois, Indiana, North Carolina, Pennsylvania, Rhode Island, Vermont, and Wisconsin.

sonable rent as determined by the going market rental for properties comparable to the leased premises.

Tenant's Obligation Not Terminated by Death The death of a tenant does not terminate a tenancy for years or a periodic tenancy and consequently the obligation to pay rent is not discharged. As is generally the case with contracts of a deceased person which are not of a personal nature, the rental agreement survives the tenant's death and the landlord's claim for rent continues against the tenant's estate, both for rent which had accrued but was unpaid at the time of the tenant's death and for rent subsequently accruing under the lease.

URLTA Position According to the Uniform Residential Landlord and Tenant Act, unless otherwise agreed by the parties, periodic rent is payable in advance at the beginning of any tenancy for a term of 1 month or less. For fixed term tenancies involving dwelling units, rent is payable in equal monthly installments at the beginning of each month in the absence of a rental agreement provision to the contrary.[13] This provision of the act is in direct conflict with the law of some states[14] which makes rent payable at the end of the term unless otherwise agreed.

Possession and Quiet Enjoyment by Tenant

Landlord's Obligation to Deliver Possession

The law implies an obligation on the part of a landlord to deliver possession of the leased premises to the tenant upon commencement of the term of the lease. The states differ, however, with respect to the scope of the landlord's obligation.

One group of states[15] applies a rule (the "American" rule) which guarantees only *legal* possession to the tenant. Under this rule, the landlord's obligation is satisfied when the tenant has the right to immediate possession free from any interference by the landlord or any person claiming under the landlord. The landlord's implied obligation to deliver possession is not breached, and hence he incurs no liability, if a new tenant is unable to enter into possession of the leased premises because a holdover tenant or some third party wrongdoer occupies the premises. According to this view, the ouster of such occupants is the responsibility of the new tenant, who meanwhile is liable to the landlord for rental payments in accordance with the terms of the lease.

Other states[16] impose a greater obligation on the landlord and apply a rule (the "English" rule) which requires the landlord to deliver not only legal possession of the leased premises but *actual* possession as well. According to this view, a tenant is entitled to occupancy of the leased premises upon commencement of the term of the lease and the tenant is not required to assume the responsibility of ousting a third party who might wrongfully occupy the premises at that time. It is the landlord's obligation to remove all obstacles to the tenant's possession when the lease period commences and his failure to do so is a breach of his implied obligation.

A landlord's failure or refusal to perform his obligation to deliver possession of the leased premises entitles the tenant to rescind the rental agreement or, if he chooses to continue the agreement, to maintain an action against the landlord for damages. Provisions in a lease that require a landlord to pay a stipulated amount of money for each day that a tenant is denied possession are upheld when interpreted as being provisions for liquidated damages but are invalid when construed as provisions for the payment of a penalty.

Implied Covenant of Quiet Enjoyment It is well established that, in the absence of an ex-

---

[13] URLTA, sec. 1.401 (c).

[14] For example, California Civil Code, sec. 1947.

[15] California, Hawaii, Illinois, Maryland, Massachusetts, Mississippi, New Hampshire, and Vermont.

[16] Alabama, Arkansas, Connecticut, Indiana, Iowa, Kentucky, Missouri, Nebraska, New Jersey, North Carolina, Oregon, and Tennessee.

press lease provision to the contrary, the landlord-tenant relationship gives rise to an implied covenant by the landlord that the tenant shall have peaceable possession and quiet enjoyment of the leased premises. This means that the tenant's occupancy and use of the premises shall be free from interference by the landlord himself, by someone acting with his authority, or by someone having a title to the property that is paramount to the title of the landlord. The landlord's implied covenant of quiet enjoyment extends to easements and other appurtenances the use of which is necessary or essential to the tenant's enjoyment of the leased premises.

With certain exceptions, and unless otherwise expressly provided in the lease or by statute, a tenant has the sole and exclusive right to occupy and use the leased premises during the term of the lease. During this period, the landlord's rights in the property are confined to his reversionary interest and, subject to certain exceptions and contrary lease provisions, the landlord has no right to enter the premises or otherwise disturb the tenant's occupancy and enjoyment of them. As a general rule, the landlord has no right to enter the leased premises during the term of the lease without the tenant's permission to make alterations or improvements, to inspect the premises for needed repairs, or even to make repairs. A landlord does, however, have a right to show the premises to prospective tenants after receiving notice from the present tenant of the termination of the tenancy, provided the right is exercised in a reasonable manner.

Unless such acts are expressly or impliedly authorized by him, a landlord is not responsible for the acts of another tenant that interfere with the quiet enjoyment of leased premises. If they are neither expressly nor impliedly authorized by the landlord, the wrongful acts of another tenant do not constitute a breach of the landlord's implied covenant of quiet enjoyment. The tenant whose peaceful and quiet enjoyment has been interfered with may have a cause of action for trespass or nuisance against the tenant whose conduct causes the interference, but not against the landlord.

When seeking to establish a breach of the landlord's implied covenant of quiet enjoyment, the complaining tenant must show that his use of the lease premises was substantially interfered with. It is essential to establishment of the breach that the acts complained of actually interfered with the tenant's use of the premises. Mere apprehension that the tenant's use and enjoyment may be interfered with in the future is not sufficient.

Unless they are expressly declared to be so by the terms of a rental agreement, the landlord's covenant of quiet enjoyment and the tenant's covenant to pay rent are not mutually dependent covenants. This lack of mutual dependency means that the tenant may not continue to occupy the premises but withhold rent payments because of the landlord's interference with his quiet enjoyment—even though what a tenant pays rent for is the beneficial use and quiet enjoyment of the leased premises. Under appropriate circumstances, however, the tenant may treat the breach of the covenant of quiet enjoyment as a constructive eviction by the landlord.

Constructive Eviction by Landlord An **eviction,** as the term is used in landlord and tenant law, may be either actual or constructive.

At early common law, to support his claim that he had been evicted from the leased premises by his landlord, the tenant had to show that he had been physically expelled from and dispossessed of the premises. A tenant's physical expulsion and dispossession by a landlord is known as an *actual* eviction. While actual evictions of tenants by landlords can and do still occur, they are not common occurrences.

It is no longer necessary that a tenant actually be ousted or physically removed from leased premises to be the victim of an eviction. In the evolution of landlord and tenant law there has developed the now well-established doctrine of constructive eviction. A **constructive eviction** results from wrongful acts on the part of a landlord, or someone acting under his authority, that interfere with the tenant's beneficial enjoyment of the leased premises. The doctrine is based on the notion that the landlord's implied covenant of quiet enjoyment is breached not only by the actual physical expulsion of the tenant, but also by such interference with the tenant's use and enjoyment of the premises that, for all practical purposes, amounts to an eviction from them. Not all wrongful acts on the part of a landlord, however, amount to constructive eviction.

For a landlord's interference with the tenant's enjoyment of the leased premises to amount to a constructive eviction, that interference must be of a serious or substantial nature and be so injurious to the tenant as to deprive him of the beneficial use and enjoyment of the premises. Furthermore, the tenant bears the burden of establishing that such interference was intentional on the part of the landlord. It is sometimes said that the landlord's intention to evict the tenant can be presumed when the results of the landlord's acts are such as to deprive the tenant of the beneficial enjoyment of the premises.

For a landlord's conduct to constitute a constructive eviction of the tenant, it is absolutely essential that the tenant vacate the leased premises because of the landlord's wrongful act and do so within a reasonable period of time after the act occurred. No matter how much a tenant's enjoyment of the rented premises may be disturbed by the landlord's act, there is no constructive eviction if the tenant continues to occupy the premises. Unless the tenant vacates the premises within a reasonable time, the tenant cannot assert the defense of constructive eviction against the landlord's claim for rent that falls due under the lease after the landlord's wrongful act has occurred. Furthermore, if the consequences of the landlord's wrong that interfered with the tenant's beneficial enjoyment cease to exist before the tenant vacates the premises, the tenant loses his right to claim a constructive eviction and to remove himself from the premises.

The tenant bears the burden of showing not only that the landlord's act was justification for the tenant's leaving the leased premises but also that his departure took place within a reasonable time after the act.

As a general rule, a claim of constructive eviction cannot be based on a landlord's mere temporary trespass on the leased premises. Although such a trespass by the landlord may entitle the tenant to recover money damages, it does not amount to an eviction. While the distinction between a trespass and an eviction is not always clear, an eviction can be said to be an aggravated form of trespass. Any conduct on the part of the landlord that would have supported the tenant's claim of constructive eviction if the tenant had vacated the premises will afford the tenant grounds for an action for trespass and consequent damages if the tenant remains in possession of the leased premises instead of vacating them.

Acts of a landlord that are of sufficient interference with a tenant's beneficial enjoyment to amount to a constructive eviction may take many forms. In the case of an apartment building, for example, interference with a tenant's right of ingress or egress by locking the door of the building, obstructing a walk or way leading to the building, or unjustifiable denial of the use of halls and passageways constitute constructive eviction. The impairment of a tenant's beneficial enjoyment of leased premises caused by a fortuitous event, such as the destruction of a leased building by fire or the elements, is not a breach of the landlord's covenant of quiet enjoyment and hence is not a constructive eviction. Nor is the landlord's covenant broken when he makes alterations and repairs on those portions of the premises which are not leased to the tenant.

It is generally held that a tenant who moves from leased premises because of a landlord's wrongful eviction is entitled to recover from the landlord as damages the necessary moving expenses incurred by him. He is also entitled to the value of the unexpired portion of his leasehold interest, any direct and reasonably certain loss of profits from a displaced business, and compensation for any other loss sustained as the direct and natural consequence of the landlord's wrongful act. If an unlawful eviction results in physical injury as well as mental anguish or humiliation to the tenant, both of these elements may be considered in determining the amount of damages recoverable by the tenant. And, as in the case of other malicious and wanton torts, if the unlawful eviction is malicious and wanton, the landlord is liable for punitive damages.

URLTA Position The Uniform Residential Landlord and Tenant Act provides that, except in the case of an emergency or the abandonment or surrender of the premises by the tenant, the landlord may not enter a leased dwelling without the consent of the tenant.[17] The tenant, on the other hand, may not unreasonably withhold consent for the landlord to enter to inspect the premises, to make necessary or agreed repairs, decorations, alterations, or improvements, to supply necessary or agreed services, or to show the dwelling unit to prospective purchasers, lenders, tenants, workmen, or contractors.[18]

If the tenant refuses to allow the landlord to enter the premises, the landlord may obtain an injunction to compel access or, if he chooses, he may terminate the rental agreement. In either case, the act provides that the landlord may recover any damages actually sustained by him plus reasonable attorney fees.[19]

The uniform act prohibits a landlord from abusing his right of access and he may not use that right to harass the tenant. Except in the case of an emergency or when it would be impracticable to do so, the landlord must give the tenant at least 2 days notice of his intent to enter the dwelling unit and may enter only during reasonable hours.[20]

If the landlord unlawfully enters the dwelling unit or enters it lawfully but in an unreasonable manner, the tenant may either obtain an injunction to prevent the recurrence of such conduct or he may terminate the rental agreement. These same remedies are available to the tenant if the landlord makes repeated demands for entry which, though otherwise lawful, have the effect of unreasonably harassing the tenant. Whichever remedy the tenant pursues, he is entitled to recover damages in an amount not less than 1 month's rent plus reasonable attorney fees.[21]

Tenant's Implied Obligations Regarding Leased Premises

Obligation Not to Commit Waste While as a general rule a tenant, in the absence of express restrictions in a lease, may use the leased premises for any lawful purpose, he is subject to certain limitations that are implied from the landlord-tenant relationship. These implied obligations are, of course, as much a part of the rental agreement as if they were set forth in express language.

The tenant is, for example, subject to an implied obligation not to commit either voluntary or permissive waste. *Waste* may briefly and generally be defined as the neglect, misuse, alteration, or destruction of premises by one lawfully in possession of them to the prejudice of the estate or interest of another person. *Voluntary waste* to leased premises arises from unreasonable or improper use by the tenant which results in substantial injury to them. *Permissive waste* results when the tenant fails to exercise the ordinary care of the prudent man for the

---

[17] URLTA, sec. 3.103(b) and (d).
[18] Id., sec. 3.103(a).
[19] Id., sec. 4.302(a).

[20] Id., sec. 3.103(d).
[21] Id., sec. 4.302(b).

preservation and protection of buildings and other structures on the leased premises. A tenant who commits waste is liable to the landlord for damages which are generally measured by the decrease in the value of the property resulting from the commission of waste.

A tenant may be held liable to the landlord for the unauthorized destruction or removal of or injury to trees or other vegetation growing on the leased premises. Liability for injury resulting from water or freezing normally depends upon whether a wrongful act or negligence on the part of the tenant was the causative factor. As a general rule, a tenant is not liable for waste when the rented premises suffer injuries from an accident occurring without fault on the part of the tenant or for damage to the premises resulting from an act of God. A tenant generally is held to be liable for the destruction of buildings by fire only in those instances where the fire and destruction are caused by his negligence or wrongful act.

URLTA Position The Uniform Residential Landlord and Tenant Act establishes minimum duties on the part of tenants consistent with public standards of health and safety by requiring a tenant in a dwelling unit to:

1 comply with all obligations primarily imposed upon tenants by applicable building and housing codes materially affecting health and safety;

2 keep that part of the premises he occupies and uses as clean and safe as the conditions of the premises permit;

3 dispose from his dwelling unit all ashes, garbage, rubbish, and other waste in a clean and safe manner;

4 keep all plumbing fixtures in the dwelling unit or used by the tenant as clean as possible;

5 use in a reasonable manner all electrical, plumbing, sanitary, heating, ventilating, air-conditioning and other facilities and appliances including elevators on the premises;

6 not deliberately or negligently destroy, deface, damage, impair or remove any part of the premises or knowingly permit any person to do so; and

7 conduct himself and require other persons on the premises with his consent to conduct themselves in a manner that will not disturb his neighbor's peaceful enjoyment of the premises.[22]

The foregoing provisions of the uniform act codify the tenant's common law duty not to commit waste on the leased premises and afford assurance to the landlord that the value of his property will not be unduly depreciated. If the tenant's failure to comply with his obligations to maintain the premises materially affect health and safety, and if the condition can be corrected by repair, replacement of a damaged item, or by cleaning, but the tenant fails to correct the condition within 14 days after receipt of the landlord's written request or as promptly as emergency conditions require, the landlord may either terminate the lease[23] or enter the premises and correct the condition himself. In the latter case, the landlord may charge the tenant for the reasonable cost of the work done and include it as an addition to the rent on the next date on which the regular rental payment is due.[24]

A novel provision of the uniform act authorizes the inclusion in rental agreements of a requirement that the tenant notify the landlord of any extended absence from the leased premises. The period suggested by the act is 7 days.[25]

If the tenant fails to notify the landlord when required to do so, and the premises are damaged during the tenant's absence, the tenant will be required to reimburse the landlord for the damages sustained by the leased premises, providing, however, that the landlord can establish that the failure to give notice was willful and that the injury would not have occurred but for the tenant's absence.[26]

Implied Limitation on Type of Use The law implies an obligation on the part of the tenant

---

[22] Id., sec. 3.101.
[23] Id., sec. 4.201(a).
[24] Id., sec. 4.202
[25] Id., sec. 3.104.
[26] Id., sec. 4.203(a).

to use the leased premises for the purpose for which they apparently were intended to be used. A tenant can neither use the premises for a purpose not contemplated by the parties at the time of the leasing nor put the building on the premises to a use that is substantially different from that for which it was constructed or for which it is adapted.

URLTA Position According to the uniform act, unless otherwise agreed in the rental agreement, a tenant may only occupy his dwelling unit as a residence and may not use it for any other purpose.[27]

Duty to Yield Possession at End of Lease Implied in every lease for a fixed or definite period of time is an obligation on the part of the tenant to yield or deliver possession of the premises to the landlord when the period of the lease expires. Upon expiration of the lease term all of the tenant's rights in the leased premises come to an end and any holding over of the premises without the landlord's agreement constitutes a legal wrong. The rights of a landlord with respect to a holding over tenant are examined later in the chapter.

Condition of Premises at End of Lease In the absence of an express lease provision to the contrary, a tenant is subject to an implied obligation to return the premises to the landlord at the end of the lease term in the same general condition they were at the time of the leasing, subject only to such general depreciation as may have been caused by reasonable use and the passage of time—frequently referred to as "ordinary wear and tear."

If during the term of the lease a tenant makes alterations or improvements to the leased premises without the landlord's knowledge and consent, the tenant must, prior to expiration of the lease, restore the premises to their original condition or be liable for breach of his implied obligation. Alterations or improvements made by the tenant with the landlord's knowledge and without objection by him are generally regarded as having been consented to by the landlord.

The tenant's implied obligation as to the condition of the premises at the expiration of the lease term generally requires him to remove all his personal property, including property of no value, from the premises. The tenant is not permitted to leave rubbish cluttering up the premises and put the landlord to the expense of having it removed. If the tenant fails to remove his personal property from the premises, the landlord has the right to do so providing he does no wanton injury to them. A landlord is under no obligation to keep a tenant's personal property and protect it until the tenant sees fit to remove it. But a landlord who removes the tenant's property in an improper manner or who negligently injures it will be liable in damages to the tenant. The landlord is entitled to recover from the tenant the reasonable cost of removing the tenant's personal property or rubbish from the premises.

According to the general rule, a tenant who fails to remove personal property from leased premises upon expiration of the lease, or within a reasonable time thereafter, does not forfeit or lose his title to that property.

Injury to Leased Premises by Third Persons

May Damage Both Leasehold and Reversion Since a landlord and a tenant have separate estates or interests in leased premises, where a third party's wrongful act causes injury to the leased premises, the landlord and the tenant both have causes of action against the third party for damage sustained by their respective interests. Wrongful acts which are injurious to the landlord's reversion commonly are also harmful to the tenant's leasehold because the acts render the leased premises less convenient or beneficial for the tenant's use, as, for example, when a third party wrongfully cuts down trees, erects fences or walls, or diverts natural watercourses and causes flooding of land. The wrongdoer, of course, is not com-

---

[27] Id., sec. 3.104.

pelled to respond twice in damages for the same injury caused by his tortious act, but simply to compensate each of the parties—the landlord and the tenant—for the amount of the injury sustained by each one's respective interest in the leased premises.

Tenant's Action for Nuisance A tenant may maintain an action for injuries to his leasehold interest caused by a nuisance, whether the nuisance was commenced during the term of the lease or whether it was already in existence at the time the tenant began his occupancy of the premises. In situations where a nuisance affects the health, comfort, or safety of a tenant in possession of leased premises, he is entitled to the same remedies and relief that are available to an occupying owner.

Measure of Damages The measure of a landlord's damages recoverable from a wrongdoing third party is the amount of the decrease in the value of his property that results from the injurious act.

Where the wrongdoer's act causes permanent injury to the tenant's leasehold interest, the measure of the tenant's damage for such injury is the amount of the diminution in the value of the leasehold interest—the difference between the "before" and "after" value of his leasehold. Where the injury to the leasehold is of a temporary nature, such as harm caused by a trespass or a nuisance that temporarily affects the tenant's use and enjoyment of the premises, the tenant's damages are measured by the decrease in value of the leasehold during the period that the wrong continues.

Habitability of Leased Dwellings

Early Common Law View When land was leased by a tenant at early common law, the lease was regarded as being equivalent to a sale of the leased premises for the period of time indicated in the lease. By virtue of the sales nature of the transaction, the tenant acquired an estate in the land and became both the owner and the occupier of it for the period of the lease. Like other purchasers at early common law, the tenant was subject to the doctrine of caveat emptor—the doctrine that says "let the buyer beware." According to the doctrine, the tenant had the responsibility of looking out for himself by ascertaining through an inspection of the premises he was about to lease that they were in fact what he hoped they would be. If the tenant failed to inspect the premises or otherwise to protect himself by obtaining an express covenant or warranty from the landlord that the premises would be tenantable, fit, or suitable for the use the tenant intended to make of them, whether for habitation, cultivation, or business, the law would not rescue him from his folly. The tenant took the leased premises as he found them, with whatever defects that might be present at the time, and he assumed the risk as to their condition and fitness. The landlord had neither the obligation to put the premises in a condition of good repair at the commencement of the lease term nor the duty of making repairs during the existence of the lease.

Implicit in the doctrine of caveat emptor as applied to leases at common law was the notion that, barring any fraud or active concealment on the part of the landlord, the tenant was as capable of knowing the condition of the premises as was the landlord.

Decline of the Doctrine of Caveat Emptor Developed in an agrarian, nonindustrial age when a prospective tenant more often than not was competent to go upon the land and determine for himself whether it was fit for his purposes, the doctrine of caveat emptor gradually came to be recognized as unsuitable in a more complex urban and industrial society. As one court put it:

> It has come to be recognized that ordinarily the lessee does not have as much knowledge of the condition of the premises as the lessor. Building code requirements and violations are known or made known to the lessor, not the lessee. He is in a better position to know of latent defects, structural and otherwise, in a building which might go unnoticed by a lessee who rarely has sufficient

knowledge or expertise to see or to discover them. A prospective lessee, such as a small businessman, cannot be expected to know if the plumbing or wiring systems are adequate or conform to local codes. Nor should he be expected to hire experts to advise him. Ordinarily all this information should be considered readily available to the lessor who in turn can inform the prospective lessee. These factors have produced persuasive arguments for re-evaluation of the *caveat emptor* doctrine and for imposition of an implied warranty that the premises are suitable for the leased purposes and conform to local codes and zoning laws.[28]

The Implied Warranty of Habitability
Courts and legislatures have created certain exceptions to the doctrine of caveat emptor with respect to leases by implying a warranty of habitability or fitness for use on the part of the landlord. The most significant exception invoking the implied warranty of habitability or fitness for use involves the leasing of residential property. The landlord who could at one time lease a ramshackle and dilapidated dwelling with impunity now leases residential property subject to an implied warranty of habitability on his part.

Rationale Underlying the Warranty The warranty of habitability, which is effective in some form in a majority of states[29] today, either by reason of statute or judicial decision, is a provision implied in rental agreements that requires landlords to provide dwelling units which are substantially in compliance with basic standards of habitability as expressed in local housing codes or as required by public policy. The courts and legislatures, in creating the implied warranty of habitability in residential leases, have rationalized their actions by reference to changing social conditions, the size and complexity of modern multifamily residences, the field of consumer protection, and, most importantly, the recognition of a lease as being a contract as well as a transfer or conveyance of an estate in land. Recognition of a lease as a contract is the necessary basis for imposing an implied obligation on the landlord to provide a dwelling that is habitable at the beginning of the term and maintaining it in that condition throughout the duration of the term.

Meaning of "Habitability" Both as an abstract definition and in its application to an actual case, "habitability" is an elusive concept. The implied warranty of habitability is not a warranty against all inconvenience and discomfort, and proof of a breach of the warranty frequently will not be an easy burden for a complaining tenant to bear. In order to reduce the uncertainty in determining whether premises are habitable or not, almost all courts that imply a warranty of habitability have used the specific and detailed requirements of applicable local housing codes as their criteria or standards. The California Supreme Court[30] stated that the implied warranty of habitability "does not require that a landlord ensure that the premises are in perfect, aesthetically pleasing condition, but it does mean that 'bare living requirements' must be maintained. In most cases substantial compliance with those applicable building and housing code standards which materially affect health and safety will suffice to meet the landlord's obligations under the common law implied warranty of habitability we now recognize."[31]

Maintenance of Habitability throughout Lease Term Judicially conceived and imposed warranties of habitability commonly require that premises used as dwellings be fit for habitation both at the beginning of the lease

---

[28] *Reste Realty Corp. v. Cooper,* 53 N.J. 444, 452, 251 A2d 268, 272 (1969).

[29] Alaska, Arizona, California, Connecticut, Delaware, District of Columbia, Florida, Hawaii, Illinois, Iowa, Kansas, Kentucky, Maine, Maryland, Massachusetts, Michigan, Minnesota, Missouri, Nebraska, New Hampshire, New Jersey, New York, Ohio, Oregon, Pennsylvania, Virginia, Washington, and Wisconsin.

[30] *Green v. Superior Court,* 10 Cal. 3d 616, 517 P2d 1168 (1974).

[31] Id., p. 637.

term and be maintained in a habitable condition by the landlord throughout the period of the lease. In what has become a frequently referenced statement of the implied warranty of habitability, the Iowa Supreme Court said that "the landlord impliedly warrants at the outset of the lease that there are no latent defects in facilities and utilities vital to the use of the premises for residential purposes and that these essential features shall continue during the entire term in such condition to maintain the habitability of the dwelling. Furthermore the implied warranty we perceive in the lease situation is a representation [by the landlord] that there neither is nor shall be during the term a violation of applicable housing law, ordinance or regulations which shall render the premises unsafe, or unsanitary and unfit for living therein."[32]

URLTA Position The Uniform Residential Landlord and Tenant Act imposes a warranty of habitability on the landlord very similar to that imposed by the courts and uses building and housing codes as its basic standard for habitability. The URLTA provision states that a landlord shall:

  1 comply with the requirements of applicable building and housing codes materially affecting health and safety;
  2 make all repairs and do whatever is necessary to put and keep the premises in a fit and habitable condition;
  3 keep all common areas of the premises in a clean and safe condition;
  4 maintain in good and safe working order and condition all electrical, plumbing, sanitary, heating, ventilating, air-conditioning, and other facilities and appliances, including elevators, supplied or required to be supplied by him;
  5 provide and maintain appropriate receptacles and conveniences for the removal of ashes, rubbish, and other waste incidental to the occupancy of the dwelling unit and arrange for their removal; and
  6 supply running water and reasonable amounts of hot water at all times and reasonable heat between [October 1] and [May 1] except where the building that includes the dwelling is not required by law to be equipped for that purpose, or the dwelling unit is so constructed that heat or hot water is generated by an installation within the exclusive control of the tenant and supplied by a direct public utility connection.[33]

The act includes a provision[34] that if the local housing code standards are more stringent or impose a greater duty than the duties imposed by the act, the housing code standards shall control.

The uniform act provides that where a rental agreement involves a single-family residence the landlord and the tenant may agree that the tenant will perform the landlord's duties set forth in items **5** and **6** above, as well as making certain repairs, performing specified maintenance tasks, making specified alterations, and remodeling. To be enforceable, such an agreement must have been made in good faith and not for the purpose of evading the landlord's obligations.[35] "Good faith" is defined in the act to mean "honesty in fact in the conduct of the transaction concerned."[36]

If the dwelling is in a multiunit building rather than being a single-family residence, the act permits a landlord and a tenant to agree that the tenant is to perform specified repairs, maintenance tasks, alterations, and remodeling, but *only if* (1) the agreement is entered into in good faith, set forth in writing, and supported by adequate consideration, (2) the work is *not* necessary to comply with health and safety requirements of building and housing codes, and (3) the agreement does not diminish the landlord's obligation to other tenants in the multiunit premises.[37]

---

[32] *Mease v. Fox* (Iowa), 200 NW2d 791, 796 (1972).
[33] URLTA, sec. 2.104(a).
[34] Id., sec. 2.104(b).
[35] Id., 2.104(c).
[36] Id., sec. 11301(5).
[37] Id., sec. 2.104(d).

Tenant's Right of "Repair and Deduct"

Nature of the Right By either legislative enactment or judicial decision, a considerable number of states[38] have granted to tenants of dwelling units the right to repair, or to hire someone to repair, minor defects in the leased premises that impair the habitability of the premises and thereafter to deduct the cost of such repairs from rent payments. This self-help remedy accorded to tenants is generally known as the tenant's right of **repair and deduct**.

Limitations on the Right A tenant's right of repair and deduct is not without limitations, some of which seem to diminish the effectiveness of the right considerably.

In the first place, repair and deduct statutes usually limit the amount that a tenant may spend for repairs and deduct from his rent payments[39] as well as restricting the frequency with which the tenant may exercise his right.[40] The effect of these restrictions, of course, is to limit the tenant's right to relatively minor and low cost repairs.

Some repair and deduct statutes and judicial decisions require the tenant to notify the landlord of defects and dilapidated conditions and give him a reasonable period of time within which to make repairs before the tenant may undertake to do so.[41] It has been suggested that tenants who are unaware of the notice requirement are apt to make needed repairs and after having done so learn that they cannot make rent deductions because they failed to give the required notice. A more significant objection to the reasonable time requirement arises from the fact that a tenant may be required to tolerate defects or dilapidations while the landlord contemplates whether to correct the condition or not.

A final but important limitation on a tenant's use of his right of repair and deduct arises from the risk that a tenant must assume when he exercises the right. The tenant runs the risk that, if the landlord sues him for the portion of the rent that the tenant deducted, the court might judge the corrected defect to have been insufficient to have justified the exercise of the right, that the tenant failed to give adequate notice, or that he failed to wait a reasonable time before making the repairs himself. Such a determination by a court would render the tenant liable for the full amount of the withheld rent as well as the cost of the repairs.

URLTA Position The Uniform Residential Landlord and Tenant Act provides that if the landlord fails to comply with the provisions of the rental agreement or the requirements of applicable building and housing codes, or fails to make all repairs necessary to keep the premises in a fit and habitable condition,[42] the tenant may take steps to correct minor defects himself.

The act provides that if the reasonable cost of correcting the landlord's failure to comply with his obligations is not more than one-half the periodic rent or $100, whichever is the greater, the tenant may correct the condition and deduct the cost from the rent. To be entitled to exercise the right of repair and deduct, however, the tenant must allow the landlord a period of 14 days to correct the condition after receipt of a written notice from the tenant indicating the tenant's intention to make the repairs at the landlord's expense.[43] A tenant who

---

[38] Alaska, Arizona, California, Colorado, Delaware, Georgia, Hawaii, Illinois, Kentucky, Louisiana, Massachusetts, Michigan, Montana, Nebraska, New Jersey, North Dakota, Ohio, Oklahoma, Oregon, South Dakota, Virginia, and Washington.

[39] Arizona, for example, limits the amount to half a month's rent or $150, whichever is the greater; California to 1 month's rent; and Massachusetts to 2 months' rent.

[40] For instance, California limits the tenant's use of the right to once in a 12-month period. (Civil Code, sec. 1942(a).

[41] A California statute requiring the tenant to give the landlord a reasonable time after receiving notice to repair dilapidations provides that "if a lessee acts to repair after the 30th day following notice, he is presumed to have acted after a reasonable time." (Civil Code, sec. 1942(b).)

[42] URLTA, sec. 2.104(a)(1) and (2).
[43] Id., sec. 4.103(a).

makes repairs after the lapse of the 14-day period must submit an itemized statement of the expenses incurred to the landlord at the time he makes his deduction from the rent payment.[44]

The act denies a tenant the right to make any repairs at the landlord's expense if the faulty condition was caused by the deliberate or negligent act or omission of the tenant, a member of his family, or someone on the premises with the tenant's consent.[45]

Retaliatory Action by Landlord

Methods of Retaliation Residential tenants who complain to public authorities about landlords' violations of the housing code or who notify their landlords of defective conditions as part of the repair and deduct procedure run the risk of incurring their landlords' displeasure and provoking retaliatory action by them. Retaliatory measures available to a landlord against a periodic tenant may take the form of increasing the monthly rent, notice to terminate the rental agreement, reduction or discontinuance of services, utility shutoffs, or other methods of harassment.

Antiretaliatory Laws Recognizing the general problem of retaliation and the need to prevent landlords from taking advantage of their position to intimidate and punish tenants, more than half of the states[46] by legislation or judicial decision protect tenants from some types of retaliatory actions by landlords. All of these jurisdictions protect tenants who report housing code violations and a majority of them also prohibit retaliatory rent increases and decreases in services.

Problem of Retaliatory Intent A major problem of any tenant who alleges an act of retaliation by his landlord is the difficult task of proving the landlord's retaliatory intent or motive. A majority of the states that have antiretaliatory legislation attempt to resolve this problem by presuming a retaliatory intent on the part of the landlord when statutorily specified action is taken by him within a certain period of time following notice or other action by the tenant.[47] The effect of the statutory presumption, of course, is to require the landlord to bear the burden of establishing the fact that his action during the statutory period was not retaliatory in character. Once the time period of the presumption runs out, however, a tenant who alleges retaliatory action has the burden of proving the landlord's retaliatory intent. Given the difficulties inherent in such proof, the protection afforded by the antiretaliatory legislation may have the effect of merely postponing retaliation by a landlord rather than preventing it.

URLTA Position The Uniform Residential Landlord and Tenant Act prohibits three common forms of retaliatory conduct by a landlord: (1) raising the tenant's rent, (2) decreasing services provided to the tenant, and (3) bringing an action for possession of the leased premises.[48]

If the landlord does any one of the foregoing things within 1 year after the tenant has (1) reported a building or housing code violation to government authorities,[49] (2) complained to the landlord about violation of his maintenance obligations imposed by the act,[50] or (3) organized or joined a tenant union,[51] the uniform act establishes the presumption that the landlord's action is retaliatory.[52] However, retaliation is not presumed when the landlord

---

[44] Id.
[45] Id., sec. 4.103(b).
[46] Alaska, Arizona, California, Connecticut, Delaware, District of Columbia, Hawaii, Illinois, Kentucky, Maine, Massachusetts, Michigan, Minnesota, Nebraska, New Hampshire, New Jersey, New York, Ohio, Oregon, Pennsylvania, Rhode Island, Tennessee, Virginia, Washington, and Wisconsin.

[47] The statutory period is often 6 months as is the case in Arizona, Connecticut, Hawaii, Maine, Massachusetts, Minnesota, and Oregon, for example.
[48] URLTA, sec. 5.101(a).
[49] Id., 5.101(a)(1).
[50] Id., 5.101(1)(2).
[51] Id., 5.101(a)(3).
[52] Id., 5.101(b).

brings an action for possession if (1) the building or housing code violation was caused primarily by lack of reasonable care by the tenant or his family,[53] (2) the tenant is in default in rent,[54] or (3) compliance with the housing code requires substantial repairs or alterations that can only be done on an empty dwelling unit.[55]

Housing Codes

Characteristics and Obligations A **housing code** is a legislative enactment that establishes minimum standards for buildings occupied by humans and creates a legal obligation on the part of landlords to comply with those standards. Although housing codes may regulate additional matters, they normally (1) require the installation of certain equipment and facilities, such as kitchen and bathroom facilities, electricity, light, and heating facilities, water supply, solid and liquid waste disposal, and ventilation, (2) set standards for proper maintenance, including cleanliness and repair, and the elimination of such unsanitary conditions as rodents and vermin, and (3) regulate the density of occupancy of buildings by establishing standards for prescribing the minimum size of dwelling units for given numbers of occupants.[56]

Exercise of Police Power The typical housing code is a municipal ordinance enacted pursuant to state enabling legislation. Because they are enacted locally, housing code standards lack uniformity even within the same state. Some states[57] have enacted state housing codes applicable either to certain cities or classes of municipalities, while other states[58] have extensive housing legislation that permits municipalities to adopt their own codes which, while they must be consistent with the state laws, may be more stringent in their requirements.

The power of a state or municipality to establish housing standards by enactment of housing codes is not open to question. The authority to impose reasonable requirements relative to housing conditions and housing maintenance is found in the state's police power to protect public order and the health, safety, and welfare of the people. Housing regulations are held to be valid by the courts as long as they bear a demonstrable relationship to the public health, safety, and welfare and do not, in violation of the Fifth Amendment, deprive an owner of housing of any property interest without due process of law.[59]

Problem of Enforcement Studies reveal that housing codes alone have done little to prevent the deterioration and dilapidation of housing.[60] The failure generally has not been attributable to the content of the codes but rather to their enforcement. The original idea was to enforce housing codes by public officials imposing criminal sanctions on owners whose violations were discovered by housing inspectors either as a result of routine inspection or in response to a complaint. Because of understaffing of inspectors, typically low fines, lack of jail sentences, etc., this method of enforcement was never successful. Recognizing the ineffectiveness of purely criminal sanctions for code violations,

---

[53] Id., 5.101(c)(1).

[54] Id., 5.101(c)(2).

[55] Id., 5.101(c)(3).

[56] Housing codes differ from building codes which are generally concerned with structural standards such as specifications for building materials and components.

[57] For example, Connecticut, Iowa, Massachusetts, Michigan, Minnesota, New Jersey, and Pennsylvania.

[58] California and New York, for example.

[59] Housing codes have frequently been attacked on grounds that newly enacted standards have a retroactive effect on existing housing that does not meet the new requirements. The courts, with isolated exceptions, have rejected contentions that such new code provisions are retroactive in the sense in which a constitutionally objectionable ex post facto law is retroactive, holding that an owner violating new housing standards is not being punished for his *past* lack of newly required facilities, but only for failing to provide such facilities *after* the effective date of the new code provision. An owner of housing does not have a vested interest in having the law applicable to his property remain unchanged.

[60] See, for example, Judah Gribetz and Frank P. Grad, *Housing Code Enforcement and Remedies,* 66 Columbia Law Review 1254 (1966).

legislatures authorized the imposition of civil sanctions in the form of cumulative penalties of so much for each day that the violation continued, ordering buildings vacated until owners complied with code provisions, appointing a receiver of rent payments and using them to correct violations, and similar economic incentives to landlords to comply with the law. Even so, the understaffed code enforcement agencies have been unable to employ civil sanctions any more effectively than they can use criminal sanctions.

Because of the ineffectiveness of traditional housing code enforcement techniques, several states have passed legislation permitting tenants to take steps that serve to enforce housing code provisions by authorizing a tenant (1) to repair any code violation that makes the premises "untenantable" and deduct the cost from the rent,[61] or (2) to withhold payment of rent if the landlord, after having received a certified notice of code violation from an enforcement agency, fails to make the required repairs within a reasonable period of time.[62] By means of these statutory techniques, the tenant exerts a certain economic pressure on the landlord to maintain the premises in good repair.

Despite the fact that housing codes have not been particularly successful in maintaining or upgrading urban housing, they have played a useful role in the court's recognition of a landlord's implied warranty of habitability by their imposing on landlords an obligation to maintain leased properties in a safe, sanitary, and livable condition.

URLTA Position While the Uniform Residential Landlord and Tenant Act does not contain a housing code, it does provide that a landlord shall "comply with the requirements of applicable building and housing codes materially affecting health and safety."[63] The act defines building and housing codes as including "any law, ordinance, or governmental regulation concerning fitness for habitation, or the construction, maintenance, operation, occupancy, use, or appearance of any premises or dwelling unit."[64]

Holding Over by Tenant

Status of Tenant Determined by Landlord A tenant who holds over or remains in possession of leased premises without permission of the landlord is a wrongdoer because his former right to occupy the premises has expired. Despite his wrongful possession, however, for technical reasons the holding over tenant does not immediately become a trespasser. The tenant only becomes a trespasser if and when the landlord chooses to treat him as such. The landlord is given the choice of either treating the tenant as a trespasser or waiving the wrong arising from the holding over and accept him as a tenant occupying the premises. While the landlord has this choice of alternatives available to him, the tenant does not. The legal status of the tenant who holds over after expiration of the lease term is whatever the landlord elects to make it.

Liability to Landlord in Damages A tenant who wrongfully withholds possession of leased premises is liable to the landlord in damages. The measure of the tenant's liability to the landlord is the reasonable rental value of the premises for the period of the wrongful withholding. The amount of the reasonable rental value may be the same, greater, or less than the contract rental the tenant previously paid during the term of the lease. In addition to the reasonable rental value, the landlord has been permitted to recover the costs and expenses of a lawsuit to regain possession, including reasonable attorney fees. Statutes in some states also

---

[61] See, for example, California Civil Code, sec. 1942.
[62] See, for example, New York Real Property Actions, sec. 755, New York Mult. Dwelling Law, sec. 302(a). Most such statutes require the tenant to pay the withheld rent into an escrow account.

[63] URLTA, sec. 2.104(a)(1).
[64] Id., 1.301(2).

provide for the payment of punitive damages by a tenant who *willfully* withholds possession from the landlord.

Like the parties to any contract, a landlord and a tenant may provide in their rental agreement for a stipulated amount of liquidated damages which will be paid by the tenant in lieu of damages measured by the reasonable rental value of the premises. Where the courts determine that such a stipulation is in fact a provision for the payment of liquidated damages and is not a penalty imposed on the tenant, the provision generally is held to be valid and will be enforced.

Renewal or Extension of Landlord-Tenant Relationship Instead of treating a tenant who holds over after expiration of the lease term as a trespasser and taking steps to remove him from the premises, the landlord may elect to treat him as a tenant. The landlord's right to treat the holdover as a tenant instead of a trespasser is not dependent upon the length of time that the tenant wrongfully holds over, and the holdover may be held liable as a tenant for a further term without reference to his wishes. The type of tenant the holdover becomes is to a large extent dependent upon the nature of the landlord's assent to the holding over and his treatment of the holdover.

The general rule is that if, after the expiration of the lease, the holding over tenant tenders payment of rent to the landlord and he accepts it, the landlord will be held to have consented to a renewal or extension of the landlord-tenant relationship. Some states[65] have enacted statutes providing that where a tenant, with the assent of the landlord, holds over after expiration of a tenancy for 1 or more years, he shall be deemed to be a tenant from year to year. Statutes in other states[66] provide that a holding over after the expiration of a lease for any definite or fixed term gives rise to a periodic tenancy from month to month.

The covenants and other terms that govern the landlord-tenant relationship resulting from a tenant's holding over may be derived either from an express provision in the original lease, from a new arrangement entered into by the landlord and the tenant, or from the provisions of a statute. In the absence of any of these, the amount of and time for the rental payment are generally held to be the same as those provided for in the parties' previous rental agreement.

Tenant at Sufferance Until a landlord does something that can be construed as recognition of a renewal or extension of the landlord-tenant relationship, the tenant holding over is considered to be a tenant at sufferance. During the period that the holdover is regarded as such a tenant, the landlord is free to decide whether to allow or refuse to allow him to remain on the premises. Statutes in some jurisdictions provide that the landlord, as a prerequisite to bringing an action to oust a tenant at sufferance, must give him notice to vacate the premises,[67] but in the absence of such a statute the tenant is not entitled to notice.

Some statutes provide that a tenant at sufferance is liable for rent equal to that stipulated in the original lease,[68] while others hold him liable for the reasonable rental value of the premises during his occupancy of the premises at sufferance.[69]

Tenant at Will Statutes in some states[70] declare that a tenant who holds over without objection by the landlord is a tenant at will and the courts in other states[71] adopt the same view. Other states do not favor tenancies at will and

---

[65] For example, Kansas, Oklahoma, and Wisconsin.
[66] For example, Arizona, Delaware, and New Jersey.
[67] For example, the District of Columbia requires 30 days' notice; Kentucky, 1 month.
[68] Statutes in Alabama and Massachusetts, for example, so provide.
[69] For example, Mississippi and New Jersey have statutes providing for the payment of reasonable rent.
[70] For example, Florida and Oklahoma.
[71] For example, Alabama and Massachusetss.

imply a more permanent type of tenancy when a landlord permits a holding over tenant to remain on the premises.

URLTA Position The Uniform Residential Landlord and Tenant Act provides that if a tenant remains in possession of the leased premises after termination of the lease without the landlord's consent, the landlord may bring an action to obtain possession.[72] The act further provides that if the tenant's holding over is willful and not in good faith, the landlord may recover either 3 months' rent or three times the actual damages sustained by him, whichever is the greater, plus reasonable attorney's fees.[73]

QUESTIONS

1. How is the landlord-tenant relationship created? What are the respective property interests of a landlord and a tenant?
2. Distinguish between the rights of a tenant and those of a licensee.
3. What is meant by the statement that a lease impliedly transfers everything that is appurtenant to the leased premises?
4. Explain how a tenancy for years differs from a periodic tenancy.
5. What is a tenancy at sufferance? What courses of action are available to a landlord with respect to a tenant at sufferance?
6. What is a percentage lease of real estate? What is the theory on which it is based?
7. Discuss the circumstances in which a court will enforce an agreement that a security deposit shall serve as liquidated damages for a tenant's breach of covenant.
8. Explain the manner in which an option to purchase leased premises operates. What if the landlord dies before the option is exercised?
9. What are the stated purposes of the Uniform Residential Landlord and Tenant Act?
10. Explain how the so-called American and English rules regarding delivery of possession of leased premises by a landlord to a tenant differ.
11. How does an actual eviction of a tenant by a landlord differ from a constructive eviction of the tenant?
12. Distinguish between "voluntary waste" and "permissive waste" as those terms are used in connection with the landlord-tenant relationship.
13. As used in connection with the renting of premises for residential purposes, what is the meaning of the word "habitability"? What is the nature of the implied warranty of habitability?
14. Describe a tenant's right of "repair and deduct" as granted by statutes or judicial decisions in a considerable number of states.
15. What kind of conduct by a landlord is considered to be retaliatory? What kinds of protection have a majority of states afforded tenants against such conduct?
16. What kinds of matters are commonly regulated by housing codes? How do they differ from building codes?
17. What is the legal status of a tenant who holds over or remains in possession of leased premises after his lease has expired?

[72] URLTA, sec. 4.301(c).
[73] Id.

Chapter 24

Landlord and Tenant— Part II

TORT LIABILITY OF LANDLORD AND TENANT

Landlord's Liability for Defective Premises
The rules of law that govern a landlord's **tort liability** for injuries resulting from defects in leased premises are largely the result of the common law's characterization of a lease as a conveyance of real property rather than a contract. Aside from the exceptions hereinafter noted, a landlord as the conveyor of an estate in real property is immune from any liability for personal injury or property damage resulting from the defective condition of the leased premises. Like the seller of real estate, a landlord at common law is entitled to invoke the doctrine of caveat emptor to immunize himself against tort liability.

Because a tenant has the right and the opportunity to inspect premises before he leases them, he is considered at common law to have assumed the risk of any personal injury or property damage that might result from a defective condition of the premises that existed and was reasonably discoverable by him at the time the lease commenced. Furthermore, once the tenant acquires possession and control of the leased premises, the landlord at common law is not liable to persons other than the tenant who might be injured because of defective conditions that were in existence at the time the lease began. In addition, since the common law makes it the duty of the tenant to repair the leased premises after he takes control of them, the landlord is immune from liability to both the tenant and to third persons for injuries caused by defects in the leased premises that arise during the term of the lease.

With the increase in migration of population from rural to urban areas, and as a result of pressure to shift responsibility for repairs and

393

liability for failure to make them from the tenant to the landlord, a number of exceptions to the rule of caveat emptor have been developed by the courts. These exceptions which render a landlord liable for injuries sustained by the tenant or other persons because of the defective condition of the premises include (1) the landlord's concealment of a known latent defect existing at the time of the leasing; (2) the landlord's breach of warranty of habitability implied by some courts with respect to short-term leases of furnished dwellings; (3) the landlord's failure to perform his covenant to repair the leased premises; (4) the landlord's failure to discharge a statutorily imposed duty to repair; (5) the landlord's failure to maintain the common areas under his control in good repair; (6) the landlord's negligence in making repairs undertaken by him; and, (7) the landlord's failure to put premises intended for use by the public in safe condition.

Concealment of Known Latent Defect One of the earliest exceptions to the landlord's immunity from tort liability recognized by the common law involved injury resulting from a latent defect in the leased premises that the landlord knew about at the time of the leasing but which he failed to disclose to the tenant. This exception does not free the tenant from the burden of examining the premises at the time of the leasing to discover any defects that could be detected by a reasonable inspection. The landlord is under no duty to inform a tenant of conditions of the premises which are apparent nor is the landlord liable for injury resulting from latent or hidden defects of which he had no knowledge at the beginning of the lease. If, however, at the time of the leasing the landlord is or should be aware of dangerous or unhealthful conditions of the premises arising from latent defects, he is under a duty to disclose that fact to the tenant. His failure to do so or his concealment of the fact constitutes fraud or negligence which will render him liable to the tenant, members of the tenant's family, and other persons rightfully on the leased premises.

Although a majority of courts originally imposed liability only when it was established that the landlord had actual knowledge of the latent defect, many courts today hold the landlord liable if it is shown that he had knowledge of facts that would lead a reasonable man to suspect that defective conditions did exist.[1] It obviously is difficult for a tenant as plaintiff to show that the landlord had reason to know of a defective condition of the premises without at the same time establishing facts that show contributory fault on the part of the tenant. Because of this difficulty, this exception to the landlord's immunity from liability is one of the least used exceptions. The exception tends to be most successful for the tenant when he proceeds on the theory that the landlord had *actual* knowledge of the dangerous condition of the leased premises that caused the harm of which the tenant complains.

Breach of Implied Warranty When Dwelling Is Furnished A minority of courts have permitted a tenant to recover for personal injuries or property damage by implying a warranty of habitability by a landlord who leases a *furnished* dwelling for a short period of time. This view has been adopted primarily by those jurisdictions that require actual knowledge of a latent defect by a landlord before imposing liability on him.

This exception to a landlord's immunity from liability, like the foregoing exception, applies only to defective conditions of the leased premises that were in existence when the lease commenced—not to those defects that arise after the tenant has taken possession.

Failure to Perform Covenant to Repair While the courts have been sharply divided as to whether to impose tort liability on a landlord for personal injuries or property damage resulting from the breach of his covenant to repair, a

---

[1] This latter position has been adopted by the Restatement of Torts (2d), sec. 358.

majority of jurisdictions does impose such liability.[2] The majority takes the view that the landlord's covenant to repair is sufficient to impose tort liability on him and that his contractual duty to repair both creates and defines the nature of his tort duty of care. The significance of this view is that the landlord is held liable to both the tenant and third parties for all damages resulting from the breached covenant, instead of being liable only to the tenant for the cost of repair or loss of rental value of the leased premises as would be the case if the landlord's liability for damages were measured by breach of contract rules. By way of justification for this exception to a landlord's immunity from tort liability, the courts emphasize the fact that if a landlord voluntarily chooses to enter into a contract to make repairs, he should not be permitted to avoid the operation of the principle of negligence law that imposes liability for breach of a contractual obligation.

The landlord's obligation under a covenant or contract to repair the leased premises is to exercise a reasonable standard of care and the specific nature of his duty is dependent upon the terms of his agreement. When the covenant is a part of the original lease made before the tenant enters into possession, the landlord has the duty of inspecting the premises before transferring them to the tenant. Unless the landlord's covenant provides that he will inspect the leased premises periodically after the tenant enters into possession, the landlord is obligated to make repairs only after he has received notice of the dangerous or defective condition. On the other hand, if the landlord's covenant provides that he will periodically inspect the leased premises to determine the need for repairs, he will be liable for injuries resulting from defective conditions that would have been discovered by a reasonable inspection by him.

Failure to Perform Statutory Duty to Repair None of the housing codes enacted by the various state legislatures creates a cause of action against a landlord for personal injury or property damage resulting from a violation of the housing legislation. As a consequence, in response to appeals by injured persons, the courts have created an exception to a landlord's immunity that is based on the widely accepted tort principle that a statute may establish the standard of conduct for a negligence action.[3]

A large number of jurisdictions adopt the view that the violation of a housing code is either negligence per se or evidence of negligence which gives rise to tort liability on the part of the landlord. These jurisdictions generally hold that the landlord's duty of care created by a housing code extends not only to the tenant but also to anyone who is lawfully on the leased premises.

In those jurisdictions that impose tort liability for the violation of a housing code, it is generally agreed that liability may be based on the landlord's *constructive* notice of statutory violations in the common areas of the premises that are under his control. The landlord is considered to have constructive notice of a defect if the party injured by the defective condition proves that the landlord had a reasonable opportunity and time to inspect the area and discover the defect and correct it. Where the defect that violates the housing code occurs in the leased portions of the premises that are not under the landlord's control, the courts have been faced with a dilemma. In a growing number of jurisdictions, the courts have held it to be the duty of the landlord to inspect sanitary, heating, water and lighting systems on the theory that they are actually under his control.

Failure to Maintain Common Areas One of the most frequently invoked exceptions to a landlord's immunity from tort liability arises in connection with areas of multiunit dwellings and office buildings that are used in common by all tenants and possession and control of

---

[2] The Restatement of Torts (2d), sec. 357 represents the majority view.

[3] See Restatement Torts of (2d), secs. 285(b), 286–288B.

which are said to be retained by the landlord. The common areas for use by all tenants include such things as approaches and entrances to the leased premises, lobbies, elevators, stairways, hallways, fire escapes, storage and utility rooms, garages, recreational areas, as well as heating, plumbing, and electrical systems, and such appliances as washing machines and dryers furnished for the tenants' common use. Because the landlord is in possession and control of these common areas, he owes all tenants and other persons who are lawfully on the premises the duty of exercising reasonable care and diligence in maintaining those areas in a safe condition.[4]

With respect to defective conditions of the common areas of which a landlord has either actual or constructive notice, his duty of reasonable care requires that he either give tenants, their families, and their guests sufficient warning to avoid the risk of harm or that he repair the dangerous condition within a reasonable period of time.

Negligence in Making Repairs Regardless of whether a landlord repairs defective conditions gratuitously or pursuant to the covenant to repair, if he makes repairs and does so in a negligent manner, he will be liable for any resulting personal injury or property damage. Virtually every jurisdiction recognizes this exception to the landlord's immunity from tort liability. Liability is imposed on the landlord, not because of the landlord-tenant relationship itself, but because the landlord, in negligently making repairs, breached his general duty to avoid creating unreasonable risk of harm to others by his affirmative conduct. Since the basis of the landlord's liability is negligence, there must be a causal connection between the act of negligence and the injury sustained.

The landlord's liability, arising as it does from his duty to exercise due care, extends to anyone who is lawfully on the leased premises.

Leased Premises Intended for Public Use A final exception to a landlord's immunity from tort liability arises in connection with leased premises that the landlord knows will be opened by the tenant to use by the public. Typical of such premises are amusement parks, sport arenas, theaters, hotels, restaurants, public garages, and similar places that are open to the public.

The landlord is under a duty to exercise reasonable care in inspecting such premises, prior to the transfer of possession to the tenant, to discover defects that might be present. The landlord's liability extends only to the public, not to the tenant, and his liability is based on a theory of negligence. As far as the landlord's liability for injuries resulting from his negligence is concerned, it is immaterial whether the tenant charges for admission to the leased premises or collects any money by way of sale or otherwise from members of the public entering the premises.

Exculpatory Clauses in Leases Standard lease forms frequently contain a clause which exculpates or absolves a landlord from liability for any personal injury or property damage sustained by a tenant as a result of negligence on the part of the landlord or his agents. By means of such a clause, the tenant agrees to assume the risk of what would ordinarily be a breach of duty by the landlord.

In situations other than the landlord-tenant relationship, such as contracts between employer and employee and contracts between one who performs a public service[5] and a member of the public, for example, the courts have often held exculpatory clauses to be void on the grounds that it would be against public policy to enforce them. The courts have not, however,

---

[4] The Restatement of Torts (2d), at sec. 360–361, adopts this exception to the landlord's immunity from tort liability.

[5] Such as an innkeeper, a bailee, a common carrier, or a public utility.

as a general rule applied the same reasoning to exculpatory clauses in leases, rationalizing that a lease is an agreement relating exclusively to the private affairs of the landlord and the tenant and not a matter of public interest. Based on that rationale and the doctrine of freedom of contract, the courts in a number of jurisdictions[6] have held that, in the absence of a statute to the contrary, exculpatory clauses providing that a landlord shall not be liable for damages arising from certain specified causes or from all causes to be valid and enforceable.

In order to soften the impact of the general rule that exculpatory clauses in leases are valid, the courts are inclined to construe such clauses very strictly. The courts have also begun to recognize that in certain circumstances the landlord-tenant relationship can be a matter of public interest, as where public housing leases are involved or where a severe housing shortage has placed the landlord and tenant in unequal bargaining positions. There is also considerable support today for the view that a lease for a *dwelling* is not purely a matter of private interest controlled by the principle of freedom of contract.

A few states[7] have enacted legislation declaring exculpatory clauses in leases to be invalid.

Tenant's Liability for Defective Premises

In an earlier chapter[8] we examined the nature of the obligation owned by the occupier of land to persons who come upon his property. As noted in that chapter, the obligation is owed whether the occupier of real property is a fee simple owner or someone, like a tenant, with a lesser interest in the property. In order that a tenant's tort liability for the condition of the premises he occupies may be placed in its proper setting, a tenant's obligation as an occupier of real property is briefly repeated here.

Subject to certain exceptions, at common law it is the tenant and not the landlord who is liable for injuries to third parties caused by the condition or the use of the leased premises. Once possession and control of the leased premises have passed to the tenant, visitors, customers, employees, etc., coming upon the premises are normally not there for any purpose related to the landlord. As far as third persons or the public are concerned, a tenant in control of leased premises is regarded as the owner.

It is well settled that a tenant occupying leased premises who directly or by implication invites or induces others to come upon the premises owes such persons the duty of having the premises in a reasonably safe condition and to warn them of latent or concealed defects. A tenant in complete control of premises occupied by him owes the same duty to persons coming there, at his express or implied invitation, to keep the premises in reasonably safe condition as he would if he were the fee simple owner rather than a tenant.

The tenant's duty is limited to persons who are invited and he has no duty to keep the premises safe for trespassers or intruders who come upon them without invitation or right.

As we saw above, when a landlord knows that the premises are leased for use by the public and he knows, or through the exercise of reasonable diligence should know, that the premises are not safe for such use, he will be liable to members of the public for injuries caused by the dangerous condition. This so-called public purpose rule imposes upon the landlord the duty to make the leased premises safe for the purpose for which they are intended to be used. The landlord's liability is limited, however, to defective conditions in existence at the time of leasing. The tenant as occupier of the premises is liable for injuries resulting from defective conditions arising after the term of the lease commences.

---

[6] For example, Alabama, California, Colorado, District of Columbia, Georgia, Illinois, Indiana, Iowa, Kansas, Kentucky, Maryland, Massachusetts, and Washington.

[7] Among them Illinois, Maryland, Massachusetts, and New York.

[8] Chapter 7, "Incidents of Ownership."

TRANSFER OF LEASED PROPERTY

Landlord's Interest Freely Transferable

A landlord's interest in leased property—the reversion—is freely transferable by him at any time without regard to whether the term of the tenant's lease has expired. The landlord may transfer his reversion by deed during his lifetime or by will upon his death. The landlord's right freely to transfer his interest in the leased property is, of course, simply a property right that is an incident of his ownership.

Transferee Becomes New Landlord

When the landlord transfers ownership of the leased property, the transferee takes the place of the original landlord and becomes the tenant's new landlord. Once the tenant has been notified of the transfer of ownership and the identity of the new landlord, his obligation to pay rent is thereafter owed to the new landlord, not the original one. Payment of rent to the original landlord after having received notice of the change in ownership of the leased premises will not relieve the tenant of his obligation to the new owner.

It is well settled that rent yet to accrue under a rental agreement is an incident to and accompanies a transfer of the reversion even though no mention is made of it in the document of transfer. Therefore, unless the transfer document expressly provides to the contrary, the transferee of the reversion is entitled to receive all rent that accrues after the effective date on the transfer.

Transfer upon Death of Landlord

The death of the landlord during the term of the lease does not terminate it nor are the tenant's rights under the lease in any way affected. Upon the death of the landlord, the reversion passes to his devisees by will or to his heirs by intestate succession, subject to the tenant's rights under the lease which still remains in effect.

Effect on Tenant's Interest

In the absence of a contrary provision in a lease, the landlord's transfer of the reversion neither terminates the tenant's leasehold interest nor deprives him of any rights that he acquired by the provisions of the lease. It is not uncommon, however, for a lease to provide that upon the sale of the leased premises the landlord shall have the option of terminating the lease. A tenant who accepts such a provision in a rental agreement must, of course, be prepared to accept the consequences of the landlord's election to exercise his right of termination.

The transferee of leased property, whether he acquires that property by gift, purchase, or inheritance, takes the property subject to any rights of the tenant of which the transferee has notice or knowledge. As we previously observed, notice to a transferee may be either actual or constructive, with constructive notice arising either from the fact that the tenant's lease has been recorded or because of the tenant's occupancy of the leased premises.

Where a lease contains an express covenant by the landlord to make repairs to the leased premises, the obligation resulting from that covenant runs with the land and is imposed upon the landlord's transferee.

TRANSFER OF TENANT'S INTEREST

Tenant's Right to Assign or Sublease

In the absence of a provision in a lease prohibiting such action, a tenant may either (1) assign his leasehold interest or (2) sublease the leased premises. This right on the part of the tenant is simply the application of the rule that favors the free alienability or transferability of estates in real property. As a result of this predilection of the law, provisions in rental agreements that restrict a tenant's right to assign or sublease are strictly construed and narrowly limited by the courts. Hence, a provision in a lease prohibiting an assignment by the tenant does not affect his right to sublease, nor does a provision against subleasing prohibit the right to assign.

The determination as to whether a particular transaction is an assignment or a sublease may be of considerable importance. For example, we have seen that leases sometimes contain a provision giving the tenant an option to purchase the leased premises. The courts generally have held that an assignee of a lease containing such a provision has the right to exercise the option, while a sublease does not.

A provision in a lease that prohibits an assignment or sublease by the tenant without the written consent of the landlord will be enforced by the courts. The majority of states hold that when such a provision is present in a rental agreement, the landlord may withhold his consent for any reason or for no reason at all.

Assignment of the Leasehold Interest

Nature of an Assignment An **assignment** of a leasehold is a transaction in which a tenant transfers his entire interest in the leased premises for the unexpired period of the lease.

In an assignment there is a complete substitution of a new tenant, the **assignee,** for the original one, the **assignor.** As a consequence of the assignment, the landlord acquires a right of action directly against the assignee on the covenant to pay rent or any other covenant that runs with the land. The assignee is presumed to know the terms and conditions of the lease that has been assigned to him and consequently he acquires no greater rights with respect to the leased premises than the original tenant had prior to the assignment.

Limiting the Right to Assign Unless a lease contains a provision expressly restricting such right, a tenant under a lease for a fixed or definite period has, as an incident of his leasehold interest, the right to assign his interest in the leased premises without the need to obtain the consent of the landlord.

It is universally recognized that an owner of real property may include in a lease for a fixed term a provision prohibiting an assignment of the leasehold interest without first obtaining the consent of the landlord. The prohibition may include a provision for the forfeiture of the tenant's leasehold interest in the event the tenant violates the prohibition against assignment.

The reasoning behind the landlord's being able to prohibit an assignment by the tenant is that it is reasonable that an owner of property should be entitled to decide who shall be permitted to occupy and use his property. Despite such reasoning, however, restraints or limitations on a tenant's right to assign are not favored by the law and consequently provisions preventing assignment will not be implied by the courts. Moreover, since an express restriction in a lease against assignment is a restraint on alienation of the tenant's interest, the courts will strictly construe the provision against the landlord.

Leases commonly contain a covenant on the part of the tenant not to assign his interest without the express consent of the landlord. If, despite such a covenant, the tenant makes an unauthorized assignment and thus breaches the covenant, the landlord ordinarily may declare a forfeiture of the lease by the tenant and terminate it. But unless the landlord takes timely steps to terminate the lease, the assignment will be valid regardless of the lack of express consent by the landlord. The landlord's right to declare a forfeiture of the lease and terminate it is deemed to be waived if he accepts rental payments from the assignee.

A leasehold interest, we have seen, does not terminate upon the death of the tenant but instead passes to his personal representative, an executor or administrator, by operation of law. Such a transfer is not considered to be a breach of a covenant in the lease restricting assignment of the leasehold interest.

Continuing Liability of Assignor In the absence of a release of liability from the landlord, an assigning tenant continues to be liable on his express covenant to pay rent even though the assignment was made with the consent of the landlord. If the person to whom the leasehold was assigned fails to make rental payments in accordance with his agreement with the original tenant when the assignment was made, the landlord may sue either the original tenant or the assignee or he may sue both at the same time, but of course he can only recover one satisfaction. If the original tenant is compelled to pay the rent, he is entitled to be indemnified for such payment by the assignee.

The original tenant's continuing liability to the landlord is not limited merely to the payment of rent. None of the tenant's covenants set forth in the lease are affected by his assignment. In other words, the contract between the landlord and the tenant is neither superseded nor altered by the tenant's assignment of his leasehold interest, whether with or without the consent of the landlord.

Sublease of Rented Premises

Nature of Sublease A **sublease** is a transfer by a tenant of an interest in leased premises that is less than the tenant's entire leasehold interest.

A sublease gives rise to a new landlord-tenant relationship between the original tenant, the **sublessor,** and a new tenant, the **sublessee.** The distinction between an assignment of a leasehold interest and the subletting of the leased premises turns on the interest that passes rather than on the extent of the premises involved. If the transferring tenant retains to himself any reversionary interest, however small it may be, the transaction is a sublease and not an assignment. Unlike an assignment in which a tenant transfers his entire estate in the rented premises, a sublessor always transfers a lesser interest than he owns and thus retains a reversion.

Limiting the Right to Sublease It is a well-settled rule that, in the absence of a contrary provision in a lease or a statutory prohibition, a tenant with a lease for a fixed or definite period may sublet the leased premises in whole or in part. Like his right to assign, a tenant's right to sublease is an incident or attribute of the estate he has in the leased property.

While a tenant's right to sublease, like his right to assign, may be prohibited by an express covenant or stipulation against subletting, since such restrictions are restraints on alienation they are not regarded with favor by the courts. Because a sublease of leased premises is distinct from an assignment of a tenant's leasehold interest, it is well settled that a covenant in a lease not to assign is not broken by a tenant's subletting the leased premises.

Rights Acquired by Sublessee Whatever rights a sublessee acquires in the premises he subleases are derived from the terms of his rental agreement with the sublessor. These rights of course, can be no greater than those which the sublessor himself acquired in his original lease with the landlord. The original lease sets the limits to the rights that a sublessee can acquire in the leased premises from the sublessor. The sublessor, for example, cannot sublet the premises for a longer period of time than that provided for in the original lease. The sublessee's right of possession terminates with the expiration of the term provided in the original lease despite an agreement between the sublessor and sublessee for a longer term. And the sublessor cannot, of course, confer upon the sublessee any right or privilege that is in conflict with express restrictions set forth in the original lease.

Continuing Liability of Sublessor A subletting by a tenant does not in any way affect his liability to the landlord for payment of rent or the performance of any of the covenants contained in the original lease. Consequently, the sublessor is liable to the landlord for the violation of any of the covenants by the sublessee, whether the sublessor knew of the violation or not. And because of the sublessor's implied obligation to exercise reasonable care in the use of the leased property, he is liable to the landlord for any injury to the leased premises resulting from the sublessee's negligence or willful act.

Sublessee's Obligations to Sublessor Where it can be established that the sublessee either (1) expressly assumed the obligations of the sublessor's covenants in the original lease, (2) agreed to comply with those covenants, or (3) had actual knowledge of them, the sublessee is under an obligation to the sublessor to perform in accordance with such covenants. If, in any of the foregoing situations, the sublessee fails to perform as required by a covenant and thus renders the sublessor liable to the landlord for the breach, the sublessor has a cause of action against the sublessee for breach of his obligations arising under the sublease.

Relationship between Landlord and Sublessee A sublessee does not, merely because of the subletting, incur any liability directly to the landlord. In the absence of an express assumption by him in the sublease, a sublessee is under no obligation to the landlord to pay the rent stated in the original lease or to perform any covenants on behalf of the sublessor. However, if the sublessor fails to pay the rent required by the original lease, the landlord has the same right to dispossess the sublessee from the leased premises that he would have to dispossess the sublessor were he still in possession.

Where the sublessee in his rental agreement with the sublessor expressly assumes the sublessor's obligations arising from the original lease, the landlord may sue the sublessee directly for any breach of an assumed obligation on the theory that the rental agreement between the sublessor and sublessee is a third party beneficiary contract with the landlord being the beneficiary.

TERMINATION OF THE LANDLORD-TENANT RELATIONSHIP

The landlord-tenant relationship may come to an end in a number of ways and for a number of reasons, significant among which are the following.

Expiration of Lease for Fixed Period

Termination without Notice A lease that transfers the right of possession of designated premises to a tenant for a fixed or definite period of time will terminate automatically, without the need for any notice to be given, when the stipulated period of the lease expires. Upon termination of the lease, the landlord-tenant relationship which was created by the lease also termineates and the tenant's right to possession of the premises comes to an end. Any holding over by the tenant thereafter gives rise to the alternative causes of action by the landlord that were previously examined.

Leases for a stipulated period of time frequently contain provisions that give the tenant the option of renewing the lease. As is true of any agreement, an option affording the tenant the right to renew the lease should be precise and unambiguous as to the steps that a tenant must take to effect the renewal of the terms and conditions that will govern the continuing landlord and tenant relationship.

Provision for Automatic Renewal Rental agreements sometimes provide that a fixed term lease will be *automatically* renewed for an additional term unless the tenant notifies the landlord of his intent not to renew at a certain time prior to the expiration of the lease term. Because of the possibility that the provision for an automatic renewal might go unnoticed among the many provisions of some leases, some states have statutes[9] designed to protect tenants which require that provisions for automatic renewal must be made to stand out from other lease provisions so as to be readily observable by tenants when signing leases.

---

[9] For example, California Civil Code, sec. 1945.5 requires that any provision in a lease "which provides for the automatic renewal or extension of the lease for all or part of the full term of the lease if the lessee remains in possession after expiration of the lease or fails to give notice not to renew or extend before expiration of the lease shall be null and void *unless the renewal or extension provision appears in at least eight-point boldface type,* if the lease is printed, in the body of the lease agreement *and a recital of the fact that such provision is contained in the body of the agreement appears in at least eight-point type,* if the contract is printed, *immediately prior to the place where the lessee executes the agreement."* (Emphasis added.)

Notice of Termination Given by Parties

Required for Periodic Tenancies Both at common law and by statute, the landlord and the tenant are required to give each other notice in order to terminate periodic tenancies. Because of the indefiniteness and uncertainty of periodic tenancies, it is considered desirable that notice be given in order to protect each of the parties from the capriciousness of the other. While the common law does not require notice to be in writing, some statutes do.[10] Even where not required, a written notice may be a highly desirable piece of evidence when one of the parties seeks to prove that he in fact gave notice of termination to the other.

Period between Notice and Termination Statutes usually specify the period of time between the giving of notice and termination of a periodic tenancy.[11] In the absence of statute, the common law rule requires 1 month's notice in the case of a month-to-month tenancy and a week's notice where the tenancy is from week to week.

Rights of Landlord Following Notice by Tenant Upon receiving notice of termination from the tenant, the landlord has the right to enter the leased premises in a reasonable manner and during reasonable hours to show the premises to prospective tenants. Thus, where a month-to-month tenant gives the required month's notice to terminate, the tenant is under a duty to provide the landlord with reasonable opportunities to show the premises to potential tenants and the tenant will be liable to the landlord for any unreasonable refusal to provide such an opportunity. Similarly, a tenant who has given notice of his intention to terminate the landlord-tenant relationship cannot be heard to object to a "for rent" sign being placed on the premises by the landlord, nor does the tenant have any right to remove the sign.

No Reason for Termination Required Under a month-to-month rental agreement, the landlord has the right to terminate the lease simply by giving the required notice, without any need to give the tenant a reason why he chose to terminate the landlord-tenant relationship. However, we have seen that some courts, observing that this simple termination procedure was in some instances being used by landlords to retaliate against tenants for reporting housing code violations or exercising the right to repair and deduct, have held that proof by a tenant of the landlord's retaliatory intent is a good defense against the landlord's attempt to terminate the lease. A few states, as noted above, have enacted legislation that adopts this judicial point of view.

URLTA Position Except for the Uniform Residential Landlord and Tenant Act's "good faith" provision, the act permits periodic tenancies from week to week and from month to month to be terminated at the landlord's pleasure after the giving of appropriate notice.[12] The "good faith" requirement in the URLTA provides that "Every duty under this Act and every act which must be performed as a condition precedent to the exercise of a right or remedy under the Act imposes an obligation of good faith in its performance or enforcement."[13] According to the act, "'Good faith' means honesty in fact in the conduct of the transaction concerned."[14] Even recognizing the tenant's problem of proving lack of good faith, it would appear that the act's "good faith" clause limits the landlord's right arbitrarily to terminate a periodic tenancy.

---

[10] For example, California Civil Code, sec. 1946 requires written notice to be sent by certified or registered mail.

[11] For example, California Civil Code, sec. 1946 requires at least 30 days' written notice unless the parties have previously agreed to a lesser period, which in no event may be less than 7 days.

[12] URLTA, sec. 4.301(a) and (b). The act suggests at least 10 days' notice for week-to-week tenancies and 60 days where the tenancy is from month to month.

[13] Id., sec. 1.302.

[14] Id., sec. 1.301(4).

Termination for Breach of Covenant

A much litigated area of landlord and tenant law, especially where tenancies from year to year for a period of years are concerned, is the right of one of the parties to terminate the tenancy because of the breach of a covenant by the other party to the lease. The right to terminate upon violation of a covenant by one of the parties may either be expressly provided for in the lease or it may be implied. Depending upon which one of them breached the covenant in question, either the landlord or the tenant may exercise the right of termination.

Breach by Tenant and Forfeiture of Leasehold In the absence of an express lease provision to the contrary, the general rule is that the breach of a covenant in the lease by the tenant does not work a forfeiture of his leasehold and entitle the landlord to remove the tenant from the premises. In the absence of an express forfeiture provision in the lease, the landlord's remedy for the tenant's breach is an action for damages resulting from that breach. Because of its drastic consequences, the courts look upon a provision for forfeiture of the tenant's leasehold with disfavor and strictly construe it against the landlord seeking to invoke it. Not only must the landlord's right to declare a forfeiture be unmistakably provided for in the lease, but proof of the happening of the event giving rise to the exercise of the right must also be clear, and the landlord must exercise his right promptly.

Despite the fact that courts do not favor forfeiture provisions, such clauses are perfectly legal and the parties may lawfully provide for forfeiture of the tenant's leasehold interest upon his breach of a covenant or a condition contained in the lease. The courts will not hesitate to give effect to a forfeiture provision when the provision clearly reflects the intent of the landlord and the tenant.

Landlord's Waiver of Right to Forfeit The choice as to whether to proceed with a forfeiture following a tenant's breach rests entirely with the landlord. Since the breach does not in and of itself terminate the lease, the landlord must indicate his election to enforce his right to forfeit by some unequivocal act.

The landlord's right of forfeiture, once it has arisen, may be waived by him either by an express waiver or by a waiver implied by his conduct. Generally speaking, any recognition of the continuance of the tenancy by the landlord after he has learned of the breach that gives rise to the right of forfeiture will be construed as a waiver. For example, where the landlord with full knowledge of the tenant's breach of covenant accepts rent from him, the landlord's conduct will be deemed to be a waiver of his right of forfeiture. Furthermore, an unreasonable delay in declaring a forfeiture by the landlord following the tenant's breach will also be deemed a waiver of the landlord's right of forfeiture.

Effect of Forfeiture of Leasehold The forfeiture of a leasehold does not release the tenant from any liabilities under the lease which had accrued at the time of the forfeiture. Any rent that had accrued and was unpaid at the time of forfeiture remains due and payable by the tenant. But all covenants and stipulations in the lease that are dependent upon continuance of the term of the lease are terminated when the landlord elects to exercise his right of forfeiture.

An act by a sublessee of the premises or an assignee of the leasehold that breaches a covenant in the original lease, such as his using the premises for an unlawful or prohibited purpose, works a forfeiture of the tenant's original lease the same as if the breach were the act of the tenant himself.

Landlord's Breach as Constructive Eviction As we previously observed, a wrongful act or breach of a covenant by the landlord that interferes with the tenant's beneficial enjoyment of the leased premises may amount to a constructive eviction of the tenant by the landlord. Not every breach of covenant by a landlord, however, amounts to a constructive eviction by him. For a landlord's breach to constitute a constructive eviction, the interference with the tenant's use of the leased premises must be of such a serious and substantial nature as to deprive him of the beneficial use and enjoyment of the leased premises and cause him to vacate them.

URLTA Position

Noncompliance by Tenant Where there has been a "material noncompliance" with the terms of the rental agreement by the tenant or a noncompliance with the maintenance obligations imposed on him by the act[15] "materially affecting health and safety," the Uniform Residential Landlord and Tenant Act permits the landlord to terminate the rental agreement if the tenant fails to correct the condition after receiving notice of noncompliance from the landlord. Under the act, the landlord may terminate the rental agreement 30 days after written notice to the tenant pointing out the nature of the tenant's noncompliance and the landlord's intention to terminate if the condition is not corrected by the tenant within 14 days following receipt of the notice.[16] If the tenant corrects the condition complained of within the 14-day period, the noncompliance is cured and the landlord no longer has the right to terminate the rental agreement.

If substantially the same act or omission which constituted a prior noncompliance by the tenant occurs within 6 months, the landlord may terminate the rental agreement after giving the tenant 14 days' notice. In such a case, the tenant cannot prevent termination by correcting the noncomplying condition.[17]

The uniform act provides[18] that the landlord waives his right to terminate the rental agreement because of the breach of a covenant by the tenant if the landlord accepts rent from the tenant after the landlord has knowledge of the tenant's breach.

Noncompliance by Landlord When the landlord fails to comply with the terms of the rental agreement or with maintenance and service obligations imposed on him by the uniform act, the tenant has a choice of several remedies, depending upon the nature of the landlord's noncompliance.[19]

Where there has been a "material noncompliance" with the terms of the rental agreement by the landlord or with the maintenance and service obligations imposed on him by the act[20] "materially affecting health and safety," the tenant may terminate the rental agreement if the landlord fails to satisfy his obligation after receiving a written notice of his noncompliance from the tenant. The act permits the tenant to terminate the rental agreement 30 days after written notice pointing out to the landlord the nature of his noncompliance and indicating the tenant's intention to terminate the lease if the noncompliance is not corrected by the landlord within 14 days after receipt of the notice.[21] If the landlord corrects the condition complained of by the tenant within the 14-day period, the noncompliance is cured and the tenant no longer has the right to terminate.

If the same act or omission which constituted a prior noncompliance by the landlord recurs within 6 months, the tenant may terminate the rental agreement after giving the landlord 14 days' notice. In this instance, the landlord's correction of the noncompliance apparently will not prevent termination by the tenant.[22]

The tenant may not terminate the rental agreement for a condition of the premises caused by the deliberate or negligent act of the tenant or a member of his family or by other persons on the premises with his consent.[23]

Effect of Surrender or Abandonment of Premises

Surrender of Premises by Tenant A lease is terminated when the tenant surrenders leased premises to the landlord.

---

[15] Id., sec. 3.101(1)–(7).
[16] Id., sec. 4.201(a).
[17] Id.
[18] Id., sec. 4.204.
[19] Id., secs. 4.101–4.107.
[20] Id., sec. 2.104(a)(1)–(6).
[21] Id., sec. 4.101(a)(1).
[22] Id., sec. 4.101(a)(2).
[23] Id., sec. 4.101(a)(3).

A *surrender* can occur either by means of an express agreement between a landlord and a tenant or by operation of law. A surrender by operation of law occurs when the conduct of the parties is inconsistent with the continuance of the landlord-tenant relationship, such as the relinquishment of possession of the leased premises by the tenant and the resumption of possession of them by the landlord. Whether it is the result of an express agreement or the operation of law, a surrender extinguishes all of the tenant's interest in the leased premises and at the same time releases him from any obligation under the lease, including liability for rent accruing after the surrender. The tenant is not relieved, however, from liability for any past breaches of covenants or for rent that is accrued but unpaid.

Surrender Requires Offer and Acceptance A tenant's giving up of possession will not amount to a surrender unless the landlord accepts the tenant's offer to release possession of the premises to him. Whether there has been an acceptance of the offer to surrender or not depends on the landlord's intention, which he can manifest either by an express agreement or by implication from his conduct with respect to the premises vacated by the tenant. The question as to whether the landlord's conduct reflects an intent to accept is one of fact for jury determination. A tenant who contends that the landlord accepted his offer bears the burden of establishing that fact.

An offer to surrender and the acceptance of it occur, and the parties' rights and obligations under the lease thus terminate, when the landlord enters into possession of the premises vacated by the tenant and treats them as though the landlord-tenant relationship no longer existed.

There is a difference of opinion among the states as to whether a landlord's reletting of the vacated premises constitutes an acceptance of the tenant's offer to surrender. One view holds that there has been an acceptance of a surrender when a landlord relets the premises unless he notifies the tenant of his refusal to accept and states that the reletting of the premises is for the account of the tenant. Other cases appear to hold that the reletting of the vacated premises constitutes an acceptance of a surrender of the premises and terminates the lease as a matter of law. It can generally be said, however, that if the landlord relets the vacated premises for the account of the tenant, there is no acceptance of the offer to surrender and, conversely, if the landlord relets on his own account, there is an acceptance.

Abandonment of Premises by Tenant A surrender of leased premises by a tenant which terminates a rental agreement must be distinguised from abandonment by a tenant, which does not. An *abandonment* occurs when a tenant wrongfully vacates the leased premises with the intention of no longer abiding by his obligations under the rental agreement.

According to the rule prevailing in most jurisdictions, a landlord is under no obligation to endeavor to relet the abandoned premises but may allow them to lay idle and continue to be entitled to recover rent from the tenant for the remainder of the lease term. Under this prevailing view, a tenant who wrongfully abandons premises cannot impose on the landlord the duty to relet the vacated premises for the tenant's benefit and thus lessen the damages resulting from the tenant's wrong.

It is generally recognized that, in case of a tenant's abandonment of leased premises, the landlord may enter the premises for the purpose of protecting them and making necessary repairs without such action being construed as an acceptance of the tenant's offer to surrender and thus relieve him of liability for rent as it accrues. If, however, the landlord makes improvement or extensive repairs not required for the preservation of the abandoned premises, his action will usually be construed as being an acceptance of the tenant's offer to surrender the leased premises.

URLTA Position The Uniform Residential Landlord and Tenant Act reverses the rule prevailing in the majority of the states that says the landlord is under no duty to mitigate the damages that result from a tenant's wrongful abandonment of leased premises. While a landlord may recover damages resulting from the tenant's abandonment of the premises during the lease term, the uniform act requires the landlord to mitigate his damages by making a reasonable effort to rent the premises at a fair rental.[24] The prevailing view is further altered by the act's provision that if the landlord fails to make a reasonable effort to rent the abandoned premises, the rental agreement is considered as having been terminated by the landlord as of the date that he first had notice of the tenant's abandonment.[25]

Termination by Merger

A person cannot be both a landlord and a tenant of the same property at the same time. Therefore, when a tenant acquires ownership of the reversion in the leased property or the landlord acquires the leasehold interest, a *merger* is said to occur and the landlord-tenant relationship comes to an end.

Foreclosure of Mortgage on Leased Premises

The effect that the foreclosure of a mortgage or deed of trust will have on a tenant's leasehold interest is determined, as we saw in an earlier chapter, by the relative priority between the mortgage and the lease.

A mortgage or deed of trust on leased premises that was recorded before the tenant recorded his lease or took possession of the premises has priority over the lease. Consequently, a foreclosure sale of the leased premises will terminate the tenant's leasehold interest, providing the tenant was made a party to the foreclosure proceeding, as he ordinarily would be.

On the other hand, a lease that was executed and recorded before the mortgage or deed of trust is not affected by a foreclosure of the leased premises.

Condemnation of Leased Premises

Total Taking According to the prevailing rule, if the entire leased premises is taken under the right of eminent domain, the rental agreement between a landlord and tenant is terminated and the tenant's liability for rent accruing thereafter ceases. The condemnation of the leased premises does not, however, have any effect on the liability of the tenant for rent that accrued before the property was taken for a public use.

Partial Taking If only a part of the leased premises is taken by condemnation, the lease is not terminated and the tenant remains liable for the full amount of the rent called for in the lease. When this is the case, the tenant will share with the landlord in the compensation awarded for the portion of the leased premises that is taken.

Damage to Premises by Fire or Casualty

Common Law Rule According to the common law as declared by the courts, where leased premises are damaged by fire or other casualty, the tenant remains liable for the full amount of the agreed rent if any portion of the premises remains in existence and is capable of being occupied. Therefore, in the absence of a statute or a provision in the lease to the contrary, damage to buildings during the term of the lease caused by fire, the violence of nature, an inevitable accident, or a public enemy, which damage is not so great as to deprive the tenant of occupancy of any remaining part of it does not relieve the tenant of his obligation to pay rent nor does it entitle him to proportional abatement of the agreed rent.

If, however, the damage or destruction of the leased premises is complete with no part of the premises left that the tenant can occupy, the lease terminates and the tenant's liability for rent ceases.

Some states[26] have adopted legislation reliev-

---

[24] Id., secs. 1.105(a) and 4.203(c).
[25] Id., sec. 4.203(c).

[26] For example, Arizona, Connecticut, Michigan, Minnesota, West Virginia, and Wisconsin.

ing the tenant from the harshness of the common law rule. The legislation provides that if the premises are destroyed or injured to the point of being untenantable or unfit for occupancy, the tenant may vacate the premises.

URLTA Position Under the Uniform Residential Landlord and Tenant Act, alternative courses of action are available to a tenant when the premises he leases are damaged by fire or other casualty to such an extent that the enjoyment of a dwelling unit is substantially impaired.

The act permits the tenant, if he chooses to do so, to vacate the leased premises immediately following the damage or destruction and within 14 days thereafter to notify the landlord of his intention to terminate the rental agreement. Where this is done, the termination of the rental agreement is effective as of the date on which the premises were vacated.[27]

Providing continued occupancy of the damaged premises is lawful, the tenant has the alternative choice of vacating any part of the dwelling unit that is rendered unusable by the fire or casualty and having his liability for rent reduced in proportion to the decrease in the fair rental value of the dwelling.[28]

Doctrine of Commercial Frustration

The doctrine of **commercial frustration** is a contract law concept that sometimes permits changed conditions that occur during the term of a contract to excuse any further performance of the contract. The rationale underlying the doctrine is that the contract contains an implied provision that changed conditions of the type that occurred will excuse performance. The doctrine has been sustained as a defense even though the condition that developed was not such that it rendered performance entirely impossible but simply frustrated the purpose of the contract. According to the doctrine, therefore, a subsequent event which substantially frustrates the purpose contemplated by the parties when they entered into their agreement will excuse nonperformance of the contract.

Some courts have permitted termination of leases on grounds of commercial frustration, but it has been said that if the doctrine is to be applied to leases, it should be limited to those cases where the law or regulations make the business contemplated by the parties illegal or prohibits it absolutely. The mere fact that a law or regulation merely makes the business unprofitable does not excuse payment of rent under the doctrine of commercial frustration.

LANDLORD'S REMEDIES TO REGAIN POSSESSION OF PREMISES

The remedies available to a landlord for regaining possession of leased premises upon termination of a lease include (1) a peaceable entry of the premises by the landlord without legal process or proceedings, (2) a retaking of possession under court authority following an action in ejectment, and (3) an entry of the premises as the result of an unlawful detainer action or similar summary proceeding granted by statute.

Retaking Possession without Legal Process

The courts in some states[29] permit a landlord who is wrongfully kept out of possession of leased premises by an overstaying tenant to regain possession without resorting to legal proceedings, providing he does so by peaceable means. For example, where the tenant's right of possession has ended, a landlord in those states may peaceably enter the premises and retake possession during the tenant's absence without being subjected to liability for wrongful entry and damages.

Other courts[30] have held that, in the absence of a statute, a landlord who is entitled to pos-

---

[27] URLTA, sec. 4.106(a)(1).
[28] Id., 4.106(a)(2).

[29] Among them Alabama, Arkansas, District of Columbia, Indiana, Kansas, Louisiana, Michigan, Missouri, New York, Oregon, and Vermont.
[30] Including those in Maine, Maryland, Massachusetts, Montana, New Hampshire, New Jersey, Ohio, Pennsylvania, Rhode Island, South Carolina, and Wyoming.

session of leased premises may enter and expel an overstaying tenant by using such force as may be reasonably necessary to overcome the tenant's resistance. However, since the right to take forcible possession of premises is not conducive to public peace and order, the courts in some states[31] have held that the force used by the landlord must stop short of personal violence. Furthermore, an increasing number of cases[32] adopt what appears to be the modern doctrine and hold that a landlord who is entitled to possession must, upon refusal of the tenant to surrender possession of the leased premises, resort to the remedy given the landlord by statute, where there is one, or be liable for using force or deception to regain possession.

Some states[33] have statutes that make forcible entry by a landlord unlawful and impose liability on him even though the tenant's possession of the leased premises is wrongful and no breach of the peace is committed by the landlord.

In those instances where the landlord is permitted to use reasonable force to dispossess a tenant, it is generally agreed that he may render the premises uninhabitable, as by shutting off the heat, and thus effectively deprive the tenant of the premises.

Action in Ejectment

Both at common law and as modified by statute, **ejectment** is a legal action in which the right to possession of real property is tried and possession of that property is obtained. An action in ejectment is brought for the purpose of regaining possession of premises that are wrongfully withheld from the plaintiff. The primary issue in an ejectment action involves the present right of the complainant to occupy, use, and enjoy the particular property in dispute.

[31] For example, Illinois, New York, Texas, and Virginia.
[32] In California, Connecticut, Delaware, Florida, Georgia, Illinois, Louisiana, Nebraska, Ohio, and Utah, for example.
[33] For example, California, Delaware, Florida, Illinois, Indiana, New Jersey, and Vermont.

As a general rule, ejectment is an appropriate type of legal action for a landlord to pursue to regain possession when a tenant wrongfully retains the leased premises after the lease has expired or where the lease expressly provides that the landlord shall have the right to re-enter the premises upon nonpayment of rent or the breach of a covenant.

Statutes that provide a landlord with some form of summary proceeding for the recovery of possession generally do not deny him his common law right to bring an action in ejectment instead. The modern action in ejectment is essentially the same as any other civil action.

Summary Actions for Possession

Under a variety of names, statutes in practically all states, following a more or less common pattern, provide summary proceedings to which a landlord may resort in order to recover possession of leased premises that are wrongfully withheld from him by a tenant. These summary actions are variously called "summary ejectment,"[34] "summary process,"[35] "dispossessory warrant proceedings,"[36] "forcible entry and detainer,"[37] "forcible entry and detention,"[38] and "unlawful detainer."[39] Because a larger number of states use the term "unlawful detainer" than any other single designation, we shall employ that term in our discussion of the nature of a landlord's summary legal proceeding to regain possession of leased premises.

Unlawful Detainer Actions The objective of unlawful detainer statutes is to provide the landlord with a remedy against a tenant who wrongfully withholds possession that is speedi-

[34] In North Carolina, for example.
[35] In Connecticut and Massachusetts.
[36] In Georgia.
[37] In Alaska, Illinois, Ohio, Oregon, South Dakota, and Texas.
[38] In Arizona, Kansas, Kentucky, and North Dakota.
[39] In Alabama, Arkansas, California, Colorado, Florida, Idaho, Mississippi, Missouri, Montana, Oklahoma, Utah, Washington, Wisconsin, and Wyoming.

er than the cumbersome, dilatory, and generally expensive action in ejectment. An action for possession of real property in the nature of unlawful detainer is a purely statutory proceeding that is limited exclusively to those situations expressly provided for in the statutes creating the summary remedy. These statutes include, and very commonly are limited to, possessory disputes that arise between a landlord and a tenant. Unlawful detainer statutes free a landlord from the necessity to which he was subject at common law of bringing an action in ejectment with its attendant delays and expense.

The characteristic feature of a "summary action" is that it is designed to examine a single issue. Affirmative defenses, cross-complaints, or counterclaims that are irrelevant to that particular issue are not permitted to be introduced at the proceeding. In summary proceedings in the nature of unlawful detainer actions, the sole issue involved is the right to possession of the leased premises and any defense the tenant may have that is not directly related to the issue of possession is excluded from consideration. The objective of the unlawful detainer proceedings is to enable the landlord quickly to regain possession of the rented premises and litigation of issues raised by counterclaims and so forth would defeat the speedy relief intended by the statute creating the summary remedy.

Although unlawful detainer statutes commonly authorize a court to enter a judgment for rent due and for damages, the recovery of these items is incidental to the principal purpose of the proceeding, the restoration of possession. The objective of the unlawful detainer is not to collect rent even in those cases where the tenant's failure to pay rent is claimed by the landlord as the ground for instituting the summary proceedings.

URLTA Position The Uniform Residential Landlord and Tenact Act provides that "If the rental agreement is terminated, the landlord has a claim for possession and rent and a separate claim for actual damages for breach of the rental agreement and reasonable attorney's fees."[40] There is no provision in the act, however, for any proceeding such as unlawful detainer by which the landlord may speedily regain possession of the leased premises upon termination of the lease.

Forcible Entry and Detainer Actions A forcible entry and detainer action is a summary proceeding provided by statute whose purpose is to obtain the speedy return of possession by a person who has been unlawfully deprived of that possession. In such an action, the only issue is the plaintiff's right to present possession of real property. In addition to establishing that the premises were forcibly entered and detained by the defendant, the plaintiff is required to show that, at the time of the forcible entry or detainer, he was either in actual possession of the premises or that he was at the time entitled to possession of them. The general objective of forcible entry and detainer statutes is to ensure that, regardless of the actual condition of title to property or the right to possession of it, an occupant who is in peaceable and quiet possession of premises shall not be turned out by violence or terror. It is also the intent of the statutes to prevent breaches of the peace which are always threatened when a party seeking possession of property resorts to self-help measures.

Generally speaking, statutes provide that a person is guilty of forcible *entry* if, either by breaking in or using violence or terror, he enters upon real property or if he causes the party in possession to leave because of force or fear induced by threats or menacing conduct. Statutes in some states[41] provide that a forcible entry means any entry against the will or merely without the permission of the party in posses-

---

[40] URLTA, sec. 4.206.
[41] For example, Arizona, Illinois, Kentucky, Mississippi, New Mexico, and Oklahoma.

sion. Forcible entry has also been found to exist when, without the use of physical force or threats, a landlord locked the tenant out of the leased premises.[42]

Statutes commonly provide that a person is guilty of forcible *detainer* if he wrongfully retains possession of real property by force or threats of violence, whether possession was obtained peaceably or otherwise, or if he unlawfully enters the premises in the absence of the occupant and refuses to restore possession to the former occupant upon demand.

In the context of the landlord-tenant relationship, forcible entry and forcible detainer commonly involve situations in which the landlord has resorted to self-help rather than legal proceedings to regain possession of the leased premises following a real or imagined breach of the rental agreement or a holding over by the tenant.

URLTA Position In providing that "A landlord may not recover or take possession of the dwelling unit by action or otherwise . . . except in the case of abandonment, surrender, or as otherwise permitted in this Act,"[43] the Uniform Residential Landlord and Tenant Act would appear to rule out self-help by the landlord in removing a tenant and regaining possession of the leased premises.

Under the uniform act, if the landlord unlawfully removes or excludes the tenant from the premises, or if he willfully decreases services to the tenant causing the interruption of heat, running water, hot water, electric, gas, or other essential services, the tenant has the choice of recovering possession of the premises or terminating the rental agreement. Whichever alternative the tenant elects, he may recover from the landlord an amount that is not more than 3 months' rent or three times the actual damages sustained by him, whichever is the greater, plus reasonable attorney's fees.[44]

QUESTIONS

1 What is a latent defect in leased premises? What is the nature of a landlord's obligation with respect to such a defect?
2 What is the significance of the majority view that imposes tort liability on a landlord who breaches his covenant to repair leased premises?
3 Discuss the nature of a landlord's liability with respect to the common areas in leased premises.
4 What is an exculpatory clause in a lease? How have such clauses in leases been treated by courts and legislatures?
5 Explain what happens to a tenant's rights when the landlord sells the leased premises before the tenant's lease has expired. What happens if the landlord dies instead of selling the property?
6 Distinguish between an assignment of a leasehold and a sublease.
7 Compare the manner in which leases for a fixed period and periodic tenancies terminate.
8 What rights, if any, does a landlord have with respect to leased property during the period between his receipt of a tenant's notice of termination and the tenant's leaving the premises?
9 How does the surrender of leased premises by a tenant differ from abandonment of the premises by him?
10 What effect does a mortgage foreclosure sale of leased premises have on a tenant's lease?
11 What is the nature of the doctrine of commercial frustration? How does it apply to the landlord-tenant relationship?
12 Discuss the differing attitudes of the courts with respect to the retaking of possession of leased premises by a landlord without resorting to legal process.
13 What is an unlawful detainer action? How does it differ from an ejectment action brought by a landlord?
14 What is a forcible entry and detainer action? What is a forcible entry? What is forcible detainer?

[42] *Lamey v. Masciotra,* 273 CA2d 709 (1969).
[43] URLTA, sec. 4.207.
[44] Id., sec. 4.107.

Index

Index

Abandonment:
  of easement, 109
  of leased premises, 405
Abstract of title, 211–213
  contents of, 211–212
  nature of, 211
Abstracter:
  function of, 211
  liability of, 212
Acceleration clause, 228–231
  defined, 228, 411
  types of, 229–231
    due on default, 229
    due-on-encumbrance, 230–231
    due-on-sale, 230
Acceptance:
  communication of, 120
  defined, 119, 411
  methods of: by an act, 119–120
    by a promise, 119
  of surrender by tenant, 305

Accretion, 181–182
Acknowledgment:
  of deed, 141
  form of, 205
  method of, 204
  prerequisite to recording, 204
Action to quiet title, 217
Actual, notice, 206
Adhesion contract, 127
Adverse possession:
  elements of, 175–179
    claim of right, 177
    color of title, 177–178
    hostile and adverse, 176–177
    open, notorious, and visible, 175–176
    payment of taxes, 179
    uninterrupted and continuous, 178–179
  future interests, 175, 180

Adverse possession:
  general characteristics, 174
  nature of title acquired by, 179–180
  objective of law, 175
  public property, 175
Adverse user, 104
Affirmative easement (*see* Easement)
Agreed boundary doctrine, 93–94
Agreement for deed (*see* Installment sale contract)
Air pollution, control of, 335
Air Quality Act, 335
Air quality standards:
  primary, 335
  secondary, 335
Airspace:
  invasions of, 14
  ownership of, 14

433

Airspace:
  separation from surface: by condemnation, 15–16
  by sale or lease, 15
  by subdivision, 15
Alienate, 8
Alienation (*see* Restraint on alienation)
Alluvion, 181
American Land Title Association (ALTA), 216
Annual percentage rate (*see* Truth in Lending Law)
Anticipatory breach, 126
Antideficiency legislation, 257–258
  Uniform Land Transactions Act position, 258
Appraisal:
  highest and best use, 357–358
  techniques of, 159–160, 357
    capitalization of income approach, 160
    cost of reproduction approach, 159
    market comparison approach, 159
  (*See also* Real property tax)
Appurtenances, nature of, 22
Appurtenant easement (*see* Easement)
Assault, nature of, 82*n*.
Assessed value (*see* Real property tax)
Assessment (*see* Real property tax)
Assignment:
  of lease, 399
  of nonnegotiable debt, 246
Attestation, 141
  of deeds, 141
  meaning of, 141
  of wills, 148
Attractive nuisance doctrine, 95–96
Auction sale, 118
  without reserve, 118
Avulsion, 181

Balancing equities, 86
Balancing hardships, 86
Balloon payment, 225
Base line, 30
Battery, nature of, 82*n*.
Bequest, 148
Bilateral contract, 115, 120
Bona fide purchaser, 144
Boundary disputes, 83
Boundary lines:
  adverse possession, 180–181
  agreed boundary doctrine, 93–94
  ascertaining location of, 93
  mistaken, 180–181
  trees near, 91
  trees on, 91
Branches, overhanging, 90
Breach, 125–126
  anticipatory, 126
  of contract, 125–126
  of covenant, 138
Building codes, 330–331
  nature of, 330
  objective of, 330
Building permits, 330–331

Capacity, legal, 122
Chain of title, 203–204
Chattel real, 56, 63
Claim of right, 177
Closing (*see* Title closing)
Closing costs, 183
Cloud on title, 217
Coastal Zone Management Act, 343–344
  coastal zone defined, 343
  purpose of, 343
Codicil, 140
Color of title, 177–178
Commercial frustration, doctrine of, 407
Common enemy doctrine, 91
Common law, 2
Community property, 75–77
  division of, 77
  presumption of, 76
  simultaneous death, 79

Compensation, just, 153, 158–160
  constitutional requirement, 158
  indemnity compared, 160
  market value as, 158
  how determined, 158–160
Competency to contract, 122–123
Condemnation:
  eminent domain distinguished, 152
  excess, 157
  theories of, 157–158
  inverse, 153
  of leased premises, 406–407
  nature of, 153
  necessity for, 156–157
  taking of restrictive covenants, 308
Condition:
  consequence of breach of, 313
  in contract: concurrent, 12
    precedent, 125
    subsequent, 125
  created by deed provision, 306
  defined, 304
  termination of, 313
Condition precedent, 65, 125, 312
Condition subsequent, 125, 312
Condominium, 15
Consent:
  apparent, 123
  real, 123
Consideration:
  act as, 122
  adequacy of, 121
  benefit or detriment, 121
  forebearance as, 122
  nature of, 121
  not required in deed, 141
  promise as, 121–122
Constructive eviction (*see* Landlord and tenant)
Constructive notice:
  of easement, 108
  nature of, 207
  other than from recording, 209
  from recording, 206–207, 211
  theory underlying, 207

INDEX

Contingent remainder, 67
Contract for deed (*see* Installment sale contract)
Contract rent, 164
Contractor (*see* Mechanics' lien)
Contracts:
  adhesion, 127
  classification of: bilateral, 115
    executed, 115
    executory, 115
    express, 115
    implied, 115
    unenforceable, 116
    unilateral, 115
    valid, 115
    void, 116, 122–123
    voidable, 116, 122–123
  defined, 114, 414
  distinguished from deed, 127
  elements of, 116–125
    capacity of parties, 122–123
    consideration, 121–122
    legal object, 124–125
    mutual assent, 116–121
      acceptance, 119–121
      offer, 116–119
    reality of consent, 123–124
  performance of, 125–126
    anticipatory breach, 126
    breach, 126
  of purchase and sale, 126, 130–132, 136
    option compared, 133
    standardized, 131–132
Contribution, right of, 72–73
Conventional mortgage, 220
Co-ownership:
  forms of, 70–77
    community property, 75–77
    joint tenancy, 70–71
    tenancy:
      in common, 71–72
      by entirety, 75
  nature of, 69–70
Correction lines, 30
Correlative rights, 18
  oil and gas, 18
Cost approach (*see* Appraisal)

Council on Environmental Quality, 346
  role of EPA compared, 347
Counteroffer as rejection, 119
Covenant:
  in deed, 137
  defined, 304, 415
  in lease, 371–376
  running with land, 309–310
Covenants of title, types of, 137
  freedom from encumbrances, 137
  quiet enjoyment, 137
  right to convey, 137
  seisin, 137
  warranty, 137
Courtesy, 78–79
  consummate, 78
  initiate, 78

Damages, consequential, 155
Deed:
  acceptance of, 143
  acknowledgment of, 141
  attestation by witnesses, 141
  characteristics of, 136
  condition in, 143
  conditional delivery of, 143
  covenant in, 143
  elements of, 139
  function of, 136
  legal delivery of, 142–143
    presumptions concerning, 142
  in lieu of foreclosure, 258–259
    Uniform Land Transactions Act, provisions, 253, 258
  parties to, 136
  reservation in, 143
  sales contract merged into, 132
  special clauses, 143
  of trust, 236–237
    mortgage compared, 236
    parties to, 236
  types of, 136–139
    quitclaim deed, 138–139
    special warranty deed, 138
    warranty deed, 137–138

Deed:
  void, 144–145
    effect of, 144
    types of, 144
      deed by incompetent grantor, 144
      forged deed, 144
  voidable, 144–145
    effect of, 144
    types of, 144–145
      deed acquired by duress, 145
      deed by incompetent grantor, 144
      deed induced by fraud, 144
      deed procured by undue influence, 144–145
Deficiency judgment, 256–258
  antideficiency legislation, 257–258
  Uniform Land Transactions Act, provisions, 258
Delivery (*see* Deed)
Descent and distribution, law of (*see* Intestate succession)
Description:
  ambiguities, clarification of, 27
  in deeds, 140–141
  function of, 26
  sufficiency of, 26–27
  types of, 28
    metes and bounds, 28
    rectangular survey system, 29
    reference to recorded map, 36
Development planning, 316
  general plan, 316
  implementation of, 316
  nature of, 316
Devise, 148
Displaced person, defined, 165
Division fence, 88
Documentary transfer tax, 205
Dominant estate, 100
Donee, 145
Donor, 145
Dower, 77
  consummate, 77
  inchoate, 77

Due on default clause, 229
Due-on-encumbrance clause, 230–231
Due-on-sale clause, 230, 244
Due process of law:
  in condemnation proceedings, 153–154
  constitutional provisions, 10
  police power, limiting of, 317
  procedural, 10
  real property tax, 359–360
  substantive, 10–11
  tax sale, 362
Duress, 124
  deed acquired by, 144
  nature of, 124
Duty, legal, 1, 81

Easement:
  extent or scope of, 105–107
  general characteristics, 99
  license distinguished, 112
  methods of creation, 101–104
    by condemnation, 104, 162
    by express grant, 101
    by express reservation, 101
    by implied grant, 102
    by implied reservation, 102
    by necessity, 103
    by prescription, 104
  methods of termination, 108–111
    by abandonment, 109
    by destruction of servient tenement, 110–111
    by estoppel, 110
    by fulfillment of purpose, 108
    by lapse of time, 108
    by merger, 109
    by nonuse, 109
    by prescription, 110
    by release, 108–109
  in party wall, 89
  repair and maintenance of, 107
  rights of owner, 106
    interference with, 107
    secondary or incidental, 107
  taking by eminent domain, 162
  transfer of, 107–108

Easement:
  types of: affirmative, 100
    appurtenant, 100
    in gross, 101
    negative, 100, 307
    prescriptive, 104–105
  valuation of, 162
Economic rent, 164
Ejectment, 408
Eminent domain:
  compensation for taking, 158–162
    how determined, 158–160
    indemnity compared, 160
    market value as, 158
    meaning of, 158
    partial taking, 161–162
      general benefits, 161
      special benefits, 161–162
  condemnation distinguished, 153
  consequential damages, 155
  constitutional limitations, 153
    just compensation, 153
    public use, 153
  defined, 152
  delegation of power, 157
  due process of law, 153–154
  easement: creation of, 162
    taking of, 162
  excess condemnation:
    protective theory, 157
    recoupment theory, 157
    remnant theory, 157–158
  interest taken, 154
  necessity for taking, 156–157
  noncompensable items, 160–161
    attorney fees, 161
    expert witness fees, 161
    loss of goodwill, 161
  partial taking, 161–162
  police power distinguished, 154
  public use, 155–156
    meaning of, 155–156
    presumption of, 156
  restrictive covenants, taking of, 162–163
  taking for future requirements, 158

Eminent domain:
  taking leased property, 163–165
    compensation for partial taking, 164–165
    compensation for total taking, 164
    landlord's interest, 163–164
    tenant's interest, 163–164
  taking less than fee interest, 162–163
  taking versus damaging, 154–155
  who may condemn, 154
Environment:
  air pollution, control of, 335
  biological features, 332
  coastal zone conservation and management, 342–344
  coastal zone defined, 343
  cultural features, 332
  defined, 332, 416
  federal legislation, 334
  impact on (*see* Environmental impact statement)
  national environmental policy, 344–345
  noise pollution, 336–338
    control of, 336–338
    effect of, 336–338
    nature of, 336–338
  physical features, 332
  solid waste disposal, 338
  state legislation, 350–352
    model act, 350
  water pollution, control of, 335–336
Eminent Domain Code, 171–173
  acquisition of real property, 172
  compensation for taking, 173
  compensation standards, 172–173
  relocation assistance, 172
Environmental impact statement, 345, 347–350
  contents of, 348
  draft statements, 349–350
    public hearings, 349
    review of comments, 349
  environmental impact, defined, 347
  guidelines for preparation, 347

Environmental law, 333–334
  development of, 333–334
  objective of, 333
Environmental Protection
    Agency, 346–347
  functions of, 346
  role of Council on
      Environmental Quality
      compared, 347
Equal Credit Opportunity Act,
    269–273
  adverse action, defined, 269*n*.
  denial or revocation of credit,
      269–272
    statement of reasons, 269–272
  enforcement of, 270
  implemented by Regulation B,
      269
  purpose of, 269
Equal protection of laws:
  constitutional provision, 11
  effect on police power, 317
  meaning of, 11
Equitable conversion, 260
Equitable servitude, 310
Equity of redemption, 254–255
  nature of, 254
  termination of, 254
  Uniform Land Transactions
      Act, provisions, 255
Escheat, 150
Escrow:
  nature of, 184
  operation of, 189
  requirements for, 185–187
  rights and duties of parties,
      187–188
    buyer, 188
    escrow holder, 188
    seller, 188
  why used, 185
Escrow account, 232–234
  interest on, 233–234
  nature of, 232
  Real Estate Settlement
      Procedures Act,
      provisions, 194, 234
Escrow agent, 126, 184, 187
Escrow agreement, 185

Escrow holder, 184
  agent of parties, 187
Escrow instructions, 126, 185
Estate, meaning of, 55
Estate at sufferance, 64
Estate at will, 64
Estate in fee simple, 56
Estate in fee tail, 62–63
Estate from period to period, 64
Estate for years, 63
Estates, classification of, 56
  freehold, 56
  nonfreehold, 56
Estoppel, doctrine of, 110
Estoppel certificate, 246
Excess condemnation (*see*
    Eminent domain)
Exculpatory clause (*see* Lease)

Federal environmental legislation,
    334–346
Federal Ocean Dumping Act,
    335–336
Federal Water Pollution Control
    Act, 335
Federally related mortgage loan,
    192
Fee, 57
Fee simple, 57
Fee simple absolute, 56–57
  presumption of, 57
  required by sales contract,
      131
  right to transfer, 8
Fee simple defeasible, 57–59
  characteristics of, 57–58
  object of, 58
  types of, 58–59
    fee simple determinable,
        59
    fee subject to condition
        subsequent, 58–59
      forfeiture of, 58–59, 313
    fee subject to executory
        limitation, 59
Fee tail, estate in, 62–63
Fence, 87–89
  barbed wire, 88
  division, 88

Fence:
  duty to construct, 87
  exterior, 88
  as nuisance, 88–89
  spite, 88
  statutes regulating, 87
Fence viewers, 88
Feudalism, 56
FHA-insured mortgage, 220
Fiduciary, 128
  broker as, 128
Fiduciary relationship, nature of,
    128
Finance charge (*see* Truth in
    Lending Law)
Fixtures, 19–20
  importance of intent, 19–20
  mechanic's lien, 278
  nature of, 19
Forcible entry and detainer, 409–410
Forebearance, 122
  as consideration, 122
Foreclosure, 248–254
  deed in lieu of, 253
    Uniform Land Transactions
        Act, provisions, 253
  by judicial sale, 249
    Uniform Land Transactions
        Act, provisions, 253
  leased premises, 406
  nature of, 248
  by power of sale, 251
    Uniform Land Transactions
        Act, provisions, 253
  strict foreclosure, 252
  types of, 249
    Uniform Land Transactions
        Act, provision, 252–254
Forfeiture:
  enforceability of provision for,
      262
  of fee subject to condition
      subsequent, 59, 313
  of leasehold, 403
Fraud:
  deed induced by, 144
  defined, 124, 418
  elements of, 124

Future advances, 238–240
  agreements for, 238
  obligatory, 239
  optional, 239–240
Future interest, 60, 64–67
  transferability of, 67–68
  types of, 65–67
    remainder, 66–67
      contingent, 66–67
      vested, classes of, 67
    reversionary interests, 65–66
      possibility of reverter, 66
      power of termination, 65–66
      reversion, 65–66

Gadsden Purchase, 41
Gift, 145
  elements of, 145
  executed, 145
  promise to make, 145
Good faith, meaning of, 21, 418
Good faith improver, 21–22
  rights and equities of, 22
    right of removal, 22
    right of setoff, 22
Good title, meaning of, 131
Grant, 101
  express, 101
  nature of, 101
Grantee, 139–140
  identification of, 139–140
  legal capacity, 140
Grantor, 139
  identification of, 139
  legal capacity, 139
Grantor-grantee index system, 206
Guide meridian, 30

Habitability (see Landlord and tenant)
Headright system, 38
Highest and best use, 357–358
Holder in due course, 246n.
Holographic will, 148

Home Mortgage Disclosure Act, 220–222
  purpose of, 221
Homestead:
  acquisition of, 295–296
    by occupancy alone, 295
    by occupancy and declaration, 296
  declaration, 296
    form of, 297
  defined, 292, 419
  encumbrance of exempt property, 299
  limits on size and value, 294
  objective of, 292–293
  operation of exemption, 296
  persons entitled to, 293
    head of family, 293
    married person, 293
    unmarried person, 293
  physical property subject to, 294
    permanent residence, 294
      combined residence and business, 294
      condominium and cooperative apartment, 294
      single-family dwelling, 294
  priority of exemption, 296–299
    as to creditors' liens, 298
    as to debts arising from tort claims, 299
    as to mechanics' liens, 298
    as to mortgages and deeds of trust, 298
    as to taxes and assessments, 299
    as to unsecured debts, 296
  probate, 301
    creation of, 301
    duration of, 301
    termination of, 301
  property interest subject to, 294
    equitable interest, 294
    fee simple, 294
    less than fee, 294
  rights of survivors, 299

Homestead:
  sale of property, 295
    forced sale, 295
    voluntary sale, 295
  termination of, 299–300
    by abandonment, 300
    by conveyance, 300
    by death, 300
    by expiration of estate, 300
    transfer of exempt property, 299
  types of, 293
  value exceeding exemption, 295
Homestead Act of 1862, 50
Housing codes:
  attacks on, 389n.
  building codes compared, 389n.
  characteristics of, 389
  enforcement problems, 389–390
  exercise of police power, 389
  tort liability for violation, 395

Improvements, 19, 21
Incapacity, 122–123
  to contract, 122–123
  due to intoxication, 123
  due to minority, 122–123
  due to unsound mind, 123
Income approach (see Appraisal)
Inheritance, law of (see Intestate succession)
Initial point, 29
Installment contract, 190
  escrow involving, 190
Installment sale contract, 259–263
  alternative to purchase money mortgage, 260
  forfeiture provisions, 262
  liquidated damages provisions, 262
  long-term arrangement, 259
  nature of, 259
  possession of premises, 260–261
  purchaser's risks, 259–260
  retention of legal title, 260

INDEX

Insurable interest, 245–246
   mortgagee's, 246
   mortgagor's, 245
   nature of, 245
Intention, 191
   how ascertained, 191
Inter vivos, meaning of, 145
Interest, 227–228
   contract rate, 227
   market rate, 227
   maximum rate, 227–228
   variable rate, 227
Interpleader:
   by escrow holder, 188
   by mortgagee, 251
Intestate, meaning of, 149
Intestate succession, 147, 149–150
   purpose of, 149
Inverse condemnation, 153
Invitee, 96
   defined, 96, 420
   occupier's duty toward, 96

Joint tenancy, 70–75
   common law unities, 71
   general characteristics, 70–71
      right of survivorship, 70
   simultaneous death, 79
   termination of, 73–75
Joint tenant, 72–73
   rights and duties of, 72–73

Laborer (*see* Mechanic's lien)
Laches, 311
   terminates restrictive covenant, 311
Land, components of, 13
Land contract (*see* Installment sale contract)
Land Ordinance of 1785, 42
Land survey (*see* Survey)
Landlocked land, 103
Landlord and tenant:
   abandonment of leased premises, 405

Landlord and tenant:
   defective premises: landlord's tort liability for, 393–396
      breach of covenant to repair, 394–395
      breach of statutory duty to repair, 395
      breach of warranty of habitability, 394
      common law rule, 393
         exceptions to, 394
      concealment of latent defect, 394
      failure to maintain common areas, 395–396
      negligence in making repairs, 396
      premises leased for public purpose, 396
      tenant's liability for, 397
   eviction, 379–381
      actual, 379
      constructive, 380–381, 403
   habitability of dwelling, 384–386, 394
      continuation during lease term, 386
      early common law rule, 384
      implied warranty of, 385, 394
         rationale underlying, 385
      meaning of "habitability," 385
   holding over by tenant, 390–391
      damages for, 390–391
      status of tenant, 390–391
      tenant at sufferance, 391
      tenant at will, 391
   injury to premises, 383–384
      measure of damages, 384
   landlord's lien, 374–375
   option to purchase, 375–376
      death of parties, effect of, 375
      exercise of, 375–376
      sale of reversion, effect of, 375
      termination of, 375
      transferability of, 375

Landlord and tenant:
   relationship of, 365–367
      created by contract, 365
         lease or rental agreement, 366
      nature of interests, 366
         leasehold, 366
         reversion, 366
      other relationships distinguished, 366–367
   remedies to regain possession, 408–410
      action in ejectment, 408
      summary actions, 408–410
         forcible entry and detainer, 409–410
         unlawful detainer, 408–409
      without legal process, 407–408
   reservation of easement, 373
   retaliatory action, 388
      antiretaliatory laws, 388
      methods of retaliation, 388
      problem of retaliatory intent, 388
   rights and obligations:
      expressly created by lease, 371–373
         not to compete, 371
         to pay rent, 372
         to pay taxes and assessments, 372–373
         to repair or rebuild, 372–373
      implied by operation of law, 376–387
         commission of waste, 381–382
         at common law, 376–377
         condition of premises, 383
         delivery of possession, 378, 383
         limitation on use, 382–383
         quiet enjoyment, 378–379
         regarding rent, 377–378
         repair and deduct, 387
   security deposits, 373–374
      interest on, 373–374

Landlord and tenant:
  security deposits: as liquidated damages, 374
    statutory regulation of, 373–374
  surrender of premises, 404–405
    effect of, 404–405
  termination of relationship, 401–407
    by breach of covenant, 403
      constructive eviction, 403
      forfeiture of leasehold, 403
    by commercial frustration, 407
    by condemnation, 406
    by damage due to casualty, 406
    by expiration of lease, 401
      automatic renewal provisions, 401
    by merger, 406
    by mortgage foreclosure, 406
    by notice, 402
    by surrender of premises, 404–405
      abandonment compared, 405
  transfer of leased property, 398
  transfer of tenant's interest, 398–401
    assignment of leasehold, 399–400
      assignor's continuing liability, 399–400
      limitations on right, 399
      nature of, 399
    interpretation of lease provisions, 398–399
    sublease of leased premises, 400–401
      landlord-sublessee relationship, 401
      limitations on right, 400
      nature of, 400
      sublessee's obligations, 400–401
      sublessee's rights, 400
      sublessor's continuing liability, 400

Landslides, 89–90
  retaining wall, 90
Lateral support, 91–92
  common law rule, 92
  statutory provisions, 92
Law, 1–2
  common, 2
  defined, 1, 420
  function of, 1
  real estate, 2
    function of, 2
    sources of, 2
Lease:
  automatic renewal clause, 401
  characteristics of, 367–369
    conveyance and contract, 367–368
  exculpatory clause, 396–397
  form and contents of, 368
  inclusion of appurtenances, 368–369
  interpretation of provisions, 368
  license distinguished, 112, 366–367
Leased fee, 163
  condemnation of, 163
  meaning of, 163
Leasehold:
  assignment of leasehold interest, 399–400
    liability of assignor, 399–400
    limitations on right, 399
    nature of, 399
  condemnation of, 163–165
  tenant's interest, 366
    injury to, 383
  types of, 369–370
    periodic tenancy, 369–370
    tenancy at sufferance, 370
    tenancy at will, 370
    tenancy for years, 369
Legal delivery, 142–143
License:
  coupled with interest, 112
  defined, 111, 420
  easement distinguished, 112
  implied, 90
  irrevocable, 112
  lease distinguished, 112

Licensee:
  defined, 96, 420
  occupier's duty toward, 96
  rights of, 111–112
  tenant compared, 366–367
Licensor, 111–112
Life estate, 59–62
  methods of creation, 60
  pur autre vie, 59–60
  termination of, 62
Life tenant, 59–61
  duties and liabilities of, 61
  rights of, 61
Line trees, 90
Liquidated damages, 262–263
  penalty compared, 262
  security deposit as, 374
  Uniform Land Transactions Act, provisions, 262–263
Listing agreement, 126, 128–130
  nature of, 128
  types of, 129–130
    exclusive agency listing, 129
    exclusive authorization and right to sell listing, 129–130
    multiple listing, 130
    net listing, 129–130
    open listing, 129
Louisiana Purchase, 39

Malice, defined, 89
Market approach (*see* Appraisal)
Market value, 158
  how determined, 158
  just compensation as, 158
  of taxable property, 357
Marketable title, 131
Materialism (*see* Mechanic's lien)
Mechanic's lien:
  claimant must have contract, 276–277
    express or implied, 277
    substantial performance of, 277
  defined, 274, 421
  encumbrance on property, 274–275
  enforcement of, 289
    period for, 289

INDEX

Mechanic's lien:
  extinction of, 286–288
    by expiration of time, 288
    by payment of debt, 288
    by posting surety bond, 287
    by release, 286
      form of, 288
  improvements by tenant, 277–278
    lien on landlord's interest, 278
    lien on tenant's interest, 277–278
  notice of cessation, 284
    form of, 285
  notice of completion, 283
    form of, 284
  notice of nonresponsibility, 278
    form of, 279
  operation and effect of, 285–286
    amount secured by, 285
    duration of lien, 286
    when lien attaches, 285
  persons entitled to, 275–276
    contractor, 275
    laborer, 276
    materialman, 276
    subcontractor, 275–276
  physical property subject to, 278
  prevention of, 286
    by contract, 286
    by waiver, 286
      form of, 287
  priority of, 289–291
  procedure for obtaining, 279–283
    preliminary notice, 280–281
      form of, 281
      purpose of, 280
      time for giving, 280
      who must give, 280
    recording claim of lien, 280–283
      contents of claim, 283
      effect of, 280
      form of claim, 282–283
      time for recording, 283

Mechanic's lien:
  property interest subject to, 277–278
    fee simple, 277
    less than fee, 277–278
Merger:
  terminates easement, 109
  terminates lease, 406
  terminates life estate, 62
  terminates restrictive covenants, 310
Metes and bounds, 28
  description by, 28
  meaning of, 28
Mineral rights, 16
Minerals, solid, ownership of, 16
Minor, 122
  contract by, 123
  deed by, 139, 144
Misrepresentation, 124
  fraudulent, 124
  innocent, 124
  intentional, 124
  unintentional, 124
Mistake, 123
  mutual, 123
  nature of, 123
  unilateral, 123
Mistaken boundary, 180–181
Mistaken improver, 21–22
  willful trespasser, 22
  (*See also* Good faith improver)
Model State Environmental Policy Act, 350–352
  environmental impact statements, 351
  purpose of, 351
Monument, 27–28
Mortgage:
  conventional, 220
  deed of trust compared, 236
  FHA-insured, 220
  function of, 224, 234
  minimum requirements, 236
  parties to, 235
  purchase money, 237–238
    nature of, 237
    priority of, 237–238
      as to homestead exemption, 298

Mortgage:
  release of, 245
  securing future advances, 239–241
    obligatory advances, 239
    optional advances, 239–240
    Uniform Land Transactions Act, provisions, 240–241
  termination of, 236
  theories of, 235
    lien theory, 235
    title theory, 235
  VA-guaranteed, 220
Mortgage market, 219–220
  primary, 220
  secondary, 220
Mortgaged property:
  encumbrance of, 244
  lease of, 242
  possession of, 241
  sale of, 242–244
    assumption of debt, 243
    subject to mortgage, 242
  use of, 241
Mortgagee, 235
  rights of, 245–247
Mortgagor, 235
  rights of, 241–245

National Environmental Policy Act, 344–346
  declaration of national policy, 344–345
  enforcing compliance, 345
  procedures to implement, 345
  purposes of, 344
Natural flow doctrine, 91
Navigable waters, 182
Necessity, 156–157
  legislative determination, 156
  for taking private property, 156–157
Negligence, 83, 85
  basis of, 83
  defined, 83, 422
  distinguished from nuisance, 85
  lack of intent, 83
Net lease, 373

Noise Control Act, 337
Noise pollution, 336–337
  control of, 337
  effect of, 336–337
  nature of, 336
Nonconforming use (*see* Zoning)
Nonnavigable waters, 182
Northwest Territory, 39
Notice, 206–207
  actual, 206
  constructive, 206–207
  nature of, 206
Notice of nonresponsibility (*see* Mechanic's lien)
Nuisance:
  action by tenant, 384
  attractive nuisance doctrine, 95–96
  branches and roots, 90–91
  characteristics of, 83
  continuing, 87
  defenses to nuisance actions, 86
  defined, 84, 422
  distinguished from negligence, 85
  distinguished from trespass, 85
  nonconforming use as, 328–329
  permanent, 87
  private, 84
    remedies for, 85
  public, 84
    remedies for, 85
  spite fence as, 88
  zoning compared, 315
Nuisance in fact, 84
Nuisance per accidens, 84
Nuisance per se, 84
Noncupative will, 149

Offer, 116–119
  distinguished from, 117
    advertisements, 117
    catalogues, 117
    price lists, 117
    solicitation for bids, 116
  as element of contract, 116
  how manifested, 116–117

Offer:
  methods of termination, 118–119
    conditional acceptance, 119
    counteroffer, 119
    death, 119
    destruction of subject matter, 119
    insanity, 119
    lapse of time, 118
    rejection, 118–119
    revocation, 118
Oil and gas, 17–19
  correlative rights, 18
  lease, 18–19
  nonownership theory, 17
  ownership in place theory, 17
  rule of capture, 17
Option, 132–134, 375–376
  characteristic feature of, 133
  contract of sale compared, 133
  defined, 132, 422
  to purchase leased premises, 375–376
  right of preemption distinguished, 133–134
Oregon Compromise, 41
Ownership, 4–10
  defined, 4, 423
  nature of, 5
  private, 9
    theories of, 9
  protection of, 10
  rights and duties of, 5
  transfer of, 8
    voluntary or involuntary, 8

Pacific Railroad Act, 48
Parol evidence, 27
  deed descriptions, 27
Partition, 74
Party wall, 89
  agreement, 89
  characteristics of, 89
  cross-easements, 89
  ownership of, 89
Passersby, occupier's duty toward, 97–98

Penalty, 262
  liquidated damages compared, 262
Percentage lease, 372
Percolating waters, 25
Periodic tenancy, 64, 369–370, 402
  creation of, 369
  termination of, 370, 402
Permissive waste, 62
Personal property, 2, 4, 16
  derivation of term, 2
  mined ores and minerals, 16
  nature of, 4
Points, 244
Police power, 7–8, 317, 389
  eminent domain distinguished, 154
  housing codes, 389
  limitations on, 8, 317
  nature of, 7, 317
  scope of, 317
  source of zoning authority, 317
  standard by which tested, 7
Possession, 5–6, 55–56
  incident of ownership, 5
  present versus future, 6
  right of, 55–56
Possibility of reverter, 59, 66
Power of termination, 58, 65
Preemption, 43
  right of, 133–134
Preemption Act, 43
Prepayment clause, 231
Prescription, 104–106
  defined, 104*n.*, 423
  easement by, 104–106, 110
    requisites for acquiring, 104–105
    scope or extent of, 106
    termination of easement, 110
Prescriptive right, 24–25, 104
  how acquired, 24–25
  to water, 24
Primary mortgage market, 220
Principal meridian, 30
Prior appropriation, 23–24
  acquisition of right, 24

INDEX

Priorities, 207, 237, 296
  established by recording, 207, 237
  homestead exemption, 296
Privacy, right of, 11
Private nuisance, 84
Private property, 10
  constitutional protection of, 10
  (*See also* Ownership, private)
Probate, 146
Probate homestead (*see* Homestead)
Profit or profit a prendre, 111
  extraction of minerals, 16
Promise, 115–116, 122
  conditional, 116
  defined, 115, 423
  illusory, 122
  offer as, 116
Promissory note, 224–232
  common provisions, 226–232
    acceleration clauses, 228–231
    interest provisions, 227–228
    prepayment clauses, 231–232
  general characteristics, 224
  types of, 224–226
    installment, 225–226
    straight, 224–225
Property:
  meaning of, 2
  privateness of, 9
  real (*see* Real property)
Protected party, defined, 223, 424
Protective theory (*see* Eminent domain)
Public domain:
  acquisition of, 38
  states created from, 44
Public nuisance, 84
Public use, 155–156
  meaning of, 155–156
  presumption of, 156
Publication of will, 148
Purchase money mortgage (*see* Mortgage)

Quitclaim deed, 138
  termination of easement, 109
Quitrent, 38

Range lines, 31
Ranges, 31, 33
Real Estate Settlement Procedures Act, 184, 190–200
  implementation of, 191
    Regulation X, 191
  lenders covered by, 192
  necessity for, 190–191
  purpose of, 191
  regulation of escrow accounts, 194
  scope of, 192
Real property, 2–4
  derivation of term, 2
  nature of, 3
  synonymous terms, 4
Real property tax:
  ad valorem, 354
  appraisal, 357–359
    cyclical reappraisal, 358
    highest and best use, 357
    preferred approach, 357
    taxpayer's protest, 359
    traditional approaches, 357
  assessed value, meaning of, 358
  assessment, 355, 358–360
    defined, 355, 412
    fractional, 358–359
    to owner of record, 359
    presumption of correctness, 355, 359
    review of, 359–360
  collection of, 360–362
  delinquency and penalty, 360–361
  due process of law, 359–360
  exemptions, 355–356
    federal property, 355
    in lieu payments, 356
    institutional property, 356
    state and local government property, 356
    veterans and home owners, 356
  nature of, 354–355
    not based on benefits, 354–355
    not personal obligation, 355, 362
    requirement of uniformity, 355

Real property tax:
  power to tax, 353
    delegation of, 353–354
  preferential taxation, 356
  tax deed, 363–364
    conveys new title, 363
    statements in, 363–364
  tax-delinquent property, 362–364
    sale of, 362–363
      certificate of sale, 363
      defeasible title, 363
      due process of law, 362
      proceeds of, 362
      redemption from, 362–363
  tax levy, 360
  tax lien, 361–362
    foreclosure of, 362
    priority of, 361
    removal of, 361–362
    security for debt, 361
  tax rate, 359–360
    calculation of, 359
    setting rate, 360
  unpopularity of, 354
Record title, 204
Recording:
  defined, 201, 424
  effects of, 202
  mechanics of, 204–206
  nature of, 201
  order of priorities, 207–208
    notice-type statute, 208
    race-notice-type statute, 208
    race-type statute, 207–208
  place of, 203
  time for, 205
Recording laws, 202–203
  objective of, 202
  parties protected by, 202–203
Recording system, 201–208
  Real Estate Settlement Procedures Act, provisions, 200
Recoupment theory (*see* Eminent domain)
Rectangular survey system, 29–36
Redemption (*see* Equity of redemption; Right of redemption)

Redlining, 220–221
  concept of, 220
  what constitutes, 221
Regulation B (*see* Equal Credit Opportunity Act)
Regulation X (*see* Real Estate Settlement Procedures Act)
Regulation Z (*see* Truth in Lending Law)
Reliction, 181
Remainder, 65–67
  contingent, 67
  vested, 66
  classes of, 67
Remainderman, 66
Remnant theory (*see* Eminent domain)
Rental agreement (*see* Lease)
Rescission, 123
  for mistake, 123
  under Truth in Lending Law, 266–268
Reservation, 101, 143
  in deed, 143
  of easement, 101
  express, 101
  nature of, 101
Resource Conservation and Recovery Act, 339–342
  congressional findings, 339–340
  objectives of, 340–341
Restraint on alienation, 8–9, 399–400
  meaning of, 8
  permissible restraints, 9
    against assignment of leasehold, 399
    against subletting, 400
  unreasonable, example of, 8
Restrictions:
  benefit-burden effect of, 305–306
  effect on value, 304–305
  methods of creating, 306–307
    contract between parties, 306
    deed to single parcel, 306
    general plan of development, 307

Restriction:
  privately imposed, 304
    condition, defined, 304
    covenant, defined, 304
  publicly imposed, 303–304
  typical enforceable restrictions, 304
  typical unenforceable restrictions, 305
  (*See also* Restrictive covenants; Zoning)
Restrictive covenants:
  benefit-burden effect of, 305–306
  breach of, 308
  defined, 306, 425
  effect on value, 305
  effect of zoning on, 312
  enforcement of, 308–310
    as equitable servitude, 310
    who may enforce, 309
  general characteristics, 307–308
    affirmative covenant, 307
    interest in land, 308
    negative covenant, 307
    similarity to negative easement, 307
  methods of creating, 306–307
    by contract, 306
    deed to single parcel, 306
    general plan of development, 307
  personal covenant, 309
  remedies for breach, 308
  running with land, 309–310
  taking by eminent domain, 162–163, 308, 312
  termination of, 310–312
    by acquiescence, 311
    by agreement, 311
    by changed neighborhood conditions, 311–312
    by condemnation, 312
    by laches, 311
    by lapse of time, 310
    by merger, 310
    by release, 311
    by waiver, 311

Restrictive covenants:
  zoning compared, 315
  (*See also* Restrictions)
Retaining wall, 90
Retaliatory action (*see* Landlord and tenant)
Reversion, 65, 163
  landlord's interest, 366
    injury to, 383
  sublessor's interest, 400
  transfer of, 67–68, 398
Reversionary interest, 63
  types of, 65–66
    possibility of reverter, 66
    power of termination, 65–66
    reversion, 65–66
Reversioner, 65
Right, legal: characteristics of, 2
  defined, 1, 5*n*., 425
  reciprocal of legal duty, 8
Right of entry, 58
Right of preemption, 133–134
Right of redemption, 255–256, 262–263
  features of, 256,
  nature of, 255, 262
  operation of, 263
Right of repair and deduct (*see* Landlord and tenant)
Right of survivorship, 70, 74–75
Riparian lands, 23
Riparian rights, 23
  natural flow theory, 23
  nature of, 23
  reasonable use theory, 23
Roots, intruding, 90
Rule of capture, 17
Rule of reason, 106

Safe Drinking Water Act, 336
Seal, 142
Search and seizure, 11–12
Secondary mortgage market, 220
Section, 34–35
  identification of, 35
  size of, 34
  subdivision of, 35

INDEX

Section lines, 34
Security agreement, defined, 237, 426
Security deposit:
  by tenant, 373–374
    interest on, 373–374
    as liquidated damages, 374
    statutory regulation of, 373–374
Self-help:
  to abate nuisance, 85
  as defense against trespass, 82
    degree of force permitted, 82
    self-defense compared, 82
  removal of branches, 90–91
  removal of obstructions to easement, 107
  resort to, 15
  right of repair and deduct, 387
Separate property, 76
Servient estate, 100
  rights of owner, 107
Settlement, meaning of, 183, 190, 234n.
Settlement costs, 183, 190
Settlement Costs—A HUD Guide, 195
Settlement costs worksheet, 195–196
Settlement services, 190
Settlement statement, 195, 197–199
Severalty, meaning of, 69
Severance, right of, 73
Severance damages, 157
Simultaneous death, 79
Social guest, status of, 96
Solid Waste Disposal Act, 338
Special information booklet, 194–195
Spite fence, 88
Squatters, 43
Standard parallel, 30
Standard State Zoning Enabling Act, 316
Stare decisis, doctrine of, 2
State environmental legislation, 350–352

Statute of frauds, 125
  boundary line agreements, 94
  nature of, 125, 366
  objective of, 125
Statute of limitations, 174
  in adverse possession, 174, 178
Subcontractor (*see* Mechanics' lien)
Subjacent support, 92
Sublease (*see* Landlord and tenant)
Subordination agreement, 238
Subsurface of land, ownership of, 16
Succession, law of (*see* Intestate succession)
Surface entry, right of, 16–17, 19
Surface water, 91
  common enemy doctrine, 91
  defined, 91, 427
  natural flow doctrine, 91
Survey, 27
  location of boundary lines, 93
  original, 27
  resurvey, 27
Survivorship, right of, 70
  co-ownership terminated by, 74
  simultaneous death, 79
Swamp Lands Act, 46

Tax levy (*see* Real property tax)
Tax lien (*see* Real property tax)
Tax sale (*see* Real property tax)
Taxes (*see* Real property tax)
Tenancy (*see* Leasehold)
Tenancy:
  in common, 71, 73–75
  entirety, 75
    simultaneous death, 79
  from period to period, 64, 369–370
  at sufferance, 64, 370, 391
  at will, 64, 370, 391
  for years, 63, 369
Tenant in common, rights and duties of, 72–73
  boundary line trees, 90

Tender, meaning of, 126
Tenement, 100
  dominant, 100
  servient, 100
    destruction of, 110–111
Tenure, 56
Testamentary capacity, 146
  mental competency, 146
  minimum age, 146
Testamentary disposition (*see* Will)
Testamentary intent, 148
Testator, 146
Tiers, 33–34
Title:
  abstract of, 211–213
  acquisition by adverse possession, 179–180
  as evidence of ownership, 5
  good or marketable, 131, 180
  guaranty of, 215–216
  signifies ownership, 5
Title closing, 126, 183
  meaning of, 183
  nature of, 126
Title examiner, 212–213
  attorney as, 212
  liability of, 212–213
Title insurance:
  attorney's opinion compared, 216
  coverage, 216–217
    common exclusions, 216
    standardization of, 216
  nature of policy, 214
  transferability of, 214
  operation of companies, 214
  regulation of companies, 214
Title of record, 204
Title plant, 212–215
  abstracter's, 212
  title insurer's, 214–215
  contents of, 215
  nature of, 214
Title registration (*see* Torrens system)
Title search, 201
Torrens system, 209–210
  nature of, 209

Torrens system:
  objective of, 210
  operation of, 210
Tort, defined, 14, 428
Township, 30, 33–34
  identification of, 34
  size of, 34
Township lines, 33
Tract book system, 215
Tract index system, 206
Trade fixtures, 20–21
  nature of, 20
  removal of, 21
Treaty of Guadalupe Hidalgo, 40
Trees, 90
  near boundary lines, 90
  on boundary lines, 90
  branches, removal of, 90
  roots, removal of, 90
Trespass, 14, 82
  defense of property against, 82
  defined, 14, 429
  described, 82
  distinguished from nuisance, 85
  trespasser's intent, 82
Trespasser, 95
  defined, 95, 429
  discovered trespasser, 95
  expulsion of, 82
  mistaken improver as, 21
  occupier's duty toward, 95
  tolerated intruder, 95
  trespassing children, 95
Trust deed (*see* Deed, of trust)
Truth in Lending Law, 263–269
  annual percentage rate, 264–266
    disclosure of, 266
    nature of, 264
  disclosure statement, 265–266
  finance charge, 264–266
    costs excluded from, 264
    costs included in, 264
    nature of, 264
    statement of total, 266
  implemented by Regulation Z, 263

Truth in Lending Law:
  objective of, 263
  penalties for noncompliance, 269
  real property transactions, 263–264
    defined, 263
    regulation of, 263–264
  right of rescission, 266–268
    effect of rescission, 268
    exception to, 267
    nature of, 266
    notice of, 267–268
    time limitation on, 268
    to whom applicable, 264

Undue influence, 124
  deed procured by, 144–145
  nature of, 124
Uniform Land Transactions Act, 222–224
  objectives of, 222
Uniform Relocation Assistance and Real Property Acquisition Policies Act, 165–171
  purpose of act, 165
  real property acquisition policies, 169–171
    acquisition by negotiation, 170
    appraisal before negotiation, 170
    avoidance of inverse condemnation, 170
    expenses incidental to title transfer, 171
    litigation expenses, 171
    notice to vacate dwelling, 170
    offer of full market value, 170
    taking of uneconomic remnants, 170–171
  relocation assistance, 165–169
    advisory services, 169
    need for legislation, 165

Uniform Relocation Assistance and Real Property Acquisition Policies Act:
  relocation assistance: persons displaced from business or farm, 168–169
    actual direct losses of personal property, 168
    expenses in searching for replacement, 169
    loss of net earnings, 168
    moving expenses, 168
  persons displaced from dwellings, 166–168
    moving expenses, 166
    replacement housing: for owners, 166–167
    for tenants, 168
Uniform Residential Landlord and Tenant Act:
  abandonment by tenant, 405–406
  adoption of, 377
  building and housing code compliance, 390
  damage to premises by fire or casualty, 407
  holding-over tenant, 392
  landlord's right of entry, 381
  noncompliance with lease provisions, 404
  notice of termination, 402
  payment of rent, 378
  purposes of, 377
  regaining possession of premises, 410
  repair and deduct, 387–388
  retaliatory conduct, 388–389
  warranty of habitability, 386
  waste by tenant, 382
Uniform Simultaneous Death Act, 79
Uniform Vendor and Purchaser Risk Act, 261
Unilateral contract, 115, 121–122
Unlawful detainer, 408–409

INDEX

447

Unreasonable search and seizure, 11–12
   administrative inspections, 12
   constitutional provision, 11
Usury, 227–228

VA-guaranteed mortgage, 220
Variable interest rate, 227
Variance, 324
Vested remainder, 66–67
   classes of, 67
Void contract, 116, 122–123
Void deed, 144–145
Voidable contract, 116, 122–123
Voidable deed, 144–145

Warranty (*see* Covenant; Covenants of title)
Warranty deed, 137–138
   short form, 137
   special, 138
Waste:
   by co-owner, 73
   impairment of security, 241, 245
   by life tenant, 61
   by mortgagor, 229, 241
      rights of mortgagee, 245

Waste:
   permissive, 62
   by tenant, 381–382
Water pollution, 335–336
   control of, 335–336
   types of, 335
      biological, 335
      chemical, 335
Water rights, 23–24
Watershed, 23
Will, 145–149
   defined, 145, 430
   formalities of execution, 147
   right to change, 146
   types of, 147–149
      holographic, 148
      noncupative, 149
      witnessed, 147
   when effective, 146

Zoning:
   aesthetic, 321–322
   boundary lines, 322
   comprehensive, 311–319
   constitutionality of, 318
   cumulative, 320
   enforcement, 329
   exclusionary, 321
   exercise of police power, 317

Zoning:
   interim or hold, 322
   nature of, 315
   nonconforming use, 326–329
      amortization of, 328
      nature of, 326
      termination of, 327
      types of, 326
   noncumulative, 320
   nuisance compared, 315
   procedures, 322–323
   regulation of intensity of use, 320–321
      floor area ratio, 321
      height and bulk limitations, 321
      minimum lot size, 321
   regulation of type of use, 320
      categories of use, 320
      restrictiveness of use, 320
   relief from, 323–326
      administrative relief, 324–325
         special permit, 324–325
         variance, 324
      judicial relief, 325–326
      legislative relief, 323
         rezoning by amendment, 323
   restrictive covenants compared, 315